# GUIDE TO COLLEGE VISITS

## Planning Trips to Popular Campuses in the Northeast, Southeast, West, and Midwest

# GUIDE TO COLLEGE VISITS

## Planning Trips to Popular Campuses in the Northeast, Southeast, West, and Midwest

The Staff of The Princeton Review

Random House, Inc.
New York
PrincetonReview.com

The Princeton Review, Inc.
2315 Broadway
New York, NY 10024
E-mail: bookeditor@review.com

© 2007 by The Princeton Review, Inc.

Excerpts from Fodor's travel guides courtesy of Fodor's Travel, a division of Random House, Inc.

ISBN 978-0-375-76600-8

Publisher: Robert Franek
Editor: Adrinda Kelly
Designer and Production Manager: Scott Harris
Production Editor: Christine LaRubio

Printed in the United States of America.

9  8  7  6  5  4  3  2

2007 Edition

# CONTENTS

# ACKNOWLEDGEMENTS

This book would not have been possible without the contributions of several members of the Book Publishing team here at The Princeton Review. Robert Franek lent his support and expertise to the development of this book; Christine LaRubio and Scott Harris were charged with the unenviable task of wading through the raw manuscript to transform it into the book now in your hands; Suzanne Podhurst also merits special thanks for all the valuable input she provided along the way.

Other contributors include Tom Meltzer, Chris Maier, and Otilia Mirambeaux, all excellent writers whose talents forged the book's introduction and school profiles. A very special thanks goes to Andrea Kornstein, who wore many hats throughout the development of this project, from profile writer to administrative support. Finally, a sincere appreciation is reserved for my amazingly talented colleague, Adam Davis, who helped me meet more than one pressing deadline throughout this book's development.

Gratitude is also reserved for Tom Russell, who was instrumental in securing our use of the Fodor's material quoted in the school profiles; thanks also to the team behind the Fodor's guidebooks, whose excellent work makes the Fodor's blurbs such a great addition.

Finally there is no way you would be holding this book right now if it were not for the extraordinary help of the numerous media relations folks and institutional researchers at the 371 colleges profiled within its pages. Although I can't name them all here, I owe each one many thanks.

—Adrinda Kelly

# PLANNING YOUR COLLEGE VISIT

## WHY VISIT COLLEGE CAMPUSES?

If you're like most college-bound students, you lead a pretty busy life. You've got a full slate of demanding academic courses, an equally jam-packed schedule of school-related extracurriculars, and an active life outside of school that involves family, friends, and community activities. You don't have a lot of free time to go gallivanting around the country to look at a bunch of ivy-covered buildings and sit in on a bunch of classes you'll be taking next year anyway. So why visit college campuses?

The fact that you're reading this book suggests that you already have some pretty good reasons. You realize that you'll soon choose the place where you'll study, socialize, work, shop, eat, sleep, and live for a substantial and important part of your life, and that the day when you have to make that choice is fast approaching. It's a big decision, and you'll want to base it on as much available information as you can.

A campus visit won't tell you everything you need to know about life at your prospective college, but it will give you a richer, more detailed view than you can get from surfing websites, browsing brochures, watching videos, or reading college guides. Every school has its own culture, its own unique way of doing things. You can't divine it from a brochure, though. Truth be told, you won't learn all there is to know from a brief visit. A visit will, however, give you a sense of the "big picture" issues that define life on a campus. You'll probably get enough of a sense of those issues to determine whether the school is a good fit for you.

Spend a weekday on campus while classes are in session and you'll get a feel for the rhythm of life there, the attitudes of the students towards their studies, and—if you get the chance to attend a few classes—some idea of the atmosphere in the school's classrooms. Visit over a weekend and you'll experience the school's social life (or lack thereof). You'll also find students relaxing and taking it easy, making it easier to approach them with any questions about the school that you may have.

Let's look at some of the benefits of a campus visit:

## You'll get a feel for academic life

Academics are the primary reason you're attending college, so you want to know whether you and the school you're considering are a good academic fit. The quality of the school's academic life and the intensity of student-teacher relationships will strongly impact your experience at college. Look for clues about both during your campus visit.

If possible, attend a class or two during your visit (make sure to arrange this with the Admissions Office well in advance of your visit). If asked for your preference, request to sit in on a class that is required for all freshmen so that you'll get a better sense of what your first year will be like. Are the classes huge or small? Is the teacher a full professor or a graduate student? Is the class format lecture, lab, discussion, or a hybrid of several formats? Are students' contributions to the class interesting? Are students furiously scribbling notes? Are they asking questions? Is "Will this be on the test?" the only question any of them asks? Answer these questions and you'll get a pretty good sense of how students approach their studies at the school, and whether you'll be comfortable with that approach.

If you can't attend a class, at least take time to walk around campus and observe the students and faculty. Pay close attention to students as they travel to and from class. Are they in a hurry? Do they look stressed? Or are they walking at a leisurely pace, conversing and laughing? Do faculty members talk with students as they walk across campus? Do you even see faculty members walking across campus, or are they missing from the picture? If faculty members are conspicuously absent, it could mean that they have numerous commitments off campus (e.g., conferences, serving on corporate boards, or teaching at more than one school) that would leave them less time to devote to undergraduates on campus.

## You'll get a feel for the type of student who attends the school

For many, whom they go to school with is just as important as where they go to school and what they study. You may think this is a frivolous concern, but it's not: Your fellow students will be your peers, friends, and, in some cases, rivals throughout your tenure at the school. If you're a bad fit with the student body, you could be in for four miserable years (fewer, probably, because most "bad fits" eventually transfer out; regardless, being the "sore thumb" at a school is an unpleasant scenario that you'll probably want to avoid).

There are lots of different issues to consider as you assess a student body. First, note the degree of similarity among students. Do they all look alike, or is the population diverse? Consider not just racial diversity but also economic diversity, religious diversity, and diversity of personality types. Are you more comfortable surrounded by people just like yourself, or do you want a college that will give you the opportunity to encounter people with different backgrounds and perspectives? More specifically, think about:

- **Class/Status:** Is the parking lot filled with new Beemers and SUVs? Or are most of the cars junkers (if they are, make sure you haven't stumbled onto the faculty parking lot by mistake!)? Do students dress as though they do all their shopping at Abercrombie? Do the men and women seem especially fashion-conscious (e.g., popped collars, Prada bags, Ugg boots, Versace shades)? Or are they outfitted in nice but affordable clothing, stuff you could buy at Marshall's or Sears? Ask yourself, "Can I envision myself a part of this community?" For many students, answering this question means having to think about class issues and the social circles they feel most comfortable navigating.

- **Personality type:** The way students dress can tell you about more than their economic status; it can also tell you about the group or personality type with which they associate. Do you see lots of students in sweats and sneakers? Or are most students decked out in Peruvian alpaca sweaters, balloon pants, and Birkenstocks? Is the campus an ocean of polo shirts with popped collars? You'll probably be surprised at how many students you will immediately identify as jocks, hippies, preps, and nerds. You've probably encountered most of these personality types in high school. Which type reigns supreme on campus? Is this a group you're comfortable spending four years among? Keep in mind, of course, that you can't judge a book entirely by its cover. Before you draw any definitive conclusions about students' personalities, talk with some students. You may well find that college students don't fit your assumptions as neatly as do your peers in high school.

- **Intellectualism:** Observe students in class, at the library, and in conversation as they walk across campus. Do you get the sense that students study primarily for the sake of learning? Or is their primary goal to score a high-paying job? If you're the type who wants to stay up all night discussing Plato, you won't likely be happy at a school full of pre-professionals with little interest in pure academics. Conversely, if your only goal is to get great grades in order to get into the best med, law, or b-school, you probably won't be happy at a school with a bunch of philosophizing dreamers.

- **Religion:** Are students religious? Are there frequent and obvious demonstrations of religious belief across campus? Deeply religious students may find the rampant secularism of many college campuses off-putting. Students with a more secular bent will likely have a hard time adjusting to life on deeply religious campuses, particularly those with strict behavioral codes or those where students openly proselytize.

- **Sexuality/Gender Climate:** To what extent do couples display affection on campus? Do you see indicators of an active and accepted gay community (e.g., posters for GLBT events)? Here's another area where you want to find a good personal fit. Socially conservative students may be uncomfortable on a campus with a large and active gay community, such as New York University or Smith. Conversely, gay students may be uncomfortable on campuses with profoundly conservative social attitudes.

While it's important for the school's academic program to be the right fit for you, it's just as important for the campus community to be a good fit. A college visit, even a brief one, will give you a good sense of who your classmates will be and whether you'll be comfortable among them.

## GETTING THE REAL SCOOP ON CAMPUS LIFE

While you won't be able to truly grasp a college's atmosphere until you become immersed in campus life, there are some things you can do to get the real scoop on life at that college.

1. **Go to the source.** Current students are your absolute best resource for juicy info on campus life. And we've already done the legwork for you in the profiles of our book *Best 361 Colleges*, chock-full of student opinion on the school's academics, student body, and campus life.

2. **Ask your guidance counselor.** He or she may have some good insight on schools, especially ones that are popular with your high school's graduates. In addition, your guidance counselor may be able to put you in touch with students she has worked with in years past who are now attending the schools in which you're interested. Making a quick call or whipping off a short e-mail to these current students is an easy way to score the kind of firsthand feedback you're after.

3. **Stats are stats.** Numbers on diversity, campus safety, enrollment, selectivity—those are solid facts. Investigate the numbers and compare them to your expectations. For example: How many sororities and fraternities are there? How many students live on campus? What majors attract the most students? What's the student/teacher ratio, especially for freshmen classes?

4. **Read college newspapers online.** In addition to the news on campus, don't forget about the editorial page, events section, city news, and even the types of ads. These are all clues to how the campus and town function on a day-to-day basis.

5. **Know your priorities.** Exactly what type of "atmosphere" are you looking for? Urban or rural? Big or small? Getting a handle on what specifically is going to make you a happy individual at college is half the battle.

Yes, it is true: You really can't know *exactly* what a school is going to be like until you get there. Even your own opinion of your college experience will change as you grow more accustomed to being on campus. In the meantime, as you're searching, trust your instincts. The real "scoop" lies not so much in the specific information you receive, as in the applicability of the information to your interests, needs, and preferences.

## You'll get a feel for extracurricular life

Your college experience will consist of more than studying and hanging out with friends. There will be all sorts of clubs and organizations available for you to participate in, and you may want to join one or more. That's why it's important to explore the extracurricular life of a school. What do students do when they're not in class, in the library, or hanging around the dorms with friends? A campus visit can give you an idea, especially if you plan an overnight stay. As you make your observations, look for evidence of the following:

- **Active clubs and organizations:** All schools have some clubs and organizations, but what those are exactly will vary from school to school. You can find out which clubs are registered on campus by visiting the student activity center, where a list of the school's organizations is usually posted. You'll also find a similar list in the school yearbook, which should be available at the Admissions Office. In addition, most schools list all their clubs and organizations on their websites; many provide separate sites for each group. Look for posters announcing meetings and events to determine which groups are most active.

- **Greek organizations:** Does the school have a Greek scene? How active is it? Is it simply one aspect of campus life, or is it the dominant feature? You can find this information in any good college guide—we recommend the *Best 361 Colleges* (Princeton Review)—but you'll also find plenty of evidence on campus. Are lots of students wearing t-shirts and sweatshirts emblazoned with the names of their houses? Are there posters around campus announcing upcoming parties at Greek houses? Ask students—Greeks and independents alike—about the school's fraternity and sorority scene. Their answers will reveal what you can expect from the social scene on campus.

- **The party scene:** The Greek scene and the party scene are synonymous at some schools, but not at all of them. Some schools have no Greek organizations. Others place strict restrictions on Greek parties, forcing the party scene elsewhere. At many schools the Greek houses are the locus of parties for underclassmen, while students of drinking age prefer local bars or even smaller parties at their apartments or houses. And some schools have minimal party scenes: military academies, single-sex schools, and religious schools are the most obvious candidates, but small schools with large commuter populations or a large in-state population (at some schools, in-state students leave campus for the weekend immediately after their last class of the week) can also be relatively party-free. Whether you're looking for a year-round Mardi Gras, a cloister, or something in between, you should consider the school's party scene when choosing your undergraduate institution. Even if you have no interest in party-ing—*especially* if you have no interest in partying, really—the intensity of the party scene will have a big impact on your life at school. Don't wait until your roommate is vomiting on your bed to figure this out! During your visit, survey the campus for evidence of an active party scene: dumpsters full of empties, posters advertising huge blowout parties, bleary-eyed students in pajamas straggling across campus in the early afternoon, etc. Better still, schedule a weekend visit so you can experience the party scene firsthand.

- **The arts:** Some schools house well-known museums and frequently host touring theatrical, musical, and dance productions. Others host regular student theatrical and musical productions, galleries displaying student and faculty art, and a steady diet of movies old and new. Still others have practically no arts scene at all; there's no interest on campus, so it doesn't exist. If your idea of fun is a Truffaut double feature or a night of experimental theater, make sure you find a school that can accommodate you. Scan the bulletin boards for notices about upcoming arts events. Survey the campus map for evidence of student galleries, art and dance studios, concert halls, etc.

- **Athletics:** Most schools have some form of an athletic program, but the degree to which athletics are a major campus focal point varies greatly from school to school. At some schools, football or basketball season is *the* high point of the school year; students are passionate about their teams and build their schedules around games, camping out to get tickets and tailgating enthusiastically for hours before the start of an event. You'll see evidence of students' devotion at these sports-happy schools in the form of banners, pennants, bumper stickers, and t-shirts. At other schools, athletics are an afterthought, and if you ask students about the football team they're likely to respond, "We *have* a football team?" If college athletics are important to you, you probably shouldn't attend such a school.

- **The neighborhood around campus and the school's hometown:** Try to save time to tour the town or city in which the school is located. If you can't, at least take a walk around the surrounding neighborhood to see what sort of off-campus housing, restaurants, clubs, and retail shops are easily accessible. If you visit enough schools, you'll probably notice that campus life is generally much more active in schools located in smaller towns. At big-city schools—schools in New York City, Boston, and Chicago, for example—students tend to seek their fun off-campus, and for good reason: Few schools could compete with all the options that a big city offers.

You won't get an accurate picture of the academic life, extracurricular life, and the student body from the school's promotional material; you'll get an idealized version, but that's not what you want. You can learn something about campus life from college guide books, particularly those books that are based on interviews with over 115,000 undergraduates (hint, hint). A campus visit, however, is the best way to learn about a school to see whether it's the sort of place where *you* will feel at home for four years.

## THE VIRTUAL VISIT

First impressions count, and a school's website is usually the first glimpse a student gets of their potential *alma mater*, so even the oldest, most traditional schools have had to jump to the forefront of Web technology in order to compete for today's students. Regardless of a website's content, a sleek, Flash-enhanced homepage exudes a certain aesthetic that says that if a school has devoted such time and resources to its online presentation, then the campus itself must be equally well-kept. In a similar vein, the quality of organization and ease of navigation can be indicative of how smoothly the school's administration runs. Problems such as outdated statistics, buried information, and broken links that aren't repaired within 24 hours may indicate an inattention to details; cluttered, shoddy pages and poor navigation reveal just how much effort the school is putting into connecting with its students.

One of the greatest things about having access to a school's website is that you're able to see the kinds of services available to students. Tech-heavy and career-oriented schools tend to have a stronger online presence and may offer online blackboards and forums for classes, online bill payment and class registration, web hosting for personal and student-activity homepages, and web-mail access for when a student wants to access their e-mail remotely (such as over winter vacation or from a friend's dorm room).

Many schools offer an online application process, a far cry from the typewritten pages of yesterday. Having this instant access is handy; you can tell a lot about a school by its application and application policy. A school's website should also provide links to companies, sites, and organizations that acquaint you with the town and what is has to offer—knowing the local culture and the available amenities is a crucial decision-making factor when deciding where to go, and the school should be well aware of this.

A school's website should be designed as if it were the only available means of seeing the campus, so that a student who paid the campus an in-person visit has only a slight advantage over a student who was only able to cyber-visit. Many of the pages you visit as a prospect will be revisited as an enrolled student through different eyes, so keep track of the location of things that you find helpful. A virtual campus may not look as pretty when the leaves fall, but it's not a bad day trip!

## WHEN IS THE BEST TIME TO VISIT?

The best time to visit a school is when the school is in session. Yes, it's probably easier to visit schools during the summer when you are on vacation. The trouble is that the school is on break then, too. You'll be able to see the campus and take a tour, but you won't be able to attend classes (summer classes are nothing like classes held during the regular academic year) and you won't get to see what the campus looks like when it's full of students. You won't get to see the students (or most of the professors and administrators, for that matter), so you won't be able to get a sense of how well you'll fit into the campus community. You won't get a good *feel* for the school, so you'll be missing out on the most important part of your campus visit.

During the school year, avoid visiting during school holidays such as Thanksgiving and Spring Break. Check the school's academic calendar (you can find it on the school's website or in its catalogue) before planning your visit. Also, try not to visit during exam periods or during the reading period that precedes final exams. It'll be difficult (perhaps impossible) to attend a class during those times, and students will be preoccupied with exams and probably a little frazzled. They won't be in the mood to chat with you about their school, because they won't have the time. Visit during these periods and you'll get a skewed impression of the school. You'll probably walk away thinking the students are all basket cases!

Exploit your vacation time and off days. When is your spring break? Use it to visit colleges that aren't on break at the same time. Check your high school's calendar for three-day weekends; some colleges don't observe national holidays, meaning you can use those weekends for a Sunday overnight visit and attend some college classes on Monday. Remember that overnight visits should be scheduled well in advance, as they require extra planning both on your part and on the part of the school.

When is the best time in your high school career to visit colleges? Any time after you start seriously considering college choices is good. During your sophomore year and the autumn semester of your junior year, try to visit lots of different types of schools—big schools, small schools, urban campuses, suburban/rural campuses, private liberal arts schools, public universities—to see what options are available to you. Intensify your efforts during the spring semester of junior year and throughout senior year, and also intensify your focus; hone in on those schools about which you are most serious. While you're a junior and during the autumn semester of senior year, you should try to pay daytime visits to all the schools on your short list, and you should try to schedule overnight visits for at least some of the schools that interest you most.

When you reach the end of your visits and it comes time to compare the schools you visited, remember to take into account the time of year of your visit. Most campuses are at their most alluring in the early autumn and late spring. Conversely, some schools can be pretty austere, even forbidding, in the height of winter. Don't let the season of your visit unduly influence your final decision positively or negatively.

## MAKING THE CAMPUS VISIT AFFORDABLE

With college tuition through the roof, the prospect of spending money to tour the campus of a school you may or may not attend can be very off-putting. But think about it this way: A campus visit now can save you time and money later by increasing the likelihood that you'll choose the right college for you and successfully obtain your degree in four years. Travel costs can get pricey though, and with the cost of gas through the roof, even road trips to colleges within a hundred miles of where you live can be prohibitively expensive. Fortunately, there are some things you can do to cut down on the costs of your campus visits:

Only visit the schools on your short list. Instead of trying to see every college you ever thought about attending, make a short list of 3–4 schools that match up well with your interests, goals, and preferences. Do research online and check out colleges' brochures and virtual tours to determine the schools on your short list.

Piggyback on a friend's visit. Chances are you and your friends will be interested in some of the same schools. You can help each other by sharing rides and splitting the cost of gas when checking out colleges. You'll also have someone to swap impressions with.

Make it a campus visiting vacation. Many great schools are in large cities or in other high-interest areas. By making those destinations the site of your next vacation, you'll kill two birds with one stone. Even though the idea of a "working vacation" may seem off-putting, the fact is that having your family along on a campus tour will make it that much more fun—not to mention cheaper.

Call your recruiter. If you are being actively recruited by a school and money is a prohibiting factor, call the Admissions Office. Often they're willing to pay for a plane ticket if it means enticing you to attend their school.

Research college touring programs. There are many special college touring programs out there and some of them are free for students who show financial need. Check out our Appendix for a list of popular programs.

## WHAT CAN I EXPECT FROM MY COLLEGE VISIT?

Your college visit experience will depend on the type of visit you make. There are three basic types of college visit.

- Daytime visits

- Overnight visits

- Open House and 'special event' visits

Here's what to expect for each.

## Daytime Visits

A daytime visit is optimal for students who are trying to cram a number of campus visits into an abbreviated period. It's also a good choice when you're visiting a safety school or a school that's not on your "short list." Although a daytime visit won't yield as much or as varied information as an overnight visit will, it will allow you to get a feel for the campus and its community. Don't underestimate the value of setting foot on your prospective campuses, even if it's only for a brief time. *Washington Post* commentator Bob Levey observes that many visiting students intuitively sense whether they are a good fit for a school almost immediately upon arriving on campus; he refers to this phenomenon as "the First Golden 30 Seconds."

Most daytime visits begin with a stop at the Admissions Office. There you and other prospective students will meet up with a guide who will lead you on a campus tour. Arrive early to give yourself plenty of time to collect brochures, catalogues, copies of the school newspaper, and any other information you think will be helpful. Sign a guestbook or check in some other way so that your visit is documented; the fact that you visited will work in your favor when the school makes its admissions decisions. You will probably not get to meet with an admissions officer unless you scheduled an interview, which you will need to do well in advance of your visit as interview sessions fill up quickly. Schedule your interview several months in advance, if possible.

Your tour will no doubt be planned to show you the best side of the school. If the school has run-down dormitories, out-of-date classrooms, or an open sewage lagoon, the tour guide will *not* be showing them to you. The quality of tour guides varies from school to school and from individual to individual. Some will recite a script word for word and will get flustered and lose their place if you ask a question. Some are much more at ease in front of a crowd and will deliver an informative and entertaining tour. Remember that the tour guide's job is to depict the school in as positive a light as possible. Guides will rarely lie to you, but they generally engage in a benign form of propaganda, presenting all facts that promote the school and ignoring those that are less flattering. Try to keep your impressions of the school separate from your impressions of the tour guide. Remember, you're choosing a school, not a tour guide. Don't allow yourself to be overly persuaded by the charm (or lack thereof) of your host.

The tour is typically followed by an information session (note that some schools reverse the itinerary, starting with the information session and then offering the campus tour). Information sessions take a variety of formats. More formal sessions are held in a lecture format in an auditorium with an admissions officer, some other school official, or a student offering a presentation and answering questions. Less formal sessions may take place in a student lounge and may take the form of back-and-forth "bull sessions" comprised primarily of conversation and question-and-answer segments. If the number of visitors on the day you arrive is small, your information session may involve a one-on-one sit down with an admissions officer, but don't count on it.

No matter how the information session is organized, at some point you will get a chance to ask questions. Do so; it gives you a chance to learn about something that truly interests you and it provides an opportunity to impress the session leader with what an articulate and thoughtful person you are. Reread "Why Visit College Campuses?" in this book to get some ideas about questions you might ask. Here are a few rules of thumb:

- **Ask about something that is of particular interest to *you*.** Do you hope to study abroad in a particular country? Ask about the availability of international education programs. Are you interested in pursuing independent study in a particular field? Ask about the opportunities and resources that will be available to you. Would you like to get related work/internship experience while at school? Ask about available cooperative learning programs.

- ***Don't* ask about data and other information that can be easily found in the school's promotional material.** Asking about average SAT scores, the number of volumes in the school library, or the student/teacher ratio communicates that you are too lazy to find this readily accessible information yourself. It also suggests that you're asking a question simply for the sake of asking a question, which fails to demonstrate genuine interest in attending that particular school.

- **If you are accompanied by your parents, politely suggest that they keep quiet and let you ask the questions.** The school is considering you for admission, not your parents. Parents who ask long-winded questions designed mostly to show off how much they know about the school may think they are making a good impression, but their effect is quite the opposite.

- **Be polite.** Present yourself well; don't slouch, don't chew gum, don't say "ain't," etc. If your parents have accompanied you, don't bicker with them; be on your best behavior. Don't tell the person conducting the information session that the school is your "safety" or that you'll only attend if you receive a monster scholarship (true stories). In other words, be tactful.

Leave time after the tour/information session to walk around campus on your own. Although the promotional material, the tour, and the information session will all be helpful, they all represent an image of the school packaged by public relations professionals. You want to spend some time seeing the school without that filter. Visit whatever buildings you can access without school identification. High on your list of "must-visit" places should be the main freshman dormitory (you'll probably be living there if you attend), the dining hall (buy lunch and try to imagine eating this food every day of the week; also, try to work your way into a group of current students chatting among themselves on campus so you can ask them about the school); finally, make sure you visit the general information library (this is where books for required courses will be on reserve and thus is a place where you could spend a lot of your freshman year). You should also check out the student union, the athletic facilities, and any other facilities you expect to use. Are all these facilities up to date and well maintained? Can you imagine yourself happy in this setting? You should also spend some time exploring the neighborhood around campus.

Finally, you should try to attend at least one class while on campus. This will require some extra planning, as you will probably need to schedule your classroom visit in advance with the Admissions Office. Ideally, the school will send you to a class that's required for all freshmen. Unless the professor calls specifically on you, do *not* try to participate in the class. You are just there to observe, not to overwhelm your future classmates with your brilliance. Stay for the entire class no matter how boring it is; it's rude to get up and leave a class that's in session. And for Pete's sake, *turn off your cell phone before you enter the classroom!*

That's a whole lot of activity to cram into one visit, which is one of the reasons admissions professionals advise against visiting more than two campuses in one day. The other reason is sensory overload; visit more than two schools in a day and they all start to blend into one amorphous blob-school. Take notes during your visits (or immediately after) so that you can remember what you liked and disliked about each school. If you visit a lot of schools you will have a hard time remembering which details pertain to which school if you don't take notes.

## CHECKLIST: REMEMBER TO ASK ABOUT

Your campus visit presents an incredible opportunity to get the skinny on life at college from the real experts—the students in attendance. Don't be shy about going up to a student and asking them the tough questions—you'll be happy you did. Here's a list to get you started.

1. Is the campus safe and secure? Is there a blue-light system or a late-night escort system available?

2. Is it easy to register for classes?

3. Do students hang out on campus on the weekends, or do they hit up local venues?

4. Is there a Greek scene on campus? Does it dominate campus social life?

5. Who are the best professors? Are professors required to teach undergraduate courses or do they mostly focus on research?

6. What percentage of classes is taught by TAs?

7. What are the most popular student groups on campus?

8. Is it easy to get face-time with administrators?

9. What research opportunities are available for undergraduates?

10. What is the quality of the student advising?

## Overnight Visits

Daytime campus visits can be very informative, but they can feel a little rushed, especially when you're trying to visit two or more campuses in the same day. The feeling of being rushed is not an issue with overnight visits, which ensure plenty of time to relax, chat with students, collect your thoughts, and soak in the campus vibe.

An overnight visit should include all the daytime visit activities, including a campus tour, information session, and a class visit. It will probably also include dinner and breakfast in the school dining facilities; please note that some schools require visiting students to pay for their food, while others provide complimentary meals. It also typically includes an overnight stay with a host student in the dorms (in such cases you will probably be required to bring a sleeping bag and a pillow), although some schools put visitors up in separate guest facilities. The former is preferable, since it ensures you'll have time to chat at length with at least one current student.

Most schools schedule overnight visits Sunday (or Monday) through Thursday; Friday night stay-overs are usually reserved for special recruiting events (see "Special Events Visits", below). While the school provides accommodations for the visiting student, it rarely provides them for parents accompanying the student; they'll have to stay at a nearby hotel or motel. Here are some items you might want to bring along on your overnight visit.

- A sleeping bag and pillow (usually required, unless you want to sleep on your host's ratty old couch)

- Toiletries (soap, toothbrush, shampoo, a bath towel)

- Workout clothing (in case you want to go to the fitness center)

- A book or homework (to keep yourself occupied while your host is studying)

- A camera (so you can take pictures of the buildings on campus and all the great students you'll meet!)

Note that schools have widely varying policies about who can visit overnight. Some will allow any high school junior, senior, or potential transfer to visit. Others limit overnight visits to high school seniors and transfers only. Others are even more selective, offering overnight visits only to applicants who have been admitted to the school. Schools generally do not offer overnight stays during the summer or during midterm or final exam periods.

If you want to visit a campus overnight, make sure to schedule your visit well in advance. Most schools require at least two weeks' advance booking, but since space is limited and visits are booked on a first-come, first-served basis, you should confirm your plans at least one month ahead of time.

## Open Houses and Special Events Visits

Many schools offer weekend recruiting events several times a year; these are usually called "Open Houses." They are more elaborately planned than your standard weekday campus visit. They typically include multiple tours (e.g., a general tour of the campus, a tour of athletic facilities, a tour of the dorms), admissions and financial aid information sessions, presentations by different academic departments, and other organized activities. Open houses draw larger crowds than do weekday tours, and you'll get to meet representatives from most academic departments. Of course, you'll also be vying for attention with a much larger group of prospective students, which isn't so good. Because of the number of visitors on campus during these events, admissions interviews are seldom available on Open House days. Open House events are typically four to six hours long.

Some campuses schedule special-event visits for select groups. These may include weekend-long events devoted to applicants who have been admitted but who have not yet decided to attend, or special-interest groups such as children of alumni, homeschoolers, students with physical or learning disabilities, and minority students. The details of these events vary widely. Check with your prospective schools to see which, if any, are available.

## CHOOSING YOUR TRAVELING COMPANIONS

Even if you're an experienced traveler, chances are that you've never taken a trip quite like a campus visiting trip. Unlike a vacation or a visit to family, a college visit isn't for the purpose of recreation; rather, your goal will be to gather information and to provide your prospective schools with information about yourself. The primary purpose of a college visit is educational, but unlike other education-related trips you've taken, on this trip you won't be chaperoned by a teacher and you probably won't be traveling with a large group of students you know. You'll either be traveling with your parents, traveling with a few friends, or traveling alone.

With whom should you travel? There's no correct answer for everyone. Some students prefer the support and direction that parents provide. Others relish the chance to travel independently and can handle the responsibilities of managing an itinerary, monitoring expenses, and gathering information about their prospective schools. Some can travel with friends without turning the trip into a free-for-all; others can't. You have to think about what will work best for you. As you decide, remember that it's okay to have fun on your college visits but that fun is not the purpose of the trip. Choose travel arrangements that will facilitate your research into prospective schools.

Traveling with your parents has many advantages. They can keep the itinerary, handle all the driving, and dole out the funds. In short, they can deal with all the drudge work so you can concentrate on the meat of your visit—getting a feel for campus life. They can also collect supplementary information for you; they're probably better equipped to meet with financial aid officers than you are, for example, since they're typically the ones who handle the family finances. Finally, they can serve as an extra set of eyes and ears, giving you additional perspective on the campuses.

### GUIDELINES FOR PARENTS

- **Be supportive, be positive, be patient:** A college visit is a stressful time for everyone. Behave in a way most likely to minimize stress.

- **Schedule plenty of extra time in the itinerary:** Nothing creates stress more effectively than running late for important appointments. Plan to spend at least three hours on each campus you visit. Build *plenty* of buffer time into your travel plans to and from campuses and to and from appointments on campus. Follow these guidelines and you shouldn't find yourself constantly rushing from one place to the next. Worst-case scenario, you have some extra time on one of the campuses you're visiting—that's a win-win. Use the extra time to check out popular campus hangout spots.

- **Don't try to run the show:** From the planning of the trip through its execution, consult with your child about the itinerary. Is s/he ready for on-campus interviews? How many campuses does s/he feel capable of assimilating in one day? Once on campus, resist the temptation to advocate for your child or to manage your child's on-campus experience. Give your child plenty of opportunities to explore on his or her own. And under no circumstances should you try to participate in your child's on-campus interview. It sends a terrible message to the school (i.e., our child is not self-sufficient enough to handle this experience) and almost always produces bad results.

- **Utilize your child's free time efficiently:** While your child is exploring the campus on his or her own, make your own inquiries. Check out the surrounding area to see whether it looks safe. Search for reasonably priced restaurants and shopping near campus. Visit dormitories, dining halls, computer labs, science labs, arts facilities, and whatever else might be of interest to your child.

- **Take pictures:** Let's face it—this is way too dorky for your kid to be seen doing (your students will be focused on *fitting in*, not standing out!), but you, on the other hand, can snap away without any embarrassment. These photos will go a long way toward helping your child compare schools later.

- **Talk to other parents:** Find out what other parents think about the school, what concerns they have, and what their questions are. Listening to them will help clarify some of your own concerns—you may even learn about a new scholarship, a new college financing program, or the name of another great school for your child to consider!

Traveling with friends has its advantages, too. Friends can create a cozy and supportive environment, reducing the "high stakes" anxiety that some students feel during college visits. Also, because your friendship is probably based on mutual interests and attitudes, friends are a natural sounding board for your observations and feelings about each campus. On the downside, an unchaperoned trip with friends can quickly turn into a party. Worse still, crises may arise (e.g., someone gets completely stressed out, someone suddenly gets appendicitis) that your group is unequipped to deal with on your own. Traveling on your own poses similar risks, although it too is not without its advantages. For the truly independent, the ability to set and pursue one's own itinerary at one's own pace is an enjoyable and rewarding experience.

## GUIDELINES FOR STUDENTS

- **Set goals in advance:** What exactly do you hope to learn from your visit? Know before you go and you'll get a lot more out of it. Make a list of questions you want to answer during your trip. You may not get to ask all your questions, but just having listed them will help focus your observations while on campus.

- **Wear comfortable shoes but dress nicely:** You'll be doing a lot of walking, so choose shoes that won't turn your feet into hamburger meat. Otherwise, dress nicely; remember, you're a guest in someone else's home and you should carry yourself accordingly. That means behaving in a respectful manner, which includes dressing well. A presentable outfit is especially important if you've scheduled an on-campus interview.

- **Don't be afraid to ask questions during your tour:** Don't be shy. You're on campus to find out what you need to know; asking questions is the best way to get that done. Don't hog the tour guide's attention, but don't be a wallflower either.

- **Don't be unduly influenced by the tour guide:** Your tour guide may seem really cool, or he/she may seem like a total dork. Either way, the guide is just one of many students who attend the school; don't judge the school based on this one person. Try to meet as many other students as you can to get a broad picture of the student body. Visit the student center and the dining hall. Introduce yourself to students and ask if they wouldn't mind answering questions. If possible, schedule an overnight visit.

- **Keep a journal:** You don't have to take notes while you're visiting campus, although it's not a bad idea. However, you should record your observations and insights about each campus you visit at the end of each day of visiting. You'll probably be visiting a lot of campuses. A journal will help you remember what you liked and didn't like about each school you visited.

## BEFORE YOU GO CHECKLIST

Whether you're flying, driving, or taking the bus, there are things each parent and student can do to prepare to go college visiting. Certainly, organizing a multi-destination, extended trip is no easy endeavor. Planning ahead will help alleviate some of the stress involved in this high-stakes process, and may even allow you time to build in a family mini-vacation. With this in mind, approach the following to-do's as a series of "must-do's" to cross off your checklist before you even think about packing a suitcase, gassing the van, or trying to make that train connection to College Station. If you do the following, in your own order and according to your own timeline, you will be prepared to experience some enjoyable and productive campus visits:

- **Figure out when you are free to take a trip.** Check your school calendar to figure out when you have weeks off, three-day weekends, etc. If you plan to miss a day or two of school in order to accommodate your trip, figure out when your exams are scheduled and make sure you're not traveling during those days or during the week before.

- **Identify all the schools you want to visit.** Visit the websites of your schools of interest and check their academic calendars (while you're there, take a look at their events calendar too!). Select schools for your visiting loop based on their relative proximity to each other, whether regular classes will be in session when you're on campus, and on the availability of on-campus appointments and tours. Try to avoid visiting campuses during holidays (e.g., Thanksgiving, Christmas, Spring Break), reading periods, and exam periods—yours and theirs.

- **Create an itinerary.** Map the schools you plan to visit. Try to map a course that covers a lot of ground as efficiently as possible. Build in enough time between schools for a little bit of "down time" in which you can explore the surrounding area and check out points of interest (the Fodor's blurbs in each school's profile can assist you with this). In general, plan to visit no more than two schools per day. Quality of visit, not quantity is what you're going for.

- **Tinker with the itinerary.** Now that you know where you're going, look closely at the mileage matrices included in this book. Are there other schools you might consider that are along your route? Make a note to squeeze in a quick visit to one or more schools. Also, take time to find out whether there are some fun sights to see along your route. Yeah, this trip is about seeing schools, but that doesn't mean you can't have a *little* fun, time permitting.

- **Call the Admissions Offices of the schools you plan to visit.** Admissions Officers like to roll out the red carpet for prospective students, so why not ensure that you get your royal due by calling the Admissions Office in advance to let them know you're coming? The Admissions Office can also help you with things like finding a hotel, arranging rides from the airport, scheduling a class visit, etc. You can even schedule an interview if you choose to. Don't forget to inquire about when the tours begin and end.

- **Put it in your planner.** In order to create a schedule for your campus visits, start with the appointments you've made. Then figure out when you have to arrive and leave each school in order to make it to all your appointments. Use an online itinerary planner (such as RandMcNally.com or MapQuest.com) to estimate your travel time between schools. You'll want to make sure to build in enough time at each school that you have a chance to wander around campus and talk with students. This is the best way to get a true feel for campus life.

- **Make your overnight arrangements.** Find places to stay. If you're planning on staying on campus, make sure to contact the school and make arrangements at least two weeks in advance. Calling a month in advance is better, two months in advance better still. If you travel with your parents, they will probably need to find a place to stay off campus. Contact the school to ask for recommendations. Schools sometimes have prearranged discount rates with local hotels and motels.

- **Write out or print out your entire itinerary.** Be sure it includes maps to and from schools and hotels, driving directions, all the phone numbers you may need, etc. Research any local dining and shopping establishments you're interested in visiting and print out their names, addresses, and telephone numbers.

- **Write out or print out a list of questions you want to ask at the schools.** This is the only way to avoid that "Rats, I wish I'd asked about…" feeling that comes about an hour after you've left the campus. See our "Remember to Ask" checklist for question ideas.

Often the best resource for planning your campus visit, are the colleges' websites themselves. That should be your very first stop, as soon as you determine that a college visit is in your future. A campus visit is just the beginning of a challenging and rewarding process, and the best thing about it is that you won't be riding shotgun—you're in the driver's seat on the road to college, so enjoy the ride!

## VISITING TIP: CHECK OUT YOUR STATE SCHOOLS

Don't dismiss your local state school as being low on prestige or lacking the academic rigor of a private school. Many state universities are highly regarded and extremely competitive. If you are seeking an additional challenge, research the honors programs offered at your local state school. Selecting and getting into the right program can make all the difference.

# HOW TO USE THIS BOOK

## HOW THIS BOOK IS ORGANIZED

*Guide to College Visits: Planning Trips to Popular Campuses in the Northeast, Southeast, West, and Midwest* is organized alphabetically by region. Why organize the book by region? Because most college-bound students choose schools relatively close to home. The Princeton Review's 2006 "Our College Hopes and Worries Survey," which polled about 4,000 students, revealed that about one in five students prefers a college less than 100 miles from home. Another 42 percent prefer a school that is less than 500 miles from home. This means that about two-thirds of college students would like to stay within a reasonable driving distance of the place where they grew up. A *Pittsburgh Post-Gazette* survey revealed an even more parochial trend among the city's college-bound: Over two-thirds of the members of the class of 2005 surveyed chose colleges within 100 miles of Pittsburgh.

There are a lot of good explanations for this trend. Many are economic. Some students choose nearby schools so they can live at home, thereby saving money on dormitories and meal plans. Those who choose to live on campus still realize big savings on travel to and from home; a bus, train, or car trip is typically a lot cheaper than a long-distance flight. They can also come home more frequently for free meals, laundry, and other economically advantageous perks. Some choose to live close to home simply so they can enjoy the comforts of familiar surroundings and old friends. And some choose to attend local schools because they can't get in to the high-profile colleges most likely to lure a student across the country. Whatever their reason, more students are choosing to stay close to home than have in the past. That's why we've organized this book regionally.

## SAMPLE PROFILE

Each of the colleges and universities listed in this book has its own one-page profile. At the top of the profile is a banner that provides the name of the school, its location, contact information for the Admissions Office, and Admissions' office hours. Each profile contains a grey sidebar (the narrow column on the outside of the page which consists mainly of statistics and appointment info) divided into the categories of School At A Glance, Freshman Profile, On-Campus Appointments, and Campus Tours. The profile's main body text or "write-up" contains five headings called "Students Say," "Fodor's Says," "About the School," "Getting There," "Where to Stay," and "Campus at Its Best!" Here's what each part contains:

## The Sidebars

- **School at a Glance:** The type of school (private or public), the school's environment (urban, rural, metropolis, town), the school's annual tuition, total undergraduate enrollment, percent male/femal, and the student/faculty.

- **Freshman Profile:** The average high school GPA and middle 50 percent range of test scores for entering students.*

- **On-Campus Appointments:** Information about arranging an on-campus appointment and/or class visit with a member of the Admissions Office staff.

- **Campus Tours:** Information about available dates and times for guided campus tours.

## The Write-up

- **Students Say:** Quotes from students about life at their schools collected via our annual student survey found online at http://survey.review.com.

- **Fodor's Says:** Quotes from the bestselling Fodor's guidebooks, highlighting attractions near campus.

 Fodor's Travel is a division of Random House, Inc., a subsidiary of Bertelsmann AG, one of the world's largest media companies. Covering over 300 destinations worldwide, Fodor's guidebooks are written for a variety of travelers who have one thing in common—they are seeking the best travel options available within their budget, including the best places to stay, eat, shop, and see. A complete list of Fodor's travel guides can be found at Fodors.com, along with up-to-the-minute trip planning information, bargains, and advice from the most knowledgeable travel community on the web.

- **About the University** offers some fun, interesting facts about the school. It may include some rankings for our Best 361 Colleges, it may include some trivia, or it may just include an overview of the school's environment and reputation.

- **Getting There** provides directions for transportation by air, train, bus, car, and, where applicable, local mass transit.

- **Where to Stay** lists some nearby accommodations in different price ranges. [Cost key: $ = less than $100; $$ = between $100–$199; $$$ = more than $200]

- **Campus at Its Best!** lists one or two special events on campus; visit during these events to see what the school is like in full celebration mode. It also lists some attractions near campus: historic landmarks, amusement parks, museums, and facilities for outdoor activities.

## REGIONAL INTRODUCTION

The schools profiled in each region are preceded by an introduction describing the region's geography, climate, and culture, followed by a mileage matrix that provides distances between major cities in the region. This section also includes sample itineraries.

## Before You Go...

All right, you've got your school profiles, you've got directions, and you've even got a sample itinerary. You're ready to hit the road, right? Not quite yet. Take some time to read and reread the introductory section of this book first. It contains a lot of tips that will help you make the most of your campus visits.

When you finally hit the road, don't forget to enjoy yourself! Yes, college visits are important and should be taken seriously, but they are also wonderful adventures to new and exciting places. Soak it all in and be grateful that you're smart enough and capable enough to be looking forward to a college education. So don't be afraid to have a little fun on your trip; you've earned it!

\* In March 2005, the College Board made significant changes to the SAT exam, which included the addition of a new Writing section, and the reconstitution of the Verbal section into a new Critical Reading component. As of the date of this publication, we are still collecting data from colleges and universities on students' score ranges for the new version of the exam. In the interim, many colleges have treated scores on the new Critical Reading portion of the exam as comparable to scores from the old Verbal section. For that reason, this books lists an SAT Critical Reading score range but no Writing score range.

Since we did not want to date ourselves in this biannual guide, we decided not to report projected score ranges, as that data will be available in a few short months following the publication of this book. We gave each school in the book an opportunity to provide us with the most updated statistics for their SAT Critical Reading and Math score ranges during the profile review process. While we strive to provide the most current statistics available, we recommend that you double-check these figures with each institution for the latest and most accurate information.

# THE NORTHEAST

While there's a tendency to equate New York with New York City, the Empire State actually provides something for everyone. If you long to live in a great metropolis, there's no place like the Big Apple. But if big-city life makes you want to run for the hills, head upstate to see amazing mountains (the Adirondacks and the Catskills), lakes (the Finger Lakes and Lake George, for example), and many smaller towns and cities. And, believe it or not, New Jersey isn't simply a bedroom community for folks who work in Manhattan, nor is it called the Garden State as part of a cruel joke. Once you travel beyond New Jersey's NYC suburbs, you'll reach the Jersey Shore (pack your sunscreen) and the Delaware Water Gap (home of canoeing, kayaking, and white-water rafting).

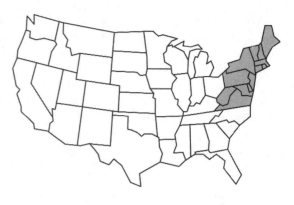

Southern Delaware and the Eastern Shore of Maryland consist primarily of flat farmland. Sitting between the Chesapeake Bay and the Atlantic Ocean, their shared peninsula provides ample opportunity to bum around on the beach, fish on the bay, and explore back country roads.

Central Maryland contains both Maryland's largest city, Baltimore, as well as its quiet and quaint historic state capital, Annapolis, along with acres of horse country. Delaware sits smack in the middle of everything, offering easy access to major metropolitan areas along the eastern seaboard: Philadelphia, New York City, Washington, DC, and Baltimore are all within a two-hour train ride.

The state of Pennsylvania can really be split into two distinct sections: Western and Eastern Pennsylvania. Western PA is anchored by the steel town of Pittsburgh and surrounded by the Allegheny Plateau to the west of the Appalachians. Here you'll find Frank Lloyd Wright's spectacular "Falling Water," as well as some water that will make you want to grab a canoe. Eastern PA is Philadelphia-centric, rich in history and the arts, and is more metropolitan than its western counterpart.

As you head north into New England, you'll find beautiful countryside and more quaint towns than you can count. Despite the commonly held notion that Connecticut is all suburbs and small cities, the state does contain large tracts of forested land, much of which is protected as state parks and state forests. Gorgeous hilly countryside abounds in the Berkshires of Western Massachusetts, while Eastern Massachusetts has Boston and the seashore, including Cape Cod, Martha's Vineyard, and Nantucket. The Appalachian Trail—a backpacker's paradise stretching from Georgia to Maine—meanders through every state in this region except Delaware, Washington, DC, and Rhode Island. While it may be the littlest state in the Union, Rhode Island boasts some of the prettiest shoreline around (and the resort prices to prove it!).

Way up north you'll find smaller and fewer cities and much wilder terrain. The Green Mountains stand majestically in Vermont, while the White Mountains cover parts of New Hampshire. Maine has mountains of its own, plus miles of rocky Atlantic coastline, stunning Acadia National Park, and many islands to explore. Last, but not least, one thing all of the Northeastern states have in common is amazing fall foliage and a full four-season calendar.

Arts and culture flourish in the Northeastern region. World-class museums, operas, symphonies, dance companies, and theaters dot the cities of the Northeast. But the region's culture extends beyond formal institutions. To get to know the region well, it's important to venture off the beaten path into eclectic neighborhoods and lesser-known locales.

If you're interested in government, you will be hard pressed to find a more appropriate region to spend four years. But even if you aren't, there's enough going on to keep you busy (and take your mind off politics!). And don't forget the bonus of that big, beautiful stretch of Atlantic coastline.

While many folks equate Connecticut with *Martha Stewart Living*, New York with high society, and Massachusetts with Yankee ingenuity, the region's culture has been impacted as much by the waves of immigrants that have entered the United States through Ellis Island and other port cities as it has by the original settlers. While nine of the original thirteen colonies are included in this region, there is no shortage of vibrant ethnic communities to explore and enjoy as well.

The Northern states tend to attract outdoorsy types who love to ski and snowboard, hike, bike, and climb. As you head further south, "getting outdoors" often means summer weekends at the shore. We all know about Washington, DC's political hyper-consciousness. But as you move further away from DC, the culture of the residents becomes less political. The Dutch-German ancestry of many in the Philadelphia region is still noticeable. The pace of things slows considerably when you arrive in Lancaster County, PA, where the Amish still live in large numbers and tourists flock to watch the horse-and-buggies. DC offers great ethnic food for the sophisticated palates of its resident diplomats, Baltimore showcases fresh seafood, and Pennsylvania's signature fare ranges from Scrapple to beloved Philly cheese-steaks.

From lobstermen (and women) working their traps off the rocky coast of Maine to the shipbuilders and fishermen of Massachusetts and Connecticut to the farmers of upstate New York and the maple syrup purveyors of Vermont, from Wall Street to the White House, the Northeast truly offers a bit of something for everyone.

# NORTHEAST MILEAGE MATRIX

| | Washington | Baltimore | College Park, | New Brunswick | Newark | New York City | Westbury | Poughkeepsie | Ithaca |
|---|---|---|---|---|---|---|---|---|---|
| Washington, DC | — | 44 | 9 | 196 | 219 | 225 | 252 | 330 | 345 |
| Baltimore, Maryland | 44 | — | 33 | 158 | 181 | 187 | 214 | 285 | 302 |
| College Park, Maryland | 9 | 33 | — | 190 | 213 | 219 | 246 | 317 | 335 |
| New Brunswick, New Jersey | 196 | 158 | 190 | — | 28 | 36 | 63 | 127 | 220 |
| Newark, New Jersey | 219 | 181 | 213 | 28 | — | 11 | 38 | 89 | 212 |
| New York City | 225 | 187 | 219 | 36 | 11 | — | 28 | 84 | 222 |
| Westbury, New York | 252 | 214 | 246 | 63 | 38 | 28 | — | 92 | 249 |
| Poughkeepsie, New York | 330 | 285 | 317 | 127 | 89 | 84 | 92 | — | 183 |
| Ithaca, New York | 345 | 302 | 335 | 220 | 212 | 222 | 249 | 183 | — |
| Rochester, New York | 400 | 358 | 390 | 330 | 323 | 332 | 390 | 301 | 89 |
| Albany, New York | 381 | 343 | 375 | 192 | 146 | 150 | 170 | 80 | 164 |
| Syracuse, New York | 385 | 340 | 363 | 239 | 237 | 246 | 277 | 220 | 57 |
| Binghamton, New York | 303 | 271 | 303 | 187 | 167 | 176 | 203 | 137 | 49 |
| Buffalo, New York | 456 | 485 | 455 | 419 | 388 | 408 | 455 | 363 | 172 |
| Pittsburgh, Pennsylvania | 245 | 247 | 244 | 346 | 358 | 367 | 410 | 405 | 334 |
| Philadelphia, Pennsylvania | 136 | 99 | 131 | 59 | 88 | 101 | 123 | 188 | 229 |
| University Park, Pennsylvania | 216 | 172 | 204 | 233 | 226 | 235 | 262 | 257 | 178 |
| Providence, Rhode Island | 404 | 367 | 399 | 215 | 190 | 184 | 185 | 193 | 325 |
| Wilmington, Delaware | 108 | 71 | 436 | 92 | 117 | 126 | 151 | 224 | 250 |
| Hartford, Connecticut | 343 | 305 | 337 | 154 | 129 | 122 | 123 | 99 | 276 |
| New Haven, Connecticut | 304 | 266 | 298 | 115 | 90 | 83 | 84 | 77 | 258 |
| Bar Harbor, Maine | 724 | 686 | 718 | 535 | 510 | 503 | 500 | 485 | 646 |
| Brunswick, Maine | 566 | 528 | 560 | 377 | 352 | 346 | 345 | 331 | 462 |
| Portland, Maine | 541 | 503 | 353 | 352 | 327 | 321 | 320 | 306 | 437 |
| Burlington, Vermont | 538 | 497 | 526 | 331 | 303 | 307 | 324 | 243 | 327 |
| Manchester, New Hampshire | 495 | 455 | 487 | 304 | 281 | 275 | 288 | 258 | 309 |
| Concord, New Hampshire | 436 | 398 | 431 | 247 | 222 | 216 | 216 | 202 | 328 |
| Cambridge, Massachusetts | 392 | 354 | 386 | 203 | 178 | 171 | 172 | 134 | 262 |
| Amherst, Massachusetts | 432 | 394 | 426 | 243 | 218 | 212 | 212 | 197 | 323 |
| Boston, Massachussetts | 440 | 406 | 434 | 250 | 226 | 214 | 219 | 205 | 330 |

# NORTHEAST MILEAGE MATRIX

| | Rochester | Albany | Syracuse | Binghamton | Buffalo | Pittsburgh | Philadelphia | University Park | Providence |
|---|---|---|---|---|---|---|---|---|---|
| Washington, DC | 400 | 381 | 385 | 303 | 456 | 245 | 136 | 216 | 404 |
| Baltimore, Maryland | 358 | 343 | 340 | 271 | 485 | 247 | 99 | 172 | 367 |
| College Park, Maryland | 390 | 375 | 363 | 303 | 455 | 244 | 131 | 204 | 399 |
| New Brunswick, New Jersey | 330 | 192 | 239 | 187 | 419 | 346 | 59 | 233 | 215 |
| Newark, New Jersey | 323 | 146 | 237 | 167 | 388 | 358 | 88 | 226 | 190 |
| New York City | 332 | 150 | 246 | 176 | 408 | 367 | 101 | 235 | 184 |
| Westbury, New York | 390 | 170 | 277 | 203 | 455 | 410 | 123 | 262 | 185 |
| Poughkeepsie, New York | 301 | 80 | 220 | 137 | 363 | 405 | 188 | 257 | 193 |
| Ithaca, New York | 89 | 164 | 57 | 49 | 172 | 334 | 229 | 178 | 325 |
| Rochester, New York | — | 225 | 87 | 160 | 73 | 284 | 340 | 235 | 386 |
| Albany, New York | 225 | — | 146 | 140 | 289 | 511 | 252 | 324 | 163 |
| Syracuse, New York | 87 | 146 | — | 73 | 149 | 359 | 253 | 234 | 306 |
| Binghamton, New York1 | 60 | 140 | 73 | — | 222 | 393 | 183 | 208 | 314 |
| Buffalo, New York | 73 | 289 | 149 | 222 | — | 216 | 428 | 224 | 449 |
| Pittsburgh, Pennsylvania | 284 | 511 | 359 | 393 | 216 | — | 304 | 137 | 561 |
| Philadelphia, Pennsylvania | 340 | 252 | 253 | 183 | 428 | 304 | — | 224 | 275 |
| University Park, Pennsylvania | 235 | 324 | 234 | 208 | 224 | 137 | 224 | — | 414 |
| Providence, Rhode Island | 386 | 163 | 306 | 314 | 449 | 561 | 275 | 414 | — |
| Wilmington, Delaware | 357 | 282 | 270 | 200 | 430 | 297 | 29 | 185 | 303 |
| Hartford, Connecticut | 336 | 113 | 256 | 234 | 399 | 500 | 213 | 352 | 86 |
| New Haven, Connecticut | 373 | 151 | 302 | 212 | 436 | 461 | 174 | 313 | 103 |
| Bar Harbor, Maine | 667 | 453 | 587 | 589 | 730 | 937 | 589 | 745 | 329 |
| Brunswick, Maine | 523 | 300 | 443 | 432 | 586 | 751 | 433 | 564 | 181 |
| Portland, Maine | 498 | 270 | 418 | 407 | 561 | 689 | 408 | 539 | 156 |
| Burlington, Vermont | 352 | 151 | 271 | 291 | 414 | 625 | 378 | 496 | 274 |
| Manchester, New Hampshire | 447 | 149 | 367 | 361 | 510 | 680 | 365 | 526 | 127 |
| Concord, New Hampshire | 388 | 165 | 308 | 303 | 415 | 593 | 306 | 437 | 51 |
| Cambridge, Massachusetts | 323 | 100 | 243 | 238 | 386 | 552 | 262 | 404 | 89 |
| Amherst, Massachusetts | 384 | 161 | 304 | 299 | 447 | 589 | 302 | 432 | 47 |
| Boston, Massachussetts | 391 | 168 | 310 | 306 | 453 | 596 | 310 | 439 | 50 |

# NORTHEAST MILEAGE MATRIX

| | Wilmington | Hatford | New Haven | Bar Harbor | Brunswick | Prtland | Burlington | Manchester | Concord |
|---|---|---|---|---|---|---|---|---|---|
| Washington, DC | 108 | 343 | 304 | 724 | 566 | 541 | 538 | 481 | 495 |
| Baltimore, Maryland | 71 | 305 | 266 | 686 | 528 | 503 | 493 | 440 | 455 |
| College Park, Maryland | 436 | 337 | 298 | 718 | 560 | 353 | 525 | 475 | 487 |
| New Brunswick, New Jersey | 92 | 154 | 115 | 535 | 377 | 352 | 310 | 289 | 304 |
| Newark, New Jersey | 117 | 129 | 90 | 510 | 352 | 327 | 304 | 264 | 281 |
| New York City | 126 | 122 | 83 | 503 | 346 | 321 | 308 | 206 | 275 |
| Westbury, New York | 151 | 123 | 84 | 500 | 345 | 320 | 323 | 273 | 288 |
| Poughkeepsie, New York | 224 | 99 | 77 | 485 | 331 | 306 | 233 | 243 | 258 |
| Ithaca, New York | 250 | 276 | 258 | 646 | 462 | 437 | 327 | 372 | 309 |
| Rochester, New York | 357 | 336 | 373 | 667 | 523 | 498 | 352 | 432 | 447 |
| Albany, New York | 282 | 113 | 151 | 453 | 300 | 270 | 154 | 212 | 149 |
| Syracuse, New York | 270 | 256 | 302 | 587 | 443 | 418 | 270 | 352 | 367 |
| Binghamton, New York | 200 | 234 | 212 | 589 | 432 | 407 | 291 | 346 | 361 |
| Buffalo, New York | 430 | 399 | 436 | 730 | 586 | 561 | 415 | 493 | 510 |
| Pittsburgh, Pennsylvania | 297 | 500 | 461 | 937 | 751 | 689 | 624 | 629 | 680 |
| Philadelphia, Pennsylvania | 29 | 213 | 174 | 589 | 433 | 408 | 378 | 351 | 365 |
| University Park, Pennsylvania | 185 | 352 | 313 | 745 | 564 | 539 | 496 | 511 | 526 |
| Providence, Rhode Island | 303 | 86 | 103 | 329 | 181 | 156 | 275 | 112 | 127 |
| Wilmington, Delaware | — | 168 | 203 | 625 | 465 | 440 | 432 | 378 | 393 |
| Hartford, Connecticut | 168 | — | 39 | 381 | 228 | 203 | 236 | 140 | 154 |
| New Haven, Connecticut | 203 | 39 | — | 417 | 264 | 239 | 273 | 178 | 193 |
| Bar Harbor, Maine | 625 | 381 | 417 | — | 135 | 175 | 328 | 268 | 288 |
| Brunswick, Maine | 465 | 228 | 264 | 135 | — | 28 | 239 | 119 | 134 |
| Portland, Maine | 440 | 203 | 239 | 175 | 28 | — | 257 | 94 | 109 |
| Burlington, Vermont | 431 | 235 | 272 | 328 | 234 | 257 | — | 166 | 152 |
| Manchester, New Hampshire | 393 | 154 | 193 | 288 | 134 | 109 | 152 | 18 | — |
| Concord, New Hampshire | 339 | 98 | 134 | 282 | 133 | 108 | 217 | 52 | 68 |
| Cambridge, Massachusetts | 292 | 52 | 89 | 353 | 199 | 174 | 197 | 92 | 96 |
| Amherst, Massachusetts | 335 | 94 | 129 | 291 | 141 | 116 | 219 | 56 | 71 |
| Boston, Massachussetts | 338 | 101 | 136 | 280 | 132 | 107 | 216 | 53 | 68 |

# NORTHEAST MILEAGE MATRIX

|  | Cambridge | Amherst | Boston |
|---|---|---|---|
| Washington, DC | 436 | 392 | 440 |
| Baltimore, Maryland | 398 | 354 | 406 |
| College Park, Maryland | 431 | 386 | 434 |
| New Brunswick, New Jersey | 247 | 203 | 250 |
| Newark, New Jersey | 222 | 178 | 226 |
| New York City | 216 | 171 | 214 |
| Westbury, New York | 216 | 172 | 219 |
| Poughkeepsie, New York | 202 | 134 | 205 |
| Ithaca, New York | 328 | 262 | 330 |
| Rochester, New York | 388 | 323 | 391 |
| Albany, New York | 165 | 100 | 168 |
| Syracuse, New York | 308 | 243 | 310 |
| Binghamton, New York | 303 | 238 | 306 |
| Buffalo, New York | 415 | 386 | 453 |
| Pittsburgh, Pennsylvania | 593 | 552 | 596 |
| Philadelphia, Pennsylvania | 306 | 262 | 310 |
| University Park, Pennsylvania | 437 | 404 | 439 |
| Providence, Rhode Island | 51 | 89 | 50 |
| Wilmington, Delaware | 339 | 292 | 338 |
| Hartford, Connecticut | 98 | 52 | 101 |
| New Haven, Connecticut | 134 | 89 | 136 |
| Bar Harbor, Maine | 282 | 353 | 280 |
| Brunswick, Maine | 133 | 199 | 132 |
| Portland, Maine | 108 | 174 | 107 |
| Burlington, Vermont | 217 | 197 | 216 |
| Manchester, New Hampshire | 68 | 96 | 53 |
| Concord, New Hampshire | — | 91 | 68 |
| Cambridge, Massachusetts | 91 | — | 69 |
| Amherst, Massachusetts | 7 | 86 | 94 |
| Boston, Massachussetts | 3 | 94 | — |

# NORTHEAST SAMPLE ITINERARIES

There are tons of schools in the Northeast region, and most of the major cities are located within convenient driving distance of one another. So planning a travel itinerary for your campus visits should be relatively easy. The itineraries below assume a Point A to Point B trajectory, involving several overnight stays. Before you head out, be sure to gather maps to and from schools and hotels, driving directions, and all the phone numbers you may need. Research any local dining and shopping establishments you're interested in visiting and print out their names, addresses, and telephone numbers. Finally, be realistic: You're not going to cover all the ground you want to cover in just a few days. In general, try not to see more than two (three at most) colleges a day; too many visits in one day and your brain will start to atrophy. The itineraries listed below are just suggestions—you can and should modify them to suit your individual needs.

## IF YOU'VE GOT SEVEN DAYS:

**Starting Point:** Washington, DC

**Saturday:** American University, The Catholic University of America
Georgetown University, Howard University
Stay overnight in Washington, DC.

**Sunday:** University of Maryland—College Park, Johns Hopkins University, Goucher College, Loyola College in Maryland
Drive to Philadelphia. Stay overnight in Philadelphia.

**Monday:** Swarthmore College, Temple University, University of Pennsylvania, Haverford College
Stay overnight in Philadelphia.

**Tuesday:** Franking and Marshall College, Pennsylvania State University
Drive to New York City. Stay overnight in New York City.

**Wednesday:** Columbia University, Fordham University, New York University, Eugene Lang College, Parsons School of Design
Stay overnight in New York City.

**Thursday:** Vassar College, Hofstra University
Drive to Hartford, CT area.

**Thursday PM:** Wesleyan University, Trinity College
Drive to Boston. Stay overnight in Boston.

**Friday:** Boston University, Northeastern University, Emerson College, Harvard University, Tufts University
Head home.

## IF YOU'VE GOT THREE DAYS:

**Starting Point:** Boston, Massachusetts

**Friday:** Boston College, Boston University, Northeastern University, Massachusetts Institute of Technology, Harvard University, Franklin W. Olin College of Engineering
Stay overnight in Boston.

**Saturday:** Wellesley College, University of Massachusetts—Amherst, Amherst College, Smith College, Hampshire College
Stay overnight in Hartford, Connecticut.

**Sunday:** Trinity College, Wesleyan University, Yale University, Brown University
Stay overnight in Providence, Rhode Island.

# NORTHEAST SCHOOLS

# ALBRIGHT COLLEGE

PO Box 15234, Thirteenth and Bern Streets, Reading, PA 19612-5234
**Telephone:** 610-921-7799 • **E-mail:** admission@albright.edu
**Website:** www.albright.edu

## STUDENTS SAY

"This school fosters such a healthy, close-knit relationship that you will very frequently find students taking other students 'under their wing.'"

## FODOR'S SAYS

"Pennsylvania's 116 state parks have more than 7,000 campsites."

## ABOUT THE SCHOOL

Albright's small class sizes ensure a great deal of interaction between students and professors. Additionally, the Experience Program extends learning beyond the classroom. A mandatory component of every student's curriculum, the program requires undergrads to attend lectures, debates, and films on current issues. Outside of academics, students avail themselves of numerous extracurricular activities, especially Greek life and athletics.

## GETTING THERE

**BY AIR:** Visitors can fly into Philadelphia International Airport, roughly an hour and a half from Reading.

**BY TRAIN:** The nearest Amtrak stations are located in Coatesville and Downingtown, both approximately 25 miles away. Take a taxi to get to campus.

**BY BUS:** Reading can be reached by Greyhound, Bieber, and Capitol Trailways Bus Lines. The terminal is just five minutes from campus.

**BY CAR:** From the South: Follow the Baltimore and Washington, DC (Interstate 83 North) to York (Route 30 East) and Lancaster (Route 222 North). Take the Baltimore Beltway (Interstate 695) to Interstate 83 North, getting off at Exit 21A. Continue on to Route 30 East. This will take you to 222 North. Proceed on the new road into the Reading area. As you enter a commercial area, there will be an exit for 222 North to Allentown. Do not exit. Proceed straight ahead onto Route 12 East. Follow 12 East for roughly two and a half miles to the 11th Street Exit. Take the exit ramp to your right and get onto 11th Street. At the traffic light (about two blocks), take a left onto Rockland Street. Drive to the next traffic light (two blocks), and make a right onto 13th Street. At the first stop sign (two blocks), take a left onto Bern Street. You'll then need to take an immediate right, turning into a campus parking lot. At the far end of the lot there will be signs for Admission guests. From the East via PA Turnpike (I-76 West): Take the Pennsylvania Turnpike, 76 West to Exit 298 (Morgantown). Follow the signs to Interstate 176 North. From 176 North you'll proceed to 422 West (Reading). Follow 422 West for roughly two miles, taking the 12 East (Pricetown) Exit. Note: Do not take the Business Exit. (You will pass exits for West Reading and the North Wyomissing Boulevard prior to the 12 East Exit.) Continue on 12 East for around two and a half miles to the 11th Street Exit. Follow "From the South" directions above.

**LOCAL:** For local taxi service call Reading Metro Taxi (610-374-5111).

## WHERE TO STAY

For hotel accommodations, try: Inn at Reading (610-372-7811, $–$$), Wyndham Reading (610-372-3700, $$), or Sheraton Reading Hotel (610-376-3811, $$).

## CAMPUS AT ITS BEST!

When Albright students decide to put down the books and relax they don't have to look far for fun and distraction. The student activities calendar is always teeming with social options. You can attend a salsa dancing party, see Chinese dragon dancers perform, or experience Oozeball, a raucous game of volleyball with a little mud thrown in for good measure. Conversely, if you're in search of some of alone time, consider stopping by Sylvan Chapel. The oldest building on campus, Sylvan is currently open for meditation. There's a charming pond adjacent to the building and it's an Albright tradition for classmates celebrating birthdays to be thrown in.

# ALFRED UNIVERSITY

Alumni Hall, One Saxon Drive, Alfred, NY 14802-1205
**Telephone:** 607-871-2115 • **E-mail:** admissions@alfred.edu
**Hours:** Monday–Friday, 8:30 A.M.–4:30 P.M.; Saturday, 9:00–NOON and by appointment

## STUDENTS SAY

"The diverse community of Alfred . . . makes life very interesting and fun here."

## FODOR'S SAYS

"The westernmost section of New York State is bordered by Lake Erie on the west and Lake Ontario on the north. This Niagara River, which connects the two lakes, and Niagara Falls—both shared by the United States and Canada—are in the northwest corner of the region."

## ABOUT THE SCHOOL

Located in the rolling landscape of western New York, Alfred University is home to 2,000 undergrads who reap the benefits of an intimate, student-centered learning environment. While city living in Rochester and/or Buffalo is a few hours away, students at Alfred have become skilled at finding fun in their rural setting.

## GETTING THERE

**BY AIR:** Buffalo Niagara International and Greater Rochester International airports are each two hours away. They can be accessed through a combination of bus and taxi. The university offers limited shuttle service to both airports during official breaks.

**BY TRAIN:** Amtrak services Buffalo, Rochester, and Syracuse. Car and bus are the best options for accessing the stations.

**BY BUS:** Numerous bus lines stop at or near campus. These include Greyhound (Alfred station), the Adirondack Transit Lines, and ShortLine buses. The Alfred Travel Center also runs daily trips between Alfred and New York City.

**BY CAR:** From I-90 West (Buffalo): I-90 is also called the New York State Thruway. Take this to Exit 54, which puts you onto Route 400 South. As you travel Route 400 South, it will change to Route 16, Route 39 (East), and finally Route 98. From Route 98, turn onto Route 293 until you reach Belmont. At Belmont, make a left onto Route 244 East, which leads to Alfred. From I-390 South (Rochester): Follow I-390 South. Turn right onto Route 36 (Exit 4), which is the second Dansville exit. Drive through Arkport. Get onto Route I-86 West. Take exit 33 in Almond, where you'll see signs for the university. Follow the signs to Route 21 South. Then turn onto Route 244, which leads to Alfred. From Route 15 North: Follow Route 15 North to Corning, where you'll turn onto I-86/Route 17. Travel west to Almond, Exit 33. Follow the signs to Route 21 South. Then turn onto Route 244, which leads to Alfred.

**LOCAL:** Green Dot Taxi service (607-201-0200) operates out of nearby Hornell. Allegany County Transit (800-284-2415) provides local bus service.

## WHERE TO STAY

Saxon Inn (607-871-2600, $$–$$$) is the university's on-campus hotel that has 25 rooms and is open to all visitors. Other lodging options include the Country Cabin Manor Bed and Breakfast (607-587-8504, $$–$$$) and Economy Inn (607-587-9555, $).

| SCHOOL AT A GLANCE | |
| --- | --- |
| Type of School | Private |
| Environment | Rural |
| Tuition | $21,250 |
| Enrollment | 1,971 |
| % Male/Female | 51/49 |
| Student/Faculty Ratio | 12:1 |

| FRESHMAN PROFILE | |
| --- | --- |
| Range SAT | |
| Critical Reading | 500–610 |
| Range SAT Math | 500–610 |
| Range ACT Composite | 20–26 |

| ON-CAMPUS APPOINTMENTS | |
| --- | --- |
| Advance Notice | Yes, other |
| Appointment | Required |
| Saturdays | No |
| Average Length | 60 min |
| Info Sessions | Yes |
| Class Visits | Yes |

| CAMPUS TOURS | |
| --- | --- |
| Appointment | Required |
| Dates | Year Round |
| Times | 9:00 A.M.–3:00 P.M. |
| Average Length | 60 min |

---

## CAMPUS AT ITS BEST!

Consider visiting Alfred on Discovery Day in April—a day set aside specifically for high school students looking to experience everything the campus has to offer. After you work up an appetite at the new, state-of-the-art Equestrian Center, enjoy a fine dining experience at Alfred's nationally-recognized Cultural Café, specializing in the world's food and culture. Finally, venture just off campus to stop by The Schein-Joseph International Museum of Ceramic Art and view the over 8,000 glass and ceramic objects in their collection.

# ALLEGHENY COLLEGE

Admissions Office, Box 5, 520 North Main Street, Meadville, PA 16335
**Telephone:** 814-332-4351 • **E-mail:** admissions@allegheny.edu
**Website:** www.allegheny.edu • **Hours:** Monday–Friday, 9:00 A.M.–3:00 P.M.; Saturday, 8:30 A.M.–11:30 A.M.

## STUDENTS SAY

"Allegheny's strengths are its ample amounts of opportunity [for students] to excel both in and outside of the classroom. The college provides numerous internship opportunities."

## FODOR'S SAYS

"Allegheny National Forest in the northwestern part of the state has hiking and cross-country skiing trails, three rivers suitable for canoeing, and stream fishing."

## ABOUT THE SCHOOL

With 2,100 undergrads, Allegheny College is a liberal arts school known for attracting students with unusual combination of interests, skills, and talents. Located in northwestern Pennsylvania, 90 miles away from big cities like Pittsburgh and Cleveland, students have plenty of time to tackle their heavy school loads during the week. Hard work is the norm, and on-campus activities are plentiful.

## GETTING THERE

**BY AIR:** Erie International Airport is closest to campus. From there, you can connect with Greyhound bus lines or rent a car for the 45-minute trip to Meadville. Prospective students can arrange to have a school representative meet them at the Erie airport. Students may also fly into Pittsburgh International Airport, just 90 minutes away.

**BY TRAIN:** The closest Amtrak train stations are in Erie, Pittsburgh, or Cleveland. However, it is much more convenient to rent a car from the airport to get to campus.

**BY BUS:** Greyhound bus lines service Meadville daily. There is also local bus service from the Meadville Greyhound station to Allegheny departing at nine minutes past the hour Monday–Saturday, 9:00 A.M.–5:30 P.M., with earlier and later departures some days. Contact Crawford Area Transportation Authority at 814-336-5600 for complete schedule information.

**BY CAR:** From I-79: Travel on I-79 to Exit 147A. Continue on Route 322 East, from which you take the Park Avenue Exit. Follow Park Avenue for six traffic lights to Chestnut Street and turn right. At the next light, turn left around Diamond Park. At the end of the park, veer right onto North Main Street. After two lights on North Main Street, bear right up the hill. After passing campus, turn left onto Allegheny Street. At the first stop sign, turn left onto Park Avenue. After passing three large buildings, take the first left into the Admissions parking area. The Admissions Office is located in Schultz Hall, the first building below the parking area.

**LOCAL:** Corey Transportation (814-336-5000) provides shuttle service to the college, and the Crawford Area Transportation Authority provides bus service in the area. Call Lafayette Taxi Service at 814-724-8600 if you'd rather take a taxi around campus.

## WHERE TO STAY

Among the many area accommodations are Motel 6 (814-724-6366, $), Holiday Inn Express (814-724-6012, $$), and Bethaven Inn (814-336-4223, $).

## CAMPUS AT ITS BEST!

Prospective students will get to see Allegheny from an interesting vantage point if they choose to walk across the Rustic Bridge. It's a school tradition for freshmen to race and see who can steal the 13th plank. Don't worry—maintenance always keeps a supply of replacement planks on hand so you are guaranteed safe crossing. Next, make your way to Ford Chapel, a venue frequently used for lectures and concerts. The Single Voice Reading Series and the Alexander String Quartet perform here.

# AMERICAN UNIVERSITY

4400 Massachusetts Avenue, Northwest, Washington, DC 20016-8001
**Telephone:** 202-885-6000 • **E-mail:** admissions@american.edu
**Website:** www.american.edu • **Hours:** Monday–Friday, 9:00 A.M.–5:00 P.M.; Saturday, 9:00 A.M.–1:00 P.M.

## STUDENTS SAY

"AU is about the international awareness, political engagement, and altruistic ambition of its students."

## FODOR'S SAYS

"Just across the street from the Fashion Centre at Pentagon City—a destination in itself for shoppers—is the DEA Museum, within the U.S. Drug Enforcement Administration's headquarters. It explores the effect of drugs on American society."

## ABOUT THE SCHOOL

Located in northwest Washington, DC, American University is home to more than 5,000 undergrads. AU's location—in a major urban area that just happens to be the nation's capital—guarantees that students have remarkable access to leaders in government, business, and the arts.

## GETTING THERE

**BY AIR:** The airports closest to campus are Dulles International Airport, Baltimore-Washington International Airport, and Ronald Reagan Washington National Airport. All airports can be reached by public transportation including subway and taxi. (AU provides a shuttle bus to transport students to and from the nearest Metro subway station, running at 15 minute intervals.)

**BY TRAIN:** Amtrak operates out of Union Station in downtown Washington, DC.

**BY BUS:** Greyhound services Union Station and Washington Station, both in downtown DC.

**BY CAR:** From I-495 (Capital Beltway): From I-495 take Exit 39, following the signs for River Road (also called Maryland Route 190) East toward Washington, DC. At the fifth traffic light, make a right onto Goldsboro Road (Maryland Route 614). Turn left at the first traffic light (Massachusetts Avenue, or Maryland Route 396). Follow Massachusetts Avenue for two miles. Pass through the Westmoreland Circle. Approximately a mile later, you'll come to a second traffic circle called Ward Circle. Enter the circle and take the first right turn onto Nebraska Avenue. The AU campus is on your right. To reach I-495 from Northeast of Washington: Take I-95 South to I-495 West toward Silver Spring. To reach I-495 from Northwest of Washington: Take I-270 South. Eventually, I-270 divides; veer right toward Northern Virginia (not toward Washington, DC) until it merges with I-495. To reach I-495 from South or West: Depending on the starting point, take either I-95 North or I-66 East. Both highways lead to I-495. Merge onto I-495 North.

**LOCAL:** Metro, Washington, DC's public transportation system, offers citywide bus and subway service. The closest subway stop is at Tenley Circle, less than a mile from campus, at the corner of Albemarle and 40th Street. The subway can be accessed by foot, car, taxi, bus, or AC shuttle service.

## WHERE TO STAY

Among the many area accommodations are Savoy Suites Georgetown (202-337-9700, $$$+), Woodley Park Guest House (202-667-0218, $$$), and Days Inn (202-244-5600, $$).

| SCHOOL AT A GLANCE | |
| --- | --- |
| Type of School | Private |
| Environment | Metropolis |
| Tuition | $29,206 |
| Enrollment | 5,788 |
| % Male/Female | 38/62 |
| Student/Faculty Ratio | 14:1 |

| FRESHMAN PROFILE | |
| --- | --- |
| Range SAT | |
| Critical Reading | 600-690 |
| Range SAT Math | 580-670 |
| Range ACT Composite | 26-30 |
| Average HS GPA | 3.5 |

| ON-CAMPUS APPOINTMENTS | |
| --- | --- |
| Advance Notice | Yes, 2 weeks |
| Appointment | Required |
| Saturdays | Sometimes |
| Average Length | 45 min |
| Info Sessions | Yes |
| Class Visits | Yes |

| CAMPUS TOURS | |
| --- | --- |
| Appointment | Preferred |
| Dates | Year Round |
| Times | M–F 10:00 A.M., |
| | 12:00 P.M., 1:00 P.M., 3:00 P.M. |
| Average Length | 60 min |

## CAMPUS AT ITS BEST!

When visiting AU, be sure to check out the Katzen Arts Center. Whether hosting a dance ensemble, the AU Symphony, or a lecture from a museum curator, the Center always has something great on the program. Sample the university's wide variety of culinary options at Bon Appetit, the on-campus eating facility. And make sure you set aside time to get off campus and explore our nation's capital. The International Spy Museum is an exciting destination.

# AMHERST COLLEGE

Campus Box 2231, PO Box 5000, Amherst, MA 01002
**Telephone:** 413-542-2328 • **E-mail:** admission@amherst.edu • **Website:** www.amherst.edu
**Hours:** Monday–Friday, 8:30 A.M.–4:30 P.M.; Saturday, 9:00 A.M.–NOON

## SCHOOL AT A GLANCE

| | |
|---|---|
| Type of School | Private |
| Environment | Town |
| Tuition | $34,280 |
| Enrollment | 1,612 |
| % Male/Female | 52/48 |
| Student/Faculty Ratio | 8:1 |

### FRESHMAN PROFILE

| | |
|---|---|
| Range SAT | |
| Critical Reading | 670–780 |
| Range SAT Math | 680–780 |
| Range ACT Composite | 29–33 |

### ON-CAMPUS APPOINTMENTS

| | |
|---|---|
| Info Sessions | Yes |
| Class Visits | Yes |

### CAMPUS TOURS

| | |
|---|---|
| Appointment | Not Required |
| Dates | Varies |
| Times | Varies |
| Average Length | 60 min |

## STUDENTS SAY

"The close proximity of four other colleges adds a lot of life to the area. The athletic facilities are top-notch and the dorms are palatial."

## FODOR'S SAYS

Amherst is home to the "Emily Dickinson Museum. The famed Amherst poet lived here her entire life, and many of her belongings are contained within (though her manuscripts are housed elsewhere)."

## ABOUT THE SCHOOL

Amherst College is renowned as one of the nation's leading liberal arts institutions—a reputation that, time and again, students assure us is well deserved. An hour and a half from Boston, Amherst offers an idyllic setting in easy reach of urban enticements. With four other colleges in the area, Amherst occupies a notably academic corner of western Massachusetts.

## GETTING THERE

**BY AIR:** Bradley International Airport is 45 minutes from campus. Boston's Logan Airport is two hours away. Valley Transport (413-253-1350) and Seemo Shuttle (413-549-7433) offer regular shuttle service to and from both airports.

**BY TRAIN:** Amtrak runs limited service through Amherst. Regular service operates out of Springfield, Massachusetts, located half an hour from campus.

**BY BUS:** Peter Pan Bus Lines, a partner of Greyhound, operates regularly from Amherst (800-237-8747).

**BY CAR:** From I-90 West: Follow I-90 (Mass Turnpike) to I-91, Exit 4. Turn onto Route 9, Exit 19. Take Route 9 East to Route 116 South. At the intersection of Routes 9 and 116, you'll see the campus straight ahead. From I-91 South: Take I-91 to Exit 19 which turns into Route 9 East. Take Route 9 East to Route 116 South. These roads intersect at a stoplight at the top of a hill where you'll see Amherst College buildings in front of you. From I-91 North: Take I-91 to Exit 20, which turns into Route 9 East. Take Route 9 East to Route 116 South. These roads intersect at a stoplight at the top of a hill where you'll see Amherst College buildings in front of you. From I-95 South: Take I-95 to I-495 South. Take I-495 South to Exit 29B (Route 2 West). Take Route 2 West to Route 202 South. Take Route 202 South to Amherst Road in Pelham; turn right. Take Amherst Road toward Amherst. (The road changes names to Pelham Road and then to Main Street.) In downtown Amherst, turn left on South Pleasant Street. Continue for two blocks to the stoplight at the intersection with Route 116. Proceed straight through the light—most Amherst College buildings are in front of you.

**LOCAL:** The University of Massachusetts Transit System runs local service, including transportation between the Five Colleges.

## WHERE TO STAY

You'll find many lodging options in Amherst, including the Amherst Hotel (413-256-8122, $), University Lodge (413-256-8111, $), Hampton Inn (413-586-4851, $$), and the Yankee Peddler Inn and Hotel (413-532-9494, $$). The Lord Jeffrey Inn, adjacent to campus, offers rooms at a broad range of rates, depending on the time of year (413-253-2576).

## CAMPUS AT ITS BEST!

With over 16,000 works from American and European masters, Amherst's Mead Art Museum is not to be missed. The city of Amherst also houses the renowned Emily Dickinson Museum. Located in the center of town, it honors the life and work of the respected poet. Those touring the college in the summer should catch a show at the Ko Festival of Performance. This theater festival has been presented on Amherst's campus for the past 15 years.

# BABSON COLLEGE

Lunder Hall, Babson Park, MA 02457
**Telephone:** 781-239-5522 • **E-mail:** ugradadmission@babson.edu
**Hours:** Monday–Friday and Saturday, 8:30 A.M.–4:30 P.M. and by appointment

## STUDENTS SAY

"Everyone at Babson is convinced they will become millionaires by the time they hit 30."

## FODOR'S SAYS

"The dazzling foliage and cool temperatures make fall the best time to visit western Massachusetts."

## ABOUT THE SCHOOL

Babson College, a school best known for its business programs and entrepreneurship training, draws many of its students for the hands-on management experience it offers. During freshman year, all students take a Foundations of Management and Entrepreneurship (FME) course series in which they conceive and launch a small business.

## GETTING THERE

**BY AIR:** Logan International Airport is the closest airport to campus. From Logan, take a taxi to campus. Students may also take the Logan Express bus to Framingham, and then transfer to a taxi to get to campus.

**BY TRAIN:** Amtrak stops at South Station in Boston. From there, take the Framingham/Worcester commuter rail to Wellesley Hills. Then take a short cab ride to Babson's campus.

**BY BUS:** Take a nonexpress Peter Pan or Greyhound bus to the Riverside MBTA terminal. The fare is about $8. Then take a taxi to Babson. The fare will be about $15 plus tip.

**BY CAR:** From Boston: Take the Massachusetts Turnpike (I-90) to Exit 15. After the toll, go South on I-95 (Route 128) to Exit 20B (Route 9 West). Continue on Route 9 West to the Route 16 Exit. Turn left onto Route 16 West (also called Washington Street). Follow Route 16 West to Forest Street. Turn left on Forest Street and follow it to the main entrance to the college. From the West: Take the Massachusetts Turnpike to Exit 14. After the toll, go South on I-95 (Route 128) to Exit 20B (Route 9 West). Continue on Route 9 West to the Route 16 Exit. Turn left onto Route 16 West (also called Washington Street). Continue to follow "From Boston" directions above. From South of Boston and Cape Cod: Take Interstate 95 (Route 128) North to Exit 20B (Route 9 West) and continue on Route 9 West to the Route 16 Exit. Turn left onto Route 16 West (also called Washington Street). Continue to follow "From Boston" directions above. From North of Boston: Take Interstate 95 (Route 128) South to Exit 20B (Route 9 West) and continue on Route 9 West to the Route 16 Exit. Turn left onto Route 16 West (also called Washington Street). Continue to follow "From Boston" directions above.

**LOCAL:** Take the Blue Line "T" inbound four stops to Government Center. Walk upstairs and take the Green Line outbound Riverside D train to Woodland, the next to last stop on the D line. Then, from Woodland, take a taxi to Babson College. Local taxi service includes Wellesley Veteran's Taxi (781-235-1600) and Wellesley Transportation (781-235-2200.)

## WHERE TO STAY

The best places to crash near campus are the Travelodge (508-655-2222, $), Babson Executive Conference Center (781-239-4000, $$), DoubleTree Guest Suites (781-890-6767, $$$), and The Four Seasons Hotel (617-338-4400, $$$).

| SCHOOL AT A GLANCE | |
| --- | --- |
| Type of School | Private |
| Environment | Village |
| Tuition | $32,256 |
| Enrollment | 1,725 |
| % Male/Female | 61/39 |
| Student/Faculty Ratio | 14:1 |

| FRESHMAN PROFILE | |
| --- | --- |
| Range SAT | |
| Critical Reading | 570-660 |
| Range SAT Math | 610-690 |

| ON-CAMPUS APPOINTMENTS | |
| --- | --- |
| Advance Notice | Yes, 2 weeks |
| Appointment | Required |
| Saturdays | No |
| Average Length | 30 min |
| Info Sessions | Yes |
| Class Visits | No |

| CAMPUS TOURS | |
| --- | --- |
| Appointment | Not Required |
| Dates | Year Round |
| Times | 10:00 A.M. and 2:00 P.M. |
| Average Length | 60 min |

## CAMPUS AT ITS BEST!

Consider visiting during one the school's specially designated Preview Days. Held throughout the fall and spring, you are guaranteed to learn a good deal about life at Babson. Of course, with Babson's close proximity to Boston, you'll probably want to explore the city as well. IMAX movies at the Museum of Science and Red Sox games are popular entertainment options.

# BARD COLLEGE

Office of Admissions, Annandale-on-Hudson, NY 12504
**Telephone:** 845-758-7472 • **E-mail:** admission@bard.edu
**Hours:** Monday–Friday, 9:00 A.M.–5:00 P.M.

## STUDENTS SAY

"Bard College is all about taking academics seriously, but understanding that social growth is just as important."

## FODOR'S SAYS

"Annandale-on-Hudson is home to the beautiful Bard College campus and its famous Fisher Center for the Performing Arts. Take the scenic route by traveling north to campus via River Road, or head to Tivoli, on Route 9G two miles north of Bard, [which] is known for its restaurants, artistic community, and active nightlife."

## ABOUT THE SCHOOL

A stalwart in American liberal arts education, Bard College champions the life of the mind. The college's out-of-the-way location in New York's scenic Hudson Valley provides an ideal haven for the pursuit of a rigorous education. Robust intellectual debates, regular ventures into the great outdoors, and frequent jaunts to NYC keep Bard students sharp, focused, and energized.

## GETTING THERE

**BY AIR:** Albany International is the nearest airport to campus (50 miles). New York City airports are also an excellent option. Also worth mentioning is Stewart International Airport in New Windsor.

**BY TRAIN:** Amtrak runs from New York City or Albany to Rhinecliff, nine miles from campus. Metro-North offers service from New York City to Poughkeepsie (half an hour south of Bard).

**BY BUS:** Greyhound and Short Line bus services stop in Rhinebeck, several miles south of Annandale-on-Hudson.

**BY CAR:** From I-84 West: Turn off I-84 West at Taconic State Parkway. Follow Parkway North until Red Hook/Route 199 exit. Go West on Route 199, passing through Red Hook. At Route 9G, turn right and drive North. Bard is less than two miles ahead. From I-90 West (Massachusetts Turnpike): Continue on I-90 into New York. Take Exit B-2 (Taconic Parkway). Follow Parkway South to Red Hook/Route 199 exit. Go West on Route 199, passing through Red Hook. At Route 9G, turn right and drive North. Bard is less than two miles ahead. From I-87 North (New York Thruway): Take I-87 North to Kingston, Exit 19. Follow Route 209 (which changes to Route 199 when you reach the Hudson River) over the Kingston-Rhinecliff Bridge. At the second light, make a left onto Route 9G and proceed North. Bard is less than four miles ahead. From I-87 South (New York Thruway): Take I-87 South to Kingston, Exit 19, and proceed according to the directions listed above for I-87 North; or take the New York State Thruway to Catskill, Exit 21. Make a left after the toll plaza onto Route 23B. Next, turn left onto Route 23 East. Once you cross the Rip Van Winkle Bridge, take a right onto Route 9G South. Bard is 15 miles South.

**LOCAL:** Local cab companies include Red Hook Taxi Service (845-758-1478), Rhinebeck Taxi (845-876-2010), and Horseless Carriage (845-757-2900).

## WHERE TO STAY

Most nearby lodging is located in the neighboring towns of Saugerties and Kingston. Options include the Holiday Inn, Kingston (845-340-1908, $$), Marriott Hotel, Kingston (845-382-2300, $$), and Sparrow Hawk Bed & Breakfast, Kingston (845-687-4492, $$$).

## CAMPUS AT ITS BEST!

Bard offers exceptional programs in the arts and interested visitors should visit the Richard B. Fisher Center for the Performing Arts, designed by renowned architect Frank Gehry. If you're touring the college in August, stick around for a performance during the annual Bard Music Festival. For a pre/post-performance snack, stop by the Root Cellar, a popular campus mainstay, which includes an organic coffee shop, a natural foods co-op, and an impressive collection of magazines.

# BARNARD COLLEGE

3009 Broadway, New York, NY 10027
**Telephone:** 212-854-2014 • **E-mail:** admissions@barnard.edu • **Website:** www.barnard.edu
**Hours:** Monday–Friday and Saturday, 9:00 A.M.–5:00 P.M.

## STUDENTS SAY

"Barnard provides the best environment for a woman who values her education, wants to make friends with other intelligent, creative women, and [wants to] explore the wonder that is New York City!"

## FODOR'S SAYS

"Idealistically conceived as an American Acropolis, the cluster of academic and religious institutions that developed in Morningside Heights managed to keep these blocks stable during years when neighborhoods on all sides were collapsing. This is an Uptown student neighborhood—less hip than the Village, but friendly, fun, and intellectual."

## ABOUT THE SCHOOL

A longtime affiliate of Columbia University, Barnard sits among America's elite women's liberal arts colleges. While this highly selective school offers the intimate experience of a small college, cross registration with neighboring Columbia means that students enjoy all the benefits of a large university. And having the vibrancy of New York City at their doorstep ain't so bad either.

## GETTING THERE

**BY AIR:** All three major airports in the New York City metro area (John F. Kennedy International Airport, LaGuardia Airport, and Newark International Airport) offer extensive flight options. Transportation from the airports to campus includes bus, taxi, and train/subway.

**BY TRAIN:** Amtrak services Penn Station (7th Avenue and 34th Street). Take taxi, bus, or subway from the station to campus.

**BY BUS:** Greyhound operates numerous stations in NYC, including the main station at Port Authority in Times Square.

**BY CAR:** From I-95 South or I-87 South: Exit at the Cross Bronx Expressway East toward the George Washington Bridge. As you come to the bridge, bear right and take the exit for the Henry Hudson Parkway South. Get off the Parkway at the 96th Street Exit (West Side Highway). Travel two blocks East to Broadway and turn left (uptown). Follow Broadway to the entrance to the Barnard campus at 117th Street. From I-95 North or I-80 East: Follow signs to the George Washington Bridge. Just before the bridge, I-95 and I-80 combine. Just after the bridge, follow the Henry Hudson Parkway South. Get off the Parkway at the 96th Street Exit (West Side Highway). Travel two blocks East to Broadway and turn left (uptown). Follow Broadway to the entrance to the Barnard campus at 117th Street. Parking: Limited street parking is available in the surrounding neighborhood, though these spots can be difficult to find. Numerous parking garages are close to campus as well.

**LOCAL:** NYC's Metropolitan Transit Authority (MTA) offers 24-hour subway and bus service to all areas of the city. To reach Barnard's campus by subway, take the 1 train to the 116th street station. The four MTA bus lines that stop close to campus are the M4, M5, M11, and M104. Subway and bus fare is $2.00 per ride.

## WHERE TO STAY

Lodging options in New York City are plentiful. Among those in Manhattan's Upper West Side—Barnard's neck of the woods—are the Millburn Hotel (212-362-1006, $$), the Quality Hotel (212-866-6400, $$), Hotel Belleclaire (212-362-7700, $$$), and the Mayflower Hotel (212-265-0060, $$$+).

---

## CAMPUS AT ITS BEST!

Reflecting its metropolitan surroundings, cultural, and entertainment options abound on Barnard's campus. If you're visiting between 12:30 P.M. and 1:30 P.M., you'll have the opportunity to attend one of the daily Lunchtime Music Series concerts. And if you're in the mood for sightseeing, take a short walk over to the Cathedral of St. John the Divine (Amsterdam Avenue and 113th Street), the largest cathedral in the world.

# BATES COLLEGE

23 Campus Avenue, Lindholm House, Lewiston, ME 04240

**Telephone:** 207-786-6000 • **Website:** www.bates.edu

**Hours:** Monday–Friday, 8:00 A.M.–5:00 P.M.; Saturday, 9:00 A.M.–NOON

## STUDENTS SAY

"In one sentence, Bates is all about getting a fantastic education, meeting a ton of amazing people, and having a really great time."

## FODOR'S SAYS

"Fall foliage can be brilliant in Maine and is made even more so by its reflection in inland lakes or streams off the ocean."

## ABOUT THE SCHOOL

Bates College is one of the three members of Maine's liberal arts powerhouse. With top-notch professors, a plethora of personal attention, and enough extracurricular activities to keep their heads spinning for years, Bates offers students a college experience that is academic, active, and (according to many of its students) just plain fun!

## GETTING THERE

**BY AIR:** Numerous major airlines operate out of the Portland International Jetport, located about 35 miles from campus. Bus transportation between the Jetport and the town of Lewiston is provided by Vermont Transit. For more extensive airline service, look at Logan International Airport in Boston. Logan is about two and a half hours south of Bates.

**BY TRAIN:** Amtrak services several nearby towns, including Portland and Bath.

**BY BUS:** Greyhound runs out of Lewiston. Regional bus service is available through Mermaid Transportation (207-885-5630) and Vermont Transit (800-552-8737).

**BY CAR:** From I-95 North: Follow I-95 to Exit 80. Take a left onto Alfred A. Plourde Parkway. Stay on Plourde, passing through the stoplight at the intersection of Plourde and Pleasant. About half a mile after this stoplight you'll come to a light at the intersection of Plourde and Webster Street. Turn left onto Webster. After a mile, you'll come to a stoplight at Farwell Street. Turn right onto Farwell. Continue until the road turns into Russell Street. Follow Russell for about a mile until you come to the third traffic light. Make a left onto College Street. At the second blinking stoplight, take a left onto Campus Avenue. At the next right, turn onto Wood Street. The Admissions parking lot will be ahead on your right. From I-95 South: Take Exit 80 and bear right onto Alfred A. Plourde Parkway. Stay on Plourde, passing through the stoplight at the intersection of Plourde and Pleasant. About half a mile after this stoplight you'll come to a light at the intersection of Plourde and Webster Street. Turn left onto Webster. After a mile, you'll come to a stoplight at Farwell Street. Turn right onto Farwell. Continue until the road turns into Russell Street. Follow Russell for about a mile until you come to the third traffic light. Make a left onto College Street. At the second blinking stoplight, take a left onto Campus Avenue. At the next right, turn onto Wood Street. The Admissions parking lot will be ahead on your right.

**LOCAL:** CityLink bus service operates regularly in the Lewiston-Auburn area.

## WHERE TO STAY

Accommodations in Lewiston and nearby Auburn include the Motel 6 (207-782-6558, $), the Hilton Garden Inn (207-784-4433, $$), and the Ware Street Inn (207-783-8171, $$$).

---

## CAMPUS AT ITS BEST!

Bates' Carnegie Science Hall boasts some impressive resources. While touring the facility, be sure to check out the planetarium and the rooftop greenhouse. If the weather's nice, take some time to relax at Keigwin Amphitheater, overlooking Lake Andrews. This favorite study spot is also host to a variety of on-campus performances. Those touring the school during the winter might be lucky enough to catch Winter Carnival, an annual event that features a multitude of activities. Summer visitors will be thrilled to attend the Bates Dance Festival, a nationally recognized dance festival that takes place right on Bates' campus.

# BENNINGTON COLLEGE

Office of Admissions and Financial Aid, Bennington, VT 05201
**Telephone:** 800-833-6845 • **E-mail:** admissions@bennington.edu • **Website:** www.bennington.edu
**Hours:** Monday–Friday, 9:00 A.M.–5:00 P.M.;  Saturday by appointment, 10:00 A.M.–2:00 P.M.

## STUDENTS SAY

"The greatest strength of Bennington is the intellectual freedom the school allows its students."

## FODOR'S SAYS

"While you're there, check out the Bennington Museum. The museum displays the largest collection of Grandma Moses, the popular self-taught folk artist who lived and painted in the area."

## ABOUT THE SCHOOL

This tiny college of just 620 students is a haven for students seeking an excellent education in a liberal and unconventional environment. Students can eschew the traditional grading system in favor of final projects with written evaluations, and the student/teacher ratio is a cozy 7:1.  Undergraduates live in actual houses rather than dorms, some of which have even been photographed for magazines.

## GETTING THERE

**BY AIR:** Albany International Airport (ALB) is about 45 miles away. Transportation from the airport is limited: take a cab from Albany airport to the Albany Greyhound Station. Then take a Yankee Trails bus to Bennington. From there, the Bennington College campus van will pick up students who call in. (Plan carefully: Yankee Trails and the college vans both have very limited schedules.) Students may also take a taxi directly to campus (approximately $60–$70 plus tip).

**BY TRAIN:** The closest Amtrak station is 30 miles away in Pittsfield, MA. Many students take the train to Albany. Take a car or taxi to campus.

**BY BUS:** Yankee Trails stops in Bennington and connects to Greyhound in Albany. The nearest Greyhound Station is in Pittsfield, MA. Take a cab or call a Bennington College student transport van for travel to and from Bennington.

**BY CAR:** From the South: Take I-87 to I-787 North (Exit 23). Take Exit 9E (Troy/Bennington) and follow Route 7 East toward Vermont. After passing turnoffs for New York Route 22 (South and North), at the second set of flashing yellow lights, follow Vermont Route 279 East. Take the Bennington/North Bennington Exit for Route 67A/Route 7A. At the end of the exit ramp take a left onto Route 67A North. After the second set of lights, the college entrance is on the right. From the East via Massachusetts Turnpike (I-90): Take I-90 West to Lee/Lenox, MA (Exit 2). Follow signs to Route 7/20 North to Pittsfield. Take U.S. Route 7 North to Bennington. At the intersection of Route 7 and Route 9 stay straight on Route 7 North. Continue on Route 7 North through two sets of lights; after the second set of lights, continue straight through on Route 7 North. Take the first left to Route 67A and exit right to Route 67A (Bennington/North Bennington). At the end of the exit ramp, take a left onto Route 67A North. After the second set of lights, the college entrance is on the right. From the West via New York State Thruway (I-90): Take the New York State Thruway (I-90) East toward Albany. Take Exit 24, which will leave you on I-90. Immediately take Exit 1 (I-87 North). Take Exit 7 and follow Route 7 East toward VT. After passing the turnoffs for NY Route 22 (South and North), at the second set of flashing yellow lights, follow VT Route 279 East. Take the Bennington/North Bennington Exit for Route 67A/Route 7A. At the end of the exit ramp, take a left onto Route 67A North. After the second set of lights, the college entrance is on the right. From the North: Take U.S. Route 7 South to Bennington. Take the exit for Route 67A (North Bennington). At the end of the exit ramp take a left onto Route 67A North. After the second set of lights, the college entrance is on the right.

**LOCAL:** Call Walt's Taxi service: (802-442-9052), D&H Taxi (802-447-1182), or Red Top Cab Company (802-442-8141).

## WHERE TO STAY

There are many hotels right in Bennington and nearby. The Alexandra Bed and Breakfast is about 10 minutes away (888-207-9386, $$). Also convenient to Bennington College's campus are the Knotty Pine Motel (802-442-5487, $) and The Four Chimneys Inn (802-447-3500, $$$).

### SCHOOL AT A GLANCE

| | |
|---|---|
| Type of School | Private |
| Environment | Town |
| Tuition | $34,340 |
| Enrollment | 571 |
| % Male/Female | 34/66 |
| Student/Faculty Ratio | 7:1 |

### FRESHMAN PROFILE

| | |
|---|---|
| Range SAT | |
| Critical Reading | 610-700 |
| Range SAT Math | 540-640 |
| Range ACT Composite | 25-28 |
| Average HS GPA | 3.63 |

### ON-CAMPUS APPOINTMENTS

| | |
|---|---|
| Advance Notice | Preferred |
| Appointment | Required |
| Saturdays | Sometimes |
| Average Length | 45 min |
| Info Sessions | Yes |
| Class Visits | Yes |

### CAMPUS TOURS

| | |
|---|---|
| Appointment | Preferred; interviews available |
| Dates | Year Round |
| Times | During Admissions Office hours |
| Average Length | 60 min |

# CAMPUS AT ITS BEST!

Since Visual Arts is one of Bennington's strongest programs, entertainment on campus often consists of attending the performances and screenings of fellow students. Try to attend one of the independent film screenings or stand-up comedy shows during your visit. Off campus, the town of Bennington plays host to the Bennington Museum, a treasure trove of early Americana.

# BENTLEY COLLEGE

175 Forest Street, Waltham, MA 02452-4705
**Telephone:** 781-891-2244 • **E-mail:** ugadmission@bentley.edu
**Hours:** Monday–Friday and Saturday by appointment, 8:30 A.M.–4:30 P.M.

## STUDENTS SAY

"Bentley College provides the best possible technology-based business education in a beautiful and close-knit environment."

## FODOR'S SAYS

Nearby "Boston is meant for walking. Most of its historical and architectural attractions are in neighborhoods that are easy to explore on foot."

## ABOUT THE SCHOOL

Located in the suburbs of Boston, Bentley is a small school with a big focus on business. The college's 4,200 undergrads benefit from a career-oriented education that keeps them up on the latest technology and theories. And as their four years at Bentley near an end, students enjoy an impressive recruitment program and extensive alumni network.

## GETTING THERE

**BY AIR:** Boston's Logan International Airport sees traffic from all the major airlines. The easiest way to get from the airport to campus is via taxi. Public bus service is also available.

**BY TRAIN:** Amtrak's Back Bay and North stations in Boston are each about 10 miles from campus. They can be accessed by taxi or bus. Commuter rail, operated by the Massachusetts Bay Transportation Authority (MBTA), also services a range of regional destinations.

**BY BUS:** Greyhound operates from its station in downtown Boston.

**BY CAR:** From the North: Follow Route 95/128 South to Trapelo Road (Exit 28). At the top of the exit ramp, make a left. Stay on Trapelo Road for 2.6 miles, driving toward Belmont. Make a right onto Forest Street. Bentley is a mile ahead on your left. From the South: From Route 95/128 follow signs for Totten Pond Road (Exit 27A). Take a right at the end of the exit ramp and follow Totten Pond Road for 1.2 miles. When the road ends, make a right onto Lexington Street. Soon after, turn left onto Beaver Street. Stay on Beaver Street for 1.5 miles, including passing through a rotary. Bentley is on the left. From the East: Follow either Storrow Drive (West) or Memorial Drive (West), following signs toward Arlington. As the road comes to an end, bear left at a sign reading "To 16 S Watertown/Waltham." Follow for half a mile, then turn right onto Belmont Street. Remain on Belmont Street until it intersects with Trapelo Road. Bear right onto Trapelo Road. After 1.7 miles, you'll come to a light; make a left, following a sign reading "60 Waltham to Route 20." This is Waverley Oaks Road (Route 60). At the next traffic light, take a right onto Beaver Street. Follow Beaver Street until it meets the Bentley campus. Go right at College Drive to enter the campus. From the West: From the Massachusetts Turnpike (I-90) West, take Exit 14. Follow signs to Route 95/128 North. Follow Route 95/128 to Trapelo Road (Exit 28). At the top of the exit ramp, make a right. Stay on Trapelo Road for 2.6 miles, driving toward Belmont. Make a right onto Forest Street. Bentley is a mile ahead on your left.

**LOCAL:** Among the Boston area's many taxi companies is Waltham Taxi, which specializes in service to and from Logan Airport (781-647-1117).

## WHERE TO STAY

Accommodations close to campus include Best Western TLC Hotel (781-890-7800, $$), Home Suites Inn (781-890-3000, $$), and Westin Hotel (781-290-5600, $$).

## CAMPUS AT ITS BEST!

Bentley College is known for its business program, and visitors should stop by the Trading Room, located in the Hughley Center for Financial Services. The facility features 15 trading desks, a business suite, and access to an array of financial information including Bloomberg, DataStream, and Morningstar.

# BOSTON COLLEGE

140 Commonwealth Avenue, Devlin Hall 208, Chestnut Hill, MA 02467-3809
**Telephone:** 617-552-3100 • **Website:** www.bc.edu
**Hours:** Monday–Friday and Saturday by appointment; see website for hours

## STUDENTS SAY

"BC is a great mix of strong academics and social justice awareness."

## FODOR'S SAYS

"Bostonians often find their city to be too hot and humid in July and August, but if you're visiting from points south, the cool evening coastal breezes might strike you as downright refreshing."

## ABOUT THE SCHOOL

Boston College offers stellar academics, top-rate athletics, and a vibrant campus life just a stone's throw away from the bustle of Beantown. And the college's devotion to Jesuit principles ensures that students seeking a strong spiritual life need look no further.

## GETTING THERE

**BY AIR:** More than 30 airlines service Logan International Airport. Use local taxi or subway for easy travel to and from the airport.

**BY TRAIN:** Amtrak operates Boston's primary train service.

**BY BUS:** Regular bus service in and out of Boston's South Station is offered by Greyhound (800-231-2222) and Peter Pan (800-343-9999).

**BY CAR:** From I-95 North/South: Follow I-95 (Route 128) to Exit 24 (Route 30). Travel East on Route 30 (also called Commonwealth Avenue) for five miles until you reach the Boston College campus. From I-90 East: Take I-90 (Massachusetts Turnpike) to Exit 17. At the first set of lights after the exit ramp, turn right onto Centre Street. Four stoplights later, turn left onto Commonwealth Avenue. Stay on Commonwealth Avenue for about one and a half miles until you reach Boston College. From downtown Boston: Follow I-90 (Massachusetts Turnpike) to Exit 17. After passing the Sheraton Tara Hotel, take a left over the bridge. Make your first right onto Center Street. Take a left over the bridge after passing the Sheraton Tara Hotel. Take the first right onto Centre Street. Four stoplights later, turn left onto Commonwealth Avenue. Stay on Commonwealth Avenue for about one and a half miles until you reach Boston College.

**LOCAL:** Boston's subway—commonly known as the "T"—services the Boston College campus. Take the Green Line's "B" train to its terminus at Boston College. On leaving the subway station, cross the street, passing St. Ignatius Church and following the perimeter road around to the campus entrance. The BC Shuttle Bus also offers free transportation in and around the Boston College campus. Taxi services include Veteran's Taxi Service (617-527-0300) and Bay State Taxi (617-566-5000).

## WHERE TO STAY

Lodging options in the vicinity of Boston College includes the Sheraton Tara Newton (617-969-3010, $$), Best Western Terrace Inn (617-566-6260, $$$), and Courtyard by Marriott, Brookline (617-734-1393, $$$+). Be sure to inquire about discounts for Boston College visitors, which some local hotels offer.

| SCHOOL AT A GLANCE | |
| --- | --- |
| Type of School | Private |
| Environment | City |
| Tuition | $33,000 |
| Enrollment | 9,019 |
| % Male/Female | 48/52 |
| Student/Faculty Ratio | 13:1 |

| FRESHMAN PROFILE | |
| --- | --- |
| Range SAT | |
| Critical Reading | 610-700 |
| Range SAT Math | 640-720 |

| ON-CAMPUS APPOINTMENTS | |
| --- | --- |
| Info Sessions | Yes |
| Class Visits | Yes |

| CAMPUS TOURS | |
| --- | --- |
| Appointment | Not Required |
| Dates | Varies |
| Times | Varies |
| Average Length | 120 min |

## CAMPUS AT ITS BEST!

Among BC's countless academic resources is the John J. Burns Library of Rare Books and Special Collections, where some 12 million manuscripts and archival items are held. When you're done perusing the collection, meander over to lunch in Corcoran Commons, where students are especially fond of the grilled sandwiches and pizza.

# BOSTON UNIVERSITY

121 Bay State Road, Boston, MA 02215
**Telephone:** 617-353-2300 • **E-mail:** admissions@bu.edu • **Website:** www.bu.edu
**Hours:** Monday–Friday, 8:30 A.M.–5:00 P.M.; Saturday, 9:00 A.M.–1:00 P.M. and by appointment

## STUDENTS SAY

"BU is a great place to learn, be independent, and enrich your life."

## FODOR'S SAYS

"Boston's cemeteries [are] among the most picturesque and historic in America." If you found a resting place at the Granary Burial Ground, "chances are your headstone was eloquently ornamented and your neighbors mighty eloquent, too: Samuel Adams, John Hancock, Benjamin Franklin's parents, and Paul Revere."

## ABOUT THE SCHOOL

Visit BU and the first thing you'll notice is its fortuitous setting on the banks of the Charles River. The university takes full advantage of its location in one of the East Coast's major urban centers. Professors often use the city as a classroom, and students benefit from the wide range of internships and alumni networks that permeate Boston.

## GETTING THERE

**BY AIR:** Boston's Logan International Airport is serviced by more than 30 airlines. To reach the university, take a taxi or the subway.

**BY TRAIN:** Amtrak offers Boston's primary train service. Amtrak's Acela Express provides high-speed travel between Boston, New York, Philadelphia, and Washington, DC. Amtrak's Downeaster allows easy access from Maine.

**BY BUS:** For bus service to and from Boston, contact Greyhound (800-231-2222) or Peter Pan (800-343-9999).

**BY CAR:** From Kenmore Square: At the first set of traffic lights, make a right onto Beacon Street. As the road forks, follow the right fork onto Bay State Road. Bay State Road leads you to the Office of Admissions. From I-90 East: Follow I-90 (Massachusetts Turnpike) East to Exit 18, Brighton/Cambridge. (This is a left exit.) Following signs to Cambridge, proceed to the second set of lights. Make a right onto Soldiers Field Road/Storrow Drive. Stay on Storrow Drive until you turn off at the Kenmore Exit. See "From Kenmore Square" directions above. From I-93 North: Travel on I-93/Route 3 (Southeast Expressway) North toward Boston. Take the Storrow Drive Exit. Follow Storrow Drive to the Kenmore Square Exit. See "From Kenmore Square" directions above. From I-93/Route 1 South: I-93 and Route 1 combine. Exit onto Storrow Drive. Follow Storrow Drive to the Kenmore Square Exit. See "From Kenmore Square" directions above.

**LOCAL:** Boston's subway—called the T—provides several Boston University stops. From all lines, transfer to the Green Line "B" train. For MBTA bus service, take Route 8, 57, 60, 65, or 8A to Kenmore Square, then transfer to the T's Westbound "B" train (Green Line). Taxicabs abound in Boston. Among the taxi companies are Red Cab (617-734-5000) and Green Cab (617-625-5000).

## WHERE TO STAY

Lodging options in the vicinity include Days Hotel (617-254-1234, $$), Midtown Hotel (617-262-1000, $$), and Hotel Commonwealth (617-933-5000, $$$+).

---

## CAMPUS AT ITS BEST!

Budding historians and literary scholars visiting BU should head over to the Howard Gotlieb Archival Research Center. Among the collections housed here are works from Walt Whitman, Robert Frost, and Theodore Roosevelt. Those looking for more physical stimulation might be impressed by the 35-foot-by-45-foot climbing wall found in the fitness center. After all that exertion, relax by catching a screening at the Redstone Film Festival. This annual event organized by the Department of Communications features the best films produced by BU undergrads and graduate students.

# BOWDOIN COLLEGE

5000 College Station, Bowdoin College, Brunswick, ME 04011-8441
**Telephone:** 207-725-3100 • **E-mail:** admissions@bowdoin.edu
**Website:** www.bowdoin.edu • **Hours:** Monday–Friday, 8:30 A.M.–5:00 P.M.; Saturday by appointment

## STUDENTS SAY

"It's nearly impossible to find a Bowdoin student who isn't smart, motivated, and ultra-involved on campus."

## FODOR'S SAYS

The nearby "General Joshua L. Chamberlain Museum displays memorabilia and documents the life of Maine's most celebrated Civil War hero." The general "served as president of Bowdoin College" from 1871–1883.

## ABOUT THE SCHOOL

With legendary alumni like Nathaniel Hawthorne and Henry Wadsworth Longfellow, Bowdoin is a pillar among American liberal arts institutions. Known for its top-notch academics, Bowdoin offers an enviable location as well. A five-minute drive will take you to the rocky shores of the Atlantic, and the wharfs of downtown Portland are only a half hour away.

## GETTING THERE

**BY AIR:** The Portland International Jetport, about half an hour from campus, is serviced by six airlines. Travel by car, taxi, or shuttle from the airport. For more extensive options, try Logan International Airport in Boston, two hours from Bowdoin. Mermaid Transportation provides daily shuttle service to both the Portland and Boston airports (206-885-5630).

**BY TRAIN:** Amtrak services Brunswick with connecting bus service. Direct train service is available in several nearby towns, including Portland and Bath.

**BY BUS:** Greyhound offers limited bus service in Brunswick; regular service is available a half hour south in Portland. Regional bus service is available through Mermaid Transportation (207-885-5630), Vermont Transit (800-552-8737), and Concord Trailways (800-639-3317).

**BY CAR:** From the South: Follow I-95 (Maine Turnpike) North to Exit 6A (I-295). Follow I-295 around Portland; it will reconnect with I-95. Turn at Exit 28 for Bath-Brunswick/Coastal Route 1. Travel on Route 1/Pleasant Street, following signs toward Maine Street. Turn right when Pleasant Street ends at Maine Street. Stay on Maine Street for a half-mile. Bear right as the road forks. Bowdoin is on your left. From the North: Travel along I-95 South to Exit 28 for Bath-Brunswick/Coastal Route 1. Travel on Route 1/Pleasant Street, following signs toward Maine Street. Turn right when Pleasant Street ends at Maine Street. Stay on Maine Street for a half mile. Bear right as the road forks. Bowdoin is on your left.

**LOCAL:** Cab service is offered by Brunswick Taxi (207-729-3688).

## WHERE TO STAY

Brunswick's accommodations include the Econo Lodge (207-729-9991, $), the Captain Daniel Stone Inn (207-725-9898, $$), and Brunswick Bed and Breakfast (207-729-4914, $$$).

### SCHOOL AT A GLANCE

| | |
|---|---|
| Type of School | Private |
| Environment | Village |
| Tuition | $34,280 |
| Enrollment | 1,730 |
| % Male/Female | 49/51 |
| Student/Faculty Ratio | 10:1 |

### FRESHMAN PROFILE

| | |
|---|---|
| Range SAT | |
| Critical Reading | 650–750 |
| Range SAT Math | 650–730 |

### ON-CAMPUS APPOINTMENTS

| | |
|---|---|
| Advance Notice | Yes, 3 weeks |
| Appointment | Required |
| Saturdays | Sometimes |
| Average Length | 45 min |
| Info Sessions | Yes |
| Class Visits | Yes |

### CAMPUS TOURS

| | |
|---|---|
| Appointment | Not Required |
| Dates | Year Round |
| Times | M–F 9:30 A.M., 11:30 A.M., |
| | 1:30 P.M.; Sat 11:30 A.M. |
| Average Length | 60 min |

## CAMPUS AT ITS BEST!

Bowdoin is home to some amazing resources, including the Peary-MacMillan Museum. Its impressive collection features exploration gear, natural history specimens, and anthropological materials. For great food on campus, visit Thorne Dining Hall. This newly renovated facility is the college's largest. Finally, if you're planning a trip in the spring, be sure to check out "Museum Pieces," an annual, outdoor dance performance sponsored by the Department of Theater and Dance.

# BRANDEIS UNIVERSITY

415 South Street, MS003, Waltham, MA 02454-9110

**Telephone:** 781-736-3500 • **E-mail:** admissions@brandeis.edu

**Hours:** Monday–Friday, 9:00 A.M.–5:00 P.M.

## STUDENTS SAY

"Brandeisians are very warm and inviting, and it is extremely difficult to feel like an outsider."

## FODOR'S SAYS

Nearby "Boston has many high-quality shops, especially in the Newbury Street and Beacon Hill neighborhoods."

## ABOUT THE SCHOOL

Put 3,000 undergrads on an über-friendly, academically intense campus on the skirts of Boston and what do you get? A Brandeis student, of course. Mixing the emphasis on research of a large university with the emphasis on student learning of a small college, Brandeis is a Jewish-sponsored (though nonsectarian) school that offers a well-rounded education to its very satisfied student body.

## GETTING THERE

**BY AIR:** The nearest airport is Logan International Airport. For the most direct transportation to the Brandeis campus, take a taxi or a shuttle service such as The Airporter (781-899-6161).

**BY TRAIN:** Amtrak offers Boston's primary train service. Take a taxi, the bus, or the subway to get to the Brandeis campus in Waltham.

**BY BUS:** Regular bus service in and out of Boston is offered by Greyhound (800-231-2222) and Peter Pan (800-343-9999).

**BY CAR:** From I-90 (Massachusetts Turnpike) East: From I-90 take Exit 14 to I-95/Rt 128. After paying the toll, merge left for 95/Route 128 North. On the exit ramp, exit immediately onto Exit 24 (Route 30). Go left onto Route 30. At the first light, turn right onto River Road. Remain on River Road for one and a half miles, at which point it turns into South Street. Brandeis is half a mile ahead on the left of South Street. From I-90 (Massachusetts Turnpike) West: From I-90 take Exit 15 for I-95/Route 128 and Route 30. Go straight for Route 30 after the toll. Turn right at end of the ramp, and then right again at the first traffic light onto Route 30. Turn left at the next traffic light onto River Road. Stay on this for one and a half miles, where it turns into South Street. Brandeis is half a mile ahead on the left of South Street. From I-95 South: Follow I-95/Route 128 South to Exit 24 for Route 30. At the end of the ramp, go through the traffic light (across Route 30). Now you're on River Road (which becomes South Street). Brandeis is two miles ahead on the left side of South Street. From I-95 North: Follow I-95/Route 128 North to Exit 24 for Route 30. Because Route 30 is one of several possibilities, follow signs carefully at this exit. Make a left at the top of the ramp onto Route 30. Turn right at the traffic lights. This is South Street, and Brandeis is two miles ahead on the left.

**LOCAL:** From Boston's North Station take the Fitchburg/South Acton commuter rail line to access campus. Local cab companies include Waltham Taxi, which specializes in service to and from Logan Airport (781-647-1117).

## WHERE TO STAY

Accommodations close to campus include the Best Western TLC Hotel (781-890-7800, $$), Home Suites Inn (781-890-3000, $$), and Westin Hotel (781-290-5600, $$).

---

## CAMPUS AT ITS BEST!

Stopping by Usen Castle is a must for anyone touring Brandeis. This dorm for upperclassmen, now a national historic landmark, features a number of architectural quirks (including stairways that lead nowhere). Afterwards, stroll over to the Rose Art Museum where you can view seminal works from artists such as Willem de Kooning, Jasper Johns, Andy Warhol, and Cindy Sherman. If time permits, catch one of the "Stein Nights" evening performances peppered throughout the semester. These events range from live music performances to stand-up comedy.

# BROWN UNIVERSITY

Box 1876, 45 Prospect Street, Providence, RI 02912

**Telephone:** 401-863-2378 • **E-mail:** admission_undergraduate@brown.edu • **Website:** www.brown.edu
**Hours:** Monday–Friday, 8:30 A.M.–5:00 P.M.; Saturday, 9:00 A.M.–NOON

| SCHOOL AT A GLANCE | |
| --- | --- |
| Type of School | Private |
| Tuition | $32,264 |
| Enrollment | 5,927 |
| % Male/Female | 47/53 |
| Student/Faculty Ratio | 9:1 |
| **FRESHMAN PROFILE** | |
| Range SAT | |
| Critical Reading | 660-760 |
| Range SAT Math | 670-770 |
| Range ACT Composite | 27-33 |
| **ON-CAMPUS APPOINTMENTS** | |
| Advance Notice | 3 weeks |
| Appointment | Required |
| Saturdays | No |
| Class Visits | No |
| **CAMPUS TOURS** | |
| Times | M–F 10:00 A.M., 11:00 A.M., 1:00 P.M., 3:00 P.M., 4:00 P.M.; Sat 10:00 A.M.–NOON |

## STUDENTS SAY

"Brown is relaxed and friendly, with a complete lack of competitiveness and cliques. The greatest strength of Brown is that all students are welcomed, accepted, and embraced by all others."

## FODOR'S SAYS

The Federal Hill neighborhood is "vital to Providence's culture and sense of self." The neighborhood "shines during the Federal Hill Stroll (usually held in the beginning of June) when festival goers enjoy music and sample cuisine at 20 eateries."

## ABOUT THE SCHOOL

Intellectual freedom and academic exploration—these are important phrases around the Brown campus. Keeping company among the nation's elite Ivy League schools, Brown boasts an "open curriculum" that allows undergrads to blaze their own educational paths while taking advantage of the university's top-notch faculty and cutting-edge facilities.

## GETTING THERE

**BY AIR:** T.F. Green Airport is 10 miles South of campus in Warwick. To get to campus, take a cab or the Airport Limousine Co. shuttle service, which travels between the airport and campus every hour.

**BY TRAIN:** Amtrak services downtown Providence. Less than a mile from campus, the station can be accessed by bus or cab.

**BY BUS:** The Greyhound station is located in downtown Providence and the Bonanza Bus Lines station is just North of downtown.

**BY CAR:** From I-95 North/South: Traveling either direction on I-95, keep your eyes open for I-195 East. As soon as you get on the I-195 East exit ramp, move to the far right-hand lane as quickly as possible. Take Exit 1 for Downtown Providence. Proceed to the first light, where you turn right onto Dyer Street. Three lights later make a right onto College Street. Continue through the next light and up the hill. On top of the hill, where College and Prospect Streets intersect, you can see Brown's Van Wickle Gates. Make a left onto Prospect Street, a right onto Waterman Street, and then another right onto Brook Street. Visitor parking is on your left. From I-195 West: Proceed on I-195 West until you reach Exit 2 for South Main Street. Drive down South Main Street to the first light (at College Street). Turn right onto College Street. Continue through the next light and up the hill. On top of the hill, where College and Prospect Streets intersect, you can see Brown's Van Wickle Gates. Make a left onto Prospect Street, then a right onto Waterman Street, and then another right onto Brook Street. Visitor parking is on your left.

**LOCAL:** Rhode Island Public Transit Authority, or RIPTA, offers regular, citywide bus service. Providence taxi companies include Laurel Sweeney Taxi Company (401-521-4200), Airport Taxi (401-737-2868), and Yellow Cab, Inc. (401-941-1122).

## WHERE TO STAY

A wide range of hotels and B&Bs are available in and around Providence, including the Sheraton Providence Airport Hotel (401-738-4000, $$), Christopher Dodge House Bed and Breakfast (401-351-6111, $$), and Hotel Dolce Villa (401-383-7031, $$$).

## CAMPUS AT ITS BEST!

As one of the country's premier universities, it's no surprise that Brown offers its students some impressive resources. For example, the multimedia studios in the Steinert Building provide equipment for video and audio processing, motion-sensing systems, new controllers, sound synthesis, and interactive and automated installations, among other things. Visitors who want to get a feel for day-to-day life at Brown should wander over to Thayer Street. This strip, which runs along the eastern side of campus, is home to numerous stores, restaurants, and coffee shops frequented by students.

# BRYN MAWR COLLEGE

101 North Merion Avenue, Bryn Mawr, PA 19010-2859
**Telephone:** 610-526-5152 • **E-mail:** admissions@brynmawr.edu • **Website:** www.brynmawr.edu
**Hours:** Monday–Friday, 9:00 A.M.–5:00 P.M.; Saturday, 9:00 A.M.–1:00 P.M.

## STUDENTS SAY

"The Bryn Mawr woman is focused and a little bit quirky. I have not met a single person here that I am not intrigued by."

## FODOR'S SAYS

"There is no sales tax on clothing, medicine, or food bought in stores. Otherwise, Pennsylvania has a 6 percent sales tax."

## ABOUT THE SCHOOL

This small, prestigious all-women's college offers an extremely rigorous academic program and a self-governing association in which students have a big say in how their school is run. The school's much-respected Honor Code gives students a lot of latitude when it comes to managing their academic lives and is one of the college's many treasured traditions.

## GETTING THERE

**BY AIR:** Philadelphia's International Airport is the closest airport. Take SEPTA's Airport Line (also known as the R-1) to 30th Street Station in Philadelphia. Catch the R-5 (Paoli/Thorndale) commuter train to Bryn Mawr.

**BY TRAIN:** Amtrak stops at Philadelphia's 30th Street Station. There you can transfer to a direct commuter SEPTA train to Bryn Mawr. Take the R5 (Paoli/Thorndale) to Bryn Mawr station.

**BY BUS:** Greyhound Bus Lines stops at Philadelphia's 30th Street Station. There you can transfer to a direct commuter SEPTA train to Bryn Mawr. Take the R5 (Paoli/Thorndale) to Bryn Mawr station.

**BY CAR:** From the North/East: Take the N.J. Turnpike (I-95) to Exit 6 (Pennsylvania Turnpike (276) Exit). Take the Pennsylvania Turnpike (I-276) to Exit 20. Follow the sign for I-476 South (toward Chester). Go South on I-476 to Exit 13 (St. Davids/Villanova). Follow Route 30 (Lancaster Avenue) East through Villanova for 2.4 miles. Make a left onto Morris Avenue and stay on this street until you see the school. From the South: Take I-95 North toward Philadelphia/New York and take Exit 7 (I-476 North toward Plymouth Meeting). Follow I-476 North about 12 miles to Exit 13 (St. Davids/Villanova). Follow "From the North/East" directions above. From the West: Take the Pennsylvania Turnpike (I-76) East to the Valley Forge interchange at Exit 326. Follow sign to I-76 East (Schuylkill Expressway). Take I-76 to Exit 331A for I-476 South (toward Chester). Go South on I-476 to Exit 13 (St. Davids/Villanova). Follow "From the North/East" directions above.

**LOCAL:** Local taxi service includes Main Line Taxi Co. (610-664-0444) and Bennett Taxi Service (610-525-1770).

## WHERE TO STAY

Lodging accommodations in the area include the Comfort Inn Downtown (877-424-6423, $$), Sheraton Suites Philadelphia Airport (215-492-0400, $$), and the Residence Inn by Marriott—Conshohocken (610-828-8800, $$$).

---

## CAMPUS AT ITS BEST!

Bryn Mawr's Thomas Library encloses an open courtyard commonly referred to as "the Cloisters." The Cloisters fountain is a great place to study or relax, although the occasional student skinny-dipping in the fountain might distract you. Carpenter Library, home to the school's art and archeology resources, is another remarkable campus facility. The building has plenty of inviting study areas in the three-story atrium. It also offers small exhibition spaces for student-curated shows.

# BUCKNELL UNIVERSITY

Freas Hall, Bucknell University, Lewisburg, PA 17837
**Telephone:** 570-577-1101 • **E-mail:** admissions@bucknell.edu
**Website:** www.bucknell.edu • **Hours:** Monday–Friday, 8:30 A.M.–4:30 P.M.; Saturday, 8:30 A.M.–NOON

## STUDENTS SAY

"A beautiful place to get a top-notch education while having a great social life even if you are stuck in the middle of Pennsylvania."

## FODOR'S SAYS

"The Pennsylvania Dutch aren't Dutch; the name comes from Deutsch (German). In the eighteenth century, this rolling farmland 65 miles west of Philadelphia became the home of the Amish, the Mennonites, and other German and Swiss immigrants escaping religious persecution."

## ABOUT THE SCHOOL

Bucknell, which calls itself a "small college with the academic resources of a large university," is one of America's premier liberal arts institutions. The 3,300-plus undergrads at Bucknell appreciate a college experience steeped in rich traditions and cutting-edge academic studies. Personal attention is the trademark of a Bucknell education.

## GETTING THERE

**BY AIR:** Larger flights land frequently at Harrisburg International and at Wilkes-Barre/Scranton airports. Commuter flights operate out of the closer Lycoming County Airport via Allegheny Commuter (USAir).

**BY TRAIN:** Amtrak service runs regularly to Harrisburg, approximately 60 miles from Lewisburg.

**BY BUS:** Susquehanna Trailways bus line stops three blocks from campus.

**BY CAR:** From I-83 North: Merge from I-83 North onto I-81 South; turn from I-81 South onto Route 322 West; turn onto Route 11/15 North; when Routes 11 and 15 split, follow Route 15 North (there will be a K-Mart on your left at this point); you'll arrive at a stoplight nearly seven miles after Selinsgrove/Shamokin Dam; Bucknell will be on your right. From the Pennsylvania Turnpike Northeast Extension and/or I-80: Turn onto I-80; take I-80 West to Exit 210A, or Route 15 South; follow Route 15 South; at the eleventh traffic light, turn left into Bucknell. From Route 22 East: Take Route 22 East to I-99 North (also called Route 220); merge onto Interstate 80 East; follow this to Exit 210A, or Route 15 South; at the eleventh traffic light, turn left into Bucknell. From Route 422 West: Take Route 422 West to Route 61 North; turn from Route 61 North onto Route 54 West; turn onto Route 642 West; turn onto Route 45 West; this will take you over a bridge and into Lewisburg; turn left on 7th Street, which will lead directly to campus.

**LOCAL:** Taxi service available through Aurora Taxi (570-523-1400).

## WHERE TO STAY

Lodging options in Lewisburg include the Lewisburg Hotel (570-523-7800, $$$), Days Inn (570-523-1711, $$), and All Suites Inn (570-523-8882, $).

| SCHOOL AT A GLANCE | |
|---|---|
| Type of School | Private |
| Environment | Village |
| Tuition | $35,802 |
| Enrollment | 3,460 |
| % Male/Female | 49/51 |
| Student/Faculty Ratio | 11:1 |

| FRESHMAN PROFILE | |
|---|---|
| Range SAT | |
| Critical Reading | 600-680 |
| Range SAT Math | 630-710 |
| Range ACT Composite | 27-30 |

| ON-CAMPUS APPOINTMENTS | |
|---|---|
| Advance Notice | Yes, 2 weeks |
| Appointment | Required |
| Saturdays | Yes |
| Average Length | 45 min |
| Info Sessions | Yes |
| Class Visits | Yes |

| CAMPUS TOURS | |
|---|---|
| Appointment | Not Required |
| Dates | Year Round |
| Times | M–F 9:30 A.M.–3:30 P.M.; |
| | Sat 10:30 A.M–NOON |
| Average Length | 60 min |

---

## CAMPUS AT ITS BEST!

Bucknell provides some great outlets for escaping academic stress. The Craft Center offers students the chance to get creative (and get their hands dirty) with classes in ceramics, stained glass, and digital film. You can also relax at the Uptown, an on-campus nightclub that opened in 2000. The club, which features both student bands and nationally touring groups, has netted performers like Maroon 5, Fallout Boy, and Phantom Planet. To get a greater sense of social life on campus, try to visit during the Chrysalis Ball gala, an annual event that brings the entire Bucknell community together.

# CANISIUS COLLEGE

2001 Main Street, Buffalo, NY 14208

**Telephone:** 716-888-2200 • **E-mail:** inquiry@canisius.edu • **Website:** www.canisius.edu

**Hours:** Monday–Friday and Saturday, 8:00 A.M. to 5:00 P.M. and by appointment

### SCHOOL AT A GLANCE

| | |
|---|---|
| Type of School | Private |
| Environment | Metropolis |
| Enrollment | 3,395 |
| % Male/Female | 44/56 |
| Student/Faculty Ratio | 13:1 |

### FRESHMAN PROFILE

| | |
|---|---|
| Range SAT | |
| Critical Reading | 470-630 |
| Range SAT Math | 480-650 |
| Range ACT Composite | 20-28 |
| Average HS GPA | 3.5 |

### ON-CAMPUS APPOINTMENTS

| | |
|---|---|
| Advance Notice | Yes, 1 week |
| Appointment | Required |
| Saturdays | Sometimes |
| Average Length | 30 min |
| Info Sessions | Yes |
| Class Visits | Yes |

### CAMPUS TOURS

| | |
|---|---|
| Appointment | Required |
| Dates | Year Round |
| Times | See website |
| Average Length | 60 min |

## STUDENTS SAY

Canisius offers "challenging classes with professors who understand and always are willing to help."

## FODOR'S SAYS

"The twentieth-century art is well represented" at the Albright-Knox Art Gallery, whose "collections are especially rich in postwar American and European art, including Jackson Pollock, Jasper Johns, and Andy Warhol. [There are also] works by Pablo Picasso, Vincent van Gogh, Claude Monet, Henri Matisse, and Pierre-Auguste Renoir. On Sunday afternoons in July and August, free jazz performances are held on the massive front steps."

## ABOUT THE SCHOOL

As a Jesuit institution, Canisius expects its students to have a broad depth of knowledge. Their mandatory core curriculum is designed to have undergrads grapple with the great philosophical questions of mankind, honing their critical thinking and writing skills. Of course, students are allowed to carve their own academic path, and with over 70 majors and minors, they are sure to find something of interest.

## GETTING THERE

**BY AIR:** The nearest airport is Buffalo/Niagara International, which is served by eight major carriers and eight commuter carriers.

**BY TRAIN:** Visitors can take Amtrak to either Buffalo or Depew, NY. Those who take the train directly into Buffalo can ride the local Metro rail to reach campus.

**BY BUS:** Both Greyhound and New York Trailways provide service to the Buffalo Metropolitan Transportation Center. If you walk two blocks west, you'll be able to connect with local rail service.

**BY CAR:** From the East: Follow I-90 West to Exit 51 West (NY 33 West). Proceed on NY 33 West until you hit NY 198 West. Take this to the Main Street (NY 5) Exit (first exit on your right). When you reach the stop sign, take a left (onto Kensington Avenue). At the light, make a left onto Main Street. When you hit the first light, take a right. You'll find the Admissions Office in Lyons Hall. From the West: Follow I-90 East to Exit 51 West (NY 33 West). NY 33 West will take you to NY 198 West. See above for the remainder of the directions. From the South: Follow U.S. 219 North to I-90 East (Buffalo and Albany). Continue on I-90 East to Exit 51 West (NY 33 West). See above for the remainder of the directions.

**LOCAL:** Visitors to campus can take the Metro Rail to the Humboldt-Hospital Metro Rail Station. Take the first set of escalators on your right and go up the second escalator. Exit the station from the left, heading towards Main Street. The Admissions Office is located one block south, on the right side of the street. Alternately, you can also take these local buses: Number 8: Main, Number 13: Kensington, Number 18: Jefferson, Number 26: Delavan, or Number 29: Wohlers.

## WHERE TO STAY

These lodging options all offer a special rate to Canisius guests: Holiday Inn (716-886-2121, $), University Inn (716-636-7500, $), or Adam's Mark Buffalo Niagara Hotel (800-444-2326, $$).

## CAMPUS AT ITS BEST!

For a taste of Canisius' impressive resources, simply remain in Lyons Hall. Home to the Communication Studies department, this facility is equipped with audio production and closed-circuit television studios, a multimedia production lab, and three video editing suites. Those touring the campus on a Friday or Saturday should attend an event at Penfold Commons. Luring students in with the promise of free food and entertainment, undergrads partake in anything from Spa Night to salsa dancing to sumo and sushi.

# CARNEGIE MELLON UNIVERSITY

5000 Forbes Avenue, Pittsburgh, PA 15213
**Telephone:** 412-268-2082 • **E-mail:** undergraduate-admissions@andrew.cmu.edu
**Website:** www.cmu.edu • **Hours:** Monday–Friday and Saturday, 8:30 A.M.–5:00 P.M. and by appointment

## STUDENTS SAY

"We are an arts school as well as a tech school so there is a very 'split personality' evident in the student body. Somehow it works and it makes the campus a way cooler place."

## FODOR'S SAYS

"One of America's oldest amusement parks and a National Historic landmark, Kennywood contains water rides and several roller coasters—including three of wooden construction dating from the 1920s. The park is 10 miles southeast of downtown."

## ABOUT THE SCHOOL

Research is the name of the game at Pittsburgh's Carnegie Mellon. While professors are reputedly stellar teachers, they are also actively engaged in their fields—and this adds a welcome dimension to the CMU experience. In addition, top-notch facilities, the latest equipment, and cutting-edge theories combine to give CMU's ambitious undergrads the high quality education they're after.

## GETTING THERE

**BY AIR:** Pittsburgh International Airport is 45 minutes from campus. Taxi services offer the most convenient transit between CMU and the airport, though the cost will range between $45 and $50. If you're staying at a hotel, check to see if complimentary shuttle service is offered.

**BY TRAIN:** Downtown Pittsburgh's Amtrak station is four miles from campus.

**BY BUS:** Greyhound services downtown Pittsburgh. The station is four miles from CMU.

**BY CAR:** From I-76 (Pennsylvania Turnpike) West: Follow I-76 East to Exit 57 for Pittsburgh/Monroeville/I-376. Take I-376 West to Exit 7 for Edgewood/Swissvale. At the end of the ramp make a right onto Braddock Avenue and continue to the intersection with Forbes Avenue. Go left onto Forbes Avenue and follow Forbes Avenue approximately three miles to campus. From I-76 (Pennsylvania Turnpike) East: Follow I-76 West to Exit 28 for Perry Highway. Exit here and merge onto I-79 South. Turn off I-79 South at Exit 72, and proceed on I-279 South. Follow signs toward the Fort Duquesne Bridge. After crossing the bridge, turn onto I-376 East. Take Exit 2A for Forbes Avenue/Oakland. Remain in the right-hand lanes as you follow Forbes Avenue for a little more than a mile. After passing through Oakland's business district you'll come to campus. From I-79 North: Follow I-79 North to I-279 North (toward Pittsburgh). Continue on I-279 North through the Fort Pitt Tunnel and onto the Fort Pitt Bridge. On the bridge, get into the far right lanes and follow signs for I-376 East/Monroeville. Take Exit 2A for Forbes Avenue/Oakland. Remain in the right-hand lanes as you follow Forbes Avenue for a little more than a mile. After passing through Oakland's business district you'll come to campus.

**LOCAL:** Port Authority Transit (PAT) offers regular bus service around campus and the greater Pittsburgh area. City taxi companies include Yellow Cab (412-665-8100), Peoples Cab (412-681-3131), and Checker Cab (412-381-5600).

## WHERE TO STAY

The Shadyside Inn (412-441-4444, $$), the Inns on Negley (412-661-0631, $$$), and the Sunnyside Boutique Hotel and Tea Room (412-683-5014, $$$) are each less than a mile from campus.

| SCHOOL AT A GLANCE | |
|---|---|
| Type of School | Private |
| Environment | Metropolis |
| Tuition | $33,050 |
| Enrollment | 5,494 |
| % Male/Female | 60/40 |
| Student/Faculty Ratio | 10:1 |

| FRESHMAN PROFILE | |
|---|---|
| Range SAT | |
| Critical Reading | 610-710 |
| Range SAT Math | 680-760 |
| Range ACT Composite | 28-32 |
| Average HS GPA | 3.57 |

| ON-CAMPUS APPOINTMENTS | |
|---|---|
| Advance Notice | Yes, 3 weeks |
| Appointment | Required |
| Saturdays | No |
| Average Length | 45 min |
| Info Sessions | Yes |
| Class Visits | Yes |

| CAMPUS TOURS | |
|---|---|
| Appointment | Not Required |
| Dates | Year Round |
| Times | M–F 9:30 A.M., 11:30 A.M., |
| | 1:30 P.M., and 3:30 P.M. |
| Average Length | 60 min |

---

## CAMPUS AT ITS BEST!

The Fence is a longstanding Carnegie Mellon tradition. Standing between Forbes Avenue and Hunt Library, the Fence is a huge billboard for student groups. However, there is a caveat. Those wishing to advertise on the board must paint it at night and then stand guard until morning to ensure the message does not get erased. If that doesn't satiate your taste for tradition, attend a football game. There you'll witness a performance by Carnegie Mellon's Kiltie Band. Dressed in full Scottish regalia, including kilts and knee socks, the band plays at every home game.

# THE CATHOLIC UNIVERSITY OF AMERICA

Office of Undergraduate Admissions, 620 Michigan Avenue, Northeast, Washington, DC 20064
**Telephone:** 202-319-5305 • **E-mail:** cua-admissions@cua.edu
**Website:** www.cua.edu • **Hours:** Monday–Friday, 10:30 A.M. and 2:00 P.M.

## Students Say

"CUA allows each person to develop fully: academically, emotionally, and most importantly, spiritually."

## Fodor's Says

"Before heading to the Capitol, pay a little attention to the grounds, landscaped in the late noneteenth century by Frederick Law Olmsted, a co-creator of New York City's Central Park. On these 68 acres are both the city's tamest squirrels and the highest concentration of TV news correspondents."

## About the School

At the Catholic University of America (CUA), undergrads grow both spiritually and academically. On the academic side, CUA mixes small-school intimacy with big-school resources (especially in fields like engineering, architecture, nursing, and music). When CUA's students don't have their noses in the books, they enjoy a campus life of seemingly endless events and activities.

## Getting There

**BY AIR:** Ronald Reagan National Airport is the most convenient airport to campus. SuperShuttle service is available to campus (800-258-3826). Students can also fly in to Dulles International Airport or Baltimore/Washington International Airport. A combination of bus and Metro will get you from Dulles as well as BWI.

**BY TRAIN:** Amtrak operates from downtown's Union Station. Take Metro (red line three stops to Brookland-CUA station) or a taxi to get to campus.

**BY BUS:** The Greyhound station is about two and a half miles South of campus. Greyhound also offers limited service at Union Station.

**BY CAR:** From I-95 North: Take I-95 North until it intersects with the Capital Beltway in Springfield, Virginia, and then follow I-395 North. Cross the Potomac River. Take the exit for "12th Street L'Enfant Promenade." Remain to the left and follow signs for 12th Street. After the tunnel, go right onto Constitution Avenue and make a left on 6th Street, Northwest. Turn right on East Street, Northwest. Turn left on North Capitol Street and proceed for two miles. Make a right onto Michigan Avenue, Northeast. The university is ahead on your left. From I-95 South: Travel along I-95 South to Exit 52 for the Baltimore/Washington Parkway. Go South on the Parkway to the Route 50 West Exit. Route 50 turns into New York Avenue. Take the South Dakota Avenue Exit. About a mile later, make a left onto Monroe Street. When Monroe Street ends, bear left onto Michigan Avenue. A university entrance will be ahead on your right.

**LOCAL:** Metro (DC's subway) has a Brookland-CUA stop on the red line. Local taxi services include Atlantic Cab (202-488-0609) and Yourway Taxi Cab (202-488-0609).

## Where to Stay

Some hotels in northeast Washington, DC offer discounted rates for CUA visitors and easy Metro access to campus. These include Sheraton Four Points (202-289-7600, $$), Phoenix Park Hotel (202-638-6900, $$$), and Hyatt Regency (202-787-1234, $$–$$$).

## CAMPUS AT ITS BEST!

The Edward J. Pryzbyla University Center is the nucleus of student life at Catholic University. Students congregate here to enjoy a meal, attend a club meeting, or listen to a stirring political debate. To see school spirit in action, think about participating in Cardinal Kickoff. This annual event, often held in conjunction with the first football game of the season, involves an abundance of food and live music. Students also have Washington, DC at their fingertips; a quick ride on the Metro will bring you to the steps of the Capitol Building and the Library of Congress.

# CHATHAM COLLEGE

Woodland Road, Pittsburgh, PA 15232
**Telephone:** 412-365-1290 • **E-mail:** admissions@chatham.edu
**Hours:** Monday–Friday, 9:00 A.M.–5:00 P.M.; Saturday, 10:00 A.M.–1:00 P.M. by appointment

## STUDENTS SAY

"The greatest strength about Chatham is its location. It's conveniently located between Squirrel Hill, Shadyside, and Oakland, but it's secluded in its own land of trees and mansions."

## FODOR'S SAYS

"Pittsburgh lies where the Allegheny and Monongahela rivers meet to form the Ohio River, in the hills of southwestern Pennsylvania. From its beginnings as an eighteenth-century French fortress and trading post, Fort Duquesne, and then as the British Fort Pitt, the city emerged as an industrial powerhouse in the 1800s, largely due to iron and steel production."

## ABOUT THE SCHOOL

Chatham, one of the oldest women's colleges in the country, remains committed to strong academics and the liberal arts. With an undergraduate population hovering around 800 and almost 800 coeducational graduate students, students are guaranteed small classes and an intimate learning environment. This closeness permeates virtually all aspects of life on campus and students are surrounded by people who want to see them succeed.

## GETTING THERE

**BY AIR:** Pittsburgh International Airport is only 23 miles from Chatham's campus.

**BY TRAIN:** Amtrak provides service to downtown Pittsburgh. Call a taxi for transportation to campus. For airport limousine service, call Airline Transportation Company at 412-471-8900.

**BY BUS:** Greyhound also provides service to downtown Pittsburgh. To reach campus (or your final destination), it's probably most convenient to call a cab.

**BY CAR:** From the Pennsylvania Turnpike (East or West): Take Exit 57 (only 12 miles from campus) and proceed to I-376 (the Parkway) West in the direction of Pittsburgh. Follow the Parkway through the Squirrel Hill tunnel and exit immediately after the tunnel at Exit 5/Squirrel Hill (old Exit 8). Merge to the extreme left and follow the exit ramp to the left toward Squirrel Hill. Drive to the multi-way intersection (Forward and Murray Avenues), bearing left onto Murray Avenue. Continue to the end of Murray Avenue where it meets with Wilkins Avenue. Make a right onto Wilkins and within one-half block make a left onto Woodland Road. Woodland will lead you directly to campus. From the North: Follow I-79 to I-279. Remain on 279 until you reach I-376 (the Parkway) to Monroeville. Continue on the Parkway to Exit 5. Follow "From the Pennsylvania Turnpike" directions above. From the South: Take I-79 to I-279. On the downtown side of the Fort Pitt Tunnel, I-279 becomes I-376. Follow I-376 to Exit 5. Follow "From the Pennsylvania Turnpike" directions above.

**LOCAL:** Port Authority Transit (PAT) provides bus service around the greater Pittsburgh area. For cab service consider: Yellow Cab (412-665-8100), Peoples Cab (412-681-3131), and Checker Cab (412-381-5600).

## WHERE TO STAY

These delightful hotels are all great options for your overnight stay: Best Western—Oakland (800-245-4444, $$), Sunnyledge Hotel (412-683-5014, $$–$$$), Courtyard By Marriott (412-683-3113, $$–$$$).

## CAMPUS AT ITS BEST!

Chatham is a college ripe with traditions. Every year students look forward to "The Battle of the Classes". The annual Airband Contest is another highly anticipated event. During this kickoff to Spring Fling, students lip-synch their hearts out in the hopes of winning a cash prize. There are several lovely neighborhoods within walking distance of campus. Self-professed shopaholics might enjoy Shadyside, which has a strip of trendy stores. Squirrel Hill offers a selection of delectable kosher delis and cozy coffee shops.

# CITY UNIVERSITY OF NEW YORK— QUEENS COLLEGE

65-30 Kissena Boulevard, Flushing, NY 11367

**Telephone:** 718-997-5600 • **E-mail:** admissions@qc.edu • **Website:** www.qc.cuny.edu

## STUDENTS SAY

"A very diverse student body that reflects the global population and the population of the great city [in] which it is located."

## FODOR'S SAYS

"Queens Botanical Gardens: Built for the 1939 World's Fair, these 39 acres include gardens of roses and herbs, an arboretum, and plantings especially designed to attract bees and birds. Plans slated for completion in 2006 will bring a new environmentally friendly visitor center that will use solar energy and water-filtering plants in its design."

## ABOUT THE SCHOOL

Queens College's appeal lies in its strong academic reputation and affordable education. Requirements emphasize the liberal arts and ensure that all QC grads are well rounded. New York City's resources help to compensate. A large percentage of students are commuters, but a plethora of extracurricular activities engender a feeling of community.

## GETTING THERE

**BY AIR:** New York is accessible via three major airports: Newark, LaGuardia, and JFK.

**BY TRAIN:** A number of train lines offer service to both Penn Station (Amtrak, New Jersey Transit, LIRR) and Grand Central Station (Metro-North).

**BY BUS:** A number of major and regional bus lines provide service to New York's Port Authority Terminal.

**BY CAR:** From Long Island and Points East: Follow the Long Island Expressway, heading Westbound. Watch for Queens College signs. For the Main Gate on Kissena, take Exit 24 (Kissena Boulevard). Make a left at the light, taking the overpass onto Kissena Boulevard. For Colden parking, take Exit 23 and make a left onto the Main Street overpass. Watch for Queens College signs to Colden parking. From Manhattan and Points West: Follow the Long Island Expressway, heading Eastbound. Watch for signs for Queens College. Take Exit 24 (Kissena Boulevard). For the Main Gate on Kissena, proceed down the service road until the first traffic light (Kissena Boulevard). Turn right onto Kissena Boulevard. For Kupterberg Arts Center parking, watch for signs as soon as you exit the expressway.

**LOCAL:** There's a cornucopia of both subway and bus service that will get you to Queens College. Via Forest Hills: Take the E, F, G, or R train to the 71st and Continental Avenue, Forest Hills stop. Follow the exit marked "North Side 70th Avenue and 108th Street." At the corner, take the Q65A bus to Kissena Boulevard and Jewel Avenue. The bus will drop you off one block south of campus. Via Flushing: Take the Long Island Railroad or 7 train to Main Street, Flushing. At Main Street, board the Q25, Q25-34, Q34, or Q17 bus. Via Kew Gardens: Take the E or F train to Union Turnpike. Next, board the Q74 Vleigh Place shuttle to the main gate.

## WHERE TO STAY

For hotels in Queens try the Comfort Inn (718-291-7500, $$), Quality Inn (718-523-8383, $$), or Howard Johnson (718-426-6200, $$).

## CAMPUS AT ITS BEST!

Jazz fans will want to pay a visit to the Louis Armstrong Archives. This unique facility serves to promote and preserve Armstrong's legacy. Visitors to the archive can listen to Louis' home-recorded tapes and read his personal manuscripts. Afterwards, those touring the school on a Tuesday should purchase tickets to Queens College Evening Readings, which have featured luminaries such as Tom Stoppard, E.L. Doctorow, and Salman Rushdie.

# CLARK UNIVERSITY

950 Main Street, Worcester, MA 01610-1477
**Telephone:** 508-793-7431 • **E-mail:** admissions@clarku.edu
**Hours:** Monday–Friday, 9:00 A.M.–5:00 P.M.; Saturday, 10:00 A.M.–2:00 P.M. and by appointment

## STUDENTS SAY

"Clark University is about high academic integrity with a twist of liberal understanding."

## FODOR'S SAYS

"Massachusetts invented the fried clam, [and] creamy clam chowder is another specialty. Eating seafood 'in the rough'—from paper plates in shack-like buildings—is a revered local custom.

## ABOUT THE SCHOOL

"Challenge Convention, Change Our World" isn't just a motto at Clark. It's a way of learning and living at a university that values hands-on learning to help solve real-world problems, experiencing diverse cultures, and making a positive difference in the world.

## GETTING THERE

**BY AIR:** Both Logan International Airport in Boston and T.F. Green International Airport near Providence are an hour from campus. The easiest transport to and from the airports is offered by Worcester Airport Limousine (800-660-0992).

**BY TRAIN:** Regional Amtrak service and MBTA commuter trains from Boston arrive at Worcester's station, which is three miles from campus. Take a taxi from the station to Clark.

**BY BUS:** Greyhound and Peter Pan bus lines offer direct service to Worcester. Take a taxi from the station to Clark.

**BY CAR:** From I-90 (Massachusetts Turnpike): Follow I-90 to Exit 10 for I-290 East toward Auburn/Worcester. Exit I-290 East at College Square/Federal Square (Exit 11) and continue straight toward Federal Square/Downtown. At Cambridge Street, turn left. Stay on Cambridge Street until it ends a mile later. Here, veer right onto Main Street. Then go left onto Maywood Street. University parking is just ahead on the left. From I-290 West: Leave I-290 West at Exit 18 for Route 9 toward Framingham/Ware. Go right at the bottom of the exit ramp. Follow signs toward Lincoln Square to the left. Turn right onto Highland Street. Then go left on Park Avenue. Six traffic lights later, make a left onto Maywood Street. After the stop sign, you'll see university parking to the right. From I-91 South: Follow I-91 South to Route 2 East. Follow Route 2 across the state until exiting onto I-190 South. Take I-190 South to I-290 West. See directions for I-290 West above.

**LOCAL:** The Worcester Regional Transit Authority (WRTA) offers regular bus service from campus to many local destinations. Campus bus stops are serviced by the 19S, 26S, and 33 lines. For taxi service, try Yellow Cab (508-754-3211) or Red Cab (508-792-9999).

## WHERE TO STAY

Worcester has no shortage of places to stay. Nearby hotels include Holiday Inn (508-852-4000, $$), Hampton Inn (508-757-0400, $$), and Beechwood Hotel (508-754-5789, $$$).

| SCHOOL AT A GLANCE | |
| --- | --- |
| Type of School | Private |
| Environment | City |
| Tuition | $31,200 |
| Enrollment | 2,069 |
| % Male/Female | 40/60 |
| Student/Faculty Ratio | 10:1 |
| **FRESHMAN PROFILE** | |
| Range SAT | |
| Critical Reading | 560-660 |
| Range SAT Math | 540-650 |
| Range ACT Composite | 24-28 |
| Average HS GPA | 3.44 |
| **ON-CAMPUS APPOINTMENTS** | |
| Advance Notice | Yes, 2 weeks |
| Appointment | Required |
| Saturdays | Sometimes |
| Average Length | 30 min |
| Info Sessions | Yes |
| Class Visits | Yes |
| **CAMPUS TOURS** | |
| Appointment | Not Required |
| Dates | Year Round |
| Times | Call for times |
| Average Length | 60 min |

---

## CAMPUS AT ITS BEST!

Students who want to glimpse the academic atmosphere at Clark should think about visiting on Spree Day. This annual April event offers students the opportunity to display their work via presentations, discussion panels, and exhibits. To further investigate the academic life on campus, stop by the George Perkins Marsh Institute. This facility features one of the country's most substantial research collections on environmental risks and hazards.

# CLARKSON UNIVERSITY

Box 5605, Potsdam, NY 13699

Telephone: 315-268-6479 • E-mail: admission@clarkson.edu

Website: www.clarkson.edu • Hours: Monday–Friday and Saturday by appointment, 8:00 A.M.–4:30 P.M.

## STUDENTS SAY

"Instead of just being a face in the crowd, students are able to actually build relationships with professors because of the smaller class sizes."

## FODOR'S SAYS

"The annual Saranac Lake Winter Carnival, held for 10 days starting in early February, is the oldest winter carnival in the country. It includes a lighted ice palace, fireworks, and a costume parade. Inner-tube and ski races, hockey tournaments, and snowshoe-softball games are among the sporting events."

## ABOUT THE SCHOOL

Clarkson is a tech-heavy school with the majority of undergrads majoring in science or engineering. The challenging curriculum provides ample opportunity for teamwork, and demands that students be focused in order to keep up with the demanding workload. Many of Clarkson's students major in the sciences, and the university tends to enroll a disproportionate amount of men. The rural setting is a plus for outdoor enthusiasts but offers few other distractions.

## GETTING THERE

**BY AIR:** Served by a number of airlines, Ottawa International and Montreal-Dorval Airports are the closest major airports, but remember to bring proof of U.S. citizenship (a passport or birth certificate will suffice).

**BY TRAIN:** Take the Amtrak to Lake Placid, approximately 55 miles from Potsdam, but from there, alternate transportation will be required.

**BY BUS:** Adirondack Trailways Bus Line provides service to Potsdam. Visitors should take a taxi to reach campus.

**BY CAR:** From Albany: Take Interstate 87 North to Exit 23 (Warrensburg). Take Route 9 North to the Route 28 intersection. Follow Route 28 to Indian Lake. Take Route 30 North to Tupper Lake. Pick up Route 3 West. Route 3 intersects with Route 56 North, which goes into Potsdam. Turn left onto Route 11 South in Potsdam. After crossing the river, campus is the first left after the traffic light. Total travel time is approximately four hours. From Syracuse: Take Interstate 81 North to Exit 48 (Route 342) North of Watertown. Route 342 East intersects with U.S. Route 11. Follow U.S. Route 11 North to Potsdam. Immediately after entering Potsdam, take second Clarkson entrance on right. Total travel time is approximately three hours. From Burlington: Take Interstate 89 North to Exit 21 (Swanton). Follow Route 78 West to Rouses Point (Route 78 merges with Route 2). Follow U.S. Route 11 South to Malone; turn left onto Route 30 South; take first right (Route 11B South) to Potsdam. Go straight onto Route 11 South in Potsdam. After crossing the river, campus is the first left after the traffic light. Total travel time is approximately three hours. From Utica: Take Route 12 North to Lowville. Then follow Route 26 North to U.S. Route 11 at Evans Mills; turn right and follow Route 11 North to Potsdam. Immediately after entering Potsdam, take the second Clarkson entrance on the right. Total travel time is approximately three hours.

**LOCAL:** Potsdam Taxi (315-268-8868).

## WHERE TO STAY

There are a number of fine establishments, including Misty Meadows located in Canton (315-379-1563, $), The Clarkson Inn (315-265-3050, $$), and Brambles Inn & Garden (315-268-0936, $$).

---

## CAMPUS AT ITS BEST!

Clarkson prides itself on creating a welcoming environment for students. Consider Our Place, the university's newest dining facility where students enjoy leisurely meals while relaxing by a fireplace. After dinner, venture to the edge of campus and visit the Adirondack House. Used as headquarters for a variety of outdoor activities, the facility comes complete with a charming chalet-like ambience. Those staying for the weekend should check out a comic or musical performance at Club '99, a student coffeehouse and pub.

---

# COLBY COLLEGE

4000 Mayflower Hill, Waterville, ME 04901-8848

**Telephone:** 207-872-3168 • **E-mail:** admissions@colby.edu • **Website:** www.colby.edu

**Hours:** Monday–Friday, 8:30 A.M.–4:30 P.M.; Saturday, 8:00 A.M.–NOON

## STUDENTS SAY

"Great place to have fun, meet great people, and learn a lot if you can bear the cold weather."

## FODOR'S SAYS

"For an authentic, Maine-style lobster dinner, you must go to a lobster pound. Generally these places are rustic and simple. Hundreds of freshly caught lobsters of varying sizes are kept in pens, waiting for customers."

## ABOUT THE SCHOOL

At Colby, 185 is an important number. Why? Because that's the combined total of majors (53), varsity sports teams (32), and student-run organizations (100) offered to the small pool of 1,800 undergrads. At this liberal arts leader, rigorous academics and an all-encompassing sense of community help create a dynamic college experience for these appreciative students.

## GETTING THERE

**BY AIR:** The most extensive regional service is available through the Portland International Jetport, a little more than an hour South. Bangor International Airport, an hour North, is serviced by five airlines with direct flights to eight U.S. cities. U.S. Air offers commuter flights to closer Augusta State Airport. Call Colby's campus services (207-859-4030) for info on shuttles. The college subsidizes shuttle fares to and from major regional airports.

**BY TRAIN:** Amtrak's Downeaster line runs from Boston to Portland. Take a shuttle or bus from there.

**BY BUS:** Vermont Transit/Greyhound runs daily service out of Waterville (207-872-5000).

**BY CAR:** From I-95 North: Follow I-95 North to Exit 127 for Routes 11 and 137 toward Waterville/Oakland. Make a right onto Kennedy Memorial Drive, then a quick left onto Washington Street. After about one and a half miles, bear right onto the Colby campus. From I-95 South: Take I-95 South to Exit 130 for Route 104 toward Waterville/Winslow. Soon after exiting, turn left onto Main Street. After half a mile, make a right at Eustis Parkway. As Eustis Parkway ends, turn right onto North Street, which turns into Mayflower Hill Drive. Colby is ahead on your right.

**LOCAL:** Shuttle service to and from regional airports is provided by several companies, including Mermaid Transportation (800-696-2463) and Moonlight Limousine Service (207-547-4184). For local taxi service, try Elm City Cab (207-872-0202) or Elite Taxi (207-872-2221).

## WHERE TO STAY

Waterville and the surrounding area offer a range of budget hotels, cozy cottages, and B&Bs. Among the most conveniently located options are the Budget Host Airport Inn (207-873-3366, $), the Lake Bed and Breakfast (207-465-4900, $$), and the Pressey House Lakeside Bed and Breakfast (207-465-3500, $$). Visitors should note that prices can vary significantly depending on whether "off season" or "in season" (usually May through October) rates apply.

### SCHOOL AT A GLANCE

| | |
|---|---|
| Type of School | Private |
| Environment | Town |
| Enrollment | 1,868 |
| % Male/Female | 47/53 |
| Student/Faculty Ratio | 10:1 |

### FRESHMAN PROFILE

| | |
|---|---|
| Range SAT | |
| Critical Reading | 640-720 |
| Range SAT Math | 640-710 |
| Range ACT Composite | 27-31 |

### ON-CAMPUS APPOINTMENTS

| | |
|---|---|
| Advance Notice | Yes, 2 weeks |
| Appointment | Required |
| Saturdays | Sometimes |
| Average Length | 45 min |
| Info Sessions | Yes |
| Class Visits | Yes |

### CAMPUS TOURS

| | |
|---|---|
| Appointment | Not Required |
| Dates | Year Round |
| Times | Varies |
| Average Length | 60 min |

---

# CAMPUS AT ITS BEST!

The Colby Museum of Art is a must-see on campus and boasts a remarkable collection of works by artists like Mary Cassatt, Gilbert Stuart, Georgia O'Keeffe, and Chuck Close. For on-campus fun, check out one of the Student Programming Board's many activities. Some of the more popular events include Disco on Ice, an Iron Chef competition, an all-campus BBQ, and the Colby Short Film Festival.

# COLGATE UNIVERSITY

13 Oak Drive, Hamilton, NY 13346
**Telephone:** 315-228-7401 • **E-mail:** admission@mail.colgate.edu
**Hours:** Monday–Friday, 8:30 A.M.–5:00 P.M.; select Saturdays, 9:00 A.M.–NOON

## STUDENTS SAY

"Colgate is about studying hard and playing hard. For the difficulty of the classes and the amount of reading we have, the weekends don't come soon enough."

## FODOR'S SAYS

"At the weeklong Herkimer County Fair, held in mid-August, you can take in many daily shows, including a demolition derby, beauty pageants, the Wild West Follies and Amateur Radio Club demos, and fireworks that round out the event. Games, rides, farming and livestock displays, tractor pulls, an ice-cream eating contest, and other diversions keep the kids busy."

## ABOUT THE SCHOOL

A bustling campus in a sleepy corner of upstate New York, Colgate sits among the heavy hitters of the Northeast's liberal arts institutions. When these undergrads aren't hitting the books, they have no trouble finding a club, sport, or an old-fashioned get-together to occupy their time.

## GETTING THERE

**BY AIR:** The Syracuse Hancock International Airport is about an hour from campus and hosts seven airlines.

**BY TRAIN:** The Amtrak station in Utica is about 25 miles away. The Syracuse station is 35 miles away.

**BY BUS:** Shortline/Coach USA bus lines stop in Hamilton. Adirondack Trailways and Greyhound operate out of nearby towns.

**BY CAR:** From I-90 West: Follow I-90 (New York State Thruway) West to Exit 25A, where you turn onto I-88 South. At the first exit, turn onto Route 20 West. Then go left on Route 12B toward Hamilton. From I-90 East: Follow I-90 (New York State Thruway) East to Exit 33 onto Route 365 West toward Vernon. In Oneida, turn onto Route 5 West, shifting quickly to the left lanes so that you can join Route 46 South. Continue on Route 46 South (passing over Route 20) for about 14 miles. Route 46 South turns into Route 12B South. This leads you into Hamilton. From I-81 North: Follow I-81 North to Binghamton, where you turn at Exit 6 for Route 12 North toward Sherburne. At Sherburne, bear left onto Route 12B North. This takes you into Hamilton.

**LOCAL:** The small town of Hamilton (population around 3,800) offers little by way of public transit. For convenient travel to nearby destinations, try one the area's taxi companies, which include Community Taxi (315-824-2227), and Hamilton Taxi (315-824-8294).

## WHERE TO STAY

Visitors can try staying at the elegant Colgate Inn (315-824-2300, $–$$), which offers rooms at a wide range of prices. The Sherburne Motel (607-674-5511, $) is 15 minutes south in Sherburne and the historic Ye Olde Landmark Tavern (315-893-1810, $$) is 10 minutes north in Bouckville. For B&B info, please check the Colgate University website.

## CAMPUS AT ITS BEST!

Colgate is home to an eclectic and remarkable number of artifacts. The Robert M. Linsley Museum houses one of the first dinosaur eggs ever discovered. If you're ready for a turkey, stop by the Reid Athletic Center and play a frame on one of the lanes at the bowling alley. In addition, the Colgate Activities Board (CAB) always has some sort of activity planned. From frequent movie screenings to Winterfest, there's always something going on.

# COLLEGE OF THE ATLANTIC

105 Eden Street, Admission Office, Bar Harbor, ME 04609
**Telephone:** 207-288-5015 • **E-mail:** inquiry@coa.edu
**Website:** www.coa.edu • **Hours:** Monday–Friday, 8:00 A.M.–4:00 P.M.

## STUDENTS SAY

"College of the Atlantic is a journey. Beyond the classrooms, students learn so much about humanity and their peers."

## FODOR'S SAYS

"At the College of the Atlantic, the George B. Dorr Museum of Natural History has wildlife exhibits, a hands-on discovery room, interpretive programs, and summer field studies for children."

## ABOUT THE SCHOOL

The College of the Atlantic, a small school of fewer than 300 students, is dedicated to social activism and the environment, and has a very engaged and active student body. A definite sense of community permeates the campus and undergrads are heavily involved in determining school policy. Indeed, freedom is a key component of a COA education; with only a few distribution requirements to fulfill, students here are able to explore their academic interests.

## GETTING THERE

**BY AIR:** Visitors can fly into either Bar Harbor or Bangor International Airport. You'll need to rent a car or take a taxi service to reach campus.

**BY TRAIN:** The nearest Amtrak station is approximately 36 miles away in Searsport. Visitors will need to take a taxi or private car service for the last portion of their trip.

**BY BUS:** Bus service is available to both Bangor and Ellsworth. Visitors will need to take a taxi or rent a car for the remainder of the trip.

**BY CAR:** From Boston: Follow Interstate 95 North to Interstate 395 in Bangor. Proceed to Route 1A from Bangor to Ellsworth. From Ellsworth: Take Route 3 East all the way to Bar Harbor. Cross the bridge onto Mount Desert Island, making sure to bear left. Make a left at the COA entrance and park in the designated areas. The Admission Office is located in Kaelber Hall. This is the building with the arch overlooking the water.

**LOCAL:** Local taxi companies include: At Your Service Taxi Co. (207-288-9222) and Mount Desert Island Taxi (207-288-3333). The Island Explorer also offers free shuttle service to a variety of points on Mt. Desert Island.

## WHERE TO STAY

Bar Harbor is home to a number of inns and B&Bs. Try the Atlantic Oakes (800-336-2463, $–$$), Aurora Inn (800-841-8925, $–$$) or Seacroft Inn (800-824-9694, $–$$).

### SCHOOL AT A GLANCE

| | |
|---|---|
| Type of School | Private |
| Environment | Rural |
| Tuition | $27,705 |
| Enrollment | 295 |
| % Male/Female | 35/65 |
| Student/Faculty Ratio | 10:1 |

### FRESHMAN PROFILE

| | |
|---|---|
| Range SAT | |
| Critical Reading | 560-670 |
| Range SAT Math | 530-630 |
| Range ACT Composite | 23-28 |
| Average HS GPA | 3.58 |

### ON-CAMPUS APPOINTMENTS

| | |
|---|---|
| Advance Notice | Yes, 1 week |
| Appointment | Required |
| Saturdays | No |
| Average Length | 45 min |
| Info Sessions | No |
| Class Visits | Yes |

### CAMPUS TOURS

| | |
|---|---|
| Appointment | Preferred |
| Dates | Year Round |
| Times | Varies |
| Average Length | 60 min |

---

## CAMPUS AT ITS BEST!

If you'd like to kick back with some COA students, simply head to the Rathskeller. This comfortable venue often sponsors pool tournaments and has an open mic night almost every Tuesday. Guests should also take advantage of the surrounding area. Acadia National Park is within walking distance of campus and has numerous trails enjoyable even to the novice hiker.

# COLLEGE OF THE HOLY CROSS

Admissions Office, 1 College Street, Worcester, MA 01610-2395
**Telephone:** 508-793-2443 • **E-mail:** admissions@holycross.edu
**Website:** www.holycross.edu • **Hours:** Monday–Friday, 8:30 A.M.–5:00 P.M.

## STUDENTS SAY

"Deeply steeped in tradition, Holy Cross provides an excellent education to students with a work hard/play hard mentality."

## FODOR'S SAYS

"If you plan to travel around a sizable portion of New England, a car or car rental is a must. Frequent rail connections exist only within Amtrak's Northeast Corridor and regional travel by air is limited.

## ABOUT THE SCHOOL

Students come to Holy Cross for a lot of reasons: the high caliber of the academics, personal attention from the professors, the beauty of the campus, and the list could go on and on. This all contributes to the towering expectations and tight sense of community that makes this liberal arts school a gem and a badge of honor in the eyes of current undergrads and alums.

## GETTING THERE

**BY AIR:** Try Logan International Airport in Boston or T.F. Green International Airport near Providence, both about an hour from campus. Worcester Airport Limousine (800-660-0992) offers easy transport to and from the airports.

**BY TRAIN:** Regional Amtrak service and MBTA commuter trains from Boston arrive at Worcester's station, just two miles from campus. For convenience, take a taxi from the station to campus.

**BY BUS:** Greyhound and Peter Pan bus lines offer direct service to Worcester. Use a taxi to get to campus.

**BY CAR:** From I-290: Turn off I-290 at Exit 11 for College Square/Southbridge Street. At the end of the ramp, shift quickly to the right lane and turn right onto College Street. As you drive up the hill, turn left onto Linden Lane and continue through the campus gates. From I-90 (Massachusetts Turnpike): Follow I-90 to Exit 10 for I-290 East, which takes you into Worcester. Follow "From I-290" directions above. From I-495 South: Take I-495 South to Exit 25B onto I-290 West. Follow "From I-290" directions above. From Route 146 North: Follow Route 146 North to Route 20 West. From Route 20 West, turn onto I-290 East toward Worcester. Follow "From I-290" directions above.

**LOCAL:** The Worcester Regional Transit Authority (WRTA) provides regular bus service throughout Worcester. The #10 bus runs between campus and downtown. The Student Government Association (SGA) Van Line offers free rides to all students traveling within 15 minutes of campus (508-733-8686). Taxi companies include Yellow Cab (508-754-3211) or Red Cab (508-792-9999).

## WHERE TO STAY

Worcester hotels include Holiday Inn (508-852-4000, $$), Hampton Inn (508-757-0400, $$), and Beechwood Hotel (508-754-5789, $$$).

## CAMPUS AT ITS BEST!

Holy Cross' Dinand Library is home to the Hiatt Holocaust Collection. This substantial collection focuses primarily on the activities of the Roman Catholic Church during the Nazi period. Guests are encouraged to peruse the museum's artifacts and periodicals. Take a break from trying to digest all that history with a quick visit to the Pub, located on the ground level of the Hogan Campus Center. Visit on a Friday, and you can eat for free.

# COLUMBIA UNIVERSITY

212 Hamilton Hall MC 2807, 1130 Amsterdam Avenue, New York, NY 10027
**Telephone:** 212-854-2522
**Website:** www.studentaffairs.columbia.edu/admissions/

## STUDENTS SAY

"Columbia is about gaining a well-rounded education in a city that forces you to be resourceful and independent."

## FODOR'S SAYS

"Long and narrow, tree-lined Riverside Park runs along the Hudson River between West 72nd and West 159th streets. From the corner of West 72nd Street and Riverside Drive—where the statue of Eleanor Roosevelt stands at the park's entrance—head down the ramp to the 70th Street Boat Basin, a rare spot in Manhattan where you can walk right along the river's edge, watch a flotilla of houseboats bobbing in the water, and take in an open-air meal at the Boat Basin Café."

## ABOUT THE SCHOOL

The intellectual crème de la crème of a very sophisticated city, Columbia University offers an academic experience that, some say, is second to none. And with New York City at the university's doorstep, students can count on both Columbia's Ivy League classrooms and the cultural riches of the Big Apple to give them a first-rate education.

| SCHOOL AT A GLANCE | |
| --- | --- |
| Type of School | Private |
| Environment | Metropolis |
| Tuition | $33,664 |
| Enrollment | 5,400 |
| % Male/Female | 50/50 |
| Student/Faculty Ratio | 7:1 |
| **FRESHMAN PROFILE** | |
| Range SAT | |
| Critical Reading | 670-770 |
| Range SAT Math | 680-790 |
| Range ACT Composite | 31-34 |
| **ON-CAMPUS APPOINTMENTS** | |
| Class Visits | Yes |
| **CAMPUS TOURS** | |
| Appointment | Not Required |
| Dates | Year Round |
| Times | M–F: 10:00 A.M.–11:00 A.M.; |
| | some Saturdays |
| Average Length | 120 min |

## GETTING THERE

**BY AIR:** All three major airports in the New York City metro area (John F. Kennedy International Airport, LaGuardia Airport, and Newark International Airport) offer wide-ranging flight options. Transportation options from the airports to campus include bus, taxi, and train/subway.

**BY TRAIN:** Amtrak services Penn Station (7th Avenue and 34th Street). Take taxi, bus, or subway from the station to campus.

**BY BUS:** Greyhound runs a number of limited service stations in NYC, as well as its primary station at Port Authority about four miles South. Take bus, taxi, or subway from the station to campus.

**BY CAR:** From I-95 South or I-87 South: Exit at the Cross Bronx Expressway East toward the George Washington Bridge. As you come to the bridge, bear right and take the exit for the Henry Hudson Parkway South. Get off the Parkway at the 96th Street Exit (West Side Highway). Travel two blocks East to Broadway and turn left (uptown). Follow Broadway to the entrance to the Columbia campus at 116th Street. From I-95 North or I-80 East: Follow signs to the George Washington Bridge. Just before the bridge, I-95 and I-80 combine. Just after the bridge, follow the Henry Hudson Parkway South. Get off the Parkway at the 96th Street Exit (West Side Highway). Travel two blocks East to Broadway and turn left (uptown). Follow Broadway to the entrance to the Columbia campus at 116th Street.

**LOCAL:** The five Metropolitan Transit Authority (MTA) bus lines that stop close to campus are the M4, M5, M11, M60, and M104. Bus fare is $2.00 per ride (pay with coins or MetroCard only). If you're traveling by subway, take the 1 train to the 116th Street stop.

## WHERE TO STAY

There's no shortage of lodging options in NYC. Among those on Manhattan's Upper West Side—Columbia's general neighborhood—are the Millburn Hotel (212-362-1006, $$), the Quality Hotel (212-866-6400, $$), Hotel Belleclaire (212-362-7700, $$$), and the Mayflower Hotel (212-265-0060, $$$+).

---

## CAMPUS AT ITS BEST!

You don't need to travel to Paris to catch a glimpse of Rodin's "The Thinker." Posed outside the entrance of Columbia's Philosophy Hall, the statue is an authentic bronze casting of the famed statue. Columbia's Butler Library was modeled on the Parthenon in Greece, while the steps of Low Library have been called one of the great meeting places of the world, and served as a backdrop for a recent *Spiderman* film. If you're anxious to explore the neighborhood, grab a cup of coffee at Tom's, the diner featured in *Seinfeld*.

# CONNECTICUT COLLEGE

270 Mohegan Avenue, New London, CT 06320
**Telephone:** 860-439-2200 • **E-mail:** admission@conncoll.edu
**Hours:** Monday–Friday, 8:30 A.M.–4:00 P.M.; Saturday, 8:30 A.M.–3:30 P.M.

## SCHOOL AT A GLANCE

| | |
|---|---|
| Type of School | Private |
| Environment | Town |
| Enrollment | 1,778 |
| % Male/Female | 41/59 |
| Student/Faculty Ratio | 10:1 |

### FRESHMAN PROFILE

| | |
|---|---|
| Range SAT | |
| Critical Reading | 630–700 |
| Range SAT Math | 620–700 |
| Range ACT Composite | 26–29 |

### ON-CAMPUS APPOINTMENTS

| | |
|---|---|
| Advance Notice | Yes |
| Appointment | Recommended |
| Saturdays | Sometimes |
| Average Length | 30–45 min |
| Info Sessions | Yes |
| Class Visits | Yes |

### CAMPUS TOURS

| | |
|---|---|
| Appointment | Not Required |
| Dates | Year Round |
| Times | Varies |
| Average Length | 60 min |

## STUDENTS SAY

"Our strict honor code is one of the best things going for our school. The honor code applies socially and academically, making this a very safe and honest campus."

## FODOR'S SAYS

"Connecticut College's Palmer Auditorium plans a full schedule of dance and theater programs."

## ABOUT THE SCHOOL

Connecticut College is a liberal arts school that brings out the best in its students, both inside and outside of the classroom. Challenging course work, dedicated professors, and an unbending sense of community contribute to a student body looking to have an impact on the world around it.

## GETTING THERE

**BY AIR:** The closest airports are T.F. Green Airport in Providence, Rhode Island (50 miles from campus) and the Bradley International Airport outside of Hartford (63 miles). Take a car, shuttle, or taxi to campus.

**BY TRAIN:** Amtrak's Acela Express and Regional lines stop at New London's Water Street station, two miles from campus. Grab a cab for the easiest transportation to campus.

**BY BUS:** New London's Greyhound station, just several doors down from the Amtrak station, is two miles South of campus. Take a taxi from the station to campus.

**BY CAR:** From I-91 South: Take I-91 South to Hartford, where you'll pick up Route 2 South toward New London/Norwich. Then turn onto I-395 South. From I-395 South, take Exit 78 for Route 32 South. Go straight for three miles. The campus entrance is on your right. From I-95 North: Follow I-95 North to Exit 83. At the end of the exit ramp, continue up the hill to the traffic light. Turn right onto Route 32 North. Drive one mile. The college entrance is on your left. From I-95 South: Follow I-95 South until you pass over the Groton Gold Star Bridge, where you turn at Exit 84 onto Route 32 North. Drive one mile. The college entrance is on your left. From I-395 South: Proceed on I-395 South to Exit 78 for Route 32 South. Go straight for three miles. The campus entrance is on your right.

**LOCAL:** New London's taxi options include Aloha Taxi (860-442-5642) and Port City Taxi (860-444-9222).

## WHERE TO STAY

Looking for a place to spend the night? Try the Radisson Hotel (860-443-7000, $$), the Holiday Inn (860-442-0631, $$), or the Lighthouse Inn Resort (860-443-8411, $$–$$$).

---

## CAMPUS AT ITS BEST!

Educational opportunities abound at Conn College, as evidenced by a trip to the observatory in Bill Hall. This facility houses an historic Alvan Clark refractor telescope. When Conn students want a break from academics, they head over to the Ad Astra Garden. This spot, overlooking the College Green, is a great place to read or converse with friends. Residential life offers additional options for both socializing and intellectual debate. Every October, students compete in the Camelympics, a two-day competition that pits residential houses against each other.

# THE COOPER UNION FOR THE ADVANCEMENT OF SCIENCE AND ART

30 Cooper Square, Office of Admissions and Records, New York, NY 10003
Telephone: 212-353-4120 • E-mail: admissions@cooper.edu

## STUDENTS SAY

"Blood, sweat, and tears; but you come out of school prepared for anything and everything."

## FODOR'S SAYS

"Jutting out as if it were Manhattan's green toe, Battery Park (so named because a battery of 28 cannons was placed along its shore in colonial days to fend off the British) is built on landfill and is the take-off point for ferries to the Statue of Liberty and Ellis Island. Climb the steps of the East Coast Memorial for a fine view of the main features of New York Harbor, from left to right: Governors Island, a former Coast Guard installation whose future is somewhat undecided; hilly Staten Island in the distance; the Statue of Liberty, on Liberty Island; Ellis Island, gateway to the New World for generations of immigrants; and the old railway terminal in Liberty State park, on the mainland in Jersey City, New Jersey."

## ABOUT THE SCHOOL

You'll be hard pressed to find a better deal than Cooper Union. Everyone enrolled receives a full tuition scholarship at a first-class institution. The school has an extremely narrow academic focus, only offering programs in art, architecture, and engineering. Students almost unanimously agree that the workload is extremely demanding yet highly rewarding, though when not busy in the lab or studio, many undergrads unwind in New York City.

## GETTING THERE

**BY AIR:** Visitors traveling by air have the option of flying into three major airports: Newark, JFK, or LaGuardia. Taxis, rental cars, and shuttle buses are all available for transportation to the city.

**BY TRAIN:** Both Penn Station and Grand Central Station are serviced by a number of train lines. Visitors can easily hop onto a subway or into a cab and quickly make their way to Cooper Union. A taxi should cost around $5.00.

**BY BUS:** All major bus lines provide service to New York's Port Authority Terminal. Visitors can easily hop onto a subway or into a cab and quickly make their way to Cooper Union. A taxi should cost around $7.00.

**BY CAR:** From the West Side of Upper Manhattan: Drive South on the West Side Highway to 56th Street. Proceed South on 12th Avenue (note: this becomes West Street). When you reach 12th Street, make a left and take 12th Street to Third Avenue. Take a right on Third Avenue and continue to Cooper Square, which begins at 7th Street. From the East side of Manhattan: Take the East River Drive to Houston Street. Continue on Houston traveling Westbound to Bowery. Turn right (North) on Bowery and drive to Cooper Square. Cooper Square begins on 7th Street.

**LOCAL:** Subway: Guests can either take the R or W subway lines to 8th Street or take the 6 train to Astor Place. Bus: Take any of the following buses and ask the driver to let you off nearest Astor Place or Cooper Square: The M1 (5th and Madison Avenues), the M15 (First and Second Avenues), the M6 (7th Avenue/Broadway and Avenue of the Americas), the M101 or M102 (3rd and Lexington Avenues).

## WHERE TO STAY

Visitors will no doubt find an abundance of accommodations in New York. Here are but a few of your options: Union Square Inn (212-614-0500, $$), Hotel Wolcott (212-268-2900, $$), or the Library Hotel (212-983-4500, $$$+).

## SCHOOL AT A GLANCE

| | |
|---|---|
| Type of School | Private |
| Environment | Metropolis |
| Tuition | $30,000* |
| Enrollment | 929 |
| % Male/Female | 64/36 |
| Student/Faculty Ratio | 7:1 |

### FRESHMAN PROFILE

| | |
|---|---|
| Range SAT | |
| Critical Reading | 610-690 |
| Range SAT Math | 600-760 |
| Average HS GPA | 3.6 |

### ON-CAMPUS APPOINTMENTS

| | |
|---|---|
| Advance Notice | Yes, 2 weeks |
| Appointment | Required |
| Saturdays | No |
| Average Length | 45 min |
| Info Sessions | Yes |
| Class Visits | Yes |

### CAMPUS TOURS

| | |
|---|---|
| Appointment | Required |
| Dates | Academic Year |
| Times | Varies |
| Average Length | 60 min |

*All students receive a full tuition scholarship. Tuition is listed so that students are eligible to apply for additional forms of financial aid.

## CAMPUS AT ITS BEST!

The Great Hall at Cooper Union has long existed as a forum for free speech and an exchange of ideas. Many leaders and power brokers have graced the stage of this famed auditorium including Theodore Roosevelt, Woodrow Wilson, and Bill Clinton. After stopping at the Great Hall, move on to the School of Art and take in the current exhibition on display. Past shows have featured a virtual dance installation choreographed by Bill T. Jones and the photography of Jules Backus.

# CORNELL UNIVERSITY

Undergraduate Admissions, 410 Thurston Avenue, Ithaca, NY 14850
**Telephone:** 607-255-5241 • **E-mail:** admissions@cornell.edu
**Hours:** Monday–Friday, 8:00 A.M.–4:30 P.M.

## STUDENTS SAY

"On how many campuses do you get to walk over a 100-foot deep gorge filled with rushing water-falls every morning on the way to class? If Cornell doesn't have the greatest campus in the country, it's certainly got the greatest one this side of California."

## FODOR'S SAYS

"With its historic buildings, weave of natural and man-made spaces, Cayuga Lake views, and two spectacular gorges, the campus of this private university is considered one of the most beautiful in the country. Four miles of trails lead through the 220-acre Sapsucker Woods Sanctuary, part of the Cornell Lab of Ornithology (159 Sapsucker Woods Road), which features a computer touch screen that leads you through interpretive displays."

## ABOUT THE SCHOOL

One of America's eight elite Ivies, Cornell is a hefty research institution that doesn't skimp on the resources. The campus, which is host to a world famous library and a cast of major academic prize winners (Nobel, Pulitzer, MacArthur, Turing—you name it), mixes the best in progressive thought with the rich traditions of one of America's oldest educational institutions.

## GETTING THERE

**BY AIR:** Ithaca Tompkins Regional Airport hosts US Airways and Northwest/KLM. Also, Syracuse Hancock International Airport and Greater Rochester International Airport are each less than two hours away.

**BY TRAIN:** Syracuse, 58 miles north of Ithaca, offers the closest Amtrak rail stop.

**BY BUS:** Ithaca's downtown bus terminal is serviced by Greyhound, Shortline, New York Trailways, Swarthout Coaches, and CU Transit. Hop on TCAT lines #14, 20, or 21 to go from the station to campus.

**BY CAR:** From I-81 South: Take I-81 South to Exit 12 for Route 281 toward Cortland/Homer. Turn off Route 281 South onto Route 13 South. As you come into Ithaca, make a left onto Route 366 (West). Then turn right onto Hoy Road, which leads you to campus. From I-90 (New York State Thruway) West: Follow I-90 West until merging onto I-88 West. After 76 miles, take the Bainbridge Exit (Exit 8) and proceed onto Route 206 West. Go 25 miles before turning onto Route 79 West at Whitney Point. About 35 miles later, Route 35 West turns into State Street as you enter Ithaca. Turn right onto Mitchell Street. On top of the hill, bear left onto Ithaca Road, which soon turns into Dryden Road. Turn from Dryden Road onto Hoy Road and follow this onto campus. From I-81 North: Follow I-81 North to Exit 8 toward Whitney Point. Turn onto Route 79 West and pick up directions from Whitney Point in "From I-90" section above.

**LOCAL:** Tompkins Consolidated Area Transit (TCAT) provides bus service for the city and campus. More than a dozen TCAT buses service the university. Local taxi companies include University Taxi (607-277-7777) and Finger Lakes Taxi (607-277-0611).

## WHERE TO STAY

Lodging includes Econo Lodge (607-257-1400, $–$$), Downtown Holiday Inn (607-272-1000, $$), and the Statler Hotel at Cornell University (607-257-2500, $$–$$$).

## CAMPUS AT ITS BEST!

If natural beauty has a name, it's Cornell. Cascadilla Gorge, the boundary between central campus and Collegetown, is breathtaking. An upperclass residence hall even backs up to the trail entrance. Crave something less rustic? Meander over to Ho Plaza, the social center of campus, where students post announcements, stage stunts to publicize events, hold fundraisers, and even occasionally engage in step-dancing competitions. Otherwise there's always the annual Rocky Horror Picture Show, the Johnson Museum, or films at Cornell Cinema.

# DARTMOUTH COLLEGE

6016 McNutt Hall, Hanover, NH 03755

**Telephone:** 603-646-2875 • **E-mail:** admissions.office@dartmouth.edu • **Website:** www.dartmouth.edu •
**Hours:** Monday–Friday, 8:00 A.M.–4:30 A.M.; Saturday, 8:00 A.M.–NOON

## STUDENTS SAY

"Dartmouth is a fast-paced place for those who want to work hard, play hard, party hard, and fall in love with their school."

## FODOR'S SAYS

"Ledyard Canoe Club of Dartmouth provides canoe rentals and kayak rentals and classes on the swift-flowing Connecticut River, which isn't suitable for beginners and is safest after mid-June."

## ABOUT THE SCHOOL

Dartmouth earns raves from students for having great food, a great library, and an overall great quality of life—and, well, they get a nod for their great parties, too. This New Hampshire Ivy Leaguer has a reputation for its outstanding academics and its outdoorsy student body; from what we can tell, it's well deserved.

## GETTING THERE

**BY AIR:** The Lebanon Regional Airport, about 15 minutes from campus, offers USAir Express connecting flights. For a greater airline selection, check out Logan International Airport. From there, take Vermont Transit or Dartmouth Coach buses to get to campus.

**BY TRAIN:** Amtrak's "Vermonter" line makes daily stops in White River Junction, VT, several miles from Hanover.

**BY BUS:** Vermont Transit Lines (800-552-8737) stop in neighboring White River Junction, VT, with connecting service to campus. Dartmouth Coach (603-448-2800) runs primarily between campus and points in Boston. Advance Transit (802-295-1824) provides free regional bus service in the New Hampshire/Vermont Upper Valley region.

**BY CAR:** From I-93 North: Follow I-93 North to I-89 North, which you stay on until Exit 18 for Lebanon/Dartmouth College/Route 120. From the exit, go right (North) on Route 120. After four miles, the road forks; bear right and continue as Route 120 merges with South Park Street. At the second light, make a left onto East Wheelock Street. Campus is just ahead. From I-91 North: Follow I-91 North, approaching Norwich, VT. Take Exit 13, bearing right and crossing the Connecticut River. You are on West Wheelock Street. Less than a mile ahead, at the town center, is the Dartmouth campus. From I-89 South: Follow I-89 South to White River Junction, VT, which neighbors Hanover. Here you merge onto I-91 North. Then use "From I-91 North" directions above.

**LOCAL:** For taxi service, contact Big Yellow Taxi (603-643-8294) or P & PS Twin State Taxi (802-295-7878).

## WHERE TO STAY

A healthy number of lodging options are sprinkled throughout Hanover, White River Junction, and Lebanon. These include Fairlee Motel and Drive-In Theatre (yes, that's right, one of only two motel/drive-in combos around: 802-333-9192, $), Residence Inn by Marriott (603-643-4511, $$), and the on-campus Hanover Inn (603-643-4300, $$$).

| SCHOOL AT A GLANCE | |
|---|---|
| Type of School | Private |
| Environment | Village |
| Tuition | $33,297 |
| Enrollment | 3,993 |
| % Male/Female | 50/50 |
| Student/Faculty Ratio | 8:1 |

| FRESHMAN PROFILE | |
|---|---|
| Range SAT | |
| Critical Reading | 670-770 |
| Range SAT Math | 680-780 |
| Range ACT Composite | 29-34 |
| Average HS GPA | 3.75 |

| ON-CAMPUS APPOINTMENTS | |
|---|---|
| Advance Notice | Yes, 3 weeks |
| Appointment | Required |
| Saturdays | Sometimes |
| Average Length | 30 min |
| Info Sessions | Yes |
| Class Visits | Yes |

| CAMPUS TOURS | |
|---|---|
| Appointment | Not Required |
| Dates | Year Round |
| Times | Varies |
| Average Length | 60 min |

## CAMPUS AT ITS BEST!

Dartmouth's impressive resources extend beyond campus boundaries. Traveling a mere three miles north, visitors will hit the Dartmouth Organic Farm. This student-run garden provides students with hands-on experience with sustainable food and energy systems. Head an additional 12 miles north and you'll arrive at the Dartmouth Skiway. The Skiway is home to the college's alpine ski team, and during the season, shuttles run daily between campus and the trails.

# DICKINSON COLLEGE

PO Box 1773, Carlisle, PA 17013-2896

**Telephone:** 717-245-1231 • **E-mail:** admit@dickinson.edu • **Website:** www.dickinson.edu

**Hours:** Monday–Friday, 8:30 A.M.–4:30 P.M.; Saturday, 9:00 A.M.–NOON

## STUDENTS SAY

"Dickinson attracts students who work hard, who want to have lots of study abroad/off-campus study options, and who want all the benefits of a small, private liberal arts school."

## FODOR'S SAYS

"Hickory Run State Park offers fishing, camping, and Boulder Field, an area of rock formations dating to the Ice Age."

## ABOUT THE SCHOOL

One of America's oldest colleges, Dickinson has long stood among the leaders in liberal arts education. Challenging academics, small classes, and seemingly endless opportunities to study abroad have made this campus in central Pennsylvania an academic powerhouse.

## GETTING THERE

**BY AIR:** Harrisburg International Airport, half an hour away from campus, is serviced by seven airlines. Taxi or limousine service is the best transportation option to campus.

**BY TRAIN:** Amtrak operates daily out of the Harrisburg Transportation Center, about half an hour from campus. Use taxi or limousine service to get to campus.

**BY BUS:** Amtrak and Trailways bus lines service the Pilot Travel Center on the edge of town.

**BY CAR:** From I-76 (Pennsylvania Turnpike) East/West: Follow I-76 to Exit 226 for Carlisle. After paying the toll, move quickly to the right lane and continue onto Route 11 South (Harrisburg Pike). As you near downtown Carlisle, Route 11 becomes Hanover Street. In the historic downtown, turn right onto High Street. The Dickinson campus is a few blocks ahead on High Street. From I-83 North: Travel on I-83 North to Exit 39B for I-76 (Pennsylvania Turnpike). Get on I-76 West toward Pittsburgh. Proceed according to "From I-76" instructions above. From I-81 North: Take I-81 North to Exit 47 for Hanover Street. At the stop sign, make a left and proceed straight. In Carlisle's historic downtown, turn left onto High Street. The Dickinson campus is a few blocks ahead on High Street. From I-81 South: Follow I-81 South to Exit 49 for High Street/Route 641. At the end of the exit ramp, make a right onto High Street. Continue through downtown until you come to campus.

**LOCAL:** Limited regional bus transportation services Carlisle through Harrisburg's Capital Area Transit (717-238-8304). For taxi or airport limousine service, try West Shore Taxi Company (717-795-8294) or Airport Limousine (717-944-4017).

## WHERE TO STAY

For lodging just a stone's throw from campus, try downtown's new Comfort Suites (717-960-1000, $$) or its historic Carlisle House Bed and Breakfast (717- 249-0350, $$–$$$). Other nearby options includes the Econo Lodge (717-249-7775, $) and the Clarion (717-243-1717, $$).

## CAMPUS AT ITS BEST!

Dickinson's West College (referred to as "Old West" by students) certainly exudes a sense of history. It is the oldest standing structure on campus and a registered Historic Landmark. When you're done ruminating on the past, head over to the Holland Union Building. This facility, affectionately known as the HUB, is the center of campus activity. You'll find everything here, from a dining hall and coffee shop to computer labs, lounges, and even a meditation room.

# DREW UNIVERSITY

Office of College Admissions, Madison, NJ 07940-1493
**Telephone:** 973-408-3739 • **E-mail:** cadm@drew.edu
**Website:** www.drew.edu

## Students Say

"People are really accepting of everything. Professors are totally cool with transgendered students, as are peers. Also, as a student body goes, we're really quite smart."

## Fodor's Says

"Although Newark International Airport is all some travelers experience of this part of the state, a wealth of activities are available to those who care to linger. Among the suburban bedroom communities of Manhattan-bound commuters are parks, performing arts venues, museums, great shopping, and some of the state's finest restaurants and lodgings."

## About the School

The self-described "close-knit" community at Drew University is home to 1,600 undergrads who enjoy small classes, constant attention from their professors, and a strong sense of individual value. Students boast that this is more than just your typical liberal arts college; with a strong study abroad program and NYC less than an hour away, Drew's students have the world at their fingertips.

## Getting There

**BY AIR:** Newark Liberty International Airport is about 17 miles from campus. Take a car or taxi to campus. Be aware that the cab fare will cost around $50.

**BY TRAIN:** New York City's Penn Station sees heavy Amtrak traffic. From Penn Station, use the New Jersey Transit (regional train service) Morris-Essex line traveling toward Dover. Take this train to the Madison stop.

**BY BUS:** Lakeland bus lines service Summit, NJ, about 15 minutes from Madison, including travel to and from New York City. From Summit, take a taxi or hop aboard the NJ Transit Morris-Essex line (toward Dover) as described above.

**BY CAR:** From I-287 South: Follow I-287 South to Exit 35 for Madison Avenue/Route 124. After climbing the exit ramp, turn right onto Route 124 East. Drive three miles into Madison. Drew is on your right. From I-80 East/West: Travel on I-80 to Exit 43 for I-287 South toward Morristown. From here, see "From I-287 South" directions above. From I-287 North: Take I-287 North to Exit 35 for South Street/Route 124. Make a left at the end of the exit ramp, then a very quick right onto Route 124 East. Drive three miles into Madison. Drew is on your right. From I-78 East: From I-78 East, merge left onto I-287 North. From here, see "From I-287 North" directions above. From New Jersey Turnpike North: Follow the New Jersey Turnpike North to Exit 10 for I-287 North. From here, see "From I-287 North" directions above. From the Garden State Parkway North: Follow the Garden State Parkway North to Exit 127 for I-287 North. From here, see "From I-287 North" directions above.

**LOCAL:** For taxi/limousine service, try P & P Taxi Service (973-377-2693), Airport Express Limousine (973-701-7884), or Madison Livery (973-377-6843).

## Where to Stay

Most area lodging is located in towns around Madison. Options include the Sheraton Parsippany Hotel (973-515-2000, $$), the Old Mill in Basking Ridge (908-221-1100, $$), and the Madison Hotel in Morristown (973-285-1800, $$–$$$).

### SCHOOL AT A GLANCE

| | |
|---|---|
| Type of School | Private |
| Environment | Village |
| Tuition | $32,508 |
| Enrollment | 1,561 |
| % Male/Female | 42/58 |
| Student/Faculty Ratio | 12:1 |

### FRESHMAN PROFILE

| | |
|---|---|
| Range SAT | |
| Critical Reading | 550-660 |
| Range SAT Math | 540-650 |
| Range ACT Composite | 24-27 |
| Average HS GPA | 3.32 |

### ON-CAMPUS APPOINTMENTS

| | |
|---|---|
| Advance Notice | Yes, 2 weeks |
| Appointment | Required |
| Saturdays | Yes |
| Average Length | 30 min |
| Info Sessions | Yes |
| Class Visits | Yes |

### CAMPUS TOURS

| | |
|---|---|
| Appointment | Not Required |
| Dates | Year Round |
| Times | Varies |
| Average Length | 60 min |

## CAMPUS AT ITS BEST!

When touring Drew, be sure to stop by the F.M. Kirby Shakespeare Theatre. This facility, which seats over 300, is home to the renowned Shakespeare Theatre of New Jersey. It is also used for large-scale student productions. Those who visit the school in the early fall might get a chance to attend FAP (First Annual Picnic). This annual event features games, music, food, and a beer garden (for those of legal age, of course).

# DREXEL UNIVERSITY

3141 Chestnut Street, Philadelphia, PA 19104
**Telephone:** 215-895-2400 • **E-mail:** enroll@drexel.edu • **Website:** www.drexel.edu
**Hours:** Monday–Friday, 9:00 A.M.–5:00 P.M.; Saturday, 10:00 A.M., by appointment only

## STUDENTS SAY

"For six months out of the year nearly every student is able to see their major in action. It has been very useful to help guide students in the direction of what they truly want to do when they leave."

## FODOR'S SAYS

"Stately Independence Hall, opened in 1732 as the state house for the colony of Pennsylvania, was the site of many historic events: the Second Continental Congress, convened on May 10, 1775; the adoption of the Declaration of Independence a year later; the signing of the Articles of Confederation in 1778; and the formal signing of the Constitution by the Framers on September 17, 1787."

## ABOUT THE SCHOOL

Drexel, an urban university with a business and technological bent, mixes rigorous academics with real-world experience. The university gets rave reviews for its co-op program, which provides students the chance to alternate between periods of classroom study and full-time professional employment. Hometown Philly provides plenty of options for fun when students need a break—South Street on Saturday night is a popular destination for students looking for a place to unwind.

## GETTING THERE

**BY AIR:** Philadelphia International Airport is the nearest option. Southeastern Pennsylvania Transportation Authority, or SEPTA, runs from the airport to Philadelphia's 30th Street Station, just a few blocks from campus. Take the R1 train line.

**BY TRAIN:** Amtrak stops at the city's 30th Street Station, just a few blocks from campus.

**BY BUS:** Greyhound's main station on Filbert Street offers service to and from destinations across the country. Limited service is also available to the 30th Street Station. Contact Greyhound for more info (800-231-2222).

**BY CAR:** From I-95 South: Follow I-95 South to Exit 22 for I-676 West toward Central Philadelphia. Turn from I-676 West onto I-76 East toward the airport. Turn off I-76 East at Exit 345 for 30th Street/University City. At the top of the exit ramp, make a right and continue around 30th Street Station to campus. From I-95 North: Proceed on I-95 North to Exit 22 (a left exit) for I-676 West toward Central Philadelphia. From there, use "From I-95 South" directions above. From the New Jersey Turnpike South: Follow the New Jersey Turnpike South to Exit 4 for Route 73 North. Take Route 73 North to the Betsy Ross Bridge (this is a left exit), which will lead you to I-95 South. From there, use "From I-95 South" directions above. From I-76 (Pennsylvania Turnpike) East: Stay on the Pennsylvania Turnpike to Exit 326 for Valley Forge. Pay the toll and continue on I-76 East toward I-476/Philadelphia/U.S. 202/Valley Forge. Turn off I-76 East at Exit 345 for 30th Street/University City. At the top of the ramp, make a right and continue around 30th Street Station to campus.

**LOCAL:** Take SEPTA's Market-Frankford Line (or Blue Line) for bus service to nearby 30th or 34th streets. SEPTA's Green Line trolleys also stop at 30th and 34th streets. For taxi service, try Liberty Cab (215-389-8000) or Quaker City Cab (215-728-8000).

## WHERE TO STAY

Hotels near Drexel include Sheraton University City (877-459-1146, $$–$$$) and Hilton Inn at Penn (215-222-0200, $$–$$$). For a less expensive option, try the Best Western Center City (215-568-8300, $). Be sure to inquire about discounts for campus visitors.

---

## CAMPUS AT ITS BEST!

Prospective Drexel students should think about visiting during Discover Drexel Days. Students who visit on these specially designated days will get to meet students and faculty, tour dorms, explore sports and performance arts groups, and participate in any special events happening that day. No matter what day you're visiting, make sure you stop by the James Creese Student Complex to sample some dining hall food while you investigate the campus radio station. Also, consider touring the 424-seat Mandell Theater. This facility always has a packed schedule, hosting guest lectures, multiple film series, and numerous student performances.

# DUQUESNE UNIVERSITY

600 Forbes Avenue, Pittsburgh, PA 15282
**Telephone:** 412-396-6222 • **E-mail:** admissions@duq.edu
**Website:** www.duq.edu • **Hours:** Monday–Friday, 8:30 A.M.–4:30 P.M.

## STUDENTS SAY

"People at Duquesne are open-minded and accepting, smart but not cocky, dedicated, and looking to have fun in college."

## FODOR'S SAYS

"East of downtown, Oakland has many of the city's cultural, educational, and medical institutions. The Carnegie is an opulent cultural center, with the Museum of Art, the Museum of Natural History, the Music Hall, and the Carnegie Library all under one Beaux-Arts roof."

## ABOUT THE SCHOOL

Catholic values and a commitment to personal attention are the trademarks of a Duquesne education. The school itself guarantees, "you'll feel at home at Duquesne University." But this doesn't mean there's no excitement. Located in the heart of uptown Pittsburgh, Duquesne spoils its students with easy access to all that Pittsburgh has to offer.

## GETTING THERE

**BY AIR:** Fly into the Pittsburgh International Airport South of town. For $2.25, hop aboard the Port Authority's West Busway line 28X (Airport Flyer) and enjoy a cheap, if slow, ride to campus. Cabs and shuttles are also available at the airport.

**BY TRAIN:** The Amtrak station is about half a mile from campus. Take a cab to campus. Or, if your bags aren't too heavy, use those legs.

**BY BUS:** The Greyhound terminal is a stone's throw South of campus.

**BY CAR:** From I-79 South: Follow I-79 South to Exit 72 for Pittsburgh/I-279 South. Turn off I-279 South at Exit 8A for I-579 South/Veteran's Bridge. Follow signs for Mellon Arena before turning right on Washington Place. Two blocks later make a right onto Forbes Avenue. Go straight until turning right into the Duquesne parking garage. I-79 North: Follow I-79 North to Exit 59A for Pittsburgh/I-279 North. As you come to the Fort Pitt Tunnel, get in the right lane. Just after the tunnel, turn right at the exit for Monroeville/I-376. Soon after, use Exit 1C (on the left) to get onto Grant Street. Five traffic lights later, turn right onto Forbes Avenue and continue half a mile to the Duquesne parking garage. From I-76 (Pennsylvania Turnpike) West: Take I-76 to Exit 57 for Pittsburgh-Monroeville/I-376. Follow I-376 West to Exit 2B for Boulevard of the Allies. When Boulevard of the Allies forks at Mercy Hospital, bear right. Continue straight to campus.

**LOCAL:** Port Authority of Allegheny County offers service throughout the city. Take lines 61 or 71 for Forbes Avenue stops close to campus. Local taxi companies include Yellow Cab (412-321-8100) and Peoples Cab Co. (412-466-8300).

## WHERE TO STAY

Pittsburgh's many lodging options include Holiday Inn Express (412-488-1130, $$), the riverfront Sheraton Station Square (412-261-2000, $$$), and, just two blocks from campus, the Pittsburgh Marriott City Center (412-471-1234, $$$).

### SCHOOL AT A GLANCE

| | |
|---|---|
| Type of School | Private |
| Environment | Metropolis |
| Tuition | $20,855 |
| Enrollment | 5,678 |
| % Male/Female | 42/58 |
| Student/Faculty Ratio | 15:1 |

### FRESHMAN PROFILE

| | |
|---|---|
| Range SAT | |
| Critical Reading | 510-600 |
| Range SAT Math | 520–620 |
| Range ACT Composite | 21-26 |
| Average HS GPA | 3.65 |

### ON-CAMPUS APPOINTMENTS

| | |
|---|---|
| Advance Notice | Yes, 2 weeks |
| Appointment | Preferred |
| Saturdays | Rarely |
| Average Length | 45 min |
| Info Sessions | Yes |
| Class Visits | Yes |

### CAMPUS TOURS

| | |
|---|---|
| Appointment | Preferred |
| Dates | Year Round |
| Times | M–F 9:00 A.M., NOON, |
| | 3:00 P.M.; Sat varies |
| Average Length | 60 min |

## CAMPUS AT ITS BEST!

Duquesne University is home to a very unique ensemble, the Tamburitzans. This group is dedicated to the performance and preservation of music and dances from Eastern Europe. They also maintain a cultural center complete with a film library, rare recordings, a collection of working instruments, and costume pieces. For a glimpse of campus social life, stop by the Duquesne Union NiteSpot. This student favorite offers Internet access, a comfortable lounge area, billiards, skee-ball, ping-pong, and video game consoles. It also hosts late-night activities like "Casino Night" and "Tournament Night." Most importantly, these events typically feature free snacks and beverages.

# ELMIRA COLLEGE

One Park Place, Elmira, NY 14901
**Telephone:** 607-735-1724 • **E-mail:** admissions@elmira.edu
**Website:** www.elmira.edu

## STUDENTS SAY

"Elmira College is about challenging oneself with academics in a very open environment where you know almost everyone."

## FODOR'S SAYS

"Elmira's most famous resident, Samuel Clemens (aka Mark Twain), spent more than 20 summers at Quarry Farm, which belonged to his wife's family. The city has also been known as the 'soaring capital of America,' since it hosted the first national soaring contest in 1930."

## ABOUT THE SCHOOL

Tucked away in the breathtaking Finger Lakes Region, Elmira offers students some impressive academic opportunities. Their distinctive curriculum requires undergrads to complete internships and perform community service. These experiences allow for practical application of classroom teachings. Additionally, their unique third term (a six-week mini-semester in April and May) provides students with travel, independent research, and innovative courses.

## GETTING THERE

**BY AIR:** Guests can opt to fly into the Elmira-Corning Regional Airport, 10 miles from campus. The airport receives daily flights from several major cities using US Air and Northwest Airlines. Taxi service is available from the airport.

**BY TRAIN:** There is no direct train service to Elmira. The closest Amtrak station is located in Syracuse, approximately 75 miles away.

**BY BUS:** Adirondack Trailways, Short Line, and Greyhound all provide service to the Elmira area. The station is less than a mile from campus.

**BY CAR:** From Exit 56: Take Route 352 (Church Street) to North Main Street, making a right on North Main Street. You'll bear slightly left at McDonald's and proceed straight to the college. From Route 13 Southbound (from Ithaca, Cortland, Syracuse): Take Route 13 South to the junction with Route 17 (Interstate 86), heading Eastbound to Exit 56 (Route 352—Church Street). See above for the remaining directions. Route 17 (Interstate 86) Westbound (from Binghamton, Albany, NYC, New England): Take Exit 56 (Route 352—Church Street). See above for the remainder of the directions. Route 17 (Interstate 86) Eastbound (from Corning, Rochester, Buffalo, Pittsburgh, Ohio): Exit 56 (Route 352—Church Street). See above for the remainder of the directions.

**LOCAL:** For local taxi service, try Totem Taxi, Inc. (607-734-6161).

## WHERE TO STAY

For an overnight stay, consider: Econo Lodge (607-739-2000, $), Comfort Inn (607-962-1515, $$), or The Painted Lady—Bed & Breakfast (607-732-7515, $$–$$$), the Hilton Garden Inn (607-795-1111, $$–$$$), and the Holiday Inn (607-739-3681, $–$$$).

## CAMPUS AT ITS BEST!

The Mark Twain Study, built by his sister-in-law, is where Twain wrote many of his famed works, including *Huckleberry Finn* and *Tom Sawyer*. For a sumptuous meal after visiting the Study, you won't have to travel far to Simeon's Restaurant, located in the Campus Center (reservations required). To cap off your day, visit the Clemens Center. This venue hosts a variety of performances throughout the year, including musicals like *Hairspray*, comedians, and silent movies with live organ music.

# EMERSON COLLEGE

120 Boylston Street, Boston, MA 02116-4624
**Telephone:** 617-824-8600 • **E-mail:** admission@emerson.edu
**Hours:** Monday–Friday, 9:00 A.M.–5:00 P.M.; Saturday by appointment

## STUDENTS SAY

"Emersonians are the most talented group of oddball, leftist, free-thinking individuals I've ever come across, with some mercilessly vapid yuppies thrown in for good measure."

## FODOR'S SAYS

"Boston's many students, artists, academics, and young professionals have made the town a haven for the arts, international cinema, late-night bookstores, ethnic food, alternative music, and unconventional politics."

## ABOUT THE SCHOOL

If you're into communications or the arts, then you'll be into Emerson. With a curriculum focused around these two areas of specialization, Emerson is a creative haven situated in one of America's most popular college towns. As if this isn't enough, a seasoned and accessible faculty is in place to make sure the academics are top-notch.

## GETTING THERE

**BY AIR:** Book a flight to Logan International Airport. From there, take a taxi or subway to get to campus.

**BY TRAIN:** Amtrak's Acela Express provides high-speed travel between Boston, New York, Philadelphia, and Washington, DC. Amtrak's Downeaster allows easy access from Maine. Take a taxi, the bus, or the T to Emerson.

**BY BUS:** Greyhound and Peter Pan bus lines service Boston's South Street station.

**BY CAR:** From I-95 North/South and I-93 North/South: Take I-95 North/South and merge onto I-93 North/South toward Boston. Follow I-93 to Exit 26 for Storrow Drive/Cambridge and continue until the left exit for Copley/Back Bay. As the ramp ends, make a left onto Beacon Street. Just after turning onto Beacon Street, make a right onto Arlington Street. Proceed straight to the fifth light, where you make a left onto Stuart Street. Parking can be tough, so as you hit Stuart Street, begin checking for vacancies in area garages. Turn left onto Charles Street for more options. From I-90 (Massachusetts Turnpike) East: Follow I-90 East into Boston, then take Exit 22 for Prudential/Copley Square. Shift to the right lane quickly to go toward Copley Square. As you come above ground, continue ahead to Stuart Street. Parking can be tough, so as you hit Stuart Street, begin checking for vacancies in area garages. Turn left onto Charles Street for more options. If traveling by car, be aware that street parking is limited. Visitors should head to one of several nearby parking facilities before making the short walk to the campus and Admission Visitor Center. The Motor Mart and Radisson Hotel Parking Garages are located at 201 and 200 Stuart Street and the Boston Common Parking Garage is located at Zero Charles Street.

**LOCAL:** The College is best accessed by Boston's subway system—the "T"—at Boylston Station on the Green Line. (Visitors can transfer to the Green Line from the Red, Orange, or Blue lines at several downtown T stations.)

## WHERE TO STAY

Boston boasts plenty of beds for visitors, and Emerson is located in the heart of Boston's Theatre District. Close to campus are the Sheraton Park Plaza (800-225-2008, $$$), Courtyard Boston Tremont Hotel (800-331-9998, $$), and Radisson-Boston (617-482-1800, $$).

### SCHOOL AT A GLANCE

| | |
|---|---|
| Type of School | Private |
| Environment | Metropolis |
| Tuition | $24,064 |
| Enrollment | 3,165 |
| % Male/Female | 44/56 |
| Student/Faculty Ratio | 14:1 |

### FRESHMAN PROFILE

| | |
|---|---|
| Range SAT | |
| Critical Reading | 590-670 |
| Range SAT Math | 560-650 |
| Range ACT Composite | 25-29 |
| Average HS GPA | 3.57 |

### ON-CAMPUS APPOINTMENTS

| | |
|---|---|
| Advance Notice | Yes, 2 weeks |
| Appointment | Required |
| Saturdays | Sometimes |
| Average Length | 30 min |
| Info Sessions | Yes |
| Class Visits | No |

### CAMPUS TOURS

| | |
|---|---|
| Appointment | Required |
| Dates | Year Round |
| Times | Varies |
| Average Length | 60 min |

## CAMPUS AT ITS BEST!

Prospective Emerson students should definitely explore the Ansin Building, the college's academic hub. With its collection of film and video editing rooms, a digital audio recording studio, and a DVD authoring suite, the Ansin Building is a great example of the kind of facilities to which you'll have access. The building is also home to the school's award-winning radio station, WERS-FM. The college recommends you book your visit to Emerson online at http://visit.emerson.edu.

# ENDICOTT COLLEGE

376 Hale Street, Beverly, MA 01915
**Telephone:** 978-921-1000 • **E-mail:** admissio@endicott.edu
**Website:** www.endicott.edu

## STUDENTS SAY

"The academics are really strong here."

## FODOR'S SAYS

"Seascapes and fall foliage are the most commonly photographed subjects in New England. Remember that saltwater and autumn leaves photograph better when something else is included in the picture."

## ABOUT THE SCHOOL

Prospective students looking for a nurturing environment in which to learn should explore Endicott. The majority of classes are capped at 20 students, and personal attention is par for the course. The college's philosophy is deeply embedded in the principles of applied learning, and all undergraduates are required to complete internships. Endicott's close proximity to Boston grants students access to unparalleled cultural and professional opportunities.

## GETTING THERE

**BY AIR:** Boston's Logan International Airport is the closest airport to Beverly. Taxis, car rentals, shuttles, and even limos are all available to get to campus.

**BY TRAIN:** Amtrak trains provide service to Boston's South Station. From there, visitors can take a commuter rail out to Beverly.

**BY BUS:** Greyhound, Peter Pan, and Concord Trailways all have routes to Boston's South Station. Taxis and commuter rails are available for further transport to campus.

**BY CAR:** From Route 128 North (Exit 45 on Route 95): Take Exit 17 (Grapevine Road, Beverly Farms). Make a right off the exit ramp. Drive for another mile and a half and then take another right onto Haskell Street. Follow this road to the end. When you reach the stop sign, make a right onto Hale Street, Route 127. This will take you directly to Endicott College. The main entrance will be the second entrance on your right. From I-84, Hartford, New York City, or I-90, Albany: Follow the Mass Pike to Exit 14, Weston. From here take I-95 North to Exit 45. Proceed to Route 128 North toward Gloucester. Follow "From Route 128 North" directions above. From Boston: Take Route I-93 North to Route I-95 North, getting off at Exit 45. Follow "From I-84" directions above. From Vermont, New Hampshire: Take Route 89 to Route 93 South. Continue on to Route 95 North. Follow "From Route 128 North" directions above.

**LOCAL:** The MBTA (Massachusetts Bay Transportation Authority) provides commuter rail service out to Beverly.

## WHERE TO STAY

Think about staying in one of these charming inns: Beverly Farms Bed & Breakfast (978-922-6074, $–$$), Lakeview Motor Lodge (978-922-7535, $–$$) or the Vine and Ivy Inn (978-927-2917, $$).

## CAMPUS AT ITS BEST!

To get a sense of the campus atmosphere, consider visiting the Lodge. Designed in an old New England style (with post and beam construction), this is a popular student gathering space. It is even equipped with barbeque pits! Endicott also manages to attract some unbelievable lecturers and performers. Music sensation Gavin Degraw and captivating speaker Alina Fernandez, Castro's daughter, have graced the campus. Finally, sports enthusiasts might want to attend the college's annual Regatta, sure to draw large crowds.

# EUGENE LANG COLLEGE—
# THE NEW SCHOOL FOR LIBERAL ARTS

65 West Eleventh Street, New York, NY 10011
**Telephone:** 212-229-5665 • **E-mail:** studentinfo@newschool.edu
**Hours:** Monday–Friday, 9:00 A.M.–5:00 P.M.

## STUDENTS SAY

"Lang is about academic freedom: you can be a total slacker or a devoted academic and you'll be in good company either way."

## FODOR'S SAYS

Visit the "Theodore Roosevelt Birthplace National Historic Site where the 26th U.S. president—the only one from New York City—was born in 1858. The original 1848 brownstone was demolished in 1916, but this Gothic Revival replica, built in 1923, is a near-perfect reconstruction of the house where Teddy lived until he was 15 years old."

## ABOUT THE SCHOOL

Eugene Lang College is a nontraditional school for students who are self-motivated and independent. After learning lessons in the classroom, students take to the streets of New York City where even more adventure can be found.

## GETTING THERE

**BY AIR:** Three major airports service the New York metropolitan area: John F. Kennedy International Airport, LaGuardia International Airport, and Newark International Airport.

**BY TRAIN:** Amtrak and New Jersey Transit stop at Pennsylvania Station (34th Street) in Manhattan.

**BY BUS:** Greyhound and New Jersey Transit stop at Port Authority (42nd Street).

**BY CAR:** From the North: Take I-95 to the Triborough Bridge. Follow the FDR Drive downtown. Exit at 14th Street. Travel East to 6th Avenue. Make a left. Turn left onto 12th Street. From the South: Take the New Jersey Turnpike North to the Holland Tunnel to Canal Street. Continue on Canal Street to 6th Avenue (Avenue of the Americas). Go North on 6th Avenue (turn left) to 12th Street and turn right. From the Lincoln Tunnel: Follow the signs to 39th or 40th Streets and head East (one block) to 9th Avenue. Travel South on 9th Avenue to 14th Street. Make a left turn on to 14th Street and continue to 6th Avenue. Turn left and continue to 12th street. From the East: Take the Long Island Expressway (I-95) West to the Midtown Tunnel. From the Tunnel, follow signs to 34th Street and the FDR Drive. Take the Drive South to the 15th Street Exit and continue South to 14th Street. Make a left on 14th Street and continue to 6th Avenue. Turn left on 6th Avenue and continue to 12th Street.

**LOCAL:** For subway travel, take the 1, 2, or 3 trains to 14th Street. Walk East to 6th Avenue and make a right. Walk to 12th Street and turn left onto 66 West 12th Street. PATH trains from Newark, Jersey City, or Hoboken in New Jersey stop at 9th Street and 6th Avenue. Walk North to 12th Street, then East (turn right).

## WHERE TO STAY

New York City offers a variety of housing options, and none of them come cheap. For hotels close to campus, check out the Wolcott Hotel (212-268-2900, $$), Howard Johnson Express Inn (212-358-8844, $$$), and Clarion Hotel Park Avenue (212-532-4860, $$$).

### SCHOOL AT A GLANCE

| | |
|---|---|
| Type of School | Private |
| Environment | |
| Tuition | $24,920 |
| Enrollment | 887 |
| % Male/Female | 31/69 |
| Student/Faculty Ratio | 16:1 |

### FRESHMAN PROFILE

| | |
|---|---|
| Range SAT | |
| Critical Reading | 540-660 |
| Range SAT Math | 470-590 |
| Range ACT Composite | 20-26 |
| Average HS GPA | 3.06 |

### ON-CAMPUS APPOINTMENTS

| | |
|---|---|
| Advance Notice | Yes, 1 week |
| Appointment | Not Required |
| Saturdays | Sometimes |
| Average Length | 30 min |
| Info Sessions | Yes |
| Class Visits | Yes |

### CAMPUS TOURS

| | |
|---|---|
| Appointment | Not Required |
| Dates | Academic Year |
| Times | M–F 11:00 A.M. |
| | and 2:00 P.M. |
| Average Length | 60 min |

---

## CAMPUS AT ITS BEST!

To experience life as a Eugene Lang student, you'll want to explore New York. Students quickly adopt Manhattan as their own and use the city's unmatched resources to complement their education and enhance their social activities. While you're there, visit the nearby Guggenheim Museum designed by famed architect Frank Lloyd Wright. Or revel in the city's historic music scene and attend a show at the Knitting Factory, a popular hangout for Lang students.

# FAIRFIELD UNIVERSITY

1073 North Benson Road, Fairfield, CT 06824-5195
**Telephone:** 203-254-4100 • **E-mail:** admis@mail.fairfield.edu
**Website:** www.fairfield.edu • **Hours:** Monday–Friday, 8:30 A.M.–4:30 P.M.; Saturday, 9:00 A.M.–12:30 P.M.

## STUDENTS SAY

"Life at Fairfield is pretty good. The dorms and other living facilities are good, the food is pretty good, the social life is awesome, and all other aspects of life are good too."

## FODOR'S SAYS

"The indoor walk-through South American rain forest at Connecticut's Beardsley Zoo alone justifies a visit. It's alive with dozens of species, some rare and endangered."

## ABOUT THE SCHOOL

A healthy balance of work and play is what students find at the Jesuit-affiliated Fairfield University. On the academic side of things, Fairfield dishes up healthy workloads and a very accessible faculty. On the social side of things, the university offers plenty of student clubs, events, and lots of good old-fashioned opportunities to just "hang out" with friends.

## GETTING THERE

**BY AIR:** Traffic permitting, Fairfield is less than one and a half hours from either JFK or LaGuardia airports in New York City. Westchester Airport is also one and a half hours away. Prime Time, a shuttle service, offers direct transport from either airport to campus (866-284-3247).

**BY TRAIN:** Metro-North offers service to and from NYC. Amtrak stops in Bridgeport, about 10 minutes from campus. Take a cab from the station.

**BY BUS:** Greyhound stops in Bridgeport, about 10 minutes away. Take a taxi to campus.

**BY CAR:** From I-95 North: Follow I-95 North to Exit 22 and turn left onto Round Hill Road. At Barlow Road, turn right. The university gates are ahead on your left. From I-95 South: Follow I-95 South to Exit 22 and turn right onto North Benson Road and proceed to the university entrance on the left. From Route 15 North: Follow Route 15 North to Exit 44. At the end of the ramp, turn left, and then make a quick right onto Route 58 (Black Rock Turnpike). Two miles later, turn right onto Stillson Road (Route 135). Veer left onto North Benson Road. Turn into Fairfield on your right. From I-84 West: Follow I-84 West until merging onto I-91 South. At New Haven, I-91 South and I-95 South merge. From there, follow "From I-95 South" directions above.

**LOCAL:** For local taxi service, call Fairfield Cab Company at 203-255-5797.

## WHERE TO STAY

For overnight accommodations close to campus, try Westport Inn (203-255-0491, $$) or the Black Rose Inn (203-659-2200, $$).. Nearby cities such as Bridgeport, Norwalk, Shelton, and Westport offer a substantial selection of additional lodging options.

## CAMPUS AT ITS BEST!

At Fairfield, education and intellectual debate doesn't stop when class is over. The university sponsors a number of well-attended lecture series. Consider sitting in on one of the Charles F. Dolan Series lectures featuring highly accomplished business leaders and visionaries. Afterwards, head over to the Quick Center for the Arts. This facility always delivers a packed season full of rich entertainment. Check out the Center's live radio dramas or its ever-popular International Literature Festival.

# FORDHAM UNIVERSITY

441 East Fordham Road, Duane Library, New York, NY 10458
**Telephone:** 718-817-4000 • **E-mail:** enroll@fordham.edu
**Website:** www.fordham.edu • **Hours:** Monday–Friday, 9:00 A.M.–5:00 P.M.

## STUDENTS SAY

In regards to student life, one student sums it up nicely: "It's Manhattan. It's up to you, man."

## FODOR'S SAYS

"Founded in 1804, the New York Historical Society is the city's oldest museum and one of its finest research libraries, with a collection of 6 million pieces of art, literature, and memorabilia. Highlights of the collection include George Washington's inaugural chair, 500,000 photographs from the 1850s to the present, original watercolors for John James Audubon's Birds of America, the architectural files of McKim, Mead & White, and one of the most in-depth collections of pre-twentieth-century American paintings in the world, including seminal landscapes by Hudson River School artists Thomas Cole, Asher Durand, and Frederic Church."

## ABOUT THE SCHOOL

Jesuit traditions are alive and well at Fordham University, a multi-campus institution with locations in Manhattan and the Bronx. What this means is that students receive a plethora of personal attention as the faculty guide them to becoming able scholars, successful professionals, and well-rounded individuals.

## GETTING THERE

**BY AIR:** All major NYC area airports—JFK, La Guardia, or Newark—allow easy access to Fordham's Rose Hill campus. Use Riverdale/Jitney Limo Service for direct service to campus (718-884-9400). Taxis are available at each airport as well.

**BY TRAIN:** Amtrak services NYC's Penn Station. Take a cab or subway to Grand Central and board the Metro-North Commuter Railroad and take it to the Fordham Road Station stop or board the #4 subway train north to the Fordham Road Station.

**BY BUS:** Greyhound services the Port Authority in Manhattan. Take a cab to Grand Central and follow the train/subway directions above.

**BY CAR:** From Garden State Parkway North: Follow Garden State Parkway North to Exit 159 toward George Washington Bridge/I-80 East. After the bridge, exit onto Henry Hudson Parkway North and proceed to Exit 24 for Mosholu Parkway. When Mosholu Parkway ends, take a right onto Southern Boulevard. Make a right at the third light. From I-87 (New York Thruway) South: Follow I-87 South as it combines with I-287 and crosses the Tappan Zee Bridge. Use Exit 8 for I-287 (Cross-Westchester Expressway) and take this to Exit 3 for Sprain Brook Parkway South toward New York City. After Sprain Brook Parkway turns into Bronx River Parkway, take Exit 7W for Fordham Road. Stay right as you proceed. Take a right onto Southern Boulevard/Dr. Theodore Kazimiroff Boulevard. The campus is a quarter mile ahead on your left. From I-95 South: Proceed on I-95 South until Exit 8C for Pelham Parkway West. Stay right as you proceed. Take a right onto Southern Boulevard/Dr. Theodore Kazimiroff Boulevard. The campus is a quarter mile ahead on your left.

**LOCAL:** Take the Metro-North Commuter Railroad or the subway (lines 4 or D) to nearby Fordham Road Station. Taxi services include Flash Cab Company (718-365-8888) and Tremont Dispatching (718-892-6666).

## WHERE TO STAY

Lodging close to the Rose Hill campus includes the Royal Regency Hotel (914-476-6200, $–$$), Ramada Inn (914-592-3300, $), and Hampton Inn (914-592-5680, $$).

| SCHOOL AT A GLANCE | |
| --- | --- |
| Type of School | Private |
| Environment | Metropolis |
| Tuition | $30,882 |
| Enrollment | 8,222 |
| % Male/Female | 41/59 |
| Student/Faculty Ratio | 12:1 |

| FRESHMAN PROFILE | |
| --- | --- |
| Range SAT | |
| Critical Reading | 560-660 |
| Range SAT Math | 560-650 |
| Range ACT Composite | 24-28 |
| Average HS GPA | 3.7 |

| ON-CAMPUS APPOINTMENTS | |
| --- | --- |
| Advance Notice | Yes, other |
| Appointment | Required |
| Saturdays | No |
| Average Length | 30 min |
| Info Sessions | Yes |
| Class Visits | Yes |

| CAMPUS TOURS | |
| --- | --- |
| Appointment | Preferred |
| Dates | Varies |
| Times | Varies |
| Average Length | 30 min |

## CAMPUS AT ITS BEST!

After taking in all the campus has to offer, try taking in all that surrounds it. For the nature lover, try the New York Botanical Garden with 240 acres of pristine gardens and plant collections. For the animal lover, try the Bronx Zoo for almost every type of fauna and the world's largest man-made rain forest. And finally, for food lovers, head to Arthur Avenue, the "Little Italy of the Bronx."

# FRANKLIN & MARSHALL COLLEGE

PO Box 3003, Lancaster, PA 17604-3003 • **Telephone:** 717-291-3953 • **E-mail:** admission@fandm.edu
**Website:** www.fandm.edu • **Hours:** Monday–Friday, 8:30 A.M.–5:00 P.M.; Saturday, 9:30am–NOON

## STUDENTS SAY

"The greatest strength of F&M is its rigorous academics that don't focus on vocational training, but on preparing the students for the world and teaching them how to analyze and interact in their surrounding communities."

## FODOR'S SAYS

"Lancaster, an attractive colonial city, is in the heart of Pennsylvania Dutch Country. Guides impart anecdotes about local architecture and history during the Historical Lancaster Walking Tour."

## ABOUT THE SCHOOL

Franklin & Marshall College students work hard for their grades and see the payoff when the graduate school acceptances roll in. The students at this small school of 2,000 undergraduates have little time for anything else but schoolwork from Monday to Friday, but the professors help by keeping long office hours and being generally accessible. The weekends are for partying, though, and these weekday bookworms definitely know how to live it up on their off days.

## GETTING THERE

**BY AIR:** Harrisburg International Airport (MDT) is just 30 miles away. Baltimore-Washington International Thurgood Marshall Airport (BWI) is only 87 miles from Lancaster. Take a cab or reserve independent shuttle service from the airport to get to campus.

**BY TRAIN:** Amtrak stops in Lancaster. Take the Red Rose Transit bus #3 to the Queens Street Station and transfer to the #1A, which stops at Franklin & Marshall College.

**BY BUS:** Greyhound stops in Lancaster. Take public transit to campus.

**BY CAR:** From Baltimore/Washington and South: From Baltimore Beltway (Route 695), exit onto Route 83 North. Follow Route 83 North to York, PA. Take Exit 19A (462 East, Market Street). Cross over Route 462 as you proceed through two lights and come to your third at Route 30. Turn right onto Route 30 East to Lancaster (approximately 20 miles). Take the exit for Harrisburg Pike. Turn right at the light at the top of the exit ramp and proceed toward Lancaster City. Franklin & Marshall is about one and a half miles ahead on your right. From Northeastern Pennsylvania: Follow Route 81 South and take Exit 90 (Route 72 South). Follow Route 72 South to the Lancaster area. Approximately two to three miles from the Route 30/Route 72 junction, turn right at the traffic light onto Dillerville Road. At the next light, turn left onto Harrisburg Pike. Franklin & Marshall is a half mile ahead on your right. From Western Pennsylvania: Take the Pennsylvania Turnpike to Exit 247/old Exit 19 (Harrisburg East). Take the first exit to your right immediately out of the tollbooth to get onto Route 283 East. Take Route 283 East to Route 30 West towards York. Take the first exit for Harrisburg Pike. At the top of the exit ramp, turn left onto Harrisburg Pike. Proceed one and a half miles through several traffic lights until you reach the overhead pedestrian bridge connecting College Square to the main campus. From New York City and New Jersey: Take the New Jersey Turnpike to Exit 6 (Pennsylvania Turnpike West). Take the PA Turnpike West to Exit 286/old Exit 21 (Lancaster/Reading/Route 222 South). Take Route 222 South approximately 14 miles to the Lancaster area. Stay to the right and follow signs for Route 30 West (York). Pass Oregon, Lititz, and Fruitville Pikes. Just beyond Fruitville Pike, exit to continue on 30 West (York). Take the first exit for Harrisburg Pike (The Park City Mall will be on your right). At the top of the exit ramp, turn left onto Harrisburg Pike. Proceed one and a half miles through several traffic lights until you reach the overhead pedestrian bridge connecting College Square to the main campus.

**LOCAL:** Lancaster's Red Rose Transit Authority's Route 1A bus stops on College Avenue and goes into Lancaster.

## WHERE TO STAY

Ask about special rates for Franklin & Marshall visitors before you reserve at local hotels and bed and breakfasts. Some local options include: King's Cottage Bed and Breakfast (717-397-1017, $$$), O'Flaherty's Dingeldein House Bed and Breakfast (800-779-7765, $$), and the Econo Lodge North (717-299-6900, $).

## CAMPUS AT ITS BEST!

Don't expect entertainment during the week on campus, when studying is at a fever pitch! Instead, stop by an F&M weekend off-campus Greek party, or visit a comedy show on campus. The city of Lancaster and its neighbors are Amish country, and a tour through an Amish farm is a fun activity in the area.

# FRANKLIN W. OLIN COLLEGE OF ENGINEERING

Olin Way, Needham, MA 02492-1245
**Telephone:** 781-292-2222 • **E-mail:** info@olin.edu • **Website:** www.olin.edu

## STUDENTS SAY

"A typical Olin student is smart and passionate. What they are smart in or passionate about, however, varies wildly."

## FODOR'S SAYS

Make sure to stop in Boston and visit Boston Common, "the oldest public park in the United States and undoubtedly the most famous of the town commons around which New England settlements were traditionally arranged. As old as the city around it (it dates from 1634), the spot was originally set aside as the place where farmers could graze their cattle."

## ABOUT THE SCHOOL

Franklin Olin College is still in its nascent stages and as such is continually evolving. Many students actually find this advantageous as they are given the opportunity to help shape the direction of the school. Feedback is taken seriously and this often results in collaborative work and hands-on projects. Undergrads give professors unusually high marks, stating that their passion for the subject matter is contagious.

## GETTING THERE

**BY AIR:** The nearest major airport to Olin College is Boston's Logan Airport. The easiest, albeit costliest, way to and from the airport is to take a cab.

**BY TRAIN:** Amtrak's Northeast Direct Service stops at Route 128 in Westwood, about six miles from Needham. From there, take a taxi to Olin College.

**BY BUS:** Greyhound, Peter Pan, and Concord Trailways all provide service to Boston's South Station.

**BY CAR:** From Great Plain Avenue: Follow Great Plain Avenue for one and a half miles. Olin will be on your right. You'll enter the campus at "Olin Way," which provides access to all campus buildings. The Admissions Office is in the "Olin Center," which will be the first building on your right. From the East: Proceed on the Massachusetts Turnpike to Exit 15 (Interstate 95/Route 128). After the tolls, follow the signs for Route 95/128 South. Take Exit Route 95/128 South at Exit 19B (Highland Avenue, Needham). Continue down Highland Avenue for one and a half miles. Bear right onto Chapel Street at the three-way intersection. Go right at the first light onto Great Plain Avenue/Route 135. See above for the remainder of the directions. From the West: Proceed along the Massachusetts Turnpike to Exit 14 (Interstate 95/Route 128). After the tolls, follow the signs for Route 95/128 South. Exit Route 95/128 South at Exit 19B (Highland Avenue, Needham). See above for the rest of the directions. From the North or South: Follow Route 95/128 to Exit 19B (Highland Avenue, Needham). See above for the rest of the directions.

**LOCAL:** Nearby commuter rail stops include Needham Center, Wellesley Hills, and Wellesley Square. The closest subway stops are Eliot, Riverside, or Woodland (all three are on the Green line). For taxi service, try Veteran's Taxi (781-449-8294) or Colonial Livery (508-653-5600).

## WHERE TO STAY

These hotels are all located near Olin: Sheraton—Needham (781-444-1110, $$), Babson Executive Conference Center (781-239-4000, $$), or Holiday Inn Newton (617-969-5300, $$).

## CAMPUS AT ITS BEST!

When students find themselves with a spare moment away from their studies, they don't have to look far for entertainment. Check out the Hawaiian Luau with its succulent roast pig and hula dancing. The annual student-faculty basketball game, held to raise money for Habitat for Humanity, also draws crowds looking to witness a professor getting dunked on. And Boston is relatively close, so visitors can always venture into the city. Consider shopping on Newbury Street or walking the Freedom Trail.

# THE GEORGE WASHINGTON UNIVERSITY

2121 I Street Northwest, Suite 201, Washington, DC 20052
**Telephone:** 202-994-6040 • **E-mail:** gwadm@gwu.edu
**Website:** www.gwu.edu • **Hours:** Monday–Friday, 8:30 A.M.–5:00 P.M.

## STUDENTS SAY

"Our location, our professors, and our access to internships are unbeatable if you are interested in anything remotely political."

## FODOR'S SAYS

"Near the chapel in Preble Hall is the U.S. Naval Academy Museum & Gallery of Ships, which tells the story of the U.S. Navy through displays of model ships and memorabilia from naval heroes and fighting vessels."

## ABOUT THE SCHOOL

The George Washington University is an academic paradise for undergrads looking to extend their education beyond the university walls. Internships, campus events, and visiting professorships allow GW's undergrads to rub elbows with the people who keep the nation's capital running.

## GETTING THERE

**BY AIR:** Reagan National Airport is five minutes from campus. Take a taxi or the Metro (subway) to GWU. Baltimore/Washington International and Dulles International airports offer more extensive flight options. Use Amtrak or MARC trains from BWI to DC's Union Station—a quick taxi/subway ride from campus. A combination of Metro bus and subway (orange line) offers a travel option from Dulles. Otherwise, catch a cab.

**BY TRAIN:** Amtrak services DC's Union Station. Take a taxi or subway (red line to either the orange or blue line).

**BY BUS:** DC's Greyhound station is less than two miles from campus.

**BY CAR:** From I-95 South: From I-95 South, merge onto I-495 (Capital Beltway) heading toward Silver Spring/Northern Virginia. Use Exit 33 to get onto Connecticut Avenue and proceed ahead for nine miles. After passing the Washington Hilton, make a right onto Florida Avenue, followed by a quick left onto 21st Street. Go right onto I Street and look for the parking garage between 22nd and 23rd streets. From I-95 North: Follow I-95 North to I-395, following signs to the Arlington Memorial Bridge. After crossing the bridge, veer left at the Lincoln Memorial. Make a left on 23rd Street Northwest, then take a right onto I Street. Look for the parking garage between 22nd and 23rd streets. From I-270 East: Follow I-270 East until it connects with I-495 (Capital Beltway). Take I-495 toward Silver Spring/Northern Virginia. From there, use "From I-95 South" directions above. From I-66 East: Follow I-66 East into DC and across the Theodore Roosevelt Memorial Bridge. Then turn onto E Street via left exit, and then take another left onto Virginia Avenue. Take a right onto 23rd Street, then a right onto I Street. Look for the parking garage between 22nd and 23rd streets.

**LOCAL:** The Foggy Bottom/GWU Metro stop is serviced by the orange and blue lines. Taxi options include Atlantic Cab (202-488-0609) and Yourway Taxi Cab (202-488-0609).

## WHERE TO STAY

The university sponsors One Washington Circle Hotel (202-872-1680, $$–$$$) and the George Washington University Inn (202-337-6620, $$$+). Other nearby options include Best Western New Hampshire Suites (202-457-0565, $$) and Hotel Lombardy (202-828-2600, $$–$$$).

## CAMPUS AT ITS BEST!

Ponder your impressions of GWU while relaxing on the Mid-Campus Quad. This "outdoor living room" consists of a fountain, clock, benches, and plenty of tables and chairs for studying or dining. Follow up on all that reflection by attending a reading from The Jenny McKean Moore Reading Series. This series sponsors six to eight readings a year with respected poets, novelists, and playwrights. Those touring the campus in January will be able to enjoy Winter Welcome Week. Chase away your post-holiday doldrums with ice-skating, free hot chocolate, movies, and more.

# GEORGETOWN UNIVERSITY

37th and O Streets, Northwest, 103 White-Gravenor, Washington, DC 20057

**Telephone:** 202-687-3600

**Website:** www.georgetown.edu • **Hours:** Monday–Friday, 9:00 A.M.–5:00 P.M.; Saturday, 9:00 A.M.–1:00 P.M.

| SCHOOL AT A GLANCE | |
| --- | --- |
| Type of School | Private |
| Environment | Metropolis |
| Tuition | $33,552 |
| Enrollment | 6,395 |
| % Male/Female | 46/54 |
| Student/Faculty Ratio | 11:1 |

| FRESHMAN PROFILE | |
| --- | --- |
| Range SAT | |
| Critical Reading | 640-750 |
| Range SAT Math | 650-740 |
| Range ACT Composite | 27-32 |

| ON-CAMPUS APPOINTMENTS | |
| --- | --- |
| Info Sessions | Yes |
| Class Visits | Yes |

| CAMPUS TOURS | |
| --- | --- |
| Appointment | Preferred |
| Dates | Year Round |
| Times | Varies |
| Average Length | 60 min |

## STUDENTS SAY

"Georgetown students are very politically aware and cover the whole spectrum of beliefs, but tend to be far more likely to express their beliefs by getting an internship on the Hill than by holding protests."

## FODOR'S SAYS

"Renowned for its power to evoke reflection, the Vietnam Veterans Memorial was conceived by Jan Scruggs, a former infantry corporal who had served in Vietnam. The wall is one of the most visited sites in Washington, its black granite panels reflecting the sky, the trees, and the faces of those looking for the names of friends or relatives who died in the war."

## ABOUT THE SCHOOL

The nation's oldest Jesuit university, Georgetown sticks to its roots by providing an education steeped in intellectual exploration, interpersonal collaboration, and commitment to (as the university puts it) "justice and the common good." All of this is enhanced by the rich educational and cultural opportunities afforded by the university's host city, Washington, DC.

## GETTING THERE

**BY AIR:** Reagan National Airport is close to campus. Take a taxi to Georgetown. Baltimore/Washington International and Dulles International airports offer greater flight options. Use Amtrak or MARC trains from BWI to DC's Union Station—a quick cab ride from campus. From Dulles, use shuttle service to reach downtown, and then take a cab from downtown to campus.

**BY TRAIN:** Amtrak services DC's Union Station. Use taxi service to get to campus.

**BY BUS:** DC's Greyhound station is about four miles from campus. To reach Georgetown, take a cab from the terminal.

**BY CAR:** From I-270 South: Follow I-270 South and merge onto I-495 East (Capital Beltway). Soon after merging, take Exit 34 for Wisconsin Avenue/Route 355 South. Take this to Reservoir Road and turn right. After 38th Street, turn left into campus. From I-95 South: Follow I-95 South until merging onto I-495 West (Capital Beltway) toward Silver Spring/Northern Virginia. Take Exit 34 for Wisconsin Ave/Route 355 South. Take this to Reservoir Road and turn right. After 38th Street, turn left into campus. From I-66 East: Follow I-66 East to the exit for Rosslyn/Key Bridge and proceed toward Key Bridge. Get in the second lane from the left as you cross the bridge. After crossing, make a left onto Canal Road. Campus is ahead on the right. From I-395 North: Follow I-395 North to the Washington Boulevard Exit. Proceed toward Rosslyn/Key Bridge. Get in the second lane from the left as you cross the bridge. After crossing, make a left onto Canal Road. Campus is ahead on the right.

**LOCAL:** Georgetown does not have a Metro station. The nearest stops are Rosslyn (orange and blue line) and DuPont Circle (red line). Georgetown University Transportation Shuttle (GUTS) offers rides between campus and the Metro stops. Taxi options include Atlantic Cab (202-488-0609) and Yourway Taxi Cab (202-488-0609).

## WHERE TO STAY

Nearby accommodations include the Holiday Inn Georgetown (202-338-4600, $$), the St. Regis Hotel (202-638-2626, $$$), and the Four Seasons Hotel (202-342-0444, $$$+).

## CAMPUS AT ITS BEST!

Georgetown provides plenty of opportunities for students to demonstrate their artistic talents. To get a glimpse of creative life on campus, check out GUTV's annual film festival, or hit up a Mask and Bauble performance. This drama group is the oldest continually running student theatrical society in the country. Of course, Georgetown's DC location means that historians and political junkies will also be satiated. Think about taking a tour of Congress or visiting the Smithsonian while you're there.

# GETTYSBURG COLLEGE

Admissions Office, Eisenhower House, Gettysburg, PA 17325-1484
**Telephone:** 717-337-6100 • **E-mail:** admiss@gettysburg.edu
**Website:** www.gettysburg.edu • **Hours:** Monday–Friday, 9:00 P.M.–5:00 P.M.; Saturday, 9:00 A.M.–NOON

## STUDENTS SAY

"The campus is really beautiful, and the people, while a bit on the preppy side, are for the most part friendly and fun to be around."

## FODOR'S SAYS

"The Battle of Gettysburg, fought in July 1863, was, along with Ulysses S. Grant's successful Vicksburg campaign, the turning point of the Civil War. At the Gettysburg National Military Park you can follow the course of the fighting on the 750-square-foot electric map or obtain brochures that will guide you along 18 miles of roads or various waling tails around the battleground."

## ABOUT THE SCHOOL

Gettysburg College, surrounded by Civil War battlefields, is a school rich in history and tradition. Among the foremost traditions at this liberal arts school are small class sizes, hands-on learning, a well-observed honor code, and challenging academics. In addition to these attributes, Gettysburg has a Center for Public Service that allows students to use their time and skills to help improve communities across the globe.

## GETTING THERE

**BY AIR:** Harrisburg International Airport is less than an hour from campus. Contact the Admissions Office (717-337-6100) to learn about college-sponsored transportation to and from the airport.

**BY TRAIN:** Harrisburg's Amtrak station is 45 minutes from Gettysburg. Call the Admissions Office to arrange transportation from the station to campus.

**BY BUS:** Harrisburg offers the nearest Greyhound service.

**BY CAR:** From I-83 South: Follow I-83 South to Route 581 West. At Exit 5B, turn onto Route 15 South and continue until the Gettysburg Hunterstown Exit. At the end of the ramp, make a right. Then turn left onto Business Route 15 South. After four miles, take a left onto Carlisle Street. The Admissions House is ahead on the right. From I-81 South: Follow I-81 South to I-83 South. From there, use "From I-83 South" directions above. From I-81 North: Follow I-81 North to Exit 16 for Route 30 East. In Gettysburg, turn out of the traffic circle onto Carlisle Street. The Admissions Office is at the intersection of Carlisle and Stevens Streets. From I-76 (Pennsylvania Turnpike) West: Follow I-76 West to 236 for Route 15 South. Turn off Route 15 South at the Gettysburg Hunterstown Exit. At the end of the ramp, make a right. Then turn left onto Business Route 15 South. After four miles, take a left onto Carlisle Street. The Admissions House is ahead on the right. From I-76 (Pennsylvania Turnpike) East: Follow I-76 East to Exit 226 for Route 11 South at Carlisle. Go through Carlisle, continuing ahead as Route 11 becomes Route 34 South. Eventually Route 34 turns to Carlisle Street as you enter Gettysburg. The Admissions Office is at the intersection of Carlisle and Stevens streets.

**LOCAL:** For taxi service, try Yellow Cab at 717-238-7252.

## WHERE TO STAY

The Quality Inn at General Lee's Headquarters (717-334-3141, $$), the Brafferton Inn (717-337-3423, $$), and the James Getty Hotel (717-337-1334, $$) are among the many local accommodations available.

## CAMPUS AT ITS BEST!

History buffs will definitely appreciate Gettysburg's location. The college is less than a mile from the site of the decisive Civil War battle for which the college is a namesake. To get a taste of the social atmosphere at Gettysburg, stop by The Attic. This student-designed and student-run nightclub is a popular venue for everything from concerts and dance parties to formals and sports screenings.

# GODDARD COLLEGE

123 Pitkin Road, Plainfield, VT 05667
**Telephone:** 802-454-8311 • **E-mail:** admissions@goddard.edu
**Website:** www.goddard.edu • **Hours:** Monday–Friday, 8:00 A.M.–4:30 P.M.

## STUDENTS SAY

"Everyone is on a first-name basis—the students, staff, and faculty."

## FODOR'S SAYS

"Attractions at the Rock of Ages Granite Quarry range from the awe-inspiring (the quarry resembles the Grand Canyon in miniature) to the mildly ghoulish (you can consult a directory of tombstone dealers throughout the country)."

## ABOUT THE SCHOOL

Goddard's progressive philosophy offers a great alternative to those wary of more traditional schools. Academic freedom is paramount here and students design an individual, self-directed curriculum. Indeed the education is focused on personally meaningful and socially important work. Not surprisingly, the college does not operate on a grading system and instead provides narrative evaluations. Goddard typically attracts leftist-leaning, creative individuals.

## GETTING THERE

**BY AIR:** Both Burlington International Airport (one hour away) or Manchester Airport (two hours away) are reasonable options.

**BY TRAIN:** Amtrak provides service to Montpelier, roughly 15 miles from campus. Guests traveling between Washington, DC and St. Albans, VT should look specifically for information on the "Vermonter."

**BY BUS:** Greyhound provides service to the area via their Vermont Transit Line.

**BY CAR:** From the South: Follow Interstate 89 North to Exit 7. Proceed straight off the exit ramp and follow the sign to Montpelier (to your right). Drive to the bottom of the hill, making a left. You'll reach an intersection where you will see a light in front of you, a Ford dealership on your left, and a vacant lot on the right. Make a right (before the light) onto Route 2 East. Follow Route 2 East until you reach East Montpelier. Veer right at the blinking light and continue to follow Route 2. Down the road, you'll see a sign for Plainfield. Shortly after, go left on Route 214 North. The Goddard entrance is the first driveway on the left. From the North: Take Interstate 89 South to Exit 8 (Montpelier/Route 2), placing you on Route 2 East. Drive until East Montpelier, where you'll come to a fork in the road by a flashing light. You'll see Dudley's Mobil station on your left. Remain on Route 2 East and take the right-hand fork, continuing on Route 2 East. See above for the rest of the directions. From the East: Take Route 2 through St. Johnsbury (roughly 30 miles from the New Hampshire border) and Marshfield (roughly 8 more miles). See above for the rest of the directions.

**LOCAL:** Being a small town, Plainfield doesn't offer much in the way of public transportation. However, C Taxi (802-476-0882) or Payless Taxi (802-476-4097) will take care of you just fine.

## WHERE TO STAY

Vermont features many homey and comfortable accommodations, including Marshfield Inn & Motel (802-426-3383, $), Comstock House (802-272-2693, $–$$), or Hollister Hill Bed and Breakfast (802-454-7725, $–$$).

| SCHOOL AT A GLANCE | |
| --- | --- |
| Type of School | Private |
| Environment | Rural |
| Tuition | $17,840 |
| Enrollment | 319 |
| % Male/Female | 41/59 |
| Student/Faculty Ratio | 11:1 |

| FRESHMAN PROFILE | |
| --- | --- |
| Range SAT | |
| Critical Reading | 550–680 |
| Range SAT Math | 480–590 |
| Range ACT Composite | 19–27 |
| Average HS GPA | 2.5 |

| ON-CAMPUS APPOINTMENTS | |
| --- | --- |
| Advance Notice | 2 weeks |
| Appointment | Required |
| Saturdays | Sometimes |
| Class Visits | No |

| CAMPUS TOURS | |
| --- | --- |
| Appointment | Not Required |

## CAMPUS AT ITS BEST!

The Admissions Office periodically holds "Discover Goddard Days." These events, running from morning until mid-afternoon, offer the opportunity to meet with current students, program directors, and financial aid officers. Prospective students are guaranteed to walk away with some invaluable insight into life at Goddard. Afterwards, take a stroll through the Greatwood Estate Gardens. Listed on the National Register of Historic Places, these breathtaking grounds are not to be missed. Most importantly, you can enjoy a spot of tea as you admire the natural beauty.

# GOUCHER COLLEGE

1021 Dulaney Valley Road, Baltimore, MD 21204-2794
**Telephone:** 410-337-6100 • **E-mail:** admissions@goucher.edu
**Hours:** Monday–Friday and Saturday, 9:00 A.M.–5:00 P.M. and by appointment

## STUDENTS SAY

"A plethora of idiosyncratic young adults shoved into an academic bubble."

## FODOR'S SAYS

"This star-shaped brick Fort McHenry is forever associated with Francis Scott Key and the "Star-Spangled Banner," which Key penned while watching the British bombardment of Baltimore during the War of 1812. A visit to the fort includes a 16-minute history film, guided tour, and frequent living history displays (including battle reenactments) on weekends."

## ABOUT THE SCHOOL

Goucher College is a small, formerly all-women's college in Baltimore where students receive a lot of personal attention in strong academic programs including creative writing and English. All incoming undergraduates are required to study abroad at least once before they graduate from Goucher—and just to make sure everyone does, Goucher provides each student with a $1,200 voucher to help offset expenses.

## GETTING THERE

**BY AIR:** Baltimore/Washington International Airport (BWI) is the closest airport to campus. Some other airport options include Dulles International Airport and Ronald Reagan Washington National Airport. Transportation from the BWI Airport includes the BWI Super Shuttle, 800-BLUE-VAN, Baltimore Airport Shuttle, as well as limousine and taxi service.

**BY TRAIN:** Amtrak trains operate out of Penn Station, located at 1501 North Charles Street in Baltimore. All passenger trains arrive at Pennsylvania Station in Downtown Baltimore. A taxi from the station to Goucher College takes approximately 20 minutes.

**BY BUS:** Greyhound buses and Peter Pan buses service Baltimore.

**BY CAR:** From any direction, take the Baltimore Beltway (I-695). Get off of I-695 at Exit 27A-Towson (Dulaney Valley Road South). You will see the college shortly on your left.

**LOCAL:** Mass Transit Administration (MTA) (410-539-5000) provides bus service throughout the Baltimore area. Other services include Call-A-Lift Bus Information (410-682-5438), Paratransit Service (410-727-3535), ABC Taxi Association (410-323-4222), Airport Taxi (410-859-1103), Jimmy's Cab (410-296-7200), Royal Cab (410-327-0330), and Yellow Cab (410-235-0300).

## WHERE TO STAY

If you're planning on staying overnight, some nearby hotels include Hampton Inn Hunt Valley (410-527-1500, $$), Days Inn—Towson (410-882-0900, $$), and Holiday Inn Select Baltimore (410-823-4410, $$$).

## CAMPUS AT ITS BEST!

Even if you can't make it for Explore Goucher Day (a college-sponsored event designed to introduce prospective students to their potential campus), the school has plenty to explore. Regular events include movie nights, comedic, theatrical, and musical performances, Annual Relaxation Day, and much more! Or if a cup of joe will suffice, hit the Gopher Hole Coffeehouse in the lower level of the Pearlstone Student Center. The Gopher Hole offers food, beverages, and a regular series of events.

# GROVE CITY COLLEGE

100 Campus Drive, Grove City, PA 16127-2104
**Telephone:** 724-458-2100 • **E-mail:** admissions@gcc.edu
**Website:** www.gcc.edu

| SCHOOL AT A GLANCE | |
| --- | --- |
| Type of School | Private |
| Environment | Rural |
| Tuition | $10,962 |
| Enrollment | 2,465 |
| % Male/Female | 51/49 |
| Student/Faculty Ratio | 17:1 |
| **FRESHMAN PROFILE** | |
| Range SAT | |
| Critical Reading | 576-691 |
| Range SAT Math | 589-697 |
| Range ACT Composite | 26-30 |
| Average HS GPA | 3.75 |
| **ON-CAMPUS APPOINTMENTS** | |
| Advance Notice | Yes, 1 week |
| Appointment | Required |
| Saturdays | Sometimes |
| Average Length | 30 min |
| Info Sessions | Yes |
| Class Visits | Yes |
| **CAMPUS TOURS** | |
| Appointment | Required |
| Dates | Year Round |
| Times | 8:00 A.M.–5:00 P.M. |
| Average Length | 60 min |

## STUDENTS SAY

"The campus is gorgeous, even when covered in two feet of snow for five months."

## FODOR'S SAYS

"When you book, look for nonstop flights and remember that 'direct' flights stop at least once."

## ABOUT THE SCHOOL

Grove City is deeply rooted in Christian traditions and principles. Indeed, faith tends to pervade both the classroom and the campus at large. While this sometimes makes every course feel like an ongoing theological discussion, students give professors high marks. Undergrads take their academics seriously and classes are generally demanding. When not studying, many students enjoy ice cream socials, square dancing, and good conversation.

## GETTING THERE

**BY AIR:** Visitors can fly into Pittsburgh International Airport. The facility is serviced by a number of major airlines. Car rental, taxis, and limousine services are all available for transportation from the airport.

**BY TRAIN:** The closest Amtrak station is located in Pittsburgh, PA, approximately 50 miles from Grove City.

**BY BUS:** Guests can take Greyhound directly to Pittsburgh. A local bus line, The Myers Coach Lines, offers weekday service from Pittsburgh to Grove City.

**BY CAR:** From I-79: Follow until Exit 113. From here take Route 208 East into Grove City. Head to the first traffic light and make a right onto Main Street (Route 58). Continue to the second traffic light (Liberty Avenue). You'll then turn left into the campus and drive down the road to Crawford Hall. From I-80 to Exit 24: Follow Route 173 South into Grove City. Continue on Route 173 as it winds through town. You'll make a left onto Main Street (Route 58). See above for the remainder of the directions.

**LOCAL:** For local transportation, try Eastern Taxi Service (724-458-8294).

## WHERE TO STAY

Grove City visitors might enjoy staying at: Snow Goose Inn (724-458-4644, $), Old Arbor Rose (724-458-6425, $; offers special rate to Grove City College guests), and Terra Nova House (724-450-0712, $–$$).

## CAMPUS AT ITS BEST!

Grove City students know how to have a good time. From a one-act play festival to a women's arm-wrestling competition and an impressive gala, the college ensures there are activities for all to enjoy. Visitors who'd like to explore the town should think about going to the Prime Outlets. Located only a few minutes from campus, the unbelievable bargains are guaranteed to turn everyone into shopaholics.

# HAMILTON COLLEGE

Office of Admissions, 198 College Hill Road, Clinton, NY 13323
**Telephone:** 315-859-4421 • **E-mail:** admission@hamilton.edu
**Website:** www.hamilton.edu • **Hours:** Monday–Friday, 8:30 A.M.–4:30 P.M.; Saturday, 8:30 A.M.–12:30 P.M.

## STUDENTS SAY

"Hamilton is the total package. There are no required courses, so students are in classes because they want to be there. . . . There is also a very well-rounded athletic program, and a great social life."

## FODOR'S SAYS

American Revolution buffs should visit the Oriskany Battlefield State Historic Site, which is "viewed as the key to later rebel victories. The site includes interpretive signs, an 85-foot-tall monument, and in summer, historic encampments."

## ABOUT THE SCHOOL

Hamilton calls itself "a liberal arts college focused on writing, research, and speaking." In other words, Hamilton students don't simply learn how to think, but they learn how to effectively communicate what they're thinking. Small class sizes, attentive professors, and a hands-on approach to education all contribute to the Hamilton experience.

## GETTING THERE

**BY AIR:** Serviced by seven airlines, Syracuse Hancock International Airport is 45 minutes from campus. For transportation to campus, contact Clinton Taxi (315-853-3355) or Empire Limousine Service (315-735-5991).

**BY TRAIN:** Amtrak's Empire Service, Lake Shore Limited, and Maple Leaf lines stop in Utica, less than 10 miles from campus. Taxi service is available at the station.

**BY BUS:** Greyhound and Trailways bus lines stop in Utica. Use taxi service to get to campus.

**BY CAR:** From I-90 (New York Thruway) East/West: Follow I-90 to Exit 32 for Westmoreland. After paying at the tollbooth, make a right and then a left to end up on Route 233 South. Proceed five miles to the intersection of Route 233 and College Hill Road. Take a right onto College Hill Road. Follow signs to the Admissions Office. From I-81 North: Follow I-81 North to Exit 6 for Route 12. Turn onto Route 12 North and continue ahead for 50 miles. Just north of Sherburne, make a left onto Route 12B. Travel on Route 12B North for 35 miles. A few miles after passing through Deansboro, go left onto Route 233 North. At the intersection of Route 233 and College Hill Road, turn left.onto College Hill Road.

**LOCAL:** For local transit, try the Clinton Cab Company (315-853-3355) or, out of nearby Utica, the Courtesy Cab Company (315-797-7272).

## WHERE TO STAY

Clinton is home to a number of moderately priced bed and breakfasts, including the Arbor Inn at Griffin House (315-859-1790, $$), the Artful Lodger (315-853-3672, $$), and Amidst the Hedges (315-853-3031, $$). Also worth a try is nearby Utica if you're looking for standard budget hotels.

## CAMPUS AT ITS BEST!

The Chapel, one of Hamilton's most enduring landmarks, also holds some architectural distinction. It is thought to be the only remaining example of an early three-story church structure found within the U.S. While you're on campus, be sure to check out The Little Pub. This campus hotspot, a restored stable/carriage barn, serves food and maintains a bar, game room, and dance floor along with a place to lounge with friends.

# HAMPSHIRE COLLEGE

Admissions Office, 893 West Street, Amherst, MA 01002
**Telephone:** 413-559-5471 • **E-mail:** admissions@hampshire.edu • **Website:** www.hampshire.edu
**Hours:** Monday–Friday, 8:30 A.M.–4:30 P.M.; Saturday, 9:00 A.M.–2:00 P.M.

## STUDENTS SAY

"A Hampshire education is like grad school for undergraduates. You learn more about yourself than you would almost anywhere else."

## FODOR'S SAYS

"[The] Amherst History Museum is housed in a mansion dating from the mid-1700s; this museum displays an extensive collection of household tools, furnishings, and clothing that reflects changing styles of interior decoration. Most items are Amherst originals, dating from the eighteenth to the mid-twentieth century."

## ABOUT THE SCHOOL

The spirit of independence reigns at Hampshire College. Situated in the intellectual hotbed of Amherst, Massachusetts, Hampshire is a liberal arts college that encourages each student to find an individual educational path that's heavy in independent study, interdisciplinary work, and close collaboration with members of the faculty.

## GETTING THERE

**BY AIR:** Bradley International Airport is about 45 minutes from Hampshire in Windsor Locks, Connecticut. Boston's Logan International Airport is about two hours away and offers a larger flight selection. Use Peter Pan bus lines (800-237-8747) or Valley Transporter (413-253-1350) to get to the campus.

**BY TRAIN:** Amtrak's Vermonter line stops in Amherst. Wider Amtrak service is available in Springfield, half an hour away from the campus. Arrange transportation from the Springfield station to Amherst through Peter Pan bus lines or Valley Transporter.

**BY BUS:** In conjunction with Greyhound, Peter Pan bus lines regularly services Amherst.

**BY CAR:** From I-91 North/South: Follow I-91 to Exit 19 for Northampton. Turn onto Route 9 East off the ramp. In Amherst, make a right onto Route 116 South. Continue ahead for three miles to Hampshire. From I-95 North: Follow I-95 North to New Haven, Connecticut, where you merge onto I-91 North. Proceed according to "From I-91 North/South" directions above. From I-90 (Massachusetts Turnpike) East/West: Follow I-90 to Exit 4 for I-91 North. After turning onto I-91 North, proceed according to "From I-91 North/South" directions above.

**LOCAL:** The University of Massachusetts Transit System teams up with the Pioneer Valley Transit Authority to provide easy transportation among Amherst's Five College area and nearby towns. Valley Transporter (413-253-1350) offers rides to and from regional airports and train stations. For cabs, call Celebrity Cab Company (413-253-7330) or Red Cab (413-253-3333).

## WHERE TO STAY

Amherst boasts a wide range of accommodations, from cozy B&Bs to standard corporate hotels. Those within five miles of campus include University Lodge (413-256-8111, $–$$), Birches Bed and Breakfast (413-256-6257, $–$$), Emily's Amherst Bed and Breakfast (413-549-0733, $$), and the Holiday Inn Express (413 582-0002, $$–$$$).

### SCHOOL AT A GLANCE

| | |
|---|---|
| Type of School | Private |
| Environment | Town |
| Tuition | $33,855 |
| Enrollment | 1,362 |
| % Male/Female | 41/59 |
| Student/Faculty Ratio | 12:1 |

### FRESHMAN PROFILE

| | |
|---|---|
| Range SAT | |
| Critical Reading | 600-710 |
| Range SAT Math | 560-660 |
| Range ACT Composite | 25-30 |
| Average HS GPA | 3.42 |

### ON-CAMPUS APPOINTMENTS

| | |
|---|---|
| Advance Notice | Yes, 1 week |
| Appointment | Required |
| Saturdays | Sometimes |
| Average Length | 45 min |
| Info Sessions | Yes |
| Class Visits | Yes |

### CAMPUS TOURS

| | |
|---|---|
| Appointment | Not Required |
| Dates | Year Round |
| Times | See website. |
| Average Length | 60 min |

---

## CAMPUS AT ITS BEST!

The Hampshire College Farm Center enables students to take a hands-on approach to sustainable agriculture. Be sure to ask about their programs and purchase a few of the organic vegetables they harvest. There is a multitude of entertaining options outside of campus as well. For example, you can get in touch with your inner child and visit the Dr. Seuss National Memorial in nearby Springfield. Of course, if hot metal and/or the nineteenth century are appealing to you, you can attend the annual Blacksmithing Meet at Hampshire's Lemelson Center for Design. Students have the opportunity to meet local blacksmiths and participate in workshops.

# HARTWICK COLLEGE

PO Box 4020, Oneonta, NY 13820-4020

Telephone: 607-431-4154 • E-mail: admissions@hartwick.edu

Website: www.hartwick.edu/ • Hours: Monday–Friday, 9:00 A.M.–5:00 P.M.; Saturday, 11:00 A.M.–2:00 P.M.

## STUDENTS SAY

"If you are looking for a school with small class sizes and good one-on-one time with your teachers, this is the place."

## FODOR'S SAYS

Check out the Hanford Mills Museum with its "still-functional mill, nature trails, gallery space, and picnic area. You can try your hand at ice harvesting during the annual Winter Ice Harvest, when period tools are used to cut ice from the frozen pond."

## ABOUT THE SCHOOL

Tucked away in the foothills of the Catskill Mountains, Hartwick is a great school for students looking to challenge themselves intellectually. The college's Pine Lake Environmental Campus, just eight miles from the main campus, provides a great living laboratory for science majors. Hartwick also encourages students to expand their horizons through its study abroad program.

## GETTING THERE

**BY AIR:** Albany International is the closest airport to Hartwick (78 miles). It is served by a number of major airlines.

**BY TRAIN:** Visitors can take Amtrak to Utica, approximately 45 miles from Oneonta.

**BY BUS:** Greyhound does provide service to Oneonta.

**BY CAR:** From Massachusetts: Take the Massachusetts Turnpike (I-90) West into New York state. Proceed on I-90 (New York State Thruway) to I-88 at Exit 25A. Continue on I-88 West to Oneonta. Get off I-88 at Exit 15. Make a right at the end of ramp. At the second traffic light, take a left onto Center Street. At the end of Center Street, yield right onto West Street. You'll see Hartwick College to your left. Use the second entrance. From Albany: Drive West on I-90 to I-88 at Exit 25A. Take I-88 West to Oneonta. Follow directions above. From New York City: Take the New York State Thruway (I-87) North to Exit 21, Catskill/Cairo. From there, get onto Route 23 West into Oneonta. This is the Foster/Lettis Highway. Upon reaching the McDonald's/Wendy's/Hess intersection, turn onto the Foster/Lettis Highway. Proceed down the Foster/Lettis Highway, following the signs to the college. At the second traffic light, take a left onto Center Street. Follow the directions above. From Washington, DC: Take I-95 North to I-695 (around Baltimore, MD). Continue onto I-83 North, eventually getting onto I-81 North to Harrisburg, PA. Take I-81 North to I-88 East in Binghamton. Leave I-88 at Exit 15, making a left at the end of the ramp. At the second traffic light, take a left onto Center Street. Follow the directions above.

**LOCAL:** Oneonta Public Transit maintains five bus routes throughout town. Taxi companies include Hill City Taxi (607-433-2227), Ace Taxi & Transport (607-432-8294), and A & D Transport (607-547-8777).

## WHERE TO STAY

Budget Inn Motel (607-432-5301, $), Christopher's Restaurant and Country Lodge (607-432-2444, $–$$), Clarion Hotel (607-432-7500, $$).

---

## CAMPUS AT ITS BEST!

Hartwick students have some amazing resources at their disposal. Pay a visit to the Anderson Center for the Arts for access to some unique mediums including papermaking, glassblowing, foundry work, and electronic imaging. For a taste of Hartwick social life, check out Spring Weekend. The highlight of this annual festival is Wick Wars. A time honored tradition, Wick Wars pits students against each other in team-oriented competition. Those who successfully complete the challenges win cash prizes.

# HARVARD COLLEGE

Byerly Hall, 8 Garden Street, Cambridge, MA 02138
**Telephone:** 617-495-1551 • **E-mail:** college@fas.harvard.edu
**Website:** www.fas.harvard.edu • **Hours:** Monday–Friday, 9:00 A.M.–5:00 P.M.; Saturday mornings

## STUDENTS SAY

"Harvard has distinguished faculty, an extremely accomplished and diverse student body, a million-and-one extracurriculars, and very generous alumni. What more could you ask for?"

## FODOR'S SAYS

"The richness of the East and artistic treasures of the ancient Greeks, Egyptians, and Romans fill three of the four floors of the Arthur M. Sackler Museum."

## ABOUT THE SCHOOL

In the United States, the name Harvard is synonymous with top-of-the-line education. Therefore, it's little wonder that the college makes regular appearances on the Princeton Review's "Best College Library," "Toughest to Get Into," and "Best Overall Academics" ranking lists. The oldest of the Ivies, Harvard is home to undergrads who excel inside and outside of the classroom.

## GETTING THERE

**BY AIR:** Logan International Airport, Boston's main airport, is the easiest option for air travel. Try US Shuttle (617-894-3100) for easy terminal-to-campus transportation. Cabs are available as well. The most economical if somewhat inconvenient option is the subway, or T; take the Silver Line from Logan to South Station and transfer to the Red Line outbound for Harvard Square Station.

**BY TRAIN:** In Boston, Amtrak stops at South Station, Back Bay, and North Station. South Station offers easy transit via the T; simply board the Red Line and travel six stops to Harvard Square Station.

**BY BUS:** Greyhound and Peter Pan bus lines service Boston.

**BY CAR:** From I-90 (Massachusetts Turnpike) East: Follow I-90 East to Exit 18 for Cambridge/Allston. Veer right toward Cambridge. Cross the River Street Bridge, and make a left onto Memorial Drive. After three lights, make a right onto JFK Street. Proceed ahead to Harvard Square. From I-93 South: Follow I-93 South to Exit 31 for Route 16 East toward Revere. Bear left onto Route 16 East (Mystic Valley Parkway), then quickly bear right toward Route 38/Mystic Avenue/Somerville. Mystic Valley Parkway turns into Harvard Street, which then becomes Warner Street. Then make a right onto Powder House Square, and another right onto College Avenue. Make another right onto Dover Street. Next make a left onto Massachusetts Avenue (Route 2A East) and proceed ahead for a little more than a mile to the Harvard campus. From I-95 North: Follow I-95 North to Exit 25 for I-90 East. Proceed according to "From I-90 (Massachusetts Turnpike) East" directions above.

**LOCAL:** The T's Red Line stops at Harvard Square Station. For taxi service, try Red Cab (617-734-5000) or Green Cab (617-625-5000).

## WHERE TO STAY

Boston has many lodging options. Those closest to Harvard Square include the Irving House (617-547-4600, $$), the Harvard Square Hotel (617-864-5200, $$–$$$), and the Charles Hotel (617-864-1200, $$$+).

| SCHOOL AT A GLANCE | |
| --- | --- |
| Type of School | Private |
| Environment | Metropolis |
| Tuition | $30,275 |
| Enrollment | 6,649 |
| % Male/Female | 53/47 |
| Student/Faculty Ratio | 8:1 |

| FRESHMAN PROFILE | |
| --- | --- |
| Range SAT | |
| Critical Reading | 700-800 |
| Range SAT Math | 700-790 |
| Range ACT Composite | 30-34 |

| ON-CAMPUS APPOINTMENTS | |
| --- | --- |
| Advance Notice | 2 weeks |
| Appointment | Required |
| Saturdays | No |
| Average Length | 45 min |
| Info Sessions | Yes |
| Class Visits | Yes |

| CAMPUS TOURS | |
| --- | --- |
| Appointment | Not Required |
| Dates | Varies |
| Times | Varies |
| Average Length | 60 min |

## CAMPUS AT ITS BEST!

As one of the nation's premier universities, Harvard has phenomenal resources and myriad attractions. Consider visiting the Arthur M. Sackler Museum, which houses ancient, Asian, Islamic, and Indian art. Students and visitors alike enjoy performances by the Hasty Pudding Theatricals; school-sponsored events such as the Harvard State Fair are highly anticipated as well. There, you can try your hand at the mechanical bull while you overindulge in corn dogs.

# HAVERFORD COLLEGE

370 West Lancaster Avenue, Haverford, PA 19041
**Telephone:** 610-896-1350 • **E-mail:** admission@haverford.edu
**Website:** www.haverford.edu • **Hours:** Monday–Friday, 9:00 A.M.–5:00 P.M.; Saturday, 9:00 A.M.–NOON

## STUDENTS SAY

"The typical Haverford student is friendly but not bubbly, self-motivated but not obsessive, smart but not obnoxious, slightly eccentric but not truly weird . . . we mill around the edges of the liberal arts stereotypes without quite embodying them."

## FODOR'S SAYS

"The Spirit of Philadelphia and the Liberty Belle run cruises along the Delaware River."

## ABOUT THE SCHOOL

Haverford boasts students that aren't simply good at working hard—they actually enjoy doing it. These perennially happy undergrads living it up in eastern Pennsylvania reap the benefits of top-notch programs, accessible professors, and easy access to the fun of Philadelphia.

## GETTING THERE

**BY AIR:** Philadelphia International Airport is 20 miles from campus, though travel time varies depending on traffic. For public transit, use SEPTA Airport Express to get to Philly's 30th Street Station; from there, board the R5 Paoli Local or the Bryn Mawr Local to Haverford. Call Main Line Airport Limousine Service (610-525-0513) or hail a cab at the terminal for direct transport to campus.

**BY TRAIN:** Amtrak services Philly's 30th Street Station. From there, SEPTA lines R5 Paoli Local or Bryn Mawr Local will take you to Haverford.

**BY BUS:** Greyhound offers connections to many destinations through its main Philadelphia station on Filbert Street. Limited service is also available to the 30th Street Station. Use commuter rail or taxi to get to campus.

**BY CAR:** From I-476 North/South: Follow I-476 to Exit 13 for U.S. 30/Lancaster Avenue East toward St. David/Villanova. After turning right (east) onto Lancaster Avenue, drive straight for three and a half miles until the campus is on your right. From I-76 (Pennsylvania Turnpike) East: Follow I-76 East to Exit 326 for the Valley Forge Interchange. Get onto I-76 East (Schuylkill Expressway) and proceed to Exit 331A for I-476 South. From there, use "From I-476 North/South" directions above. From the New Jersey Turnpike South: Follow the New Jersey Turnpike South to the interchange with the Pennsylvania Turnpike at Exit 6. Take the PA Turnpike West to Exit 333 for I-476 South. From there, use "From I-476 North/South" directions above. From the New Jersey Turnpike North: Follow the New Jersey Turnpike to Exit 2 for Route 322 West. After crossing the Commodore Barry Bridge, merge onto I-95 North and proceed ahead to Exit 7 for I-476 North. From there, use "From I-476 North/South" directions above.

**LOCAL:** SEPTA (Southeastern Pennsylvania Transportation Authority) services Haverford via the R5 Paoli Local and Bryn Mawr Local lines. The Haverford station is a 10-minute walk from campus. For cab service, try Maxwell Cab Company (610-896-5100).

## WHERE TO STAY

Local accommodations include the Hilton Philadelphia City Avenue (215-879-4000, $$–$$$), Wayne Hotel (610-687-5000, $$–$$$), and Radnor Hotel (610-688-5800, $$–$$$).

## CAMPUS AT ITS BEST!

Haverford is home to the western hemisphere's largest collection of cricket literature and memorabilia. Think about making a quick trek to the C.C. Morris Cricket Library and peruse one of these distinctive tomes. If cricket holds little appeal for you, take a quick trip into nearby Philadelphia. The city has a plethora of attractions, from Revolutionary War icons to fine dining and world-class museums like the Franklin Institute.

# HOBART AND WILLIAM SMITH COLLEGES

629 South Main Street, Geneva, NY 14456
**Telephone:** 315-781-3472 • **E-mail:** admissions@hws.edu
**Website:** www.hws.edu • **Hours:** Monday–Friday, 8:30 A.M.–5:00 P.M.; Saturday, 9:00 A.M.–NOON

## STUDENTS SAY

"Hobart and William Smith College is a diverse educational institution on one of the most beautiful lakes in the United States, which offers an exceptional education and an all-around great college experience."

## FODOR'S SAYS

Overlooking Seneca Lake, Rose Hill Mansion has "more than 20 rooms are open to the public, including servants' quarters, the children's playroom, the kitchen, formal dining room, and parlors. The grounds include boxwood gardens, and a Civil War reenactors' encampment is one of the summer events here."

## ABOUT THE SCHOOLS

The small classes at Hobart and William Smith Colleges help promote a sense of community among the students, professors, and administration. While the top-notch athletic program gets a lot of attention, every student has a chance to shine in the variety of activities available on campus.

## GETTING THERE

**BY AIR:** Syracuse Hancock International Airport in Syracuse and Greater Rochester International Airport in Rochester are both about an hour from campus. Taxi service and rental cars are available from the airports.

**BY TRAIN:** Amtrak stops in Syracuse. From there, visitors can transfer to the Greyhound Bus Line, which stops in Geneva.

**BY BUS:** Greyhound Bus Line services a station at 41 Lake Street in Geneva.

**BY CAR:** From the North: Take New York State Thruway (I-90) to Exit 42 and proceed right onto Route 14 South. Take Route 14 South to the first light. Turn right onto North Street. At the light in front of Geneva General Hospital, make a left onto Main Street. Stay on Main for about one mile until you reach the college. From the South/Southeast: Take the George Washington Bridge to I-80 West to I-380 in Pennsylvania. In Scranton, pick up I-81 North to Binghamton. From there, take Route 17 West. Then, take Route 96 North toward Ithaca. Follow Route 96 through Ithaca. At Ovid, take Route 96A. When 96A ends, make a left onto Routes 5 & 20. Drive past the lake and, at the top of the hill, make a left at Pulteney Street to enter the college. From the South/Southwest: Take Route 17/I-86 to Route 14 North in Elmira. Route 14 becomes South Main Street in Geneva. Take Main Street to the college.

**LOCAL:** Local taxi service includes American Way Taxi (315-789-1590) and Greene's Taxi & Airport Service (315-539-2111).

## WHERE TO STAY

Some of the best hotels in the area include the Holiday Inn (315-539-5011, $$), Ramada Inn Lakefront (315-789-0400, $$), and Hampton Inn in Geneva (315-781-2035, $$).

## SCHOOL AT A GLANCE

| | |
|---|---|
| Type of School | Private |
| Environment | Village |
| Tuition | $31,850 |
| Enrollment | 1,855 |
| % Male/Female | 46/54 |
| Student/Faculty Ratio | 11:1 |

### FRESHMAN PROFILE

| | |
|---|---|
| Range SAT | |
| Critical Reading | 530-640 |
| Range SAT Math | 540-630 |
| Range ACT Composite | 24-27 |
| Average HS GPA | 3.22 |

### ON-CAMPUS APPOINTMENTS

| | |
|---|---|
| Advance Notice | Yes, 1 week |
| Appointment | Required |
| Saturdays | Sometimes |
| Average Length | 30 min |
| Info Sessions | Yes |
| Class Visits | Yes |

### CAMPUS TOURS

| | |
|---|---|
| Appointment | Preferred |
| Dates | Year Round |
| Times | M–F 9:00 A.M.–11:00A.M., |
| | 1:00 P.M.–3:00 P.M.; |
| | Sat 9:00 A.M.–1:00 P.M. |
| Average Length | 60 min |

## CAMPUS AT ITS BEST!

The William Scandling ship is a 65-foot vessel utilized for teaching and research primarily on Seneca Lake. After exploring the boat, spend some time relaxing by the breathtaking Finger Lake. This lake plays multiple roles for the Hobart and William Smith community—living laboratory, sports facility, and recreational hub for students and faculty alike. For more indoor-related activities, consider attending one of the Campus Activities Board's many events, such as the "Mr. Hobart" pageant.

# HOFSTRA UNIVERSITY

Admissions Center, Bernon Hall, Hempstead, NY 11549
**Telephone:** 516-463-6700 • **E-mail:** admitme@hofstra.edu
**Hours:** Monday, Thursday, Friday, 9:00 A.M.–5:00 P.M.; Tuesday and Wednesday, 9:00 A.M.–7:00 P.M.;
Saturday, 9:30 A.M.–2:00 P.M

## STUDENTS SAY

"The greatest strength of Hofstra is its unique location. . . . The school also boasts strong academic programs in business, communications, education, and music."

## FODOR'S SAYS

The largest island on the East Coast, Long Island is "notable for having one of the nation's finest stretches of white-sand beaches along its South Shore, as well as one of the most congested highways, the notorious Long Island Expressway. In addition to superb beaches, nature has given Long Island bountiful harbors and coves, rich soil, and a fascinating geology, whereas its inhabitants have given it a long and distinguished history, beautiful old homes, and more recently, wonderful places to eat and stay."

## ABOUT THE SCHOOL

Long Island's Hofstra University earns high marks in areas such as business and communications. The combination of on-campus and commuter students—as well as the school's proximity to New York City—means there's a lot of coming and going at Hofstra. Though the one permanent thing, students say, is an increasingly strong academic curriculum.

## GETTING THERE

**BY AIR:** Fly into JFK, LaGuardia, or MacArthur airports. Take shuttle or taxi to campus.

**BY TRAIN:** Amtrak services NYC's Penn Station. From Penn Station, board Long Island Railroad (LIRR). LIRR's Hempstead stop is less than two miles from campus.

**BY BUS:** Greyhound's Hempstead terminal is less than two miles from campus. If you aren't up for a stroll, take a cab.

**BY CAR:** From I-495 (Long Island Expressway) East: Follow I-495 East to Exit 38 for Northern State Parkway East, which leads to Exit 31A for Meadowbrook Parkway South. At Exit M4 for Hempstead/Coliseum turn onto Route 24 (Hempstead Turnpike) West. After a mile, Hofstra is visible on each side of Route 24. From New Jersey Turnpike North: Follow the New Jersey Turnpike to Exit 13 to I-278 toward the Verrazano-Narrows Bridge. After the bridge, turn left for Belt Parkway East. At Exit 25A, turn onto Southern State Parkway East and follow this to Exit 22N for Meadowbrook Parkway North. At Exit M4 for Hempstead/Coliseum, turn onto Route 24 (Hempstead Turnpike) West. After a mile, Hofstra is visible on each side of Route 24. From the Throgs Neck Bridge: After crossing the Throgs Neck Bridge, follow Cross Island Parkway to Exit 29 for Grand Central Parkway East (which turns into Northern State Parkway). Continue ahead to Exit 31A for Meadowbrook Parkway South. At Exit M4 for Hempstead/Coliseum, turn onto Route 24 (Hempstead Turnpike) West. After a mile, Hofstra is visible on each side of Route 24.

**LOCAL:** LIRR trains stop at Hempstead, two miles from campus. Take Long Island Bus N70/71/72 or a taxi to campus. For a cab, try Ace Taxi (516-483-4433) or Hempstead Taxi (516-489-4460).

## WHERE TO STAY

The closest hotel to campus is the Long Island Marriott (516-794-3800, $$). Other nearby hotels include Red Roof Inn (516-794-2555, $$), Wingate Hotel (516-705-9000, $$), and Garden City Hotel (516-747-3000, $$$).

## CAMPUS AT ITS BEST!

Enjoy natural surroundings and priceless art inside of Hofstra's unique sculpture garden. On display are bronze works that have been commissioned from some of the twentieth century's leading artists. Reflect on these pieces as you walk through the Hofstra Labyrinth, an ornate and soothing path adapted from the Chartres Cathedral labyrinth in France. Those touring the school in the spring should visit during Greek Week to indulge in chariot races, flag football, and, of course, the mandatory toga party.

# HOOD COLLEGE

401 Rosemont Avenue, Frederick, MD 21701

**Telephone:** 301-696-3400 • **E-mail:** admissions@hood.edu

## SCHOOL AT A GLANCE

| | |
|---|---|
| Type of School | Private |
| Environment | Town |
| Tuition | $23,320 |
| Enrollment | 1,136 |
| % Male/Female | 25/75 |
| Student/Faculty Ratio | 12:1 |

## FRESHMAN PROFILE

| | |
|---|---|
| Range SAT | |
| Critical Reading | 510-600 |
| Range SAT Math | 500-600 |
| Range ACT Composite | 20-25 |
| Average HS GPA | 3.31 |

## ON-CAMPUS APPOINTMENTS

| | |
|---|---|
| Advance Notice | Yes, 1 week |
| Appointment | Preferred |
| Saturdays | Sometimes |
| Average Length | 45 min |
| Info Sessions | Yes |
| Class Visits | Yes |

## CAMPUS TOURS

| | |
|---|---|
| Appointment | Preferred |
| Dates | Year Round |
| Times | Varies |
| Average Length | 60 min |

## STUDENTS SAY

"The greatest strengths of Hood are the sense of community and the professors. Everyone here is equal; the professors here aren't hoity-toity and will eat lunch with you and take time out to help you if you genuinely want and need it."

## FODOR'S SAYS

"Some of Frederick's most famous sons and daughters rest at Mount Olivet Cemetery, including Francis Scott Key and Barbara Fritchie. The cemetery also shelters the graves of more than 800 Confederate and Union soldiers killed during the battles of Antietam and Monocacy."

## ABOUT THE SCHOOL

Hood College's impressive student/faculty ratio (11:1) ensures that no student is left behind. Low numbers allow for an intimate setting and discussion based classes, which encourage a free flow of ideas. Undergrads can also take advantage of Hood's incredible location, a mere hour from both Washington, DC and Baltimore. Not only do these cities provide a great escape from campus but they also present a number of internship options.

## GETTING THERE

**BY AIR:** Guests flying to Hood have three airport options: Dulles, Baltimore-Washington International (BWI), or National. All three are within an hour's drive from campus. The college conveniently provides transportation to and from BWI during hectic travel times.

**BY TRAIN:** Amtrak provides service to Penn Station (Baltimore), BWI Rail station, and Union Station in Washington, DC. Visitors can take either a bus or a taxi to Frederick.

**BY BUS:** Those who wish to travel by bus can take Greyhound, which provides daily service to Frederick from a variety of major cities. Additionally, visitors can use Trailways, though service to Frederick is limited.

**BY CAR:** From Points North: Follow U.S. 15 South to the Rosemont Avenue Exit. Make a right onto Rosemont Avenue. Continue for roughly half a mile, turning left at the entrance to Hood. From Points West: Follow I-70 East to the first Frederick Exit onto U.S. 40. Take U.S. 40 East to U.S. 15 North to Rosemont Avenue. See above for the remaining directions (note: you'll make a left onto Rosemont instead of a right). From Washington: Take I-270 Northwest heading toward Frederick and Gettysburg (note: avoid turning onto I-70). You'll be on I-270 when it merges into U.S. 15 North. Follow U.S. 15 North to Rosemont Avenue. See above for the remainder of the directions. From Baltimore: Follow I-70 West from Baltimore to junction with U.S. 15 North (Exit 53). See above for the remaining directions.

**LOCAL:** For taxi service, try City Cab Co. (301-662-2250), Airport Express (301-668-4000), or Henry's Airport Service (301-663-6310).

## WHERE TO STAY

While visiting Hood, guests might choose to stay in the Econo Lodge Frederick (301-698-0555, $), Courtyard by Marriott (301-631-9030, $$), or Inn at Buckeystown (301-874-5755, $$–$$$).

## CAMPUS AT ITS BEST!

Prospective students should definitely register for Discover Hood Days. Through interaction with professors and students, visitors gain detailed insight into life as a Hood student. Guests touring the campus during July and August should attempt to catch a performance at the annual Chamber Music Festival. The festival, free and open to the public, features both faculty and guest artists. Visitors might also enjoy simply strolling through downtown Frederick and admiring the renowned examples of eighteenth- and nineteenth-century architecture.

# HOWARD UNIVERSITY

2400 Sixth Street, Northwest, Washington, DC 20059
**Telephone:** 202-806-2700 • **E-mail:** admission@howard.edu
**Website:** www.howard.edu • **Hours:** Monday–Friday, 8:00 A.M.–5:00 P.M.

## STUDENTS SAY

"Howard University is about developing future leaders who have a strong sense of the struggles and history of their ancestors."

## FODOR'S SAYS

"A 30-minute drive from Washington, Maryland's National Cryptologic Museum is a surprise, telling in a public way the anything-but-public story of 'signals intelligence,' the government's gleaning of information from radio signals, messages, radar, and the cracking of other governments' secret codes. Connected to the super secret National Security Agency, the museum recounts the history of intelligence from 1526 to the present."

## ABOUT THE SCHOOL

A historically Black university located in the nation's capital, Howard enjoys a strong reputation that draws talented students and eager recruiters to its campus. In fact, the university's robust network links undergrads to an impressive spectrum of alumni, employers, and DC professionals, ensuring that Howard's benefits extend beyond the perimeter of campus.

## GETTING THERE

**BY AIR:** Reagan National Airport is less than 10 miles from campus. Catch a cab to campus or take the Metro (Yellow line to L'Enfant Plaza, then Green Line to the Shaw/Howard University stop.) Baltimore/Washington International and Dulles airports offer wider flight selections, though cab rides to campus are considerably more expensive. Use Amtrak or MARC trains from BWI to DC's Union Station—a short taxi ride from campus.

**BY TRAIN:** Amtrak services DC's Union Station. Take a taxi to campus or catch the Metro (Red Line to Green Line to Shaw/Howard University stop).

**BY BUS:** DC's Greyhound station is about two miles from campus.

**BY CAR:** From I-95 South: From I-95 South, merge onto I-495 (Capital Beltway) heading toward Silver Spring/Northern Virginia. Take Exit 31 onto Georgia Avenue South. Drive seven miles until you reach Howard Place, and then make a left. One block later, turn left onto Sixth Street. The university is ahead on your left. From I-95 North: Follow I-95 North to I-395 North. Turn off I-395 at the exit for 12th Street. Then make a right onto Constitution Avenue. At 7th Street, turn left. Continue ahead (as 7th Street becomes Georgia Avenue), and at Howard Place, turn right onto campus. From I-66 East: Follow I-66 East over the Theodore Roosevelt Memorial Bridge and onto Constitution Avenue. Proceed on Constitution Avenue to 7th Street and take a left. (Note: 7th Street becomes Georgia Avenue.) At Howard Place, take a right onto campus.

**LOCAL:** Take the Metro (subway) Green Line to the Shaw/Howard University stop. Taxi options include Atlantic Cab (202-488-0609) and Yourway Taxi Cab (202-488-0609).

## WHERE TO STAY

Among the nearby hotels recommended by the Admissions Office are Henley Park Hotel (202-414-0502, $$), Red Roof Inn (202-289-5959, $$-$$$), and Latham Hotel (202-726-5000, $$$).

---

## CAMPUS AT ITS BEST!

To get your bearings on Howard's expansive campus, spend some time on the main quad (known affectionately as "The Yard"). This area is at the center of campus life and is utilized for countless events such as concerts, job fairs, commencement activities, and occasionally even studying. After absorbing all the Yard action, head inside to WHUT-TV, the university's television station. The station broadcasts more than 3,500 hours of programming a year, and has won 11 Emmys in the process.

# INDIANA UNIVERSITY OF PENNSYLVANIA

216 Pratt Hall, Indiana, PA 15705
Telephone: 724-357-2230 • E-mail: admissions-inquiry@iup.edu
Website: www.iup.edu

## STUDENTS SAY

"IUP is an amazing, fun, beautiful school located in a small-town setting, but still close to the big city of Pittsburgh with lots to do; [at IUP] you'll make the best friends of your life!"

## FODOR'S SAYS

"Northeast of Pittsburgh, the Laurel Highlands region has Revolutionary War-era forts and battlefields, restored inns and taverns, and lush mountain scenery. The region is noted for white-water rafting, hiking, and skiing."

## ABOUT THE SCHOOL

Many students proclaim IUP's Honors College as the university's greatest asset. Undergrads enrolled in the program applaud their discussion-based classes and their intellectually-driven peers. While hometown Indiana (birth place of Jimmy Stewart!) leaves much to be desired, the university offers a range of activities to keep students entertained on campus. And when all else fails, Pittsburgh is only an hour away.

## GETTING THERE

**BY AIR:** Guests should fly into Pittsburgh International Airport. Rental cars are available from the airport.

**BY TRAIN:** Visitors can take Amtrak to Johnstown, PA, approximately 24 miles from Indiana.

**BY BUS:** Greyhound provides service to Indiana.

**BY CAR:** From the Northwest: Take Interstate 79 South to Route 422 East. Exit at Oakland Avenue (Route 286). Next, take a left on Oakland Avenue and drive roughly two miles until you see the university's archway. From the Northeast: Take Interstate 80 West to Route 220 South. Follow Route 220 to Altoona. From there take Route 22 West to Ebensburg. Proceed to Route 422 West to Indiana. You should exit at Oakland Avenue (Route 286). Make a right on Oakland Avenue. Drive for approximately two miles until you see the university's archway. From the Southwest: Take Route 22 East to the Indiana Exit (this is one exit East of Blairsville). Next, follow Route 119 North to Indiana. Continue on to Route 422 West. Exit at Oakland Avenue (Route 286). Follow "From the Northeast" directions above. From the Southeast: Take the Turnpike (Interstate 76) West to Bedford Exit 146 (old Exit 11). Continue on to Route 220 North to Altoona.

**LOCAL:** For local taxi service, call Red & White Taxi (724-463-0270).

## WHERE TO STAY

Indiana has many affordable hotels, including Best Western University Inn (724-349-9620, $), Comfort Inn (724-465-7000, $–$$), and Super 8 (724-349-4600, $–$$).

### SCHOOL AT A GLANCE

| | |
|---|---|
| Type of School | Public |
| Environment | Village |
| In-state Tuition | $5,038 |
| Out-of-state Tuition | $11,976 |
| Enrollment | 11,976 |
| % Male/Female | 45/55 |
| Student/Faculty Ratio | 18:1 |

### FRESHMAN PROFILE

| | |
|---|---|
| Range SAT | |
| Critical Reading | 480–570 |
| Range SAT Math | 470–570 |
| Average HS GPA | 3.38 |

### ON-CAMPUS APPOINTMENTS

| | |
|---|---|
| Advance Notice | Yes, 1 week |
| Appointment | Required |
| Saturdays | No |
| Average Length | 30 min |
| Info Sessions | Yes |
| Class Visits | Yes |

### CAMPUS TOURS

| | |
|---|---|
| Appointment | Required |
| Dates | Academic Year |
| Times | M–F 11:00 A.M. and 2:30 P.M. |
| Average Length | 60 min |

## CAMPUS AT ITS BEST!

IUP students certainly can't complain about boredom. From poker tournaments to a William Hung karaoke battle, there's always an event you'll want to attend. For those who enjoy the great outdoors, there are a number of activities of which to take advantage. Nearby Yellow Creek State Park has sailing facilities maintained by the Student Cooperative Association. Additionally, there are three ski resorts within an hour's drive from campus.

# IONA COLLEGE

715 North Avenue, New Rochelle, NY 10801

**Telephone:** 914-633-2502 • **E-mail:** icad@iona.edu

**Website:** www.iona.edu • **Hours:** Monday–Friday, 8:00 A.M.–6:00 P.M.; Saturday, 9:00 A.M.–2:00 P.M.

## STUDENTS SAY

"The student population is very diverse, although people tend to stick with those who they are most like. We all mingle well, though, and everyone can pretty much find a niche here."

## FODOR'S SAYS

"The lower Hudson Valley splits its allegiance between urban New York City and rural upstate, and a little of both can be found here . . . but the lower valley still has a sense of place, and its rich history has become part of everyday life. Many American Indian names, such as Nyack, Taconic, and Ramapo, remain in use today, and historical markers locate the numerous Revolutionary War battles that were fought along the Hudson."

## ABOUT THE SCHOOL

Iona is a small, Catholic college tucked away in suburban New York. Dedicated to helping students become informed, independent thinkers, they continually churn out skilled decision makers with an eye towards civic responsibility. Socially, the school has a wealth of organizations and hundreds of events to attend, and New York City is only a short train ride away.

## GETTING THERE

**BY AIR:** New York is accessible via three major airports: Newark, LaGuardia, and JFK. Direct flights are available from virtually anywhere.

**BY TRAIN:** Guests can take both Amtrak and the Metro-North New Haven Line to New Rochelle. It is recommended you take a cab from the station to Iona.

**BY BUS:** Greyhound serves New Rochelle. Travelers can also take a variety of bus lines into New York's Port Authority Terminal.

**BY CAR:** From Long Island, Queens, and Brooklyn: Take the Whitestone Bridge to the Hutchinson River Parkway. Drive North to Exit 14. Make a right on Pelhamdale Avenue and then take an immediate left onto Eastchester Road. Eastchester Road will end at North Avenue about a mile later. You'll make a right onto North, and at the second traffic light, turn left into the school's main entrance. From Yonkers: Follow the Cross County Parkway East to Exit 10, New Rochelle Road, Eastchester. At the end of the ramp, you'll want to turn right. As you drive under the underpass, be sure to stay in the left-hand lane. When you reach the second traffic light, make a left on Eastchester Road. You'll take Eastchester until its end at North Avenue. See above for the remainder of the directions. From Manhattan: Follow the Major Deegan Expressway (I-87) North to the Cross County Parkway East. See above (Yonkers) for the remainder of the directions. From New Jersey: Cross the George Washington Bridge (I-95) and continue East to the Major Deegan Expressway (I-87) North. See above for the remainder of the directions.

**LOCAL:** If you're looking for a taxi in New Rochelle, try calling United Taxi Co. (914-632-6888) or Red Fox Taxi (914-636-6006).

## WHERE TO STAY

If you're looking for hotels in Westchester, consider: Residence Inn (914-636-7888, $$), Hilton Rye Town (914-939-6300, $$), or Radisson Hotel New Rochelle (914-576-3700, $$–$$$).

## CAMPUS AT ITS BEST!

Iona students make the most of every season—even the arctic chill of the annual Winterfest doesn't dissuade them. During this event, undergrads hold snowman-building contests and make snow angels. Then when the snow melts, students eagerly anticipate Spring Carnival. This festival always promises a good time with live music, barbeques, and even a dunk tank. Visitors looking to explore New Rochelle should stop by New Roc City, an entertainment and retail complex.

# ITHACA COLLEGE

100 Job Hall, Ithaca, NY 14850-7020

**Telephone:** 607-274-3124 • **E-mail:** admission@ithaca.edu • **Website:** www.ithaca.edu

**Hours:** Monday–Friday, 8:30 A.M.–5:00 P.M.; Saturday 8:30 A.M.–1:00 P.M. by appointment

## STUDENTS SAY

"The school is small but provides many opportunities for students, as do the awesome town of Ithaca and nearby Cornell University."

## FODOR'S SAYS

"Eclectic Ithaca is the multicultural and intellectual capital of the central Finger Lakes region," and its "diverse restaurant scene and array of arts venues contribute to Ithaca's urbane air. And the setting, amid steep hills and waterfalls at the southern tip of Cayuga Lake, is spectacularly beautiful."

## ABOUT THE SCHOOL

The sound of music is not hard to come by at Ithaca College. Communications, therapy, theater, and, most definitely, music are among the more renowned programs at this mid-sized college located in upstate New York. Warning to those driving to Ithaca: Breathtaking scenery awaits.

## GETTING THERE

**BY AIR:** For proximity to campus, try Ithaca's Tompkins Regional Airport. For a wider array of carriers, Syracuse Hancock International Airport and Greater Rochester International Airport are each a few hours away.

**BY BUS:** Ithaca is serviced by Greyhound, Shortline, New York Trailways, and Swarthout Coaches.

**BY CAR:** From I-81 South: Follow I-81 South to Exit 12 toward Cortland. Merge onto Route 281 South. Take Route 13 South into Ithaca. Move left after passing Green Street; continue ahead onto Route 96B (Clinton Street). Make a right onto Aurora Street. Campus is a mile ahead on the left. From I-81 North: Follow I-81 North to Exit 8 for Whitney Point. Get onto Route 79 West. When Route 79 West comes to a T, go left onto Route 96B (Aurora Street). Campus is a mile ahead on your left. From I-90 (New York State Thruway) West: Follow I-90 West to Exit 25A for I-88. Proceed on I-88 West to Exit 8 for Bainbridge. Take Route 206 West toward Whitney Point. Turn onto Route 79 West. When Route 79 West comes to a T, make a left onto Route 96B (Aurora Street). Campus is a mile ahead on your left. From I-90 (New York thruway) East: Follow I-90 East to Exit 41 for Waterloo. After the toll, go right onto Route 414 South, then left onto Route 318 East. When the road comes to a T, make a left, then a quick right onto Route 89. Then merge onto Route 13 South. Move left after you pass Green Street, continuing ahead onto Route 96B (Clinton Street). Then make a right onto Aurora Street. Campus is a mile ahead on the left.

**LOCAL:** TCAT bus lines 11 and 12 service Ithaca College. For taxi service, try University Taxi (607-277-7777) or Finger Lakes Taxi (607-277-0611).

## WHERE TO STAY

Nearby lodging options include Econo Lodge (607-257-1400, $–$$), Downtown Holiday Inn (607-272-1000, $$), and for a more scenic option, Rice Heritage Cottage (607-387-5446, $$–$$$).

## CAMPUS AT ITS BEST!

Ithaca's School of Business features The Center for Trading and Analysis of Financial Instruments, which provides real-time streaming data from over 125 exchanges and allows students to track mock portfolios at 25 work stations. Wall Street aside, Ithaca offers a wealth of recreational opportunities such as concerts and events like Urban Cowboy, Community Plunge, and Ithaca's own version of The Dating Game.

# JOHNS HOPKINS UNIVERSITY

3400 North Charles Street, 140 Garland Hall, Baltimore, MD 21218
**Telephone:** 410-516-8171 • **E-mail:** gotojhu@jhu.edu
**Hours:** Monday–Friday, 8:30 A.M.–5:00 P.M.; Saturday, 11:00 A.M.–NOON

## STUDENTS SAY

"Hopkins is about an incredibly diverse group of people working ridiculously hard while trying ridiculously hard to have some sort of fun."

## FODOR'S SAYS

"Sherwood Gardens is a popular spring destination for Baltimore families. This 6-acre park contains more than 80,000 tulips that bloom in late April."

## ABOUT THE SCHOOL

Johns Hopkins is a leading name in U.S. higher education that earns particular praise in the sciences. Self-motivators do especially well at Hopkins because there is a high supply of valuable resources, but it's up to each student to make the most of them.

## GETTING THERE

**BY AIR:** Baltimore/Washington International Airport is about 25 minutes away from the campus, but you should definitely account for more time because of traffic. Take taxi service if you are looking to take the fastest method of transportation. You can also take the light rail to Penn Station and ride the Hopkins Shuttle from there, which is the cheaper option.

**BY TRAIN:** Eight Amtrak lines service downtown Baltimore's Penn Station. Take a taxi to campus or board the Hopkins Shuttle, which runs regularly from the station to the campus.

**BY BUS:** Greyhound stops at its Haines Street terminal near the Inner Harbor. Take a taxi to the campus.

**BY CAR:** From I-95 North/South: Follow I-95 South to Exit 53 and merge onto I-395 toward downtown Baltimore. Stay right, and when I-395 ends, make a right onto Pratt Street. After three blocks, turn left onto North Charles Street. After three miles, go left onto 29th Street. Pass through the next light and bear right onto Howard Street. Shift to the left lane quickly, and when you come to the traffic island, make a left onto Wyman Park Drive, which leads you to the campus. From Route 50 East/West: Follow Route 50 to Exit 21 for I-97 North. Proceed on I-97 North to Exit 17A for I-695 toward Baltimore/Towson. Stay on I-695 till Exit 53, which allows you to get onto I-95 North toward North Baltimore. From there, follow the "From I-95 North/South" directions above. From I-83 South: Follow I-83 South and merge onto I-695 (Baltimore Beltway) toward Towson. Get off the Beltway at Exit 25 for North Charles Street. Proceed seven miles South on North Charles Street, staying right when the road splits. Make a slight right onto 29th Street. Bear right again onto Howard Street. Shift to the left lane quickly, and when you come to the traffic island, make a left onto Wyman Park Drive, which leads you to the campus.

**LOCAL:** About 10 shuttle services operate in and around campus. MTA bus service also stops nearby. If you prefer to take a taxi, try the Water Taxi (410-563-3901).

## WHERE TO STAY

Nearby lodging includes Quality Inn Suites at the Carlyle (410-889-4500, $$), 4 East Madison Inn (410-332-0880, $$$), and Doubletree Inn at the Colonnade (410-235-5400, $$$+).

## CAMPUS AT ITS BEST!

It's not surprising that Johns Hopkins, a lacrosse powerhouse, is home to the Lacrosse Museum and National Hall of Fame. Come learn about the history of the United States' oldest sport and marvel at the vintage equipment and uniforms on display. If you're looking for other intellectual fare, try to attend the Milton S. Eisenhower Symposium. This lecture series, run entirely by undergraduates, attracts some of the world's most prominent leaders and scholars. Past speakers have included Noam Chomsky, Michael Moore, and Ralph Nader.

# THE JUILLIARD SCHOOL

60 Lincoln Center Plaza, New York, NY 10023-6588
**Telephone:** 212-799-5000 • **E-mail:** admissions@juilliard.edu
**Hours:** Monday–Friday, 9:00 A.M.–5:00 P.M.

## Students Say

"This is the hardest and best music school in the world."

## Fodor's Says

"Lincoln Center is the [Upper West Side's] cultural anchor. Flanking the central fountain are three major concert halls Avery Fisher Hall, where the New York Philharmonic Orchestra performs; the glass-fronted Metropolitan Opera House, home of the Metropolitan Opera and the American Ballet Theatre; and the New York State Theater, home of the New York City Ballet and the New York City Opera."

## About the School

Juilliard is one of the country's preeminent conservatories. The school's renowned programs in music, drama, and dance attract aspiring artists from all over the world. Hard work and passion are essential for survival, and students log many hours in rehearsal. Juilliard's incredible location, right in Lincoln Center, welcomes undergraduates into a vibrant arts community.

## Getting There

**BY AIR:** Newark, LaGuardia, and JFK airports are all very close to campus.

**BY TRAIN:** Amtrak, New Jersey Transit, and LIRR offer service to Penn Station and Metro-North stops at Grand Central Station.

**BY BUS:** A number of national and regional bus lines stop at New York's Port Authority Terminal.

**BY CAR:** From Long Island: Take the Long Island Expressway to Midtown Tunnel. Follow signs to Uptown/West Side. Drive West on 34th Street to Eighth Avenue. Turn right onto Eighth Avenue and continue to 59th Street. Turn right onto Columbus Circle, and again onto Broadway. Follow Broadway and turn left on West 62nd Street. From Southern New Jersey Via Lincoln Tunnel: Take exit toward 40th Street (Northbound). Turn left onto West 42nd Street. Turn right onto 10th Avenue. Take 10th Avenue all the way to 65th Street. Finally, turn right onto West 65th Street. From Southern New Jersey Via Holland Tunnel: Follow signs to Exit 1 (Uptown and Canal Street) onto Laight Street. Take Laight Street to West Side Highway. Continue to 56th Street (Stay to the right after 42nd Street). Turn right onto West 56th Street, and turn left onto 11th Avenue. Turn right onto West 65th Street. Lastly, cross Amsterdam Avenue. From Westchester: Drive South to get onto Route 9 South (from Saw Mill Parkway). Route 9 will turn into the Henry Hudson Parkway South/West Side Highway. Follow the Henry Hudson to the West 79th Street (Boat Basin) Exit. Take the circle and exit onto 79th street. Turn right onto West End Avenue, driving South. Turn left onto 65th Street. You will cross over Amsterdam Avenue.

**LOCAL:** For subway transit, take the 1 (to 66th), 2, 3 (to 72nd), or A, C, B, D (to 59th). The following bus lines also stop close to campus: M5, M7, M11, M20, M66, and M104.

## Where to Stay

New York City has a bounty of hotels within a wide range of rates. Three possibilities include Larchmont Hotel (212-989-9333, $–$$), Hotel Pennsylvania (212-736-5000, $$–$$$), or Le Parker Meridien (212-245-5000, $$$+).

## CAMPUS AT ITS BEST!

Unsurprisingly, Juilliard has some impressive performance facilities. Alice Tully Hall, the school's most famous auditorium, is equipped with phenomenal acoustics and a 4,192-pipe organ. When you finish your tour of Juilliard you might just want to stick around Lincoln Center. The square is great for people-watching, and you can admire the Chagalls hanging in the window of the Metropolitan Opera House. Afterward, take in a performance of the New York City Ballet.

# JUNIATA COLLEGE

1700 Moore Street, Huntingdon, PA 16652

**Telephone:** 814-641-3420 • **E-mail:** admissions@juniata.edu

| SCHOOL AT A GLANCE | |
| --- | --- |
| Type of School | Private |
| Environment | Town |
| Tuition | $26,900 |
| Enrollment | 1,379 |
| % Male/Female | 47/53 |
| Student/Faculty Ratio | 13:1 |

| FRESHMAN PROFILE | |
| --- | --- |
| Range SAT | |
| Critical Reading | 530-630 |
| Range SAT Math | 550-640 |
| Average HS GPA | 3.82 |

| ON-CAMPUS APPOINTMENTS | |
| --- | --- |
| Advance Notice | Yes, 2 weeks |
| Appointment | Preferred |
| Saturdays | Yes |
| Average Length | 60 min |
| Info Sessions | Yes |
| Class Visits | Yes |

| CAMPUS TOURS | |
| --- | --- |
| Appointment | Preferred |
| Dates | Year Round |
| Times | Varies |
| Average Length | 60 min |

## STUDENTS SAY

"There is no such thing as a typical student at Juniata. Everyone is unique and is encouraged to be so."

## FODOR'S SAYS

"To sample such regional fare as ham, buttered noodles, chowchow, and shoofly pie, eat at one of the bustling family-style restaurants where diners share tables, and the food is passed around."

## ABOUT THE SCHOOL

Juniata's distinctive approach to education is embodied within the Program of Emphasis (POE). POE allows students to combine their interests into one program, unifying a diverse course load and personalizing the educational experience. This results in students who are incredibly passionate about their studies and sparks an intellectual curiosity that extends beyond the classroom. Outside of academics, Juniata students are very active in athletics, including both varsity and club sports.

## GETTING THERE

**BY AIR:** The University Park Airport in State College is roughly 35 miles away. Take a taxi to get to the campus.

**BY TRAIN:** Amtrak serves Huntingdon twice daily, from both the East and the West. The station is only 1 mile from campus.

**BY BUS:** Guests can take Greyhound to State College, PA. Take a taxi to get to the campus.

**BY CAR:** From New York City, Connecticut, and Points Northeast: Take I-80 West to Exit 161 (I-99/220 South) and continue South on 220 for 9 miles. Merge onto U.S. 322 East, and eventually take the Boalsburg/Oak Hall PA 45 Exit and travel 6 miles. Turn left onto PA 26 South and continue 25 miles to Huntingdon. From Washington, DC and Points South: Take I-270 North to I-70 West to take I-81 North to PA 16 West or exit 5. Follow PA 16 West to PA 522 North to Mount Union and take U.S. 22 West to Huntingdon. From Philadelphia and Points East: Take the PA Turnpike (I-76) West, exit 180 (Ft. Littleton), and follow PA 522 North to US 22 West to Huntingdon. From Pittsburgh and Points West: Take I-376 East to U.S. 22 East to Huntingdon.

**LOCAL:** For local taxi service call Cranberry Taxi at 724-776-3050.

## WHERE TO STAY

Guests should consider fine accommodations at Comfort Inn (814-643-1600, $), and the Inn at Solvang (814-643-3035, $–$$).

---

## CAMPUS AT ITS BEST!

Those touring Juniata on a frigid winter's day might enjoy a visit to the Kennedy Sports and Recreation Center. The building maintains sauna facilities which are bound to make you sweat, even when the thermometer drops below the freezing mark. Furthermore, Juniata is a college with many unique traditions. The always eagerly anticipated All-Class Night brings out the inner performer in members of the student body. Every class presents skits spoofing the school, all in the hopes of winning the highly coveted All-Class Night Cup. Zany antics are par for the course, with live sheep sometimes appearing on stage and even the President belting out some tunes.

# LAFAYETTE COLLEGE

118 Markle Hall, Easton, PA 18042
**Telephone:** 610-330-5100 • **E-mail:** admissions@lafayette.edu • **Website:** www.lafayette.edu
**Hours:** Monday–Friday, 9:00 A.M.–5:00 P.M.; Saturday open only for information sessions

## STUDENTS SAY

"For the motivated, Lafayette is about unparalleled opportunities for undergrad research."

## FODOR'S SAYS

"Whether you're shopping for gifts or purchasing travel services, pay with a major credit card whenever possible, so you can cancel payment or get reimbursed if there's a problem."

## ABOUT THE SCHOOL

Though this liberal arts school is small, it holds its own among the big boys of American higher education. With top programs in math and engineering, competitive D-I sports teams, and a wealth of internship and study abroad opportunities, Lafayette has no trouble maintaining its national reputation as a favorite college choice among the best and the brightest.

## GETTING THERE

**BY AIR:** Lehigh Valley International Airport, located 20 minutes from campus, is serviced by seven airlines. Take a taxi or call Elite Limousine and Coach (484-275-6600) for transportation to the campus. Newark International Airport, about an hour's drive away, is serviced by virtually every airline.

**BY TRAIN:** Though Easton offers no direct train service, there are 29 Amtrak terminals within 80 miles of the campus. The closest is in Trenton, N.J., about 42 miles away.

**BY BUS:** Bus lines that service Easton's central bus terminal include Greyhound, Susquehanna Trailways, and Trans-Bridge Lines. The terminal is about a 15 minutes walk from campus.

**BY CAR:** From I-78 West: Follow I-78 West to Exit 3 (denoted the "Last Exit in New Jersey") for U.S. 22 West. Take U.S. 22 West across the Delaware River. After paying the toll, follow signs to the second exit ramp toward Easton and Lafayette College. Make a right onto Third Street. (This soon turns into College Street.) Make a left onto McCartney Street at the top of the hill. Then make another left onto High Street. A block and a half later, turn right into the parking area. From I-81 South: Follow I-81 South to Exit 187 for U.S. 6 East. (Note: U.S. 6 East will turn into I-380 South.) From I-380 South, take Exit 1 onto I-80 East and proceed ahead to Exit 302A. At the end of the ramp, merge onto PA 33 South. Exit on US 22 East heading toward Easton. Continue to the exit for 4th Street/Lafayette College. Turn left at the end of the ramp, then left again at the light, which will leave you on Third Street. (This soon turns into College Street.) Make a left onto McCartney Street at the top of the hill. Then make another left onto High Street. A block and a half later, turn right into the parking area.

**LOCAL:** For local taxi service, try Easton Taxi Incorporated (610-258-2888).

## WHERE TO STAY

Nearby lodging options include the Hampton Inn (610-250-6500, $$), the Seipsville Inn Bed and Breakfast (610-252-3620, $$), and the Lafayette Inn (610-253-4500, $$–$$$).

### SCHOOL AT A GLANCE

| | |
|---|---|
| Type of School | Private |
| Environment | Village |
| Tuition | $31,501 |
| Enrollment | 2,310 |
| % Male/Female | 53/47 |
| Student/Faculty Ratio | 11:1 |

### FRESHMAN PROFILE

| | |
|---|---|
| Range SAT | |
| Critical Reading | 580–670 |
| Range SAT Math | 600–700 |
| Range ACT Composite | 25–30 |
| Average HS GPA | 3.7 |

### ON-CAMPUS APPOINTMENTS

| | |
|---|---|
| Advance Notice | 3 weeks |
| Appointment | Required |
| Saturdays | Sometimes |
| Class Visits | Yes |

### CAMPUS TOURS

| | |
|---|---|
| Dates | Year-Round |
| Times | M–F 10:00 A.M., 11:00 A.M., |
| | 1:00 P.M., 2:00 P.M., and 3:15 P.M. |
| Average Length | 1 hour |

## CAMPUS AT ITS BEST!

The Allen P. Kirby Sports Center at Lafayette grants students access to some first-rate facilities. Visitors are sure to be impressed by the center's huge gymnasium, state-of-the-art fitness center, not to mention its 35-foot climbing wall. After burning some calories, stop by Colton Chapel for a moment of quiet contemplation. This striking building plays host to worship services, theater performances, and guest lectures. If you're looking for more stimulating activities, check out the Lafayette Activities Forum. This student group is continually promoting events, such as the monthly comedy acts featured at Farinon Snack Bar.

## SCHOOL AT A GLANCE

| | |
|---|---|
| Type of School | Private |
| Environment | City |
| Tuition | $33,470 |
| Enrollment | 4,743 |
| % Male/Female | 59/41 |
| Student/Faculty Ratio | 9:1 |

### FRESHMAN PROFILE

| | |
|---|---|
| Range SAT | |
| Critical Reading | 580-670 |
| Range SAT Math | 650-740 |

### ON-CAMPUS APPOINTMENTS

| | |
|---|---|
| Advance Notice | Yes, 2 weeks |
| Appointment | Required |
| Saturdays | Sometimes |
| Average Length | 45 min |
| Info Sessions | Yes |
| Class Visits | No |

### CAMPUS TOURS

| | |
|---|---|
| Appointment | Not Required |
| Dates | Varies |
| Times | Varies |
| Average Length | 75 min |

# LEHIGH UNIVERSITY

27 Memorial Drive West, Bethlehem, PA 18015

**Telephone:** 610-758-3100 • **E-mail:** admissions@lehigh.edu • **Website:** www.lehigh.edu

**Hours:** Monday–Friday, 8:30 A.M.–4:45 P.M.; Saturday, 1:00 P.M.–5:00 P.M.

## STUDENTS SAY

"We are a very involved campus. Most people do at least one activity if not more, and there is so much to take advantage of."

## FODOR'S SAYS

"A quaint and sometimes inexpensive option for those interested in getting to know the people as well as the local flavor of a town is to check into a bed-and-breakfast inn. These are often run by individuals or families who open up their homes to paying visitors."

## ABOUT THE SCHOOL

Lehigh University—known for its strong business, engineering, and liberal arts programs, its academic rigor, and its great social scene—is a midsized school in pastoral Bethlehem, Pennsylvania. With NYC and Philly each just over an hour away, students at Lehigh enjoy the best of rural and urban living.

## GETTING THERE

**BY AIR:** Lehigh Valley International Airports sees 43 daily departures via seven airlines. The airport is 10 minutes from campus and easily accessible by taxi.

**BY TRAIN:** Though Bethlehem has no Amtrak stop, there are 15 stations within an hour's drive of the campus. The nearest is in Paoli, Pennsylvania, about 40 miles away. The Paoli terminal is serviced by the Keystone and Pennsylvanian lines. Take a car or taxi to the campus.

**BY BUS:** Trans-Bridge and Greyhound bus lines service Bethlehem. Both companies stop at the Mechanic Street terminal, about half a mile from campus.

**BY CAR:** Visit Lehigh.edu/directions for detailed directions to the university. From Route 22 East/West: Follow Route 22 to the exit for Route 378 heading South. After crossing the Lehigh River, stay in the left lane and merge onto Third Street. Then make a right onto Brodhead Avenue and proceed ahead to the campus. From I-78 East: Follow I-78 East to Exit 60 for Route 309 South toward Quakertown. Proceed for less than a mile and make a left onto Center Valley Parkway East. After two miles, bear left onto Route 378 heading North. Drive nearly three miles before turning right onto Summit Street. Soon after, make a left onto Brodhead Avenue, followed by a quick right onto Memorial Drive West. From I-78 West: Follow I-78 West to Exit 67 for Hellertown/Bethlehem. Take a right onto Route 412/Hellertown Road and proceed ahead for 1.5 miles. Continue straight for another mile or so after Route 412 turns into East 4th Street, and then make a left on Webster Street followed by a quick right onto East Packer Avenue. Make another quick right onto University Drive, and a final quick right onto Memorial Drive West.

**LOCAL:** LANTA, the local transit system, offers regular bus service from campus to most regional destinations. TRACS, the university van/shuttle system, offers transportation around campus and nearby neighborhoods. For local taxi, try Lehigh Valley Taxi (610-867-5855).

## WHERE TO STAY

There are plenty of options in the Bethlehem/Allentown area, including the Hampton Inn and Suites (610-868-2442, $$), the Morning Star Inn B&B (610-867-2300, $$), and Hotel Bethlehem (610-625-5000, $$$).

---

## CAMPUS AT ITS BEST!

To see Lehigh students in their "natural habitat" make sure to visit the Quad. This picturesque portion of campus houses three co-ed residence halls—one multi-class and two strictly for first-years. Afterward, swing by the Ulrich Student Center. This building, complete with a post office and deli, houses the student senate as well as Kenner Theater, which screens recently released movies every Thursday through Sunday. Visitors who are able to stay through the evening should attend a Late Nite Lehigh event. Past entertainment has included a Last Comic Standing competition, a masquerade ball, swing dancing, and poker tournaments.

---

# LOYOLA COLLEGE IN MARYLAND

4501 North Charles Street, Baltimore, MD 21210
**Telephone:** 410-617-5012 • **Website:** www.loyola.edu
**Hours:** Monday–Friday, 9:00 A.M.–5:00 P.M.; Saturday open only for special programs

## STUDENTS SAY

"Academics are Loyola's greatest strength because professors challenge students to reach new heights. Whoever you are there is a support network available for you at Loyola."

## FODOR'S SAYS

"The 150 acres of the Maryland Zoo in Baltimore—the third-oldest zoo in the country—are natural stomping grounds for little ones seeking out the spectacle of elephants, lions, giraffes, hippos, and penguins, among the 2,000 animals that make this their home. Don't miss the warthog exhibit, said to be the nation's only dedicated environment for the bumpy beasts."

## ABOUT THE SCHOOL

At Loyola, community is the key word. This Jesuit liberal arts college encourages students to work with one another and with professors to create a dynamic and successful community. Undergrads have a healthy give-and-take relationship with host city Baltimore—performing plenty of community service while taking in the cultural pleasures of the metropolis.

## GETTING THERE

**BY AIR:** Baltimore-Washington International Airport (BWI) is 14 miles away from campus. The easiest way to get to the campus is to take a taxi. Super Shuttle service is also available (800-258-3826). Be sure to make reservations in advance.

**BY TRAIN:** Eight Amtrak lines service Penn Station, just three miles away from Loyola. Take a cab from campus or hop on a city bus heading North. (Both Penn Station and Loyola are on North Charles Street.)

**BY BUS:** Greyhound stops at its Haines Street terminal near the Inner Harbor. Take a taxi to the campus.

**BY CAR:** From I-83 South: Follow I-83 South to I-695 (Baltimore Beltway). Travel one exit East on the Beltway to Exit 25 for Charles Street. Drive South on Charles Street for seven miles until you see the main entrance to the Loyola campus. From I-95 North/South: Follow I-95 South to Exit 53 and merge onto I-395 toward downtown Baltimore. Stay right, and when I-395 ends, make a right onto Pratt Street. After three blocks, turn left onto North Charles Street. Proceed ahead on North Charles Street for about 4.5 miles until you see the campus entrance. From Route 50 East/West: Follow Route 50 to Exit 21 for I-97 North. Proceed on I-97 North to Exit 17A for I-695 toward Baltimore/Towson. Stay on I-695 until Exit 53, which allows you to get onto I-95 North toward North Baltimore. From there, continue according to the "From I-95 North/South" directions above.

**LOCAL:** Maryland Transit Authority (MTA) bus lines 33 and 11 stop in the campus area. For taxi service, call Water Taxi (410-563-3901).

## WHERE TO STAY

The hotels closest to campus are the Radisson Hotel at Cross Keys (410-532-6900, $$–$$$) and Doubletree Inn at the Colonnade (410-235-5400, $$$+). Hotels in Baltimore's Inner Harbor area include the Days Inn (410-576-1000, $$) and the Sheraton Inn (410-962-8300, $$$).

### SCHOOL AT A GLANCE

| | |
|---|---|
| Type of School | Private, HSI |
| Environment | Village |
| Tuition | $30,615 |
| Enrollment | 3,502 |
| % Male/Female | 42/58 |
| Student/Faculty Ratio | 12:1 |

### FRESHMAN PROFILE

| | |
|---|---|
| Range SAT | |
| Critical Reading | 560-650 |
| Range SAT Math | 570-650 |
| Range ACT Composite | 24-29 |
| Average HS GPA | 3.5 |

### ON-CAMPUS APPOINTMENTS

| | |
|---|---|
| Advance Notice | Yes, 1 week |
| Appointment | Required |
| Saturdays | No |
| Info Sessions | Yes |
| Class Visits | Yes |

### CAMPUS TOURS

| | |
|---|---|
| Appointment | Required |
| Dates | Year Round |
| Times | M–F 10:00 A.M. and 2:00 P.M. |
| Average Length | 60 min |

## CAMPUS AT ITS BEST!

Nestled in the dynamic city of Baltimore, Loyola's surroundings are full of entertainment and opportunity. Be sure to visit the Inner Harbor, a scenic waterfront locale with dozens of shops, restaurants, and a smattering of street performers. You should also think about making a trip to the charming neighborhood of Fells Point. With its cobblestone streets and selection of pubs you'll feel as though you're in England (almost). Of course, Loyola has plenty of activity to keep your attention focused on the campus. Students delight in annual events such as Loyolapalooza, which brings musical acts such as Blues Traveler to the school.

# MARIST COLLEGE

3399 North Road, Poughkeepsie, NY 12601-1387

**Telephone:** 845-575-3226 • **E-mail:** admissions@marist.edu

## STUDENTS SAY

"The greatest strengths at Marist would have to be its student community. . . . It's easy to become acquainted with many different people from different backgrounds. All school events get great attendance and the student activities group is always looking for new ways to keep students entertained."

## FODOR'S SAYS

"After Samuel F.B. Morse, the inventor of the telegraph, bought Locust Grove, he remodeled it into a Tuscan-style villa. It still contains the possessions and keepsakes of the family that lived here after him, and the Morse Gallery, inside the visitor center, has exhibits of telegraph equipment and paintings by Morse."

## ABOUT THE SCHOOL

Marist is an independent liberal arts college in upstate New York that is dedicated, as the college puts it, "to the development of the whole person." This means that Marist's undergraduates receive a wealth of personal attention inside the classroom as well as plenty of opportunities to grow beyond the campus walls.

## GETTING THERE

**BY AIR:** The closest option to campus is Stewart International Airport (40 minutes). Albany International Airport is a close second at an hour and a half away.

**BY TRAIN:** Several lines offer regular service to Poughkeepsie's Amtrak/Metro-North Station. The station is about two miles from campus.

**BY BUS:** Greyhound stops daily at Thrifty Check Cashing, Main Mall. Take a taxi to campus.

**BY CAR:** From I-90 West: Follow I-90 (Massachusetts Turnpike) West to the Taconic Parkway South Exit. Take the Parkway to Route 199 West toward Red Hook/Pine Plains. At the intersection of Routes 199 and 308, turn onto Route 308 West. In Rhinebeck, pick up Route 9 South. Marist is 15 miles down on the right. From I-95 South: Drive on I-95 South until merging onto I-287 West. From I-287, exit onto I-684 North and continue onto I-84 West. Leave I-84 at Exit 13 for Route 9 North. Marist is 15 miles ahead on the left. From I-84 East/West: Follow I-84 to Exit 13 for Route 9 North. Marist is 15 miles ahead on the left-hand side of the road. From I-87 (New York Thruway) South: Follow I-87 South to Exit 18 for New Paltz. Merge onto Route 299 East and continue until turning onto 9W South. Then turn onto Route 44-55, accessing the Mid-Hudson Bridge. After the bridge, take the first right, following signs for Route 9 North/Hyde Park. Drive one and a half miles ahead to Marist. From I-97 (New York Thruway) North: Follow I-87 North to Exit 17 for Newburgh. Follow I-84 East to Exit 13 for Route 9 North. Marist is 15 miles ahead on the left.

**LOCAL:** The Poughkeepsie Transit System and Dutchess County Loop system offer buses that service the area. For a cab, call Anthony's Taxi (845-485-8580).

## WHERE TO STAY

Nearby accommodations include Econo Lodge (845-452-6600, $$), the Sheraton Hotel (845-485-5300, $$), and Inn at the Falls (845-462-5770, $$-$$$).

## CAMPUS AT ITS BEST!

Did you know that Marist's 2002 crew team qualified for the Henley Cup Regatta in Oxford, England? While touring Marist, make a point to stop by its breathtaking boathouse. Overlooking the Hudson, it houses the college's sailing and rowing equipment. Marist is also situated near many historic landmarks. Franklin Delano Roosevelt's home and museum is near campus and is a must-see for any visitor.

# MARLBORO COLLEGE

PO Box A, 2582 South Road, Marlboro, VT 05344-0300
**Telephone:** 802-258-9236 • **E-mail:** admissions@marlboro.edu
**Hours:** Monday–Friday, 8:30 A.M.–4:30 P.M.

## STUDENTS SAY

"The enthusiasm of the professors and the strength of personality in the students are the best things about Marlboro. These things allow for the possibility for students to shape their education to fit their interests, and especially to enjoy their education."

## FODOR'S SAYS

"Many of the Southern Vermont towns with village greens and white-spired churches were founded in the early eighteenth century as frontier outposts and later became trading centers."

| FRESHMAN PROFILE | |
| --- | --- |
| Range SAT | |
| Critical Reading | 590-690 |
| Range SAT Math | 510-650 |
| Range ACT Composite | 24-32 |
| Average HS GPA | 3.2 |

| ON-CAMPUS APPOINTMENTS | |
| --- | --- |
| Advance Notice | Yes, 1 week |
| Appointment | Required |
| Saturdays | No |
| Average Length | 45 min |
| Info Sessions | Yes |
| Class Visits | Yes |

## ABOUT THE SCHOOL

Marlboro, a tiny school with fewer than 400 undergraduates located in rural Vermont, is known for an academic program that emphasizes closely supervised independent study and self-governance. Under this plan, students attend one-on-one tutorials with professors exploring the subjects of their interest. When they're not thinking critically inside the classroom, Marlboro students spend their time coming up with inventive ways to entertain themselves outside of class, since their secluded campus is 20 minutes away from the nearest town.

| CAMPUS TOURS | |
| --- | --- |
| Appointment | Preferred |
| Dates | Year Round |
| Times | M–F 10:00 A.M.-2:00 P.M. |
| Average Length | 60 min |

## GETTING THERE

**BY AIR:** Marlboro is an hour and a half away from Bradley International Airport in Hartford and the Albany International Airport in Albany, NY, two hours away from Logan International Airport in Boston, and four hours away from JFK Airport in New York City. The Vermont Transit (802-254-6066; 802-885-4567) offers bus service from these points to Brattleboro, Vermont. With advanced notice, the Admissions Office (800-343-0049) may be able to organize transportation for visitors from Brattleboro to the college (a 20-minute drive) during weekday business hours.

**BY TRAIN:** Amtrak makes a stop in Brattleboro. Take a taxi to get to the campus.

**BY BUS:** Greyhound stops at the Vermont Transportation Bus Depot in Brattlesboro. Take a taxi to get to the campus.

**BY CAR:** From the North, South and East: Take Exit 2 off Interstate 91 in Brattleboro, Vermont. Make a right onto Route 9 West through West Brattleboro. After passing the Marlboro Elementary School on the left (about 10 miles from the Interstate Exit), look for signs for the college. From the West: Follow Route 9 East through Bennington and Wilmington, Vermont. Watch for a sharp right turn to the village of Marlboro. Stay on the paved road through the village of Marlboro to the college (about three miles).

**LOCAL:** To get from Brattleboro to campus, visitors can take the Deerfield Valley Transit Association MOOver bus service. Brattleboro Taxi (802-254-6446) and Erins Taxi (802-579-6261) are also available for transport to campus.

## WHERE TO STAY

If you plan on spending the night, some popular hotel choices in the area include the Econo Lodge (802-254-2360, $), Latchis Hotel (802-254-6300, $$), and Colonial Motel & Spa (802-257-7733, $$).

## CAMPUS AT ITS BEST!

Simply visit the dining hall to get a sense of Marlboro students' ingenuity. Led by the campus handyman, students and faculty converted this former cow barn into an airy dining establishment. They even included a stage for concerts and cabaret performances. Afterward, head over to the Brown Science Building. Here you'll find everything from peacocks hatching in the basement, to students working with Lego robotics. Those visiting on a Monday should plan on staying into the evening. The Monday Night Lecture Series offers a variety of thought-provoking speakers, from slam poetry champions to renowned dance critics.

# MASSACHUSETTS INSTITUTE OF TECHNOLOGY

MIT Admissions Office Room 3-108, 77 Massachusetts Avenue, Cambridge, MA 02139
**Telephone:** 617-253-4791 • **E-mail:** admissions@mit.edu
**Website:** web.mit.edu • **Hours:** Monday–Friday, 9:00 A.M.–5:00 P.M.

## STUDENTS SAY

"The students are passionate about what they do, and it's very inspiring. People study hard but play hard too."

## FODOR'S SAYS

"A place where art and science meet, the MIT Museum showcases photos, paintings, and scientific instruments and memorabilia. A popular ongoing exhibit is the 'Hall of Hacks,' a look at the pranks MIT students have played over the years."

## ABOUT THE SCHOOL

A leader in scientific research, MIT sits in the upper echelons of U.S. higher education. Cutting-edge facilities, seemingly endless internship possibilities, and an overarching spirit of cooperation give shape to an MIT education. Let's not forget that the riches of Boston are right at its doorstep.

## GETTING THERE

**BY AIR:** Logan International, Boston's primary airport, is the best option for air travel. Call U.S. Shuttle (617-894-3100) to arrange easy terminal-to-campus transportation. Taxis are available as well. For the subway, or T, take the Silver Line from Logan to South Station and transfer to the Red Line outbound for the Kendall/MIT stop.

**BY TRAIN:** Amtrak stops at Boston's South Station, Back Bay, and North Station. Travel from South Station is easy via the T; simply board the Red Line and travel outbound to Kendall/MIT.

**BY BUS:** Greyhound and Peter Pan bus lines service Boston.

**BY CAR:** From I-90 (Massachusetts Turnpike) West: Take I-90 East to Exit 18 for Cambridge/Allston. Follow signs pointing toward Cambridge. After crossing the River Street Bridge, proceed straight for one mile until arriving at Central Square, where you turn right onto Massachusetts Avenue. After half a mile, MIT's main entrance is on your left. From I-93 North/South: Follow I-93 to Exit 26 for Storrow Drive West. Follow the signs toward Back Bay. Take Storrow Drive for 1.5 miles until exiting onto Route 2A—a left exit just prior to the Harvard Bridge. MIT is just across the bridge. From I-95 North: Follow I-95 North until merging onto I-93 North at Exit 12. From there, follow the "From I-93 North/South" directions above. From I-95 South: Follow I-95 South to Exit 37 for I-93 South. From there, follow the "From I-93 North/South" directions above.

**LOCAL:** The subway, known as the T to locals, offers Red Line service to MIT via the Kendall/MIT stop. The Red Line's Central Square stop is a scenic, 10-minute walk from campus. The following MBTA buses stop at campus: #1 (Dudley/Harvard Station), CT1, and CT2. If you're looking for a cab, call Red Cab (617-734-5000) or Green Cab (617-625-5000).

## WHERE TO STAY

Doubletree's Hotel at MIT (617-577-0200, $$$) is close to campus and is endorsed by MIT. Be sure to ask for MIT visitor rates. Other nearby lodging includes the Holiday Inn Express (617-864-5200, $$) and the Kendall Hotel (617-577-1300, $$$+).

## CAMPUS AT ITS BEST!

MITers definitely know how to pull off a good prank. While you're on campus, check out the record of their genius and ingenuity at the MIT Museum. In addition to renowned collections in science and technology, the museum features a Hall of Hacks, which pays tribute to some of the school's most inventive pranksters. Especially noteworthy is a rare photo of Oliver Reed Smoot Jr., a 1958 MIT Lambda Chi Alpha pledge. Smoot's eventual fraternity brothers used the small-stature pledge to measure the nearby Harvard Bridge. Every five feet or so became "one Smoot." To this day, the markings remain painted on the bridge.

# MIDDLEBURY COLLEGE

The Emma Willard House, Middlebury, VT 05753-6002
**Telephone:** 802-443-3000 • **E-mail:** admissions@middlebury.edu
**Hours:** Monday–Friday, 8:00 A.M.–5:00 P.M.; Saturday, 9:00 A.M.–NOON

## STUDENTS SAY

"The greatest strength of Middlebury is the people. Professors, administrators, students, even the custodial staff are always friendly and helpful."

## FODOR'S SAYS

"In the Masonic Hall, the Vermont Folklife Center exhibits photography, antiques, folk paintings, manuscripts, and other artifacts and contemporary works that examine facets of Vermont life."

## ABOUT THE SCHOOL

Academically one of the most rigorous programs in the country, Middlebury manages to offer the resources, facilities, and faculty excellence of a much larger school. Nationally recognized programs in theater and writing share the spotlight with a top-ranked science curriculum that has benefited from the construction of a new science center on campus. Given all this, it's no wonder that Vermont's Middlebury sits prominently among the most elite colleges in the United States.

## GETTING THERE

**BY AIR:** Burlington International Airport, less than an hour from campus, is serviced by six airlines. Take a car or taxi to campus. For shuttle/van service, try Middlebury Transit (802-388-3838).

**BY TRAIN:** Amtrak's Adirondack line stops in Port Henry, New York, and Ticonderoga, New York, each less than half an hour away. Take a cab to campus or arrange service through Middlebury Transit.

**BY BUS:** Regular, major-line bus companies do not service Middlebury. Greyhound stops in Rutland and Burlington, each about 45 minutes away from campus.

**BY CAR:** From Route 7 South: Follow Route 7 South into the town of Middlebury, where Route 7 is also called Grandview Avenue. Bear right onto Main Street (Route 30) and proceed ahead to campus. From Route 7 North: Follow Route 7 North into the town of Middlebury, where Route 7 is also called Charles Avenue. Once in town, make a left onto Seymour Street. Soon after, make another left onto Main Street (Route 30). Continue Southwest for less than a mile until coming to campus.

**LOCAL:** The Addison County Transit Resources, or ACTR, provides public bus lines. The Middlebury Shuttle Bus offers service among a range of in-town destinations, while the Tri-Town Shuttle Bus travels between Middlebury and the nearby towns of Vergennes and Bristol. (Skiers might take advantage of the Snow Bowl Shuttle Bus.) If you're looking for a taxi, try Middcab (802-388-3232). Middlebury Transit offers rides between campus and regional transportation hubs.

## WHERE TO STAY

The area's numerous accommodations include Courtyard Middlebury Marriott (802-388-7600, $$), Waybury Inn (800-348-1810, $$–$$$), Middlebury Inn (800-842-4666, $$–$$$), and Inn on the Green (888-244-7512, $$–$$$).

## CAMPUS AT ITS BEST!

Student life at Middlebury is deeply rooted in the five residential Commons. Known as living-learning communities, the Commons help students forge academic and social networks on campus. Stop by Atwater or Ross to investigate these distinctive living programs. Afterward, visit the Middlebury College Museum of Art. The museum's impressive collection includes a newly acquired fifteenth-century altarpiece from Italy.

# MORAVIAN COLLEGE

1200 Main Street, Bethlehem, PA 18018
**Telephone:** 610-861-1320 • **E-mail:** admissions@moravian.edu
**Website:** www.moravian.edu

## STUDENTS SAY

"There is no typical student at Moravian College. From scholar to athlete, cosmopolite to individualist, every student can find a niche at Moravian College."

## FODOR'S SAYS

"The Poconos, in the northeastern corner of the state, encompass 2,400 square miles of wilderness bordering the Delaware River, with lakes, streams, waterfalls, resorts, and country inns."

## ABOUT THE SCHOOL

Moravian's Learning in Common program exposes students to a multidisciplinary framework applicable to most any field. Additionally, the college is a member of the Lehigh Valley Association of Independent Colleges. This allows students to take classes and use the libraries of surrounding schools like Lafayette and Muhlenberg.

## GETTING THERE

**BY AIR:** The Lehigh Valley International Airport is a 15-minute drive from campus. Guests can also fly in to Philadelphia International Airport.

**BY TRAIN:** Visitors can take Amtrak into Philadelphia's 30th Street Station. You'll need to rent a car or order a limousine service for the remainder of your trip.

**BY BUS:** Trans Bridge, Greyhound, and Bieber all offer passenger service to the Bethlehem Bus Terminal. The station is located one mile from campus.

**BY CAR:** From Route 22: Take the exit at Center Street (Route 512), turning left off the exit ramp. Drive south for 2.4 miles and make a right onto Elizabeth Avenue. Take a left onto Main Street, followed by another left at the next corner onto Locust Street. Finally, take a right into the college parking lot. From the North: Follow I-81 South to I-380 South. I-380 will take you to I-80 East. Take Exit 302A off of I-80, getting onto Route 33 South. Continue on Route 33 to Route 22 West. This will take you into Bethlehem. Follow "From Route 22" directions above. From the South: Follow the Northeast Extension of the Pennsylvania Turnpike (I-476 North) to Lehigh Valley Exit 56. Proceed to 22 East, taking the exit at Center Street (Route 512). Follow "From Route 22" directions above. From the East: Follow I-78 West to Exit 71. Continue on to Route 33 North. This will lead to 22 West, which takes you into Bethlehem. Follow "From Route 22" directions above. From the West: Take I-78 East to Exit 51. Proceed to Route 22 East, taking this road into Bethlehem. Follow "From Route 22" directions above.

**LOCAL:** For local car service, call Lehigh Valley Taxi (610-867-5855).

## WHERE TO STAY

These hotels all offer special rates for Moravian guests: Hampton Inn and Suites (610-868-2442, $), Best Western Lehigh Valley Hotel and Conference Center (610-866-5800, $), and the Bethlehem Inn (610-867-4985, $$).

## CAMPUS AT ITS BEST!

One of the most important aspects of college life is, of course, the food. Guests should make a pit stop in the Haupert Union Building where they can feast in the dining hall or the food court. Afterwards, venture into downtown Bethlehem. The scenic city has many lovely shops to peruse. It also has a number of cultural offerings. Those who visit in May might be privy to a performance at the annual Bach Festival. Additionally, August brings the nine-day Musikfest which attracts nearly one million visitors every year.

# MOUNT HOLYOKE COLLEGE

Office of Admissions, Newhall Center, South Hadley, MA 01075
**Telephone:** 413-538-2023 • **E-mail:** admission@mtholyoke.edu
**Website:** www.mtholyoke.edu • **Hours:** Monday–Friday, 8:30 A.M.–5:00 P.M; Saturday, 9:00 A.M.–NOON

## STUDENTS SAY

"Mount Holyoke students want to learn from one another as well as from their professors. Students walk through the beautiful campus discussing ideas and politics, and as you walk past you catch bits of their conversations and smile."

## FODOR'S SAYS

"The Mount Holyoke College Art Museum contains some 11,000 works including Asian, European, and American paintings and sculpture."

## ABOUT THE SCHOOL

Founded in 1837, Mount Holyoke College is the nation's first women's college. The college is dedicated to empowering women to be stronger writers, critical thinkers, and ambitious students, and provides a quiet and nurturing atmosphere for students to learn. Holyoke's academic offerings are augmented by the school's participation in the Five College Consortium, which allows students to take classes at four other institutions in the area.

## GETTING THERE

**BY AIR:** Bradley International Airport is 30 miles south of campus. Boston's Logan International Airport is 95 miles to the east. Visitors can book reservations with Valley Transporter (800-872-8752), Michael's Limousine Service (800-533-8470), Seemo Shuttle (877-805-2600), and First Class Shuttle (413-733-4632) to get to campus.

**BY TRAIN:** The closest Amtrak station is in Springfield, Massachusetts.

**BY BUS:** Greyhound makes a stop in South Hadley. Peter Pan bus lines (800-237-8747) provides service from Boston and New York City to South Hadley, with transfers in Springfield. Take a taxi to get to the campus.

**BY CAR:** From the South and North: Take I-91 to Route 202 (Exit 16, Holyoke/ South Hadley). Go North on 202 through Holyoke across the Connecticut River and around the rotary to the South Hadley Center-Amherst Exit, Route 116 North. The college is about two miles from the exit. From the East or West: Take I-90 to Exit 5 (Holyoke/Chicopee) and bear to the right. At the end of the ramp, make a left on Route 33 for 5 miles to Route 116. Make a right onto 116, and drive about 1.5 miles North to the college.

**LOCAL:** If you don't feel like taking the bus around town, you can contact Seemo Taxi (413-582-0095) or City Cab Co. (413-734-8294).

## WHERE TO STAY

If you're planning on staying awhile, try Econo Lodge (413-582-7077, $), Holiday Inn Express (413-582-0002, $$), and Quality Inn (413-584-9816, $$), which are all nearby.

| SCHOOL AT A GLANCE | |
| --- | --- |
| Type of School | Private |
| Environment | Village |
| Tuition | $34,090 |
| Enrollment | 2,064 |
| % Male/Female | 0/100 |
| Student/Faculty Ratio | 10:1 |

| FRESHMAN PROFILE | |
| --- | --- |
| Range SAT | |
| Critical Reading | 620-710 |
| Range SAT Math | 610-690 |
| Range ACT Composite | 27-30 |
| Average HS GPA | 3.59 |

| ON-CAMPUS APPOINTMENTS | |
| --- | --- |
| Advance Notice | Yes, 2 weeks |
| Appointment | Required |
| Saturdays | Yes |
| Average Length | 45 min |
| Info Sessions | Yes |
| Class Visits | Yes |

| CAMPUS TOURS | |
| --- | --- |
| Appointment | Not Required |
| Dates | Year Round |
| Times | M–F 9:00 A.M.–3:00 P.M.; |
| | Sat 10:00 A.M. and 11:00 A.M. |
| Average Length | Varies |

## CAMPUS AT ITS BEST!

It's easy to be captivated by the natural beauty surrounding Mount Holyoke. The campus boasts three enchanting waterfalls, including the main falls, which connect the Upper and Lower Lakes. Holyoke's residences truly form the backbone of the college's social life, with every dorm sponsoring a Hall Programming Council. Each group organizes dinners, parties, tea, and fund-raising events. For a taste of campus tradition, visit the school on Founders Day. Every November, students wake up at 5:00 A.M. and indulge in ice cream at the gravesite of Mary Lyon, the woman who founded MHC.

# MUHLENBERG COLLEGE

2400 West Chew Street, Allentown, PA 18104-5596
**Telephone:** 484-664-3200 • **E-mail:** admission@muhlenberg.edu

## STUDENTS SAY

"Muhlenberg College is about being a close, caring college; they really care about their students getting a quality education."

## FODOR'S SAYS

"The Delaware Water Gap National Recreation Area, a 40-mile long preserve in the northeast corner of the state and across the Delaware River in New Jersey, has camping, fishing, river rafting, and tubing."

## ABOUT THE SCHOOL

Undergrads agree that Muhlenberg's small size is one of the college's greatest assets. Professors are very approachable and really attempt to cater to students' needs. This is especially important, since many students report demanding workloads. Hometown Allentown isn't always the most fun place to be, but students find a way to keep themselves entertained, whether through attending house parties or taking advantage of their proximity to New York and Philadelphia.

## GETTING THERE

**BY AIR:** Visitors can fly into Lehigh Valley International Airport, which is roughly 15 minutes from campus

**BY TRAIN:** The closest Amtrak station is located in Paoli, PA, roughly 40 miles from Allentown.

**BY BUS:** Bieber, Greyhound-Trailways, and Trans Bridge Lines have depot facilities in downtown Allentown. Take a taxi to get to campus.

**BY CAR:** From I-476 (Northeast Extension of the Pennsylvania Turnpike): Take this to U.S. Route 22. Proceed on U.S. Route 22 or I-78 to the Allentown exits. From Route 22: Take the Cedar Crest Boulevard Exit South (left) to third traffic light. Make a left onto Chew Street and continue for approximately one mile to the campus. From Route 78: Take the Cedar Crest Boulevard Exit North (right) and proceed for six traffic lights. Take a right onto Chew Street and follow Chew Street about one mile to the campus.

**LOCAL:** For local taxi service call Quick Service Taxi Company at 610-434-8132.

## WHERE TO STAY

Allentown has a number of affordable lodging alternatives such as: Comfort Inn (610-391-0344, $), Wingate Inn (610-366-1600, $$), and Crowne Plaza Hotel (610-433-2221, $$).

## CAMPUS AT ITS BEST!

Prospective students should pay a visit to Martin Luther Hall, an upperclassmen dorm. This facility also features The Underground, a social lounge equipped with a game room, TV, and vending machines. A number of campus events are also held here. The Muhlenberg Activities Council (MAC) continually provides students with fun entertainment options. Past MAC events have included indoor horse races, a Mardi Gras Party, and a Make Your Own Videos and Reggae Night.

# NEW YORK INSTITUTE OF TECHNOLOGY

PO Box 8000, Northern Boulevard, Old Westbury, NY 11568
**Telephone:** 516-686-7520 • **E-mail:** admissions@nyit.edu
**Website:** www.nyit.edu

## STUDENTS SAY

Students appreciate the "community involvement" and "the fact that the professors are working in the fields now as they are teaching."

## FODOR'S SAYS

"Around the turn of the twentieth century, fashionable ladies and gentlemen used to gather to see and be seen on the broad, formal walkway known as the Mall. The south end of its main path, the Literary Walk, is covered by the majestic canopy of the largest collection of American elms in North America and lined by statutes of authors and artists such as Robert Burns Shakespeare, and Sir Walter Scott."

## ABOUT THE SCHOOL

An NYIT education is a career oriented education. The school's philosophy promotes learning through technology and applications oriented research. Classes are small (never exceeding 30 students) to ensure a high level of interaction and personal attention. NYIT's three campuses (one in Manhattan, two on Long Island) offer a variety of settings in which to learn. Students are allowed to take classes on all three campuses.

## GETTING THERE

**BY AIR:** All three of NYIT's campuses are accessible from JFK, LaGuardia, and Newark Airports.

**BY TRAIN:** Take Amtrak and New Jersey Transit into Penn Station or Metro-North into Grand Central Station. The Long Island Railroad (LIRR) is also an option.

**BY BUS:** Greyhound, Peter Pan, and a number of other bus lines provide service to New York's Port Authority. For the Old Westbury campus, take the Long Island Bus service; for those heading to Central Islip, take the Suffolk County Bus.

**BY CAR:** Old Westbury (East from New York City and points West via the Long Island Expressway/I-495): Follow the Long Island Expressway (I-495) East to Exit 39, Glen Cove Road. At the end of the exit ramp, go left onto Glen Cove Road (heading North). Continue on Glen Cove Road for roughly two miles. Make a right at Northern Boulevard (Route 25A—now heading East). The Old Westbury campus entrance will be at the third traffic light on your right. Central Islip (East from New York City and points West via the Long Island Expressway/I-495): Follow the Long Island Expressway (I-495) East to Exit 56, Route 111. Following the exit ramp, make a right at the first traffic light onto Route 11 (you'll be driving south). Immediately bear to the left onto Wheeler Road/County Road 17. This will eventually become Carleton Avenue. Drive South on Carleton Avenue for roughly two and a half miles and take a left into the Central Islip campus entrance.

**LOCAL:** Take the A, C, E, or 1 train to Columbus Circle, a half block from the campus entrance. Additionally, guests can take the 57th and 66th Street crosstown buses to their respective stops on Broadway. The 57th Street bus stops three blocks away from campus and the 66th Street bus, five blocks away.

## WHERE TO STAY

Hotel options abound in the New York area. Think about making reservations here: Econo Lodge (516-433-3909, $, Hicksville), Holiday Inn Express (631-348-1400, $$, Hauppauge), or in Manhattan at the Hotel Pennsylvania (212-736-5000, $$–$$$).

### SCHOOL AT A GLANCE

| | |
|---|---|
| Type of School | Private |
| Environment | Village |
| Tuition | $16,926 |
| Enrollment | 5,141 |
| % Male/Female | 62/38 |
| Student/Faculty Ratio | 16:1 |

### FRESHMAN PROFILE

| | |
|---|---|
| Range SAT | |
| Critical Reading | 470–580 |
| Range SAT Math | 510–630 |
| Range ACT Composite | 20–27 |
| Average HS GPA | 3.1 |

### ON-CAMPUS APPOINTMENTS

| | |
|---|---|
| Advance Notice | Yes, 1 week |
| Appointment | Required |
| Saturdays | Sometimes |
| Info Sessions | Yes |
| Class Visits | Yes |

### CAMPUS TOURS

| | |
|---|---|
| Appointment | Preferred |
| Dates | Year Round |
| Times | M–F 11:00 A.M.–2:00 P.M.; |
| | Sat 11:00 A.M. |
| Average Length | 60 min |

---

## CAMPUS AT ITS BEST!

NYIT students and guests take advantage of the school's fabulous location. With the resources of Manhattan, you'll never want for entertainment or distraction. Enjoy a leisurely stroll through Central Park, minutes from campus, and visit the zoo. Perhaps take a ferry ride to Ellis Island and learn about the country's storied immigration history. Afterwards, wander over to Lincoln Center and take in a concert with the New York Philharmonic.

# NEW YORK UNIVERSITY

Jeffrey S. Gould Welcome Center, 50 West Fourth Street, New York, NY 10011
**Telephone:** 212-998-4500 • **E-mail:** admissions@nyu.edu/
**Hours:** Monday–Friday, 9:00 A.M.–6:00 P.M.

## STUDENTS SAY

"Unbeatable location and phenomenal professors provide for amazing internship possibilities and real-life experiences."

## FODOR'S SAYS

On any day or night, Washington Square Park is filled with "earnest-looking NYU students, Frisbee players, street musicians, skateboarders, jugglers, chess players, and bench warmers," but few know the park "started out as a cemetery, principally for yellow fever victims—an estimated 10,000–22,000 bodies lie below. In the early 1800s it was a parade ground and the site of public executions; bodies dangled from a conspicuous Hanging Elm that still stands at the northwest corner of the square."

## ABOUT THE SCHOOL

A hotbed of intellectualism and creativity nestled inside an urban hotbed of business and culture, NYU offers one of the richest experiences in higher education today. Situated in NYC's Greenwich Village, NYU mixes a world-class education with the whirlwind of daily life in the Big Apple.

## GETTING THERE

**BY AIR:** The three large airports in the NYC metro area (JFK, LaGuardia, and Newark international airports) offer plenty of flight options.

**BY TRAIN:** Amtrak services Penn Station (7th Avenue and 34th Street). The Long Island Railroad also stops at Penn Station.

**BY BUS:** Greyhound runs a number of limited service stations around the city, as well as its primary station at Port Authority.

**BY CAR:** From I-95 North: Proceed on I-95 North, following signs for the Holland Tunnel. Proceed onto the Pulaski Skyway and through the tunnel. After exiting the tunnel, you will come to a circle, which you'll exit onto Canal Street East. A few blocks later, go left onto West Broadway. Washington Square is right up ahead. From I-95 South: Follow I-95 South through the Bronx. Merge onto I-278 (Bruckner Expressway) toward the Triborough Bridge. After the bridge, get onto FDR Drive South. Eventually you come to Houston Street; make a right (West) onto Houston Street. Then take another right (North) onto La Guardia Place. Look for Washington Square. From I-87 (New York State Thruway) South: Continue on I-87 South as it turns into the Major Deegan Expressway in the Bronx. Cross the Triborough Bridge and get onto FDR Drive South. Eventually you come to Houston Street; make a right (West) onto Houston Street. Then take another right (North) onto La Guardia Place. When you reach Washington Square, you're at the heart of campus.

**LOCAL:** The following subway lines stop within walking distance of NYU: 6 (Astor Place); N, R, W (8th Street); A, C, E, F, V (West 4th Street, Washington Square); and the 1 and 2 (Christopher Street, Sheridan Square). Taxis are everywhere. Just raise your hand and they'll come calling.

## WHERE TO STAY

Among the many of lodging options in the area are Union Square Inn (212-614-0500, $$) and Washington Square Hotel (212-777-9515, $$$). For the quintessential New York experience, check out the New York Marriott Marquis Time Square Hotel (212-398-1900, $$$+).

---

## CAMPUS AT ITS BEST!

NYU's *Grey Art Gallery* showcases all aspects of the visual arts. Aside from its illustrious collection, which includes pieces by Picasso and Miro, the Grey also sponsors walking tours, lectures, and films. The gallery is conveniently located on the east side of Washington Square Park, in the heart of Greenwich Village. Take time out while you're there to commune with students, street performers, and legendary chess players.

# NORTHEASTERN UNIVERSITY

Admissions Visitor Center, Behrakis Center Room 110, Boston, MA 02115
Telephone: 617-373-2200 • E-mail: admissions@neu.edu • Website: www.northeastern.edu/admissions
Hours: Monday–Friday, 8:30 A.M.–4:30 P.M.; Saturday, 8:30 A.M.–1:00 P.M.

## STUDENTS SAY

"[Northeastern] incorporates classroom learning with real-world application in the middle of a great city."

## FODOR'S SAYS

"The Boston Duck Tours, which gives narrated land-water tours on a World War II amphibious vehicle, are particularly popular. After driving past several historic sights, the vehicle dips into the Charles River to offer a view of the Boston skyline."

## ABOUT THE SCHOOL

Right in the heart of Beantown, Northeastern takes advantage of its urban location by arranging big-city work experience for students while they're still enrolled in school. This cooperative education program not only lets Northeastern's undergrads test their interests but also allows them to build a network on which they can draw after they graduate.

## GETTING THERE

**BY AIR:** Boston's Logan International is about seven miles from campus. Call Knights Airport Limousine Service (800-822-5456) to arrange easy terminal-to-campus transportation. Taxis are available as well. For the subway, or T, take the Silver Line from Logan to South Station and transfer to the Red Line outbound to Park Street, and then transfer to the Green Line E train outbound to Northeastern.

**BY TRAIN:** Amtrak stops at Boston's South Station, Back Bay, and North Station. To travel from South Station on the T, take the Red Line outbound to Park Street, then the Green Line E train outbound to Northeastern.

**BY BUS:** Greyhound and Peter Pan bus lines service Boston.

**BY CAR:** From I-93 North/South: Follow I-93 to Exit 26 for Storrow Drive, and continue to the Fenway exit. Proceed toward signs for Boylston Street, and bear right onto Westland Avenue. Then make a right onto Massachusetts Avenue, and make another right onto Columbus Avenue at the third light. Drive ahead to the Renaissance Parking Garage. From I-90 (Massachusetts Turnpike) East: Follow I-90 East to Exit 22 for Copley Square, bearing right off the exit ramp. At the first light, make a right onto Dartmouth Street. A block later, turn right onto Columbus Avenue. Proceed to the Renaissance Parking Garage. From I-95 North: Follow I-95 North until merging onto I-93 North at Exit 12. From there, proceed according to "From I-93 North/South" directions above. From I-95 South: Follow I-95 South to Exit 37 for I-93 South. From there, proceed according to "From I-93 North/South" directions above.

**LOCAL:** Boston's subway, the T, offers direct service to campus via the Green Line E train, which stops at Northeastern University Station. The Orange Line's Ruggles Station is also close to campus. For taxi service, call Red Cab (617-734-5000) or Green Cab (617-625-5000).

## WHERE TO STAY

When making reservations, be sure to mention your Northeastern affiliation. Accommodations close to campus include the Midtown Hotel (617-262-1000, $$–$$$), Colonnade Hotel (617-424-7000, $$$), and Copley Square Hotel (617-536-9000, $$$–$$$+).

---

## CAMPUS AT ITS BEST!

If you attend Northeastern you'll no doubt be spending a good portion of your time at Snell Library. Check out the CyberCafe, located on the library's main floor, which helps fuel students during crunch time. Take a respite from academics and unwind at Krentzman Quad. Students often come here to relax, go to concerts, or buy items from local vendors. Of course, the vibrant city of Boston is also right at your fingertips. Consider shopping in historic Faneuil Hall Marketplace or taking in a game at Fenway Park.

---

# PACE UNIVERSITY

1 Pace Plaza, New York, NY 10038
**Telephone:** 212-346-1323 • **E-mail:** infoctr@pace.edu
**Website:** www.pace.edu

## STUDENTS SAY

"Being that Pace is in the heart of NYC, there is no such thing as 'atypical.' You get all different colors and tastes of the rainbow here . . . and everyone is accepting and respectful of other people."

## FODOR'S SAYS

"Spanning the East River, the Brooklyn Bridge connects Manhattan Island to the once-independent city of Brooklyn. Its twin Gothic-arch towers support a span of 1,595 feet, 272 feet from the river below; the bridge's overall length of 6,016 feet made it four times longer than the longest suspension bridge of its day."

## ABOUT THE SCHOOL

Pace is a comprehensive university that offers a wide range of programs and courses of study. The school remains dedicated to teaching, putting an emphasis on students and maintaining small classes. Professors focus on theory and practice to best enhance the undergraduate perspective. Although Pace is largely a commuter school, there is a strong sense of community, and many students are actively involved on campus.

## GETTING THERE

**BY AIR:** JFK, LaGuardia, and Newark International Airport are within driving distance.

**BY TRAIN:** Take Metro-North's Harlem Line to Pleasantville. During the academic year, Pace runs a shuttle bus to and from the station, running twice every hour until 6:00 P.M.

**BY BUS:** Greyhound has stops in nearby Yonkers and White Plains.

**BY CAR:** From Saw Mill River Parkway (Northbound): Drivers should take Exit 26, Taconic State Parkway. The first exit on the Taconic Parkway is for Pace University at Pleasantville—Route 117. At the end of the exit is an intersection, just beyond which is the entrance to Pace. Go right at the light and continue east on Route 117; a third entrance will be on the left that leads to the administrative buildings and residence halls. From Saw Mill River Parkway (Southbound): Drivers should take Exit 29, Manville Road/Pleasantville. At the stop sign, make a left onto Manville Road. At the next stop sign, make a right onto Route 117 (Bedford Road). The campus will be on your right-hand side. There are three entrances, marked in descending order—the third is the best. From Tappan Zee Bridge and Cross Westchester Expressway—Route 287 East: After paying the toll on the Tappan Zee Bridge, remain in the right lane and continue South on Route 87. Exit at Route 87 South/Route 119/Saw Mill Parkway North. Stay to the right as the exit splits. Follow the Saw Mill River Parkway North, and take Exit 26, Taconic State Parkway. The first exit on the Taconic Parkway is for Pace University at Pleasantville—Route 117. At the end of the exit is an intersection, just beyond which is the entrance to Pace. Go right at the light and continue east on Route 117; a third entrance will be on the left that leads to the administrative buildings and residence halls.

**LOCAL:** Take the Bee-Line Bus System into Pleasantville. Route 6, White Plains/Yonkers/Pleasantville, ends at Memorial Plaza near the Pleasantville train station, where a Pace shuttle bus makes stops twice an hour (until 6:00 P.M.).

## WHERE TO STAY

For local accommodations consider the Wellesley Inn and Suites (914-592-3300, $$), Courtyard by Marriott (914-631-1122, $$), and Westchester Marriott (914-631-2200, $$–$$$).

## CAMPUS AT ITS BEST!

Pace University knows how to keep their students entertained, presenting enlightening cultural fare and fun, stress-relieving activities. Undergrads can hear renowned poets and scholars, such as Maya Angelou, speak on campus. Additionally, events such as Wet Fete, the ultimate water balloon party, offer the opportunity to kick back (and ambush your friends). The university frequently runs trips into New York City, the entertainment capital of the world.

# PARSONS—THE NEW SCHOOL FOR DESIGN

66 Fifth Avenue, New York, NY 10011
**Telephone:** 877-528-3321 • **E-mail:** studentinfo@newschool.edu
**Website:** www.parsons.newschool.edu

| SCHOOL AT A GLANCE | |
| --- | --- |
| Type of School | Private |
| Environment | Metropolis |
| Tuition | $26,820 |
| Enrollment | 2,753 |
| % Male/Female | 21/79 |
| Student/Faculty Ratio | 12:1 |

| FRESHMAN PROFILE | |
| --- | --- |
| Range SAT | |
| Critical Reading | 460-600 |
| Range SAT Math | 490-610 |
| Range ACT Composite | 20-22 |

| ON-CAMPUS APPOINTMENTS | |
| --- | --- |
| Class Visits | No |

## STUDENTS SAY

"Parsons is extremely good at recruiting talented individuals; this challenges you and improves your work. As a result, many students excel in their fields, and it's an honor to be placed among them."

## FODOR'S SAYS

With the Flatiron Building, architect Daniel Burnham made ingenious use of the triangular wedge of land and employed a revolutionary steel frame, which allowed for its 20-story, 286-foot height. Covered with a limestone and terra-cotta skin in the Italian Renaissance style, the ship's bow-like structure appears to sail intrepidly up Fifth Avenue."

## ABOUT THE SCHOOL

From its inception, Parsons has been an innovator in design education and it remains one of the most comprehensive art schools in operation. The main campus is located in historic Greenwich Village, surrounded by galleries, coffee shops, and awash in cultural vibrancy. Indeed, the city is seen as an extension of the classroom and many professors integrate New York and its attractions into their curriculum.

## GETTING THERE

**BY AIR:** Parsons is easily reachable from JFK, LaGuardia, and Newark International Airports.

**BY TRAIN:** Visitors travel into either Penn Station (Amtrak, New Jersey Transit, LIRR) or Grand Central Terminal (Metro-North).

**BY BUS:** Many major bus lines feed into New York's Port Authority Terminal.

**BY CAR:** From South Jersey and Points South: Take the Holland Tunnel, making the first right after exiting tunnel. Proceed on Hudson Street for roughly 20 blocks and turn right on 12th Street. Drive east on 12th Street and turn left University Place. Go left on to 13th Street. You'll see a parking garage on the left. Admissions is at 65 Fifth Avenue. From North Jersey and Points Northwest: Take the George Washington Bridge to Henry Hudson Parkway South. Exit bridge into Manhattan. Follow Parkway South. Exit left at 23rd Street, then continue on 23rd Street, turning right onto Fifth Avenue. Drive South on Fifth Avenue until you reach 14th Street. Admissions is at 65 Fifth Avenue. From Westchester County and Points North: East side of the Hudson: Follow the Taconic Parkway South to Saw Mill River Parkway South. Continue until it becomes Henry Hudson Parkway. Exit the Parkway at 23rd Street. Drive East on 23rd Street and go right on Fifth Avenue. Follow Fifth Avenue to 14th Street. See above for the rest. West side of the Hudson: Take New York State Thruway (87 South) to Palisades Parkway South. Then take the George Washington Bridge to Henry Hudson Parkway South. See above for the rest.

**LOCAL:** Take the 4, 5, 6 or N, R, W to Union Square, located a short walk from the school. You can also take the A, C, E or the F, V, S, Q to 14th Street, which is equally close.

## WHERE TO STAY

These three hotel options are all in close proximity to Parsons: Larchmont Hotel (212-989-9333, $–$$), Washington Square Hotel (212-777-9515, $$$), or "W" Hotel—Union Square (212-253-9119, $$$+). New York does have a myriad of other accommodations, with an equally expansive price range.

## CAMPUS AT ITS BEST!

Parson's Fine Arts Lecture Series brings accomplished artists to campus every month. Speakers for Fall 2006 will include Brian Sholis, the managing editor at *Artforum*, and Jonathan Schipper, a celebrated sculptor. Visitors should also take advantage of all that New York City has to offer. Consider stopping by the Cooper-Hewitt National Design Museum or simply taking a stroll through Central Park.

# PENNSYLVANIA STATE UNIVERSITY— UNIVERSITY PARK

201 Shields Building, Box 3000, University Park, PA 16802-3000
Telephone: 814-865-5471 • E-mail: admissions@psu.edu

## STUDENTS SAY

"Anything that you want to do—whether it be social or academic—you can do it at Penn State. The opportunities are endless and it seems to me like it really is going to be the best four years of my life."

## FODOR'S SAYS

"Gift shops and outlet malls line U.S. 30 and [Route] 340; some have appealing discounts, but it's best to know prices before you shop."

## ABOUT THE SCHOOL

Penn State—University Park manages to instill a strong sense of pride in students who can't stop singing the school's praises. Despite the fact that it's usually either raining or snowing, the university is known as Happy Valley and keeps most of its 34,000 undergraduates very satisfied. Students happily find time outside of their course load for their two favorite extracurricular activities: rooting for Penn State football and partying.

## GETTING THERE

**BY AIR:** Private or charter aircraft may fly into University Park Airport (814-865-5511), which is five miles away from campus. Take a taxi to get to the campus.

**BY TRAIN:** Train travel to Penn State isn't very convenient. The closest stations are in Lewistown, Tyrone, Huntingdon, and Altoona. Amtrak runs from Philadelphia, with stops at Paoli, Lancaster, Harrisburg, Lewistown, Huntingdon, Tyrone, Altoona, Johnstown, Latrobe, Greensburg, and Pittsburgh.

**BY BUS:** Greyhound bus lines (814-238-7971) has connections to and from Penn State.

**BY CAR:** From the North: Take the George Washington Bridge to I-80. Take Exit 161 (Bellefonte) and follow Pennsylvania Route 220 South to State College. Take Exit 74 for Innovation Park/Penn State University. From the East: Take Philadelphia Schuylkill Expressway to the Pennsylvania Turnpike. Take the Turnpike at Exit 247 (Harrisburg East), and take I-283 to I-83. Go North on I-83 to the I-81 interchange. Then follow I-81 South to Route 322, 22 West Exit. Go West on Route 322 through Lewistown to State College Exit 74. From the West: Take Route 22 East to Duncansville, I-99/Route 220 North to Route 322 East to Mt. Nittany Expressway/State College Exit 73. From the South: Take Route 270 to Frederick, and take Route 70 to Breezewood/Pennsylvania Turnpike (Exit 12) and go one exit West to Bedford (Exit 11); Take I-99 North to Route 220 to Route 322 East to State College Exit 74.

**LOCAL:** The Capital Area Transit System provides local bus transportation around town. Fullington Trailways (814-238-1100) provides intercity bus service from Central Pennsylvania to locations in Pennsylvania and New York. For taxi service, try American Taxi (717-901-8294).

## WHERE TO STAY

The Nittany Lion Inn or The Penn Stater Conference Center Hotel are lodging options conveniently located on campus (800-233-7505, $$). Super 8 (814-237-8005, $) and Residence Inn by Marriott (814-235-6960, $$) are other popular hotel choices.

## CAMPUS AT ITS BEST!

One of Penn State's most beloved spots is the Creamery. Approximately 50,000 ice cream cones are sold there every year, along with a few other dairy products. With a refreshing treat in hand, walk West of the Kern Building to the Nittany Lion Shrine. A revered campus site, students line up there to take pictures on graduation day.

# PRINCETON UNIVERSITY

PO Box 430, Admission Office, Princeton, NJ 08544-0430
**Telephone:** 609-258-3060
**Website:** www.princeton.edu • **Hours:** Monday–Friday, 8:45 A.M.–5:00 P.M.

## STUDENTS SAY

"They spoil you with amazing resources, world-class professors, beautiful architecture, great people, fun social life, and the inability of the school to say no to anything you want."

## FODOR'S SAYS

"Washington followed his victory in Trenton with one in Princeton, to the North. The two battles were the first major victories for the Continental Army. Princeton is now a pretty university town, with upscale shops and the governor's mansion."

## ABOUT THE SCHOOL

Tight-knit, prestigious, competitive: Princeton University offers its students the type of individual attention they deserve. The university offers no medical, business, or law schools, enabling it to focus 100 percent on undergraduate education. Students have incredible access to Nobel laureates, who teach and have office hours, and enjoy ample opportunities and funding for undergraduate research.

## GETTING THERE

**BY AIR:** Newark Liberty International Airport is about 40 minutes away. New Jersey Transit train service is available at the airport. The Philadelphia International Airport is about 55 miles South. The SEPTA R1 train is accessible from the airport. Take SEPTA R1 from the airport to Philadelphia 30th Street Station. Transfer to the SEPTA R7 train. Transfer to the Northeast Corridor line Southbound at the Trenton station and take the train to Princeton Junction.

**BY TRAIN:** New Jersey Transit's Northeast Corridor Line stops at Princeton Junction between Penn Station in New York and Trenton, New Jersey. When visitors get off at Princeton Junction, they can take a single-car train operated by N.J. Transit for the five-minute ride to Princeton Station.

**BY BUS:** New Jersey Transit buses offer three stops in Princeton.

**BY CAR:** From the North/New York City: Take the N.J. Turnpike South to Exit 9 (New Brunswick). After the toll, take the first right turn onto the ramp for Route 18 North. After you enter Route 18, take the left side of a fork in the road and stay in the right lane. Immediately bear right for an exit to U.S. Route 1 South/Trenton. Drive South on Route 1 for about 18 miles to the Washington Road Exit, which is a traffic circle. Make the first right off the circle (between the gas stations) toward Princeton. The campus is located about a mile away. From the West: Drive East on Interstate 78 into New Jersey. Exit onto Southbound Interstate 287 (toward Somerville). Follow signs for Routes 202/206 South. Go South on 202 for a short distance and then follow signs to 206 South, which will take you to a traffic circle. Go South on 206 for about 18 miles to Nassau Street (Route 27) in the center of Princeton. Turn left onto Nassau Street, and follow it to the third traffic light. Turn right onto Washington Road. From the South: If you are coming from southern New Jersey, take I-295 North. Take Exit 67 to Route 1 North. Travel about three miles North on Route 1 to the Washington Road Exit, which is a traffic circle. Go three quarters of the way around the circle and turn right (between the gas stations) toward Princeton. The campus is located about a mile away. From the East: Take Interstate 195 West (toward Trenton) to the exit for I-295 North. Drive seven miles to the exit for Route 1 North (exit 67). Follow the "From the South" directions above.

**LOCAL:** For local taxi service try A-1 Limousine (800-678-2154) and Concorde Limousine (888-426-2673).

## WHERE TO STAY

Some of the most popular hotels in the area include the Best Western Manor Princeton Manor Inn & Suites (732-329-4555, $$), Holiday Inn Princeton (609-520-1200, $$$), and Residence Inn by Marriott Princeton-South Brunswick (732-329-9600, $$$).

## SCHOOL AT A GLANCE

| | |
|---|---|
| Type of School | Private |
| Environment | Village |
| Tuition | $33,000 |
| Enrollment | 4,719 |
| % Male/Female | 54/46 |
| Student/Faculty Ratio | 5:1 |

### FRESHMAN PROFILE

| | |
|---|---|
| Range SAT | |
| Critical Reading | 690-770 |
| Range SAT Math | 690-790 |
| Average HS GPA | 3.84 |

### ON-CAMPUS APPOINTMENTS

| | |
|---|---|
| Info Sessions | Yes |
| Class Visits | Yes |

### CAMPUS TOURS

| | |
|---|---|
| Appointment | Not Required |
| Dates | Year Round |
| Times | Varies |
| Average Length | 60 min |

## CAMPUS AT ITS BEST!

The Freedom Fountain in front of Princeton's Woodrow Wilson School is a testament to Wilson's vision of world peace. It's probably better known to students as the setting for bursts of jubilation. Every time the Tigers win a home football game, the Princeton University Band plays a celebratory concert from inside the fountain. Additionally, seniors are prone to jumping in after handing in their thesis.

# PROVIDENCE COLLEGE

Harkins 222, 549 River Avenue, Providence, RI 02918
**Telephone:** 401-865-2535 • **E-mail:** pcadmiss@providence.edu
**Website:** www.providence.edu

## STUDENTS SAY

"The small student body makes PC very comfortable. You never go anywhere without seeing someone you know and at the same time you are always meeting new people."

## FODOR'S SAYS

"[At the Roger Williams Park and Zoo] you can picnic, feed the ducks in the lakes, rent a paddle-boat or miniature speedboat, or ride a pony. The Museum of Natural History and Cormack Planetarium are also here, the Tennis Center has Rhode Island's only public clay courts, and more than 900 animals of 156 different species live at the zoo."

## ABOUT THE SCHOOL

Providence is a great option for students seeking a solid liberal arts college with a heavy Catholic influence. The school attracts a number of fairly religious, preppy students from New England. However, while Mass might be well attended, undergrads definitely enjoy a healthy party scene. Students also delight in spending evenings in downtown Providence and head over to Thayer Street to mix with the RISD and Brown crowd.

## GETTING THERE

**BY AIR:** T. F. Green Airport is serviced by a number of major airlines.

**BY TRAIN:** Amtrak provides direct service to Providence.

**BY BUS:** Peter Pan, Bonanza, and Greyhound bus lines all provide direct service to Providence.

**BY CAR:** From Fall River, New Bedford, and Cape Cod: Take I-195 West to I-95 North. Proceed to Rhode Island Exit 23 (State Offices). Go right onto Orms Street, veer right onto Douglas Avenue, and turn left onto Eaton Street. The campus gate is at the intersection of Eaton Street and River Avenue. From Boston and Points North using I-95: Follow I-95 South to Rhode Island Exit 23 (Charles Street). Continue right on Charles Street and make a left onto Admiral Street. Go left onto River Avenue—the campus gate will be on your left ahead. From New York, Southern Connecticut, T. F. Green Airport (PVD), and Points South: Take I-95 North to Rhode Island Exit 23 (State Offices). Turn right onto Orms Street. Follow the "From Fall River . . . " directions above. From Albany and Western Massachusetts using I-90: Take I-90 East to Exit 10A (Worcester/ Providence, Routes 146/20), which takes you to Route 146 South. Proceed on Route 146 South all the way into Providence. Take the Admiral Street exit. Follow the "From Boston . . . " directions above. From Hartford and Central Connecticut: Take I-84 to Route 2 East to Norwich, and take I-395 North. Follow to Route 6 East into Johnston, Rhode Island. Proceed along Route 6 East to Route 10 North. Take I-95 North to Rhode Island Exit 23 (State Offices). Turn right onto Orms Street. Follow the "From Boston . . ." directions above.

**LOCAL:** For local cab service call Checker Taxi (401-944-2000), Corporate Taxi (401- 231-2228), or Express Taxi (401-286-2298). Additionally, Rhode Island Public Transit Authority (RIPTA) offers regular bus service around the city.

## WHERE TO STAY

Providence is a great tourist town and provides a number of enchanting bed and breakfasts such as The Old Court B&B (401-751-2002, $$), Christopher Dodge House B&B (401-351-6111, $$), or Providence Biltmore (401-421-0700, $$$).

## CAMPUS AT ITS BEST!

Stop by McPhail's, located on the ground floor of the Slavin Center, for a milkshake and to shoot some pool. McPhail's also hosts numerous events like Rock 'n Roll Jeopardy, dances, and late night breakfasts. Things for Thursday is another fabulous entertainment program. Endeavoring to give students a break from the rigors of academics, these afternoon activities include making your own sundaes, getting Henna tattoos, and participating in hot dog-eating contests.

# QUINNIPIAC UNIVERSITY

275 Mount Carmel Avenue, Hamden, CT 06518
**Telephone:** 203-582-8600 • **E-mail:** admissions@quinnipiac.edu
**Website:** www.quinnipiac.edu

### SCHOOL AT A GLANCE

| | |
|---|---|
| Type of School | Private |
| Environment | Town |
| Tuition | $25,240 |
| Enrollment | 5,542 |
| % Male/Female | 39/61 |
| Student/Faculty Ratio | 15:1 |

### FRESHMAN PROFILE

| | |
|---|---|
| Range SAT | |
| Critical Reading | 520-590 |
| Range SAT Math | 540-610 |
| Range ACT Composite | 22-27 |
| Average HS GPA | 3.4 |

### ON-CAMPUS APPOINTMENTS

| | |
|---|---|
| Advance Notice | Yes, 2 weeks |
| Appointment | Required |
| Saturdays | No |
| Average Length | 60 min |
| Info Sessions | Yes |
| Class Visits | Yes |

### CAMPUS TOURS

| | |
|---|---|
| Appointment | Preferred |
| Dates | Year Round |
| Times | Call to confirm |
| Average Length | 60 min |

## STUDENTS SAY

"The school is small and does not have any teaching assistants. The professors can schedule time for their students and also reply to their student's e-mails. Because the school is small, classes really do not go past 35 to 40 students."

## FODOR'S SAYS

"Silver Sands State Park, with its signature beach and old-fashioned wooden boardwalk, is an inviting spot to while away an afternoon—whatever the season. You can walk out to Charles Island (where Captain Kidd is rumored to have buried his treasure) at low tide."

## ABOUT THE SCHOOL

Although a midsize university, Quinnipiac manages to provide the personal attention more often attributed to smaller schools. Indeed, many classes are no larger than 20 students. Additionally, the Learning Center offers a guiding hand for students struggling with academics. Once the weekend rolls around, undergrads are quick to trade in their books for a rowdy game of beer pong.

## GETTING THERE

**BY AIR:** Hartford's Bradley International Airport is the closest major airport to the university. Guests can also choose to fly into JFK, La Guardia, or Newark.

**BY TRAIN:** Train service to nearby New Haven is available via both Amtrak and Metro-North.

**BY BUS:** Greyhound provides service to nearby New Haven and Hartford. It is best to take a taxi from the station to the campus.

**BY CAR:** From New York City and West, via I-95: Follow I-95 to New Haven. Get onto I-91 North, and take Exit 10 (Route 40). Continue on Route 40 for roughly three miles until it ends at Whitney Avenue. Make a right onto Whitney Avenue (Route 10) and drive North for 1.4 miles. Make a right onto Mount Carmel Avenue. Drive a mere 0.3 miles and you'll reach campus. From Northern New Jersey: Take Route 287 over the Tappan Zee Bridge to Exit 8. Proceed on Route 287 to Merritt Parkway (Exit 9N). Continue on the Parkway (Route 15) to Exit 61. Make a right onto Whitney Avenue (Route 10) and continue heading North for three miles until you reach Mount Carmel Avenue. Make a right onto Mount Carmel and follow it for 0.3 miles to campus. From Hartford, Boston, and Upper New England via I-91: Follow I-91 South to Exit 10 (Route 40). Follow the "From New York City . . ." directions above. From Hartford and East, via the Merritt Parkway: Follow the Parkway (Route 15) to Exit 62. Make a right onto Whitney Avenue (Route 10). Follow the "From New York City . . ." directions above.

**LOCAL:** CT Transit provides local and express bus service around the greater Stamford, Hartford, and New Haven areas. For car service call Connecticut Limo (203-878-2222).

## WHERE TO STAY

For affordable hotels in close proximity to Quinnipiac try Days Inn of Hamden (203-288-2505, $), Clarion Hotel & Suites (203-288-3831, $$), or the Holiday Inn (203-239-4225, $$).

---

## CAMPUS AT ITS BEST!

Quinnipiac's industrious Student Programming Board continually satiates students' thirst for great entertainment. They regularly bring remarkable performers such as Dane Cook and Busta Rhymes to campus. SPB also sponsors activities such as Laser Tag and the annual Powder Puff Football game. Consider exploring the surrounding area's attractions as well. Lighthouse Point Park in New Haven and the beaches of West Haven are perfect for enjoying Connecticut's natural beauty.

# RENSSELAER POLYTECHNIC INSTITUTE

110 Eighth Street, Troy, NY 12180-3590
**Telephone:** 518-276-6216 • **E-mail:** admissions@rpi.edu
**Hours:** Monday–Friday, 8:30–5:00 P.M.; Saturday, 9:30 A.M.–3:00 P.M.

| SCHOOL AT A GLANCE | |
| --- | --- |
| Type of School | Private |
| Environment | City |
| Tuition | $32,600 |
| Enrollment | 5,148 |
| % Male/Female | 75/25 |
| Student/Faculty Ratio | 14:1 |

| FRESHMAN PROFILE | |
| --- | --- |
| Range SAT | |
| Critical Reading | 580–680 |
| Range SAT Math | 640–740 |
| Range ACT Composite | 25–29 |

| ON-CAMPUS APPOINTMENTS | |
| --- | --- |
| Info Sessions | Yes |
| Class Visits | Yes |

| CAMPUS TOURS | |
| --- | --- |
| Appointment | Preferred |
| Dates | Year Round |
| Times | M–F 11:00 A.M. and 2:00 P.M. |
| Average Length | 90 min |

## STUDENTS SAY

"Rensselaer is about being innovative, being a leader, and getting an education in technology."

## FODOR'S SAYS

"The Durham Reservoir in Grafton Lakes State Park features 20 miles of trails and a series of ponds that make this a favorite place for such warm-weather activities as picnicking, swimming, fishing, hiking, and biking. In winter, cross-country skiers, snowshoers, and snowmobilers hit the trails, and ice-skaters take to the frozen water."

## ABOUT THE SCHOOL

Though Rensselaer has recently begun to expand its focus, pouring funding into arts programs, students assert that it remains a tech-oriented school. Indeed, RPI is a math and science powerhouse, emphasizing cutting-edge innovations and research opportunities. Though the work is demanding and the concepts difficult, the learning assistance center ensures no one falls behind. The school maintains a dichotomy of computer nerds mixed with a healthy Greek population.

## GETTING THERE

**BY AIR:** Guests traveling by air should fly into Albany International Airport.

**BY TRAIN:** Visitors should take Amtrak to the Albany/Rensselaer station.

**BY BUS:** Greyhound provides service to Albany.

**BY CAR:** From the North: Follow I-87 (the Adirondack Northway) South to Exit 7 East. Proceed on Route 7 heading toward Troy, New York, and Bennington, Vermont. Cross the Collar City Bridge and follow the signs for Route 7, Hoosick Street. When you reach the fourth traffic light, take a right onto 15th Street. Drive through the third traffic light on 15th Street. Follow "Directions to Campus" below. From the South: Follow I-87 (the New York State Thruway) North to Exit 23. From Exit 23 you'll get onto I-787 North to Route 7 East. Take Exit 9E. Disregard the sign for RPI (Rensselaer) and Russell Sage College at the previous exit. Exit 9E, Route 7 East, provides an easier approach to campus. Follow the "From the North" directions above. From the East: Follow I-90 (Massachusetts Turnpike, Berkshire Spur of the New York Thruway) to Exit B1. Drive West for 13.5 miles, and take I-787 North to Route 7 East, Exit 9E. Follow the "From the South" directions above. From the West: Take I-90 (the New York State Thruway) to Exit 24. Take exit 1N of I-87 (the Adirondack Northway) North to Exit 7, heading East on Route 7 toward Troy, New York, and Bennington, Vermont. Follow the "From the South" directions above. Directions to Campus: Continue along 15th Street, make a left at the third traffic light onto Sage Avenue. You will know you're at Rensselaer when you see the large granite Rensselaer sign at the intersection of 15th Street and Sage Avenue. The Admissions Building will be directly in front of you; bear to the left of the building onto Eaton Road. The parking lot will be on your right, directly behind the Admissions Building.

**LOCAL:** For local taxi service call Black & White Cab System (518-235-4854) or Star & Strand Taxi (518-272-6961).

## WHERE TO STAY

Accommodations include the Best Western Rensselaer Inn (518-274-3210, $), Franklin Plaza Inn & Suites (518-274-8800, $$), or Albany Marriott (518-458-8444, $$).

## CAMPUS AT ITS BEST!

After all the stress and strain of the college search, you deserve a treat. Stop by the Rensselaer Union and splurge on some Ben & Jerry's. The college has the unique distinction of being the first collegiate institution to have a Ben & Jerry's on campus. Afterward, burn off your indulgence by taking in a few frames at RPI's bowling alley.

# RHODE ISLAND SCHOOL OF DESIGN

2 College Street, Providence, RI 02903
**Telephone:** 401-454-6300 • **E-mail:** admissions@risd.edu
**Website:** www.risd.edu • **Hours:** Monday–Friday, 8:30 A.M.–4:30 P.M.; Saturday by appointment

## STUDENTS SAY

"The facilities are excellent; everything you need to create is here at your fingertips. The instructors are really dedicated to helping you improve. RISD allows you to think and create freely."

## FODOR'S SAYS

"The two-term Rhode Island governor, Henry Lippit, made his fortune selling textiles to both armies during the Civil War, and he spared no expense in building his home, an immaculate Renaissance Revival mansion, in 1863. The floor of the billiard room uses nine types of inlaid wood; the ceilings are intricately hand-painted (some look convincingly like tiger maple), and the neoclassical chandeliers are cast in bronze."

## ABOUT THE SCHOOL

RISD is one of the country's premiere art schools. Offering programs in visual arts, architecture, design, and art education, students find their creativity nurtured while honing their craft. The school's curriculum impresses a global sensitivity upon undergrads, encouraging them to create works that will shape and benefit the world at large. The school believes in a holistic education, and students must take a selection of liberal arts courses as well.

## GETTING THERE

**BY AIR:** People can fly into Providence's T. F. Green International Airport or Boston's Logan International Airport. Each airport is serviced by a number of carriers.

**BY TRAIN:** Amtrak provides service to Providence. Visitors can also take the MBTA Commuter Rail between Providence and Boston on the Attleboro/Stoughton Line.

**BY BUS:** Both Greyhound and Bonanza bus lines provide direct service to Providence. Visitors can either take a taxi or local RIPTA to reach the campus.

**BY CAR:** From New York: Take I-278 East heading toward I-87 N/Bronx/Upstate New York/New England. Merge onto I-278 East/Bruckner Expressway via Exit 47 (toward New Haven). The I-278 East/Bruckner Expressway turns into I-95 North. Get on the Hutchinson Parkway North, taking Exit 9. Merge onto Hutchinson River Parkway North via the exit on the left. Proceed onto I-95 North via Exit 6 (again toward New Haven). You'll drive through Connecticut and cross into Rhode Island. Merge onto Memorial Boulevard via Exit 22A. Head toward downtown. Make a left onto Washington Place. Washington will become Waterman Street. Finally, make a left onto Prospect Street.

**LOCAL:** You can read campus via the Rhode Island Public Transit Authority (RIPTA). Take 35 RIPTA routes that access Kennedy Plaza, which will leave you a mere two blocks from RISD.

## WHERE TO STAY

Charming B&B's that are sure to enhance any visit to Providence include Annie Brownell House (401-454-2934, $$), Cady House Bed & Breakfast (401-273-5398, $$), or the Old Court Bed & Breakfast (401-751-2002, $$).

---

## CAMPUS AT ITS BEST!

When RISD students emerge from the studio they know how to have a good time. The annual Hip Hop Showdown has quickly grown in popularity. Audiences clamor to see RISD and Brown rappers, dancers, and musicians face off. The International Festival, held every spring, features food, music, and dance. The festival coincides with the open-air student art sale. Visitors wishing to find fun away from campus might enjoy seeing WaterFire, an award-winning fire installation on three rivers passing through downtown.

## SCHOOL AT A GLANCE

| | |
|---|---|
| Type of School | Private |
| Environment | City |
| Tuition | $23,949 |
| Enrollment | 12,423 |
| % Male/Female | 70/30 |
| Student/Faculty Ratio | 13:1 |

### FRESHMAN PROFILE

| | |
|---|---|
| Range SAT | |
| Critical Reading | 540-640 |
| Range SAT Math | 570-670 |
| Range ACT Composite | 23-28 |
| Average HS GPA | 3.7 |

### ON-CAMPUS APPOINTMENTS

| | |
|---|---|
| Advance Notice | Yes, 1 week |
| Appointment | Required |
| Saturdays | Sometimes |
| Average Length | 60 min |
| Info Sessions | Yes |
| Class Visits | Yes |

### CAMPUS TOURS

| | |
|---|---|
| Appointment | Preferred |
| Dates | Year Round |
| Times | M–F 10:00 A.M., NOON, and 2:00 P.M.; Sat 10:00 A.M. |
| Average Length | 60 min |

# ROCHESTER INSTITUTE OF TECHNOLOGY

60 Lomb Memorial Drive, Rochester, NY 14623-5604

Telephone: 585-475-6631 • E-mail: admissions@rit.edu

Website: www.rit.edu • Hours: Monday–Friday; Saturday, 8:30 A.M.–4:30 P.M.; 10:00 A.M.–NOON

## STUDENTS SAY

"Academics [at RIT] are second to none. If you want to learn and do nothing else RIT is for you. If you want to go to college for wild and crazy parties, RIT is not for you."

## FODOR'S SAYS

"More than 5000 years of art is contained within the 14 exhibit rooms of the Memorial Art Gallery of the University of Rochester. Egyptian coffins, medieval tapestries, impressionist paintings, European masters, and African carvings are on permanent display."

## ABOUT THE SCHOOL

Academically oriented students with a desire to succeed plus an intense quarter system equals a very busy bunch of undergrads at RIT. Praise is almost unanimous for the school's engineering and arts programs, as well as its partnerships with companies such as Bausch and Lomb and Kodak. Socially, the school has made recent strides with the addition of new venues, thus attracting more concerts and events.

## GETTING THERE:

**BY AIR:** The Greater Rochester International Airport is a mere five miles away from RIT's main campus. It is serviced by most major airlines, including United, Delta, American, and USAir.

**BY TRAIN:** Amtrak provides service to Rochester. Taxis are available at the station.

**BY BUS:** Both Greyhound and Trailways bus lines serve Rochester. Taxis are available at the station.

**BY CAR:** From the New York State Thruway: Take Exit 46 and proceed North on I-390 to Exit 13 (Hylan Drive). Take a left onto Hylan Drive, and continue North to Jefferson Road (Route 252), and make a left at the light. Proceed West a short distance to the main campus. Once entering campus at the main entrance (indicated with a very large sign that reads: Rochester Institute of Technology, Founded 1829), follow the signs to the Information Booth. The Campus Safety officer will issue a parking pass and provide directions to your desired destination. From the airport: Turn right onto Brooks Avenue, and make a quick right onto I-390 South. From 390, take the next exit (Scottsville Road) and turn right at the end of the ramp. Drive for approximately three miles and turn left onto Jefferson Road (Route 252). Proceed East a short distance to campus, RIT's main entrance will be on your right.

**LOCAL:** The Rochester Genesee Regional Transportation Authority provides bus service throughout Rochester and campus. For taxi service, try Empire Metro Taxi (585-746-0232) and Associate Taxi (585-232-3232).

## WHERE TO STAY

Rochester features a number of affordable hotels, including Microtel (800-771-7171, $), Radisson Hotel (585-475-1910, $$), and Fairfield Inn by Marriott (585-529-5000, $$).

## CAMPUS AT ITS BEST!

Consider stopping in the Ritz Sports Zone, located on the lower level of the Alumni Student Union, where students can dine in the Ritz grill, gorging themselves on famous Oscar Hot Burgers. They can also take advantage of the ESPN Sports Center Desk, performing a broadcast and sending it on to friends. Java Wally's, found in the RIT Library, is another hotspot where students enjoy a smoothie while participating in trivia or open mic nights.

# ROGER WILLIAMS UNIVERSITY

One Old Ferry Road, Bristol, RI 02809-0000
**Telephone:** 401-254-3500 • **E-mail:** admit@rwu.edu
**Website:** www.rwu.edu • **Hours:** Monday–Friday and Saturday, 8:30 A.M.–4:30 P.M.

## STUDENTS SAY

"The campus is gorgeous ... the overlook of the water is amazing, and there is a beautiful bridge. Once you settle in it feels like home."

## FODOR'S SAYS

"Smith's Castle, built in 1678 by Richard Smith Jr., is a beautifully preserved saltbox plantation house on the quiet shore of an arm of Narragansett Bay. The ground have one of the first military burial grounds (open during daylight hours) in the country: a marked mass grave holding 40 colonists killed in the Great Swamp battle of 1675, during which the Narragansetts were nearly annihilated, ending King Philip's War in Rhode Island."

## ABOUT THE SCHOOL

Roger Williams represents four years of exploration and discovery. Offering a bounty of majors, students are guaranteed to find a stimulating academic path. The university's waterfront location is put to good use by the stellar marine biology program as well as outdoor enthusiasts. Students also take advantage of the school's proximity to Providence, enjoying the city's fine shops and restaurants.

## GETTING THERE

**BY AIR:** The T. F. Green Airport, located in Warwick, Rhode Island, is served by a number of airlines. Logan Airport, though further away, is also a viable option.

**BY TRAIN:** Amtrak makes stops in Providence. The station is approximately 13 miles away from Bristol.

**BY BUS:** Both Greyhound and Bonanza bus lines provide service to Providence.

**BY CAR:** From Boston: Take Route 93 South to Route 24 South to Fall River. From Route 24 bear right onto Route 195 West to Exit 8A (Tiverton/Newport RI). Follow Route 24 South to Mt. Hope Bridge/Bristol Exit. Bear right up the hill and across Mt. Hope Bridge. The university is just after the bridge on the right. From Massachusetts and Points North: Take Route 128 South (also called 95) toward Rhode Island. Travel South on Route 95 to Route 195 East toward Cape Cod. Take Route 195 East to Massachusetts Exit 2 (Warren/Newport RI, Route 136 South). Follow 136 South—the campus is nine miles ahead. From Albany and Points West: Take Route 87 to Route 90 East (Mass Turnpike). Take Route 146 South to Route 95 South to Providence, Rhode Island. Take Route 195 East to Massachusetts Exit 2 (Warren/Newport RI, Route 136 South). Follow 136 South—the campus is nine miles ahead. From New York City and Points South: Take Route 95 North to Providence, Rhode Island. Take Route 195 East to Massachusetts Exit 2 (Warren/Newport RI, Route 136 South). Follow 136 South—the campus is nine miles ahead.

**LOCAL:** The Rhode Island Public Transit Authority operates buses throughout Bristol and Rhode Island (as well as ferry service). For a taxi, try A Taxi Service (401-285-6684).

## WHERE TO STAY

Charming hotel options include the Captain's Place (401-253-2573, $), Bristol Harbor Inn (401-254-1444, $$–$$$), and Rockwell House Inn (410-253-0040, $$$).

## SCHOOL AT A GLANCE

| | |
|---|---|
| Type of School | Private |
| Environment | Town |
| Tuition | $22,932 |
| Enrollment | 4,358 |
| % Male/Female | 51/49 |
| Student/Faculty Ratio | 16:1 |

### FRESHMAN PROFILE

| | |
|---|---|
| Range SAT | |
| Critical Reading | 490-580 |
| Range SAT Math | 500-600 |
| Range ACT Composite | 21-25 |
| Average HS GPA | 3.07 |

### ON-CAMPUS APPOINTMENTS

| | |
|---|---|
| Advance Notice | Yes, 1 week |
| Appointment | Required |
| Saturdays | No |
| Average Length | 30 min |
| Info Sessions | Yes |
| Class Visits | Yes |

### CAMPUS TOURS

| | |
|---|---|
| Appointment | Preferred |
| Dates | Academic Year |
| Times | 9:00 A.M., 11:00 A.M., 1:00 P.M. |
| Average Length | 60 min |

---

## CAMPUS AT ITS BEST!

A large portion of college life involves experiences found outside of the classroom. Roger Williams fosters this sentiment with an impressive events calendar. Past activities have included lectures on the history of hip-hop, grocery bingo, make your own license plate, and performances by slam poets. The surrounding area also offers a plethora of recreational opportunities. The nearby waters of Mt. Hope and Narragansett Bays are excellent locations for windsurfing, sailing, and jogging.

# RUTGERS, THE STATE UNIVERSITY OF NEW JERSEY—NEW BRUNSWICK/PISCATAWAY

65 Davidson Road, Piscataway, NJ 08854-8097

**Telephone:** 732-932-4636 • **E-mail:** admissions@ugadm.rutgers.edu

**Hours:** Monday–Friday, 8:30 A.M.–4:30 P.M.

## STUDENTS SAY

"Rutgers offers boundless opportunity, both educational and professional, but you have to be willing to go out and seek it."

## FODOR'S SAYS

"For Hudson River views take the Palisades Interstate Parkway North from the George Washington Bridge to the state line."

## ABOUT THE SCHOOL

At Rutgers, students know they are getting a quality education for an affordable, state-school price. The New Brunswick campus alone has more than 12 colleges, which offers students a host of different majors from which to choose, and courses that are taught by professors who are at the top of their fields. The large campus of more than 25,000 undergraduates is always busy. With no shortage of extracurricular activities from which to choose and easy access to a hip downtown area in hometown New Brunswick, the motivated self-starters at Rutgers prove that bigger is sometimes better.

## GETTING THERE

**BY AIR:** Newark Liberty International Airport is about 24 miles away from campus. New Jersey Transit train and bus service or taxi service is available from the airport.

**BY TRAIN:** Amtrak provides limited direct service to New Brunswick; however, transfers can be made via New Jersey Transit trains at the MetroPark, New York, and Trenton stations.

**BY BUS:** Greyhound stops in New York City and various locations in New Jersey. Transfer to a New Jersey Transit bus for direct service to and from campus.

**BY CAR:** From New Jersey Turnpike (North or South): Take Exit 9, and bear right after the toll. Follow signs for "Route 18 North—New Brunswick." Stay to the left so you may continue on Route 18 North. Proceed along Route 18 North. Turn off at the exit marked "George Street—Rutgers University" (approximately 2.6 miles from the turnpike). From the North: Take the Parkway South. Turn off at Exit 129 for the New Jersey Turnpike and head South. Take Exit 9 to exit the turnpike, bear right after the toll, and follow the signs for "Route 18 North—New Brunswick." Stay to the left so you may continue on Route 18 North. Proceed along Route 18 North. Turn off at the exit marked "George Street—Rutgers University" (approximately 2.6 miles from the turnpike). From the South: Take the Parkway North. Turn off at Exit 105, and follow the signs for Route 18 North. After around 24 miles, you will pass the entrance for the New Jersey Turnpike. Continue on Route 18 North. Turn off at the exit marked "George Street-Rutgers University" (approximately 2.6 miles from the turnpike).

**LOCAL:** New Jersey Transit's Northeast Corridor Line stops minutes from campus in New Brunswick with local and express service between Penn Station in New York and Trenton, New Jersey. SEPTA provides service at Trenton to and from Philadelphia. For local taxi service around New Brunswick call Contact Yellow Cab (732-246-2222).

## WHERE TO STAY

Some popular lodging choices near the campus include Howard Johnson Express Inn (800-446-4656, $), Quality Inn Somerset (732-469-5050, $$), and Residence Inn by Marriott Cranbury (609-395-9447, $$$).

## CAMPUS AT ITS BEST!

The Rutgers University Geology Museum boasts some fascinating exhibits on both geology and anthropology. It's open to the public so pay a visit and see their mastodon and Egyptian mummy. Independent film is also alive and well on campus. The Rutgers Film Co-op/New Jersey Media Arts Center has more than 100 screenings annually. Afterward, visit the Red Lion Café where you can get a $1 bottomless cup of coffee. The café also hosts Talent Tuesdays where students, faculty, and staff perform for the university community.

# RUTGERS, THE STATE UNIVERSITY OF NEW JERSEY—NEWARK

249 University Avenue, Newark, NJ 07102-1896
**Telephone:** 973-353-5205 • **E-mail:** admissions@ugadm.rutgers.edu
**Website:** www.rutgers.edu

| SCHOOL AT A GLANCE | |
| --- | --- |
| Type of School | Public |
| Environment | |
| Enrollment | 5,963 |
| % Male/Female | 42/58 |
| Student/Faculty Ratio | 11:1 |
| **FRESHMAN PROFILE** | |
| Range SAT | |
| Critical Reading | 490-590 |
| Range SAT Math | 500-620 |
| **ON-CAMPUS APPOINTMENTS** | |
| Class Visits | No |

## STUDENTS SAY

"Professors are wonderful, and the classroom sizes are great!"

## FODOR'S SAYS

"The Newark Museum has outstanding fine-arts, science, and industry collections; its restored Ballantine House, a National Historic Landmark, has two floors of Victorian period rooms and decorative arts."

## ABOUT THE SCHOOL

Rutgers—Newark is one arm of Rutgers University, New Jersey's premiere state institution. Located in Jersey's largest city, the university offers a cosmopolitan setting within a cozy campus community. Professors are approachable and the diverse student body ensures that everyone finds his or her niche. Rutgers undergrads are curious, critical thinkers who are determined to make their mark on the world.

## GETTING THERE

**BY AIR:** Rutgers's campus is only 15 minutes from Newark International Airport. Visitors can take the Air Train from the airport to Newark Penn Station.

**BY TRAIN:** New Jersey Transit, PATH, and Amtrak trains all stop at New Penn Station, approximately 10 blocks from campus. Additionally, New Jersey Transit's Morris and Essex and Midtown Direct Lines stop at the Broad Street Station.

**BY BUS:** A number of bus lines from both New York and New Jersey provide service to Newark Penn Station.

**BY CAR:** From the New Jersey Turnpike or Route 95 (North or South): Take Exit 15 West to Route 280 West. After you pass the drawbridge, take Exit 14B (Martin Luther King Jr. Boulevard). When you reach the end of the exit ramp, make a left and continue to the stop sign. At stop sign, make a left onto Martin Luther King Jr. Boulevard. From the Garden State Parkway (North or South): Take Exit 145 to Route 280 East, Newark-Harrison. Once on Route 280, stay in the right lane and follow the signs for Harrison. Get out at Exit 14B (Martin Luther King Jr. Boulevard), and turn right at the first light onto Martin Luther King Jr. Boulevard.

**LOCAL:** Guests can connect with Newark's local subway system at Penn Station. Get on for two stops, and exit at Washington Street; you'll be right on campus. Construction is currently underway for light rail service that will connect the Broad Street Station with Penn Station.

## WHERE TO STAY

Accommodations that are relatively close to campus include Robert Treat Hotel (973-622-1000, $$), Hilton Newark Gateway (973-622-5000, $$), and the Hampton Inn and Suites Newark-Harrison Riverwalk (973-483-1900, $$; ask about the Rutgers special rate).

## CAMPUS AT ITS BEST!

Although often overshadowed by New York City, Newark has some fabulous resources and amazing venues that are worth exploring. The New Jersey Performing Arts Center (NJPAC) is quickly emerging as one of the area's greatest theaters. It continually attracts a diverse group of artists such as Bob Weird, Jackie Mason, and the Alice Coltrane Quartet. The city also holds the action and excitement of professional sports. Indeed, the Newark Bears baseball team has gained a number of fans over the years. Consider catching a game at the beautiful Riverfront Stadium.

# SAINT JOSEPH'S UNIVERSITY (PA)

5600 City Avenue, Philadelphia, PA 19131
**Telephone:** 610-660-1300 • **E-mail:** admit@sju.edu

## Students Say

"The typical student at St. Joe's works to the best of his or her ability in all things and strives to become the best student he or she can be. They support one another in different things and are always ready to lend a helping hand for any cause."

## Fodor's Says

"The Gazela of Philadelphia, built in 1883, is the last of a Portuguese fleet of cod-fishing ships, known as 'The White Fleet,' and the oldest wooden square-rigger still sailing."

## About the School

Saint Joseph's is a midsize university in the heart of thriving Philadelphia. A Jesuit institution, the school promotes ethics and social awareness in students. The strong liberal arts core curriculum gives undergrads an important academic grounding in the humanities.

## Getting There

**BY AIR:** Philadelphia International is a major airport serviced by many airlines. Car rentals, taxis, and local SEPTA bus and rail service are all accessible for travel to Saint Joseph's or other points in the city.

**BY TRAIN:** Amtrak and New Jersey Transit offer service to Philadelphia's famed 30th Street Station. SEPTA trains and taxis are available for travel in and around the city.

**BY BUS:** Greyhound and Peter Pan have stops in Philadelphia.

**BY CAR:** From the North: Take New Jersey Turnpike to Exit 6 (Pennsylvania Turnpike connector). Proceed on the Pennsylvania Turnpike to Route 476 (Old Exit 25A/New Exit 20). Follow 476 South to Route 76 East (heading toward Philadelphia). Take Route 76 East to Exit 339 (Route 1, City Avenue). After two miles you'll reach Saint Joseph's. From the East: Take the Ben Franklin Bridge (via Route 676) or the Walt Whitman Bridge. Get on Route 76 West and follow the "From the North" directions above. From the South: Take Interstate 95 North to 476 North. Proceed on 476 North to Exit 5 (Route 1). Route 1 North (which you'll be on for roughly 10 miles) will take you all the way to Saint Joseph's. From the West: Take the Pennsylvania Turnpike to Old Exit 24/New Exit 326 (Valley Forge). Proceed on Route 76 East and follow the "From the North" directions above.

**LOCAL:** From the 30th Street Station Amtrak/SEPTA: Ride the R5 local Paoli/Thorndale for one stop to Overbrook train station. Saint Joseph's is a half a mile walk north from the station. **BY BUS:** Ride SEPTA's number 65 bus all the way to the campus on City Line Avenue.

## Where to Stay

For hotels near to campus, try Best Western (215-464-9500, $), Holiday Inn City Avenue (215-477-0200, $$; ask for the SJU Family Rate), and the Hilton City Avenue (215-879-4000, $$$).

---

## CAMPUS AT ITS BEST!

Saint Joseph's Student Union Board takes the lead in creating and sponsoring campus fun. Every Tuesday students screen the latest Hollywood fare at movie night. Additionally, undergrads can catch the finest local music talent at Thursday Java Jams. Hometown Philadelphia also offers a plethora of entertainment options. Consider cruising down the city's famed South Street or dining on a cheesesteak (a must for any tourist!) at Geno's Steaks.

# SARAH LAWRENCE COLLEGE

1 Mead Way, Bronxville, NY 10708-5999
**Telephone:** 914-395-2510 • **E-mail:** slcadmit@slc.edu
**Website:** www.sarahlawrence.edu • **Hours:** Monday–Friday and Saturday, 9:00 A.M.–5:00 P.M.

| SCHOOL AT A GLANCE | |
| --- | --- |
| Type of School | Private |
| Environment | Metropolis |
| Enrollment | 1,264 |
| % Male/Female | 26/74 |
| Student/Faculty Ratio | 6:1 |

| FRESHMAN PROFILE | |
| --- | --- |
| Average HS GPA | 3.6 |

| ON-CAMPUS APPOINTMENTS | |
| --- | --- |
| Advance Notice | Yes, 2 weeks |
| Appointment | Required |
| Saturdays | Sometimes |
| Average Length | 60 min |
| Info Sessions | Yes |
| Class Visits | Yes |

| CAMPUS TOURS | |
| --- | --- |
| Appointment | Required |
| Dates | Year Round |
| Times | M–F and Sat |
| | 9:00 A.M.–4:00 P.M. |
| Average Length | 60 min |

## STUDENTS SAY

"Sarah Lawrence College is about growth: personal growth, academic growth, and a growth in awareness."

## FODOR'S SAYS

"Summer and fall are the peak seasons in the valley; this is when most of the biggest festivals take place. Winter can be cold and dreary, but many of the villages look quite magical with a fresh layer of snow."

## ABOUT THE SCHOOL

Sarah Lawrence College isn't your typical school. Its students have the freedom to choose their curriculum, their advisors, and even whether or not they want to receive letter grades. They have the chance to take only courses that interest them and to bloom into a creative, intelligent adults.

## GETTING THERE

**BY AIR:** JFK, LaGuardia, and Newark Liberty International Airports are the closest airports to the campus.

**BY TRAIN:** Amtrak trains provide service at stations in Yonkers and New Rochelle, which are 20 minutes away from campus.

**BY BUS:** Greyhound bus lines provide service to nearby New Rochelle.

**BY CAR:** From the North: Take Interstate 95 South to Exit 21/Interstate 287 West, toward the Tappan Zee Bridge (the first exit in New York). Exit at Exit 9 (Hutchinson River Parkway). Go straight, looking for the Hutchinson River Parkway South (9S). Follow the Hutchinson River Parkway South into Cross County Parkway West. Take Cross County Parkway West to Exit 5, Kimball Avenue, and go right at the stop sign. Make a left at the Kimball Avenue traffic light. At the next traffic light, make a right onto Glen Washington Road. Make the first left onto Mead Way and an immediate left onto Westlands Gate. From the East and South: Take the New Jersey Turnpike and follow the signs to the lower level George Washington Bridge. Once past the bridge, take the exit on the right marked "Thru Traffic" and follow the signs to the Major Deegan Expressway/Interstate 87 North. This becomes the New York State Thruway/Interstate 87 North in Westchester County. Take Exit 4 (Cross County Parkway East), bear right at the fork in the road, and take Exit 5, Kimball Avenue. At the traffic light, take a left onto Kimball Avenue. Follow the "From the North" directions above.

**LOCAL:** Take the Metro-North Railroad Harlem Line from Grand Central Terminal to the Bronxville Station. From there, taxi service is available. Other ways to get around town include taxi or car rental services, including Bronxville Depot Taxi & Trip (914-337-8311), Hertz Local Edition (914-633-0643), and Altra Auto Rental (212-538-2271).

## WHERE TO STAY

Possible accommodations include the Ardsley Acres Hotel Westchester (914-693-2700, $$), (Wellesley Inn Elmsford (914-592-3300, $$), and Residence Inn by Marriott, New Rochelle (914-636-7888, $$$).

---

## CAMPUS AT ITS BEST!

When Sarah Lawrence students are feeling stressed they often retreat to The Teahaus, a small stone building at the center of campus that functions as an oasis for those in need of refreshments and a quiet place in which to enjoy them. It regularly hosts study groups, poetry readings, and open mics. The school is always bustling with numerous activities—whether it's a birthday party for Ella Fitzgerald, Sleaze Week, or a film celebrating Earth Week, there's always something going on.

# SIMMONS COLLEGE

300 The Fenway, Boston, MA 02115 • **Telephone:** 617-521-2051 • **E-mail:** ugadm@simmons.edu

**Hours:** Monday–Friday, 8:30 A.M.–4:30 P.M.; Saturday, 8:30 A.M.–NOON

## STUDENTS SAY

"Simmons is a small, beautiful, competitive school in the heart of Boston—perfect!"

## FODOR'S SAYS

"It is an interesting coincidence that the oldest house standing in one of the oldest sections of Boston should also have been the home of Paul Revere, patriot activist and silversmith. And it is a coincidence, since many homes of famous Bostonians have burned or been demolished over the years. It was saved from oblivion in 1902 and restored to an approximation of its original seventeenth-century appearance."

## ABOUT THE SCHOOL

Simmons, an all-female institution in the heart of Boston, typically attracts liberal, academically minded students. While the college might play into some single-gender stereotypes (an abundance of feminists for example), undergrads are quick to highlight how much confidence they gain throughout their four years at the school. Simmons women take full advantage of being in Boston, whether by going to a Red Sox game, attending the theater, or mixing with students from surrounding universities.

## GETTING THERE

**BY AIR:** Visitors can fly into Logan International, one of the country's busiest international airports. There are a variety of alternatives for getting to and from the airport. Shuttles, taxis, car rentals, and public transportation are all available.

**BY TRAIN:** Boston is accessible via Amtrak and a variety of commuter rails. These train lines provide service to South Station. Visitors can use public transportation or take taxis to reach the campus.

**BY BUS:** Concord Trailways, Bonanza, Greyhound, and Peter Pan bus lines all provide service to Boston. Busses arrive and depart from South Station.

**BY CAR:** Local Directions: Look for the "Kenmore Square, Fenway, Route 1 South" sign and exit left, following the sign for "Fenway 1 South." Do not take the Kenmore Square Exit. Stay right at the light, following the sign for "Boylston St. Outbound, Riverway 1." Get in the left lane, and proceed to first light. Turn left onto Park Drive. Follow Park Drive to the lights and cross Boylston Street and Brookline Avenue. Stay left. At the next set of lights, bear left following the "Fenway" sign to the reverse direction. At the lights, continue straight, crossing Brookline Avenue again. You will be on "The Fenway." Turn right onto Avenue Louis Pasteur after Emmanuel College. Simmons's library is on the left. From the West (including NYC and CT): Take Route 90 East (Massachusetts Turnpike) to Exit 22. Stay left and follow the signs marked "Prudential Center/West 9." Stay on Huntington Avenue West for approximately one mile. Pass the Museum of Fine Arts on the right, and turn right at the next light on Louis Prang Street. Continue through two lights. The main building of Simmons will be on left. Turn left on Avenue Louis Pasteur. Simmons's library is on the left. From the South: Take I-93 North to Exit 26, Storrow Drive. Follow "Local Directions" above. From the North: Take I-93 South to Exit 26, Storrow Drive West/North Station. Keep left on exit and follow the signs for Storrow Drive West. Follow "Local Directions" above. From Logan International Airport: Take the airport exit following signs for I-93 North. Go through tolls and into Sumner Tunnel. Get in the right lane. At end of tunnel, take the "3 North/Storrow Drive" Exit. Stay right on Storrow Drive. Follow "Local Directions" above.

**LOCAL:** Take the MBTA Green Line E train (Heath Street) to the museum stop. Turn right onto Louis Prang Street, from which you can see Simmons's green cupola. Walk past Isabella Stewart Gardner Museum on the left. Simmons College, 300 The Fenway, is on the left.

## WHERE TO STAY

As a major metropolitan area, there's certainly no shortage of lodging options in Boston. Consider Newbury Guest House (800-437-7668, $$), Best Western Terrace Inn (617-566-6260, $$), or Boston Harbor Hotel (617-439-7000, $$$+).

## CAMPUS AT ITS BEST!

Simmons students are always eager to participate in the Simmons Cup, an annual field day competition. Teaming with MIT fraternities, students vie for top honors in relay races, scavenger hunts, and volleyball matches. Another campus favorite is the Mr. Simmons Contest. Residence halls and student organizations all enter contestants and hilarity inevitably ensues. If you don't want to participate in college traditions, Boston offers a myriad of attractions. Consider heading to Chinatown for some dim sum or going to Newbury Street for some great shopping.

# SIMON'S ROCK COLLEGE OF BARD

84 Alford Road, Great Barrington, MA 01230
**Telephone:** 413-528-7312 • **E-mail:** admit@simons-rock.edu
**Website:** www.simons-rock.edu • **Hours:** Monday–Friday, 9:00 A.M.-5:00 P.M.

## STUDENTS SAY

"The typical student [at this school] is different. No one is afraid to express themselves at all. Everyone fits in because everyone is so different; it's amazing."

## FODOR'S SAYS

"Bartholomew's Cobble is a natural rock garden beside the Housatonic River (the Native American name means 'river beyond the mountains'). The 277-acre site is filled with trees, ferns, wildflowers, and five miles of hiking trails."

## ABOUT THE SCHOOL

Simon's Rock is something of an anomaly—a school geared toward exceptional high school students who'd like to begin college early. Classes are small, and students help shape the direction of their courses. While their catalog is not extensive, undergrads always find something that piques their curiosity. The social scene can be quiet, but the college does offer daily trips into town and weekend excursions.

## GETTING THERE

**BY AIR:** Try either Albany or Bradley International airports. It is best to rent a car or take a taxi into Great Barrington.

**BY TRAIN:** Take Amtrak to Hudson, New York (roughly 45 minutes away) or Metro-North to Wassaic, New York (approximately 50 minutes away).

**BY BUS:** Greyhound, Bonanza, and Peter Pan all offer service to the area. There is frequent bus service between Great Barrington and New York City, as well as between nearby Lee and Boston.

**BY CAR:** From Massachusetts and Points East: Follow the Massachusetts Turnpike (I- 90) to Exit 2 (Lee). Take Route 102 West to Stockbridge. Make a left onto U.S. 7 South to Great Barrington. This will become Main Street. Go right onto Taconic Avenue. The main entrance to the college will be ahead on your right. From Albany and Points West: Follow the New York State Thruway (I-90) to Exit B3. Take Route 22 South, turning left onto Route 102 East. Follow Route 102 to West Stockbridge. Go right onto Route 41 South to Great Barrington, which becomes Main Street. Follow the "From Massachusetts and Points East" directions above. From Connecticut: Follow I-84 or U.S. 44 to U.S. 7. Take U.S. 7 North to Great Barrington (Main Street). Turn left onto Taconic Avenue. The main entrance to the college will be ahead on your right. From New York, New Jersey, and Points South: Follow the Taconic Parkway North to the Hillsdale/Claverack Exit (Route 23). Take Route 23 East to Great Barrington. Turn left at the traffic light onto U.S. 7/23, and go left onto Taconic Avenue. The entrance to the college will be ahead on the right.

**LOCAL:** If you need a local car service consider AA Taxi (413-528-3906), Taxico (413-528-0911), or Abbott's Limousine and Livery Service (413-243-1645).

## WHERE TO STAY

For hotel accommodations call the Monument Mountain Motel (413-528-3272, $), Comfort Inn (413-644-3200, $$), or Travelodge (413-528-2340, $$).

---

### CAMPUS AT ITS BEST!

Great Barrington, in the heart of the Berkshires, offers a myriad of cultural and recreational opportunities. Bring a picnic and delight in the surrounding natural beauty as you listen to a concert at Tanglewood. The Berkshire Choral Festival is another great music event that continually draws a crowd. Guests interested in sporting events can visit nearby Lime Rock Park, an auto race track. The area also features a wide variety of hiking and skiing trails.

---

| SCHOOL AT A GLANCE | |
| --- | --- |
| Type of School | Private |
| Environment | Village |
| Tuition | $32,834 |
| Enrollment | 380 |
| % Male/Female | 43/57 |
| Student/Faculty Ratio | 8:1 |

| FRESHMAN PROFILE | |
| --- | --- |
| Range SAT | |
| Critical Reading | 580-700 |
| Range SAT Math | 530-690 |
| Range ACT Composite | 22-28 |
| Average HS GPA | 3.75 |

| ON-CAMPUS APPOINTMENTS | |
| --- | --- |
| Advance Notice | Yes, 1 week |
| Appointment | Required |
| Saturdays | No |
| Average Length | 60 min |
| Info Sessions | Yes |
| Class Visits | Yes |

| CAMPUS TOURS | |
| --- | --- |
| Appointment | Required |
| Dates | Year Round |
| Times | Very flexible |
| Average Length | 60 min |

# SKIDMORE COLLEGE

815 North Broadway, Saratoga Springs, NY 12866-1632
**Telephone:** 518-580-5570 • **E-mail:** admissions@skidmore.edu • **Website:** www.skidmore.edu
**Hours:** Monday–Friday, 8:30 A.M.–4:30 P.M.; Saturday, 8:30 A.M.–NOON

## STUDENTS SAY

"Skidmore College is about providing enormous amounts of freedom to let students grow, while giving just enough guidance so we don't freak out!"

## FODOR'S SAYS

"This four-year coeducational college, founded in 1903, sponsors year-round cultural events and entertainment, and is the summer home of the New York State Writer's Institute. The Frances Young Tang Teaching Museum and Art Gallery contains galleries large enough for oversize works and innovative installations, a 150-seat presentation room, and multimedia classrooms for lectures and film screenings."

## ABOUT THE SCHOOL

Skidmore College, a highly selective, small liberal arts college in upstate New York whose slogan is "Creative Thought Matters," is firmly committed to providing students with a superior grounding in the arts, humanities, and sciences. While business and English are its two most popular majors, the college is also known for its strong visual and performing arts and science programs.

## GETTING THERE

**BY AIR:** Albany International Airport is the closest airport near campus. From the airport, you can take a taxi, rent a car, or take the CDTC bus service to get to the campus.

**BY TRAIN:** Amtrak provides service to Saratoga Springs.

**BY BUS:** Greyhound stops in Saratoga Springs. Adirondack Trailways also stops in Saratoga Springs.

**BY CAR:** Skidmore is in Saratoga Springs, New York, which is about 30 minutes North of Albany. From the Adirondack Northway (I-87), take Exit 14 and proceed West on Union Avenue toward Saratoga Springs. When Union Avenue ends at the intersection of Circular Street, make a right. Make your first left onto Spring Street. At the top of the hill, make a right onto Broadway. Go through six traffic lights onto North Broadway to the college entrance.

**LOCAL:** Capital District Transit Authority (CDTC), a regional bus and train system in Albany and Saratoga, can easily get you around town. Upstate Tours also provides bus service throughout the local area. If you'd rather use local taxi service, contact Saratoga Taxi (518-584-2700), Saratoga Capitaland Taxi (518-583-3131), Hertz Rent A Car (518-691-0404), and Enterprise Rent-A-Car (518-587-0687).

## WHERE TO STAY

If you're planning on staying overnight, popular, nearby lodging choices include the Best Western Park Inn (518-371-1811, $$), Holiday Inn Saratoga Springs (518-584-4550, $$), and Hilton Garden Inn Saratoga Springs (518-587-1500, $$$).

## CAMPUS AT ITS BEST!

Falstaff's is a consistent favorite among Skidmore students. Owned and operated by the Student Government Association, this recently renovated venue hosts everything from raves to pub nights. With regards to social activities, Fun Day is always a highly cherished event. Celebrated campus-wide, students enjoy carnival games, cotton candy, and live music. Students also rave about hometown Saratoga Springs. Those who visit in the summer months should explore the Racetrack, which attracts the best and fastest of the equine world.

# SMITH COLLEGE

7 College Lane, Northampton, MA 01063

**Telephone:** 413-585-2500 or 800-383-3232 • **E-mail:** admission@smith.edu

**Website:** www.smith.edu • **Hours:** Monday–Friday, 8:30 A.M.–4:30 P.M.; Saturday, 9:00 A.M.–1:00 P.M.

## Students Say

"Smith College is all about accepting everyone and pushing its students to exceed in whatever they wish."

## Fodor's Says

"The cultural center of western Massachusetts is without a doubt the city of Northampton, whose vibrant downtown scene reminds many people of lower Manhattan (Hence its nickname 'Noho')."

## About the School

Smith College is a women's college in Northampton, Massachusetts known for its highly demanding courses that offers its students an incredible education so they can pursue opportunities around the world. Best of all, the school doesn't require a core curriculum, so the classes into which students are putting so much effort are classes of their own choosing.

## Getting There

**BY AIR:** Bradley International is about 35 miles South of Northampton, near Hartford, Connecticut. Another viable option is Boston's Logan Airport. Limousines, buses, and rental cars are available at the airport.

**BY TRAIN:** Amtrak provides service to Springfield. From Springfield, you can arrange for van service to Northampton from Valley Transporter (800-872-8752) or take a bus.

**BY BUS:** Peter Pan, Greyhound, and Vermont Transit service the area. Most routes go to the main bus terminal in Springfield, where you can catch another bus to Northampton. Smith is a 10-minute walk or short taxi ride from the bus station.

**BY CAR:** From the South: Take Route I-91 North at Exit 18. Follow Route 5 North into the center of town. Make a left onto Route 9. Head straight through four traffic lights until you see the college on your left. From the North: Take I-91 South, and exit at Exit 20. Follow Route 5 South into the center of town. At the intersection of Route 5 and Route 9 (Main Street), make a right onto Route 9. Follow the "From the South" directions above. From the East or West: Take the Massachusetts Turnpike to Exit 4 (Route I-91 North). Follow the "From the South" directions above once you are on Route I-91 North.

**LOCAL:** The Massachusetts Bay Transportation Authority (MBTA) provides rail, bus, and subway service in Eastern Massachusetts. Visitors looking to get around Northampton can contact The MassParadise Taxi (413-584-0055), Florence Taxi (413-586-8005), Northampton Taxi Co. (413-584-6244), or Seemo Taxi (413-582-0095).

## Where to Stay

If you decide to stay overnight, the Best Western (413-586-1500, $$) and the Clarion Hotel & Conference Center (413-586-1211, $$$) are close to campus. The Quality Inn (413-584-9816, $$) is another popular choice and is only a short drive away from campus.

---

## CAMPUS AT ITS BEST!

Bookworms delight in Smith's Mortimer Rare Book Room. The broad manuscript collection includes papers from literary greats Sylvia Plath and Virginia Woolf. Afterward, go to the typically busy campus center where you might be able to view Midday Madness, live music, or even receive a massage at a stress-free event. If you can, visit campus on the third Wednesday in February and attend Rally Day, which involves anything from debates to dramatic presentations and dancing.

# ST. BONAVENTURE UNIVERSITY

PO Box D, St. Bonaventure, NY 14778
**Telephone:** 716-375-2400 • **E-mail:** admissions@sbu.edu
**Website:** www.sbu.edu

## STUDENTS SAY

"It is a beautiful school that has awesome classes with a great party side to it."

## FODOR'S SAYS

"[Founded in 1804, Olean is home to] St. Bonaventure University, two community colleges, and manufacturers of assorted goods from Cutco knives to Drusser Rand turbines. The old public library, a National Historic Landmark facing the tree-lined town square, has been converted into a restaurant, and you can take a paved path—on foot, skates, or by bicycle—along the Allegheny River."

## ABOUT THE SCHOOL

St. Bonaventure University is a small Catholic university in a mostly freezing, very isolated area in upstate New York. Professors at Bona are known for being caring and eager to help students get the grades they deserve. The journalism program, sports, and partying are among the most popular activities at the university.

## GETTING THERE

**BY AIR:** At 78 miles, Buffalo Airport Niagara International Airport is closest to the campus.
**BY TRAIN:** Amtrak trains service Buffalo, which is almost two hours away from the campus.
**BY BUS:** Greyhound buses stop in nearby Olean.
**BY CAR:** From Buffalo: Take Route 219 South to Salamanca. Go East on I-86 (formerly Route 17) to Exit 24. From New York: Take George Washington Bridge to I-80 West. Stay on I-80 West until you reach Route 380 West. Then go North on Route I-81 to Interstate 86. Head West on I-86 to Exit 24. From Pittsburgh: Take Route 79 North to Route I-80. Go East on Route I-80 to Route 219. Take Route 219 North to Interstate 86, and go East on I-86 to Exit 24. From Rochester: Take Route I-390 South until you reach Route 36. Take Route 36 South to ArkpoRoute. Take Route I-86 West to Exit 24. From Syracuse and Utica: Go West on Route I-90 (New York State Thruway) to Route 14 South, which you take to Route 54. Take Route 54 South to I-86 West to Exit 24. From New Jersey: Take Route I-80 West to Route 380 West to Scranton, Pennsylvania. Get on Route I-81 North, and take I-86 West to Exit 24.

**LOCAL:** The Olean Area Transit System provides public bus service throughout the area. If you'd rather take a taxi or use a rental car to get around, some local companies include Enterprise Rent-A-Car (716-373-2100), Alle-Catt Taxi Svc (716-372-7171), and Silver Bird Taxi (716-373-5700).

## WHERE TO STAY

If you're planning on staying overnight, some local lodging options include the Hampton Inn (716-375-1000, $), Country Inn & Suites by Carleson (716-372-7500, $$), and Best Western (716-372-1300, $$).

## CAMPUS AT ITS BEST!

St. Bonaventure's impressive facilities afford students some fantastic hands-on experiences. The John J. Murphy Professional Building features a state-of-the-art broadcast journalism laboratory and television studio. When looking to kick back, students often head to the basement of Hickey Dining Hall, home to the Rathskeller, an on-campus club. The Rathskeller sponsors recreational sports leagues for darts, billiards, and foosball. Students also frequently gather here to watch Monday Night Football and show off their moves at late-night dance parties.

# ST. JOHN'S COLLEGE (MD)

PO Box 2800, Annapolis, MD 21404
**Telephone:** 410-626-2522 • **E-mail:** admissions@sjca.edu

## STUDENTS SAY

"You can feel the passion of the Johnnies in the air. The extreme focus on academics makes Johnnies much more focused individuals in all aspects: music, running, crew."

## FODOR'S SAYS

"A fine example of colonial five-part Georgian architecture (a single block with two connecting rooms and wings on each side), the nearby Hammond-Harwood House is the only verifiable full-scale example of William Buckland's work [and] it was also his final project, as he died the year the house was completed. Exquisite moldings, cornices, and other carvings appear throughout (note especially the garlands of roses above the front doorway), [and it is] furnished with eighteenth-century pieces, and the garden's plants are also reflective of the period."

## ABOUT THE SCHOOL

St. John's promises students a very unique and rewarding college experience. The entire curriculum is pre-determined and presents a four-year survey of intellectual history. This distinctive program elicits a (comparatively) self-selecting applicant pool, attracting students who thrive on philosophical discussion. St. Johnnies are a fairly egalitarian lot and report that the campus feels like a close-knit community.

## GETTING THERE

**BY AIR:** While visitors can fly into either into Washington National or Dulles International Airport, it is most convenient for travelers to use Baltimore-Washington International (BWI) Airport. Travelers will find private car service to Annapolis on the lower level of the terminal.

**BY TRAIN:** Amtrak provides service to Penn Station (Baltimore), BWI Rail station, and Union Station in Washington, DC. Visitors can take either a bus or taxi to Annapolis.

**BY BUS:** Several national and local companies provide service to Annapolis, though Greyhound has its own station at 308 Chinquapin Road.

**BY CAR:** From Washington, DC: Follow Route 50 East to Exit 24 (Rowe Boulevard) heading toward Annapolis. The exit splits in two, so take the right lane of the exit. From Baltimore: Follow I-97 to Route 50 East. Follow the "From Washington, DC" directions above. Once you hit Annapolis: Continue on Rowe Boulevard until you hit Calvert Street. Make a left onto Calvert. You'll go through the light, proceeding straight to St. John's Street. Make a right on St. John's Street and follow through to College Avenue. Turn left on College Avenue, driving through the intersection of College and King George Street. Make a left onto King George Street. Turn into the second driveway on your left. You'll see a sign for Iglehart Entrance. The Admissions Office is in the Carroll Barrister House, next to the Gym (Iglehart Hall). You'll need to request a parking pass from Admissions.

**LOCAL:** Annapolis Transit's Rainbow Route makes 180 stops within the city and surrounding area. Visitors can also call Annapolis Cab Co. (410-268-0022) or use Jiffy Water Taxi (410-263-0033).

## WHERE TO STAY

Lodging options include, but are not limited to, Super 8 Annapolis (410-757-2222, $), Charles Inn (410-268-1451, $$–$$$), and Annapolis Inn (410-295-5200, $$$+).

---

## CAMPUS AT ITS BEST!

The Mitchell Art Gallery extends learning beyond the classroom and helps cultivate a love of art in many patrons. The facility hosts a number of phenomenal traveling exhibits and has shown works by Rodin, Calder, Rembrandt, and Whistler. While St. John's students thrive on intellectual activity, they also understand the importance of letting loose. Dance opportunities abound, with undergrads throwing frequent rock and waltz parties. Additionally, every spring brings Reality Weekend, a festival that includes skits, picnics, and athletic games.

# ST. JOHN'S UNIVERSITY

8000 Utopia Parkway, Queens, NY 11439
**Telephone:** 718-990-2000 • **E-mail:** admissions@stjohns.edu
**Hours:** Monday–Thursday, 8:30 A.M.–4:30 P.M.; Friday, 8:30 A.M.–3:00 P.M.; Saturday, 9:30 A.M.–2:30 P.M.

## STUDENTS SAY

"It's a beautiful campus with excellent facilities, a truly diverse student body that reflects New York City, and brilliant faculty."

## FODOR'S SAYS

"New York City is one of the most exciting cities in the world. It's a national hub for banking and finance, communications, advertising, fashion, sports, and publishing. And it can rightly be called a world cultural capital: Artists, actors, musicians, writers, poets, conductors, and craftspeople all work and play here."

## ABOUT THE SCHOOL

St. John's University, a Catholic school located in diverse Queens, has a top basketball team, excellent computer facilities, and New York City in its backyard. Many students rave about the school's excellent location but complain about losing many of their classmates on the weekend when they hit the road to head home.

## GETTING THERE

**BY AIR:** La Guardia and JFK airports are the closest airports to campus at 15 and 20 minutes, respectively.

**BY TRAIN:** Amtrak trains stop in Penn Station. Visitors can take the Long Island Rail Road or subway to get to the campus.

**BY BUS:** Greyhound buses stop at Port Authority. Visitors can take the subway or local buses to the campus.

**BY CAR:** From Manhattan: Take the Queens Midtown Tunnel to the Long Island Expressway. Get off at Utopia Parkway. Stay on the service road to Utopia Parkway and make a right. Take Utopia Parkway to Union Turnpike and the college will be on your right. From Brooklyn: Take the Belt Parkway East to the Van Wyck Expressway. Exit the Van Wyck at Main Street/Union Turnpike. Go to the third traffic light and turn right onto the Grand Central Parkway service road. Make a left on Utopia Parkway (at fourth traffic light) and take this road until you see the college. From the Bronx: Take the Triborough Bridge to the Grand Central Parkway. Get off at Utopia Parkway. Make a left at the light and a left into the college. From the North: Take I-95 South to the Bruckner Expressway. Cross the Throgs Neck Bridge to the Clearview Expressway. Take Exit 2 from the Clearview and turn right onto Union Turnpike. Turn left onto Utopia Parkway and take this road until you see the college. From the South: Take I-95 North or I-80 East. Cross the George Washington Bridge and take the Cross Bronx Expressway to I-295 to the Throgs Neck Bridge. Follow the "From the North" directions above.

**LOCAL:** Queens has ample public transportation, including the New York City transit bus and subway, taxis, and the Long Island Railroad (LIRR).

## WHERE TO STAY

Some lodging accommodations include the Holiday Inn JFK (718-322-1014, $$), Wyndham Garden Hotel (718-426-1500, $$), Courtyard by Marriott/LaGuardia (800-321-2211, $$$), and Crown Plaza/LaGuardia (718-457-6300, $$$).

## CAMPUS AT ITS BEST!

Students at St. John's breathe a collective sigh of relief during Spring Fling Weekend. Celebrating the end of spring term, this festival offers one last hurrah before exams begin. Hundreds of students and staff gather on the Queens campus to ride a Ferris wheel, jump around in an inflatable maze, and dance to live music. Red Storm sports are also highly anticipated. Pay a visit to Carnesecca Arena and catch St. John's Big East Division I talented basketball team in action.

# ST. LAWRENCE UNIVERSITY

Payson Hall, Canton, NY 13617
**Telephone:** 315-229-5261 • **E-mail:** admissions@stlawu.edu • **Website:** www.stlawu.edu

## STUDENTS SAY

"I love my professors and the administration is in general fairly aware of what is happening on campus. Professors are excellent in providing necessary information about classes and requirements."

## FODOR'S SAYS

"The Traditional Arts in Upstate New York Gallery is run by a nonprofit organization dedicated to preserving North Country folk arts and traditions—everything from music and crafts to architecture and storytelling. The gallery has audiovisual displays, a photography exhibit, folk-art examples, changing exhibits, and a gift shop with local crafts and products, including rustic furniture, baskets, quilts, and maple candy."

## ABOUT THE SCHOOL

St. Lawrence's relative isolation and small student body facilitate a comfortable, homey atmosphere. Classes are dominated by discussions and allow students to develop a personal connection with their professors. The university tends to live up to its preppy reputation and students readily admit that diversity is lacking. Weekend activities typically revolve around going to the local bars and Division I hockey in winter.

## GETTING THERE

**BY AIR:** For proximity to campus (1.5 hours), head across the border to Ottawa, but don't forget your proof of U.S. citizenship (a passport or birth certificate will suffice). Otherwise, Syracuse Hancock International or Ogdensburg airports are another option.

**BY TRAIN:** The nearest Amtrak stop is in Lake Placid, 60 miles away from Canton.

**BY BUS:** Adirondack Trailways provides service to Canton from Syracuse (twice daily) as well as Port Authority in New York City, via Albany (once daily).

**BY CAR:** From Albany (also for New York metropolitan area, Western Connecticut, and Massachusetts): Take I-87 (Northway) to Exit 23 (Warrensburg). Take Route 28 to Blue Mountain Lake. This leads to Route 30 and, in turn, to Tupper Lake. Take Route 3 West to Route 56. Proceed to Route 68 to Canton. From Syracuse (also for New Jersey, Philadelphia, DC, Rochester, Buffalo, Central and Western PA, Ohio, and Lower Great Lakes Region): Follow I-81 North to Exit 48 (North of Watertown). Take Route 342 to Route 11 North, which leads to Canton. Once in Canton, follow Main Street into the center of town. Turn right onto Park Street and continue to Admissions Parking on your right. Admissions and Financial Aid offices will be across the street. From Burlington, VT (also for Northern New England, Rhode Island, Eastern MA and CT): Take 89 North to Exit 17. This will lead to Route 2. Follow signs to Grand Isle Ferry. After exiting the ferry, take Route 314 to I-87 South. Then take Exit 38 I-87 South one exit. Proceed to Route 374 West to Chateaugay. Take Route 11 South to Malone, and Route 11B to Potsdam.

**LOCAL:** For local taxi service call Potsdam Taxi (315-265-7506).

## WHERE TO STAY

Canton offers a variety of moderately priced and charming hotels such as Misty Meadows (315-379-1563, $), Felician House (315-386-4647, $), or Craftsman Suites (800-261-6292, $$).

---

## CAMPUS AT ITS BEST!

Before scheduling your visit to St. Lawrence, inquire about Admissions Visit Days. This program is highly recommended and offers guests an admissions overview, campus tour, a panel with faculty and current students, and most important, lunch. While touring, be sure to stop by Herring-Cole Hall. A favorite study spot and gathering place, the hall features exquisite woodwork and impressive stained-glass seal. Afterward, pay a visit to the Java Barn for great musical acts most Fridays and Saturdays.

# ST. MARY'S COLLEGE OF MARYLAND

Admissions Office, 18952 East Fisher Road, St. Mary's City, MD 20686-3001
**Telephone:** 800-492-7181 or 240-895-5000 • **E-mail:** admissions@smcm.edu
**Website:** www.smcm.edu

## STUDENTS SAY

"St. Mary's is a place where everyone can present their ideas, and selves, in a diverse and open atmosphere."

## FODOR'S SAYS

"Throughout historic St. Mary's City, you're encouraged to explore other sites and exhibits-in-progress, including the town center, the location of the first Catholic church in the English colonies, a 'victualing' and lodging house, and the woodland Native American hamlet."

## ABOUT THE SCHOOL

St. Mary's is a public honors college that provides a private school setting at state school prices. Indeed, undergrads continually laud the school as one of higher education's best buys. Professors always have their door open to students, often even supplying them their home phone numbers. Though some students grumble about the rural setting, the Chesapeake Bay region is breathtaking and offers great opportunities for outdoor recreation.

## GETTING THERE

**BY AIR:** Baltimore-Washington International Airport, Reagan National, and Dulles International Airports are each within two hours of the campus.

**BY TRAIN:** Take Amtrak to Baltimore's Penn Station, BWI Airport Rail Station, or Washington DC's Union Station. You'll still need to either rent a car or take a taxi to the campus.

**BY BUS:** Greyhound provides service to a number of points in Maryland (Baltimore, Annapolis, Silver Spring, Frederick). Once again, you will still need to rent a car or take a taxi to the campus.

**BY CAR:** From the North (Baltimore, Annapolis): Follow I-97 South to MD Route 3 in Bowie, Maryland. Take Route 3 to MD Route 4 in Upper Marlboro. Proceed on Route 4 South, driving through Prince Frederick. Cross the Thomas Johnson Bridge at Solomons. After the bridge, go left onto Route 235 South. Continue through Lexington Park, making a right onto Shangri La Drive. Bear left at the fork in the road on Willows Road, and go left at the stop sign at MD Route 5 South. The campus is four miles ahead. From Washington, DC: Follow the Capital Beltway (I-495/95) to Exit 11A. Take MD Route 4 South. Follow the "From the North" directions above. From the South (Richmond): Follow U.S. Route 301 North over the Potomac River Bridge. Make a right onto MD Route 234. Proceed down Route 234 for roughly 23 miles, taking it to its end at MD Route 5. Make a right on Route 5 (you'll drive through Leonardtown) and proceed for 15 miles to St. Mary's College. The campus is located on Route 5.

**LOCAL:** We recommend having a car or being very good friends with someone who has a car. If you like walking, we won't hold that against you.

## WHERE TO STAY

For accommodations that are within 15 minutes of the St. Mary's campus, try Bard's Field of Trinity Manor (301-872-5989, $), St. Michael's Manor (301-872-4025, $), or the Fairfield Inn (301-863-0203, $$).

---

## CAMPUS AT ITS BEST!

St. Mary's frequently takes advantage of its waterfront location. Recreational and instructional sailing opportunities are readily available. A variety of vessels, including ocean kayaks and keelboats, can be borrowed by both students and faculty. The Waterfront also plays host to numerous events. Throughout the year the college community enjoys concerts, department picnics, the Cardboard Boat Race, and the Governor's Cup all along the pristine banks of the St. Mary's River.

# STATE UNIVERSITY OF NEW YORK AT ALBANY

Office of Undergraduate Admissions, UAB 101, 1400 Washington Ave., Albany, NY 12222

**Telephone:** 518-442-5435 • **E-mail:** ugadmissions@albany.edu

**Hours:** Monday–Friday, 8:30 A.M.–4:00 P.M.

| SCHOOL AT A GLANCE | |
| --- | --- |
| Type of School | Public |
| Environment | City |
| In-state Tuition | $4,350 |
| Out-of-state Tuition | $10,610 |
| Enrollment | 11,680 |
| % Male/Female | 50/50 |
| Student/Faculty Ratio | 19:1 |

| FRESHMAN PROFILE | |
| --- | --- |
| Range SAT | |
| Critical Reading | 500–590 |
| Range SAT Math | 520–610 |
| Average HS GPA | 3.26 |

| ON-CAMPUS APPOINTMENTS | |
| --- | --- |
| Advance Notice | 1 week |
| Appointment | Required |
| Saturdays | Yes |
| Info Sessions | Yes |
| Class Visits | Yes |

| CAMPUS TOURS | |
| --- | --- |
| Appointment | Preferred |
| Dates | Year Round |
| Times | 11:00 A.M. and 1:00 P.M. |
| Average Length | 60 min |

## STUDENTS SAY

"We have a huge population, which means there are a lot of Student Association–sponsored clubs and organizations. No matter what you like to do, there is a social group for you."

## FODOR'S SAYS

"It took more than 30 years to complete the New York State Capitol building (1867–1899), which incorporates elaborate carvings, interesting architectural elements, and elective styles. The 45-minute guided tour highlights the ornate Great Western Staircase (aka, the Million Dollar Staircase)—which took 13 years and 600 stones carvers to complete—and right over it, a 3,000-square-foot skylight that had been covered from World War II until 2002."

## ABOUT THE SCHOOL

Albany's modest price tag and sound academics make the school an excellent choice for many New York residents. No student interest goes unmatched thanks to extensive course listings and a range of departments. To strengthen the undergraduate experience, the university recently launched a new Honors College for well-prepared students. Unfortunately, as is typical at most large state schools, undergrads can sometimes get lost in the shuffle unless they take the initiative to be recognized.

## GETTING THERE

**BY AIR:** Albany International Airport, just a few miles away from the university, is serviced by a number of major airlines.

**BY TRAIN:** The nearest Amtrak stop is the Albany-Rensselaer Station, located across the Hudson River from Albany. The station is roughly seven miles away from campus. Taxis are located at the entrance of the train station. You can get to campus either by taxi or bus.

**BY BUS:** Greyhound Bus and Adirondack Trailways serve most of the state with local and express buses.

**BY CAR:** From the South: Follow I-87 (Thruway) to Exit 24. Proceed to I-90 East and take Exit 2. You'll cross Washington Avenue and enter the campus. Make a left and you'll be on University Drive. From the West: Take I-90 (Thruway) to Exit 24. Continue on to I-90 East. Follow the "From the South" directions above. From the North: Follow I-87 (Northway) to Exit 1. Proceed onto I-90 East. Follow the "From the South" directions above. From the East: Take I-90 West to Exit 2. Make a left onto Fuller Road and another left onto Washington Avenue. Make the first right into campus.

**LOCAL:** The Capital District Transportation Authority (CDTA) has a variety of different routes for public transportation to the university and around the Albany area.

## WHERE TO STAY

Convenient accommodations include the Holiday Inn Express (518-438-0001, $), Hampton Inn & Suites (518-432-1113, $$–$$$), or Courtyard by Marriott (518-435-1600, $$).

## CAMPUS AT ITS BEST!

Politics junkies will definitely appreciate a trip to Albany. As the capitol of New York, there is a plethora of government sites and buildings to visit. Consider stopping by the Executive Mansion or the Court of Appeals and see state law makers at work. For something less political, wander back to campus and participate in Danes After Dark, a program that provides Albany students with a number of activities ranging from movies and sports tournaments to arts and crafts.

# STATE UNIVERSITY OF NEW YORK AT BINGHAMTON

PO Box 6001, Binghamton, NY 13902-6001

**Telephone:** 607-777-2171 • **E-mail:** admit@binghamton.edu • **Website:** www.binghamton.edu

**Hours:** Monday–Friday, 8:30 A.M.–5:00 P.M.; Saturday, 10:30 A.M.-1:00 P.M.

## STUDENTS SAY

"Binghamton has done a great job of incorporating the opportunities of a large school (sports, study abroad, clubs, etc.) with the intimacy and personality of a small school (small classes, attentive professors, etc.)."

## FODOR'S SAYS

"Part of New York's agricultural and dairy heartland, the region known as Leatherstocking Country epitomizes the pastoral lifestyle. Rivers, streams, and brooks glisten between vivid green hillsides; forests of hardwood and pine and fields of corn and alfalfa form a shimmering patchwork."

## ABOUT THE SCHOOL

Binghamton proves popular with students, offering a quality education at a bargain price. While professor quality can vary, undergrads praise exceptionally strong programs in management, political science, and the hard sciences. There is also a lot of ethnic diversity, including a large Asian minority. The surrounding city can be pretty quiet; therefore, the majority of the student body spends its free time drinking in the dorms and attending frat parties.

## GETTING THERE

**BY AIR:** The Greater Binghamton Airport is serviced by most major airlines. Rental cars and taxis are available for transportation to and from the airport.

**BY TRAIN:** The nearest Amtrak station is located in Syracuse, roughly 70 miles away from Binghamton.

**BY BUS:** Several bus lines, including Greyhound and Hudson Transit, provide service to Binghamton.

**BY CAR:** From Metropolitan New York/Tappan Zee Bridge: Take Thruway 87 North to the Harriman Exit, which leads to Route 17 West. Take Route 17 West to Exit 70 South. Then follow Route 201 and the SUNY signs, crossing the bridge to Route 434 East. Make the first right and you're there. Via George Washington Bridge: Take I-80 West to Route 380 North. Follow Route 380 North to I-81 North. I-81 leads to Route 17 West. Proceed on Route 17 West until you see the exit for 70 South. Follow the "From Metropolitan New York" directions above. From New Jersey: Take the New Jersey Turnpike North to Route 280 West. Proceed down I-80 West until you see the exit for Route 380 North. Follow the "From Metropolitan New York" directions above. From Southern New England and Downstate New York: Take the New York State Thruway 87 to Exit 16. Follow Exit 16 until you hit Route 17 West. Follow the "From Metropolitan New York" directions above. From Northern New England and Albany: Take I-88 West to I-81 South. Follow I-81 until you reach the exit for Route 17 West. Follow the "From Metropolitan New York" directions above.

**LOCAL:** Binghamton city buses are free with your student ID and will take you all throughout town. For taxis, call Yellow Cab (607-722-2322), Taximo (607-372-0064), or Coachmaster (607-748-2322).

## WHERE TO STAY

Hotels that are closest to Binghamton's campus include Howard Johnson (607-729-6181, $), Holiday Inn University (607-729-6371, $$), and Residence Inn Marriott (607-770-8500, $$–$$$).

## CAMPUS AT ITS BEST!

Binghamton's 190-acre nature preserve serves as a phenomenal resource for both budding scientists and outdoor enthusiasts. Functioning as a living laboratory for plant and animal life, it's a great locale for hiking and cross-country skiing. Cultural opportunities include Tamasha, an annual event that features both traditional and modern Indian dance. Students looking to kick back can attend Late Nite at Binghamton. This program provides an array of entertainment from remote control car races and dodgeball to massages and roving magicians.

# STATE UNIVERSITY OF NEW YORK AT GENESEO

1 College Circle, Geneseo, NY 14454-1401
**Telephone:** 585-245-5571 • **E-mail:** admissions@geneseo.edu

## STUDENTS SAY

"If you're the type of person who likes to go out on the town, Geneseo might not be for you. [However, there is] a great sense of community on and off of campus."

## FODOR'S SAYS

"Iroquois legend has it that the Finger Lakes were formed when the Great Spirit placed his hand in blessing on this favored land, leaving behind an imprint. Geologists offer another explanation: the intense grinding pressure of retreating ice masses gouged deep holes in the earth, creating the long, narrow lakes that lie side by side, the region's deep gorges and their rushing falls, and the wide fertile valleys that extend South for miles."

## ABOUT THE SCHOOL

Geneseo offers what many state schools can't—a small, teaching-oriented school at a bargain price. The professors are extremely dedicated and always have their door open to students. Class discussions and group work are standard in most classes. The 150-plus student organizations provide students with a wide array of extracurricular options to explore.

## GETTING THERE

**BY AIR:** The Greater Rochester International Airport is serviced by several major airlines. Car rentals and taxis are available at the terminal.

**BY TRAIN:** Guests who are interested in traveling by train can take Amtrak to Rochester (30 miles away). A bus service is available to Geneseo.

**BY BUS:** Trailway bus lines provides service to Geneseo. All lines travel through Rochester, where you might need to transfer to Empire Trailways. The Geneseo station is within walking distance of the campus.

**BY CAR:** From the West: Follow the New York State Thruway to Batavia Exit 48. Proceed to Route 63 South. Geneseo is roughly 20 miles down Route 63. Bear left at fork following the traffic light (toward 20A). Make a left at stop sign, turning onto 20A. Make the first left at the stop light onto Main Street (Route 39). Make the first left (this time off Main Street), turning onto Park Street. You can park at the visitors' circle on the right. The Admissions Office is located on the first floor of Austin W. Erwin Hall, the third building on the left. From the South: Take Route 390 North to Exit 7. Continue on to Route 63/39 North (approximately three miles). Make a left at the second traffic light onto Main Street (Route 39). Follow the "From the West" directions above. From the North and East: Follow the New York State Thruway to Rochester, taking Exit 46. Continue onto Route 390 South to Geneseo Exit 8. Take Route 20A West (you'll be on this road for approximately five miles). Make a right at the third traffic light onto Main Street (Route 39). Follow the "From the West" directions above.

**LOCAL:** For taxi rides in Geneseo call ABLE Taxi (585-663-1600).

## WHERE TO STAY

For accommodations within a mile of campus call Annabel Lee (585-243-9440, $–$$), Oak Valley Inn (585-243-5570, $$), the Big Tree Inn (585-243-5220, $$–$$$) or the Quality Inn (585-243-0500).

| SCHOOL AT A GLANCE | |
| --- | --- |
| Type of School | Public |
| Environment | Rural |
| In-state Tuition | $4,350 |
| Out-of-state Tuition | $10,610 |
| Enrollment | 5,230 |
| % Male/Female | 41/59 |
| Student/Faculty Ratio | 19:1 |

| FRESHMAN PROFILE | |
| --- | --- |
| Range SAT | |
| Critical Reading | 600-670 |
| Range SAT Math | 620-680 |
| Range ACT Composite | 27-29 |
| Average HS GPA | 3.80 |

| ON-CAMPUS APPOINTMENTS | |
| --- | --- |
| Advance Notice | Yes, 1 week |
| Appointment | Preferred |
| Saturdays | Sometimes |
| Average Length | 60 min |
| Info Sessions | Yes |
| Class Visits | Yes |

| CAMPUS TOURS | |
| --- | --- |
| Appointment | Preferred |
| Dates | Year Round |
| Times | Visit Admissions Tours and Events Calendar on website |
| Average Length | 60 min |

## CAMPUS AT ITS BEST!

Prospective students who like to remain in touch with their inner 10-year-old might want to visit the Corner Pocket, located in MacVittie College Union. This cozy venue maintains a fabulous game inventory, including Battleship, air hockey, table tennis, Dungeons & Dragons, and Dominoes. Visitors who prefer more energetic activities should inquire about Geneseo Late Knight. Held every Friday and Saturday, this always well-attended program sponsors events such as Geneseo Idol and Human Foosball.

# STATE UNIVERSITY OF NEW YORK— UNIVERSITY AT BUFFALO

17 Capen Hall, Buffalo, NY 14260-1660

**Telephone:** 716-645-6900 • **E-mail:** admissions@buffalo.edu • **Hours:** Monday–Friday, 8:30 A.M.–5:00 P.M.

## STUDENTS SAY

"My school is all about diversity, and the opportunities to get involved are just as diverse."

## FODOR'S SAYS

"After President William McKinley was assassinated at the Pan-American Exposition in Buffalo in 1901, Theodore Roosevelt was inaugurated as the nation's 26th president in the library of this Wilcox Mansion. You can take guided tours and view exhibits and gardens."

## ABOUT THE SCHOOL

Many consider Buffalo to be SUNY's flagship school, and students continually proclaim their experience to be the equivalent of a private education. Academically, the business and engineering programs garner the most respect although architecture and communications also receive rave reviews. Undergrads hail the diversity of the student body, exclaiming that the variety of personalities enhances their education.

## GETTING THERE

**BY AIR:** Buffalo/Niagara International Airport serves eight major carriers and eight commuter carriers.

**BY TRAIN:** Amtrak provides service to Buffalo. For transportation from the station guests may take a taxi or use Buffalo's public transportation.

**BY BUS:** Both Greyhound and New York Trailways provide service to the Buffalo Metropolitan Transportation Center.

**BY CAR:** From Albany: Follow Western Boulevard West to the Crosstown Arterial. Drive North on Crosstown Arterial to I-90. Drive West on I-90 (portions are a toll road) to I-290 West. Continue on I-290 (Youngmann Expressway) until Exit 5B, Millersport Highway North. As you exit onto Millersport Highway, you'll drive through one traffic light (Flint Road intersection), past the Maple Road Exit, and continue to either of the next two exits to the Flint Entrance or Coventry Entrance to UB's North Campus. From New York City: Follow the Triborough Bridge East to I-278. Drive Northeast on I-278 to the Major Deegan Expressway. Drive Northwest on the Major Deegan Expressway to I-95. Go West on I-95 to George Washington Bridge. Take the GWB to New Jersey and continue West to I-95. Drive Southwest on I-95 to I-80. Follow I-80 West to Pennsylvania. Proceed on I-80 to I-380 and onto I-81. Drive North on I-81 to New York (state) and go North on I-81 to I-690. Continue Northwest on I-690 to I-90 (New York State Thruway). You will follow the Thruway West to I-290 West. Proceed West on the I-290 (Youngmann Expressway) until Exit 5B, Millersport Highway North. Follow the "From Albany" directions above. From Syracuse: Follow I-690 Northwest to I-90. Proceed West on I-90 to I-290 West. Follow the "From Albany" directions above.

**LOCAL:** Metro rail is Buffalo's local rail service. There are also public buses available for transportation.

## WHERE TO STAY

For overnight stays consider the Comfort Inn University (716-688-0811, $), Buffalo Marriott Niagara (716-689-6900, $$), or the Residence Inn Buffalo Amherst (716-632-6622, $$).

## CAMPUS AT ITS BEST!

Buffalo's arts facilities and programs are unparalleled. Lippes Concert Hall (located in Slee Hall) is a pristine 670-seat auditorium equipped with a 2,883-pipe organ. The hall hosts a variety of events, including the annual Beethoven String Quartet Cycle and June in Buffalo Festival. Sports fans will surely want to attend the Rockin' Rally. This kickoff to the Buffalo football season includes a pep rally, concerts, and a spectacular fireworks display.

# SUSQUEHANNA UNIVERSITY

514 University Avenue, Selinsgrove, PA 17870
Telephone: 570-372-4260 • E-mail: suadmiss@susqu.edu

## STUDENTS SAY

"Susquehanna is about preparing students for the 'real world' through a well-rounded liberal arts education in a small, community-oriented environment."

## FODOR'S SAYS

"The Poconos, in the northeastern corner of the state, encompass 2,400 square miles of wilderness bordering the Delaware River, with lakes, streams, waterfalls, resorts, and country inns." The Poconos are a 90-minute drive away from Susquehanna.

## ABOUT THE SCHOOL

Susquehanna is noted for the beauty of its campus and its exceptional facilities. A new residence hall will be added the summer of 2007 and ground will be broken for a new science building in 2008. Students note that both the academics and aesthetics of the school are continually improving. Additionally, undergrads praise SU's dedication to helping students find jobs and internships. Students are able to maintain a good balance between studies and extracurricular activities, with many participating in community service and club sports.

## GETTING THERE

**BY AIR:** The Harrisburg International Airport is roughly 60 miles from Selinsgrove. Additionally, the Penn Valley Airport in Selinsgrove maintains facilities for private and charter aircraft.

**BY TRAIN:** Visitors wishing to travel by train can take Amtrak to Harrisburg. Greyhound connects to the station and taxis are also available.

**BY BUS:** Both Greyhound and Capitol Trailways provide service to Selinsgrove.

**BY CAR:** From Route 80: Take Exit 224 (formerly 33) in Danville. Proceed to Route 54 East and 11 South. Take Exit 210A (formerly 30A) in Lewisburg, continuing on to Route 15 South. Simply follow the signs to downtown Selinsgrove and Susquehanna University.

**LOCAL:** For taxi service in Selinsgrove call Paul's Cab Service (570-286-7509) or Aurora Taxi Inc. (570-523-1400).

## WHERE TO STAY

These inns are all conveniently located and include the Potteiger House Bed & Breakfast (570-374-0415, $$), River View Inn Bed & Breakfast (570-286-4800, $), and the Hampton Inn (570-743-2223, $$). A new inn in the area, Selinsgrove Inn (570-374-4100, $$), is also close to the campus.

### SCHOOL AT A GLANCE

| Type of School | Private |
|---|---|
| Environment | Town |
| Tuition | $27,300 |
| Enrollment | 2,009 |
| % Male/Female | 45/55 |
| Student/Faculty Ratio | 13.5:1 |

### FRESHMAN PROFILE

| Range SAT | |
|---|---|
| Critical Reading | 500-610 |
| Range SAT Math | 520-620 |

### ON-CAMPUS APPOINTMENTS

| Advance Notice | Yes, 1 week |
|---|---|
| Appointment | Preferred |
| Saturdays | Yes |
| Average Length | 30 min |
| Info Sessions | Yes |
| Class Visits | Yes |

### CAMPUS TOURS

| Appointment | Preferred |
|---|---|
| Dates | Year Round |
| Times | M-F 9:00 A.M.–NOON and 1:00 P.M.–4:00 P.M.; Sat 9:00 A.M.–1:00 P.M. |
| Average Length | 30 min |

## CAMPUS AT ITS BEST!

Charlie's Coffeehouse is a favorite haunt of many Susquehanna students. It's a great place to get your caffeine fix and enjoy a plate of nachos (or the sometimes free chicken wings); undergrads also congregate there to watch football on the big-screen television or demonstrate their vocal talent on karaoke night. Fall Frenzy also gets the masses out, with promises of inflatables and an all-day barbeque. Students also love November's annual "Old Skool Dodgeball" tournament. This newly minted tradition allows undergrads to revert back to their childhoods and blow off some academic stress.

# SWARTHMORE COLLEGE

500 College Avenue, Swarthmore, PA 19081
**Telephone:** 610-328-8300 • **E-mail:** admissions@swarthmore.edu
**Website:** www.swarthmore.edu • **Hours:** Monday–Friday, 8:30 A.M.–4:30 P.M.; Saturday, 9:00 A.M.–NOON

## STUDENTS SAY

"The only thing that all Swatties have in common is that they picked a school where they knew they would have to think critically and work hard. After that, there's a lot of diversity, and everyone's pretty accepting."

## FODOR'S SAYS

"Almost a century after English Quaker William Penn founded Philadelphia [just 12 miles by train from Swarthmore]…the city became the birthplace of the nation and the home of its first government. Today, Philadelphia is synonymous with Independence Hall, the Liberty Bell, cheese steaks and hoagies, ethnic neighborhoods, theaters—and city streets teeming with life."

## ABOUT THE SCHOOL

Swarthmore College, known for its intense academics, is the kind of school where A's don't come often, but when they do you can be sure they are well deserved. Students love the college's flexible curriculum in which minimal course requirements allow students to forge their own intellectual paths. Professors also receive high marks for being extremely accessible outside of class and going the extra mile to make sure students succeed.

## GETTING THERE

**BY AIR:** The Philadelphia International Airport is the closest airport to campus. From there, take the SEPTA R1 Airport Express train to Center City Philadelphia commuter stations, with connections to the SEPTA Media/Elwyn R3 rail line to Swarthmore.

**BY TRAIN:** Amtrak trains stop at Philadelphia's 30th Street Station. From there, take the SEPTA Media/Elwyn R3 rail line to Swarthmore.

**BY BUS:** The Greyhound Bus Station is at Filbert and 10th Streets in Philadelphia, and connects to the SEPTA Media/Elwyn R3 rail line to Swarthmore.

**BY CAR:** From the North: Take I-95 South to Exit 7, I-476 North/Plymouth Meeting. Take I-476 North to Exit 3, Media/Swarthmore. After the exit ramp, follow signs for Swarthmore and turn right onto Baltimore Pike. Stay in the right lane and in less than a quarter of a mile turn right onto Route 320 South. At the first light, make a right to stay on 320. Proceed through second light at College Avenue to the first driveway on your right to visitor parking at the Benjamin West House, the college's visitor center. From the South: Follow I-95 North to Exit 7 (in Pennsylvania), I-476 North/Plymouth Meeting. Take I-476 to Exit 3, Media/Swarthmore. After the exit ramp, follow the signs for Swarthmore and turn right onto Baltimore Pike. Follow the "From the North" directions above. From the East: From Exit 333, Norristown, follow the signs for I-476 South. Stay on I-476 for approximately 17 miles to Exit 3, Media/Swarthmore. After the exit ramp, follow the signs to Swarthmore and turn left onto Baltimore Pike. Follow the "From the North" directions above. From the West: From Exit 326, Valley Forge, Take I-76 East, Schuykill Expressway, about four miles to I-476 South. Take I-476 approximately 12 miles to Exit 3, Media/Swarthmore. After the exit ramp, follow the signs to Swarthmore and turn left onto Baltimore Pike. Follow the "From the North" directions above.

**LOCAL:** The SEPTA Media/Elwyn R3 commuter rail line offers service directly to Swarthmore's campus.

## WHERE TO STAY

Some of the most popular lodging options near campus include the Magnolia House (610-544-6779, $), Purcell Darrell House (610-690-4421, $), and Longfellow House (610-544-4588, $).

---

## CAMPUS AT ITS BEST!

Swarthmore is home to the Swarthmore College Peace Collection, a unique repository of materials that document nonviolent change and conflict resolution between peoples and nations. While you're on campus, stop by the Lang Center for Civic and Social Responsibility, an organization which prepares students for leadership in civic engagement, public service, advocacy and social action. You might also tune in to Swarthmore's student-run War News Radio, which fills in the gaps in the mainstream media's coverage of war in Iraq.

# SYRACUSE UNIVERSITY

200 Crouse-Hinds Hall, Office of Admissions, Syracuse, NY 13244-2130
**Telephone:** 315-443-3611 • **E-mail:** orange@syr.edu • **Website:** www.syracuse.edu
**Hours:** Monday–Friday 8:30 A.M.–5:00 P.M.; Saturday 9:00 A.M.–NOON

## STUDENTS SAY

"Life at Syracuse University is amazing! Classes are intriguing and entertaining. Every professor has a different, yet distinct personality." Or as another student mentions, "Having a good time—Orange you glad you came to 'Cuse?"

## FODOR'S SAYS

"Two centuries of building styles can be seen on the compact campus, which is crossed by city streets and includes a traditional collegiate quadrangle. A number of lectures and music performances are open to the public, as is the Lowe Art Gallery in the Shaffer Art Building, and football, basketball, and lacrosse are played in the 50,000-seat Carrier Dome."

## ABOUT THE SCHOOL

Syracuse University offers students top programs in areas such as journalism, architecture, information studies, and bioengineering, along with enough snow to become first-rate skiers. While snow sports are popular, March madness is what really gets these Orange fans excited as they root for their championship basketball team.

## GETTING THERE

**BY AIR:** Hancock International Airport is only a few miles North of downtown Syracuse, and services all the major airlines. The easiest way to get from the airport to campus is by taxi, which costs about $25 one way.

**BY TRAIN:** Amtrak train service takes you to the William F. Walsh Regional Transportation Center in Syracuse, only four miles away from campus. You can then take a taxi to campus.

**BY BUS:** Greyhound services the William F. Walsh Regional Transportation Center in Syracuse, located four miles away from campus. From there, you can take the Syracuse OnTrack to campus. Call 800-FOR-TRAIN for more information.

**BY CAR:** The university can be easily reached from Interstate 81. New York State Thruway drivers should exit at I-81 (Thruway Exit 36) and proceed South. From North and South I-81: Drivers on I-81 should exit at Adams Street (Exit 18). Continue up the Adams Street hill to the third traffic light. Go across University Avenue and make a left into the University Avenue Garage. The entrance to the main campus is two blocks from the University Avenue Garage.

**LOCAL:** CENTRO provides bus service in and around campus. Basic fare is $1.00. Local taxi options include Syracuse Area Taxi (315-478-8294), Ace Taxi Svc (315-471-7133), and AAA Carousel Taxi (315-478-8000).

## WHERE TO STAY

The Sheraton Syracuse University Hotel & Conference Center (800-395-2105, $$) is located on campus and offers easy access to the downtown business and cultural districts. Other options include Comfort Inn Syracuse (315-437-0222, $) and Embassy Suites Hotel Syracuse (315-446-3200, $$$).

### SCHOOL AT A GLANCE

| | |
|---|---|
| Type of School | Private |
| Environment | City |
| Tuition | $28,820 |
| Enrollment | 11,546 |
| % Male/Female | 44/56 |
| Student/Faculty Ratio | 13:1 |

### FRESHMAN PROFILE

| | |
|---|---|
| Range SAT | |
| Critical Reading | 570-650 |
| Range SAT Math | 570-670 |
| Average HS GPA | 3.6 |

### ON-CAMPUS APPOINTMENTS

| | |
|---|---|
| Advance Notice | Yes, 1 week |
| Appointment | Preferred |
| Saturdays | Selected |
| Average Length | 90 min |
| Info Sessions | Yes |
| Class Visits | Yes |

### CAMPUS TOURS

| | |
|---|---|
| Appointment | Required |
| Dates | Year Round |
| Times | M–F varies; Sat by appt. |
| Average Length | 60 min |

## CAMPUS AT ITS BEST!

In April, Block Party features concerts along with carnival events to celebrate the end of classes. The Westcott Street Fair is also popular with students. Attendees enjoy folk dancing, folk singing, arts and crafts, and clowns. If you can tear yourself away from all the fun, seek out the "kissing bench" on the West lawn of the Hall of Languages. University lore proclaims that couples who kiss while sitting on the bench will eventually marry.

# TEMPLE UNIVERSITY

1801 North Broad Street, Philadelphia, PA 19122-6096

**Telephone:** 215-204-7200 • **E-mail:** tuadm@temple.edu

**Hours:** Monday–Friday, 10:00 A.M.–2:00 P.M.

## STUDENTS SAY

"Temple is a very diverse school where people of all types can feel comfortable, confident, and make friends who share their beliefs as well as those who may be different. It is a great place to meet people while getting a terrific education."

## FODOR'S SAYS

"At the geographic center of Penn's original city stands City Hall—the largest city hall in the country (it has 642 rooms). For a tour of the interior and a 360-degree view of the city from the William Penn statue, go to Room 121 via the Northeast corner of the courtyard and ride the elevator to the top of the 548-foot tower."

## ABOUT THE SCHOOL

For students looking for a diverse learning experience, Temple University is the perfect fit. The university's 12 schools offer a wide variety of academic options and classes that range from large lecture courses to small seminars. While the professors are generally accessible and genuinely care about their students, the large number of undergraduates on campus means that students have to take the initiative to really take advantage of all Temple has to offer.

## GETTING THERE

**BY AIR:** Philadelphia International Airport is less than nine miles away from Temple University. Taxi and SEPTA service are available from the airport.

**BY TRAIN:** SEPTA Regional High Speed Lines stop at Temple University Station, 10th and Berks Streets.

**BY BUS:** The SEPTA C and 3 buses stop near campus.

**BY CAR:** From the Pennsylvania Turnpike: Take Exit 326 (Philadelphia/Valley Forge). Follow I-76 East (Schuylkill Expressway) about 18 miles to Exit 344 (Central Philadelphia/I-676), which is on the left. Follow I-676 about one mile to Central Philadelphia/Broad Street Exit. Take the Broad Street Exit (stay on the left). After one block, make a left onto Broad Street. Follow Broad Street to Norris Street (about two and a quarter miles). Make a left onto Norris Street. Make the next left (15th Street). The Liacouras Center parking garage is two blocks down to the right. From I-95 North: Take Exit 22 (Central Philadelphia/I-676). Follow Central Philadelphia signs to Broad Street exit. Follow the "From the Pennsylvania Turnpike" directions above. From I-95 South: Take Exit 22 (Central Philadelphia/I-676), which is on the left. I-676 West to Broad Street Exit. Follow the "From the Pennsylvania Turnpike" directions above. From the New Jersey Turnpike: Take Exit 4 to Route 73 North. Go about one mile to Route 38 West. Follow for 5.5 miles to Benjamin Franklin Bridge. Take I-676 West to Broad Street Exit. Follow the "From the Pennsylvania Turnpike" directions above.

**LOCAL:** All local Broad Street subway trains stop near campus, at the Cecil B. Moore Station (Broad and Cecil B. Moore Avenue).

## WHERE TO STAY

Some popular hotel choices include the Best Western Center City Hotel (215-568-8300, $$), Comfort Inn Downtown Philadelphia (877-424-6423, $$$), and Sheraton University City Hotel (215-387-8000, $$$).

## CAMPUS AT ITS BEST!

Liacouras Walk, which shoots through the heart of Temple's Main Campus, is constantly buzzing with activity. This area offers a range of retail and food outlets where patrons can enjoy a casual dining experience in a sunlit atrium. Afterward, you can enjoy one of the many events constantly happening around the university. Every week, the Student Center hosts Free Food and Fun Fridays, featuring tournaments like Texas Hold 'Em and Madden.

# TOWSON UNIVERSITY

8000 York Road, Towson, MD 21252-0001
**Telephone:** 410-704-2113 • **E-mail:** admissions@towson.edu
**Website:** www.towson.edu

## STUDENTS SAY

"I love the size of Towson. It is large enough to have a variety of majors, clubs, and activities. Yet it is small enough that every day I run into someone I know; professors remember my name."

## FODOR'S SAYS

"Baltimore's indoor food markets, all of which are at least 100 years old, are a mix of vendors selling fresh fish, meat, produce, and baked goods, and [there is also] a food court."

## ABOUT THE SCHOOL

Towson is Maryland's second largest public university and the largest comprehensive university in the Baltimore area. The beautifully landscaped suburban campus is an ideal environment for both studying and relaxing. Proximity to Baltimore provides students with many opportunities for real-world experience; a large number of students takes advantage of the city's resources for research, internships, and jobs.

## GETTING THERE

**BY AIR:** The closest airport to Towson University is Baltimore Washington International (BWI). Approximate travel time (non–rush hour) between BWI and the university is 45 minutes. An airport shuttle runs between the Towson Sheraton and BWI.

**BY TRAIN:** Amtrak serves Pennsylvania Station in Baltimore City. Visitors can either take taxis or public transportation to the campus.

**BY BUS:** Greyhound unfortunately does not provide direct service to Towson. Visitors can take a bus into Baltimore and transfer to local public transportation to get to campus.

**BY CAR:** From I-95 (Northbound and Southbound): Follow the Baltimore Beltway I-695 West (heading toward Towson). Use Exit 25 (Charles Street) South. Drive for roughly 1.7 miles. Make a left onto Towsontown Boulevard and continue to the first stoplight. Make a right on Osler Drive. Make the first right into the Enrollment Services Center parking lot. From I-83 (Northbound and Southbound): Follow the Baltimore Beltway I-695 East (heading toward Towson). Use Exit 25 (Charles Street) South. Drive for roughly 1.7 miles. Make a left onto Towsontown Boulevard and continue to the first stoplight. Make a right on Osler Drive. Make the first right into the Enrollment Services Center parking lot. From I-70 (Eastbound): Follow the Baltimore Beltway I-695 North (heading toward Towson). Use Exit 25 (Charles Street) South. Drive for roughly 1.7 miles. Make a left onto Towsontown Boulevard and continue to the first stoplight. Make a right on Osler Drive. Make the first right into the Enrollment Services Center parking lot.

**LOCAL:** The MTA number 11 bus runs between Penn Station and the Bosley/Allegheny Avenue intersection a few blocks from the TU campus. On weekends, visitors returning to Penn Station from Towson can take the MTA number 9 bus and transfer to either the light rail or the number 3 bus to reach the station. For local taxi service, call ABC Taxi Association (410-323-4222), Airport Taxi (410-859-1103), or Yellow Cab (410-235-0300).

## WHERE TO STAY

For hotels in Towson call the Ramada Inn (410-823-8750, $), Comfort Inn (410-882-0900, $$), or Burkshire Marriott Conference Hotel (800-435-5986, $$$).

## CAMPUS AT ITS BEST!

Towson's Programming Board works diligently to make sure all undergrads enjoy themselves. You'll want to scrap your Labor Day plans and attend Towson's annual Beach Bash, which features great food, live music, and free giveaways. Furthermore, with Baltimore in such close proximity, you should think about spending a few hours in the city. Consider visiting the American Visionary Art Museum. It is sure to revolutionize how you view contemporary art.

# TRINITY COLLEGE

300 Summit Street, Hartford, CT 06016

**Telephone:** 860-297-2180 • **E-mail:** admissions.office@trincoll.edu • **Website:** www.trincoll.edu

**Hours:** Monday–Friday, 8:00 A.M.–4:30 P.M.; Saturday 9:00 A.M.–NOON

## SCHOOL AT A GLANCE

| | |
|---|---|
| Type of School | Private |
| Environment | Metropolis |
| Tuition | $32,000 |
| Enrollment | 2,181 |
| % Male/Female | 50/50 |
| Student/Faculty Ratio | 10:1 |

### FRESHMAN PROFILE

| | |
|---|---|
| Range SAT | |
| Critical Reading | 610–700 |
| Range SAT Math | 610–700 |
| Range ACT Composite | 25–29 |

### ON-CAMPUS APPOINTMENTS

| | |
|---|---|
| Advance Notice | Recommended |
| Appointment | Required |
| Saturdays | Yes |
| Class Visits | Yes |

### CAMPUS TOURS

| | |
|---|---|
| Dates | Year-Round |
| Times | Varies |
| Average Length | 1 hour |

## STUDENTS SAY

"We are so lucky; we have awesome facilities. Our library is beautiful, and the classrooms have so much character."

## FODOR'S SAYS

"Built in 1874, the Mark Twain House & Museum was the home of Samuel Langhorne Clemens, better known as Mark Twain, until 1891. While he and his family lived in this 19-room Victorian mansion, Twain published seven major novels, including *Tom Sawyer*, *Huckleberry Finn*, and *The Prince and the Pauper*."

## ABOUT THE SCHOOL

Trinity has a well-deserved reputation as a strong and solid liberal arts college. In the past few years, the school has worked diligently to increase its academic rigor and students on campus log in long library hours. Once known as a bastion for rich, preppy undergrads, the administration has been pushing for more diversity in the student body. Given Hartford's close proximity to Boston and New York, many students head off campus on the weekends.

## GETTING THERE

**BY AIR:** Visitors can fly into Bradley International Airport, approximately 30 minutes away from Trinity by car. Car rental agencies are available at the airport.

**BY TRAIN:** Amtrak provides service to Hartford. Take a taxi to get to the campus.

**BY BUS:** Peter Pan bus lines provide service to Hartford. Take a taxi to get to the campus.

**BY CAR:** From the West (New York City via I-84, Danbury, etc.): Take I-84 East to Exit 48 (Capitol Avenue). Make a left at the traffic light at the end of the exit ramp. Go to the first traffic light (Washington Street), and make a right (there is a statue of Lafayette on a horse). Continue down Washington Street for eight traffic lights (total of 1.1 miles). You should pass a hospital complex on your left-hand side. Once you hit the eighth light, turn right onto New Britain Avenue. Proceed 0.3 miles to the next traffic light (Broad Street). Make a right onto Broad Street, look for the Trinity College gate, and turn left into the driveway. From the East (Boston, etc.): Take I-84 West. Stay to the right. Upon reaching Hartford, drive through a short tunnel. When you emerge from the tunnel take Exit 48 (Asylum Avenue). At the end of the exit, make a left onto Asylum Street. Making sure to stay in the right-hand lane, follow the roadway to the right, hugging Bushnell Park. Bear right through the brownstone arch into Trinity Street. Staying in the left lane, go to the second stoplight. Bushnell Memorial Hall is to your left. From the South (New Haven, New York, etc.): Take I-91 North to I-84 West, and follow the "From the East" directions above. From the North (Springfield, Bradley Airport, etc.): Take I-91 South to I-84 West, and follow the "From the East" directions above.

**LOCAL:** For taxi service, call either Connecticut Limousine Service at (800-472-5466) or the Yellow Cab Company at (860-666-6666).

## WHERE TO STAY

Some nearby lodging options include the Holiday Inn Express (860-525-1000, $), the Smith House (860-297-5241, $–$$), and the Crowne Plaza (860-549-2400, $$–$$$).

---

## CAMPUS AT ITS BEST!

Trinity students tend to gravitate toward Mather Hall, a center for activity and socializing. Whether it's challenging your roommate to a game of pool, grabbing a snack in the Cave, or seeing a band perform in the Underground (a coffee shop), Mather always promises fun and entertainment. Students also love hanging out at Cinestudio, the campus movie theater.

# TUFTS UNIVERSITY

Bendetson Hall, Medford, MA 02155
**Telephone:** 617-627-3170 • **E-mail:** admissions.inquiry@ase.tufts.edu
**Website:** www.tufts.edu • **Hours:** Monday–Friday, 8:30 A.M.–5:00 P.M.; Saturday mornings by appointment

## STUDENTS SAY

"At Tufts, the classes are demanding, and the students work hard, but they're all pretty down to earth, and they get their work done so they can have fun too."

## FODOR'S SAYS

"In summer and fall, boats leave Boston, Cape Cod, and Cape Ann two or more times a day to observe the whales feeding a few miles offshore. It's rare not to have the extraordinary experience of seeing several whales, most of them extremely close up."

## ABOUT THE SCHOOL

Tufts University, a small school with a reputation as a "safety" school for Ivy League applicants, places heavy demands on its students whose lives often revolve around their academics. Tuft's silver-medal standing doesn't do justice to its highly regarded offerings, which are often competitive with those of the Ivies. The international relations program is a special standout. On those rare occasions when students can pull themselves away from their studies, all the delights of Boston are only a subway ride away.

## GETTING THERE

**BY AIR:** Boston's Logan Airport is the closest airport near campus. Take a taxi to get to the campus. For public transportation from the airport, you can take the Silver Line Waterfront Bus to South Station and board the Red Line subway to Davis Square. Campus is a 15-minute walk from there, or you can take the number 94 or 96 bus.

**BY TRAIN:** Amtrak trains provide service to South Station in Boston. From there, you can board the Red Line subway to Davis Square.

**BY BUS:** Greyhound buses provide service to South Station. From there, you can board the Red Line subway to Davis Square.

**BY CAR:** From the North: Take Route 93 South to Exit 32, which is Medford Square. After the exit ramp, make the first right on to Route 60 West. At the second set of lights, bear left on Main Street and make an immediate right onto Route 16 West. Continue on Route 16. Bear left through the next traffic circle and drive up the hill on Powder House Boulevard. At the third traffic light, make a left onto Packard Avenue to enter the university campus. From the West: Take Route 95 North to Route 2 East (Exit 29A). At the junction of Routes 2 and 16, turn left through a full traffic light on Route 16 East. Stay on Route 16 through two traffic lights and look for signs directing you to the university. From the South: Take Route 3 North to Route 93 North. If you are coming from Boston, take Route 93 North to Exit 31. Follow the exit ramp to Route 16 West. Follow the "From the North" directions above.

**LOCAL:** You can get around town by taking the MBTA's Red Line subway. You could also take a taxi to get around the area. Some local possibilities include Green Cab of Medford (781-396-4040) and Yellow Cab Assoc. Medford (781-396-2400).

## WHERE TO STAY

Some popular hotel choices in the area include the Red Roof Inn (781-935-7110, $), La Quinta Inn & Suites (617-625-5300, $$), and AmeriSuites (781-395-8500, $$$).

---

## CAMPUS AT ITS BEST!

Tufts maintains a vibrant arts scene. The Aidekman Arts Center features a permanent collection of almost 2,000 works, including photographs from Walker Evans and Lee Friendlander, and paintings by Joan Miro and Alice Neel. After your trip to the museum, check out a performance by the TURBOS, Tufts' very own break-dancing team. Those with a literary bent are sure to appreciate the annual Spoken Word Night, sponsored in part by *Onyx*, Tufts's black visual arts and literary magazine.

## SCHOOL AT A GLANCE

| | |
|---|---|
| Type of School | Private |
| Environment | Town |
| Enrollment | 2,161 |
| % Male/Female | 53/47 |
| Student/Faculty Ratio | 11:1 |

### FRESHMAN PROFILE

| | |
|---|---|
| *Range SAT | |
| Critical Reading | 500–650 |
| Range SAT Math | 580–670 |
| Range ACT Composite | 24–29 |
| Average HS GPA | 3.5 |

### ON-CAMPUS APPOINTMENTS

| | |
|---|---|
| Advance Notice | Yes, 2 weeks |
| Appointment | Required |
| Saturdays | Sometimes |
| Average Length | 60 min |
| Info Sessions | Yes |
| Class Visits | Yes |

### CAMPUS TOURS

| | |
|---|---|
| Appointment | Not Required |
| Dates | Year Round |
| Times | M–F 10:00 A.M.–3:00 P.M. |
| Average Length | 60 min |

*Testing is optional.

# UNION COLLEGE

Grant Hall, Union College, Schenectady, NY 12308
**Telephone:** 888-843-6688 • **E-mail:** admissions@union.edu
**Hours:** Monday–Friday, 9:00 A.M.–4:00 P.M.; Saturday, 10:00 A.M.–1:00 P.M.

## STUDENTS SAY

"Union provides a phenomenal education and a multitude of extracurricular opportunities within a sheltered, close-knit community."

## FODOR'S SAYS

Historic Stockade District is "one of the oldest continuously occupied neighborhoods in the nation (George Washington slept here)." In September, "residents open their homes to the public for guided tours during Walkabout Weekend, and at the Stockade Villagers Art Show, painters set up easels and tents to display their works."

## ABOUT THE SCHOOL

Something of an anomaly in higher education, Union offers a solid liberal arts education as well as a renowned engineering program. Students claim that, regardless of major, your curriculum will be research- and writing-intensive. Indeed, coasting here is not an option. When the weekend rolls around, undergrads are ready to party. Social life typically revolves around the Greek system and attending football and hockey games.

## GETTING THERE

**BY AIR:** Albany Airport is approximately 15 minutes from Union. Taxis and rental cars are both available for additional transportation needs.

**BY TRAIN:** Amtrak provides service to Schenectady. The station is a 10 minute walk or quick taxi ride from the campus.

**BY BUS:** Greyhound also provides direct service to Schenectady. The station is a short cab ride or 15-minute walk from the campus.

**BY CAR:** From the North and South: Take the New York State Thruway to Exit 24. Proceed to the Northway (I-87 North), taking Exit 6 (marked "Route 7 West"). You'll continue on Route 7 West for 6.5 miles, bearing right onto Union Street. After 2.7 miles you'll see Payne Gate on your right. This is where you'll enter the campus. The Admissions Office will be the third building on your right. From the East: Take I-90 West to the New York State Thruway Exit B1. Continue on I-90 West to Exit 1. Take I-87 North (the Adirondack Northway). From there, proceed according to "From the North and South" directions above. From the West: Take Thruway Exit 26. From there proceed to I-890 East, Exit 4 (Erie Boulevard). Continue on Erie Boulevard North until you hit Union Street. You'll make a right turn onto Union, driving for one mile and Payne Gate will be on your left which is where you will turn in.

**LOCAL:** For local taxi service call New Millennium Taxi (518-459-6666) or Capitaland Taxi (518-372-7777).

## WHERE TO STAY

For lodging in Schenectady, try Holiday Inn of America (518-393-4141, $$), The Stockade Inn (518-346-3400, $$–$$$), or the Parker Inn (518-688-1001, $$–$$$).

## CAMPUS AT ITS BEST!

Visitors captivated by campus lore will definitely want to visit The Idol. Originally found in Shanghai around 1860, this statue of a lioness and cub was donated as a gift by a Union alum. It quickly became a landmark and is painted continually according to school tradition. For other campus activities check out the U-Program. This group promotes many fantastic events such as the annual Battle of the Bands contest, Midnight Breakfast, and massage workshops.

# UNITED STATES MILITARY ACADEMY

646 Swift Road, West Point, NY 10996-1905
**Telephone:** 845-938-4041 • **E-mail:** admissions@usma.edu
**Hours:** Monday–Friday, 7:30 A.M.–4:00 P.M.; Saturday, 8:00 A.M.–NOON

## STUDENTS SAY

"West Point develops leaders of character prepared to take on the challenges of the future."

## FODOR'S SAYS

"Occupying the western shore of one of the most scenic bends in the Hudson River, the academy consists of some 16,000 acres of training grounds, playing fields, and buildings constructed of native granite in the Military Gothic style. The world's oldest and largest military museum, the West Point Museum in Olmstead Hall showcases a vast collection of uniforms, weapons, flags, American military art, and other memorabilia."

## ABOUT THE SCHOOL

It takes exceptionally disciplined individuals to survive a West Point education. From day one, students follow a prescribed schedule of demanding academics and mandatory drills, lectures, and activities. Campus life is incredibly regimented, and freshmen are only allowed to leave one weekend per semester. That said, graduates emerge extraordinary leaders, equipped with an excellent—and free!—education, ready for any future challenge.

## GETTING THERE

**BY AIR:** Visitors can fly to JFK, LaGuardia, or Newark International Airport. Car rentals and taxis are both available for transportation to West Point.

**BY TRAIN:** The nearest Amtrak station to West Point is located in Croton-Harmon, approximately 15 miles away.

**BY BUS:** Greyhound provides limited service directly to West Point.

**BY CAR:** From JFK Airport: VanWyck Parkway to Bronx-Whitestone Bridge. After crossing the bridge, look for the Cross Bronx Expressway. Follow the Cross Bronx Expressway to the Bronx River Parkway North. Take the Bronx River Parkway to the left fork for the Sprain Brook Parkway. Follow Sprain Brook Parkway to Route 287, left exit to Tappan Zee Bridge and Interstate 87 (New York State Thruway). Over bridge, take Exit 13 North onto the Palisades Interstate Parkway heading North. Take the Palisades Interstate Parkway North to its end (Bear Mountain traffic circle). Follow signs for Route 9 West, North (third exit off traffic circle). Take the first "West Point, Highland Falls" Exit. This will lead you into Highland Falls, past the Visitor's Center and Museum, and through to Thayer Gate. From LaGuardia Airport: Take the Whitestone Parkway to Bronx-Whitestone Bridge. From there, proceed according to "From JFK Airport" directions above. From Newark Airport: Take Interstate 78 West to the Garden State Parkway. Take the GSP North to the end and follow signs for the New York State Thruway (I-87) South. Exit Thruway at exit 13 North onto the Palisades Interstate Parkway heading North. From there, proceed according to "From JFK Airport" directions above.

**LOCAL:** There's not much by way of public transport as most students are relegated to the campus at all times. However, for a taxi try Highland Transport Corp. (845-265-8294).

## WHERE TO STAY

Overnight visitors should consider the Five Star Inn—Army Lodging (845-446-5943, $), Bear Mountain Bridge Motel (845-258-5066, $), or The Glenwood House (845-258-5066, $$$).

## CAMPUS AT ITS BEST!

The West Point Museum is one of the country's best depositories of military artifacts. Collections encompass almost all aspects of military history, the growth of America's armed forces, and the evolution of warfare. Included in the museum's holdings are Napoleon's sword and pistols, and the safety plug removed from the Nagasaki atomic bomb. Following a visit to the museum, take in a concert by the renowned United States Military Academy Band. Music ranges from jazz to marches to Broadway tunes.

# UNITED STATES NAVAL ACADEMY

117 Decatur Road, Annapolis, MD 21402

**Telephone:** 410-293-4361 • **E-mail:** webmail@usna.com

**Hours:** Monday–Friday, 8:00 A.M.–5:00 P.M.; Saturday, 9:00 A.M.–NOON

## STUDENTS SAY

"The academic opportunities are world-class. The athletic programs are all solid. Life at the academy sets you up for success in life."

## FODOR'S SAYS

"The centerpiece of the campus is the bright copper-clad dome of the U.S. Naval Academy Chapel. Beneath it lies the crypt of the Revolutionary War naval officer John Paul Jones, who, in a historic naval battle with a British ship, uttered the inspirational words, 'I have not yet begun to fight!'"

## ABOUT THE SCHOOL

The 4,400 midshipmen at the United States Naval Academy earn every penny of the full scholarship they receive to attend. Nonstop mental, physical, and ethical training and competition starts the first day students set foot on campus and doesn't end until graduation. Life at the academy is intense: Expect a heavy academic load, mandatory athletics, and military drills. However, students say it's well worth it.

## GETTING THERE

**BY AIR:** The Baltimore-Washington International (BWI) Airport is the closest airport to campus. Amtrak and MARC commuter trains stop at the BWI and connect to Annapolis by Annapolis Transit's Sky Blue Bus Route. Shuttles are also available to take you to area hotels.

**BY TRAIN:** AMTRAK and MARC commuter trains connect to Annapolis by the Sky Blue Bus Route. Take a taxi to get to the campus.

**BY BUS:** Greyhound buses provide service to Annapolis. Take a taxi to get to the campus.

**BY CAR:** Annapolis is located 33 miles East of Washington, DC, and 30 miles Southeast of Baltimore. From Washington, DC: Take U.S. Route 50 East for 35 miles and exit at Rowe Boulevard, Exit 24. Follow Rowe Boulevard 1.6 miles to the dead-end at College Avenue, and make a left turn. Make a right turn onto King George Street. Follow King George Street until you see the academy. From Baltimore: Take either I-97 South or Maryland Route 2 South for 26 miles. Exit at Rowe Boulevard, Exit 24. Follow the "From Washington DC" directions above.

**LOCAL:** From Washington, DC, during the week, you can take the METRO rail or bus service to New Carrollton Station and catch the 921 bus into Annapolis. The Annapolis Transit (410-263-7964) provides bus service throughout Annapolis. If you'd rather catch a taxi, some local companies include Reliable Cab Co. (410-268-4714) and Annapolis Cab Co. (410-268-0022).

## WHERE TO STAY

If you plan on staying overnight, some local lodging accommodations include Comfort Inn Annapolis (410-757-8500, $$), Best Western Annapolis (410-224-2800, $$), and State House Inn (410-990-0024, $$$).

## CAMPUS AT ITS BEST!

Visitors to the United States Naval Academy could conceivably spend hours in the Armel-Leftwich Visitor Center. On display you'll find the Freedom 7 space capsule, an original Dahlgren boat howitzer, and an exhibit on John Paul Jones. The Annapolis Maritime Museum commemorates the heritage of Annapolis and the surrounding Chesapeake Bay. It also hosts an annual summer concert series featuring traditional seafaring songs, shanties, and music with a nautical twist.

# UNIVERSITY OF BRIDGEPORT

126 Park Avenue, Bridgeport, CT 06604
**Telephone:** 203-576-4552 • **E-mail:** admit@.bridgeport.edu • **Website:** www.bridgeport.edu
**Hours:** Monday–Thursday, 8:30 A.M.–5:30 P.M.; Friday, 8:30 A.M.–4:30 P.M.; Saturday, 9:00 A.M. and NOON

## FODOR'S SAYS

"The Romanesque, red-sandstone-and-brick Barnum Museum stands out in downtown Bridgeport much like P. T. Branum, the 'Greatest Showman on Earth' and former mayor of Bridgeport, did in his day. The museum depicts the life and times of Barnum, who founded his circus in 1871."

## ABOUT THE SCHOOL

The University of Bridgeport, a school with a particularly large population of international students, is dedicated to educating students from around the world. Whether they're homegrown or visiting, all Bridgeport students benefit from the school's challenging classes and wide variety of extracurricular activities.

## GETTING THERE

**BY AIR:** Bradley International Airport at Windsor Locks, Groton/New London Airport on Connecticut's Southeastern coast, and Tweed-New Haven Airport are the closest airports to campus. Taxi service is available from all three locations.

**BY TRAIN:** Metro-North Rail Service, the New Haven Line, takes passengers between New York City's Grand Central Terminal and New Haven, with connecting service to Bridgeport. Amtrak provides service to Bridgeport and several other locations in Connecticut. Take a taxi to get to the campus.

**BY BUS:** Greyhound Bus Lines provides service to Bridgeport. Bonanza bus line and Peter Pan Trailways also make regular stops in Connecticut. Take a taxi to get to the campus.

**BY CAR:** From the North: Take I-95 South, take Exit 27. Make a left onto Lafayette Street. At the first light, make a left onto South Frontage Road and go right. At the next light, make a right (by Harbor Yard Stadium and Arena) onto Broad Street. Go about one mile South and Broad Street turns right into Waldemere Avenue. At the first stop sign, make a right onto Park Avenue. Go one block and make a right on Linden Avenue and you will have reached the university. From the South: Take I-95 North. Take Exit 27 and go straight off the exit ramp. Go right. At the fourth light, make a right (by Harbor Yard Stadium and Arena) onto Broad Street. Go about one mile South and Broad Street turns into Waldemere Avenue. At the first stop sign, make a right onto Park Avenue. Go one block and make a right on Linden Avenue and you will see the university ahead.

**LOCAL:** CT Transit provides area-wide bus service. Call 860-522-8101 for route and schedule info. If you would rather take a taxi around town, call Town Taxi (203-366-8534) or Yellow Cab (203-334-2121).

## WHERE TO STAY

If you're planning on spending the night, some nearby hotel choices include the Rodeway Inn (203-377-6288, $$), Ramada Inn (203-375-8866, $$), and Holiday Inn Bridgeport (203-334-1234, $$$).

### SCHOOL AT A GLANCE

| | |
|---|---|
| Type of School | Private |
| Environment | City |
| Tuition | $19,200 |
| Enrollment | 1,676 |
| % Male/Female | 36/64 |
| Student/Faculty Ratio | 11:1 |

### FRESHMAN PROFILE

| | |
|---|---|
| Range SAT | |
| Critical Reading | 380-490 |
| Range SAT Math | 390-490 |
| Range ACT Composite | 15-20 |
| Average HS GPA | 2.79 |

### ON-CAMPUS APPOINTMENTS

| | |
|---|---|
| Advance Notice | No |
| Appointment | Preferred |
| Saturdays | Sometimes |
| Average Length | 30 min |
| Info Sessions | Yes |
| Class Visits | Yes |

### CAMPUS TOURS

| | |
|---|---|
| Appointment | Preferred |
| Dates | Year Round |
| Times | Wed 10:30 A.M. and 2:30 P.M.; |
| | Sat 10:30 A.M. |
| Average Length | Varies |

## CAMPUS AT ITS BEST!

Walking into Marina Dining Hall on the University of Bridgeport's campus the sense of history is palpable. The entrance arch once belonged to the estate of Phineas Taylor Barnum, who played a crucial role in the city's development. After enjoying a sumptuous meal, relax on the beach at nearby Seaside Park. When you've had enough sun, return to campus for the Mertens Contemporary Composers Festival. This annual event pays tribute to principal U.S. composers with lectures on and performances of their work.

## SCHOOL AT A GLANCE

| | |
|---|---|
| Type of School | Public |
| Environment | Town |
| In-state Tuition | $6,456 |
| Out-of-state Tuition | $19,656 |
| Enrollment | 15,709 |
| % Male/Female | 47/53 |
| Student/Faculty Ratio | 17:1 |

### FRESHMAN PROFILE

| | |
|---|---|
| Range SAT | |
| Critical Reading | 540-630 |
| Range SAT Math | 550-650 |
| Range ACT Composite | 23-27 |

### ON-CAMPUS APPOINTMENTS

| | |
|---|---|
| Advance Notice | Yes, 1 week |
| Appointment | Required |
| Saturdays | No |
| Average Length | 30 min |
| Info Sessions | Yes |
| Class Visits | Yes |

### CAMPUS TOURS

| | |
|---|---|
| Appointment | Required |
| Dates | Year Round |
| Times | Varies |
| Average Length | 120 min |

# UNIVERSITY OF CONNECTICUT

2131 Hillside Road, Unit 3088, Storrs, CT 06268-3088
**Telephone:** 860-486-3137 • **E-mail:** beahusky@uconn.edu • **Website:** www.uconn.edu
**Hours:** Monday–Friday, 8:00 A.M.–6:00 P.M.; Saturday–Sunday, 10:00 A.M.–4:00 P.M.

## STUDENTS SAY

"UConn's camaraderie is outstanding. I feel like I'm part of a big family."

## FODOR'S SAYS

"Scenic delights unfold on the narrow roads that wind through the Litchfield Hills in northwestern Connecticut, especially in the spring and autumn."

## ABOUT THE SCHOOL

The University of Connecticut offers more than 15,000 undergrad students a solid foundation based on research and challenging academics. UConn's amazing alumni network provides students with direct access to a variety of academic, internship, and career opportunities. With more than 100 majors and 300 clubs and activities on campus, UConn students have plenty of options both inside and outside of the classroom. Whatever their interests, the whole campus comes together to root for UConn's Division I Huskies.

## GETTING THERE

**BY AIR:** Bradley International Airport is the closest airport to the university and is about 25 miles away. Taxi, limousine, and shuttle service is available from the airport to the campus.

**BY TRAIN:** Amtrak trains provide service to Hartford, which is about 10 miles away from the university. Take a taxi to get to the campus.

**BY BUS:** Bonanza bus lines, Connecticut Transit, and Peter Pan bus lines all provide regular bus service near the university. Greyhound has limited service to the university. Take a taxi to get to the campus.

**BY CAR:** From the West: Take Interstate 84 East to Exit 68. After the exit, make a right onto Route 1-95. Drive for approximately seven miles and you will see the university ahead. From the East: Take Interstate 84 West to Exit 68. From the exit, make a left onto Route 1-95. Drive for approximately seven miles and you will see the university ahead. From the Southeast: Take Interstate 95 to 395 North. Take Exit 81 West to Route 32 North. Take Route 32 North to Willimantic. Turn right and go over the bridge. Continue straight through the light and follow 1-95 North for eight miles to campus.

**LOCAL:** The university's shuttle buses are free for visitor use. Buses operate when classes are in session during the week. For local taxi service, call Thread City Cab (860-456-2227) and Prime Cab (860-871-2255).

## WHERE TO STAY

The Nathan Hale Inn (860-427-7888, $$) is the university's on-campus hotel, which offers convenient lodging. The Best Western Regent Inn (860-423-8451, $$) and Still Waters Bed and Breakfast (860-429-9798, $$$) are other popular nearby choices.

## CAMPUS AT ITS BEST!

Take a respite from the arduous grind of college tours and treat yourself to a tasty treat at the UConn Dairy Bar. This popular campus hangout serves up ice cream in 24 tasty flavors—try the Jonathan Supreme, named after the school's mascot.

# UNIVERSITY OF DELAWARE

Admissions Office, 116 Hullihen Hall, Newark, DE 19716-6210
**Telephone:** 302-831-8123 • **E-mail:** admissions@udel.edu
**Website:** www.udel.edu • **Hours:** Monday–Friday, 8:00 A.M.–5:00 P.M.; Saturday, 9:00 A.M.–2:00 P.M.

## STUDENTS SAY

"University of Delaware has achieved the perfect balance between strong and challenging academic work and social events."

## FODOR'S SAYS

"Two nearby towns—Newark, home of the University of Delaware, and New Castle, the state's beautifully restored colonial capital—are linked to Wilmington by a few miles of neighborhoods and strip malls."

## ABOUT THE SCHOOL

A sense of engagement permeates students' academic experience at the University of Delaware. Despite the school's large enrollment, it manages to make students feel like part of a community that cares about them personally. Professors are extremely accessible and the school provides plentiful opportunities for undergraduate research. A strong study abroad program, an excellent Honors College, and tons of extracurricular activities means that UD students always have something to look forward to, both in and outside of the classroom.

## GETTING THERE

**BY AIR:** Philadelphia International Airport is 50 minutes North of the campus, and Baltimore Washington International Airport is one hour South of the campus. Ground transportation to and from the airport is provided by The Delaware Express (800-648-5466) and SuperShuttle (888-258-3826).

**BY TRAIN:** Amtrak trains stop in Wilmington. From the Wilmington train station, it is a 45-minute express bus ride to campus via the #6 DART bus. Limited Amtrak and regional rail service (SEPTA) is available to the Newark train station.

**BY BUS:** Greyhound buses travel to Wilmington. From the Wilmington train station, it is a 45-minute express bus ride to campus via the #6 DART bus. Limited Amtrak and regional rail service (SEPTA) is available to the Newark train station.

**BY CAR:** From the North: Take I-95 South to Delaware Exit 1-B. It's the exit for Route 896 North and becomes South College Avenue at the intersection of Route 4. Go straight about two miles on South College Avenue and the college will be seen. From the South: Take I-95 North to Delaware Exit 1 for Route 896 North. From there, proceed according to "From the North" directions above. From the West: Take the Pennsylvania Turnpike East to Route 283 South, which turns into Route 30 East, to Route 896 South. Turn left onto Delaware Avenue and right at the second traffic light onto South College Avenue. You will see the college shortly.

**LOCAL:** The DART, Delaware's public transit provider, can get you around the area. SEPTA trains can get you from the Philadelphia airport to Newark. For local taxi service, call City Cab (302-368-8294).

## WHERE TO STAY

If you're planning on staying awhile, some nearby hotels include Sleep Inn (302-453-1700, $$), Courtyard by Marriott (302-737-0900, $$), and Embassy Suites Hotel (302-368-8000, $$).

### SCHOOL AT A GLANCE

| | |
|---|---|
| Type of School | Public |
| Environment | Town |
| In-state Tuition | $6,980 |
| Out-of-state Tuition | $17,690 |
| Enrollment | 15,742 |
| % Male/Female | 42/58 |
| Student/Faculty Ratio | 14:1 |

### FRESHMAN PROFILE

| | |
|---|---|
| Range SAT | |
| Critical Reading | 550-640 |
| Range SAT Math | 560-660 |
| Range ACT Composite | 26-32 |
| Average HS GPA | 3.6 |

### ON-CAMPUS APPOINTMENTS

| | |
|---|---|
| Advance Notice | Yes, 3 weeks |
| Appointment | Required |
| Saturdays | No |
| Average Length | 30 min |
| Info Sessions | Yes |
| Class Visits | Yes |

### CAMPUS TOURS

| | |
|---|---|
| Appointment | Recommended |
| Dates | Year Round |
| Times | M–F 10:00 A.M., NOON, 2:00 P.M.; Sat 10:00 A.M., NOON |
| Average Length | 90 min |

## CAMPUS AT ITS BEST!

Delaware's Fred Rust Ice Arena is home to the Ice Skating Development Center. Stop by and hone your skating techniques; you just might leave with the ability to perform a triple sau cow. After all that exercise, relax with a meal at Vita Nova, a gourmet restaurant operated by students in the Department of Hotel, Restaurant, and Institutional Management. Reservations are recommended. Conclude your evening by catching some of today's best comedians perform at the Coffeehouse Series. Past comics have included Aziz Ansari and Kyle Grooms.

# UNIVERSITY OF MAINE

5713 Chadbourne Hall, Orono, ME 04469-5713

**Telephone:** 207-581-1561 • **E-mail:** um-admit@maine.edu

**Website:** www.umaine.edu • **Hours:** Monday–Friday, 8:00 A.M.–4:30 P.M.

## STUDENTS SAY

"Life is great here. There is so much to do that sometimes you have a difficult time choosing what to try."

## FODOR'S SAYS

"Moosehead Lake, Maine's largest, has rustic camps, restaurants, guides, and outfitters. Its 420 miles of shorefront are virtually uninhabited and in most places accessible only by floatplane or boat."

## ABOUT THE SCHOOL

University of Maine, to the benefit of its students, is much smaller than most flagship public universities. Undergrads don't have to worry about anonymity: They receive ample personal attention from professors and administrators. While students wish there was more ethnic diversity on campus, they maintain a wide variety of interests and activities. Whether it be supporting Black Bear hockey, rushing a fraternity/sorority, or hiking the trails near campus, there is something for everyone.

## GETTING THERE

**BY AIR:** Visitors can fly into Bangor International Airport, a relatively short trip from Orono. Nonstop flights are available from Boston, New York (La Guardia), Newark, Atlanta, Philadelphia, Cincinnati, Detroit, and Minneapolis (seasonal). There are a variety of transportation options available at the airport.

**BY TRAIN:** Amtrak provides service to Portland.

**BY BUS:** Greyhound provides limited service to Orono. Alternatively, visitors can take either Greyhound or Concord Trailways to Bangor. You will need to call a taxi to reach the campus.

**BY CAR:** From the South Exit 191 (formerly Exit 50): Coming from the South on I-95, take Kelley Road Exit 191 (formerly Exit 50). Make a right at end of the exit ramp. You'll drive one mile until you reach a red flashing light. Take a left onto Route 2, driving 2.5 miles to the third set of traffic lights. Make a left onto College Avenue. Turn right at the University of Maine sign. From the South Exit 193 (formerly Exit 51): Coming from the South on I-95, take Stillwater Avenue Exit 193 (formerly Exit 51). Turn toward Burger King and the shopping center. Make a right at the fourth traffic light by McDonald's and KFC. This is College Avenue. Take the third left onto Munson Road at the first University of Maine sign. From the North Exit 193 (formerly Exit 51): Coming from the North on I-95, take Stillwater Avenue Exit 193 (formerly Exit 51). Turn left at the end of the exit ramp. Drive one mile to the fourth set of traffic lights. Turn right onto College Avenue. Take the third left onto Munson Road at the first University of Maine sign.

**LOCAL:** For local taxi service call Old Town Taxi at 207-827-8800.

## WHERE TO STAY

When making hotel reservations for Orono consider the University Inn Academic Suites (207-866-4921, $), Best Western Black Bear Inn & Conference Center (207-866-7120, $), and Milford Motel on the River (800-282-3330, $).

## CAMPUS AT ITS BEST!

Adjacent to the Maine Center for the Arts guests will find the Rose Garden. Providing a wonderful counterpoint to the bustle of university life, visitors enjoy sculptures and flora alike. The garden is an especially popular stop when students are going to and from a performance. Of course, UM students don't just spend their time meditating in nature. For example, every Monday is game night, featuring scrabble tournaments and madcap games of Cranium. Fridays and Saturday bring the Maine Attraction, high-energy entertainment, including chainsaw jugglers, semi-formals and drive-in movies.

# UNIVERSITY OF MARYLAND— BALTIMORE COUNTY

1000 Hilltop Circle, Baltimore, MD 21250
**Telephone:** 410-455-2291 • **E-mail:** admissions@umbc.edu

## STUDENTS SAY

"The students at University of Maryland—Baltimore County are very motivated and caring individuals. We all understand the concept of hard work and integrity.'

## FODOR'S SAYS

"[At the] Contemporary Museum, new works are created expressly for the museum by artists invited from all over the world to work in residence here. The pieces must be created in collaboration with a local community or institution and be relevant to the city in some way."

## ABOUT THE SCHOOL

UMBC's strength lies within its stellar science and engineering programs. Students also applaud the university's emphasis on research, which presents tremendous academic opportunities for undergraduates. Commonly regarded as a commuter school, a growing number of students are starting to live on campus, bolstering the sense of community. There's also been a push to augment social options though many undergrads head into Baltimore or Washington, DC on the weekends.

## GETTING THERE

**BY AIR:** Baltimore-Washington Airport is a mere five minutes from campus. Guests can easily take a cab to campus.

**BY TRAIN:** Amtrak and MARC commuter trains provide service to BWI Rail Station. Take a taxi to get to campus.

**BY BUS:** Greyhound provides service into Baltimore. Take a taxi to get to campus.

**BY CAR:** From the North: Follow Interstate 95 to Route 166 (Exit 47B, Catonsville). You can also take Interstate 83 to the Baltimore Beltway (I-695, west), exiting at 12C (Wilkens Avenue, west). Follow the signs to UMBC. From the South: Proceed on Interstate 95 to Route 166 (Exit 47B, Catonsville). Follow signs to UMBC.

**LOCAL:** Baltimore has local light rail, metro, and bus transportation options which make traveling around the city easy and efficient.

## WHERE TO STAY

Among Baltimore's many lodging options are: Four Points by Sheraton—BWI Airport (410-859-3300, $$), Holiday Inn—BWI (410-694-6024, $$) or Baltimore Marriott—Inner Harbor (410-962-0202, $$$+).

| SCHOOL AT A GLANCE | |
| --- | --- |
| Type of School | Public |
| Environment | Metropolis |
| In-state Tuition | $6,484 |
| Out-of-state Tuition | $15,216 |
| Enrollment | 9,244 |
| % Male/Female | 54/46 |
| Student/Faculty Ratio | 17:1 |

| FRESHMAN PROFILE | |
| --- | --- |
| Range SAT | |
| Critical Reading | 540-650 |
| Range SAT Math | 570-670 |
| Range ACT Composite | 23-27 |
| Average HS GPA | 3.5 |

| ON-CAMPUS APPOINTMENTS | |
| --- | --- |
| Advance Notice | Yes, 1 week |
| Appointment | Not Required |
| Saturdays | No |
| Average Length | 30 min |
| Info Sessions | Yes |
| Class Visits | Yes |

| CAMPUS TOURS | |
| --- | --- |
| Appointment | Preferred |
| Dates | Year Round |
| Times | Varies |
| Average Length | 60 min |

## CAMPUS AT ITS BEST!

The Library Gallery presents engaging exhibitions throughout the year, showcasing its photography and rare books collections. Lectures, tours and publications all supplement the exhibits. The UMBC Theatre is another fabulous facility on campus. Think about seeing a performance by the Phoenix Dance Company, a professional modern dance ensemble in residence.

# UNIVERSITY OF MARYLAND— COLLEGE PARK

Mitchell Building, College Park, MD 20742-5235

**Telephone:** 301-314-8385 • **E-mail:** um-admit@uga.umd.edu

**Website:** www.umd.edu • **Hours:** Monday–Friday, 8:00 A.M.–5:00 P.M.; Saturday, 9:00 A.M.–3:00 P.M.

## STUDENTS SAY

"University of Maryland—College Park is an incredible mix of anything you could ever want—it has more people, types of people, sports, clubs, and nearby entertainment than you could ever want."

## FODOR'S SAYS

"The Wright Brothers once trained military officers to fly at College Park Airport, the world's oldest continuously operating airport, which is now affiliated with the Smithsonian Institution. The College Park Aviation Museum is a tribute to the Wright Brothers and early aviation memorabilia."

## ABOUT THE SCHOOL

The University of Maryland—College Park has it all: a beautiful campus, a diverse student body, great athletics, amazing classes, and tons of activities to get involved in. The state's flagship institution has the kind of academic reputation that you'd like to see on a resume, with particularly strong programs in engineering and business. With over 24,000 undergraduates on campus, it's easy to feel like a number, but industrious students are able to distinguish themselves from the masses by taking advantage of the university's top-notch resources and amazing research opportunities.

## GETTING THERE

**BY AIR:** The University of Maryland is served by three major airports: Reagan Washington National, Baltimore-Washington International, and Washington Dulles. Public transit, Super Shuttle (703-416-7873), and taxi service are convenient options for transport to campus.

**BY TRAIN:** Amtrak stops in Union Station and New Carrollton. Take the Washington Metrorail or a taxi to get to campus.

**BY BUS:** Greyhound and Peter Pan buses stop near Union Station. Take the Washington Metrorail or a taxi to get to campus.

**BY CAR:** From the North (via I-95): Take I-95 South to the Capital Beltway (I-495). Get off at Exit 27 and follow signs to Exit 25 (U.S. Route 1 South). Head approximately two miles on U.S. Route 1 South and follow signs for the university. From the North and South (via I-295): Take 295 (the Baltimore/Washington Parkway) to the Capital Beltway (I-95/I-495). Get off at I-95/I-495 North. Take Exit 23 and go South on 201. Make a right onto Paint Branch Parkway. Go approximately two miles to U.S. Route 1. Make a left onto US Route 1 and follow signs for the university. From the East: Take U.S. 50 West to the Capital Beltway (I-495). Head North on I-95/I-495. Take Exit 23 and follow "From the North and South" directions above.

**LOCAL:** Shuttle-UM buses serve a six-mile radius of campus. The MARC commuter trains, a part of the Maryland Transit Administration, and the Washington Metrorail subway, can get you around Maryland, Washington DC, and to and from local airports. If you'd rather take a taxi to get around the area, some local companies include Greenbelt Taxi Service (301-441-8400) and Bob's Cab Co. (301-864-7700).

## WHERE TO STAY

If you plan on spending the night, some local hotel accommodations include the Marriott's UMUC Inn and Conference Center (301-985-7300, $$) on campus, the nearby Comfort Inn (301-441-8110, $$), and the Howard Johnson Express Inn (301-513-0002, $).

## CAMPUS AT ITS BEST!

Perhaps the best introduction to the University of Maryland, College Park is to simply spend some time at the Stamp Student Union. Inside are a variety of art and entertainment venues which host numerous events. For example, stop by the Union Gallery for the Wednesday Walk and Talk. This quick 20-minute tour presents a casual forum for discussing and viewing artwork currently on display. If you're looking for something more recreational, the TerpZone offers bowling, billiards, arcade games, and a television lounge. It also sponsors tournaments every Sunday.

# UNIVERSITY OF MASSACHUSETTS— AMHERST

University Admissions Center, 37 Mather Dr., Amherst, MA 01003-9291
**Telephone:** 413-545-0222 • **Hours:** Monday–Friday, 8:30 A.M.–5:00 P.M.

## STUDENTS SAY

"I would say the many opportunities that students have is the best part of the school. You can honestly do anything here from classes to clubs to a semester abroad. There really are no limits."

## FODOR'S SAYS

"Founded in 1980 by a student on a mission to rescue Yiddish books from basements and Dumpsters, the National Yiddish Book Center has become a major force in the effort to preserve the Yiddish language and Jewish culture."

## ABOUT THE SCHOOL

As a relatively large university, UMass offers a melting pot of people and ideas. While students sometimes complain about large class sizes, they often highlight the diverse range of studies available and access to the Five College Consortium. Socially, UMass is anything but dull. The parties are extremely popular on campus, and students often head into Amherst and nearby Northampton to eat, shop, or catch a concert.

## GETTING THERE

**BY AIR:** There are several airports within a reasonable distance from Amherst. Visitors can fly into Boston's Logan International Airport, Hartford's Bradley International Airport, Manchester Airport in New Hampshire, or T. F. Green International Airport in Providence, Rhode Island. For shuttle service to Amherst from Bradley, Logan, and Providence airports call Valley Transporter (413-253-1350) or Murphy Sedan Service (413-259-2055).

**BY TRAIN:** The Amherst Amtrak station provides limited service, with one Northbound and one Southbound train a day: the Vermonter. This line runs between Washington, DC, and St. Albans, Vermont, with stops in New York City and other points. Additionally, visitors can use the Springfield Amtrak station, also a stop for the Vermonter, for regional train service. The Valley Transporter will provide shuttle service from Springfield to Amherst.

**BY BUS:** Both Peter Pan and Greyhound bus lines stop in Amherst. Additionally, the Pioneer Valley Transit Authority (PVTA) offers service throughout the region. The system is free to Five College students and employees.

**BY CAR:** From the South (Via I-91 North, Exit 19 in Northampton): From the exit ramp, make a right onto Route 9 and go approximately 4.5 miles to Route 116 North (you'll turn left at the lights). The UMass Exit will be one mile down. From the North (Via I-91 North, Exit 24 in Deerfield): Drivers will come to a stop sign at the top of the ramp. You'll need to turn right onto Routes 5 and 10, and immediately turn right again at the traffic lights onto Route 116 South. Continue eight miles to the UMass Exit. From the North (Via I-91 South, Exit 25 in Deerfield): At the end of the ramp turn left and follow the road to the intersection. Turn right onto Routes 5 and 10 South. Go one mile, and turn left onto Route 116 South. Continue eight miles to the UMass Exit. From the South (Via I-93 South): Follow I-93 to I-495 South. You'll then take I-495 South to Route 2 West. Continue on Route 2 until you hit Exit 16 (Belchertown/Amherst). Take Route 202 for roughly 15 miles to the blinking light at Route 9 and 116 Amherst Exit (Pelham). Turn right and drive for seven miles to the center of Amherst. Once you hit town, simply follow the signs to UMass. From the East or West via I-90 (Massachusetts Turnpike): Take Route 32 South to Palmer and Route 20 West to Route 181 North into Belchertown. Finally, continue on Route 9 West to Amherst. Follow the signs to UMass.

**LOCAL:** The University of Massachusetts Transit System teams up with the Pioneer Valley Transit Authority to provide easy transportation among Amherst's Five College area and nearby towns. Valley Transporter (413-253-1350) offers rides to and from regional airports and train stations. For cabs, call Celebrity Cab Company (413-253-7330) or Red Cab (413-253-3333).

## WHERE TO STAY

Given the number of schools in the area, visitors can count on plenty of hotel options, including University Motor Lodge (413-256-8111, $), the Lord Jeffery Inn (413-253-2576, $–$$$), and Allen House Victorian Inn (413-253-5000, $–$$).

## CAMPUS AT ITS BEST!

The Distinguished Visitors Program consistently brings a range of captivating lecturers to campus. Past speakers have included Henry Rollins, Nadine Strossen, Allen Ginsberg, and Kurt Vonnegut. Another great event is the annual Massachusetts Multicultural Film Festival. Free screenings are held on the various Five Colleges campuses. Hometown Amherst also provides a number of attractions. Visitors might enjoy touring the Eric Carle Museum of Picture Book Art or the National Yiddish Book Center.

# UNIVERSITY OF MASSACHUSETTS— BOSTON

100 Morrissey Boulevard, Boston, MA 02125-3393
**Telephone:** 617-287-6100 • **E-mail:** undergrad@umb.edu

## STUDENTS SAY

"The professors are among the best in the country, unusually dedicated to their fields and their students, and they are incredibly energetic."

## FODOR'S SAYS

"New England's largest and most important city—Boston—was the cradle of American independence. The city's most famous buildings are not merely civic landmarks but national icons, and its local heroes are known to the nation: John and Samuel Adams, Paul Revere, John Hancock, and many more who live at the crossroads of history and myth."

## ABOUT THE SCHOOL

UMass—Boston was established to provide a stellar education to the citizens of the greater Boston area at a modest price. The university boasts more than 100 majors for students to choose from, along with phenomenal resources (including the John F. Kennedy Library). Additionally, UMass—Boston is one of the most ethnically schools diverse in New England, providing many cultural exchanges both within and outside the classroom.

## GETTING THERE

**BY AIR:** Visitors should fly into Boston's Logan Airport. Taxis and shuttle service into the city are easily accessible.

**BY TRAIN:** Visitors can take Amtrak into South Station or local commuter rails to the JFK/UMass station on the Middleboro and Plymouth lines.

**BY BUS:** Greyhound, Peter Pan, Bonanza and Concord Trailways all provide service to Boston's South Station. Taxis, subways and local buses are all accessible from the station.

**BY CAR:** From the North: Proceed on Interstate 93 South through Boston, taking Exit 15 (JFK Library/South Boston/Dorchester) and follow the UMass—Boston signs along Columbia Road and Morrissey Boulevard to the campus. From the South: Follow Interstate 93 North to Exit 14 (JFK Library/Morrissey Boulevard). Proceed to Morrissey Boulevard North and from there to the campus. From the West: Follow the Massachusetts Turnpike (Interstate 90) East to Interstate 93. Continue on I-93 South for one mile, taking Exit 15 (JFK Library/South Boston/Dorchester). Follow the UMass—Boston signs along Columbia Road and Morrissey Boulevard to the campus.

**LOCAL:** For local subway service take the Red Line to JFK/UMass Station. A free shuttle bus will carry you to the campus. For local bus service take the number 8 to Kenmore Square or the number 16 to Forest Hills (rush hour only).

## WHERE TO STAY

Boston has numerous hotels to meet a variety of needs and budgets. These hotel options are all in downtown Boston Chandler Inn Hotel (617-482-3450, $$), Howard Johnson Inn (617-267-8300, $-$$$), and the Copley Square Hotel (617-536-9000, $$-$$$).

## CAMPUS AT ITS BEST!

Guests should take a moment to peruse Arts on the Point, a public sculpture park on UMass—Boston's campus. This phenomenal venue is a great space in which to view contemporary sculpture. In the fall, the campus comes alive with an annual party known as Fest-of-Us, which includes a big barbecue and games and music galore.

# UNIVERSITY OF NEW HAMPSHIRE

4 Garrison Avenue, Durham, NH 03824
**Telephone:** 603-862-1360 • **E-mail:** admissions@unh.edu
**Hours:** Monday–Friday, 8:00 A.M.–4:30 P.M.

## STUDENTS SAY

"People are insanely nice here; it is rare if someone doesn't go out of their way to hold the door open for you."

## FODOR'S SAYS

"The art gallery at UNH occasionally exhibits items from a permanent collection of about 1,100 pieces but generally uses the space to host traveling exhibits. Noted items in the collection include nineteenth-century Japanese wood-block prints and American landscape paintings."

## ABOUT THE SCHOOL

At University of New Hampshire, a great education is yours for the taking. The school has many excellent programs, including nursing, nutrition, business, and marine biology. Opportunities for individual projects and research grants are plentiful. UNH has an active social scene and parties can be found throughout the week.

## GETTING THERE

**BY AIR:** Guests may fly into Logan International Airport (roughly 60 miles from campus), Portland International Jetport (roughly 50 miles from campus), or Manchester Airport (roughly 50 miles from campus). Taxi and shuttle service are available from all three airports.

**BY TRAIN:** Amtrak's Downeaster line provides direct service to Durham. The train leaves from Boston and arrives in the heart of campus on Main Street.

**BY BUS:** Greyhound's Vermont Transit line makes stops in downtown Portsmouth. C&J Trailways makes stops in Denver. From both locations, visitors can take Wildcat Transit to Durham.

**BY CAR:** From I-95 South (Maine): Take Exit 5 (in NH) to the Spaulding Turnpike (Route 16N). Next, take Exit 6 West (Route 4 West) toward Durham to the exit for Route 155A. Follow directions to the Visitor Information Center. From I-95 North (MA): Take Exit 4 (in NH left-hand exit) to the Spaulding Turnpike (Route 16 North). Follow the "From I-95 South" directions above. From the West: Take Route 101 East to Exit 7 (Route 125 North). Proceed on Route 125 North to the traffic circle. Get on Route 4 East and take it to the Durham Exit (Route 155A). Follow directions to the Visitor Information Center. From Route 4 West: Take the exit for Route 155A. Make a left at the bottom of the ramp. Drive down Main Street for roughly three quarters of a mile. Take the second left on to Loop Road. When you reach the end of the street make a right. The Visitor Information Center is the second building on your left (white with green trim). From Route 4 East: Take the exit for Route 155A. When you reach the bottom of the ramp take a right. Drive down Main Street for roughly three quarters of a mile. Take the second left on to Loop Road. When you reach the end of the street make a right. The Visitor Information Center is the second building on your left (white with green trim).

**LOCAL:** UNH operates Wildcat Transit, which runs campus connector and public transit routes between Dover, Newington, Newmarket, and Portsmouth. For shuttle service from Logan and Manchester visitors can call Mermaid Transportation (207-885-5630) or C&J Trailways (800-258-7111).

## WHERE TO STAY

Possible hotel choices include the Hickory Pond Inn (603-659-2227, $–$$), Holiday Inn Express (603-868-1234, $$), or the Three Chimneys Inn (603-399-9777, $$–$$$).

---

## CAMPUS AT ITS BEST!

UNH is a hockey powerhouse, and when the season rolls around it's a safe assumption that the games will be packed. Stop by the Whittemore Center Ice Arena and see the Wildcats in action. Visitors who are avid outdoors people will be happy to know that the White Mountains are only an hour away from campus. Prospective students who enjoy some sun and sand will want to spend some time at nearby Hampton Beach.

# UNIVERSITY OF PENNSYLVANIA

1 College Hall, Philadelphia, PA 19104

**Telephone:** 215-898-7507 • **E-mail:** info@admissions.ugao.upenn.edu

**Website:** www.upenn.edu • **Hours:** Monday–Friday, 9:00 A.M.–5:00 P.M.; Saturday, 10:00 A.M.–2:00 P.M.

## SCHOOL AT A GLANCE

| | |
|---|---|
| Type of School | Private |
| Environment | Metropolis |
| Tuition | $29,030 |
| Enrollment | 9,841 |
| % Male/Female | 50/50 |
| Student/Faculty Ratio | 6:1 |

### FRESHMAN PROFILE

| | |
|---|---|
| Range SAT | |
| Critical Reading | 660-750 |
| Range SAT Math | 680-770 |
| Range ACT Composite | 28-33 |
| Average HS GPA | 3.83 |

### ON-CAMPUS APPOINTMENTS

| | |
|---|---|
| Info Sessions | Yes |
| Class Visits | Yes |

### CAMPUS TOURS

| | |
|---|---|
| Appointment | Not Required |
| Dates | Year Round |
| Times | Varies |
| Average Length | Varies |

## STUDENTS SAY

"The school is academically rigorous, and the high standards set by both the faculty and one's peers really push the students to learn, achieve, and do their best."

## FODOR'S SAYS

"The Rosenbach Museum and Library offers a 75-minute tour of its sumptuous painting, rare books (including the original manuscript of James Joyce's *Ulysses*), and *objets d'art*."

## ABOUT THE SCHOOL

The University of Pennsylvania, an Ivy League school known for its career-minded students, offers strong academic programs in many areas, particularly business. Its Wharton School of Business is world-renowned and considered by many to be the top undergraduate business program in the country. Though students at Penn put a lot of time and effort into their studies, they manage to find time on the weekend to unwind at on-campus events or in nearby Philadelphia.

## GETTING THERE

**BY AIR:** The Philadelphia International Airport is about 20 minutes from the university. Visitors can use the SEPTA or taxi to get to the campus.

**BY TRAIN:** Amtrak provides service to Philadelphia's 30th Street Station. Take a taxi to get to the campus.

**BY BUS:** Greyhound and Trailway bus lines provide service to Philadelphia. From there, you can reach the campus via the SEPTA or taxi.

**BY CAR:** From the Northeast: Take the New Jersey Turnpike South to Exit 4. Head right out of the toll, following signs for Philadelphia and Ben Franklin Bridge. After crossing the bridge take I-676 West to I-76 East, the Schuylkill Expressway. Take I-76 East to Exit 346-A, South Street and make a right onto South Street to enter the college. From the West: Take the Pennsylvania Turnpike to Exit 326, the Valley Forge Interchange. Follow I-76 East for about 17 miles to Exit 346-A, South Street. Make a right onto South Street to enter the college. From the North: Take I-95 South to the I-676/Center City Philadelphia Exit. Follow signs to I-676 West, the Vine Street Expressway. Take I-676 West to I-76 East, the Schuylkill Expressway. Take I-76 East to Exit 346-A, South Street and make a right onto South Street to enter the college. From the South: Take I-95 North to the I-676/Center City Philadelphia Exit which is about 7 miles North of the airport. Take I-676 West, the Vine Street Expressway, to I-76 East, the Schuylkill Expressway. Take I-76 East to Exit 346-A, South Street and make a right onto South Street to enter the college.

**LOCAL:** The SEPTA provides local bus, subway, train, and trolley service. If you'd rather take a taxi around town, there are local companies like Liberty Cab Co. (215-389-8000) and City Cab Co. Inc. (215-492-6500).

## WHERE TO STAY

If you're planning on staying overnight, some popular nearby hotels include the Sheraton-University City Hotel (215-387-8000, $$), The Hilton Inn at Penn (215-222-0200, $$$), and the Comfort Inn Downtown Philadelphia (1-877-424-6423, $$$).

## CAMPUS AT ITS BEST!

Aspiring anthropologists and archeologists will surely want to visit Penn's University Museum. The first anthropological museum on the campus of any American university, its collection is rich in Greek, African, Pacific, and South American artifacts. Those who happen to tour Penn on Halloween will want to saunter over to Irvine Auditorium afterward. The location for many concerts, films, and speaking engagements, Irvine annually screens a silent version of *The Phantom of the Opera*, complete with organ accompaniment.

# UNIVERSITY OF PITTSBURGH— PITTSBURGH CAMPUS

4227 Fifth Avenue, First Floor Alumni Hall, Pittsburgh, PA 15260
**Telephone:** 412-624-7488 • **E-mail:** oafa@pitt.edu
**Website:** www.pitt.edu • **Hours:** Monday–Friday, 8:30 A.M.–5:00 P.M.

## STUDENTS SAY

"The strength of the school in general has to be the opportunities for cross-cultural learning."

## FODOR'S SAYS

"The Andy Warhol Museum devotes seven floors to the work of the native Pittsburgher and pop art icon."

## ABOUT THE SCHOOL

The University of Pittsburgh, a large, public university with top programs in the sciences, offers students a wide range of courses, fantastic facilities, and a location that every student loves. Students who choose to take advantage of the ample opportunities available at the university will enjoy excellent academics, plentiful internships, not to mention great shows at nearby Carnegie Museum. And with 300 student organizations on campus, there's no shortage of stuff to do outside of class.

## GETTING THERE

**BY AIR:** Pittsburgh International Airport is the closest airport to campus. Take a taxi to get to the campus.

**BY TRAIN:** Amtrak trains stop in Pittsburgh. Take a taxi to get to the campus.

**BY BUS:** Greyhound buses stop in Pittsburgh. The Pittsburgh campus can be reached by local buses or by taxi service.

**BY CAR:** From the East: Take the Pennsylvania Turnpike (I-76) to Exit 57. Get onto I-376 West. From I-376 Parkway East, take Exit 3B onto Bates Street. Follow Bates to Bouquet Street. Make a left onto Bouquet, then turn right onto Forbes Avenue and you will see the university. From the West: Take the Pennsylvania Turnpike (I-76) to Cranberry Exit 28 and take I-79 South to I-279 South. Take I-279 to the Veteran's Bridge Exit, then get onto I-579 South. Follow I-579 to the Oakland/Monroeville Exit, and then get onto the Boulevard of the Allies. Follow the Boulevard of the Allies to the Forbes Avenue Exit on your right. Forbes Avenue then leads right into the campus. From the North: Take I-79 South to I-279 South. From there, proceed according to "From the West" directions above. From the South, including the Pittsburgh Airport: Take I-79 North to the exit for I-279 North. Take I-279 to the I-376 Monroeville Exit. Take I-376 to the Forbes Avenue-Oakland Exit. Forbes Avenue will lead you to the campus.

**LOCAL:** Port Authority of Allegheny County operates the mass transit system serving Pittsburgh, including the university. If you'd rather take a taxi to get around, some local companies include Yellow Cab (412-665-8100), Checker Cab (412-664-5600), and People's Cab (412-441-3200).

## WHERE TO STAY

If you're planning on spending the night, some nearby hotel accommodations include Hampton Inn (412-681-1000, $$), The Holiday Inn (412-682-6200, $$), and Wyndham Garden Hotel (412-683-2040, $$).

| SCHOOL AT A GLANCE | |
| --- | --- |
| Type of School | Public |
| Environment | City |
| In-state Tuition | $11,368 |
| Out-of-state Tuition | $20,686 |
| Enrollment | 16,585 |
| % Male/Female | 48/52 |
| Student/Faculty Ratio | 16:1 |

| FRESHMAN PROFILE | |
| --- | --- |
| Range SAT | |
| Critical Reading | 560-660 |
| Range SAT Math | 570-670 |
| Range ACT Composite | 24-29 |

| ON-CAMPUS APPOINTMENTS | |
| --- | --- |
| Advance Notice | Yes, other |
| Appointment | Preferred |
| Saturdays | No |
| Average Length | 60 min |
| Info Sessions | Yes |
| Class Visits | Yes |

| CAMPUS TOURS | |
| --- | --- |
| Appointment | Not Required |
| Dates | Year Round |
| Times | Varies |
| Average Length | Varies |

## CAMPUS AT ITS BEST!

Don't have a passport? Pitt's Nationality Classrooms are a great proxy for international travel. From Italy to India, the 26 classrooms allow you to explore the heritage of each particular nation. Following your cultural exchange, take a leisurely walk down Forbes Avenue. This street, running through the heart of campus, offers a number of shops, restaurants, and museums. Pittsburgh itself provides a great deal of entertainment. Those visiting during the summer might try their hand at strawberry picking or catch a movie at one of the area's drive-ins.

# UNIVERSITY OF RHODE ISLAND

Undergraduate Admissions Office, 14 Upper College Road, Kingston, RI 02881

**Telephone:** 401-874-7100 • **E-mail:** uriadmit@etal.uri.edu

**Hours:** Monday–Friday, 8:30 A.M.–4:30 P.M.

## STUDENTS SAY

"There are always opportunities to get involved and meet new people; it's just a matter of taking those opportunities and making the most of the time you've got at school."

## FODOR'S SAYS

"Packed with American history, Rhode Island holds 20 [percent] of the country's national Historic Landmarks and has more restored Colonial and Victorian buildings than anywhere else in the United States."

## ABOUT THE SCHOOL

URI offers a comprehensive academic experience. There is a diverse course selection, and popular majors including nursing, communications, psychology, pharmacy, and human development and family studies. Students laud professors' knowledge and experience. Approximately 50 percent of the students are from Rhode Island. With more than 90 student organizations on campus, students have plenty opportunities for fun. When they want to head off campus for entertainment, nearby Newport and Providence beckon.

## GETTING THERE

**BY AIR:** T. F. Green Airport is located approximately 20 miles away from campus. Car rentals, taxis, and buses are available for transportation to and from the airport.

**BY TRAIN:** Visitors can take Amtrak directly to Kingston. The station is roughly two miles away from URI.

**BY BUS:** Bonanza Bus Lines provides direct service to Kingston.

**BY CAR:** From the North: Take I-95 South to Exit 9 (Route 4 South) in Rhode Island. Follow Route 4 to Route 1 South. Stay on Route 1 until the intersection of Route 138 West. Route 138 West takes you directly to the university. From the South: Take I-95 North to Exit 3A (Route 138 East). Continue East on Route 138 to the university. From Newport: Follow Route 138 West over the Newport and Jamestown bridges to Route 1. Take Route 1 South to Route 138 West. Follow Route 138 West to the university.

**LOCAL:** Bus service to URI's Kingston campus is available on Rhode Island Public Transit Authority (RIPTA) Route 66 connecting URI to Providence. Call 401-781-9400 for route and schedule info.

## WHERE TO STAY

There are quaint and affordable accommodations close to South Kingstown, including Almost Heaven B&B (401-783-9272, $), Admiral Dewey Inn (401-783-2090, $–$$), and Eden Manor B&B (401-792-8234, $$–$$$).

## CAMPUS AT ITS BEST!

URI's remarkable facilities definitely enhance the overall learning experience. Fogarty Hall, home to the College of Pharmacy, maintains professional practice laboratories, including a model CVS. It also houses the Rhode Island State Crime Laboratory, used by the state's law enforcement community. Follow up your tour with a show at URI's Great Performances Series. Past performances have run the gamut, from music and dance of the Andes, to the famed comedy troupe Chicago City Limits.

# UNIVERSITY OF ROCHESTER

300 Wilson Boulevard, PO Box 270251, Rochester, NY 14627-0251
**Telephone:** 585-275-3221 • **E-mail:** admit@admissions.rochester.edu
**Website:** www.rochester.edu • **Hours:** Monday–Friday, 9:00 A.M.–4:00 A.M.

## STUDENTS SAY

"During the day, studies reign supreme. At night, social life does. You will have friends from all walks of life."

## FODOR'S SAYS

"More than 5,000 years of art is contained within the 14 exhibit rooms of the Memorial Art Gallery of the University of Rochester. Egyptian coffins, medieval tapestries, impressionist paintings, European masters, and African carvings are on permanent display."

## ABOUT THE SCHOOL

Rochester offers an unbeatable combination of small-school intimacy and large-university resources. The school is a math and science powerhouse, though students applaud the overall academic experience as well. Administrators are quick to respond to undergrads' needs and are frequently seen around campus. While quite studious during the week, students definitely relax on the weekend, often celebrating on the fraternity quad. During the long winter months, many choose to stay indoors and take advantage of dorm life.

| SCHOOL AT A GLANCE | |
| --- | --- |
| Type of School | Private |
| Environment | Village |
| Tuition | $30,540 |
| Enrollment | 4,532 |
| % Male/Female | 51/49 |

| FRESHMAN PROFILE | |
| --- | --- |
| Range SAT | |
| Critical Reading | 610–710 |
| Range SAT Math | 640–710 |
| Range ACT Composite | 26–30 |

| ON-CAMPUS APPOINTMENTS | |
| --- | --- |
| Class Visits | Yes |

| CAMPUS TOURS | |
| --- | --- |
| Appointment | Required |
| Dates | Year-Round |
| Times | M–F; call Admissions |
| | for times |
| Average Length | 1 hour |

## GETTING THERE

**BY AIR:** Visitors can opt to fly into the Greater Rochester International. Car rentals, taxis, shuttles, and limousines are all available for transportation to and from the airport.

**BY TRAIN:** Amtrak provides service to Rochester. Taxis are available at the station.

**BY BUS:** Both Greyhound and Trailways bus lines serve Rochester. Taxis are available at the station.

**BY CAR:** From the East: Take the New York State Thruway (I-90) to Exit 46. From here take I-390 North to Exit 16 (West Henrietta Road). Cross West Henrietta to East River Road. Turn right onto Kendrick Road and make another right onto Elmwood Avenue. Bear left onto Elmwood Avenue. Make the next right onto Wilson Boulevard. The campus is ahead. From the West: Take the New York State Thruway (I-90) to Exit 47. From there follow I-490 (East) and I-390 (South) to Exit 17 (Scottsville Road-NY 383 East). Make a left onto Scottsville and bear right onto Elmwood Avenue. From here you'll drive over a bridge. Make a left at Wilson Boulevard. The campus is ahead. From the South: River Campus: Take I-390 (North) to Exit 16 (West Henrietta Road). Cross West Henrietta to East River Road. Turn right onto Kendrick Road and bear left onto Elmwood Avenue. Finally, make a right onto Wilson Boulevard. The campus is ahead.

**LOCAL:** The RGRTA (585-654-0200) is Rochester's regional transit service. The bus has routes throughout the greater Rochester area.

## WHERE TO STAY

For comfortable and moderately priced accommodations, try East Avenue Inn (585-325-5010, $), Crown Plaza Hotel (585-546-8714, $$), and Hyatt Regency (716-546-1234, $$).

---

## CAMPUS AT ITS BEST!

Architecture buffs are sure to appreciate a stop at Wilson Commons. The facility, designed by I. M. Pei's firm, was originally designated by *The New York Times* as one of the best student unions in the country. Wilson plays host to some of the campus's Fashionably Late events—popular evening entertainment for Rochester students. Activities have included Bingo, dance lessons, and a cappella concerts. Another highly anticipated event on campus is the annual Winter Fest Weekend. Undergrads chase the seasonal doldrums away with basketball games, dances, and Casino Night.

# UNIVERSITY OF SCRANTON

800 Linden Street, Scranton, PA 18510-4699

**Telephone:** 570-941-7540 • **E-mail:** admissions@scranton.edu • **Website:** www.scranton.edu
**Hours:** Monday–Friday, 8:30 A.M.–4:30 P.M.; Saturday, 10:00 A.M.–NOON and by appointment

## STUDENTS SAY

"The typical student at this school is a well-rounded individual who has a strong sense of community and a driving desire to help others."

## FODOR'S SAYS

"Road and highway conditions [leading to Scranton] vary from state to state, depending on the climate and budget allocations of a given area. In general, interstates and parkways are well maintained through revenue generated from tolls."

## ABOUT THE SCHOOL

The University of Scranton is a Jesuit institution, and the Jesuit ideals of service to others resonate in nearly every aspect of university life. While students happily maintain that religion is not forced upon anyone, the school does challenge the undergraduate community to become better people, and many students are active in community service.

## GETTING THERE

**BY AIR:** The Scranton area is serviced by the Wilkes-Barre/Scranton International Airport, just 10 miles south of Scranton. Take a taxi to get to the campus.

**BY TRAIN:** Scranton is not located near any major train lines. It is recommended you find alternate transportation.

**BY BUS:** Greyhound provides service to Scranton. Take a taxi to get to the campus.

**BY CAR:** From the North: Take I-81 South to Exit 185. Follow the visitor parking signs to campus. The campus will be located on your right-hand side. Take the first sharp right onto Madison Avenue (this will be before the first traffic signal). Drive 1.5 blocks, past the stop sign. You'll make a right just past Brennan Hall, turning into the Parking Pavilion. You can park in Visitor Parking on the second level. From New York and Northern New Jersey: Take I-80 West to I-380 North. Continue to I-81 South, taking Exit 185. From there, proceed according to "From the North" directions above. From the West: Take I-80 East to I-81 North to Exit 185. From there, proceed according to "From the North" directions above. From Philadelphia and Southern New Jersey: Take the Northeast Extension of the Pennsylvania Turnpike (I-476) to Exit 115 (old Exit 37). Proceed to I-81 North, taking Exit 185. From there, proceed according to "From the North" directions above. From Connecticut and New England: Take I-84 West to I-81 South. From there take Exit 185. From there, proceed according to "From the North" directions above. From Baltimore and Washington, DC: Take I-83 North to I-81 North, exiting at Exit 185. From there, proceed according to "From the North" directions above.

**LOCAL:** For local taxi service guests can call Public Service Taxi Co. (570-344-5000), Posten Taxi Inc. (570-983-1111), or McCarthy Flowered Cabs (570-342-7676).

## WHERE TO STAY

Visitors can contact affordable hotels in the surrounding area, such as Econo Lodge (570-348-1000, $), Clarion Hotel (570-344-9811, $–$$), or the Hilton Conference Center (570-343-3000, $$).

## CAMPUS AT ITS BEST!

If you're seeking some on-campus entertainment, simply head over to the Wolves' Den. Most Thursday nights, the Den hosts open mics which feature a wide variety of musical talent. Additionally, every Friday the latest Hollywood blockbusters are screened. The surrounding area also offers some great attractions, including Sno Mountain Ski Resort, the AAA Affiliate New York Yankees, shopping malls, and cinemas.

# UNIVERSITY OF VERMONT

Admissions Office, 194 South Prospect Street., Burlington, VT 05401-3596
**Telephone:** 802-656-3370 • **E-mail:** admissions@uvm.edu
**Website:** www.uvm.edu • **Hours:** Monday–Friday and Saturday by appointment, 8:00 A.M.–4:30 P.M.

## STUDENTS SAY

"Students are generally friendly and outgoing. It is not at all hard to make new friends or to fit in and there is something for everyone."

## FODOR'S SAYS

"Part of the waterfront's revitalization, the ECHO Leahy Center for Lake Champlain is an aquarium and [a] science center."

## ABOUT THE SCHOOL

The perfect size of the University of Vermont is one of its best qualities. With over 9,000 undergrads, students say it's small enough to allow friendships between students and faculty and large enough to offer academic diversity. It doesn't hurt that UVM is in one of the best college towns. Burlington has something for everyone: movies, restaurants, the waterfront, and an endless array of bands.

## GETTING THERE

**BY AIR:** Burlington International Airport is the closest airport to campus (three and a half miles away). Taxi service is available from the airport.

**BY TRAIN:** Amtrak stops at the Essex train station, which is 15 minutes from Burlington.

**BY BUS:** Greyhound buses stop in Burlington. Take a taxi to get to the campus.

**BY CAR:** From I-89 North or South: Take Exit 14W. Travel one mile West on Route 2 (Williston Road turns into Main Street) to campus. From North or South on Route 7: Enter Burlington and turn onto Main Street (Route 2 East). Travel to South Prospect Street. The campus is ahead. From the Adirondack Northway (I-87): Take Exit 20. Travel North on Route 9 to Route 149, headed to Fort Ann, New York. In Fort Ann, follow Route 4 North to Route 22A in Vermont. Take Route 22A through Vergennes, and follow Route 7 North into Burlington. Make a right onto Main Street (Route 2 East). Travel to South Prospect Street. The campus is ahead.

**LOCAL:** Chittenden County Transportation Authority (CCTA) offers bus service in Burlington. The Vermont Rail System and Vermont Transit Lines provide train and bus service to the Vermont area. If you'd rather take a taxi to get around the area, call Yellow Cab & Van Service (802-862-3300) or Benway's Taxi (802-862-1010).

## WHERE TO STAY

Local hotel accommodations include University Inn & Suites (802-863-5541, $$), Comfort Inn & Suites (802-865-3400, $$), and Sheraton Burlington Hotel & Conference Center (802-865-6600, $$$).

### SCHOOL AT A GLANCE

| | |
|---|---|
| Type of School | Public |
| Environment | City |
| In-state Tuition | $9,832 |
| Out-of-state Tuition | $24,816 |
| Enrollment | 9,040 |
| % Male/Female | 45/55 |
| Student/Faculty Ratio | 15:1 |

### FRESHMAN PROFILE

| | |
|---|---|
| Range SAT | |
| Critical Reading | 530-630 |
| Range SAT Math | 540-640 |
| Range ACT Composite | 22-27 |

### ON-CAMPUS APPOINTMENTS

| | |
|---|---|
| Advance Notice | Yes, 2 weeks |
| Appointment | Required |
| Saturdays | No |
| Average Length | 30 min |
| Info Sessions | Yes |
| Class Visits | Yes |

### CAMPUS TOURS

| | |
|---|---|
| Appointment | Required |
| Dates | Year Round |
| Times | M–F 10:00 A.M. and 2:00 P.M. |
| Average Length | Varies |

## CAMPUS AT ITS BEST!

UVM's resources extend beyond Burlington's borders. Consider making a trip to nearby Underhill for a tour of the university-run Proctor Maple Research Center. Visitors are invited to this field research station to witness how maple syrup is made. Once your sweet tooth has been satisfied, return to campus for a concert sponsored by the Lane Series. This series attracts a diverse group of performers, including the acclaimed jazz/klezmer/bluegrass band the Wayfaring Strangers.

# URSINUS COLLEGE

Ursinus College, Admissions Office, Collegeville, PA 19426
**Telephone:** 610-409-3200 • **E-mail:** admissions@ursinus.edu
**Website:** www.ursinus.edu

## SCHOOL AT A GLANCE

| | |
|---|---|
| Type of School | Private |
| Environment | Metropolis |
| Tuition | $33,200 |
| Enrollment | 1,555 |
| % Male/Female | 48/52 |
| Student/Faculty Ratio | 12:1 |

### FRESHMAN PROFILE

| | |
|---|---|
| Range SAT | |
| Critical Reading | 550–660 |
| Range SAT Math | 560–670 |
| Average HS GPA | 3.5 |

### ON-CAMPUS APPOINTMENTS

| | |
|---|---|
| Advance Notice | Yes, 1 week |
| Appointment | Required |
| Saturdays | Yes |
| Average Length | 60 min |
| Info Sessions | Yes |
| Class Visits | Yes |

### CAMPUS TOURS

| | |
|---|---|
| Appointment | Required |
| Dates | Year Round |
| Times | M–F, 9:00 A.M.–11:00 A.M. |
| | and 1:00–3:00 P.M.; Sat mornings |
| Average Length | 60 min |

## STUDENTS SAY

"Everyone is very accessible—from the deans to professors and even the president—and I have found that they are all interested in me as an individual. They know my name and details about my life, and they all do what they can to help me with my goals."

## FODOR'S SAYS

Nearby "Philadelphia is synonymous with Independence Hall, the Liberty Bell, cheese steaks and hoagies, ethnic neighborhoods, theaters—and city streets teeming with life."

## ABOUT THE SCHOOL

Ursinus is a fantastic choice for college bound students interested in the sciences. The school has stellar chemistry and biology departments and boasts an impressive medical school acceptance rate. Humanities students also commend the school's excellent programs, with special praise for the history and philosophy programs. Fraternities and sororities dominate the social scene, with roughly a third of the student body pledging. Undergrads also take advantage of their close proximity to Philadelphia, often visiting the "City of Brotherly Love" on the weekends.

## GETTING THERE

**BY AIR:** Those guests wishing to travel by air should book flights into Philadelphia International Airport. The airport provides a myriad of transportation options to get to campus.

**BY TRAIN:** Amtrak provides service to Paoli, PA, approximately 10 miles from Collegeville. A taxi can provide access to the campus.

**BY BUS:** Greyhound provides service to nearby Pottstown, PA. A taxi can provide access to the campus.

**BY CAR:** From the Pennsylvania Turnpike: Take Exit 326 at Valley Forge. You'll take the second exit (just past the tollgates) and follow signs to 422 West/Pottstown. Drive roughly eight miles to the Route 29/Collegeville Exit. When you reach the bottom of the exit ramp make a right onto Route 29 North. Continue for three miles then make a left onto Main Street. You'll find the campus about half a mile up the hill on your right-hand side. Corson Hall will be the second building on your right, adjacent to the Visitor's Parking Lot. The Admissions Office is located on the first floor of Corson Hall. From Northern New Jersey: Follow Route 202 South. Approximately 40 minutes after you cross into Pennsylvania, you will cross Route 63 and arrive at Route 73 West. Make a right onto Route 73, continuing until you reach the intersection of Routes 73 and 363. Make a left onto Route 363 South. Continue on and make a turn right onto Germantown Pike. You'll stay on the Pike for several miles until you hit the Perkiomen Bridge. Cross over the bridge (making sure to stay in the left lane) and follow signs to the left for Main Street. Drive for approximately half a mile up the hill. You will see the campus on your right.. From Delaware and the Southern States: From Delaware follow Route 202 North to the exit for Route 422 West/Pottstown. From there, proceed according to "From the Pennsylvania Turnpike" directions above.

**LOCAL:** For service to and from Philadelphia International Airport call, Super Shuttle (215-633-8600) or Tropiano Transportation (610-265-3050).

## WHERE TO STAY

Overnight accommodations can be found at The French Creek Inn (800-870-5040, $), Hampton Inn (610-676-0900, $$), or the Hilton Hotel (610-337-1200, $$–$$$).

---

## CAMPUS AT ITS BEST!

Red and Gold is Ursinus's open house program that is specifically geared toward high school seniors. Visitors spend the day attending class, mingling with professors and current students, and participating in campus events. Technology fiends should request to visit Pfahler Hall of Science. It was in this very facility that Professor John Mauchly constructed key elements of ENIAC, considered to be the world's first computer.

---

# VASSAR COLLEGE

124 Raymond Avenue, Poughkeepsie, NY 12604
**Telephone:** 845-437-7300 • **E-mail:** admissions@vassar.edu
**Website:** www.vassar.edu • **Hours:** Monday–Friday, 8:30 A.M.–5:00 P.M.

## STUDENTS SAY

Students appreciate "the attention given to each student's education and general well-being, the fabulous opportunities for students with any interests, the campus, the classes, the reputation, the facilities... it's an amazing place."

## FODOR'S SAYS

"Vassar was the first college in the United States to have an art gallery; that gallery grew into the Frances Lehman Loeb Art Center, housed in a 1993 Cesar Pelli building. The center's collections amount to more than 15,000 works, from Egyptian and Asian relics to nineteenth and twentieth century paintings."

## ABOUT THE SCHOOL

Vassar College gives its academically intense students the freedom to think for themselves and doesn't require them to follow a core curriculum. When students aren't competing for the best grades, they typically find themselves frequenting different events on campus rather than searching for something to do off campus in the college's isolated Hudson Valley location.

## GETTING THERE

**BY AIR:** The Stewart International Airport in Newburgh is about 35 minutes from the campus.

**BY TRAIN:** The Metro-North Commuter Railroad connects New York City's Grand Central Terminal with Poughkeepsie. Amtrak also provides service to Poughkeepsie. Taxi service is available for the three miles from the Poughkeepsie train station to the campus.

**BY BUS:** Greyhound Bus Lines provides service to Poughkeepsie.

**BY CAR:** From the Taconic State Parkway: Exit at Route 55 West. Go six miles West and make a left turn onto Route 376 Extension/Van Wagner Road, which turns into Raymond Avenue. Go less than one mile to the college. From the New York State Thruway Northbound: Take Exit 17 (Newburgh) and follow I-84 Eastbound across the Newburgh-Beacon Bridge to Exit 13 (Route 9 North). Head 9.5 miles North from the intersection of I-84 and Route 9 toward Spackenkill Road Exit (Route 113). Go about a half a mile on Spackenkill Road. Make a left at the second traffic light onto Wilbur Boulevard. Make a right when Wilbur ends at Hooker Avenue. Make a left at first traffic light onto Raymond Avenue and you will see the college. From the New York State Thruway Southbound: Take Exit 18 (New Paltz) and go East on Route 299. Make a right onto Route 9W South, and exit onto Route 44/55 East. Cross the Mid-Hudson Bridge and continue on Route 44/55 East for about two miles. Make a right onto Raymond Avenue and you will see the college.

**LOCAL:** If you didn't bring your car to the campus, some ways to get around include Allen's Taxi (845-485–2411), Visconti Ground Transport (845-567-3560), and Anthony's Taxi (845-485-8580).

## WHERE TO STAY

If you're going to spend the night, Vassar College Alumnae House (845-437-7100, $$), located on campus, is a very convenient option. Some other popular nearby choices include the Econo Lodge of Poughkeepsie (845-452-6600, $), and the Courtyard by Marriott (845-485-6336, $$).

## CAMPUS AT ITS BEST!

Enjoy a Vassar tradition by relaxing with a spot of tea in Rose Parlor. Served every weekday at 3:00 P.M., this will also give visitors an opportunity to mingle with students and staff. For something more lively, try Founders Day, held every spring in honor of Matthew Vassar's birthday: The celebration includes carnival rides, live music, and fireworks. The surrounding Hudson Valley is also worth exploring, especially during the fall season for apple picking in Red Hook.

# VILLANOVA UNIVERSITY

800 Lancaster Avenue, Villanova, PA 19085-1672
**Telephone:** 610-519-4000 • **E-mail:** gotovu@villanova.edu
**Website:** www.villanova.edu • **Hours:** Monday–Friday, 9:00 A.M.–5:00 P.M.; Saturday, 9:00 A.M.–1:00 P.M.

## SCHOOL AT A GLANCE

| | |
|---|---|
| Type of School | Private |
| Environment | Village |
| Tuition | $33,000 |
| Enrollment | 6,802 |
| % Male/Female | 49/51 |
| Student/Faculty Ratio | 13:1 |

### FRESHMAN PROFILE

| | |
|---|---|
| Range SAT | |
| Critical Reading | 580-660 |
| Range SAT Math | 600-690 |
| Range ACT Composite | 27-30 |
| Average HS GPA | 3.69 |

### ON-CAMPUS APPOINTMENTS

| | |
|---|---|
| Saturdays | No |
| Info Sessions | Yes |
| Class Visits | Yes |

### CAMPUS TOURS

| | |
|---|---|
| Appointment | Not Required |
| Dates | Year Round |
| Times | Varies |
| Average Length | 60 min |

## STUDENTS SAY

"Villanova is a well-rounded school with top-notch academics combined with an amazing social life and location that blend together to make a wonderful college experience."

## FODOR'S SAYS

In nearby Philadelphia, "Society Hill was—and still is—Philadelphia's showplace, the city's most charming and photogenic neighborhood. Federal brick row houses and narrow streets stretch from the Delaware River to 7th Street."

## ABOUT THE SCHOOL

Villanova's well-known business program attracts a quarter of the student body to its campus. A rigorous core curriculum ensures that students receive a solid foundation in liberal arts and creative thinking, plentiful internships, and nationally-recognized service programs perfectly complement student's development both inside and outside of the classroom.

## GETTING THERE

**BY AIR:** Philadelphia International Airport is 25 minutes from Villanova. A taxi or the SEPTA train can provide access to the campus.

**BY TRAIN:** Amtrak stops in Philadelphia. Transfer to SEPTA's Regional Rail Line, R5 (Paoli Local) to Villanova Station, which is directly on the campus.

**BY BUS:** Greyhound stops at the 30th Street Station in Philadelphia. Transfer to SEPTA's Regional Rail Line, R5 (Paoli Local) to Villanova Station, which is directly on the campus.

**BY CAR:** From the North: Take the New Jersey Turnpike South (I-95) to Exit 6 (I-276). Take the Pennsylvania Turnpike (I-276) Westbound to Exit 20 (I-476 South/Chester), and follow I-476 South to Exit 13 (Villanova/St. Davids). After the ramp, turn right onto Route 30 East, (Lancaster Avenue). Go East on Route 30 for a half mile and at the fourth traffic light it will be Villanova's main parking lot on the right. From the West: Take the Pennsylvania Turnpike (76) to Valley Forge Exit 326 (formerly Exit 24). Take I-76 (Schuylkill Expressway) to Exit 331A (I-476 South/Chester) to Exit 13 (U.S. 30 St. Davids/Villanova) to Route 30 East, also known as Lancaster Avenue. From there, proceed accordingly to "From the North" directions above. From the South: Take I-95 North to Exit 7 (I-476 (Blue Route) North-Plymouth Meeting). Take I-476 (Blue Route) North to Exit 13 (Villanova/St. Davids) to Route 30 East, also known as Lancaster Avenue. From there, proceed accordingly to "From the North" directions above.

**LOCAL:** Local taxi service includes Bennett Taxi Service Inc (610-525-1770) and Main Line Taxi Co (610-525-6230).

## WHERE TO STAY

Some popular local hotels include Wayne Hotel (800-962-5850, $$), Radnor Hotel (800- 537-3000, $$$), and Courtyard Philadelphia Devon (610-687-6633, $$$).

## CAMPUS AT ITS BEST!

Included in Villanova's public art collection is a sculpture affectionately referred to by students as the "Oreo." This work is located in the plaza outside the Connelly Center, a common meeting place for students. Villanova is situated just outside Philadelphia and visitors will want to make time for a trip into the city. Consider strolling down the famed South Street, known for its eclectic shops and vibrant nightlife.

# WAGNER COLLEGE

One Campus Road, Staten Island, NY 10301-4495

**Telephone:** 718-390-3411 • **E-mail:** adm@wagner.edu • **Website:** www.wagner.edu

## STUDENTS SAY

"Wagner College, being located in one of the best spots in the country, places great emphasis on the quality of academics while providing amazing experience in the field."

## FODOR'S SAYS

Take the "Staten Island Ferry. The free 20- to 30-minute ride across New York Harbor provides great views of the Manhattan skyline, the Statue of Liberty, the Verrazano-Narrows Bridge, and the New Jersey coast."

## ABOUT THE SCHOOL

A Wagner education puts students on the path to success. The required senior year internships as well as active volunteering programs allow for impressive resume builders. The college manages to attract students with its strong arts program as well as top business, nursing and physician's assistant departments. New York City is also a huge draw, putting world-class academic and entertainment opportunities at students' fingertips.

## GETTING THERE

**BY AIR:** Newark Liberty International Airport is the closest to campus, though LaGuardia and JFK aren't too much further away.

**BY TRAIN:** Amtrak, Long Island Railroad, and New Jersey Transit trains stop at Penn Station. From there take either a taxi or the subway to the South Ferry Terminal. Take the #1 train downtown (make sure you're in the front five cars) and the last train stop is the Ferry Terminal.

**BY BUS:** A number of major bus lines, including Greyhound, Peter Pan, and Bonanza, provide service to New York City's Port Authority Terminal.

**BY CAR:** From New England: From 95 South through New York City: Follow 95 South to New York. Take Exit 14 (Whitestone Bridge/Hutchinson River Parkway South) and proceed over the Whitestone Bridge, following signs for 678 South/Van Wyck Expressway toward JFK. Follow 678 South/Van Wyck Expressway, then proceed on the Belt Parkway heading West, following signs for the Verrazano-Narrows Bridge. From 95 South through New Jersey: Take 95 South to 287, following signs for the Tappan Zee Bridge. Cross the Tappan Zee and follow signs for Garden State Parkway South. Proceed on Garden State Parkway to Route 80, then exit at 95 South/NJ Turnpike. Take NJ Turnpike to Exit 13, to get on the Goethals Bridge. From Long Island: Proceed on the Belt Parkway West or the Brooklyn-Queens Expressway to the Verrazano-Narrows Bridge. From Pennsylvania: From Northern PA: Proceed on Route 80 West to the NJ Turnpike South. Follow Turnpike to Exit 13, then head toward the Goethals Bridge. From Southern/Central PA: Take Route 78 East to New Jersey toward the New Jersey Turnpike, and follow the Turnpike South to Exit 13, heading for the Goethals Bridge.

**LOCAL:** New York City transit operates bus lines throughout Staten Island. If you are heading into Manhattan, take the Staten Island Ferry and the subways in Manhattan will provide you with your transit needs.

## WHERE TO STAY

Staten Island and the surrounding area provide a variety of lodging options. Check out The Staten Island Hotel (800-532-3532, $$), Hilton Garden Inn Staten Island (718-477-2400, $$–$$$), and the Sheraton Hotel in Edison, NJ—30 minutes from Wagner (732-225-8300, $$).

| SCHOOL AT A GLANCE | |
| --- | --- |
| Type of School | Private |
| Environment | Metropolis |
| Tuition | $27,300 |
| Enrollment | 1,962 |
| % Male/Female | 37/63 |
| Student/Faculty Ratio | 15:1 |

| FRESHMAN PROFILE | |
| --- | --- |
| Range SAT | |
| Critical Reading | 530-630 |
| Range SAT Math | 530-640 |
| Range ACT Composite | 23-27 |
| Average HS GPA | 3.52 |

| ON-CAMPUS APPOINTMENTS | |
| --- | --- |
| Advance Notice | Yes, 1 week |
| Appointment | Required |
| Saturdays | Sometimes |
| Average Length | 60 min |
| Info Sessions | Yes |
| Class Visits | Yes (Spring only) |

| CAMPUS TOURS | |
| --- | --- |
| Appointment | Required |
| Dates | Year Round |
| Times | M–F: 10:00 A.M.–3:00 P.M., |
| | Sat 11:00 A.M. |
| Average Length | 60 min |

## CAMPUS AT ITS BEST!

In addition to over 60 clubs and organizations, and a D-1 sports program, Wagner has a celebrated theater program and visitors should attempt to see one their main stage productions. The 2006–2007 season will feature *42nd Street*, *Oklahoma!*, and *Grand Hotel*. For a sampling of the social scene, try attending Wagnerstock, which features campus-wide barbeques and live music. If all else fails, there's always New York! Visit the Guggenheim Museum, or climb to the top of the Empire State Building and gain a new perspective on the city.

# WEBB INSTITUTE

298 Crescent Beach Road, Glen Cove, NY 11542
Telephone: 516-674-9838 • E-mail: admissions@webb-institute.edu
Website: www.webb-institute.edu

## SCHOOL AT A GLANCE

| | |
|---|---|
| Type of School | Private |
| Environment | Village |
| Tuition | $0 |
| Enrollment | 80 |
| % Male/Female | 80/20 |
| Student/Faculty Ratio | 8:1 |

### FRESHMAN PROFILE

| | |
|---|---|
| Range SAT | |
| Critical Reading | 660-700 |
| Range SAT Math | 720-750 |
| Average HS GPA | 3.9 |

### ON-CAMPUS APPOINTMENTS

| | |
|---|---|
| Class Visits | No |

### CAMPUS TOURS

| | |
|---|---|
| Appointment | Required |
| Dates | Year Round |
| Times | Varies |
| Average Length | 60 min |

## STUDENTS SAY

"Webb is a rigorously academic experience tempered by a spirit of cooperation among the students and professors who are always willing to help out."

## FODOR'S SAYS

"Ever since Glen Cove was established in 1668, its waterfront, woodlands, and varied topography have been constant attractions. At one time, Gold Coast mansions occupied half of the town's land; the estates of Standard Oil's cofounder, Charles Pratt, and his sons alone covered more than 1,000 acres. . . . Many of these mansions remain today in and around the more than 300 acres of nature preserves overlooking the harbor."

## ABOUT THE SCHOOL

Webb promises an unparalleled four years for students with an eye toward ship design. Providing an unbeatable combination of full-tuition scholarship and 100 percent success rate for grad school and job placement, the institute is an ideal stepping stone for ambitious individuals interested in naval architecture and marine engineering. The small student body (70 to 80) declares the workload brutal but well worth the toil.

## GETTING THERE

**BY AIR:** JFK, Newark Liberty, and La Guardia airports are all viable flight options.

**BY TRAIN:** Take Amtrak or New Jersey Transit trains into New York's Penn Station or the Metro-North line into Grand Central Station.

**BY BUS:** Unfortunately, there is no direct bus service to Glen Cove, though a variety of bus lines (including Greyhound and Peter Pan) stop at New York's Port Authority Terminal.

**BY CAR:** From the West: Follow the Long Island Expressway, taking Exit 39. You will be driving North on Guinea Woods Road, which eventually becomes Glen Cove Road, which, in turn, becomes Route 107. When you reach the end you'll see a firehouse directly across the street. Make a right onto Brewster Street and continue through three traffic lights. At the fourth light, take a left onto Dosoris Lane. Proceed down Dosoris Lane for almost a mile until you hit New Woods Road (intersects Dosoris Lane at the left only). Take a left onto New Woods Road and follow to the end. Finally, make a right onto Crescent Beach Road. This will lead you directly to Webb's main entrance. From the East: Follow the Long Island Expressway, exiting on Route 107 (going North). You will take Route 107 North to the end. As you reach the end you'll notice a firehouse directly across the street. Follow the "From the West" directions above.

**LOCAL:** The Long Island Railroad (LIRR) provides service out to Glen Cove. Visitors can connect with the LIRR at New York's Penn Station. Additionally, the LI Bus (Long Island Bus), a regional transportation system, supplies service to nearby towns like Syosset, Great Neck, and Roslyn.

## WHERE TO STAY

For hotels that are within 20 minutes of Webb, try the East Norwich Inn (516-922-1500, $–$$; inquire about the preferred rate for the Webb Institute), Harrison Conference Center (516-674-2940, $$; inquire about preferred rate for the Webb Institute), or the Fairfield Inn (516-921-1111, $$).

## CAMPUS AT ITS BEST!

Webb is equipped with state-of-the-art facilities that help students master their trade. To see for yourself, consider stopping by the fluids lab, which contains a small wind tunnel, electrolytic tank, and an oscillating table that simulates ship motions. Recreational opportunities also abound at Webb. The Student Organization sponsors many intramural events, including the annual Dalai Lama Floor Hockey Tournament and students versus faculty softball games. Many Webbies also take advantage of the school's small fleet of boats.

# WELLESLEY COLLEGE

Board of Admission, 106 Central Street, Wellesley, MA 02481-8203
**Telephone:** 781-283-2270 • **E-mail:** admission@wellesley.edu
**Website:** www.wellesley.edu • **Hours:** Monday–Friday, 8:30 A.M.–4:30 P.M.; Saturday, 8:30 A.M.–12:30 P.M.

## STUDENTS SAY

"Wellesley is a place where women who love to learn can come and be themselves."

## FODOR'S SAYS

"Massachusetts invented the fried clam, which appears on many North Shore and Cape Cods menus. Creamy clam chowder is another specialty."

## ABOUT THE SCHOOL

Wellesley women are known for being studious and loquacious. These women have a lot to say, which makes for a lively and intense experience in the classroom. The college offers its students a discussion-based curriculum centered around seminar-style classes, taught by dedicated professors who help students apply to grad schools, get internships, and make career contacts. The college seeks to educate women who will make a difference in the world, and from the looks of their alumni roster, they always succeed.

## GETTING THERE

**BY AIR:** Logan International Airport is the closest airport to campus, about an hour away. Taxi service is available from the airport.

**BY TRAIN:** Amtrak stops at South Station in Boston. From South Station, take the Framingham/Worcester Commuter Rail, which is part of the local MBTA subway service, to the Wellesley Square stop. From there, you can walk or take a taxi to the campus.

**BY BUS:** Peter Pan buses and Greyhound buses both stop at South Station. From South Station, take the Framingham/Worcester Commuter Rail, which is part of the local MBTA subway service, to the Wellesley Square stop. From there, you can walk or take a taxi to campus.

**BY CAR:** From the West: Take the Massachusetts Turnpike (I-90) to Exit 13 (Natick/Framingham/Route 30). Follow Route 30 East to the first set of lights. Make a right onto Speen Street until you hit the intersection with Route 135. Make a left onto Route 135 East and drive 3.6 miles to a traffic light, which is the main entrance to Wellesley. From the East: Take the Massachusetts Turnpike (I-90) West to Exit 15 (Weston/I-95/Route 128). Go South two miles on I-95/ Route 128 to Exit 20B (Framingham/Worcester/ Route 9 West). Head West on Route 9 for 3.9 miles. Watch for the green Weston Road/Weston sign. Get out at the exit marked Wellesley/Needham, which immediately follows that sign. At the end of the ramp, make a right onto Weston Road. Drive one mile to the traffic light at the intersection of Route 135. Make a right onto 135 West and drive half a mile to the first traffic light, which is the college's main entrance. From the North or South: Take I-95/Route 128 to Exit 20B (Framingham/Worcester/Route 9 West). Follow the "From the East" directions above.

**LOCAL:** If you don't have your car on campus, you can take the Logan Express Bus (800-23-LOGAN), which provides service to the airport and around Framingham. You can also take a taxi to check out the area. Some local companies include JFK Taxi (508-653-4500), Newton Yellow Cab (617-332-7700), and Red Cab (617-734-5000).

## WHERE TO STAY

Some popular nearby hotels include the Travelodge Boston Natick (508-655-2222, $), the Sheraton Needham Hotel (781-444-1110, $$), and the Holiday Inn (617-969-5300, $$).

| SCHOOL AT A GLANCE | |
|---|---|
| Type of School | Private |
| Environment | Town |
| Tuition | $32,384 |
| Enrollment | 2,255 |
| % Male/Female | 0/100 |
| Student/Faculty Ratio | 9:1 |

| FRESHMAN PROFILE | |
|---|---|
| Range SAT | |
| Critical Reading | 660-750 |
| Range SAT Math | 650-730 |
| Range ACT Composite | 28-31 |

| ON-CAMPUS APPOINTMENTS | |
|---|---|
| Advance Notice | Yes, 2 weeks |
| Appointment | Required |
| Saturdays | Sometimes |
| Average Length | 45 min |
| Info Sessions | Yes |
| Class Visits | Yes |

| CAMPUS TOURS | |
|---|---|
| Appointment | Not Required |
| Dates | Year Round |
| Times | M–F 9:00 A.M.–3:00 P.M. |
| | hourly; Sat 9:00 A.M., |
| | 10:00 A.M., and 11:00 A.M. |
| Average Length | 60 min |

## CAMPUS AT ITS BEST!

After making the trek up to the fourth floor of Clapp Library, visitors will encounter the Wellesley Book Arts Lab where students have the rare opportunity to learn skills in typography, letterpress printing, hand bookbinding, and using decorated papers. Afterward, visit the Collins Café located within the Davis Museum and Cultural Center. The café has been converted into a student gallery and holds juried exhibitions every semester.

# WELLS COLLEGE

Route 90, Aurora, NY 13026

**Telephone:** 315-364-3264 • **E-mail:** admissions@wells.edu

| SCHOOL AT A GLANCE | |
| --- | --- |
| Type of School | Private |
| Environment | Rural |
| Tuition | $15,580 |
| Enrollment | 407 |
| % Male/Female | 8/92 |
| Student/Faculty Ratio | 8:1 |

| FRESHMAN PROFILE | |
| --- | --- |
| Range SAT | |
| Critical Reading | 520-630 |
| Range SAT Math | 480-580 |
| Range ACT Composite | 20-26 |
| Average HS GPA | 3.5 |

| ON-CAMPUS APPOINTMENTS | |
| --- | --- |
| Advance Notice | No |
| Appointment | Preferred |
| Saturdays | Sometimes |
| Average Length | 30 min |
| Info Sessions | Yes |
| Class Visits | Yes |

| CAMPUS TOURS | |
| --- | --- |
| Appointment | Preferred |
| Dates | Year Round |
| Times | M–F 9:00 A.M.–4:00 P.M. |
| Average Length | 60 min |

## STUDENTS SAY

"The students at Wells College are generally nice people who are extremely smart and very diverse academically. They work hard and they play hard. No matter what, they always get their work done."

## FODOR'S SAYS

"Stretching nearly a mile along the east shore of Cayuga Lake, Aurora has long been one of the prettiest [nineteenth-century] villages in upstate New York. Historically sensitive renovations beginning in 2001 freshened a number of commercial and residential buildings on Main Street, where colonial, Federal, and Victorian structures mix with examples of other architectural styles."

## ABOUT THE SCHOOL

With the recent decision to go coed, Wells has faced some growing pains. The women of the college are somewhat divided in their opinions on having male peers. Luckily, the discord hasn't permeated the classroom. Students happily report intimate, discussion-based classes that encourage free thinking. Hometown Aurora is rather small and doesn't offer much in the way of entertainment, so undergrads take the initiative to liven things up.

## GETTING THERE

**BY AIR:** Ithaca's Tompkins-Cortland Regional, Syracuse's Hancock Field, or Rochester International airports provide close service to campus. The Admissions Office will arrange transportation to the campus for a fee.

**BY TRAIN:** Both Syracuse and Rochester have Amtrak stations that are within reasonable driving distance to Wells.

**BY BUS:** Major and local bus lines stop in Ithaca. The Admissions Office will arrange transportation to the campus for a fee.

**BY CAR:** From Route 17 traveling West: Take I-81 to the Homer Exit (12). Turn right at the end of the exit ramp onto Route 281 North. After turning on to 281, go left onto Route 90. Take local 90 to Aurora (40 miles). From Route 17 traveling East: Exit at Route 13 (54) North to Ithaca. Exit off Route 13 onto Route 34 North to Lansing. Go left onto Route 34B and left onto Route 90 in King Ferry (9 miles to Aurora). From Massachusetts and New England: Follow the Massachusetts Turnpike (I-90) West into New York State. Continue on I-90 (which turns into the New York State Thruway) in New York to Exit 40 (Weedsport). Turn right onto Route 34 South to Auburn. Go right onto Routes 5 and 20 West and left onto Route 326 to the village of Union Springs. Turn left on local Route 90 to Aurora. From Maryland/DC and Southern states: Follow I-95 North to I-695 around Baltimore. Take I-83 North to Harrisburg, Pennsylvania. In Harrisburg, exit from I-83 to I-81 North. Take I-81 North to the Homer, New York Exit (12). Turn right onto Route 281 North and left onto Route 90 (very soon after turning on to Route 281). Take local 90 to Aurora (40 miles).

**LOCAL:** Taxi options include American Taxi (315-568-1811), American Way Taxi (315-539-5212), and Any Taxi Services (315-252-2222).

## WHERE TO STAY

For accommodations located fairly close to campus, try the Holiday Inn in Auburn (315-253-4531, $$), Aurora Inn (315-364-8888, $$–$$$), and Dills Run B&B in Union Springs (315-889-5001, $$).

## CAMPUS AT ITS BEST!

One of Wells's most unique resources is perhaps the Book Arts Center. Instructing students in the fabrication of books, the center is equipped with a bindery, scriptorium, and paper mill. The college is rich with tradition as well. The annual Disco Dodge has students dancing the night away to 70s music in their finest bell-bottoms. Another campus favorite is the Talent Show, performed by the freshmen and sophomore class during Spring Week.

# WESLEYAN UNIVERSITY

The Stewart M. Reid House, 70 Wyllys Avenue, Middletown, CT 06459-0265
**Telephone:** 860-685-3000 • **E-mail:** admiss@wesleyan.edu • **Website:** www.wesleyan.edu/
**Hours:** Monday–Friday, 8:30 A.M.–5:00 P.M.; Saturday, 9:00 A.M.–NOON

## Students Say

"Wesleyan is where you go to work hard, learn, meet the coolest people ever, and really discover what makes you content."

## Fodor's Says

"Dinosaurs once roamed the area around Dinosaur State Park, North of Middletown. You can still see some 500 tracks, dating from the Jurassic period, 200 million years ago, preserved under a giant geodesic dome."

## About the School

Wesleyan University, a small, prestigious school in Middletown, Connecticut, tends to attract students who are creative, intelligent, and quite liberal. Wesleyan students work very hard to keep up with their rigorous academics, but they also know how to have fun, participating in the many activities around campus. The Greek scene on campus is fun but not out of hand, and the campus boasts one of the nation's most diverse student populations among highly selective universities.

## Getting There

**BY AIR:** Bradley International Airport in Windsor Locks is the closest airport near campus and is 40 minutes away from the college. The university operates a shuttle that takes visitors to and from the airport.

**BY TRAIN:** Metro-North travels from New York to New Haven; New Haven is a 35-minute drive to the campus. Amtrak trains service the Meriden train station, which is seven miles away from campus.

**BY BUS:** Greyhound and Peter Pan bus lines both provide service to Middletown. Take a taxi to get to the campus.

**BY CAR:** From the North: Take I-91 South to Exit 22 for Route 9 Southbound. At Exit 15, make a right on Route 66 West (Washington Street). Make a left on High Street. The campus is ahead. From the South: Take I-95 North to I-91 North. At Exit 18, take Route 691/66 East. Route 66 turns into Washington Street in Middletown. Make a right onto High Street. The campus is ahead. From the West: Take I-84 East. Take Exit 27 to Route 691/66 East. Route 66 turns into Washington Street in Middletown. Make a right on High Street. The campus is ahead. From the Northeast: Take the Massachusetts Turnpike (I-90) West to Exit 9 for I-84 West to Hartford. Take Exit 57 over the Charter Oak Bridge and follow signs to I-91 South. Follow I-91 South to Exit 22 for Route 9 Southbound. At Exit 15, make a right onto Route 66 West (Washington Street). Make a left on High Street. The campus is ahead.

**LOCAL:** CT Transit (860-828-0512) provides bus service for the area near the college. If you would rather take a taxi around town, try Bill's Taxi (860-559-1040), and Edie's Cab Co. (860-570-1129).

## Where to Stay

The Inn at Middletown (860-854-6300, $$$) is a convenient hotel choice because it is within walking distance from campus. Other popular nearby choices include the Super 8 Motel (860-632-8888, $) and the Hartford Marriott (860-257-6000, $$).

## CAMPUS AT ITS BEST!

Atop Wesleyan's South College is a set of 16 alloy copper bells. Rung by students every day at noon, the bells chime popular songs, ranging from the Beatles to Darth Vader's Theme. If the college search process is beginning to feel repetitive, venture out into Middletown. You can visit the Connecticut aMAIZEing Maze and get lost in the winding paths of a growing corn field. Wesleyan also hosts an annual writer's conference every June, which attracts writers from all over the world.

# WESTMINSTER COLLEGE (PA)

319 South Market Street, New Wilmington, PA 16172
**Telephone:** 724-946-7100 • **E-mail:** admis@westminster.edu
**Website:** www.westminster.edu

## STUDENTS SAY

"Music is huge on the Westminster campus, and you can always find a concert or performance of some kind being appreciated by students and faculty alike."

## FODOR'S SAYS

"The fastest way to learn about current availability in a specific town or city is to call the local chamber of commerce for a list of the names and phone numbers of B&Bs in the area."

## ABOUT THE SCHOOL

Personal attention is the bedrock of Westminster. Professors and administrators readily make themselves available to students and often treat them as though they're family. In turn, this breeds a comfortable classroom atmosphere. Undergrads assert that their academic experience expands their world view and hones their analytical skills. In recent years, the college has made strides in building a more diverse student body.

## GETTING THERE

**BY AIR:** Pittsburgh International is the closest airport to the campus. Taxis and car rentals are both available.

**BY TRAIN:** The closest Amtrak stations to New Wilmington are located in Alliance, Ohio (approximately 42 miles away), and Pittsburgh, Pennsylvania (approximately 50 miles away).

**BY BUS:** There is no direct service to New Wilmington. However, guests can take Greyhound to nearby Mercer, Pennsylvania. From there, take a taxi to the campus.

**BY CAR:** From the North (Buffalo, Erie, etc.): Go South on I-79 Exit 113 (London, Grove City) West on PA 208 (approximately nine miles). Watch in Leesburg and Volant for right turns to stay on PA 208 into New Wilmington. Turn left at stoplight onto Market Street. Go two blocks. College is on the left. From the South (Pittsburgh or PA Turnpike): North on I-79 Exit 113 (London, Grove City). Follow the "From the North" directions above. From the East (New Jersey, New England): West on I-80 Exit 15 (Mercer) South on U.S. 19 about 4 miles West on PA 208. Follow the "From the North" directions above. From the West (Cleveland, Akron, Youngstown): East on I-80 Exit 4 South PA 60 South to Route 18. Exit South on Route 18 to PA 208 (look for Cheesehouse and Amoco Gas Station near left-hand corner). Turn left (East) on PA 208. Follow 208 one mile into New Wilmington. Follow the "From the North:" directions above.

**LOCAL:** For local taxi service call Phil's Dependable Taxi at 724-981-7445.

## WHERE TO STAY

For accommodations, try the Veazey House Bed & Breakfast (724-946-2918, $), the Jacqueline House B&B (724-946-8382, $–$$), and the Comfort Inn (724-658-7700, $–$$).

## CAMPUS AT ITS BEST!

Visitors should inquire about seeing Pesed, Westminster's 2,300-year-old mummy. In the school's possession since 1885, legend has it that she frequently traveled around campus, often landing in coed's beds. Prospective students who prefer communing with the living might enjoy the school's annual Mardi Gras celebration. With fireworks and live music you are guaranteed to have a good time.

# WHEATON COLLEGE (MA)

Office of Admission, Norton, MA 02766

**Telephone:** 508-286-8251 • **E-mail:** admission@wheatoncollege.edu

**Hours:** Monday–Friday, 8:30 A.M.–4:30 P.M.; Saturday, 8:30 A.M.–2:00 P.M.

## STUDENTS SAY

"Students at Wheaton think about bridging academics with real life outside of the classroom. We have a very high number of students who participate in internships, volunteer efforts, and study abroad programs."

## FODOR'S SAYS

"Benefit Street, the centerpiece of any visit to [nearby] Providence is the 'mile of History,'" where a cobblestone sidewalk passes a row of early eighteenth- and nineteenthth-century candy-color houses crammed shoulder-to-shoulder on a steep hill overlooking downtown."

## ABOUT THE SCHOOL

Wheaton's relatively small student population is perhaps one of its greatest strengths. Students boast that personal attention defines their academic experience at the school. Wheaton does a great job of helping students pursue study abroad and internship opportunities; many undergrads develop close relationships with their professors and frequently have the chance to take on independent study. For fun, students frequently head into nearby Providence or Boston on the weekends.

## GETTING THERE

**BY AIR:** Wheaton students and guests can fly into either Boston's Logan Airport or Providence's T. F. Green Airport. Car rentals, taxis, and limousine service are all available for transportation to Norton.

**BY TRAIN:** Visitors can take Amtrak to either Boston or Providence. People who take the train into Boston's South Station can take an MBTA commuter rail to nearby Attleboro or Mansfield.

**BY BUS:** Guests can take the Bonanza bus line for round-trip service to and from Boston's Logan Airport.

**BY CAR:** From Boston and Northern New England: Proceed on Interstate 95 South to Exit 6A, and get onto Route 495 South. Continue on 495 South to Exit 11, and turn onto 140 South. Remain on Route 140 South for two and a half miles. Make a left at the intersection of Routes 140 and 123. Continue for three-tenths of a mile East on Route 123 to the visitors' parking lot. From Western Massachusetts: Follow the Massachusetts Turnpike (Route 90) to Exit 11A. Continue onto Route 495 South. Continue on 495 South to Exit 11, and turn onto 140 South. You'll remain on Route 140 South for two and a half miles. Make a left at the intersection of Routes 140 and 123. Continue for three-tenths of a mile East on Route 123 to the visitors' parking lot. From Providence and Southern New England: Take Interstate 95 North to Exit 6A. Proceed onto Route 495 South. Continue 495 to Exit 11, turning onto 140 South. You'll remain on Route 140 South for two and a half miles. Next make a left at the intersection of Routes 140 and 123. Continue for three-tenths of a mile east on Route 123 to the visitors' parking lot. From Cape Cod: Take Route 495 North to Exit 10. Proceed onto Route 123 West. Continue on Route 123 to the visitors' parking lot.

**LOCAL:** Wheaton College offers GATRA (Greater Attleboro, Taunton Regional Transit Authority) service free to students, staff, and faculty with a Wheaton ID. The GATRA service runs daily. For local taxi service call Norton Taxi Currier at 508-285-6751.

## WHERE TO STAY

Nearby lodging options include the Colonel Blackinton Inn (508-222-6022, $$), Residence Inn (508-698-2800, $$), and the Holiday Inn Mansfield (508-339-2200, $$).

## SCHOOL AT A GLANCE

| | |
|---|---|
| Type of School | Private |
| Environment | Village |
| Tuition | $34,365 |
| Enrollment | 1,559 |
| % Male/Female | 38/62 |
| Student/Faculty Ratio | 11:1 |

### FRESHMAN PROFILE

| | |
|---|---|
| Range SAT | |
| Critical Reading | 600–690 |
| Range SAT Math | 580–660 |
| Range ACT Composite | 26–30 |
| Average HS GPA | 3.45 |

### ON-CAMPUS APPOINTMENTS

| | |
|---|---|
| Advance Notice | Yes, 2 weeks |
| Appointment | Preferred |
| Saturdays | Yes |
| Average Length | 30 min |
| Info Sessions | Yes |
| Class Visits | Yes |

### CAMPUS TOURS

| | |
|---|---|
| Appointment | Preferred |
| Dates | Year Round |
| Times | M–F 9:30 A.M.–3:30 P.M., |
| | Sat 10:00 A.M.–NOON |
| Average Length | 60 min |

## CAMPUS AT ITS BEST!

Wheaton's Admissions Office holds several specially designated visit days every semester. These events offer prospective students the chance to sit in on classes, attend a hands-on lab, and meet with students and faculty. If your desire to mingle with Wheaties isn't satiated, you can always stop by the Café at the Balfour-Hood Center. This is a popular spot where students enjoy lingering over good food and even better conversation. Wheaton's events calendar usually has some thought-provoking fare on tap, including everything from 10-minute play festivals to readings by visiting poets.

# WILLIAMS COLLEGE

33 Stetson Court, Williamstown, MA 01267

**Telephone:** 413-597-2211 • **E-mail:** admission@williams.edu • **Website:** www.williams.edu

**Hours:** Monday–Friday, 8:30 A.M.–4:30 P.M.; Saturday, 9:00 A.M.–NOON

## STUDENTS SAY

"Williams is a place where you are surrounded by amazingly talented and intelligent people, but nobody cares; what you can learn is so much more important than what you know or can do."

## FODOR'S SAYS

"One of the nation's notable small art museums, the Clark Art Institute has more than 30 paintings by Renoir (among them *Mademoiselle Fleury in Algerian Costume*) as well as canvases by Monet and Pissarro."

## ABOUT THE SCHOOL

Williams is a top-rated liberal arts college renowned for its rigorous academics. Students especially laud programs within the hard sciences as well as the art history department. Although somewhat isolated, the rural setting does help foster a strong campus community. Students occupy extracurricular time with varsity or intramural athletics. Many students also take advantage of outdoor recreational opportunities in the area, especially during ski/snowboarding season.

## GETTING THERE

**BY AIR:** Visitors can fly into Albany, New York (roughly an hour away from campus), or Hartford, Connecticut (roughly two and a half hours from campus). Rental cars, taxis, limousines, and buses are all available for transportation from the airport.

**BY TRAIN:** Amtrak serves the Albany/Rensselaer, New York, station, which is approximately an hour away from campus.

**BY BUS:** Bonanza, Greyhound, and Peter Pan bus lines all provide service to Williamstown. Busses stop at the Williams Inn, next to the campus.

**BY CAR:** From New York City and Points South: Take I-87 North to I-84 East, which leads to the Taconic Parkway North. Take it to Route 295 East. Proceed onto Route 22 North. Take Route 22 North to Route 43 East. Continue to Route 7 North. Route 7 North leads to Route 2 East. You will see the campus shortly thereafter. From Boston and Points East: Drivers can either take Route 2 West all the way to Williamstown or the Mass Pike (I-90) West to Lee (Exit 2). Get on Route 20 West, and take it to Route 7 North. Route 7 North leads to Route 2 East. You will see the campus shortly thereafter. From Albany and Points West: Take Route 7 East to Route 278. Make a right on Route 278 and get onto Route 2. Turn left on Route 2 East. You will see the campus shortly thereafter. From Bennington, VT and All Points North: Take Route 7 South to Route 2. You'll need to turn left on Route 2 East. You will see the campus shortly thereafter.

**LOCAL:** Limousine service is available to and from Albany/Rensselaer, Bradley Airport (Hartford, CT), JFK/Newark/LaGuardia, and Logan/Boston. Try calling Vet's Taxi/Norm's Airport Limo Service (413-663-8300), Jenkins Livery (413-684-1893), Airport Limousine Service (from Albany, 518-869-2258), or Paladin Livery (413-663-3188).

## WHERE TO STAY

Hotels within walking distance to campus include the Maple Terrace Motel (413-458-9677, $–$$), the Williams Inn (413-458-9371, $$–$$$), and the Williamstown B&B (413-458-9202, $$–$$$).

---

## CAMPUS AT ITS BEST!

The Log, a centrally located campus pub, is a popular meeting place for students (especially given the free popcorn, chips and salsa, and soda). It also sponsors regular events such as Tuesday Irish Pub Night and Thursday Night DJ. Students searching for entertainment options beyond the Lodge should investigate ACE (All Campus Entertainment). This industrious group is continually holding some event, be it a rave party, a film screening, or comedic hypnotists. Prospective students who decide to visit campus during the summer should definitely take in a performance at the world-renowned Williamstown Theatre Festival.

# WORCESTER POLYTECHNIC INSTITUTE

100 Institute Road, Worcester, MA 01609
**Telephone:** 508-831-5286 • **E-mail:** admissions@wpi.edu • **Website:** www.wpi.edu
**Hours:** Monday–Friday, 8:30 A.M.–5:00 P.M.; Saturday, 9:00 A.M.–NOON and by appointment

## STUDENTS SAY

"WPI allows great personal attention and freedom of studies."

## FODOR'S SAYS

"November and early December are hunting season in much of New England; those who venture into the woods should wear bright orange clothing."

## ABOUT THE SCHOOL

Worcester Polytechnic Institute supplies a number of great academic opportunities. The college emphasizes theory and practice, an unbeatable combination that leads to highly capable graduates. Each student is required to complete three projects: one in the humanities, a second in their major, and a third that entails addressing (and solving) a real-world problem. Socially, students range from self-proclaimed computer nerds to those heavily involved in Greek life.

## GETTING THERE

**BY AIR:** WPI is an easy drive from Logan International Airport, T. F. Green Airport, Manchester Airport, and Bradley International Airport. Taxi and shuttle service is available from each location.

**BY TRAIN:** Amtrak provides service to Worcester from more than 500 cities nationwide. The station is approximately two miles away from campus. Additional train service is available from MBTA commuter rail. That station is a mile away from the campus.

**BY BUS:** Greyhound and Peter Pan bus lines both offer transportation to Worcester.

**BY CAR:** From the East: Take the Massachussetts Turnpike (I-90) to Exit 11A (I-495). Proceed North to Exit 25B (I-290), and go West into Worcester. Take Exit 18 (Lincoln Square, Route 9), turn right at end of ramp, and make an immediate right before next traffic light. At next light, proceed straight through, bearing to the right on Salisbury Street. At the WPI sign, turn left onto Boynton Street, then right onto Institute Road. Make your first right (Private Way). Admissions visitor parking is located on either side of Bartlett Center. Visitors should pick up a visitor parking pass at the Admissions Office to display in their windshield. From the North: Take I-495 South to I-290. Follow the "From the East" directions above. From the South and West: Take the Massachussetts Turnpike (I-90) to Exit 10 (Auburn). Proceed East on I-290 into Worcester. Take Exit 17 (Lincoln Square, Route 9), turn left at end of ramp, follow Route 9 West through Lincoln Square, straight onto Highland Street, and make a right at the light onto West Street. Travel one block and cross Institute Road (onto Private Way). Admissions visitor parking is located on either side of Bartlett Center. Visitors should pick up a visitor parking pass at the Admissions Office to display in their windshield.

**LOCAL:** Guests can ride the WRTA (Worcester Regional Transit Authority) local bus system, which offers extensive routes throughout the city. The WPI campus lies along two separate routes. For local taxi service try Yellow Cab (508-754-3211).

## WHERE TO STAY

For accommodations in Worcester, try the Crowne Plaza Hotel (508-791-1600, $$), Courtyard by Marriott (508-363-0300, $$), or the Beechwood Hotel (508-754-5789, $$–$$$).

### SCHOOL AT A GLANCE

| | |
|---|---|
| Type of School | Private |
| Environment | City |
| Tuition | $32,818 |
| Enrollment | 2,838 |
| % Male/Female | 75/25 |
| Student/Faculty Ratio | 13:1 |

### FRESHMAN PROFILE

| | |
|---|---|
| Range SAT | |
| Critical Reading | 560-670 |
| Range SAT Math | 620-710 |
| Range ACT Composite | 24-29 |
| Average HS GPA | 3.6 |

### ON-CAMPUS APPOINTMENTS

| | |
|---|---|
| Advance Notice | Yes |
| Appointment | Required |
| Saturdays | No |
| Average Length | 45 min |
| Info Sessions | Yes |
| Class Visits | Yes |

### CAMPUS TOURS

| | |
|---|---|
| Appointment | Not Required |
| Dates | Year Round |
| Times | Varies |
| Average Length | 60 min |

## CAMPUS AT ITS BEST!

Visitors who are allured by ominous names (and perhaps the occult) should stop by Skull Tomb. Constructed entirely without iron, this facility was originally used for experiments in electricity and magnetism and high voltage transformers. It is currently home to a senior honors society that holds secret meetings there. For activities that are open to the public, check out SocComm, WPI's social committee. They sponsor many events, and have brought bands such as Ben Folds and Reel Big Fish to the campus.

# YALE UNIVERSITY

PO Box 208234, New Haven, CT 06520-8234

**Telephone:** 203-432-9300 • **E-mail:** undergraduate.admissions@yale.edu
**Website:** www.yale.edu • **Hours:** Monday–Friday, 8:30 A.M.–5:00 P.M.

## STUDENTS SAY

"Though we come from different backgrounds and have different interests, it's easy to look around and imagine your classmates being the leaders of the next generation."

## FODOR'S SAYS

"Bordered on the west side by Yale's campus, the New Haven Green is a fine example of early urban planning. As early as 1638, village elders set aside the 16-acre plot as a town common."

## ABOUT THE SCHOOL

Yale University has so many strengths it's hard to name them all. Great resources, professors who are at the top of their fields, and amazing students are just some of the many great things this school has to offer. When they're not busy studying and trying to stay on top of Yale's tough academics, students are very involved in extracurricular activities on campus, and theatrical and musical events abound. And if there's ever time for a quick off-campus excursion, New York City is only an hour's train ride away.

## GETTING THERE

**BY AIR:** Tweed New Haven Airport is 10 minutes from the Yale campus by car or taxi.

**BY TRAIN:** Take Amtrak to Union Station in New Haven. Take a taxi to get to the campus.

**BY BUS:** Greyhound Bus service stops at Union Station in New Haven. Take a taxi to get to the campus.

**BY CAR:** From the North: Take I-91 North in New Haven. Take Exit 3 (Trumbull Street). Stay in the middle lane and continue straight onto Trumbull Street until the fifth traffic light. Turn left onto Prospect Street, and continue for one block. Prospect Street becomes College Street at this point. Continue for two blocks, and turn left onto Elm Street. You will see the college shortly thereafter. From the South: Take I-91 North in New Haven (left exit). Take Exit 3 (Trumbull Street). Stay in the middle lane and continue straight onto Trumbull Street until the fifth traffic light. Turn left onto Prospect Street and continue for one block. Prospect Street becomes College Street at this point. Continue for two blocks and turn left onto Elm Street. You will see the college shortly thereafter. From the West: Drive East on Route 34 (Derby Avenue) for about five miles past the Yale Athletic Fields. Turn left onto Route 10 North, Ella T. Grasso Boulevard. Proceed to the fifth traffic light and turn right onto Whalley Avenue. Whalley becomes Broadway one mile later, and Broadway becomes Elm Street in another 0.2 miles. Continue on Elm for 2.5 blocks until you see the college.

**LOCAL:** For local taxi service call City Wide Taxi (203-777-0007).

## WHERE TO STAY

Some of the most popular hotels near the college include the Days Inn New Haven (203-469-0343, $), New Haven Hotel (203-498-3100, $$), and Clarion Hotel & Suites (203-288-3831, $$).

---

## CAMPUS AT ITS BEST!

Yale's Center for British Art is certain to excite even the most staid anglophile. The museum's collection contains prominent works by Joshua Reynolds, William Hogarth, and Damien Hirst. Visitors who want a broad overview of what's happening on campus should stop by the Kiosk. This bulletin board reflects the frenetic pace of Yale's campus life, with thousands of events being advertised there throughout the year. Yale is known for its incredibly strong performing arts. Guests should aim to catch a Whiffenpoofs performance, which is perhaps the school's most storied and acclaimed a capella group.

# YORK COLLEGE OF PENNSYLVANIA

Country Club Road, York, PA 17405-7199
**Telephone:** 717-849-1600 • **E-mail:** admissions@ycp.edu
**Website:** www.ycp.edu

## STUDENTS SAY

"Professors are almost always available to talk and help students."

## FODOR'S SAYS

"If you'll be sightseeing in historic cities, you'll spend a lot of time walking, so bring sturdy, well-fitting flat-heeled shoes."

## ABOUT THE SCHOOL

With a student population hovering around 4,500, York is large enough to appeal to a wide range of personalities and small enough to cater to the needs of individual students. State-of-the-art facilities and a rigorous curriculum challenge undergraduates to reach their full potential. The college attracts energetic, engaged students who participate in the many extracurricular activities available. Additionally, Baltimore and Lancaster are only a short drive away for off-campus excursions.

## GETTING THERE

**BY AIR:** Visitors should fly into either Baltimore Washington International (BWI) or Harrisburg International Airport. York is approximately 45 minutes away from Harrisburg and an hour from Baltimore.

**BY TRAIN:** The nearest train station is located in Elizabethtown, approximately 14 miles from York. Take a taxi to get to the campus.

**BY BUS:** Greyhound stops in York. Take a taxi to get to the campus.

**BY CAR:** From Harrisburg, PA: Take I-83 South to Exit 16B (Route 74 North/Queen Street). Proceed on Queen Street to the third traffic light and take a left onto Rathton Road. Drive straight through the second light onto Country Club Road. You'll find the entrance to the college a short distance down, on the right-hand side. From New York City: Follow I-80 West to Route 287 South. Proceed on Route 22/78 West (Clinton), taking it to I-81 South. I-81 will take you to Harrisburg. Follow the "From Harrisburg" directions above. From Lancaster, PA: Follow Route 30 West to I-83 South. Take I-83 to Exit 16B (Route 74 North/Queen Street). Follow the "From Harrisburg" directions above. From Philadelphia, PA: Follow the Pennsylvania Turnpike West to Exit 21 (new Exit 286). Proceed to route 222 South to Lancaster. Follow the "From Lancaster" directions above. From Baltimore, MD: Take I-83 North to Exit 16B (Route 74 North/Queen Street). Follow the "From Harrisburg" directions above. Follow the "From Harrisburg" directions above.

**LOCAL:** If you're looking for local taxi service, try Capital City Cabs (717-845-2798) or American Taxi (717-846-8294).

## WHERE TO STAY

Try making reservations at the Econo Lodge (717-846-6260, $), Super 8 Motel (717-852-8686, $), or the Yorktowne Hotel (717-848-1111, $$).

### SCHOOL AT A GLANCE

| | |
|---|---|
| Type of School | Private |
| Environment | Town |
| Tuition | $10,160 |
| Enrollment | 5,664 |
| % Male/Female | 41/59 |
| Student/Faculty Ratio | 15:1 |

### FRESHMAN PROFILE

| | |
|---|---|
| Range SAT | |
| Critical Reading | 500-600 |
| Range SAT Math | 490-590 |
| Range ACT Composite | 18-24 |
| Average HS GPA | 3.1 |

### ON-CAMPUS APPOINTMENTS

| | |
|---|---|
| Advance Notice | Yes, 1 week |
| Appointment | Required |
| Saturdays | No |
| Average Length | 30 min |
| Info Sessions | Yes |
| Class Visits | Yes |

### CAMPUS TOURS

| | |
|---|---|
| Appointment | Required |
| Dates | Year Round |
| Times | M–F 10:00 A.M., 11:30 A.M., 1:30 P.M. |
| Average Length | 75 min |

## CAMPUS AT ITS BEST!

If you'd like to see York students in their native habit, you should stop by Sparks Den. It's a popular hangout, and you'll likely be able to see some of your potential future peers perform at open mic night or the student showcase. If you're interested in seeing some of York's finest traditions, try to attend the annual Mr. and Miss YCP pageant or Fall Fest.

# THE SOUTHEAST

From the Louisiana bayou to the barrier islands off the Carolinas to the urban metropolis of Atlanta and the rural mountains of West Virginia, the Southeastern landscape is as varied as you'll find anywhere in the rest of the United States.

South Carolina is home to fancy resort islands such as Kiawah and Hilton Head, small historic cities such as Charleston, and over 300 golf courses (now that's a lot of golf). North Carolina is a bit more high-tech and fast-paced; the Research Triangle connecting the three cities (and their three universities) of Durham, Chapel Hill, and Raleigh is an area that has seen tremendous growth over the past 10 years: It is now the nation's second largest baking center (after New York City). Mountains are plentiful in the Carolinas, Virginia, and West Virginia. And West Virginia, in particular—with its state slogan "Wild and Wonderful"—attracts outdoor enthusiasts for hiking, biking, skiing, and white water rafting.

Florida alone contains miles of beaches, the Florida Keys, the Panhandle, and Everglades National Park—the only subtropical preserve in North America. In Arkansas, you can explore hot springs and the Ozarks. Intrepid explorers can investigate the canyons and caves of Alabama. Mississippi offers its own set of barrier islands in the Gulf of Mexico. Georgia's got some too, along with rivers and swamps of its very own.

The culture of the Southeast is just as varied as its landscape; Orlando, Florida is home to Walt Disney World, a subculture to experience in its own right. Cuban-American culture thrives in Miami, giving the city a profoundly Latin flavor, while Creole and Cajun cultures (and cuisine!), keep Southern Louisiana life spicy. Bring your fancy hat (and your wallet) if you're headed to the Kentucky Derby.

The region is rich in American musical traditions. Jazz got its start in New Orleans, the blues reign supreme in Memphis, bluegrass came from Kentucky, and good ol' country still rules Nashville. The Southeast's literary legacy is also impressive. Ernest Hemingway spent years living, drinking, and fishing in the Florida Keys. Eudora Welty, Walker Percy, Zora Neale Hurston, William Faulkner, and Flannery O'Connor—along with many others—represent Southern literature at its best.

Southern plantation life, Civil War history, and the Civil Rights Movement are just some aspects of the past here, all which continue to influence the region's culture to this day. The Louisiana Purchase celebrated its 200th anniversary in 2003. Historical sites and landmarks can be found throughout the region—Colonial Williamsburg in Williamsburg, Virginia, is the world's largest living history museum, and aims to transport visitors back to the eighteenth century.

Not exactly cosmopolitan, the Southeast still has pockets of modern life aplenty. And outdoor adventurers find that the region is one big playground, filled with expanses for hunting, fishing, sailing, swimming, horseback riding, and camping. If you choose to head to the Southeast, you're certain to encounter a mix of culture, characters, history, and charm, whichever state you choose. But be ready to take it slow! Pour yourself some lemonade, take a stroll, and stay a while.

# SOUTHEAST MILEAGE MATRIX

| | Montgomery | Mobile | Birmingham | Tuscaloosa | Fayetteville | Little Rock | Tallahassee | Miami | Sarasota |
|---|---|---|---|---|---|---|---|---|---|
| Montgomery, Alabama | — | 168 | 93 | 133 | 647 | 466 | 210 | 720 | 497 |
| Mobile, Alabama | 168 | — | 258 | 225 | 755 | 574 | 243 | 786 | 566 |
| Birmingham, Alabama | 93 | 258 | — | 58 | 559 | 377 | 303 | 814 | 591 |
| Tuscaloosa, Alabama | 133 | 225 | 58 | — | 549 | 368 | 344 | 855 | 632 |
| Fayetteville, Arkansas | 647 | 755 | 559 | 549 | — | 190 | 1054 | 1430 | 1378 |
| Little Rock, Arkansas | 466 | 574 | 377 | 368 | 190 | — | 677 | 1250 | 1030 |
| Tallahassee, Florida | 210 | 243 | 303 | 344 | 1054 | 677 | — | 470 | 292 |
| Miami, Florida | 720 | 786 | 814 | 855 | 1430 | 1250 | 470 | — | 229 |
| Sarasota, Florida | 497 | 566 | 591 | 632 | 1378 | 1030 | 292 | 229 | — |
| Orlando, Florida | 464 | 497 | 558 | 599 | 1308 | 1128 | 259 | 234 | 131 |
| Tampa, Florida | 457 | 514 | 551 | 616 | 1326 | 978 | 277 | 279 | 58 |
| Atlanta, Georgia | 160 | 327 | 146 | 202 | 780 | 523 | 270 | 661 | 505 |
| Macon, Georgia | 185 | 352 | 229 | 285 | 789 | 605 | 194 | 584 | 428 |
| Athens, Georgia | 230 | 398 | 216 | 272 | 832 | 652 | 286 | 676 | 520 |
| Savannah, Georgia | 334 | 540 | 393 | 449 | 953 | 769 | 300 | 483 | 388 |
| Louisville, Kentucky | 457 | 620 | 365 | 420 | 620 | 553 | 691 | 1082 | 926 |
| Frankfort, Kentucky | 497 | 663 | 408 | 463 | 674 | 563 | 677 | 1101 | 911 |
| New Orleans, Louisiana | 309 | 144 | 343 | 291 | 631 | 452 | 385 | 859 | 709 |
| Baton Rouge, Louisiana | 364 | 199 | 398 | 346 | 619 | 433 | 441 | 915 | 759 |
| Jackson, Mississippi | 312 | 232 | 237 | 185 | 450 | 344 | 532 | 1042 | 851 |
| Asheville, North Carolina | 367 | 534 | 354 | 410 | 822 | 642 | 473 | 787 | 708 |
| Greensboro, North Carolina | 494 | 658 | 480 | 535 | 1007 | 827 | 637 | 818 | 726 |
| Raleigh, North Carolina | 573 | 737 | 558 | 614 | 1086 | 906 | 616 | 797 | 702 |
| Winston Salem, North Carolina | 485 | 649 | 467 | 523 | 978 | 798 | 624 | 805 | 713 |
| Clemson, South Carolina | 289 | 456 | 275 | 331 | 891 | 711 | 395 | 768 | 629 |
| Charleston, South Carolina | 477 | 639 | 469 | 525 | 1103 | 845 | 399 | 583 | 487 |
| Columbia, South Carolina | 366 | 533 | 358 | 414 | 992 | 812 | 452 | 633 | 538 |
| Nashville, Tennessee | 281 | 447 | 192 | 247 | 529 | 349 | 492 | 910 | 782 |
| Memphis, Tennessee | 331 | 439 | 242 | 234 | 318 | 137 | 542 | 1083 | 1063 |
| Fairfax, Virginia | 808 | 976 | 724 | 782 | 1177 | 997 | 866 | 1047 | 955 |
| Richmond, Virginia | 696 | 860 | 684 | 740 | 1139 | 948 | 769 | 944 | 855 |
| Morgantown, West Virginia | 807 | 973 | 721 | 780 | 1021 | 911 | 925 | 1146 | 1090 |
| Charleston, West Virginia | 651 | 817 | 565 | 624 | 865 | 755 | 769 | 990 | 894 |

# SOUTHEAST MILEAGE MATRIX

| | Orlando | Tampa | Atlanta | Macon | Athens | Savannah | Louisville | Frankfort | New Orleans |
|---|---|---|---|---|---|---|---|---|---|
| Montgomery, Alabama | 464 | 457 | 160 | 185 | 230 | 334 | 457 | 497 | 309 |
| Mobile, Alabama | 497 | 514 | 327 | 352 | 398 | 540 | 620 | 663 | 144 |
| Birmingham, Alabama | 558 | 551 | 146 | 229 | 216 | 393 | 365 | 408 | 343 |
| Tuscaloosa, Alabama | 599 | 616 | 202 | 285 | 272 | 449 | 420 | 463 | 291 |
| Fayetteville, Arkansas | 308 | 1326 | 780 | 789 | 832 | 953 | 620 | 674 | 631 |
| Little Rock, Arkansas | 1128 | 978 | 523 | 605 | 652 | 769 | 553 | 563 | 452 |
| Tallahassee, Florida | 259 | 277 | 270 | 194 | 286 | 300 | 691 | 677 | 385 |
| Miami, Florida | 234 | 279 | 661 | 584 | 676 | 483 | 1082 | 1101 | 859 |
| Sarasota, Florida | 131 | 58 | 505 | 428 | 520 | 388 | 926 | 911 | 709 |
| Orlando, Florida | — | 84 | 438 | 361 | 453 | 279 | 911 | 897 | 633 |
| Tampa, Florida | 84 | — | 456 | 380 | 472 | 336 | 877 | 863 | 652 |
| Atlanta, Georgia | 438 | 456 | — | 84 | 70 | 248 | 421 | 407 | 467 |
| Macon, Georgia | 361 | 380 | 84 | — | 91 | 166 | 504 | 490 | 492 |
| Athens, Georgia | 453 | 472 | 70 | 91 | — | 224 | 480 | 400 | 537 |
| Savannah, Georgia | 279 | 336 | 248 | 166 | 224 | — | 658 | 609 | 642 |
| Louisville, Kentucky | 911 | 877 | 421 | 504 | 480 | 658 | — | 55 | 705 |
| Frankfort, Kentucky | 897 | 863 | 407 | 490 | 400 | 609 | 55 | — | 748 |
| New Orleans, Louisiana | 633 | 652 | 467 | 492 | 537 | 642 | 705 | 748 | — |
| Baton Rouge, Louisiana | 694 | 707 | 542 | 547 | 612 | 697 | 759 | 802 | 80 |
| Jackson, Mississippi | 785 | 799 | 381 | 464 | 451 | 629 | 587 | 630 | 186 |
| Asheville, North Carolina | 583 | 660 | 208 | 286 | 162 | 310 | 360 | 312 | 694 |
| Greensboro, North Carolina | 614 | 672 | 331 | 379 | 286 | 342 | 491 | 443 | 799 |
| Raleigh, North Carolina | 593 | 650 | 410 | 418 | 364 | 321 | 571 | 523 | 877 |
| Winston Salem, North Carolina | 601 | 658 | 321 | 366 | 273 | 329 | 463 | 414 | 789 |
| Clemson, South Carolina | 564 | 557 | 129 | 177 | 84 | 291 | 439 | 391 | 596 |
| Charleston, South Carolina | 379 | 435 | 323 | 265 | 274 | 116 | 616 | 568 | 781 |
| Columbia, South Carolina | 429 | 485 | 212 | 195 | 189 | 156 | 507 | 459 | 674 |
| Nashville, Tennessee | 687 | 706 | 250 | 337 | 306 | 497 | 174 | 218 | 531 |
| Memphis, Tennessee | 796 | 845 | 384 | 467 | 516 | 632 | 384 | 427 | 402 |
| Fairfax, Virginia | 843 | 901 | 646 | 672 | 600 | 570 | 612 | 563 | 1068 |
| Richmond, Virginia | 740 | 803 | 533 | 583 | 488 | 473 | 560 | 512 | 1000 |
| Morgantown, West Virginia | 942 | 999 | 659 | 708 | 614 | 670 | 402 | 354 | 1065 |
| Charleston, West Virginia | 786 | 882 | 503 | 582 | 458 | 514 | 246 | 198 | 908 |

# SOUTHEAST MILEAGE MATRIX

| | Baton Rouge | Jackson | Asheville | Greensboro | Raleigh | Winston Salem | Clemson | Charleston | Columbia |
|---|---|---|---|---|---|---|---|---|---|
| Montgomery, Alabama | 364 | 312 | 367 | 494 | 573 | 485 | 289 | 477 | 366 |
| Mobile, Alabama | 199 | 232 | 534 | 658 | 737 | 649 | 456 | 639 | 533 |
| Birmingham, Alabama | 398 | 237 | 354 | 480 | 558 | 467 | 275 | 469 | 358 |
| Tuscaloosa, Alabama | 346 | 185 | 410 | 535 | 614 | 523 | 331 | 525 | 414 |
| Fayetteville, Arkansas | 619 | 450 | 822 | 1007 | 1086 | 978 | 891 | 1103 | 992 |
| Little Rock, Arkansas | 433 | 344 | 642 | 827 | 906 | 798 | 711 | 845 | 812 |
| Tallahassee, Florida | 441 | 532 | 473 | 637 | 616 | 624 | 395 | 399 | 452 |
| Miami, Florida | 915 | 1042 | 787 | 818 | 797 | 805 | 768 | 583 | 633 |
| Sarasota, Florida | 759 | 851 | 708 | 726 | 702 | 713 | 629 | 487 | 538 |
| Orlando, Florida | 694 | 785 | 583 | 614 | 593 | 601 | 564 | 379 | 429 |
| Tampa, Florida | 707 | 799 | 660 | 672 | 650 | 658 | 557 | 435 | 485 |
| Atlanta, Georgia | 542 | 381 | 208 | 331 | 410 | 321 | 129 | 323 | 212 |
| Macon, Georgia | 547 | 464 | 286 | 379 | 418 | 366 | 177 | 265 | 195 |
| Athens, Georgia | 612 | 451 | 162 | 286 | 364 | 273 | 84 | 274 | 189 |
| Savannah, Georgia | 697 | 629 | 310 | 342 | 321 | 329 | 291 | 116 | 156 |
| Louisville, Kentucky | 759 | 587 | 360 | 491 | 571 | 463 | 439 | 616 | 507 |
| Frankfort, Kentucky | 802 | 630 | 312 | 443 | 523 | 414 | 391 | 568 | 459 |
| New Orleans, Louisiana | 80 | 186 | 694 | 799 | 877 | 789 | 596 | 781 | 674 |
| Baton Rouge, Louisiana | — | 173 | 750 | 876 | 937 | 844 | 672 | 837 | 754 |
| Jackson, Mississippi | 173 | — | 607 | 715 | 793 | 702 | 513 | 704 | 593 |
| Asheville, North Carolina | 750 | 607 | — | 171 | 251 | 145 | 90 | 267 | 158 |
| Greensboro, North Carolina | 876 | 715 | 171 | — | 80 | 29 | 225 | 274 | 183 |
| Raleigh, North Carolina | 937 | 793 | 251 | 80 | — | 110 | 304 | 278 | 225 |
| Winston Salem, North Carolina | 844 | 702 | 145 | 29 | 110 | — | 212 | 286 | 171 |
| Clemson, South Carolina | 672 | 513 | 90 | 225 | 304 | 212 | — | 248 | 139 |
| Charleston, South Carolina | 837 | 704 | 267 | 274 | 278 | 286 | 248 | — | 114 |
| Columbia, South Carolina | 754 | 593 | 158 | 183 | 225 | 171 | 139 | 114 | — |
| Nashville, Tennessee | 586 | 414 | 294 | 480 | 559 | 452 | 317 | 551 | 442 |
| Memphis, Tennessee | 389 | 210 | 504 | 690 | 769 | 662 | 575 | 787 | 653 |
| Fairfax, Virginia | 1124 | 961 | 452 | 274 | 275 | 306 | 539 | 528 | 475 |
| Richmond, Virginia | 1060 | 920 | 374 | 209 | 163 | 233 | 427 | 431 | 391 |
| Morgantown, West Virginia | 1128 | 959 | 448 | 402 | 480 | 373 | 553 | 627 | 511 |
| Charleston, West Virginia | 1005 | 803 | 292 | 245 | 324 | 216 | 398 | 471 | 355 |

# SOUTHEAST MILEAGE MATRIX

| | Nashville | Memphis | Fairfax | Richmond | Morgantown | Charleston |
|---|---|---|---|---|---|---|
| Montgomery, Alabama | 281 | 331 | 808 | 696 | 807 | 651 |
| Mobile, Alabama | 447 | 439 | 976 | 860 | 973 | 817 |
| Birmingham, Alabama | 192 | 242 | 724 | 684 | 721 | 565 |
| Tuscaloosa, Alabama | 247 | 234 | 782 | 740 | 780 | 624 |
| Fayetteville, Arkansas | 529 | 318 | 1177 | 1139 | 1021 | 865 |
| Little Rock, Arkansas | 349 | 137 | 997 | 948 | 911 | 755 |
| Tallahassee, Florida | 492 | 542 | 866 | 769 | 925 | 769 |
| Miami, Florida | 910 | 1083 | 1047 | 944 | 1146 | 990 |
| Sarasota, Florida | 782 | 1063 | 955 | 855 | 1090 | 894 |
| Orlando, Florida | 687 | 796 | 843 | 740 | 942 | 786 |
| Tampa, Florida | 706 | 845 | 901 | 803 | 999 | 882 |
| Atlanta, Georgia | 250 | 384 | 646 | 533 | 659 | 503 |
| Macon, Georgia | 337 | 467 | 672 | 583 | 708 | 582 |
| Athens, Georgia | 306 | 516 | 600 | 488 | 614 | 458 |
| Savannah, Georgia | 497 | 632 | 570 | 473 | 670 | 514 |
| Louisville, Kentucky | 174 | 384 | 612 | 560 | 402 | 246 |
| Frankfort, Kentucky | 218 | 427 | 563 | 512 | 354 | 198 |
| New Orleans, Louisiana | 531 | 402 | 1068 | 1000 | 1065 | 908 |
| Baton Rouge, Louisiana | 586 | 389 | 1124 | 1060 | 1128 | 1005 |
| Jackson, Mississippi | 414 | 210 | 961 | 920 | 959 | 803 |
| Asheville, North Carolina | 294 | 504 | 452 | 374 | 448 | 292 |
| Greensboro, North Carolina | 480 | 690 | 274 | 209 | 402 | 245 |
| Raleigh, North Carolina | 559 | 769 | 275 | 163 | 480 | 324 |
| Winston Salem, North Carolina | 452 | 662 | 306 | 233 | 373 | 216 |
| Clemson, South Carolina | 317 | 575 | 539 | 427 | 553 | 398 |
| Charleston, South Carolina | 551 | 787 | 528 | 431 | 627 | 471 |
| Columbia, South Carolina | 442 | 653 | 475 | 391 | 511 | 355 |
| Nashville, Tennessee | — | 212 | 648 | 600 | 566 | 410 |
| Memphis, Tennessee | 212 | — | 859 | 830 | 774 | 618 |
| Fairfax, Virginia | 648 | 859 | — | 98 | 211 | 366 |
| Richmond, Virginia | 600 | 830 | 98 | — | 307 | 314 |
| Morgantown, West Virginia | 566 | 774 | 211 | 307 | — | 156 |
| Charleston, West Virginia | 410 | 618 | 366 | 314 | 157 | — |

# SOUTHEAST SAMPLE ITINERARIES

Many of the colleges and universities clustered within the nation's Southeastern states are known for their great athletics, warm hospitality, and amazing traditions. Some of the nation's top Historically Black Colleges and Universities (HBCUs) can be found in this region, along with two of the most competitive state-school systems in the country (North Carolina and Florida). While you're visiting, be sure to set aside some time to explore the region's great restaurants and gorgeous historical landmarks. Charleston, South Carolina alone boasts over 3,000 historic sites.

The itineraries below assume a linear trajectory, and involve several overnight stays. Before you head out, be sure to gather maps to and from schools and hotels, driving directions, and all the phone numbers you may need. Research any local dining and shopping establishments you're interested in visiting and print out their names, addresses, and telephone numbers. Finally, be realistic: You're not going to cover all the ground you want to cover in just a few days. In general, try not to see more than two (three at most) colleges a day; too many visits in one day and your brain will start to atrophy. The itineraries listed below are just suggestions—you can and should modify them to suit your individual needs.

## IF YOU'VE GOT SEVEN DAYS:

**Starting Point:** Durham, North Carolina

**Saturday:** Duke University, University of North Carolina at Chapel Hill, University of North Carolina at Greensboro, Elon University
Drive to Asheville, North Carolina. Stay overnight in Asheville.

**Sunday:** University of North Carolina at Asheville
Drive to Columbia, South Carolina.

**Sunday PM:** University of South Carolina—Columbia
Drive to Charleston, South Carolina. Stay overnight in Charleston.

**Monday:** College of Charleston, The Citadel
Drive to Atlanta, Georgia. Stay overnight in Atlanta.

**Tuesday:** Emory University, George Institute of Technology, Ogelthorpe University, Georgia State University
Stay overnight in Atlanta.

**Wednesday:** Spelman College, Morehouse College, Clark Atlanta University, Agnes Scott College
Drive to Auburn, Alabama. Stay overnight in Auburn.

**Thursday:** Auburn University
Drive to Tuscaloosa, Alabama.

**Thursday PM:** University of Alabama at Tuscaloosa
Drive to New Orleans, Louisiana. Stay overnight in New Orleans.

**Friday:** Tulane University, Loyola University—New Orleans, University of New Orleans
Head home.

## If You've Got Three Days:

**Starting Point:** Tallahassee, Florida

**Friday:** Florida State University, Florida A&M University
Drive to Gainesville, Florida.

**Friday PM:** University of Florida.
Drive to Orlando. Stay overnight in Orlando.

**Saturday:** University of Central Florida, Rollins College
Drive to Sarasota, Florida. Stay overnight in Sarasota.

**Sunday:** Eckerd College, New College of Florida
Head Home.

# SOUTHEAST SCHOOLS

# AGNES SCOTT COLLEGE

141 East College Avenue, Atlanta/Decatur, GA 30030-3797
**Telephone:** 404-471-6285 • **E-mail:** admission@agnesscott.edu
**Website:** www.agnesscott.edu • **Hours:** Monday–Friday, 8:30 A.M.–4:30 P.M.

## SCHOOL AT A GLANCE

| | |
|---|---|
| Type of School | Private |
| Environment | Metropolis |
| Tuition | $25,100 |
| Enrollment | 875 |
| % Male/Female | 0/100 |
| Student/Faculty Ratio | 10:1 |

## FRESHMAN PROFILE

| | |
|---|---|
| Range SAT | |
| Critical Reading | 570-685 |
| Range SAT Math | 540-650 |
| Range ACT Composite | 24-29 |
| Average HS GPA | 3.72 |

## ON-CAMPUS APPOINTMENTS

| | |
|---|---|
| Advance Notice | Yes, 1 week |
| Appointment | Required |
| Average Length | 30 min |
| Info Sessions | Yes |
| Class Visits | Yes |

## CAMPUS TOURS

| | |
|---|---|
| Appointment | Preferred |
| Dates | Year Round |
| Times | M–F 10:00 A.M. |
| | and 2:00 P.M.; Sat 10:00 A.M. |
| Average Length | 60 min |

## STUDENTS SAY

"ASC is about women who are less concerned about how men perceive them and more concerned about how they themselves can affect the world."

## FODOR'S SAYS

"Constructed in 1823," the Decatur Historical Courthouse "now houses the DeKalb History Center. It's right in the midst of shops, coffeehouses, and cafés of Decatur's quaint main square."

## ABOUT THE SCHOOL

Agnes Scott College ranks among America's top liberal arts colleges for women. Located 15 minutes from downtown "Hot-lanta," Agnes Scott offers the cozy atmosphere of a tight-knit community along with all the thrills of city living. While there's certainly fun to be had on campus and off, students assure us that academics come first at Agnes Scott.

## GETTING THERE

**BY AIR:** Thirty airlines operate out of the large Hartsfield-Jackson Atlanta International Airport. Taxi fare from the airport to campus is $30.

**BY TRAIN:** Amtrak operates out of Atlanta's central train/bus terminal located on Peachtree Street, about eight miles from campus.

**BY BUS:** The Greyhound station in downtown Atlanta can be reached by car or taxi.

**BY CAR:** From I-75: Follow I-75/85 to the Freedom Parkway exit. Stay on the Freedom Parkway for approximately two miles until it ends at Ponce de Leon Avenue. Turn right onto Ponce de Leon Avenue, toward Decatur. After a few miles, Ponce de Leon Avenue will bear to the right. Turn right onto West Trinity Place and after about half a mile, turn right on to North McDonough Street. Agnes Scott College is less than half a mile ahead. From the North on I-85: From I-85, take the Clairmont Road exit. Turn left onto Clairmont Road. Five miles later, make a right onto Commerce Drive. Then turn left onto West Trinity Place, and after about half a mile, turn right onto North McDonough Street. Agnes Scott College is less than half a mile ahead. From the East on I-285 or I-20: Take I-285 to Stone Mountain Freeway, Highway 78 exit; follow Highway 78 West. Highway 78 will eventually turn into Scott Boulevard. Drive down Scott Boulevard for four miles, and then turn left on Clairmont Road. Less than one mile later, turn right onto Commerce Drive. Then turn left onto West Trinity Place and after about half a mile, turn right onto North McDonough Street. Agnes Scott College is less than half a mile ahead.

**LOCAL:** The East-West line of MARTA, Atlanta's public transportation system, offers subway service within three blocks of campus. MARTA also offers local bus service to South Decatur via Route 18. See station agent for details.

## WHERE TO STAY

A limited number of rooms are available on campus through the Agnes Scott College Alumnae House (404-471-6329, $). Hotels in Decatur include the Atlanta Marriot Century Center (404-325-0000, $$) and the Hampton Inn/North Druid Hills (404-320-6600, $$).

---

## CAMPUS AT ITS BEST!

If you're visiting ASC in September, check out Bonfire or Junior Production during Black Cat Week, and witness a long-time ASC ritual for inducting first-years into the campus community. And don't miss out on a walk through ASC's new Science Center and newly renovated Planetarium. For students who want to check out the scene off campus, the Martin Luther King Memorial, the new Georgia Aquarium, and many other attractions are only a stone's throw away in downtown Atlanta.

# APPALACHIAN STATE UNIVERSITY

Office of Admissions, PO Box 32004, Boone, NC 28608-2004
**Telephone:** 828-262-2120 • **E-mail:** admissions@appstate.edu
**Website:** www.appstate.edu

## STUDENTS SAY

"The mountain location is cool, so those into outdoor stuff are really happy here. Also, the huge variety of student clubs is great."

## FODOR'S SAYS

Hometown Boone houses the Daniel Boone Native Gardens, highlighting "local plants and trees in a setting of quiet beauty. The wrought-iron gate to the gardens was a gift of Daniel Boone VI, a direct descendant of the pioneer."

## ABOUT THE SCHOOL

Appalachian State University is a midsize school located in a mountain city just smaller than the university's own population of 15,117. ASU boasts four colleges and a school of music with an emphasis on international programs. Hometown Boone is surrounded by the Blue Ridge Mountains, allowing students plenty of options for fun outside of the classroom, including skiing, fishing, and white-water rafting.

## GETTING THERE

**BY AIR:** ASU is about two hours from the Charlotte-Douglas International Airport and the Piedmont Triad International Airport located in Greensboro. The university's Plemmons Student Union hosts a "Ride Share Board" that makes transportation arrangements for currently enrolled students; otherwise, a [rented] car is your best option for getting to the campus.

**BY TRAIN:** Amtrak services a station in Winston-Salem, approximately 80 miles from campus. From there, connect to the Piedmont Authority for Regional Transportation (PART) bus service for easiest transport to campus.

**BY BUS:** The local PART bus service in Boone makes regular trips to Winston-Salem and Greensboro, the sites of the closest Greyhound stations.

**BY CAR:** From Northbound: Take Highway 421 North into Boone. At the intersection of Highway 421 and Highway 321 South/Hardin Street, make a left to approach the campus. At the second stoplight, turn right onto Rivers Street and proceed to Hill Street—then turn left. After turning left onto Hill Street, you'll see a small gated lot on the right, adjacent to the John Thomas Building. This is visitor parking. Press the button on the call box for parking gate access. From Southbound: Take Highway 421/321 Southbound into Boone. Continue on Highway 321 South /Hardin Street to approach the campus area. At the first stoplight on Highway 321/Hardin Street, turn right onto Rivers Street and proceed to Hill Street—then turn left. After turning left onto Hill Street, you'll see a small gated lot on the right, adjacent to the John Thomas Building. This is visitor parking. Press the button on the call box for parking gate access.

**LOCAL:** Students with a valid University ID ride free on the AppalCART, which services all of Boone and Watauga County, including Appalachian State University.

## WHERE TO STAY

Visitors can stay at the Broyhill Inn and Conference Center (800-951-6048, $), conveniently located on campus. Other nearby lodging options include Crestwood (877-836-5046, $$) and the Blowing Rock Victorian Inn (828-295-0034, $$$).

## SCHOOL AT A GLANCE

| | |
|---|---|
| Type of School | Public |
| Environment | Rural |
| In-state Tuition | $2,221 |
| Out-of-state Tuition | $11,963 |
| Enrollment | 15,117 |
| % Male/Female | 48/52 |
| Student/Faculty Ratio | 17:1 |

### FRESHMAN PROFILE

| | |
|---|---|
| Range SAT | |
| Critical Reading | 510-600 |
| Range SAT Math | 530-620 |
| Range ACT Composite | 20-25 |
| Average HS GPA | 3.74 |

### ON-CAMPUS APPOINTMENTS

| | |
|---|---|
| Advance Notice | Yes |
| Appointment | Preferred |
| Saturdays | No |
| Average Length | 30 min |
| Info Sessions | Yes |
| Class Visits | Yes |

### CAMPUS TOURS

| | |
|---|---|
| Appointment | Preferred |
| Dates | Year Round |
| Times | Varies |
| Average Length | 120 min |

## CAMPUS AT ITS BEST!

Appalachian State is home to several museums and art galleries dedicated to presenting and preserving the rich cultural traditions of the region. While you're on campus, check out exhibits at the Turchin Center for the Visual Arts for insight into the people and history of the area. For students visiting in the summer, the nationally-regarded Appalachian Summer Festival is a must-see. The festival boasts numerous exhibits and performances from artists across the country.

# AUBURN UNIVERSITY

108 Mary Martin Hall, Auburn, AL 36849-5149
**Telephone:** 334-844-4080 • **E-mail:** admissions@auburn.edu
**Hours:** Monday–Friday, 8:00 A.M.–4:45 P.M.

## STUDENTS SAY

"Auburn is about football, drinking, and George W."

## FODOR'S SAYS

"The best times to visit the South are spring and fall, when temperatures are in the 70s and 80s."

## ABOUT THE SCHOOL

Making regular appearances on The Princeton Review's annual ranking list of top "Jock Schools," Auburn is a place where extracurriculars are taken seriously. But, as students are quick to point out, this is also one of the top research institutions in the South, and students pack the library as often as they do the football stadium.

## GETTING THERE

**BY AIR:** Smaller flights land at the Columbus Metropolitan Airport about 45 minutes from campus. The Hartsfield-Jackson Atlanta International Airport, one hour and 45 minutes away from campus, is serviced by all major airlines.

**BY TRAIN:** Amtrak operates out of Atlanta (one hour and 45 minutes away) and Birmingham (two hours away).

**BY BUS:** Greyhound operates a bus station in neighboring Opelika. The Express 85 charter bus service offers daily runs between Atlanta and East-Central Alabama (334-741-0916).

**BY CAR:** From I-85 North (Montgomery): Follow I-85 North to Exit 51. At the light, make a left onto College Street. Continue on College Street for four miles, at which point you'll see university buildings on both sides of the street. From I-85 South (Atlanta): Follow I-85 South to Exit 57. At the light, make a left onto Glenn Avenue. Continue on Glenn Avenue for about four miles, passing through four traffic lights. At the fifth traffic light, College Street, turn left. The next traffic light sits at Toomer's Corner. You will see Auburn University on the far right-hand side of this intersection. From U.S. 280 East (Birmingham): Turn right off U.S. 280 East onto AL-147 South (keep an eye out for the Conoco station at the intersection). Follow AL-147 for about five miles, driving into the Auburn city limits. Eventually, AL-147 will turn into College Street. Take College Street across the railroad tracks and into Auburn's downtown. Go through the first light at Glenn Avenue. At the next intersection (with Magnolia Avenue) you will see the Auburn campus on the far right-hand side of the intersection.

**LOCAL:** The Lee County Transit Agency (LETA) provides local bus service throughout Auburn and neighboring Opelika. Cabs and vans are available through Auburn Taxi Service (334-887-9356).

## WHERE TO STAY

Auburn offers hotels galore. Among the options are the Knights Inn (334-749-8377, $), the Best Western (334-821-7001, $$), the Hotel at Auburn University (334-821-8200, $$$), and, for golf lovers, the Auburn-Opelika Marriott at Grand National (334-741-9292, $$$).

## CAMPUS AT ITS BEST!

Those considering Auburn should try to visit the campus during War Eagle Days, one of 12 days during the academic year specifically set aside for visits from prospective students. If you're visiting the campus in the fall, you won't want to miss the Beat Bama Parade, an annual pep rally event to fire up Auburn fans before their big game against long-time rival University of Alabama. For off-campus fun, head to the Southeastern Raptor Center dedicated to rehabilitating birds of prey, or the air traffic control simulation facility operated by the Department of Aviation Management and Logistics.

# BELLARMINE UNIVERSITY

2001 Newburg Road, Louisville, KY 40205
**Telephone:** 502-452-8131 • **E-mail:** admissions@bellarmine.edu
**Website:** www.bellarmine.edu

## STUDENTS SAY

"Bellarmine is a small private university that has small classes and very personal professors who care about each student."

## FODOR'S SAYS

"Historic sites abound in the heart of Louisville. West Main Street has more examples of nineteenth century cast-iron architecture than anyplace else in the country except New York City's SoHo."

## ABOUT THE SCHOOL

Bellarmine is a liberal arts college located on a picturesque campus in one of the nation's most vibrant cities. Bellarmine takes pride in an expanding curriculum that allows undergrads to mix a classical education with specific training in professional fields. The faculty here are experts in their fields, and passionate about teaching and research.

## GETTING THERE

**BY AIR:** Most major airlines service the Louisville International Airport. The airport, just five miles from campus, can be easily accessed by bus, taxi, or car.

**BY TRAIN:** Amtrak stops at the train/bus station in downtown Louisville. The station can be reached by bus, taxi, or car.

**BY BUS:** Greyhound, which shares a station with Amtrak, operates out of downtown Louisville.

**BY CAR:** From I-71 South: Take I-71 South to I-264 West (Watterson Expressway). Follow I-264 West to Newburg Road North (Exit 15A). Stay on Newburg Road for one and a half miles until you reach Bellarmine. From I-64 West: Stay on I-64 West until you reach I-264 (Watterson Expressway). Go west on I-264 until you come to the exit for the Newburg Road North (Exit 15A). Follow the Newburg Road for one and a half miles until you reach Bellarmine. From I-64 East: From I-64 East turn onto I-264 East (Watterson Expressway) soon after the Ohio River Bridge. Follow I-264 to Newburg Road (Exit 15). Turn left at the end of the exit ramp and stay on Newburg Road for one and a half miles until you arrive at Bellarmine. From I-65 South: Take I-65 South across the Kennedy Bridge. Exit at I-264 (Watterson Expressway) and go east. Remain on I-264 until you come to Newburg Road (Exit 15). Take this exit, turning left at the end of the ramp. Follow Newburg Road for one and a half miles until you reach Bellarmine.

**LOCAL:** The Transit Authority of River City (TARC) offers extensive bus service throughout Louisville.

## WHERE TO STAY

Hotels within five miles of campus include Holiday Inn (502-452-6361, $), Executive West Hotel (502-367-2251, $), Courtyard by Marriott (502-368-5678, $$), and Candlewood Suites (502-357-3577, $$).

### SCHOOL AT A GLANCE

| | |
|---|---|
| Type of School | Private |
| Environment | Village |
| Tuition | $24,180 |
| Student/Faculty Ratio | 13:1 |

### FRESHMAN PROFILE

| | |
|---|---|
| Range SAT | |
| Critical Reading | 500-618 |
| Range SAT Math | 520-628 |
| Range ACT Composite | 22-27 |
| Average HS GPA | 3.5 |

### ON-CAMPUS APPOINTMENTS

| | |
|---|---|
| Advance Notice | Yes, 1 week |
| Appointment | Preferred |
| Saturdays | Yes |
| Average Length | 45 min |
| Info Sessions | Yes |
| Class Visits | Yes |

### CAMPUS TOURS

| | |
|---|---|
| Appointment | Preferred |
| Dates | Year Round |
| Times | Varies |
| Average Length | 60 min |

## CAMPUS AT ITS BEST!

Café Ogle is a popular study break destination for Bellarmine students. The jukebox and specialty drinks provide a much-needed antidote to academic pressures. Students also take advantage of all the cultural and recreational opportunities available in Louisville. Whether you're interested in attending a performance at The Actors Theatre, a sporting event like the Kentucky Derby, or spending the day at The Louisville Slugger Museum or The Muhammad Ali Center, the city of Louisville offers many options to enhance your visit (and your college experience).

# BEREA COLLEGE

CPO 2220, Berea, KY 40404

**Telephone:** 859-985-3500 • **E-mail:** admissions@berea.edu
**Website:** www.berea.edu

## STUDENTS SAY

"Berea strives to make students more aware of opportunities to help, how to become involved, and what service to others means."

## FODOR'S SAYS

Check out "Boone Tavern. Dating from 1909, this grand old Colonial-style hotel is operated by Berea College and outfitted with furniture handmade by students. The restaurant—which requires men to wear a jacket and tie—is famous for its spoon break, chicken flakes in bird's nest, and Jefferson Davis pie."

## ABOUT THE SCHOOL

Berea is member of a select group of colleges that offer tuition-free education for all undergraduates. Students "earn" their keep through a mandatory work-study program. Of course, hard work outside the classroom doesn't translate into an academic cakewalk. Professors demand a good deal and students log many hours in the library. When undergrads do find a free moment, they often do contra and swing dance, attend Bible study, or simply enjoy the company of their peers.

## GETTING THERE

**BY AIR:** Visitors can fly into Blue Grass Airport in Lexington. The airport provides nonstop flights from 13 different cities including Atlanta, Dallas, Cleveland, New York, and Washington, DC. Rental cars and taxis are both available for transportation to and from the airport.

**BY TRAIN:** The nearest Amtrak station is located almost 80 miles away in Maysville, KY. You will most likely need to rent a car for the remainder of your journey.

**BY BUS:** Greyhound provides direct service to Berea. To reach campus, it is best to call a taxi.

**BY CAR:** From the South via I-75: Take the first Berea exit, #76. Make a right off the exit ramp. You'll follow this road through several traffic lights until you pass the Berea City Hall and fire department on your left and the El Rio Grande Mexican Restaurant on your right. Here you'll see the edge of the Berea College campus. Drive past the large stone and brick Berea College sign (on your right) through campus, remaining on U.S. 25 North. From the North via I-75: Take the second Berea exit, #76. Follow "From the South" directions above.

**LOCAL:** For local cab service, call P Cab Co. (859-986-1111).

## WHERE TO STAY

These hotels all offer discount rates to Berea guests: Comfort Inn and Suite (859-985-5500, $), Fairfield Inn and Suite (859-985-8191, $–$$) or the Holiday Inn (859-985-1901, $–$$).

## CAMPUS AT ITS BEST!

While touring the campus, spend some time perusing the Log House Craft Gallery. Here you'll find tangible evidence of Berea ingenuity and creativity as student crafts are both on display and available for purchase.

# BIRMINGHAM-SOUTHERN COLLEGE

900 Arkadelphia Road, BirminghA.M., AL 35254
**Telephone:** 205-226-4696 • **E-mail:** admission@bsc.edu
**Website:** www.bsc.edu

## STUDENTS SAY

"Southern's about learning what makes a difference in this world and then going out and making it."

## FODOR'S SAYS

"Sloss Furnaces, a National Historic Landmark, is a massive, 32-acre ironworks that from 1882 to 1971 produced pig iron from ore dug up from the hills surrounding Birmingham. Retired blast-furnace workers sometimes conduct tours of the plant. At other times tours are self-guided."

## ABOUT THE SCHOOL

Birmingham-Southern College is a small school with a strong sense of community, nestled in the heart of a large, bustling city. Students love their close proximity to downtown Birmingham, and engage in the city's cultural offerings and nightlife without having to travel far from their dormitory.

## GETTING THERE

**BY AIR:** The Birmingham International Airport is only a 10-minute drive from the college. The school will make arrangements to meet students if requested. Otherwise, take a cab, shuttle or limousine service car. The shuttle and limousine service cars must be reserved beforehand: Try Airport Express (205-591-7770), Birmingham Door to Door (205-591-5550), or eShuttle (205-702-4566).

**BY TRAIN:** Birmingham's Amtrak station is only three miles from the BSC campus. Take a cab or MAX (Birmingham's Metro Area Express) service to campus.

**BY BUS:** Greyhound has a terminal in downtown Birmingham. Take a cab or MAX service to campus.

**BY CAR:** From East or West (via I-20/59): Take I-20/59 to Exit 123/Arkadelphia Road. From I-20 East/I-59 North, turn right onto Arkadelphia Road. From I-20 West/I-59 South, turn left onto Arkadelphia Road. Drive over the interstate overpass. Birmingham-Southern will be on the right as you top the hill. From North or South (via I-65): Take I-65 to the junction of I-20/59 and proceed on I-20 West/I-59 South (toward Tuscaloosa) to Exit 123/Arkadelphia Road. Turn left and drive over the interstate overpass. Birmingham-Southern will be on the right as you top the hill.

**LOCAL:** BJCTA (Birmingham Jefferson County Transit Authority) and its Metro Area Express buses (MAX) serve the Birmingham-Southern College campus via the #6 Pratt/Ensley bus. For cab service in the Bennington area call Meteors (205-980-1083), American Cab Co. (205-322-2222), or Baseemah Taxi Service (205-592-9410).

## WHERE TO STAY

Birmingham offers many hotel options. The Days Inn is in downtown Birmingham, near many of the city's sights and attractions (205-822-6030, $). The Wynfrey Hotel, at the edge of Birmingham, is attached to a retail emporium (800-476-7006, $$$). Also convenient to the BSC campus is the Hampton Inn—Mountain Brook (205-967-0002, $$).

## CAMPUS AT ITS BEST!

Since more than half of Birmingham-Southern College's students join a fraternity or sorority, Greek events make up a large part of the social life on campus. Drop in on BSC's common hour events, an engaging series of art, culture, and politics lectures and performances held on Tuesdays and Thursdays all year throughout the campus. If you're into film, consider planning your visit around Birmingham's acclaimed Sidewalk Moving Picture Festival, held in late September.

# CATAWBA COLLEGE

2300 West Innes Street, Salisbury, NC 28144

**Telephone:** 704-637-4402 • **E-mail:** admission@catawba.edu

**Website:** www.catawba.edu • **Hours:** Monday–Friday, 8:00 A.M.–5:00 P.M.

## STUDENTS SAY

"The theater department and athletics are very good and very popular here."

## FODOR'S SAYS

"You might want to forgo a modern hotel in favor of a historic property—there are dozens of fine old hotels, many of them fully restored and quite a few offering better rates than chain properties with comparable amenities."

## ABOUT THE SCHOOL

With only about 1,350 undergrads, Catawba students enjoy small classes and lots of one-on-one attention from professors. Catawba has particularly strong programs in theater, environmental science, and athletic training, and one of the school's most enduring characteristics is the devotion of its faculty to the liberal arts.

## GETTING THERE

**BY AIR:** Charlotte Douglas International Airport (CLT) is 47 miles away, and the Piedmont Triad International Airport (GSO) is 56 miles away. A rented car or airport shuttle is your best bet for transport to campus.

**BY TRAIN:** Amtrak has a station about two miles from campus at 215 Depot Street. Take a taxi to campus, or hop on the Salisbury Transit bus.

**BY BUS:** Greyhound services a station located six miles from campus. Take a taxi to campus or hop on the Salisbury Transit bus.

**BY CAR:** From East and Northeast: Take I-85 South. Exit on I-85, Exit 76 (Salisbury, Catawba College). Bear right at end of exit ramp onto Innes Street. Drive straight through downtown, continuing approximately three miles to the Catawba campus. From West and Northwest: Take I-40 East to I-77 South. Get off I-77 at Exit 49A (Garner-Bagnal Boulevard), turn right at end of exit ramp onto Highway 70 East. Continue for approximately 30 miles. In Salisbury, 70 East is renamed Statesville Boulevard. Continue straight on Statesville Boulevard to the intersection with Innes Street. Turn left onto Innes Street and continue four blocks to Catawba College. From South: Take I-85 North to Exit 76 (Salisbury, Catawba College). Bear left at the stop sign at the end of the exit ramp onto Innes Street. Drive straight through downtown, continuing approximately three miles to the Catawba campus.

**LOCAL:** The best way to get around is via car or cab, but the Salisbury Transit System operates buses that stop a few blocks from several points on campus. Fare is 60 cents within Salisbury and $1.20 for points outside the city. For local cab service, try Safety Taxi (704-633-7217), Phase II Taxi (704-636-4112), or Town and Country Limousine (704-638-0503).

## WHERE TO STAY

Salisbury has hotels and bed and breakfasts for every budget. Try the Holiday Inn (704-637-3100, $), the Turn of the Century Victorian Bed & Breakfast (704-642-1660, $$), and the Rowan Oak House Bed & Breakfast (800-786-0437, $$).

## CAMPUS AT ITS BEST!

When visiting Catawba College, be sure to take in of one of the college's many lively student-run theater productions. Walk the self-guided African American Heritage Tour and don't miss the revolving exhibits at the Waterworks Visual Arts Center in nearby downtown Salisbury.

# CENTRE COLLEGE

600 West Walnut Street, Danville, KY 40422
**Telephone:** 1-800-423-6236 • **E-mail:** admission@centre.edu
**Hours:** Monday–Friday, 8:30 A.M.–5:00 P.M.; Saturday, 9:00 A.M.–NOON

## STUDENTS SAY

"Centre is challenging. The academics are tough, the atmosphere forces you to grow as a person, and after the week is over there is something for everyone to do to relax and have fun."

## FODOR'S SAYS

"West of Danville on U.S. 150 and north on U.S. 68 is Perryville Battlefield, the site of Kentucky's most important (and bloodiest) Civil War battle, where 4,241 Union soldiers and 1,822 Confederates were killed or wounded."

## ABOUT THE SCHOOL

Centre College is the perfect place for undergrads who appreciate guarantees. What kind of guarantees? The college promises that each student will land a discipline-specific internship, will be able to study abroad, and will have that diploma in hand within four years. All this adds up to what the college calls "the Centre Commitment."

## GETTING THERE

**BY AIR:** The airports closest to campus are the larger Louisville International Airport (85 miles from campus) and the smaller Blue Grass Airport in Lexington (35 miles). Transportation to and from the airport can be arranged in advance through the Admissions Office.

**BY TRAIN:** There is no nearby train service, though Amtrak does offer thruway bus service from regional train destinations to downtown Louisville.

**BY BUS:** Greyhound services Lexington, about half an hour from campus.

**BY CAR:** From I-65 North: From I-65 North, exit onto Cumberland Parkway. Take this to U.S. 127/Hustonville Road, which goes into Danville 47 miles later. As the road splits, stay on 3rd Street. Make a right onto Maple Avenue. Then take a left onto Perryville Street. Campus parking is just ahead. From I-75 South: Take I-75 South to Route 922 (Exit 115). Bear right and go one and a half miles to New Circle Road and turn right. Four miles later, exit at Versailles Road and go West. Turn onto Bluegrass Parkway (Exit 72) and follow to U.S. 127 South (Exit 59). After 28 miles, go left onto U.S. 127 Business/Maple Avenue. Two miles later, turn right onto Perryville Street. For parking, turn left at the second driveway.

**LOCAL:** For cabs, try Danville/Boyle County Taxi Service (859-236-4443).

## WHERE TO STAY

Danville offers a number of budget hotels, including the Holiday Inn Express (859-236-8600, $) and Comfort Suites (859-936-9300, $). Among a range of cozy B&Bs around Danville are the Lincliff Guesthouse (859-236-0185, $$) and Country Lane Bed and Breakfast (866-761-7336, $$).

### SCHOOL AT A GLANCE

| | |
|---|---|
| Type of School | Private |
| Environment | Village |
| Tuition | $23,110 |
| Enrollment | 1,122 |
| % Male/Female | 49/51 |
| Student/Faculty Ratio | 11:1 |

### FRESHMAN PROFILE

| | |
|---|---|
| Range SAT | |
| Critical Reading | 580-678 |
| Range SAT Math | 600-670 |
| Range ACT Composite | 25-29 |
| Average HS GPA | 3.7 |

### ON-CAMPUS APPOINTMENTS

| | |
|---|---|
| Advance Notice | Yes, 1 week |
| Appointment | Required |
| Saturdays | Sometimes |
| Average Length | 60 min |
| Info Sessions | Yes |
| Class Visits | Yes |

### CAMPUS TOURS

| | |
|---|---|
| Appointment | Required |
| Dates | Year Round |
| Times | M–F 10:00 A.M., 1:00 P.M., and 3:00 P.M.; Sat 10:00 A.M. |
| Average Length | 60 min |

## CAMPUS AT ITS BEST!

Prospective students looking to gain insight into daily campus life should visit the Combs Student Center. This building, listed in the National Register of Historic Places, is a popular gathering place for students. Among its many amenities are pool tables, a performance space, an Internet center, and a café. Visitors should also stop by the Norton Center for the Arts, an internationally recognized facility that hosts a number of impressive performers each year, including David Copperfield, the Boston Pops, and Garrison Keillor. Finally, those touring the campus in June might want to check out the Great American Brass Band Festival, held annually in hometown Danville.

# THE CITADEL—THE MILITARY COLLEGE OF SOUTH CAROLINA

171 Moultrie Street, Charleston, SC 29409
**Telephone:** 843-953-5230 • **E-mail:** admissions@citadel.edu
**Website:** www.citadel.edu

## STUDENTS SAY

"The Citadel takes motivated undergraduates and turns them into professional, reliable, and positive all-around leaders for any aspect of life."

## FODOR'S SAYS

"On a man-made island in Charleston Harbor, Confederate forces fired the first shot of the Civil War on April 12, 1861. After a 34-hour bombardment, Union forces surrendered and Confederate troops occupied Sumter, which became a symbol of Southern resistance. The Confederacy held the fort, despite almost continual bombardment, for nearly four years; when it was finally evacuated, the place was a heap of rubble. Today, the National Park Service oversees the Fort Sumter National Monument complex."

## ABOUT THE SCHOOL

The Citadel is a state-supported comprehensive military college and one of the region's finest institutions. Undergraduates are welcomed into a residential Corps of Cadets that emphasizes discipline, unity, and loyalty. Teamwork is also highly valued, and cadets report strong feelings of camaraderie with their classmates.

## GETTING THERE

**BY AIR:** Visitors may fly into Charleston International Airport. Taxis, shuttles, and rental cars are all available for transport to the campus.

**BY TRAIN:** Guests may take Amtrak directly into Charleston. To reach the Citadel from the station it's best to take a taxi.

**BY BUS:** Greyhound also offers service to Charleston. For additional transportation needs you'll want to call a taxi or rent a car.

**BY CAR:** From Interstate 26 Eastbound: Take the Rutledge Avenue Exit (219-A). Proceed on Rutledge Avenue for approximately 1.2 miles, and make a right onto Moultrie Street. Continue down Moultrie Street until it ends at Lesesne Gate, which is the main entrance to the Citadel. From U.S. 17 Southbound: Cross the Ravenel Bridge and proceed along U.S. 17 South. Make a right onto Hagood Avenue. Drive past the football stadium and enter the Citadel through the Hagood Gate. Should you find Hagood Gate closed, make a right onto Huger Street, a left onto Elmwood Street, and another left at the following block so you enter the Citadel through Lesesne Gate. From U.S. 17 Northbound: After you pass the round Holiday Inn and cross the Ashley River Bridge, you exit U.S. 17 toward the right (you need to stay in the exit ramp's left-hand lane until you reach the traffic light). Make a left onto Lockwood Drive, proceed 0.5 miles, and then make another right onto Fishburne Street. Drive another 0.3 miles, and make a left at the stop sign onto Hagood Avenue. Follow "From U.S. 17 Southbound" directions above.

**LOCAL:** For local taxi service call Express Cab Company (843-577-8816), North Area Taxi (843-554-7575) or Lee's Limousine (843-797-0041).

## WHERE TO STAY

Charleston has a wide variety of hotel accommodations, including the Sleep Inn (843-556-6959, $), Kings Courtyard Inn (843-723-7000, $$–$$$), and Planters Inn (800-845-7082, $$$+).

---

## CAMPUS AT ITS BEST!

Summerall Field is decorated with various military monuments representative of the four service branches. Stroll around the grounds, and you'll be able to see a Marine Landing Craft, an army Sherman tank, an army missile, an AH-1 Cobra helicopter, an air force jet, and a navy anchor. Prospective students visiting on a Friday will want to remain on the field. You'll be able to witness a Citadel parade, considered by some to be the best free show in Charleston.

# CLARK ATLANTA UNIVERSITY

223 James P. Brawley Drive at Fair Street, Atlanta, GA 30314
**Telephone:** 404-880-8000 • **E-mail:** admissions@panthernet.cau.edu
**Hours:** Monday–Friday, 9:00 A.M.–5:00 P.M.

## STUDENTS SAY

"The greatest strength of the school is the networking opportunities."

## FODOR'S SAYS

"Atlanta's lack of a grid system confuses many drivers—even locals. Before setting out anywhere, get the complete street address of your destination, including landmarks, cross streets, or other guideposts, as street numbers and even street signs are hard to find."

## ABOUT THE SCHOOL

Clark Atlanta University is a small, historically Black college in Atlanta that puts a strong emphasis on academic excellence, building character, and service to others. The university is home to nationally renowned marching band the Mighty Marching Panther Band, which was featured in the movie Drumline.

## GETTING THERE

**BY AIR:** The South/Hartsfield International Airport (ATL) is the closest airport to campus and services all the major airlines. Take a taxi or the local MARTA Rail to get to campus.

**BY TRAIN:** Amtrak services a station on Peachtree Street in Atlanta. Take a taxi or the local MARTA Rail to get to campus.

**BY BUS:** Greyhound stops at a station on Forsyth Street in Atlanta. Take a taxi or the local MARTA Rail to get to campus.

**BY CAR:** From I-75/85 North or South: Take I-20 West. Get off at Joseph Lowery Boulevard. Make a right onto Joseph Lowery Boulevard until you reach Fair Street. Make a right onto Fair Street until you reach James P. Brawley Drive. The campus is ahead. From I-20 East: Exit at Joseph Lowery Boulevard. Make a right onto Joseph Lowery Boulevard until you reach Fair Street and stay on it until you reach James P. Brawley Drive. The campus is ahead. From I-20 West: Exit at Joseph Lowery Boulevard. Make a left onto Joseph Lowery Boulevard until you reach Fair Street and stay on it until you reach James P. Brawley Drive. The campus is ahead. From Downtown Atlanta: Take Centennial Olympic Drive to Martin Luther King Jr. Drive. Turn right onto Martin Luther King Jr. Drive. Then turn left onto Northside Drive. Finally, turn right onto Fair Street (South) and continue until you reach James P. Brawley Drive. The campus is ahead.

**LOCAL:** Visitors can take the local train, the MARTA Rail, to the Vine City or West End station. From there a shuttle from the college takes you directly to the campus. If you'd rather take a taxi, some local companies include Cascade Cab Co (404-758-5521) and City Wide Cab Co (404-875-1223).

## WHERE TO STAY

Some popular hotel choices in Atlanta include the Stratford Inn Atlanta (404-607-1010, $), Atlanta Days-Inn Downtown (404-523-1144, $$), and the Hilton Atlanta (404-659-2000, $$$).

| SCHOOL AT A GLANCE | |
| --- | --- |
| Type of School | Private |
| Environment | Metropolis |
| Tuition | $14,522 |
| Enrollment | 3,667 |
| % Male/Female | 30/70 |
| Student/Faculty Ratio | 16:1 |
| **FRESHMAN PROFILE** | |
| Range SAT | |
| Critical Reading | 330-593 |
| Range SAT Math | 360-580 |
| Range ACT Composite | 14-25 |
| Average HS GPA | 3.10 |
| **ON-CAMPUS APPOINTMENTS** | |
| Advance Notice | 1 week |
| Appointment | Required |
| Saturdays | No |
| Class Visits | No |
| **CAMPUS TOURS** | |
| Appointment | Required |
| Dates | Varies |
| Times | M–F 10:00 A.M. |
| | and 2:00 P.M. |
| Average Length | 60 min |

## CAMPUS AT ITS BEST!

The art galleries of Clark Atlanta University offer some of the most extensive collections of African American art in the country. The holdings include pieces by Hale Woodruff, Jacob Lawrence, and Romare Bearden. Visitors to campus in the fall should try to attend CAU's homecoming football game. This popular event draws alums, current students, and local Atlantans to CAU's campus where the Mighty Marching Panther Band always puts on a great show.

# CLEMSON UNIVERSITY

105 Sikes Hall, Box 345124, Clemson, SC 29634-5124

**Telephone:** 864-656-2287 • **E-mail:** cuadmissions@clemson.edu • **Website:** www.clemson.edu

**Hours:** Monday-Sunday, 8:00 A.M.–4:30 P.M.

## STUDENTS SAY

"At Clemson life is very happy-go-lucky. People are in a seemingly good mood all of the time because they love their university."

## FODOR'S SAYS

"Wondering about the hand-lettered signs advertising 'Hot Boiled Peanuts' on display in nearly every gas station, convenience store, and roadside stand?" Simmered in brine, they are "a slightly slippery, but never slimy treat."

## ABOUT THE SCHOOL

One of the nation's premier public universities, Clemson offers students great academics and professors who go the extra mile to make sure their students are engaged in the classroom. The social life on campus also receives a lot of kudos from students. Clemson football is a unifying force in this small college town, and brings students and locals together in a mass show of school spirit.

## GETTING THERE

**BY AIR:** The Greenville-Spartanburg International Airport (GSP), located in Upstate South Carolina, is less than an hour from Clemson. Take a taxi to get to campus.

**BY TRAIN:** Amtrak stops at Calhoun Memorial Highway and College Avenue in Clemson. Take a taxi to get to campus.

**BY BUS:** Greyhound stops at 203 West Earl Street in Anderson, located 20 miles from Clemson. Take a taxi to get to campus.

**BY CAR:** From the South: Take I-85 North toward Charlotte, NC. Take Exit 19B to U.S. 76 West to Clemson. From the North: Take I-85 South toward Atlanta, GA. Take Exit 19B to U.S. 76 West to Clemson. From the East: Take I-126 West to I-26 West toward Spartanburg, SC. Take the exit for I-385 West to Greenville, SC. Take the exit for I-85 South toward Atlanta, GA. Take Exit 19B to US 76 West to Clemson.

**LOCAL:** For local taxi service, try Rochester Cab Co. (864-882-8787).

## WHERE TO STAY

The university offers lodging on campus at the James F. Martin Inn (888-654-9020, $). Two popular choices near the college include Comfort Inn (864-653-3600) and Lake Hartwell Inn (864-654-4450, $$).

## CAMPUS AT ITS BEST!

Hit the links on Clemson's picturesque John E. Walker Sr. Golf Course. Home to the university's 2003 NCAA championship team, the course is open and available to the public year round. Following your 18 holes, celebrate nineteenth-century America by visiting Fort Hill. This was the home of John C. Calhoun, the prominent South Carolina statesman. Finally, complete your tour with a stop at the Garrison Livestock Arena. This facility hosts numerous events, ranging from horse shows and bull sales to rodeos.

# COLLEGE OF CHARLESTON

66 George Street, Charleston, SC 29424
**Telephone:** 843-953-5670 • **E-mail:** admissions@cofc.edu
**Website:** www.cofc.edu • **Hours:** Monday–Friday, 9:00 A.M.–5:00 P.M.; Saturday by appointment

## STUDENTS SAY

"C of C is a wonderful place to live, study, work, and play, set in a magical city in the charming Old South."

## FODOR'S SAYS

"Drive along U.S. 17 North to find the basket ladies set up at rickety roadside stands, weaving sweet-grass, pine-straw, and palmetto leaf baskets. Baskets typically cost less on this stretch than in downtown Charleston."

## ABOUT THE SCHOOL

Personal attention is the name of the game at the College of Charleston. C of C students love the fact that at this midsized school (which has an undergrad population of about 10,000) they get to know their professors as people as well as teachers. And they also love the fact that they live in the heart of Charleston, a thriving Southern city just 15 minutes from the beach.

## GETTING THERE

**BY AIR:** More than 100 flights operate daily out of Charleston International Airport, which is about 13 miles from campus. The easiest way to get to campus is to hop in a cab.

**BY TRAIN:** The Amtrak station in North Charleston is less than 10 miles from campus. Take a cab from the station to campus.

**BY BUS:** Greyhound offers regular service to Charleston. The station is six miles North of campus.

**BY CAR:** From I-26: Take I-26 to the Meeting Street exit. Make a right and stay on Meeting Street until you come to Calhoun Street, where you'll make another right. When you get to St. Philip Street, you're on campus. From Highway 17 South: Follow Highway 17 South to the right exit for Lockwood Drive. Going South on Lockwood Drive, make a left onto Calhoun Street. When you get to St. Philip Street, you're on campus. From Highway 17 North: Take Highway 17 North, passing over the Ravenel Bridge and exiting at Meeting Street. Turn left onto Meeting Street and go straight. At Calhoun Street, make a right. When you get to St. Philip Street, you're on campus.

\* Note that the college cannot validate parking. Instead, it recommends that visitors park in one of the nearby city parking garages.

**LOCAL:** Students ride free on Charleston Area Regional Transit Authority buses and shuttles. CARTA's DASH shuttle service operates rides directly to downtown. Bus Route 210 runs directly through campus. Taxi choices included Express Cab Company (843-577-8816) and Yellow Cab (843-577-6565).

## WHERE TO STAY

Charleston has plenty of accommodations to offer the overnight visitor. Options near campus in Charleston's posh historic district include the Holiday Inn (843-805-7900, $$$) and Charleston Place (843-722-4900, $$$+). More economical options are available in nearby areas such as Mount Pleasant and West Ashley.

---

## CAMPUS AT ITS BEST!

The College of Charleston's Beatty Center is a prime example of one of the school's state-of-the-art facilities. Visitors will think they're on Wall Street when they enter the "real-time" investment trading room. After taking a hit on a stock trade, take a stroll down Fountain Walk and enjoy the city of Charleston's beautiful scenery.

# THE COLLEGE OF WILLIAM & MARY

PO Box 8795, Williamsburg, VA 23187-8795
**Telephone:** 757-221-4223 • **E-mail:** admiss@wm.edu
**Website:** www.wm.edu • **Hours:** Monday–Friday; 8:00 A.M.–5:00 P.M.; Saturday, 9:00 A.M.–NOON

## STUDENTS SAY

"Big-time reputation, rigorous academics, and powerful professors make the William & Mary experience unforgettable."

## FODOR'S SAYS

"Dining rooms within walking distance of Colonial Williamsburg's restored area are often crowded, and reservations necessary."

## ABOUT THE SCHOOL

Undergrads at William & Mary enjoy a combination of innovation and tradition. Situated on the edge of historic Williamsburg, Virginia, William & Mary boasts top-of-the-line academic programs and rigorous standards that have landed the college among America's most elite institutions. An added bonus: Men and women in colonial costume can often be seen on the streets of town while a flurry of student activity enlivens the campus.

## GETTING THERE

**BY AIR:** The nearest airport is the Newport News-Williamsburg International Airport about 20 minutes from campus. In addition, Richmond's Byrd International Airport and the Norfolk International Airport are each an hour from campus. Take a taxi or limousine service from the airport to campus.

**BY TRAIN:** Williamsburg's Amtrak station is less than a mile from campus.

**BY BUS:** Amtrak and Greyhound use the same depot, less than a mile from campus.

**BY CAR:** From I-64: Follow I-64 (North or South) to Exit 238 at Williamsburg onto Route 143 East. Half a mile later, turn right onto Route 132 South. Merge onto Bypass Road and take this until it ends at the intersection with Richmond Road. Make a left onto Richmond Road. When you reach the third traffic light, Zable Stadium is on your right. The Admissions Office is on the other side of the light on the right-hand side of the street.

**LOCAL:** Williamsburg Area Transport provides bus service for Williamsburg, James City County, and part of York County. The Green Line runs through campus. Also, taxi service is available through Colonial Cabs of Williamsburg (757-713-3440), Williamsburg Taxi Service (757-254-2190), and Yellow Cab of Williamsburg (757-722-1111).

## WHERE TO STAY

Colonial Williamsburg and the surrounding area offer a bounty of overnight accommodations. These include the White Lion Motel (757-229-3931, $), the Black Badger Inn Bed and Breakfast (757-253-0202, $$), and, considered one of the nation's top hotels, the Colonial Williamsburg Inn (757-220-7978, $$$+). Also, across the street from campus is the Williamsburg Hospitality House (757-229-4020, $$), which boasts excellent accommodation and a convenient location.

---

## CAMPUS AT ITS BEST!

William & Mary is the perfect campus for the budding historian. The Wren Building, the oldest academic structure in the nation, is believed to have been designed by Christopher Wren, architect of St. Paul's Cathedral in London. Another favorite locale is the Sunken Garden, an area conceived by Thomas Jefferson. Students flock there to study...and to play the occasional game of Frisbee or soccer. Before visiting, research the performance schedule for the Lively Arts Series. Past performers have included the Golden Dragon Acrobats and The Glenn Miller Orchestra.

# DAVIDSON COLLEGE

Box 7156, Davidson, NC 28035-5000
**Telephone:** 800-768-0380 • **E-mail:** admission@davidson.edu • **Website:** www.davidson.edu
**Hours:** Monday–Friday, 8:30 A.M.–5:00 P.M.; Saturday, 10:30 A.M.–1:00 P.M. and by appointment

## STUDENTS SAY

"We're a close-knit community. With only 1,600 students, we feel a strong sense of what it means to be a Davidsonian—which we like to explain as a condition characterized by constant exhaustion, five or more serious extracurricular activities, and ambition that would stun a yak."

## FODOR'S SAYS

"Want a guaranteed one-word conversation starter in any gathering of North Carolinians? Say 'barbecue.' The state's barbecue tradition is so revered that it has inspired place names such as Barbecue Presbyterian Church."

## ABOUT THE SCHOOL

It's all about challenging academics and intellectual integrity at this top-notch liberal arts college. Well, that's almost what it's all about. With downtown Charlotte just 20 minutes away and everything from the Atlantic Ocean to the Appalachian Mountains within a two-hour drive, the Davidson experience has its perks inside and outside of the academic halls.

## GETTING THERE

**BY AIR:** Douglas International Airport in Charlotte is about half an hour from campus. Travel to campus by car or taxi.

**BY TRAIN:** Amtrak rail service operates out of Kannapolis and Charlotte, each less than half an hour from campus. The easiest transport to campus is via car or taxi.

**BY BUS:** Greyhound's Charlotte hub is 22 miles south of campus. To get to campus, take a car or a cab.

**BY CAR:** From I-77 North: Proceed on I-77 North until you reach Exit 30. At the end of the ramp, turn right onto Griffith Street and drive straight ahead until you reach campus. From I-77 South: Proceed on I-77 South until you reach Exit 30. At the end of the ramp, turn left onto Griffith Street and drive straight ahead until you reach campus. From I-85 North: Take I-85 North to Exit 38 for I-77 North toward Statesville. Proceed on I-77 North until you reach Exit 30. At the end of the ramp, turn right onto Griffith Street and drive straight ahead until you reach campus. From I-40 West: Drive on I-40 West to Exit 152A for I-77 South toward Charlotte. Proceed on I-77 South until you reach Exit 30. At the end of the ramp, turn left onto Griffith Street and drive straight ahead until you reach campus.

**LOCAL:** The Charlotte Area Transit System (CATS) offers bus service in Davidson via the North Mecklenburg Village Rider. Use line 96 (Village Rider—Davidson). Local taxi companies include A Taxi (704-777-2000), Terry's Taxi Service (704-663-9812), and Yellow Cab of Lake Norman (704-662-9222).

## WHERE TO STAY

The elegant on-campus Carnegie Guest House has limited space for campus visitors. For information, call 704-894-2127. Other local options include the Comfort Inn Suites—Lake Norman (704-896-7622, $), Hampton Inn—Lake Norman (704-892-9900, $$), and the Davidson Village Inn (704-892-8044, $$).

## SCHOOL AT A GLANCE

| | |
|---|---|
| Type of School | Private |
| Environment | Village |
| Tuition | $29,119 |
| Enrollment | 1,683 |
| % Male/Female | 50/50 |
| Student/Faculty Ratio | 10:1 |

## FRESHMAN PROFILE

| | |
|---|---|
| Range SAT | |
| Critical Reading | 650-750 |
| Range SAT Math | 650-740 |
| Range ACT Composite | 28-32 |
| Average HS GPA | 3.96 |

## ON-CAMPUS APPOINTMENTS

| | |
|---|---|
| Advance Notice | Yes, 2 weeks |
| Appointment | Preferred |
| Saturdays | Sometimes |
| Info Sessions | Yes |
| Class Visits | Yes |

## CAMPUS TOURS

| | |
|---|---|
| Appointment | Preferred |
| Dates | Year Round |
| Times | Varies |
| Average Length | 60 min |

## CAMPUS AT ITS BEST!

For a taste of Davidson's academic life, guests should tour the Baker-Watt Science Complex. This facility grants students access to incredible, state-of-the-art equipment, such as a scanning electron microscope, a UV-visible spectrophotometer, and laser systems. While you're on campus, inquire about the monthly musical interlude concerts sponsored by the ever-active music department, a favorite among students. Fraternities and social/dining clubs are prevalent on Davidson's campus. Therefore, visitors might want to stop by Patterson Court and investigate residential Greek life.

# DUKE UNIVERSITY

2138 Campus Drive, Box 90586, Durham., NC 27708-0586
**Telephone:** 919-684-3214 • **Website:** www.admissions.duke.edu
**Hours:** Monday–Friday, 8:00 A.M.–5:00 P.M.; Saturday, 10:00 A.M.–1:00 P.M.

### SCHOOL AT A GLANCE

| | |
|---|---|
| Type of School | Private |
| Environment | City |
| Tuition | $32,850 |
| Enrollment | 6,330 |
| % Male/Female | 52/48 |
| Student/Faculty Ratio | 11:1 |

### FRESHMAN PROFILE

| | |
|---|---|
| Range SAT | |
| Critical Reading | 690-770 |
| Range SAT Math | 690-800 |
| Range ACT Composite | 29-34 |

### ON-CAMPUS APPOINTMENTS

| | |
|---|---|
| Advance Notice | Yes |
| Appointment | Required |
| Saturdays | No |
| Average Length | 30 min |
| Info Sessions | Yes |
| Class Visits | Yes |

### CAMPUS TOURS

| | |
|---|---|
| Appointment | Not Required |
| Dates | Year Round |
| Times | Varies |
| Average Length | 60 min |

## STUDENTS SAY

"Duke is the whole package—superb academics, vibrant social life, beautiful campus, engaging students, and bountiful extracurricular offerings."

## FODOR'S SAYS

"Named for the kind of tobacco once manufactured in the old warehouses here, Brightleaf Square, with its flowering courtyard, striking turn-of-the-twentieth-century architecture, upscale shops, and restaurants, is the shining star of a downtown revitalization effort" in hometown Durham.

## ABOUT THE SCHOOL

The South's answer to the Ivy League, Duke University promotes tradition and personal attention while providing all the benefits of a cutting-edge research institution. Students should be aware, however, that life at Duke is not exactly easy-breezy. At this perennial academic powerhouse, high achievement is prompted by high expectations and precipitated by a lot of hard work.

## GETTING THERE

**BY AIR:** Fly into Raleigh-Durham International Airport, which is serviced by about 20 airlines. To get to campus—located less than half an hour from the airport—use a cab or limousine service.

**BY TRAIN:** Durham's Amtrak station is just a mile and a half from campus. Take a cab for quick and easy transit to campus.

**BY BUS:** The Greyhound terminal is a five-minute drive from campus. Use a taxi to get there.

**BY CAR:** From I-40 West: Take I-40 West to Exit 279 for the Durham Freeway (Route 147) North. Follow the Durham Freeway North to Exit 14 for Swift Avenue. At the end of the ramp, go left. After passing through a traffic light, make a right onto Campus Drive. The Admissions Office is less than a mile ahead on your right. From I-85 South: Follow I-85 South to Exit 174B for 15-501 South By-Pass/Duke University/Chapel Hill. After two miles, turn left onto Highway 751/Cameron Boulevard and proceed for a mile. At the fourth light, make a left onto Duke University Road. Make a left on Chapel Drive less than a mile later. In the traffic circle, take the first right onto Campus Drive. The Admissions Office is just ahead. From I-85 North: Follow I-85 North to Exit 170 for Highway 70 East toward NC 751/Duke University. A little more than a mile later, turn right onto Highway 751. Nearly five miles later, turn left onto Duke University Road. Then make a left onto Chapel Hill Drive. In the traffic circle, take the first right onto Campus Drive. The Admissions Office is just ahead.

**LOCAL:** Taxi companies that offer fares to/from the airport and around town include Durham's Best (919-680-3330), Charlene's Safe Ride (919-309-7233), and J.M.T. Taxi Service (919-417-7033). Triangle Transit Authority (919-549-9999) and Duke University Transit (919-684-2218) offer extensive bus service to Duke and the surrounding area. Call for schedule info.

## WHERE TO STAY

Durham accommodations include La Quinta Inn (866-725-1661, $–$$), Residence Inn by Marriott (800-331-3131, $$), and Washington Duke Inn and Golf Club (800-443-3853, $$$).

---

### CAMPUS AT ITS BEST!

Science buffs will especially appreciate the Sara P. Duke Gardens, covering 55 acres in the heart of Duke's West Campus. This popular botanical garden sees over 300,000 visitors a year and provides a great place for education and discovery. After communing with nature, make your way over to The Duke Lemur Center, the world's largest sanctuary for rare and endangered prosimian primates. Students visiting during fall term might be able to attend the annual Oktoberfest. This popular outdoor festival typically hosts an array of entertainment, and includes craft vendors and international food stations.

---

# EAST CAROLINA UNIVERSITY

Office of Undergraduate Admissions, 106 Whichard Building, Greenville, NC 27858-4353
**Telephone:** 252-328-6640 • **E-mail:** admis@ecu.edu

## STUDENTS SAY

"From the moment you get here, you feel right at home—like you have been here for years."

## FODOR'S SAYS

"Forced to name North Carolina's top agricultural crop, most people would likely respond with tobacco. But, in fact, it's grapes that are on the rise—grapes and their glamorous first cousins—wineries."

## ABOUT THE SCHOOL

East Carolina University is best known for its nursing, premed, fine arts and music, and special needs education programs, but offers many other degree options in its many undergraduate colleges. Students here are pleased with the accessibility of the faculty, and outside of the large "core" courses, class size is rarely larger than 25 students. The beautiful weather, natural scenery of the region, and proximity to bustling Raleigh are all reasons students choose ECU.

## GETTING THERE

**BY AIR:** US Airways services Pitt-Greenville Airport (PGV), seven miles away, and Craven County Regional Airport (EWN), 46 miles away. Raleigh/Durham International Airport is the nearest international airport—about 95 miles away. Greenville Public Transit goes to Pitt-Greenville Airport and stops three blocks from the ECU campus. Otherwise, take a cab or shuttle service to get to campus.

**BY TRAIN:** The nearest Amtrak station is 35 miles away in Wilson, NC. Take a cab to campus.

**BY BUS:** Carolina Trailways and Greyhound Bus Lines run scheduled buses to and from the Greenville terminal at 310 Martin Luther King Jr. Drive. Ride the East Carolina University Student Transit Authority (ECUSTA) or Greenville Public Transit to campus from the terminal.

**BY CAR:** From the West via 264: Travel on 264 East to Greenville. After mile marker 73, you will see a sign for East Carolina University. Continue straight, pass under the overpass with the sign pointing to downtown Greenville. You are on Stantonsburg Road. As you cross Memorial Drive, Stantonsburg Road becomes Farmville Boulevard. Continue on Farmville Boulevard. Turn right onto 14th Street. Continue to Charles Boulevard. Turn left onto Charles Boulevard. Charles Boulevard becomes Cotanche Street. Turn right onto Reade Circle. Turn right onto 5th Street. Continue six blocks to the first light. After the first light you will make a left onto Harding Street. The Admissions Office is across the street from the Visitor Parking Lot. From The South via I-95: Take Exit 119A to 264 East and follow directions above for "From the West via 264." From the North via I-95: Follow I-95 to Rocky Mount to 64 East to Exit 496 (Highways 11 and 13 South). Take 11/13 South. Turn right on 264 East towards Washington. 264 becomes Greenville Boulevard. Turn right on 10th Street (at Hastings Ford). Stay in the right lane and continue on to 5th Street at the fork. Go about one mile. Campus will be on your left. From the North via 11: Follow 11 South to Farmville Boulevard. Turn left onto Farmville Boulevard. Turn right onto 14th Street. Turn left onto Charles Boulevard. Charles Boulevard becomes Cotanche Street. Turn right onto Reade Circle. Turn right onto 5th Street. Continue six blocks to the first light. After the first light you will make a left onto Harding Street. The Admissions Office is across the street from the Visitor Parking Lot. From the South via 11: 11 North intersects 264 Alternate. Turn right onto Greenville Boulevard. Continue to Charles Boulevard. Turn left onto Charles Boulevard. Charles Boulevard becomes Cotanche Street. Turn right onto Reade Circle. Turn right onto 5th Street. Continue six blocks to the first light. After the first light you will make a left onto Harding Street. The Admissions Office is across the street from the Visitor Parking Lot.

**LOCAL:** East Carolina University Student Transit Authority (ECUSTA) transports students and staff around campus and to/from off-campus housing areas and several shopping areas.

## WHERE TO STAY

Try the Fifth Street Inn right across the street (252-355-0699, $$). The Best Western Suites—Greenville is only one and a half miles from the ECU campus and has an airport shuttle (252-752-2378, $). Other options include the Pettigru Place Bed & Breakfast (864-242-4529, $$).

| SCHOOL AT A GLANCE | |
| --- | --- |
| Type of School | Public |
| Environment | City |
| In-state Tuition | $2,335 |
| Out-of-state Tuition | $12,849 |
| Enrollment | $18,587 |
| % Male/Female | 40/60 |
| Student/Faculty Ratio | 21:1 |

| FRESHMAN PROFILE | |
| --- | --- |
| Range SAT | |
| Critical Reading | 460-560 |
| Range SAT Math | 480-570 |
| Range ACT Composite | 18-22 |
| Average HS GPA | 3.22 |

| ON-CAMPUS APPOINTMENTS | |
| --- | --- |
| Advance Notice | Yes, 2 weeks |
| Appointment | Preferred |
| Saturdays | No |
| Average Length | 30 min |
| Info Sessions | Yes |
| Class Visits | Yes |

| CAMPUS TOURS | |
| --- | --- |
| Appointment | Preferred |
| Dates | Year Round |
| Times | 10:30 A.M. and 2:30 P.M. |
| Average Length | 60 min |

## CAMPUS AT ITS BEST!

Greenville was named "Sportstown USA" by *Sports Illustrated* magazine, and the small town is a mecca of sports activities and events. While you're there, take in one of ECU Pirates' football games, or play at one of the many luxury golf courses in the area. Visit the Raleigh International Festival in November, featuring performers and food from a vast array of countries.

# ECKERD COLLEGE

4200 Fifty-fourth Avenue South, St.Petersburg, FL 33711

**Telephone:** 727-864-8331 • **E-mail:** admissions@eckerd.edu

**Hours:** Monday–Friday, 8:30 A.M.–5:00 P.M.; Saturday, 9:30 A.M.–NOON

## STUDENTS SAY

"Eckerd College is an ideal place to learn how to accomplish anything that you desire; no idea is too outlandish."

## FODOR'S SAYS

Check out St. Petersburg's Salvador Dali Museum for "the world's most comprehensive collection of originals by Spanish surrealist Salvador Dali. The collection includes 95 oils, more than 100 watercolors and drawings, and 1,300 graphics, sculptures, photographs, and *objets d'art*."

## ABOUT THE SCHOOL

Where Eckerd's campus ends, the waters of Florida's Gulf Coast begin. Eckerd College's coastal location in the city of St. Petersburg makes it a pretty nice place to be. Add to this strong academics, plenty of attention from professors, and an emphasis on hands-on learning, and it's easy to see why students at Eckerd have so much school pride.

## GETTING THERE

**BY AIR:** The pristine Tampa International Airport is about 20 miles from Eckerd. For easy transit to campus, use SuperShuttle (800-282-6817). Be sure to call a day in advance to make reservations. Taxi service is available at the airport as well.

**BY TRAIN:** Amtrak's Silver Service/Palmetto line runs from New York City to Miami with a scheduled stop in Tampa, about half an hour from campus. Travel by car or taxi to campus.

**BY BUS:** Greyhound stops in central St. Petersburg, less than 10 minutes from campus.

**BY SEA:** Traveling along the main shipping channel (Marker #1—Egmont Lighthouse), go East five nautical miles along Mullet Key Channel. Turn to the North prior to the Sunshine Skyway and take the Skyway Channel for more than five nautical miles. At the mouth of Frenchman's Creek (Marker #8), idle motor and proceed to the Eckerd College Waterfront Complex. Visitors may use temporary docking.

**BY CAR:** From I-75 South: Follow I-75 South until merging onto I-275 South North of Tampa. Cross Tampa Bay using the Howard Frankland Bridge and continue on I-275, passing all exits for downtown St. Petersburg. Bear right onto Exit 17 for Pinellas Bayway/St. Petersburg Beach. Eckerd is just ahead on your left. From I-75 North: Take I-75 North to I-275 North/Sunshine Skyway. After crossing the Sunshine Skyway Bridge, bear left for Exit 17 toward Pinellas Bayway/St. Petersburg Beach. At the light, turn left onto 54th Avenue South. The campus entrance is a half-mile ahead.

**LOCAL:** For local taxi service, try Blue Star Cab (727-327-4104) and Indian Rocks Yellow Cab Company (727-821-7777).

## WHERE TO STAY

St. Petersburg, located on Florida's popular Gulf Coast, has plenty of hotels. Those within five miles of campus include Holiday Inn SunSpree (727-867-1151, $$), Sirata Beach Resort (727-363-5170, $$–$$$), and Don CeSar Beach Resort (727-360-1881, $$$+).

## CAMPUS AT ITS BEST!

Eckerd College takes full advantage of its Gulf Coast location, as a visit to the Marine Mammal Pathobiology Lab will demonstrate. This lab, run in conjunction with the Florida Marine Research Institute, boasts a notable Manatee Salvage Program. Of course, students also use the water for recreational purposes. The waterfront program maintains the Wallace Boathouse and the Activities Center, where students have access to the school's collection of sailboats, sea kayaks, and powerboats. Not a water enthusiast? Not a problem. There's always an event happening on campus, ranging from book readings and community service events to socials with free food and live music.

# ELON UNIVERSITY

100 Campus Drive, Elon, NC 27244-2010
**Telephone:** 336-278-3566 • **E-mail:** admissions@elon.edu • **Website:** www.elon.edu/admissions
**Hours:** Monday–Friday, 8:00 A.M.–5:00 P.M.; Saturday, 9:00 A.M.–NOON

## STUDENTS SAY

"Elon is small enough to know people, large enough to not be confining, [and] a great place to party, but also a challenging institution."

## FODOR'S SAYS

"North Carolina was home to the nation's first cultivated grape and, for a while, grew more wine grapes than all other states combined."

## ABOUT THE SCHOOL

Elon University prides itself on giving students a hands-on education, both inside the classroom and out. The university goes far beyond its 48 majors, state-of-the-art facilities, and historic campus to actively facilitate internships, study abroad programs, and community service. Students in engineering benefit from a program offered in conjunction with other colleges that allows them to graduate with a degree from both schools. Nearby Raleigh and Greensboro provide entertainment when students need a change from the tiny town of Elon.

## GETTING THERE

**BY AIR:** Piedmont Triad International Airport (GSO) is 35 miles and a 30-minute drive away. Raleigh/Durham International Airport (RDU) is 53 miles and an hour's drive away. The school provides a shuttle ($35–$45) to both around break times, but reservations must be made in advance (336-278-7215). Take a cab or reserve independent shuttle service from the airport to the Elon U campus.

**BY TRAIN:** The closest Amtrak station is four miles away in Burlington, NC at 101 North Main Street. Take a taxi to campus.

**BY BUS:** Greyhound's nearest station is in nearby Burlington at 314 West Harden Street. Drive or take a taxi to campus.

**BY CAR:** Take Interstate 85/40 to Exit 140 (University Drive). From Southbound 85/40: Exit right and turn right. From Northbound 85/40: Exit right and turn left. At the first stoplight (shopping center entrance), turn right onto St. Mark's Church Road. Follow this road for 2.6 miles. Note that the name of the road changes to Williamson Avenue after you cross South Church Street. You will cross railroad tracks as you enter the campus area. Turn right at the stoplight on Haggard Avenue. Turn left at the stoplight on North O'Kelly Avenue. Take the first left into the Visitors Parking Lot at Moseley Center.

**LOCAL:** With a reservation, the Alameda County Transportation Authority (ACTA) can arrange to pick up residents, but the schedule is limited. The Elon University Transportation System and E-ride shuttles students to on-campus destinations and off-campus housing only. Taking cabs and driving your own car are the most convenient options for getting around.

## WHERE TO STAY

The Acorn Inn is two blocks from Elon University (336-585-0167, $$), but has limited availability around commencement and the beginning of the school year. Ten minutes away in Burlington is the Best Western Inn (336-584-0151, $). The O. Henry Hotel in Greensboro is about 20 miles away (336-854-2000, $$$).

| SCHOOL AT A GLANCE | |
|---|---|
| Type of School | Private |
| Environment | Town |
| Tuition | $20,441 |
| Enrollment | 4,849 |
| % Male/Female | 41/59 |
| Student/Faculty Ratio | 14:1 |

| FRESHMAN PROFILE | |
|---|---|
| Range SAT | |
| Critical Reading | 560-650 |
| Range SAT Math | 570-660 |
| Range ACT Composite | 23-28 |
| Average HS GPA | 3.9 |

| ON-CAMPUS APPOINTMENTS | |
|---|---|
| Appointment | Preferred |
| Saturdays | Yes |
| Average Length | 120 min |
| Info Sessions | Yes |
| Class Visits | Yes |

| CAMPUS TOURS | |
|---|---|
| Appointment | Preferred |
| Dates | Year Round |
| Times | 9:00 A.M., 11:00 A.M., |
| | 1:00 P.M. or 2:30 P.M. |
| Average Length | 120 min |

---

## CAMPUS AT ITS BEST!

Sit in on one of the many fascinating guest lectures held at Elon U. Recent speakers have included Queen Noor of Jordan, Desmond Tutu, Sandra Day O'Connor, and Walter Cronkite. Check the "cultural calendar" online for dates (Elon.edu/e-net/cultural). If you'd like to explore the nearby cities, visit the Raleigh International Festival in November, featuring performances and food from a vast array of countries.

## SCHOOL AT A GLANCE

| | |
|---|---|
| Type of School | Private |
| Environment | Metropolis |
| Tuition | $32,100 |
| Enrollment | 6,378 |
| % Male/Female | 42/58 |
| Student/Faculty Ratio | 7:1 |

### FRESHMAN PROFILE

| | |
|---|---|
| Range SAT | |
| Critical Reading | 640-730 |
| Range SAT Math | 660-740 |
| Range ACT Composite | 29-33 |
| Average HS GPA | 3.8 |

### ON-CAMPUS APPOINTMENTS

| | |
|---|---|
| Info Sessions | Yes |
| Class Visits | Yes |

### CAMPUS TOURS

| | |
|---|---|
| Appointment | Required |
| Dates | Varies |
| Times | M–F, Sat by appt. |
| Average Length | 60 min |

# EMORY UNIVERSITY

Boisfeuillet Jones Center, Atlanta, GA 30322

**Telephone:** 404-727-6036 • **E-mail:** admiss@emory.edu

**Website:** www.emory.edu • **Hours:** Monday–Friday, and Saturday, 8:00 A.M.–5:00 P.M. and by appointment

## STUDENTS SAY

"Emory's greatest strengths are the diverse student population and the way the students are able to balance academics and partying."

## FODOR'S SAYS

"Although the author of *Gone With the Wind* detested the turn-of-the-twentieth century apartment house (she called it 'the Dump') in which she lived, when she wrote her masterpiece, determined volunteers got back to restoring the house and open it to the public. To many Atlantans, the Margaret Mitchell House is a lightening rod, symbolizing the conflict between promoting the city's heritage and respecting its varied roots."

## ABOUT THE SCHOOL

Whether sitting in a campus classroom or completing an internship in downtown Atlanta, students quickly realize that the Emory experience is all about learning something new at every turn. The university is recognized internationally for its outstanding liberal arts college and superb professional programs. An administration that's eager to listen and a faculty that's always ready to help lend a small-school feel to this university in the heart of the South.

## GETTING THERE

**BY AIR:** Hartsfield Atlanta International Airport is half an hour away, traffic willing. Budget-minded travelers should use MARTA (Metro Atlanta Rapid Transit Authority) to get to campus. Take any of MARTA's Northbound trains and get off at the Lindbergh Station. Transfer to the #6/Emory bus to get to campus. Taxi service is also available at the airport.

**BY TRAIN:** Amtrak operates out of a station located in downtown Atlanta on Peachtree Street, about five miles from campus. Use a cab to get to Emory.

**BY BUS:** Greyhound services its downtown Atlanta station. The easiest transport to campus is by cab.

**BY CAR:** From I-20 East/West: Follow I-20 to Exit 60B for Moreland Avenue North. Make a right onto Moreland. You'll be on this road for about five miles, though its name changes from Moreland to Briarcliff. Take a right onto North Decatur Road until it intersects with Oxford Road. From I-75 North/South: Follow I-75 to Exit 248C for the Freedom Parkway. As the road splits, bear left. Turn right onto Ponce de Leon Avenue. Next make a left on Briarcliff Road. After two miles, turn right onto North Decatur Road and continue until it intersects with Oxford Road. From I-85 North: I-85 North combines with I-75 North. Follow "From I-75 North/South" directions above. From I-85 South: Follow I-85 South to Exit 91 for Clairmont Road. Make a left onto Clairmont Road, traveling three miles. Go right onto North Decatur Road and take this one mile to campus.

**LOCAL:** MARTA provides commuter train/bus service to Atlanta. Take trains to the Lindbergh or Candler stations and transfer to the #6 bus to campus; take trains to the Arts Center or Avondale stations to take the #36 bus to campus. For taxi service, try Atlanta Checker Cab Company (404-351-1111) or Royal Cabbies (404-584-6655).

## WHERE TO STAY

The university-owned Emory Inn (800-933-6679, $$), the Emory Conference Center Hotel (800-933-6679, $$–$$$), and the University Inn (800-654-8591, $$–$$$) are each within a half mile of campus. Within 10 miles of campus, a wide variety of budget hotels, luxury hotels, and B&Bs are available.

## CAMPUS AT ITS BEST!

The Michael C. Carlos Museum is one of Emory's preeminent attractions. Inside you'll find the country's largest private collection of sub-Saharan African art. After your tour through the museum, make a pit stop at the DownUnder Lounge. A student favorite, the lounge is equipped with a 42-inch plasma TV, an Xbox, and several karaoke machines. The city of Atlanta supplies students with plenty of entertainment as well. While in town, think about catching a Falcons game or seeing a show at the Georgia Shakespeare Festival.

# FISK UNIVERSITY

1000 Seventeenth Avenue North, Nashville, TN 37208-3051
**Telephone:** 615-329-8665 • **E-mail:** admissions@fisk.edu
**Website:** www.fisk.edu

## STUDENTS SAY

"Fisk University is a family of college-educated (mostly African American) students who believe in the empowerment of our race and our generation through higher education."

## FODOR'S SAYS

"Two miles west of downtown in Centennial Park—built for the 1897 Tennessee Centennial Exposition—stands the Parthenon, an exact copy of the Athenian original [that is] now used as an art gallery."

## ABOUT THE SCHOOL

One of America's premier HBCUs (Historically Black Colleges or Universities), Fisk is a school that expects a lot from its students. The school's demanding curriculum supplements each undergrad's studies with lessons on African American heritage. And all of this takes place in one of the South's great cultural cities: Nashville, Tennessee.

## GETTING THERE

**BY AIR:** Fisk is less than a 10-minute drive from Nashville International Airport. Use taxi service to get to campus.

**BY TRAIN:** Amtrak does not service Nashville. The nearest Amtrak stop is in Fulton, Kentucky, about two hours away.

**BY BUS:** Greyhound stops in downtown Nashville, less than two miles from campus. For the easiest trip to campus, take a cab.

**BY CAR:** From I-24 East: Follow I-24 East until merging onto I-65 South toward Memphis/Huntsville/I-40 West. At Exit 84B, turn onto I-65 South/I-40 East toward Knoxville/Huntsville. Take Exit 209 for U.S. 70/Charlotte Avenue. Make a left onto Charlotte Avenue. Then turn right onto Dr. DB Todd Jr. Boulevard. Make another right onto Jackson Street. Fisk is ahead to the left. From I-24 West: Follow I-24 West to Exit 211A for I-40 West/I-65 South toward Memphis/Huntsville. Get onto I-40 West and continue to Exit 209 for Church Street/Charlotte Avenue. Make a left onto Charlotte Avenue. Then take a right onto Dr. DB Todd Jr. Boulevard. Take another right onto Jackson Street. The campus is to your left. From I-65 South: Follow I-65 South to Exit 84B where you merge onto I-40 East/I-65 South toward Knoxville/Huntsville. Take Exit 209 for U.S. 70/Charlotte Avenue. Make a left onto Charlotte Avenue. Then turn right onto Dr. DB Todd Jr. Boulevard. Make another right onto Jackson Street. Fisk is ahead to the left. From I-65 North: Follow I-65 North to Exit 82B (left exit) for I-40 West. Continue on I-40 West to Exit 209 for Church Street/Charlotte Avenue. Make a left onto Charlotte Avenue. Then take a right onto Dr. DB Todd Jr. Boulevard. Take another right onto Jackson Street. The campus is to your left.

**LOCAL:** Nashville MTA operates bus service around the city. Lines 19, 25, and 29 stop at Fisk. For travel by taxi, try Diamond Cab Company (615-254-6596) or Grand Old Taxi (615-868-8080).

## WHERE TO STAY

Nearby lodging includes the Baymont Inn and Suites (615-376-4666, $; mention you're with Fisk for special rates), Hampton Inn & Suites (615-320-6060, $$), and Millennium Maxwell House (615-259-4343, $$).

| SCHOOL AT A GLANCE | |
|---|---|
| Type of School | Private |
| Environment | Metropolis |
| Tuition | $12,480 |
| Enrollment | 812 |
| % Male/Female | 0/0 |
| Student/Faculty Ratio | 12:1 |

| FRESHMAN PROFILE | |
|---|---|
| Range SAT | |
| Critical Reading | 395-650 |
| Range SAT Math | 365-620 |
| Range ACT Composite | 17-29 |
| Average HS GPA | 3.0 |

| ON-CAMPUS APPOINTMENTS | |
|---|---|
| Advance Notice | Yes, 2 weeks |
| Appointment | Required |
| Saturdays | Sometimes |
| Average Length | 60 min |
| Info Sessions | Yes |
| Class Visits | Yes |

| CAMPUS TOURS | |
|---|---|
| Appointment | Required |
| Dates | Varies |
| Times | MWF 1:00 P.M. and 3:00 P.M.; T, Th; 11:00 A.M. and 2:00 P.M. |
| Average Length | 60 min |

## CAMPUS AT ITS BEST!

Fisk University is home to the renowned Jubilee Singers. These student vocalists have performed worldwide and were even featured in the PBS series *The American Experience*. Try to attend one of their concerts while you're on campus. If you are unable to see them perform, stop by their on-campus namesake, Jubilee Hall. This dormitory, one of Fisk's most striking buildings, was constructed with proceeds from the Jubilee Singers' historic 1871 tour. It has been designated a National Historic Landmark since 1976.

# FLORIDA A&M UNIVERSITY

Suite G-9, Foote-Hilyer Administration Center, Tallahassee, FL 32307
**Telephone:** 850-599-3796 • **E-mail:** adm@famu.edu
**Website:** www.famu.edu

| SCHOOL AT A GLANCE | |
|---|---|
| Type of School | Public |
| In-state Tuition | $2,702 |
| Out-of-state Tuition | $11,765 |
| Enrollment | 10,592 |
| % Male/Female | 43/57 |
| Student/Faculty Ratio | 22:1 |

| FRESHMAN PROFILE | |
|---|---|
| Range SAT | |
| Critical Reading | 440-550 |
| Range SAT Math | 440-550 |
| Range ACT Composite | 19-22 |
| Average HS GPA | 3.18 |

| ON-CAMPUS APPOINTMENTS | |
|---|---|
| Advance Notice | Yes, 2 weeks |
| Appointment | Required |
| Saturdays | Sometimes |
| Average Length | 30 min |
| Info Sessions | No |
| Class Visits | Yes |

| CAMPUS TOURS | |
|---|---|
| Appointment | Required |
| Dates | Year Round |
| Average Length | 120 min |

## STUDENTS SAY

"Life at FAMU is an adventure. There is always something to do, always something new to get involved in. We do just about anything to have fun."

## FODOR'S SAYS

Check out the Museum of Florida History. "If you thought Florida was founded by Walt Disney, stop here. Covering 12,000 years, the displays explain Florida's past by highlighting the unique geological and historical events that have shaped the state."

## ABOUT THE SCHOOL

FAMU, a historically Black college in Tallahassee, is known for its academic programs in pharmacy, business, and journalism; its outstanding marching band team; and its highly competitive football team. It seeks to provide a caring and nurturing environment to educate its students through inspirational teaching as well as meaningful values.

## GETTING THERE

**BY AIR:** Tallahassee Regional Airport is the closest regional airport to campus. Take a car or taxi to campus.

**BY TRAIN:** Amtrak trains stop in Tallahassee. Take a car or taxi to campus.

**BY BUS:** Greyhound buses service Tallahassee. Take a car or taxi to campus.

**BY CAR:** From the North (via I-75 South): Take I-75 South to I-475 South. Take Route 300 (the Georgia-Florida Parkway) South until you reach Route 319 South. Take Route 319 to Route 61 South. Route 61 becomes Route 27. Make a right on West Pensacola Street. Make a left on South Macomb Street. South Macomb Street turns into Railroad Avenue, which turns into Wahnish Way. From the South (via I-75 North): Take I-75 North to I-10 West. Get off of I-10 at Exit 203, onto Route 61 South. Follow "From I-75 South" directions above. From the East (via Route 17 North): Take Route 17 North to I-95 South. Get off of I-95 at Exit 351B onto I-10 West. Get off of I-10 at Exit 209A onto Route 90 West. Get off of Route 90 at Macomb Street. Make a left on Macomb Street and follow it until you see the university.

**LOCAL:** StarMetro, formerly known as TalTran, provides bus service throughout Tallahassee. If you'd rather take a taxi, some local companies include City Taxi (850-562-4222), and Yellow Cab (850-575-1022).

## WHERE TO STAY

If you're planning on staying overnight, some nearby hotel options include Best Western Pride Inn & Suites (850-656-6312, $), Tallahassee Days Inn University Center (850-222-3219, $), and Park Plaza Hotel Tallahassee (850-224-6000, $$).

## CAMPUS AT ITS BEST!

Florida A&M students eagerly anticipate Homecoming. Occurring every fall, the celebration is always based around a theme and features a concert with a popular performer. The FAMU Essential Theater is also very popular. The season typically features African American playwrights and new interpretations of classics. Be sure to take advantage of all that the city of Tallahassee has to offer. Bradley's 1927 Country Store, listed on the National Register of Historic Places, is well known for its homemade sausage and a variety of Southern goods.

# FLORIDA INSTITUTE OF TECHNOLOGY

150 West University Boulevard, Melbourne, FL 32901-6975
**Telephone:** 321-674-8030 • **E-mail:** admission@fit.edu
**Hours:** Monday–Friday, 8:00 A.M.–5:00 P.M.

## STUDENTS SAY

"Florida Tech is a place where motivated students learn the sciences from talented instructors."

## FODOR'S SAYS

"It took 20,000 volunteers two weeks to turn 56 acres of forest and wetlands into the Brevard Zoo, the only American Zoo and Aquarium Association–accredited zoo built by a community."

## ABOUT THE SCHOOL

Florida Institute of Technology understands how to maximize its phenomenal location, creating unparalleled research opportunities for undergraduates. The university is a mere 50 minutes from the Kennedy Space Center, and students can enroll in onsite classes there. Additionally, marine biologists can take advantage of the school's close proximity to both the Atlantic Ocean and Indian River, studying everything from manatee distribution to reef structures.

## GETTING THERE

**BY AIR:** Visitors have the option of flying into either Orlando International Airport or Melbourne International Airport. Melbourne, a mere five minutes from campus, is only served by Delta. However, all major airlines fly into Orlando, which is only an hour from Florida Tech.

**BY TRAIN:** The nearest Amtrak station is located in Kissimmee, FL, roughly 50 miles from campus. If you decide to travel via train it is recommended that you rent a car for the final portion of your trip.

**BY BUS:** Visitors can take Greyhound to Melbourne International Airport. If you'd like to go directly to campus, you can either catch a cab or use local transit.

**BY CAR:** From Orlando: Follow Highway 528 (also known as Beachline Expressway) East to Interstate 95 South. Continue on I-95 to Exit #176, Palm Bay Road. When you reach the end of the ramp, make a left and drive East for roughly two miles. At the intersection of Palm and Babcock Street, take a left onto Babcock. Drive for another two miles until you hit University Boulevard. You will make a left onto University. Continue to the first intersection at Country Club Road and make a right. The Office of Undergraduate Admission is located in the Jerome P. Keuper Administration Building on Country Club Road. From Highway U.S. 1: Drive West onto Palm Bay Road and continue for roughly two miles to the intersection at Palm Bay Road and Babcock Street. Follow "From Orlando" directions above.

**LOCAL:** Melbourne does have its very own bus system, Space Coast Area Transit. Numerous routes provide access to many local attractions.

## WHERE TO STAY

Guests planning on staying overnight can find lodging here: Suburban Hotels (321-768-9777, $), Hampton Inn (321-956-6200, $$), or the Courtyard by Marriott (321-724-6400, $$–$$$).

## SCHOOL AT A GLANCE

| | |
|---|---|
| Type of School | Private |
| Environment | Town |
| Tuition | $27,540 |
| Enrollment | 2,337 |
| % Male/Female | 69/31 |
| Student/Faculty Ratio | 13:1 |

### FRESHMAN PROFILE

| | |
|---|---|
| Range SAT | |
| Critical Reading | 500–620 |
| Range SAT Math | 550–660 |
| Range ACT Composite | 22–29 |
| Average HS GPA | 3.49 |

### ON-CAMPUS APPOINTMENTS

| | |
|---|---|
| Advance Notice | Yes, 2 weeks |
| Appointment | Preferred |
| Saturdays | No |
| Average Length | 30 min |
| Info Sessions | No |
| Class Visits | Yes |

### CAMPUS TOURS

| | |
|---|---|
| Appointment | Preferred |
| Dates | Academic Year |
| Times | M–F 10:00 A.M. and 2:00 P.M. |
| Average Length | 60 min |

---

## CAMPUS AT ITS BEST!

When visiting Florida Tech, prospective students will have the opportunity to travel back in time. The Historic School House, located in the breathtaking Botanical Garden, was built in 1883 and served as the first public school for families in the Melbourne area. For those who are happy in the present, the Campus Activities Board provides many opportunities for amusement and relaxation. Consider joining the fun on Casino or Karaoke Night, or catching one of the comedians who frequently performs on campus.

# FLORIDA INTERNATIONAL UNIVERSITY

University Park, PC 140, Miami, FL 33199
Telephone: 305-348-2363 • E-mail: admiss@fiu.edu
Website: www.fiu.edu • Hours: Monday–Thursday, 8:00 A.M.–7:00 P.M.; Friday, 8:00 A.M.–5:00 P.M.

## SCHOOL AT A GLANCE

| | |
|---|---|
| Type of School | Public, HSI |
| Environment | Metropolis |
| In-state Tuition | $2,696 |
| Out-of-state Tuition | $12,162 |
| Enrollment | 28,491 |
| % Male/Female | 43/57 |
| Student/Faculty Ratio | 17:1 |

## FRESHMAN PROFILE

| | |
|---|---|
| Range SAT | |
| Critical Reading | 520–590 |
| Range SAT Math | 510–590 |
| Range ACT Composite | 21–25 |
| Average HS GPA | 3.60 |

## ON-CAMPUS APPOINTMENTS

| | |
|---|---|
| Advance Notice | Yes, 1 week |
| Appointment | Not Required |
| Saturdays | No |
| Info Sessions | Yes |
| Class Visits | No |

## CAMPUS TOURS

| | |
|---|---|
| Appointment | Required |
| Dates | Varies |
| Times | Mon and Wed 9:30 A.M.; Fri 3:00 P.M. |
| Average Length | 60 min |

## STUDENTS SAY

"Florida International University is a very diverse school that is still trying to heighten its status in the college world, which it will probably achieve in the years to come."

## FODOR'S SAYS

"The focus of the Holocaust Memorial is a 42-foot-high bronze arm rising from the ground, with sculptured people climbing the arm seeking escape. Don't stare from the street; enter the courtyard to see the chilling memorial wall and hear the eerie songs that seem to give voice to the victims."

## ABOUT THE SCHOOL

With two campuses stretching out over a combined 544 acres, Florida International University offers students some incredible resources. The university places an emphasis on research, giving students a competitive advantage. Furthermore, FIU has emerged as a cultural asset to Southern Florida, attracting a variety of artists and performers. When students do look to get off campus, they have the city of Miami as their playground.

## GETTING THERE

**BY AIR:** Guests traveling by plane should fly into Miami International Airport. Car rentals, taxis, and shuttle service are all available for further transportation. Local bus and rail systems are also accessible.

**BY TRAIN:** Amtrak does offer direct service to Miami. Cabs and public transit are both available for additional transportation needs.

**BY BUS:** Greyhound stops in several locations within the Miami area. Guests looking for supplementary transportation may either take a taxi or use local transit.

**BY CAR:** University Park Campus—from I-95, Downtown Miami, Fort Lauderdale, and West Palm Beach: Follow I-95 to I-836 West. Take I-836 to the Florida Turnpike South.

Continue on the turnpike until you reach the Tamiami Trail Exit (Southwest 8th Street). Proceed on Southwest 8th Street. You will see the university on your right, before Southwest 107th Avenue. From the Florida Turnpike North, Western Palm Beach/Broward County: Follow the Florida Turnpike South to the Tamiami Trail exit (Southwest 8th Street). See above for the remainder of the directions. Biscayne Bay Campus—from Miami: Follow I-95 North to 135th Street. Next, drive East to U.S. 1. Continue driving North to 151st Street and make a right turn. Proceed down the road (heading East). You will see the campus on your left. From Fort Lauderdale: Follow I-95 South to 163rd Street. Drive East to U.S. 1. Drive South until you reach 151st Street. You will make a left and continue down (heading East). You will find the campus on your left-hand side.

**LOCAL:** Miami-Dade County has convenient local transportation including bus service, metro-rail (providing service around the county), metro-mover (providing service around downtown), and the tri-rail (a commuter train service offering transportation from the airport to Broward and Palm Beach Counties).

## WHERE TO STAY

For University Park: Baymont Inns and Suites (305-871-1777, $–$$) or Doral Resort and Country Club (305-592-2000, $$–$$). For Biscayne Bay: Sheraton Bal Harbour (305-865-7511, $$) or the Sea View Hotel (305-866-4441, $$–$$$).

## CAMPUS AT ITS BEST!

FIU's Wolfsonian museum promotes the understanding and preservation of the decorative arts. Patrons can explore how design influences and reflects our daily experiences. Once you've had your fill of the collection, take in a presentation from Writers on the Bay, which offers lectures from illustrious authors such as Elmore Leonard, Marge Piercy, and Gay Talese. The South Beach Wine and Food Festival also attracts the masses. Those in attendance are privy to delectable culinary tastings and seminars.

# FLORIDA STATE UNIVERSITY

2500 University Center, Tallahassee, FL 32306-2400
**Telephone:** 850-644-6200 • **E-mail:** admissions@admin.fsu.edu
**Website:** www.fsu.edu • **Hours:** Monday–Friday, 8:00 A.M.–5:00 P.M.

## STUDENTS SAY

"FSU is about tradition, honoring the past, preparing for the future . . . and football!"

## FODOR'S SAYS

Lake Jackson Mounds Archaeological State Park has "waters to make bass anglers weep. For sight-seers, Indian mounds and the ruins of an early nineteenth-century plantation built by Colonel Robert Butler, adjutant to General Andrew Jackson during the siege of New Orleans, are found along the shores of the lake."

## ABOUT THE SCHOOL

What do you get when you mix world-class research opportunities with nonstop sunshine? That's exactly what FSU offers its 30,000 undergrads. Located on the eastern edge of Florida's panhandle, FSU boasts a wide range of courses, majors, and top-notch facilities. And when it's time to put the books away, great beaches and powerhouse NCAA sports are just a stone's throw away.

## GETTING THERE

**BY AIR:** The Tallahassee Regional Airport is about five miles from FSU. Flights arrive from about a dozen cities. Use taxi service to get to campus.

**BY TRAIN:** Typically Amtrak's Sunset Limited line services Tallahassee and offers limited stops in New Orleans, Jacksonville, Orlando, and Miami.

**BY BUS:** Tallahassee's Greyhound station is less than a mile from campus. Use a taxi or bus to get to campus.

**BY CAR:** From I-10 East: Follow I-10 East to Exit 192 for U.S. 90. Take U.S. 90 East for seven miles until turning right onto Ocala Road. Half a mile later, turn left onto Pensacola Street. After another half mile, make a right onto Stadium Drive. At the next light, take a left onto Hendry Street. Proceed to the stop sign and make a right onto Champions Way. Continue to the second parking lot entrance, which is on your right. Take a left into visitor parking. From I-10 West: Both I-95 and I-75 intersect with I-10 West. Follow I-10 West to Exit 209A for U.S. 90 West (or Tennessee Street). After eight miles, turn left onto Monroe Street (Highway 27). Proceed several blocks on Monroe Street before turning right onto College Avenue. Half a mile later, when College Avenue ends, make a left onto Copeland Street. Go two blocks and take a right onto Pensacola Street. Proceed to Stadium Drive and make a left. Following Stadium Drive to the right, proceed for half a mile to Hendry Street and turn right. At the stop sign, make a right into the parking area. At the second lot entrance, turn right. Then make a left for visitor parking.

**LOCAL:** StarMetro operates citywide bus services. Lines stopping at FSU include 3, 9, 15, 17, 20, 23, and 29. For taxi service, try Yellow Cab at 850-580-8080.

## WHERE TO STAY

Area lodging includes La Quinta North (850-385-7172, $), Allison House Inn (850-875-2511, $$), and Homewood Suites by Hilton (850-402-9400, $$–$$$).

---

## CAMPUS AT ITS BEST!

Visit the FSU Reservation and take a minute to soak up some sun. The "Rez," a lakeside recreation complex, often hosts picnics, musical events, and even water skiing competitions. When you're ready to head indoors, stop by Crenshaw Lanes, located in Oglesby Student Union, for bowling, billiards, and chilling. Before you head home, try to see FSU's Flying High Circus perform. This student-run troupe—the only one in the nation—is a crowd-pleaser with its entertaining acts.

# FURMAN UNIVERSITY

3300 Poinsett Highway, Greenville, SC 29613

**Telephone:** 864-294-2034 • **E-mail:** admissions@furman.edu • **Website:** www.furman.edu •
**Hours:** Monday–Friday and Saturday, 9:00 A.M.–5:00 P.M. and by appointment

## STUDENTS SAY

"The campus is gorgeous and the academics are first-rate."

## FODOR'S SAYS

"Devil's Fork State Park, on Lake Jocasse, has luxurious villas and camping facilities, hiking, boating, and fishing. Lower Whitewater Falls plunges more than 200 feet over huge boulders to splash into the lake waters."

## ABOUT THE SCHOOL

Just because Furman is a small school with an attentive faculty doesn't mean that the expectations aren't high. In other words, hard work is par for the course at Furman. If students ever feel like getting away from campus for a while, the top-notch study abroad program offers plenty of options.

## GETTING THERE

**BY AIR:** Fly into the Greensville-Spartanburg International Airport. The airport is about 20 miles from campus. Take a cab to campus.

**BY TRAIN:** Amtrak's Crescent line stops near downtown Greenville, about five miles from campus. Take a cab to campus.

**BY BUS:** Greyhound operates out of its terminal on West McBee Avenue in downtown Greenville. Take a cab to campus.

**BY CAR:** From I-85 South: Follow I-85 South to I-385 North, which heads toward downtown Greenville. Stay on this road, which changes to Beattie Place and then to College Street. Veer right onto U.S. 276 West and stay on it for five miles to the Furman exit. From I-85 North: Follow I-85 North to Exit 42 for I-185 North toward downtown Greenville. Stay on I-185 North, which changes to Mills Avenue and then to Church Street. Turn left at Beattie Place, which changes to College Street. Veer right onto U.S. 276 West and stay on it for five miles to the Furman exit. From I-26 North: Follow I-26 North to I-385 North, and stay on I-385 North for 43 miles. In downtown Greenville, I-385 North changes to Beattie Place, which changes to College Street. Veer right off College Street onto U.S. 276 West and stay on it for five miles to the Furman exit. From I-26 South: Follow I-26 South to Hendersonville, North Carolina, where you pick up U.S. 25 South. Before reaching Greenville, veer left onto U.S. 276 East. Travel on U.S. 276 East for a mile and exit on Furman.

**LOCAL:** Looking for a cab? Check out Yellow Cab of Greenville (864-233-6666), Budget Cab Company (864-233-4200), and A Cab Company (864-233-6099).

## WHERE TO STAY

Greenville's overnight accommodations include the Phoenix Greenville's Inn (864-233-4651, $–$$), La Quinta Inn and Suites (864-233-8018, $–$$), and the Westin Poinsett (864-421-9700, $$–$$$).

---

## CAMPUS AT ITS BEST!

If you're looking to mingle with Furman students, visit the Tower Café located in the University Center. This campus hotspot is outfitted with a lakeside patio complete with wireless Internet access. Afterward you can try your luck at a Texas Hold 'Em tournament sponsored by the Student Activities Board.

# GEORGE MASON UNIVERSITY

Undergraduate Admissions Office, 4400 University Drive MSN 3A4, Fairfax, VA 22030-4444
**Telephone:** 703-993-2400 • **E-mail:** admissions@gmu.edu • **Website:** www.gmu.edu

## STUDENTS SAY

"Diversity is one of the greatest strengths of George Mason University because it allows us to grow culturally [while] interacting with so many different people."

## FODOR'S SAYS

"The National Rifle Association's National Firearms Museum has exhibits on the role guns have played in the history of America. The permanent collection includes muzzle-loading flintlocks used in the Revolutionary War, high-tech pistols used by Olympic shooting teams, and weapons that once belonged to American presidents, including Teddy Roosevelt's .32-caliber Browning pistol and a Winchester rifle used by Dwight Eisenhower."

## ABOUT THE SCHOOL

George Mason University offers a program for every student's preference: an Honors General Education Program, an interdisciplinary, self-designed degree from the New Century College, and a large selection of traditional majors. Students learn in small classes from top-notch professors. GMU's proximity to the DC area provides internships and research opportunities with noteworthy organizations and companies.

## GETTING THERE

**BY AIR:** The best options are Reagan National Airport (20 miles), Dulles International Airport (15 miles), and Baltimore Washington International Airport (55 miles).

**BY TRAIN:** Take the Amtrak red line from Union Station in Washington, DC to Metro Center and transfer to the Orange line going to Vienna to the Vienna Stop. At Vienna Station, take a GMU CUE bus to campus.

**BY BUS:** Greyhound stops at Union Station in DC.

**BY CAR:** From the Capital Beltway (I-495): Take Exit 54, Braddock Road (Route 620), then the Westbound fork. Follow Braddock Road West for approximately six miles, turning right at Roanoke River Road. Bear right at the fork in the road. Go left onto Mason Pond Drive. Via I-66 East from Front Royal and Fairfax County Parkway: Exit at Fairfax County Parkway South (Route 7100). Take the Parkway at Braddock Road, and turn left onto Braddock Road. Take the first left past Route 123 (Ox Road) onto Roanoke River Road. See above for the rest of the directions. Via I-66 West from Washington, DC or Arlington: Take Exit 60 at Route 123 South, Chain Bridge Road. Follow Route 123 through Fairfax, and turn left at University Drive. Go right onto Occoquan River Lane, then right again onto Patriot Circle. At the pond, bear left to stay on Patriot Circle. Go left on Mason Pond Drive to the Parking Deck. From I-95 (North or South): From points North on I-95, take Exit 27 (I-495 West), then follow the directions "from the Capital Beltway (I-495)." From points South on I-95, take Exit 160B (Route 123 North) at Lake Ridge/Occoquan. Follow Route 123 North, turning right on Braddock Road. At the first signal, turn left on Roanoke River Road. See above for the rest of the directions.

**LOCAL:** George Mason University's CUE bus goes to the DC Metro Vienna Station on the Orange Line. Take the orange line into DC for transfer to other DC trains.

## WHERE TO STAY

George Mason University's CUE bus provides transportation between the Fairfax campus and several nearby hotels. Options include Best Western Fairfax (703-591-5500, $$), the Bailiwick Inn (703-691-2266, $$$), and the Comfort Inn Fairfax (703-591-5900, $$).

| SCHOOL AT A GLANCE | |
|---|---|
| Type of School | Public |
| Environment | City |
| In-state Tuition | $4,356 |
| Out-of-state Tuition | $15,636 |
| Enrollment | 17,529 |
| % Male/Female | 46/54 |
| Student/Faculty Ratio | 15:1 |

| FRESHMAN PROFILE | |
|---|---|
| Range SAT | |
| Critical Reading | 490-600 |
| Range SAT Math | 510-610 |
| Range ACT Composite | 20-24 |
| Average HS GPA | 3.36 |

| ON-CAMPUS APPOINTMENTS | |
|---|---|
| Advance Notice | Yes, 2 weeks |
| Appointment | Required |
| Saturdays | Sometimes |
| Average Length | 30 min |
| Info Sessions | Yes |
| Class Visits | Yes |

| CAMPUS TOURS | |
|---|---|
| Appointment | Preferred |
| Dates | Year Round |
| Times | M–F 10:15 A.M., 2:15 P.M.; Sat 10:00 A.M. and 11:30 A.M. |
| Average Length | 60 min |

## CAMPUS AT ITS BEST!

Only a quarter of George Mason undergraduates live on campus, so weekends can be pretty uneventful, unless you take the Metro into DC and see where many of the students disappear to. During the week, attend a basketball game on campus—many of the GMU students support the team, so you'll be able to see the campus come alive!

## SCHOOL AT A GLANCE

| | |
|---|---|
| Type of School | Public |
| Environment | Metropolis |
| In-state Tuition | $3,892 |
| Out-of-state Tuition | $19,238 |
| Enrollment | 12,103 |
| % Male/Female | 72/28 |
| Student/Faculty Ratio | 14:1 |

### FRESHMAN PROFILE

| | |
|---|---|
| Range SAT | |
| Critical Reading | 570–680 |
| Range SAT Math | 650–730 |
| Range ACT Composite | 26–30 |
| Average HS GPA | 3.7 |

### ON-CAMPUS APPOINTMENTS

| | |
|---|---|
| Class Visits | No |

### CAMPUS TOURS

| | |
|---|---|
| Appointment | Not Required |
| Dates | Year Round |
| Times | M–F 11:00 A.M. and 2:00 P.M. |
| Average Length | 60 min |

# GEORGIA INSTITUTE OF TECHNOLOGY

225 North Avenue, Northwest, Atlanta, GA 30332-0320
**Telephone:** 404-894-4154 • **E-mail:** admission@gatech.edu
**Website:** www.gatech.edu • **Hours:** Monday–Friday, 8:00 A.M.–5:00 P.M.

## STUDENTS SAY

"Georgia Tech is about learning everything you can about your chosen subject from the bottom up."

## FODOR'S SAYS

"Centennial Olympic Park was the central venue for the 1996 Summer Olympics. The park's Fountain of Rings (the world's largest using the Olympic symbol) centers a court of 24 flags, each of them representing the Olympic Games as well as the host countries of the modern Games."

## ABOUT THE SCHOOL

While earning a degree in the unofficial "Capital of South" has its perks, undergrads at Georgia Tech don't have time for many distractions. Towering expectations and mountainous workloads keep these students busy from sun up to sun down. The payoff, of course, is a degree from a top-notch science and technology powerhouse.

## GETTING THERE

**BY AIR:** Fly into Hartsfield-Jackson Atlanta International Airport. Take a cab from the airport to the campus. Fare runs about $30. You can also take a MARTA train from the airport to the North Avenue station; from there, take a #13 bus to campus.

**BY TRAIN:** Amtrak services Atlanta's central station, about 2.5 miles from campus. Take a cab to Georgia Tech.

**BY BUS:** Greyhound services its downtown Atlanta station. It's easiest to take a taxi to the campus.

**BY CAR:** From I-75 South: Follow I-75 South to Exit 249D for North Avenue. As the ramp ends, make a right onto North Avenue. At Cherry Street, make a right. Go left onto Ferst Drive, and find visitor parking (A03) ahead on your right. From I-85 South: Follow I-85 South to I-75 South. Proceed according to "From I-75 South" directions above. From I-75 North: Follow I-75 North to Exit 250 for 10th and 14th Streets. At the end of the ramp, make a left onto 10th Street. At State Street, make a left. Turn right at Ferst Street, and after passing over Means Street, turn left into visitor parking (A03). From I-85 North: Follow I-85 North until it combines with I-75 North and proceed according to the "From I-75 North" directions above.

**LOCAL:** MARTA rail service does not stop at Georgia Tech. However, the Tech Trolley offers transportation between campus and the Midtown MARTA Station. Stinger Bus Service offers three routes (red, green, and blue loops) that service Georgia Tech. For taxi service, try Atlanta Checker Cab Company (404-351-1111) or Royal Cabbies (404-584-6655).

## WHERE TO STAY

There is a Holiday Inn Express is just across the street from campus (404-881-0881, $–$$; ask for Georgia Tech rate). Other nearby options include the Marriott Residence Inn—Historic Midtown (404-872-8885, $$) and the Georgia Tech Hotel and Conference Center (800-706-2899, $$$).

---

## CAMPUS AT ITS BEST!

Be careful not to confuse Georgia Tech's Campus Rec Center with an amusement park. One of the pools boasts an impressive waterslide open to all staff, faculty, and student members of CRC. Musicians should investigate Under the Couch, a prime venue for rock bands and a meeting place for the Musicians Network. Try to plan your Georgia Tech visit to coincide with the annual CultureTech event. Students especially enjoy the Fall Food Fair, which enables them to sample food from around the globe.

# GEORGIA STATE UNIVERSITY

PO Box 4009, Atlanta, GA 30302-4009
**Telephone:** 404-651-2365 • **E-mail:** admissions@gsu.edu
**Website:** www.gsu.edu/index.htm

### SCHOOL AT A GLANCE

| | |
|---|---|
| Type of School | Public |
| Environment | Metropolis |
| Enrollment | 18,480 |
| % Male/Female | 39/61 |
| Student/Faculty Ratio | 20:1 |

### FRESHMAN PROFILE

| | |
|---|---|
| Range SAT | |
| Critical Reading | 490-590 |
| Range SAT Math | 500-590 |
| Range ACT Composite | 19-24 |
| Average HS GPA | 3.30 |

### ON-CAMPUS APPOINTMENTS

| | |
|---|---|
| Class Visits | No |

## Students Say

"GSU is as close to real life as possible with students and professors from all walks of life."

## Fodor's Says

"Asa G. Candler, founder of the Coca-Cola Company, engaged the local firm of Murphy & Stewart to design the splendid terra-cotta and marble Candler Building in 1906. The ornate bronze and marble lobby shouldn't be missed."

## About the School

GSU, the second largest university within Georgia, is a leader in research, teaching, and service. With enrollment over 27,000, you'll interact with a highly diverse student body. The university offers over 250 fields of study—enough to satiate even the most intellectually curious! Additionally, Georgia State's Atlanta location provides students with a myriad of cultural and professional resources.

## Getting There

**BY AIR:** Those traveling via plane should fly into Hartsfield-Jackson Atlanta International Airport. A major hub, Hartsfield-Jackson receives flights from all over the world. Car rentals, shuttles, taxis, and local public transit are available for further transportation.

**BY TRAIN:** Visitors wishing to travel by train can take Amtrak directly into Atlanta. Public transportation and taxis are both accessible for additional travel.

**BY BUS:** Greyhound provides service to several points throughout Atlanta, including Georgia State. Please note that the GSU stop only receives limited service.

**BY CAR:** From I-75/85 Northbound: Take Exit #246 (Central Avenue/Fulton Street). Follow the signs to Fulton Street. When you reach the light at the end of the ramp, make a right onto Fulton. At the next light, take a left onto Capitol Avenue. Cross MLK Jr. Drive. At this point, Capitol Avenue turns into Piedmont Avenue. Piedmont passes through campus. From I-75/85 Southbound: Take Exit #249A (Courtland Street/Georgia State University). This is a one-way street that will take you directly to the campus. From I-20 Eastbound: Take Exit #56B (Windsor/Spring Street). Drive straight to the third traffic light, turning left onto Central Avenue. Central will take you directly to the campus. From I-20 Westbound: Take Exit #58A (Capitol Avenue) and take a right at the light. See "Northbound" for the remainder of the directions.

**LOCAL:** MARTA (Metropolitan Atlanta Rapid Transit Authority): Ride the East/West Rapid Rail line to the Georgia State Station (E1). Exit the station onto Piedmont Avenue and take a right.

## Where to Stay

For a convenient location to campus, try AmeriSuites (404-577-1980, $–$$), Fairfield Inn (404-659-7777, $–$$), or the Atlanta Hilton Hotel (404-659-2000, $$–$$$).

## CAMPUS AT ITS BEST!

For a taste of Georgia State's social scene try attending the Panther Prowl. This monthly event guarantees to be a great time. It typically features food, music, and novelty acts like bumper cars and even an oxygen bar. If you're looking to explore Atlanta, think about visiting AeroBalloon. This hot air balloon facility will allow you to soar high above the city and admire Atlanta from a unique vantage point.

# GUILFORD COLLEGE

5800 West Friendly Avenue, Greensboro, NC 27410
**Telephone:** 336-316-2100 • **E-mail:** admission@guilford.edu
**Hours:** Monday–Friday, 8:30 A.M.–5:00 P.M.; Saturday, 8:30 A.M.–NOON

## STUDENTS SAY

"The classes are incredible. The woods are beautiful. The people are endlessly entertaining. Need I say more?"

## FODOR'S SAYS

"Guilford Courthouse National Military Park, the nation's first Revolutionary War park, has monuments, military memorabilia, and more than 200 acres with wooded hiking trails."

## ABOUT THE SCHOOL

The classes at Guilford College are challenging and reading-intensive. Students work hard during the semester to keep up but still find time to participate in the numerous activities and community service groups on campus. Guided by its egalitarian philosophy and known for its tight-knit, familial atmosphere on campus, Guilford College is the kind of place where it's not uncommon for entire classes to be invited over to professors' houses for dinner at the end of the semester.

## GETTING THERE

**BY AIR:** Piedmont Triad International Airport in Greensboro and the Raleigh/Durham International Airport are the closest airports to the campus. Taxi service or car rentals are both convenient ways to get from the airport to the college.

**BY TRAIN:** Amtrak stops at Gaylon Transportation Center in Greensboro. Take a taxi to get to the campus.

**BY BUS:** Greyhound stops at the Gaylon Transportation Center in Greensboro. Take a taxi to get to the campus.

**BY CAR:** From the West: Take I-40 East to Exit 213. Turn right onto Guilford College Road. Go about one mile, and turn right on West Market Street. At the first stop light, turn left on Dolley Madison. Go to the end of the street and make a left on Friendly Avenue. The college is on your right. From the East: Take I-40 West/I-85 South toward Greensboro/ Winston-Salem. Take I-40 West to Exit 213, Guilford College/ Jamestown. Turn right onto Guilford College Road and follow "From the West" directions above. From the South: Take I-85 North to Exit 87, Highway 52/ Lexington/ Winston-Salem. Take Highway 52 North to I-40 East. Take I-40 East toward Greensboro. Take Exit 213 off of I-40, Guilford College/ Jamestown. Follow "From the West" directions above. From the North: Take I-85 South/I-40 West toward Greensboro/Winston-Salem. Take I-40 West to Exit 213. Follow "From the West" directions above.

**LOCAL:** Some local taxi companies include A-1 Transportation (336-574-2240), Blue Bird Taxi Greensboro (336-272-5112), and Daniel-Keck Taxi Co. Inc. (336-275-6337).

## WHERE TO STAY

Some lodging choices near the college include the Red Roof Inn Coliseum (336-852-6560, $), AmeriSuites (336-852-1443, $$), and Courtyard by Marriott (336-294-3800, $$).

---

## CAMPUS AT ITS BEST!

Guilford's hometown of Greensboro offers a plethora of activities to interest students and tourists alike. Those interested in U.S. history will want to investigate the International Civil Rights Center and Museum. Also popular is the Germanton Art Gallery and Winery, where you take in contemporary art while sipping the finest Chardonnay (only if you're of age, of course!). Visitors should also try to attend a lecture sponsored by the Bryan Series during their visit. Recently invited guests include historian David McCullough, renowned literary figure Toni Morrison, and Mary Robinson, the first female president of Ireland.

# HAMPDEN-SYDNEY COLLEGE

PO Box 667, Hampden-Sydney, VA 23943-0667
**Telephone:** 434-223-6120 • **E-mail:** admissions@hsc.edu
**Website:** www.hsc.edu

## STUDENTS SAY

"Hampden-Sydney College is one of the last places that tradition thrives and honor lives."

## FODOR'S SAYS

"Twenty-five miles east of Lynchburg, the village of Appomattox Court House has been restored to its appearance of April 9, 1865—the day that the Confederate General Lee surrendered the army of Northern Virginia to General Grant. A highlight is the reconstructed McLean House, in whose parlor the articles of surrender were signed."

## ABOUT THE SCHOOL

Hampden-Sydney College is a man's world, literally. This all-male liberal arts school is steeped in tradition ranging from a cherished honor code to deep devotion to classical learning. Proper manners, conservative ideologies, and good ol' Southern fun are par for the course at Hampden-Sydney.

## GETTING THERE

**BY AIR:** Lynchburg Regional Airport is about an hour from campus and is serviced by Delta/Atlantic Southeast connections from Atlanta and US Airways Express/Piedmont connections from Charlotte. Richmond International Airport, an hour and a half from Hampden-Sydney, provides a more extensive flight selection. The college offers a student-run shuttle service ($50 each way) for those students who are traveling alone and arriving in Richmond or Lynchburg. Rental cars are available at the airport.

**BY TRAIN:** Amtrak has several stations within an hour of the college. Lynchburg is serviced by Amtrak's Crescent Line. Charlottesville is serviced by the Crescent and Cardinal/Hoosier State lines. Petersburg is serviced by the Carolinian/Piedmont and Silver Service/Palmetto lines. And Richmond is serviced by the Carolinian/Piedmont, Silver Service/Palmetto, and the Regional lines. Take a taxi to campus.

**BY BUS:** Greyhound stops in Farmville, a few miles North. Take a taxi to campus.

**BY CAR:** From Route 460 West: Follow Route 460 West. Turn off Route 460 West at the second Farmville Exit and make a left onto Route 15 South. Four miles later, take a right onto Route 133. Soon after getting onto Route 133, bear right at the Y and continue onto campus. From Route 460 East: Follow Route 460 East to the first exit for Farmville and make a right onto Route 15 South. Four miles later, take a right onto Route 133. Soon after getting onto Route 133, bear right at the Y and continue onto campus. From Route 60 East/West: Follow Route 60 to the exit for Route 15 South. Follow Route 15 South to the exit for Route 133 and go right. Soon after getting onto Route 133, bear right at the Y and continue onto campus.

## WHERE TO STAY

Overnight accommodations in the vicinity include Days Inn, Farmville (434-392-6611, $–$$), Comfort Inn, Burkesville (434-767-3750, $–$$), and the Comfort Inn, Farmville (434-392-8163, $–$$).

| SCHOOL AT A GLANCE | |
| --- | --- |
| Type of School | Private |
| Environment | Rural |
| Tuition | $26,889 |
| Enrollment | 1,100 |
| % Male/Female | 100/0 |
| Student/Faculty Ratio | 10:1 |

| FRESHMAN PROFILE | |
| --- | --- |
| Range SAT | |
| Critical Reading | 520-630 |
| Range SAT Math | 530-640 |
| Range ACT Composite | 21-27 |
| Average HS GPA | 3.32 |

| ON-CAMPUS APPOINTMENTS | |
| --- | --- |
| Advance Notice | Yes, 1 week |
| Appointment | Preferred |
| Saturdays | Yes |
| Average Length | 45 min |
| Info Sessions | No |
| Class Visits | Yes |

| CAMPUS TOURS | |
| --- | --- |
| Appointment | Preferred |
| Dates | Year Round |
| Times | M–F 9:00 A.M.–3:30 P.M.; |
| | Sat 9:00 A.M.–NOON |
| Average Length | 60 min |

## CAMPUS AT ITS BEST!

For an intriguing juxtaposition of past and present, check out the Carriage House, a nineteenth century building that houses the campus radio station, WWHS-FM. With one in three students belonging to a Greek organization, you might want to stop by Fraternity Circle to investigate. Hampden Sydney's amazing location affords plenty of off-campus action as well. The historic town of Appomattox, a mere 37 miles away, offers music and craft festivals throughout the year, as well as vineyards you can tour.

# HAMPTON UNIVERSITY

Office of Admissions, Hampton University, Hampton, VA 23668
Telephone: 757-727-5328 • E-mail: admit@hamptonu.edu
Website: www.hamptonu.edu

## STUDENTS SAY

"Hampton University is about an education for life, providing academic and social growth to each person making them a valuable asset to the workforce and community."

## FODOR'S SAYS

"The Virginia Air and Space Center traces the history of flight and space exploration. The nine-story, futuristic, $30 million center is the official repository of the NASA Langley Research Center. Its space artifacts include a 3-billion-year-old moon rock, the Apollo 12 command capsule, and lunar lander."

## ABOUT THE SCHOOL

Hampton University is a historically Black college near the beautiful Virginian coastline that offers students a rigorous academic experience, with standout programs in communications, psychology, and business. The school successfully instills an admirable sense of school spirit and pride in its students. Despite HU's strict rules on everything from conduct to dress, students can't stop singing the university's praises. The vast social opportunities created by the college's location near the sea are nothing to frown about either.

## GETTING THERE

**BY AIR:** Norfolk International Airport is 30 minutes away from the campus, and the Newport News/Williamsburg Airport is 20 minutes away. Visitors can take a taxi to get to the school.

**BY TRAIN:** Amtrak stops in Newport News. Visitors can take a taxi to get to the school.

**BY BUS:** Greyhound stops in Hampton and Newport News. Visitors can take a taxi to get to the school.

**BY CAR:** Hampton University is near Exit 267 on I-64 in Virginia. From the West: Take I-64 East to the Settlers Landing Road Exit and go straight through the light onto Tyler Street. The college is ahead. From the East: Take I-64 West to the Woodland Road/Downtown Hampton Exit, and turn left at the next light onto Tyler Street. The college is ahead. From the South: Take I-85 North to South Hill, Virginia. Exit at U.S. 58 East Travel to Suffolk, Virginia. Exit at I-64 East, and follow I-64 East. Exit at Exit 267. The college is ahead. From the Northeast: Take I-95 South to Richmond, Virginia. Exit at I-295 South Beltway to I-64 East. Exit at Exit 267. The college is ahead.

**LOCAL:** For local taxi service call Checker Cab Co. (757-727-4504), Harvest Taxicab Co. (757-723-7922), and Arrington's Taxi Service (757-827-9300).

## WHERE TO STAY

Some local accommodations include the Days Inn (757-826-4810, $), La Quinta Inn (757-827-8680, $), and Quality Inn & Suites (757-838-5011, $$).

## CAMPUS AT ITS BEST!

Hampton University's Emancipation Tree has a sense of history and significance that is palpable. As the site of the first Southern reading of the Emancipation Proclamation, it's no surprise that many newly freed men and women sought an education beneath the shade of this very oak. Those who enjoy tapping into their inner child should visit the Hampton Carousel. Within walking distance from campus, this antique ride proudly displays its original mirrors and oil paintings. Afterward, go back to Hampton and attend one of the many events, which range from DJs spinning the latest tracks to basketball tournaments and even a car show.

# HOLLINS UNIVERSITY

PO Box 9707, Roanoke, VA 24020-1707
**Telephone:** 540-362-6401 • **E-mail:** huadm@hollins.edu
**Hours:** Monday–Friday, 8:30 A.M.–4:30 P.M.; Saturday, 9:00 A.M.–NOON

## Students Say

"The personal community is definitely the greatest strength at Hollins. A picturesque atmosphere is complemented by a friendly student body as well as an involved and accessible faculty."

## Fodor's Says

"Dixie Caverns is unusual in that, rather than descending into the cave, you first must walk upstairs into the heart of a mountain. The Spacious Cathedral Room, formations dubbed Turkey Wing and Wedding Bell, and an earthquake fault line are among the sights."

## About the School

Students at Hollins say small classes, attentive faculty, and an all-female undergrad population make the university a comfortable place to pursue a challenging education. A handful of other perks—the famous equestrian team, the successful internship program, the breathtaking outdoors of western Virginia, to name a few, give Hollins its own special zest.

## Getting There

**BY AIR:** Nearby Roanoke Regional Airport receives flights from 30 airports and about half a dozen carriers. The Smart Way Bus runs regularly between the airport and downtown Roanoke. The Hollins Express links the campus and the airport.

**BY TRAIN:** Clifton Forge, a little more than half an hour away, is serviced by Amtrak's Cardinal/Hoosier State line. Take a taxi to the campus.

**BY BUS:** Greyhound stops at Swanson Transportation Services in Roanoke.

**BY CAR:** From I-81 North: Follow I-81 North to Exit 146, where you make a left onto Plantation Road. At the stoplight, go left onto Williamson Road (Route 11 North). Half a mile later, you will see the campus entrance on your left. From I-81 South: Follow I-81 South to Exit 146, where you make a right onto Plantation Road. At the stoplight, go left onto Williamson Road (Route 11 North). Half a mile later, you will see the campus entrance on your left. From Route 220 North: Follow Route 220 North until merging onto I-581 North. Drive a little more than five miles on I-581 North and turn onto I-81 North. From there, follow "From I-81 North" directions above. From Route 220 South: Follow Route 220 South to the intersection with Route 11. Make a right onto Route 11 South and continue ahead for 3.5 miles until you see the campus on your right.

**LOCAL:** Valley Metro's Hollins Express links campus to downtown and the airport. For taxi service, call Liberty Cab (540-344-1776), Yellow Cab (540-345-7711), or Quality Transportation Service (540-265-0467).

## Where to Stay

Hollins University offers limited lodging through its Barbee Guest House (540-362-6225, $). Be sure to book well in advance. Other nearby options include the Hampton Inn (540-563-5656, $–$$), and the Country Inn and Suites (540-366-5678, $$).

## CAMPUS AT ITS BEST!

Prospective students should saddle up and visit Hollins' Riding Center. This state-of-the-art facility includes both an outdoor and indoor ring as well as two stables. When you've had your fix of all things equestrian, take a stroll past the Dana Science Building and stop at The Rock. Students use this boulder as a sounding board, painting it in times of celebration and to voice opinions on important issues. If you want to partake in some university traditions, tour the campus on Tinker Day. Every October, the president cancels class and the entire Hollins community hikes up Tinker Mountain in outrageous costumes for a picnic.

# JAMES MADISON UNIVERSITY

Sonner Hall, MSC 0101, Harrisonburg, VA 22807
**Telephone:** 540-568-5681 • **E-mail:** admissions@jmu.edu

## STUDENTS SAY

"James Madison University is a school made up of well-rounded students who study a variety of exceptionally strong majors, participate in rewarding field work experiences, and enjoy an all-around positive atmosphere."

## FODOR'S SAYS

"At the Virginia Quilt museum, you can see examples of quilts made throughout the mid-Atlantic region and learn about the international heritage of quilting."

## ABOUT THE SCHOOL

James Madison is a state-run university with a healthy course selection. Despite its size—about 15,000 undergrads—JMU offers a comfortable environment in which students can get to know their professors and classmates on a personal level. The school is located at the edge of the Appalachians and just two hours away from DC.

## GETTING THERE

**BY AIR:** The Shenandoah Valley Regional Airport, about 20 minutes away from campus, is serviced by U.S. Air connector flights. Airport Shuttle offers transportation to campus (540-234-8304). The Charlottesville–Albermarle Airport is 45 minutes away from campus and is serviced by four airlines. Dulles and Richmond international airports are each two hours away.

**BY TRAIN:** Amtrak's Cardinal/Hoosier State line stops in Staunton, about 25 miles away from campus. Take a taxi to the campus.

**BY BUS:** Greyhound services Charlottesville, a little more than half an hour away. Take a taxi to the campus.

**BY CAR:** From I-81 North: Follow I-81 North to Exit 245 for Port Republic Road. At the end of the ramp, make a left onto Port Republic Road. At the second light, turn right onto the campus. From I-81 South: Follow I-81 South to Exit 245 for Port Republic Road. At the end of the ramp, make a right onto Port Republic Road. Drive to the first light, and make a right onto campus. From I-64 East: Follow I-64 West to Lexington, where you merge onto I-81 North. From there, follow the "From I-81 North" directions above. From I-64 West: Follow I-64 West to Waynesboro, where you merge with I-81 North. From there, follow the "From I-81 North" directions above. From I-66 West: Follow I-66 West. When the road comes to an end at Front Royal, take I-81 South in the direction of Roanoke. From there, follow the "From I-81 South" directions above.

**LOCAL:** Harrisonburg Transit bus service operates lines 2, 3, 4, 7, and 9 through campus. You can also try Fiesta Cab (540-438-5900) or Yellow Cab (540- 434-2515) for taxi service.

## WHERE TO STAY

Lodging options within a mile of the JMU campus include the Days Inn (540-433-9353, $), the Village Inn (540-434-7355, $), and the Joshua Wilton House (540-434-4464, $$).

## CAMPUS AT ITS BEST!

The James Madison Center, conveniently located on JMU's campus, honors the legacy of our fourth president. The center operates as a repository for information on both Madison and the Federalist era. All that political discourse will leave you wanting a front seat to the Madison Cup, a debate competition that coincides with the university's annual celebration of its namesake's birthday. Afterward, enjoy a meal at the Festival Student and Conference Center. This facility includes an array of dining services and recreational and meeting spaces.

# LOUISIANA STATE UNIVERSITY— BATON ROUGE

110 Thomas Boyd Hall, Baton Rouge, LA 70803
**Telephone:** 225-578-1175 • **E-mail:** admissions@lsu.edu
**Website:** www.lsu.edu • **Hours:** Monday–Friday, 7:30 A.M.–5:00 P.M.

## STUDENTS SAY

"Our school is all about the Purple and Gold, football, southern tradition, and striving for excellence in every area."

## FODOR'S SAYS

"After an extensive two-year restoration that involved peeling multiple layers of paint off the walls to reveal original colors and handsome frieze work, the Old Governor's Mansion is again worth a visit. Built in 1930, during Huey Long's administration, the mansion has memorabilia that pertains to every governor that has served since the house was built."

## ABOUT THE SCHOOL

Research is the name of the game at LSU. Undergrads have no problem getting their hands on the cutting-edge equipment in the labs and up-to-date resources in the immense library. Because the campus is so large, self-motivators with lots of initiative tend to thrive in this pocket of the South.

## GETTING THERE

**BY AIR:** Baton Rouge Metropolitan Airport is serviced by four airlines. Located less than 10 minutes from the airport, LSU is an easy taxi ride away. The Louis Armstrong New Orleans International Airport, a little over an hour away, has more flight options.

**BY TRAIN:** New Orleans and New Iberia, each about 80 miles from Baton Rouge, are serviced by Amtrak.

**BY BUS:** Greyhound runs regular service in Baton Rouge through its Florida Avenue terminal. Take a taxi to the campus.

**BY CAR:** From I-10 East: Proceed on I-10 East to Exit 157B and make a right onto Acadian Thruway. (Note: Acadian Thruway becomes Stanford Avenue, which becomes LSU Avenue.) Continue on LSU Avenue until you arrive at the intersection with Highland Drive and turn right onto Highland Road. The Visitor Information Center is at the corner of Highland Road and Dalrymple Drive. From I-10 West: Proceed on I-10 East to Exit 157B and make a left onto Acadian Thruway. (Note: Acadian Thruway becomes Stanford Avenue, which becomes LSU Avenue.) Continue on LSU Avenue until you arrive at the intersection with Highland Drive and turn right onto Highland Road. The Visitor Information Center is at the corner of Highland Road and Dalrymple Drive.

**LOCAL:** About a dozen CATS bus lines service LSU, providing transportation to and from most local destinations around the campus. A taxi can be found through Yellow Cab (225-926-6400) or Mackie's Airport Cab Service (225-357-4883).

## WHERE TO STAY

Baton Rouge offers plenty of hotels for overnight visitors. Among the options are La Quinta Inn (225-924-9600, $$), Comfort Inn University Center (225-927-5790, $$), and Baton Rouge Marriott (225-924-5000, $$).

### SCHOOL AT A GLANCE

| | |
|---|---|
| Type of School | Public |
| Environment | Metropolis |
| In-state Tuition | $2,981 |
| Out-of-state Tuition | $11,281 |
| Enrollment | 25,301 |
| % Male/Female | 48/52 |
| Student/Faculty Ratio | 22:1 |

### FRESHMAN PROFILE

| | |
|---|---|
| Range SAT | |
| Critical Reading | 520-630 |
| Range SAT Math | 540-660 |
| Range ACT Composite | 22-27 |
| Average HS GPA | 3.47 |

### ON-CAMPUS APPOINTMENTS

| | |
|---|---|
| Saturdays | No |
| Info Sessions | Yes |
| Class Visits | Yes |

### CAMPUS TOURS

| | |
|---|---|
| Appointment | Preferred |
| Dates | Year Round |
| Times | M–F 10:00 A.M. or by appt. |
| Average Length | 120 min |

## CAMPUS AT ITS BEST!

Contemplating going to school in Louisiana? Then perhaps you'd like to take a closer look at the culture of this colorful state by visiting LSU's Rural Life Museum. The museum includes exhibits on Louisiana Folk architecture as well as nineteenth-century plantation life. To experience the university social life, simply stop by the LSU Union where you can catch a show by the Great Performance Theater Series. Prospective students staying overnight should also attend one of the "Tigers After 10" events. Past activities have included LSU Idol, sumo wrestling, a freestyle rap competition, and bull riding.

# LOYOLA UNIVERSITY—NEW ORLEANS

6363 St. Charles Avenue, Box 18, New Orleans, LA 70118-6195
Telephone: 504-865-3240 • E-mail: admit@loyno.edu
Website: www.loyno.edu

## SCHOOL AT A GLANCE

| Type of School | Private |
| --- | --- |
| Environment | Metropolis |
| Tuition | $23,954 |
| Enrollment | 3,618 |
| % Male/Female | 39/61 |
| Student/Faculty Ratio | 13:1 |

### FRESHMAN PROFILE

| Range SAT | |
| --- | --- |
| Critical Reading | 570-680 |
| Range SAT Math | 560-660 |
| Range ACT Composite | 24-29 |
| Average HS GPA | 3.70 |

### ON-CAMPUS APPOINTMENTS

| Advance Notice | Yes, 2 weeks |
| --- | --- |
| Appointment | Preferred |
| Saturdays | No |
| Average Length | 30 min |
| Info Sessions | Yes |
| Class Visits | Yes |

### CAMPUS TOURS

| Appointment | Required |
| --- | --- |
| Dates | Year Round |
| Times | M–F 11:30 A.M. and 3:30 P.M. |
| Average Length | 60 min |

## STUDENTS SAY

"New Orleans gets named for being the party place, [though] it's so beyond that. Yes, we know how to have fun, but we also know what is important in life . . . and that became especially apparent to us during Hurricane Katrina. And I can say that I am a better person after being at Loyola, especially in the times of hardship."

## FODOR'S SAYS

"An ideal time for a first visit to New Orleans is Spring Fiesta (the weekend following Easter) when the city is dressed in springtime finery and many of the handsome homes are open for tours."

## ABOUT THE SCHOOL

Undergraduates are the clear priority at Loyola University—New Orleans. Professors and administrators are very responsive to students' needs and even the president is frequently seen chatting with undergrads. Class discussions are encouraged and one-on-one contact with teachers is the norm. Hometown New Orleans provides plenty of fun outside of class, with the French Quarter and Bourbon Street only a short streetcar ride away.

## GETTING THERE

**BY AIR:** Louis Armstrong New Orleans International Airport is the closest airport to campus. It is recommended that you take a taxi or shuttle to Loyola.

**BY TRAIN:** Amtrak trains stop in New Orleans. Take a taxi or local transportation to get to campus.

**BY BUS:** Greyhound buses stop at the Downtown Bus Station in New Orleans. Local buses and taxis can take you to your ultimate destination.

**BY CAR:** From I-10 West: Follow the signs toward the Central Business District. Use Exit 232, the Carrollton Avenue exit. Proceed on South Carrollton until it ends in a left-hand curve and turns into St. Charles Avenue. The main campus will be on your left, across from Audubon Park, at 6363 St. Charles Avenue. You'll find the Broadway campus located at 7214 St. Charles Avenue (at the corner of Broadway). From I-10 East: Upon entering the downtown area, follow the signs to Highway 90 Business/West Bank. Use the exit at St. Charles Avenue/Carondelet Street (Note: Do not cross the bridge). When you hit the second traffic light, turn right onto St. Charles Avenue. Continue on St. Charles Avenue for four miles; Loyola's main campus will be on your right.

**LOCAL:** New Orleans Regional Transit Authority offers bus and streetcar service throughout the city. If you're in search of a local cab company consider Coleman Cab Company (504-586-0222) or United Cabs Inc (504-522-9771).

## WHERE TO STAY

For hotels within close proximity to campus try: Hotel Intercontinental (504-585-4345, $$), Sheraton New Orleans (504-525-2500, $$) or Loews New Orleans Hotel (504-636-3300, $$–$$$).

## CAMPUS AT ITS BEST!

On beautiful days, Loyola's Peace Quad doubles as a magnet, pulling students into its lush field. A popular spot for studying or merely relaxing with friends, the Quad also frequently hosts barbecues, crawfish boils, and small concerts. Visitors interested in staying through the evening should investigate Loyola After Dark. This program sponsors a variety of activities ranging from Wiffle ball tournaments and fashion shows, to a ghost/cemetery tour.

# MERCER UNIVERSITY—MACON

Admissions Office, 1400 Coleman Avenue, Macon, GA 31207-0001
**Telephone:** 478-301-2650 • **E-mail:** admissions@mercer.edu
**Website:** www.gomercer.com

## STUDENTS SAY

"Mercer is a great place to go if you are looking for a fairly small community of students and faculty. We also have a good service learning program that is making a commendable effort to reach out to the community of Macon."

## FODOR'S SAYS

"The Tubman African American Museum honors the former slave who led more than 300 people to freedom as one of the conductors of the Underground Railroad. A mural depicts several centuries of Black culture. The museum also has an African artifacts gallery."

## ABOUT THE SCHOOL

Guided by Baptist principles of religious faith and moral behavior, Mercer University is a great choice for spiritually minded students who are looking for a rigorous education among like-minded individuals. The school is fairly small with only 4500 undergrads; students benefit from classes that are always taught by actual professors, who are by all accounts extremely intelligent and accessible. Social activities on campus are plentiful, and the cities of Macon and Atlanta (one hour away) provide endless options for culture and entertainment.

## GETTING THERE

**BY AIR:** Mercer University is about 81 miles from Atlanta's Hartsfield-Jackson, the second busiest airport in the world. Macon's own Middle Georgia Regional Airport is 18 miles away, but all flights connect from the Atlanta Airport via shuttle. Your best options to get to the campus are a rental car or shuttle.

**BY TRAIN:** Amtrak does not have a station in Macon, but it does provide bus service to and from Atlanta's Brookwood Amtrak station.

**BY BUS:** There is a Greyhound station near downtown Macon. Take a taxi to get to the campus.

**BY CAR:** From I-75, heading North (from Florida): Take I-75 North to Exit #164 (Hardeman Avenue/Forsyth Street). Turn right at top of exit ramp and proceed to the second traffic light and turn right onto College Street. Follow College Street to the North entrance of the campus. Enter North entrance and proceed to the three-way stop. Turn left onto Elm Street. The University Welcome Center will be on the right. From I-75, heading South (from Atlanta): Take I-75 South to Exit #164 (Hardeman Avenue/Forsyth Street). Take ramp off the interstate, and follow the road to the second light. Turn left at the second light, and proceed to the third traffic light. Turn right onto College Street, and follow the "From I-75" directions above. From I-16, heading West (from Savannah): Take I-16 West until it merges with I-75 South. Take I-75 South to Exit #164 (Hardeman Avenue/Forsyth Street). Take ramp off the interstate, and follow the road to the second light. Turn left at the second light, and proceed to the third traffic light. Turn right onto College Street, and follow the "From I-75" directions above.

**LOCAL:** The MTA (Macon Transit Authority) serves Macon and Bibb County and stops at Mercer University. For local taxi service try Yellow Cab Inc. (478-785-1124) and Radio Cab, Inc. (478-781-6052).

## WHERE TO STAY

The affordable Crowne Plaza Hotel is in downtown Macon, close to the university (877-227-6963, $). In North Macon, hotel options include the Courtyard by Marriott (478-477-8899, $$) and the 1842 Inn (877-452-6599, $$$).

## SCHOOL AT A GLANCE

| | |
|---|---|
| Type of School | Private |
| Environment | City |
| Tuition | $25,056 |
| Enrollment | 2,355 |
| % Male/Female | 45/55 |
| Student/Faculty Ratio | 13:1 |

### FRESHMAN PROFILE

| | |
|---|---|
| Range SAT | |
| Critical Reading | 530-640 |
| Range SAT Math | 550-640 |
| Range ACT Composite | 22-27 |
| Average HS GPA | 3.6 |

### ON-CAMPUS APPOINTMENTS

| | |
|---|---|
| Advance Notice | Yes, 1 week |
| Appointment | Preferred |
| Saturdays | Yes |
| Average Length | 60 min |
| Info Sessions | Yes |
| Class Visits | Yes |

### CAMPUS TOURS

| | |
|---|---|
| Appointment | Preferred |
| Dates | Year Round |
| Times | 9:00 A.M., 11:00 A.M., 2:00 P.M. |
| Average Length | 60 min |

---

## CAMPUS AT ITS BEST!

Macon is the Cherry Blossom capital of the world, so don't miss the annual Cherry Blossom festival in March. It features fashion shows, a marathon, air shows, evening concerts, and street parties. If you're there in the fall, try to check out the Mercer University homecoming parade. At this annual event, the entire campus and local community comes together in support of the school.

# MILLSAPS COLLEGE

1701 North State Street, Jackson, MS 39210-0001
**Telephone:** 601-974-1050 • **E-mail:** admissions@millsaps.edu
**Hours:** Monday–Friday, 8:00 A.M.–4:30 P.M.

## SCHOOL AT A GLANCE

| | |
|---|---|
| Type of School | Private |
| Environment | Metropolis |
| Tuition | $20,660 |
| Enrollment | 1,065 |
| % Male/Female | 51/49 |
| Student/Faculty Ratio | 12:1 |

## FRESHMAN PROFILE

| | |
|---|---|
| Range SAT | |
| Critical Reading | 538-683 |
| Range SAT Math | 540-650 |
| Range ACT Composite | 23-30 |
| Average HS GPA | 3.55 |

## ON-CAMPUS APPOINTMENTS

| | |
|---|---|
| Advance Notice | Yes, 1 week |
| Appointment | Preferred |
| Saturdays | Sometimes |
| Average Length | 30 min |
| Info Sessions | Yes |
| Class Visits | Yes |

## CAMPUS TOURS

| | |
|---|---|
| Appointment | Preferred |
| Dates | Year Round |
| Times | M–F 9:30 A.M. and 1:30 P.M. |
| Average Length | 60 min |

## STUDENTS SAY

"Millsaps is an engaging academic experience, [with a] beautiful campus, close-knit community, caring faculty, and [is an] excellent place for intellectual and personal growth."

## FODOR'S SAYS

"The Russell C. Davis Planetarium offers breathtaking science and nature adventures every day (except Monday). The planetarium's McNair Space Theater has a 60-foot domed screen (the largest in the mid-South), and a full complement of star, slide, special effect, and video shows."

## ABOUT THE SCHOOL

Little more than a thousand students populate this small, Methodist liberal arts college in Jackson, Mississippi. Millsaps places a strong emphasis on individual thinking, community participation, and writing. And we mean a lot of writing. (The college's core curriculum program includes a substantial writing component.) Students get to experience all of this in the heart of the South.

## GETTING THERE

**BY AIR:** Jackson-Evers International Airport, 14 miles from campus, offers flights to and from 11 cities. Limousine/shuttle service can be arranged in advance through companies such as Act One Limousine (601-952-0000) and Go-Fer Girls (601-638-2574). Otherwise, catch a cab to campus.

**BY TRAIN:** Amtrak's famed City of Orleans line stops in Jackson, fewer than three miles from campus. Take a taxi to campus.

**BY BUS:** Jackson's Greyhound terminal is only about two miles from Millsaps. Taxis offer the easiest transit to campus.

**BY CAR:** From I-55 North/South: Follow I-55 to Exit 98A and proceed West on Woodrow Wilson Drive. Continue on Woodrow Wilson Drive to the second traffic light, where you should make a left turn onto North State Street. Millsaps College will be on your right-hand side. You may enter campus at either the North Security Gate entrance or the Whitworth Circle entrance.

**LOCAL:** Jackson's local bus service, JATRAN, runs 13 lines that service the local area. The city offers a number of options by way of taxi, including Citi-Cab Company (601-355-8319), Deluxe Cab Company (601-948-4761), and Yellow Cab Company Inc. (601-922-3782).

## WHERE TO STAY

Among the local hotels that offer discounted rates to Millsaps visitors—don't forget to mention that you're visiting the campus!—are Cabot Lodge Millsaps (located right at the edge of campus; 800-874-4737, $$) and Hampton Inn and Suites, Jackson—Coliseum (601-352-1700, $$). In addition, there is a range of other nearby hotels such as the Red Roof Inn—Coliseum (601-969-5006, $), the Clarion Hotel and Suites (601-366-9411, $$), and the elegant Fairview Inn (888-948-1098, $$–$$$), an 18-room bed and breakfast in a Colonial Revival mansion.

## CAMPUS AT ITS BEST!

As the oldest building on campus, the James Observatory is a prominent Millsaps landmark. Inside you'll find a six-inch Warner Swayze refracting telescope which was originally installed in 1901. After all that star-gazing, you can pay your respects to the Millsaps founder. That's right—near the center of campus is the tomb of Major R.W. Millsaps and his wife. The mausoleum boasts a stunning stained-glass window, selected by the Major himself. To gain an idea of the many cultural opportunities available at Millsaps, try to attend the annual Multicultural Festival. This event typically includes dancing, martial arts demonstrations, and succulent ethnic food.

# MISSISSIPPI STATE UNIVERSITY

PO Box 6334, Mississippi State, MS 39762
**Telephone:** 662-325-2224 • **E-mail:** admit@msstate.edu
**Website:** www.msstate.edu

| SCHOOL AT A GLANCE | |
| --- | --- |
| Type of School | Public |
| Environment | Town |
| In-state Tuition | $4,596 |
| Out-of-state Tuition | $10,552 |
| Enrollment | 12,555 |
| % Male/Female | 52/48 |
| Student/Faculty Ratio | 14:1 |
| **FRESHMAN PROFILE** | |
| Range ACT Composite | 19-27 |
| Average HS GPA | 3.18 |
| **ON-CAMPUS APPOINTMENTS** | |
| Class Visits | Yes |
| **CAMPUS TOURS** | |
| Appointment | Preferred |
| Dates | Year Round |
| Times | Varies |
| Average Length | Varies |

## STUDENTS SAY

"The student body at MSU is the friendliest group of people and most will stop to help a complete stranger with anything."

## FODOR'S SAYS

"Locals say that if you find yourself in Mississippi and you're looking for a great juke joint, you might just check out the telephone poles. Over the years, they've proven to be a good informational source, since ads for the so-called 'chitlins circuit' are often posted there."

## ABOUT THE SCHOOL

Mississippi State, a public land-grant institution, strives to provide affordable and accessible education to those around the state and around the world. Engaging professors foster the exploration of ideas and encourage students to apply lessons learned in the classroom. MSU has particularly strong programs in agriculture, natural resources, and engineering. Athletics are extremely popular and Bulldog spirit is contagious, especially during football season.

## GETTING THERE

**BY AIR:** Mississippi State is approximately 15 minutes from the Golden Triangle Regional Airport. Flights are available via Delta Connection/Atlantic Southeast Airlines. MSU is also accessible from Jackson International and Tupelo Regional Airports.

**BY TRAIN:** The closest Amtrak stations are located in Tuscaloosa, AL and Meridian, MS, both approximately 75 miles from Mississippi State.

**BY BUS:** Visitors may take Greyhound to either Jackson, MS or Tupelo, MS. For additional transportation to campus it is recommended that you rent a car.

**BY CAR:** From Birmingham, AL: Proceed Southwest on I-59 to Exit 68 (Black Warrior Parkway). Continue Northwest on Black Warrior Parkway to U.S. Highway 82. You will then drive West on Highway 82 to the Mississippi state line. Continue on Highway 82 to Mississippi Highway 182. Travel West on Highway 182 to Mississippi Boulevard. Finally, take a left onto Mississippi Boulevard (MSU North entrance road). From Jackson, MS: Proceed Northeast on Mississippi Highway 25 (from I-55) to Mississippi Highway 12. Continue East on Highway 12 to Collegeview Street. You will exit onto Collegeview Street. From Memphis, TN: Proceed Southeast on U.S. Highway 78 to U.S. Highway 45. Continue South on Highway 45 to U.S. Highway 45 Alternate. Drive South on Highway 45 Alternate to U.S. Highway 82. See above for the remainder of the directions.

**LOCAL:** For local cab service, visitors may call McClain Taxi Service (662-323-9530) or Dogs Patrol Cab Co. (662-648-9818).

## WHERE TO STAY

These hotels are all within a mile from campus: Microtel Inn and Suites (662-615-0700, $), Hotel Chester (662-323-5005, $–$$), or the Ramada Inn (662-323-6161, $–$$). The Butler Guest House on campus (662-325-4140, $) is another popular lodging option.

## CAMPUS AT ITS BEST!

Voracious readers and fans of literary legal thrillers will want to take a gander at the John Grisham Room (an MSU alum), located in Mitchell Memorial Library. Featured among the room's collection is the original manuscript of his first novel, *A Time to Kill*, photographs from his legislative days, and personal correspondence. Prospective students interested in Mississippi State tradition should attend the annual Bulldog Bash, the largest free outdoor music festival in the state. The festivities also include face painting, karaoke, and pep rallies.

# MOREHOUSE COLLEGE

830 Westview Drive, Southwest, Atlanta, GA 30314
**Telephone:** 404-215-2632 • **E-mail:** janderso@morehouse.edu
**Website:** www.morehouse.edu • **Hours:** Monday–Friday, 9:00 A.M.–5:00 P.M

## STUDENTS SAY

"The school stresses that it is each student's responsibility to support and encourage [his or her] fellow students. This notion fosters a brotherhood [among] students that can be felt throughout the campus."

## FODOR'S SAYS

"Underground Atlanta—This six-block entertainment and shopping district, dotted with historic markers, was created from the web of underground brick streets, ornamental building facades, and tunnels that fell into disuse in 1929 when the city built viaducts over the train tracks."

## ABOUT THE SCHOOL

Morehouse College is a historically Black liberal arts college for men that offers its students a challenging and rigorous academic program, while promoting social awareness, integrity, and leadership skills. Professors get involved in students' lives, serving as mentors, academic advisors, and career counselors. For fun, students frequent downtown Atlanta, the "Capital of the South," for great restaurants, nightlife, and entertainment.

## GETTING THERE

**BY AIR:** The South/Hartsfield International Airport is the closest airport to campus. Take a taxi or local public transportation to get to the campus.

**BY TRAIN:** Amtrak stops on Peachtree Street in Atlanta. Take a taxi or local public transportation to get to the campus.

**BY BUS:** Greyhound stops on Forsyth Street in Atlanta. Take a taxi or local public transportation to get to the campus.

**BY CAR:** From the North/Downtown: Take I-75/85 South to I-20 West. Take Exit 55B (Lee Street). Turn right at the traffic light onto Westview Drive and go two blocks to the campus. From the East: Take I-20 West to Exit 55B (Lee St). Turn right at the traffic light onto Westview Drive and go two blocks to the campus. From the West: Take I-20 East to Exit 55A, which is Ashby Street/West End. Turn left onto Ashby Street and go through four traffic lights. At the fourth traffic light, turn right onto Westview Drive and proceed toward campus.

**LOCAL:** Visitors can take the local train, the MARTA Rail, to the Vine City or West End station. From there, a shuttle from the college can take you directly to the campus. For local taxi service call Cascade Cab Co. (404-758-5521) and City Wide Cab Co (404-875-1223).

## WHERE TO STAY

Some popular hotel choices in Atlanta include the Stratford Inn Atlanta (404-607-1010, $), Atlanta Days-Inn Downtown (404-523-1144, $$), and the Hilton Atlanta (404-659-2000, $$$).

---

## CAMPUS AT ITS BEST!

To gain a good understanding of life at Morehouse, simply stop by the Kilgore Campus Center. This multipurpose building includes the President's Dining Room, a snack bar, a game room, and a student lounge. A visit to Sale Hall should also be on your agenda. This building features the Chapel for the Inward Journey and the Thurman Meditation Room.

# NEW COLLEGE OF FLORIDA

5800 Bay Shore Road, Sarasota, FL 34243
**Telephone:** 941-487-5000 • **E-mail:** admissions@ncf.edu
**Website:** www.ncf.edu • **Hours:** Monday–Friday, 8:00 A.M.–5:00 P.M.

## STUDENTS SAY

"You will never want for intellectual conversation during your undergraduate experience if New College is your choice. Everyone can learn something from everyone here."

## FODOR'S SAYS

"On display at the Sarasota Classic Car Museum are 100 restored antique, classic, and muscle cars—including Rolls-Royces, Pierce Arrows, and Auburns. The collection includes rare cars and vehicles that belonged to famous people, such as John Lennon and John Ringling."

## ABOUT THE SCHOOL

At the New College of Florida, students enjoy the freedom to study whatever they want. New College's innovative curriculum allows students to design their own curriculum (after consulting with faculty advisors) and plot out a distinctive course of study that will satisfy their academic goals and interests. Since there are no grades (only written evaluations from professors), students have to be truly self-motivated to be successful.

## GETTING THERE

**BY AIR:** New College of Florida is less than a mile from Sarasota-Bradenton International Airport. Visitors can also fly into Tampa International Airport, which is an hour's drive away from campus. Students can take the Sarasota-Tampa Express (800-326-2800) or the Greyhound Bus from Tampa to Sarasota.

**BY TRAIN:** Amtrak makes two stops in Sarasota. Take a taxi to get to campus.

**BY BUS:** Greyhound Bus Lines stops in Sarasota. Take a taxi to get to campus.

**BY CAR:** From I-75: Take Exit 213, the University Parkway, from I-75. Go seven miles West on University Parkway, until it intersects with U.S. 41 (North Tamiami Trail). Make a right at this intersection. Turn left at the next stoplight onto College Drive. At the next stop sign, go straight.

**LOCAL:** Sarasota County Area Transit (SCAT) offers bus service around town. Call 941-861-1234 for route and schedule information. If you don't feel like taking the bus to get around town, call Yellow Cab of Siesta Key (941-955-3341) or Emerald Green Cab Taxi (941-922-6666) for taxi service.

## WHERE TO STAY

Popular hotel choices include the Comfort Inn (941-921-7750, $), Best Western Golden Host Resort (941-355-5141, $$), and Hyatt Sarasota (941-953-1234, $$$).

### SCHOOL AT A GLANCE

| | |
|---|---|
| Type of School | Public |
| Environment | Town |
| In-state Tuition | $3,734 |
| Out-of-state Tuition | $19,964 |
| Enrollment | 761 |
| % Male/Female | 39/61 |
| Student/Faculty Ratio | 11/1 |

### FRESHMAN PROFILE

| | |
|---|---|
| Range SAT | |
| Critical Reading | 630–720 |
| Range SAT Math | 580–670 |
| Range ACT Composite | 25–29 |
| Average HS GPA | 3.96 |

### ON-CAMPUS APPOINTMENTS

| | |
|---|---|
| Advance Notice | No |
| Appointment | Required |
| Saturdays | No |
| Average Length | 60 min |
| Info Sessions | Yes |
| Class Visits | Yes |

### CAMPUS TOURS

| | |
|---|---|
| Appointment | Preferred |
| Dates | Year Round |
| Times | M–F 11:00 A.M. and 3:00 P.M. |
| Average Length | 60 min |

## CAMPUS AT ITS BEST!

Among New College of Florida's many distinct attributes is the Pei Residence Hall. Conceived by eminent architect I.M. Pei, this quirky dormitory is designed so that no student can walk anywhere in a straight line. If that proves too dizzying, you can easily make your way to Crescent Beach. Taking advantage of its close proximity to campus, students often enjoy a refreshing dip in the Atlantic while they play in the famed white powder sand.

# NORTH CAROLINA STATE UNIVERSITY

Box 7103, Raleigh, NC 27695
**Telephone:** 919-515-2434 • **E-mail:** undergrad_admissions@ncsu.edu
**Hours:** Monday–Friday, 8:00 A.M.–5:00 P.M.

## STUDENTS SAY

"At school, life is very laid-back and very demanding. The course load can somewhat be hard, but on the weekends and even during the week, students like to go out and have a good time with their friends."

## FODOR'S SAYS

"At 20,000 square feet, the North Carolina Museum of Natural Sciences is the largest of its kind in the Southeast. Permanent exhibits and dioramas celebrate the incredible diversity of species in the state's three regions, along with enough live animals and insects to qualify as a small zoo...The pièce de résistance, however, is the 'terror of the South' exhibit, featuring the dinosaur skeleton of 'Acro,' a giant carnivore that lived in the region 110 million years ago."

## ABOUT THE SCHOOL

As with many large universities, it can be easy to get lost in the fray at NC State. Of course, as you progress, the system becomes infinitely more manageable. The university is primarily recognized as an engineering and agriculture school, though humanities students are quick to applaud their programs as well. Undergrads are passionate about sports, especially during football season when tailgating becomes a way of life.

## GETTING THERE

**BY AIR:** Raleigh-Durham International Airport receives from major airlines such as Delta, jetBlue, US Airways, and United. Rental cars, taxis, and public buses are all available for any other travel needs.

**BY TRAIN:** Take an Amtrak train into Raleigh. Taxis and local buses may be used for additional transport.

**BY BUS:** Greyhound also provides service to Raleigh. Local buses and taxis can be taken to reach campus.

**BY CAR:** From Durham via U.S. 70: Follow U.S. 70 to downtown Raleigh. (Note: U.S. 70 will become Glenwood Avenue.) Proceed on Glenwood Avenue to Oberlin Road. You will take a right onto Oberlin Road and make another right onto Hillsborough Street. You'll then need to make an immediate left at Pullen Road. Follow signs to the Visitor Information Booth on Stinson Drive (at the traffic circle). From New York, Pennsylvania, Maryland, and Virginia via I-95 South: Follow I-95 South to I-85 South. Proceed to U.S. 1 (which ultimately becomes Capital Boulevard) to downtown Raleigh. Make a right onto Edenton Street. This will merge with Hillsborough Street. See above for the rest of the directions. From Florida via I-95 North: Follow I-95 North to I-40 West. Continue on I-40 West (this will take you into Raleigh) to Gorman Street, Exit 295. Make a right at the stoplight onto Gorman Street and continue to the second traffic light. Make a right onto Avent Ferry Road. Next you will make a right onto Western Boulevard. Finally, take the first left onto Pullen Road. See above for the rest of the directions.

**LOCAL:** The Triangle Transit Authority provides local bus service around Raleigh, Durham, Chapel Hill, and RTP. Additionally, the university offers the Wolfline Transit System for transportation around all three campuses.

## WHERE TO STAY

Overnight guests might consider: Hampton Inn and Suites (919-233-1798, $), Candlewood Suites Raleigh/Crabtree (919-789-4840, $), or the Sheraton Capital Center Hotel (919-834-9900, $).

---

## CAMPUS AT ITS BEST!

Those looking for a healthy arts and culture scene certainly won't be disappointed by NC State. Film buffs will be glad to learn that the school is equipped with its own cinema (complete with digital surround sound), located in Witherspoon Student Center. Screenings range from the latest blockbusters to little-known independent flicks. Additionally, Center Stage, the university's premiere performing arts series, brings impressive acts such as the Actor's Gang and the East Village Opera to campus.

# OGLETHORPE UNIVERSITY

4484 Peachtree Road Northeast, Atlanta, GA 30319
**Telephone:** 404-364-8307 • **E-mail:** admission@oglethorpe.edu
**Website:** www.oglethorpe.edu • **Hours:** Monday–Friday, 8:30 A.M.–5:00 P.M.; Saturday, 9:00 A.M.–NOON

## STUDENTS SAY

"The typical student at Oglethorpe is friendly, open-minded, independent, opinionated, and completely dedicated to [his or her] education."

## FODOR'S SAYS

"World of Coca-Cola Pavilion: At this three-story, $15 million special exhibit facility, you can sip samples of 38 Coca-Cola products from around the world and study memorabilia from more than a century's worth of corporate archives."

## ABOUT THE SCHOOL

Oglethorpe University is a small school of only 900 undergraduates located in the heart of Atlanta that offers its students a solid foundation through its innovative core curriculum in the concepts that have shaped Western civilization. Small class sizes and extremely accessible professors ensure that students receive a lot of personal attention. When class is over, students take advantage of the amazing resources and opportunities Atlanta has to offer.

## GETTING THERE

**BY AIR:** Atlanta Hartsfield-Jackson International Airport is the closest airport to campus. Visitors can take Metropolitan Atlanta Rapid Transit Authority (MARTA) trains or a taxi to get to the campus.

**BY TRAIN:** Amtrak makes a stop in Atlanta. Take a taxi to get to the campus.

**BY BUS:** Greyhound makes several stops in Atlanta. Take a taxi to get to the campus.

**BY CAR:** From I-85: Take Exit 89 (North Druid Hills Road). Go West about two miles, where North Druid Hills Road meets Peachtree Road. Make a right onto Peachtree Road, and continue on it until you reach the university. From I-285: Take Exit 31-A, Peachtree Industrial Boulevard South. Go South on Peachtree Industrial Boulevard for about four miles until you reach the college. From GA-400: Take GA-400 to I-285 East. Take I-285 East to Exit 29, Ashford-Dunwoody Road. Make a right onto Ashford-Dunwoody Road, and continue until the road meets Peachtree Road. Make a right on Peachtree Road, and you will see the college shortly.

**LOCAL:** Visitors can take the MARTA to Brookhaven station to reach Oglethorpe University. Call 404-848-5000 for route and schedule info. For local taxi service, call American Cab Co. (404-873-1410) and Atlanta Lenox Taxi (404-872-2600).

## WHERE TO STAY

If you're planning on spending the night, nearby hotel choices include La Quinta Inn & Suites (770-350-6177, $), Sheraton Buckhead (404-261-9250, $$), and Courtyard by Marriott Buckhead (404-869-0818, $$$).

## CAMPUS AT ITS BEST!

Interested in seeing a place where the past and the future collide? Stop by Oglethorpe University's Crypt of Civilization, a time capsule sealed in 1940. Listed in the Guinness Book of World Records, the crypt contains a record of customs from ancient times through the middle of the twentieth century. Afterward, pay a visit to the Conant Performing Arts Center. This state-of-the-art facility includes a 500-seat main stage theater, rehearsal spaces, a small library, and a covered veranda for receptions. It's also home to the popular Georgia Shakespeare Festival. Visitors should try to secure tickets to a performance.

# RANDOLPH MACON COLLEGE

PO Box 5005, Ashland, VA 23005
**Telephone:** 804-752-7305 • **E-mail:** admissions@rmc.edu
**Website:** www.rmc.edu • **Hours:** Monday–Friday, 8:30 A.M.–5:00 P.M.

### SCHOOL AT A GLANCE

| Type of School | Private |
|---|---|
| Environment | Village |
| Tuition | $24,710 |
| Enrollment | 1,146 |
| % Male/Female | 46/54 |
| Student/Faculty Ratio | 11:1 |

### FRESHMAN PROFILE

| Range SAT | |
|---|---|
| Critical Reading | 510-600 |
| Range SAT Math | 500-580 |
| Average HS GPA | 3.27 |

### ON-CAMPUS APPOINTMENTS

| Advance Notice | Yes, 1 week |
|---|---|
| Appointment | Required |
| Saturdays | Sometimes |
| Average Length | 30 min |
| Info Sessions | Yes |
| Class Visits | Yes |

### CAMPUS TOURS

| Appointment | Preferred |
|---|---|
| Dates | Year Round |
| Times | 11:00 A.M., 2:00 P.M. |
| Average Length | 60 min |

## STUDENTS SAY

"Small class size, excellent professors who love to teach, and the train that runs through campus is charming."

## FODOR'S SAYS

"[At the Museum and White House of the Confederacy,] the 'world's largest collection of Confederate memorabilia' includes artifacts such as the sword Robert E. Lee wore to the surrender at Appomattox. During the 45-minute guided tour, you see the entry hall's period nine-foot-tall French rococo mirrors and its floor cloth, painted to resemble ceramic tiles."

## ABOUT THE SCHOOL

Randolph Macon College, a small school just North of Richmond, offers its students the chance to pursue a great education as well as a great social life. It offers the broadest liberal arts core curriculum of any college in Virginia and a social setting that fraternities and sororities dominate.

## GETTING THERE

**BY AIR:** The closest major airport near college is Richmond International, which is less than 30 minutes away from campus. Dulles International and Washington's National Airport are both less than two hours away. Taxi and car rental services are available at all three locations.

**BY TRAIN:** An Amtrak station is adjacent to the campus in Ashland. If you decide to get out at the Richmond station, the college is only a short taxi ride away.

**BY BUS:** Greyhound provides bus service to Richmond.

**BY CAR:** Take I-95 to Central Virginia. Take Exit 92B, Route 54 West. Follow Route 54 across Route 1. Make a right onto Henry Street and you will see the college shortly thereafter.

**LOCAL:** Washington Metropolitan Area Transit Authority provides rail and bus service in Washington, DC, Maryland, and Virginia. It connects with the Virginia Railway Express, a local train system. You can also consider taking a taxi. Some local companies include Public Cab Inc. (804-248-0021), A-Broad St Cab (804-216-7383), and A-Action Cabs (804-218-8294).

## WHERE TO STAY

Some popular nearby hotel choices include Budget Inn (804-798-9291, $), Days Inn (804-798-4262 or 800-329-7466, $), and Ashland Inn (804-752-7777 or 877-888-2466, $$).

---

## CAMPUS AT ITS BEST!

Students curious about Randolph-Macon College will greatly benefit from attending Macon Days. People who participate in this program are "adopted" by current students and spend the day sitting in on classes, dining and, visiting with their hosts. Afterward, take advantage of the surplus of attractions in the outlying area. Nearby James River Park offers an array of activities such as white-water rafting and tubing. Busch Gardens, an amusement park in Williamsburg, is also a frequent destination.

# RANDOLPH COLLEGE

2500 Rivermont Avenue, Lynchburg, VA 24503-1526
**Telephone:** 434-947-8100 • **E-mail:** admissions@randolphcollege.edu
**Website:** www.randolphcollege.edu • **Hours:** Monday–Friday and Saturday, 9:00 A.M.–5:00 P.M.

## STUDENTS SAY

"Our school is about traditions—it's what binds us all together; all of us girls from different backgrounds and upbringings are all tied together by the love of our alma mater."

## FODOR'S SAYS

"Twenty-five miles east of Lynchburg, the village of Appomattox Court House has been restored to its appearance on April 9, 1865. It was on that day that the Confederate General Lee surrendered the Army of Northern Virginia to General Grant."

## ABOUT THE SCHOOL

Now a coeducational institution, Randolph College is all about tradition; traditions that begin in the classroom and last long after graduation. The curriculum here is writing-intensive and quite challenging, with the dance and riding programs receiving especially high marks from students. Over 45 countries are represented on Randolph's diverse campus.

## GETTING THERE

**BY AIR:** Lynchburg Regional Airport is 6 miles away from downtown Lynchburg and is served by Delta Connection and US Airways Express. Airport limousine and taxi service to the college is available from the airport.

**BY TRAIN:** Amtrak stops in Lynchburg. Take a taxi to get to campus.

**BY BUS:** Greyhound stops in Lynchburg. Take a taxi to get to campus.

**BY CAR:** From Charlotte (via I-85 North): Take I-85 North to Greensboro. Exit on 29 North to Danville, VA. Just past the Lynchburg Airport take the exit for 29 North/460 East. Take the left exit for 501 North (Buena Vista/Candlers Mountain Road). After exiting, stay in the right hand lane. After the second light, take the exit for 29 North Business (Charlottesville). Take Exit 1A (Main Street) and follow through downtown. After crossing 5th Street, Main Street becomes Rivermont Avenue. Continue on Rivermont Avenue approximately 2 miles until you see the college entrance on your right. From Richmond (via I-64): Follow I-64 to Charlottesville. Exit onto 29 South. Stay on 29 South. Exit onto Route 210 West (Historic Downtown Lynchburg). Turn right at the stop sign at the end of the ramp. Turn left at the traffic light onto Highway 163 South. Go down a hill and across the bridge. Turn right at the 2nd traffic light (Rivermont Avenue/Main Street). Follow "From Charlotte" directions above. From Washington, DC (via I-66 West): Follow Route I-66 West to Route 29 South near Gainesville. (Please Note: You will pass an earlier exit for Route 29, which you should not take; wait for the later exit.) Continue on Route 29 South past Charlottesville. Stay on 29 South until the Route 210 West (Historic Downtown Lynchburg) Exit. Turn right at the stop sign at the end of the ramp. Turn left at the 4th traffic light left on to Highway 163 South. Go down a hill and across the bridge. Turn right at the 2nd traffic light (Rivermont Avenue). Follow "From Charlotte" directions above.

**LOCAL:** For local taxi service call Hill City Cab at 434-845-8554.

## WHERE TO STAY

The Holiday Inn Express—Lynchburg offers affordable lodging close to campus  434-237-7771, $). Best Western of Lynchburg (434-237-2986, $) and the Wingate Inn Lynchburg (434-845-1800, $$) are some other nearby options.

| SCHOOL AT A GLANCE | |
|---|---|
| Type of School | Private |
| Environment | City |
| Tuition | $23,900 |
| Enrollment | 715 |
| % Male/Female | 0/100 |
| | (coed as of Fall 07) |
| Student/Faculty Ratio | 9:1 |

| FRESHMAN PROFILE | |
|---|---|
| Range SAT | |
| Critical Reading | 540-670 |
| Range SAT Math | 510-630 |
| Range ACT Composite | 23-29 |
| Average HS GPA | 3.4 |

| ON-CAMPUS APPOINTMENTS | |
|---|---|
| Advance Notice | Yes, 1 week |
| Appointment | Preferred |
| Saturdays | Sometimes |
| Average Length | 30-45 min |
| Info Sessions | No |
| Class Visits | Yes |

| CAMPUS TOURS | |
|---|---|
| Appointment | Preferred |
| Dates | Year Round |
| Times | M–F 9:00 A.M.–4:00 P.M.; |
| | Sat 10:00 A.M.–4:00 P.M. |
| Average Length | 60 min |

## CAMPUS AT ITS BEST!

Traditions abound on campus and no matter what time of year you plan your visit, chances are you'll get to see at least one of them in action. If you're visiting in the spring, maybe you'll be lucky enough to catch "MacDoodle Day," a day of pure fun and community-building activities on campus whose exact date is kept a secret up until the time the activities start. If you miss this event, you'll have no trouble finding plenty of other things to check out on campus; stop by the Maier Museum of Art to see works by nineteenth- and twentieth-century American artists.

# RHODES COLLEGE

Office of Admissions, 2000 North Parkway, Memphis, TN 38112
**Telephone:** 901-843-3700 • **E-mail:** adminfo@rhodes.edu
**Website:** www.rhodes.edu • **Hours:** Monday–Friday, 8:30 A.M.–5:00 P.M.; Saturday, 9:00 A.M.–11:30 A.M.

## SCHOOL AT A GLANCE

| | |
|---|---|
| Type of School | Private |
| Environment | Metropolis |
| Tuition | $26,798 |
| Enrollment | 1,677 |
| % Male/Female | 42/58 |
| Student/Faculty Ratio | 11:1 |

### FRESHMAN PROFILE

| | |
|---|---|
| Range SAT | |
| Critical Reading | 580-680 |
| Range SAT Math | 580-670 |
| Range ACT Composite | 25-30 |
| Average HS GPA | 3.61 |

### ON-CAMPUS APPOINTMENTS

| | |
|---|---|
| Advance Notice | Yes, 1 week |
| Appointment | Required |
| Saturdays | Yes |
| Class Visits | Yes |

### CAMPUS TOURS

| | |
|---|---|
| Appointment | Required |
| Dates | Year Round |
| Times | Varies |
| Average Length | Varies |

## STUDENTS SAY

"The students have the mentality of 'work hard, play hard,' yet also devote an extreme amount of time to the service of others, as well as general awareness of the diversity of the world around them.

## FODOR'S SAYS

"Graceland, the estate once owned by Elvis Presley, is 12 miles south of downtown. A guided tour of the mansion, automobile museum, and burial site reveals the spoils of stardom. Reservations are recommended especially in August during 'Elvis Week.'"

## ABOUT THE SCHOOL

For the ambitious undergraduate already thinking about grad school, Rhodes College offers the perfect college experience. The school stresses preparedness for grad school, and professors give students detailed feedback on papers with an eye toward strengthening their research and writing skills. "Rhodents" are often sleep deprived, but studying isn't the only cause: Nearby Memphis is a center of culture and entertainment, and students get very involved in activities both on and off campus.

## GETTING THERE

**BY AIR:** Rhodes College is only seven miles away from Memphis Airport and with advance notice the college can arrange transportation to campus for students.

**BY TRAIN:** Amtrak stops at the Memphis Central Station. Take a car or taxi to the campus.

**BY BUS:** Greyhound's station is located in downtown Memphis at 203 Union Street. Take a car or taxi to the campus.

**BY CAR:** From the North (Chicago, Kansas City, and St. Louis): Take I-55 South to West Memphis, Ark. Make connections with I-40 East going toward Memphis. Exit at Danny Thomas Boulevard North (Exit 1B), and make the first right onto North Parkway. Turn left at University to Phillips Lane Entrance. From the South (New Orleans, Mobile, and Jackson): Take I-55 North to Memphis and merge with I-240 North. Exit at Union Avenue East. Turn left onto East Parkway and left at North Parkway. Turn right at University to Phillips Lane Entrance. From the East (New York, Miami, Atlanta, Louisville, and Nashville): Take I-40 West to Memphis. At I-240, continue straight through the interchange onto Sam Cooper Boulevard, and turn right onto East Parkway. Make the first left onto North Parkway and right at University to Phillips Lane Entrance. From the West (Dallas, Denver, Oklahoma City, and Little Rock): Take I-40 East to Memphis. Take I-55 South to West Memphis, AR. Make connections with I-40 East going toward Memphis. Exit at Danny Thomas Boulevard North (Exit 1B), and make the first right onto North Parkway. Turn left at University Street to Phillips Lane Entrance.

**LOCAL:** Your best bets for getting around are take rent a car or take taxi service, as the MATA (Memphis Area Transit Authority) does not directly service the campus. For local cab service try Checker Cab (800-796-7750), Yellow Cab Co. (901-577-7777), and Memphis Shuttle Svc. (901-523-8608).

## WHERE TO STAY

Rhodes College has discount agreements with many local hotels, so call ahead for the code before reserving. In downtown Memphis some lodging options include the Comfort Inn Downtown (910-526-0583, $), The Spring Hill Suites by Marriott (901-522-2100, $$), and the Madison Hotel (901-333-1200, $$$).

## CAMPUS AT ITS BEST!

With 100 acres of well-maintained campus grounds, a $22 million recreation center, and cable in every dorm room, Rhodes students couldn't be more comfortable. Weekend entertainment options abound, from plays at the McCoy theater and trips into Memphis to enjoy the local culture and nightlife, to parties at the many on-campus Greek organizations. If you're visiting in the fall, check out GARBA, an Indian festival in which students come together to dance.

# ROLLINS COLLEGE

Campus Box 2720, Winter Park, FL 32789-4499
**Telephone:** 407-646-2161 • **E-mail:** admission@rollins.edu
**Website:** www.rollins.edu • **Hours:** Monday–Friday and Saturday, 8:30 A.M.–5:00 P.M. and by appointment

## STUDENTS SAY

"Life is what you make it. You can party every weekend or study. The location of Winter Park is perfect—close to movies, shopping, parks, museums, and nightlife in downtown Orlando."

## FODOR'S SAYS

"Where the tannin-stained Wekiva River meets the crystal-clear Wekiwa headspring, you'll find the 6,400-acre Wekiwa Springs State Park good for camping, hiking, picnicking, swimming, canoeing, fishing, and watching for alligators, egrets, and deer. Although it can be crowded on weekends, on weekdays it's Walden Pond, Florida style."

## ABOUT THE SCHOOL

Rollins College is the perfect place for students who are seeking a small school with solid academics and a country club attitude. The professors at Rollins give a lot of personal attention to the 1,759 students, and administrators hold open meetings every week to address student suggestions and complaints. The ritzy Winter Park, Orlando, setting provides great shopping, dining, and entertainment opportunities nearby.

## GETTING THERE

**BY AIR:** Orlando International Airport is about 30 minutes away. Take a taxi to the campus.

**BY TRAIN:** Amtrak stops right in Winter Park at 150 West Morse Boulevard. You can either walk or take a taxi to the campus.

**BY BUS:** Greyhound has a depot at 555 North John Young Parkway at the corner of Business Center Boulevard, about six miles away from the Rollins campus.

**BY CAR:** From Orlando International Airport: Take State Road 436 (Semoran Boulevard) North from the Airport to the intersection of State Road 436 and Aloma. Make a left at Aloma, another left on Park Avenue, and an immediate right into the Rinker Building parking lot. The Office of Admission is located in the Marshall & Vera Lea Rinker Building. From the Northeast: Take Interstate 95 South to Interstate 4 West to the Fairbanks Avenue Exit (Exit 87). Turn left onto Fairbanks, and turn right onto Park Avenue. Follow the "From Orlando International Airport" directions above. From the Northwest: Take Interstate 75 heading Southeast to the Florida Turnpike. Follow the Turnpike Southeast to Interstate 4 East. Continue on Interstate 4 East, turning right onto Fairbanks. Follow the "From Orlando International Airport" directions above. From the Southeast: Take Interstate 95 North to the Highway 528 West (Beeline). Take 528 West to the Semoran/Highway 436 exit. Go North on Semoran/Highway 436, and turn left onto Aloma. At the Park Avenue intersection, turn left onto Park Avenue, and make an immediate right into the Rinker Building parking lot. From the Southwest: Take Interstate 4 East to the Fairbanks Avenue Exit (Exit 87). Turn right onto Fairbanks. Follow the "From Orlando International Airport" directions above.

**LOCAL:** Most students drive their own cars, since Orlando's public transportation is limited (GoLynx.com). Yellow Cab of Orlando is an option for taxi service (407-422-2222).

## WHERE TO STAY

Options for lodging near Rollins College include the Comfort Inn (407-629-4000, $$), Marriott Springhill Suites (888-287-9400, $$), and the Park Plaza Hotel (407-849-6614, $$).

## CAMPUS AT ITS BEST!

Rollins College students spend most of their free time off campus, so make sure you get to know Winter Park and downtown Orlando when you visit. A good place to start is the Disney Boardwalk, where families, students, and tourists can be found enjoying the view and multitude of restaurants.

# SAMFORD UNIVERSITY

800 Lakeshore Drive, Birmingham, AL 35229
**Telephone:** 205-726-3673 • **E-mail:** admiss@samford.edu
**Website:** www.samford.edu

## STUDENTS SAY

"Sometimes life at SU is so perfect it can appear to be almost surreal and nothing like the real world."

## FODOR'S SAYS

"The Southern Museum of Flight, near the airport, has the Alabama Aviation Hall of Fame, the first Delta Airlines plane, and World War II training planes. In addition to housing artifacts, this museum specializes in painstakingly renovating old aircraft."

## ABOUT THE SCHOOL

Prospective students in search of a school with a conservative Christian atmosphere might be intrigued by Samford. Small classes foster a nurturing environment, and undergrads laud the nursing, business, and journalism departments. The student body is predominantly Southern and Baptist, and proud of their religious principles. Campus rules are strict and many choose to head home or into Birmingham on the weekends.

## GETTING THERE

**BY AIR:** Guests should fly into Birmingham International Airport, approximately 10 miles from Samford. Eight major airlines operate out of BHM, including American, Delta, and Northwest. Shuttles, rental cars, and taxis are all available at the airport.

**BY TRAIN:** Amtrak has a station in Birmingham. Taxis and local buses are available for further transport to campus.

**BY BUS:** Greyhound offers transportation to Birmingham. To reach your ultimate destination visitors may either take a taxi or use the local bus system.

**BY CAR:** From Birmingham International Airport: Drive Southwest on Messer Airport Highway toward Tower View Drive. Merge onto I-20 West/I-59 South heading toward Tuscaloosa/Downtown. Proceed onto U.S. 31 South/AL-3 South via Exit 126A. Continue onto Lakeshore Drive/AL-149 North. Make a U-turn onto Lakeshore Drive/AL-149 South, which leads you to campus.

**LOCAL:** You can take airport shuttle service (205-591-5550). For taxi service, call American Cab Co. (205-322-2222). Additionally, Birmingham maintains its own bus system, MAX (metro area express), which offers service around Birmingham and Jefferson County.

## WHERE TO STAY

Hotels within five miles of Samford include La Quinta Inn and Suites (205-290-0150, $–$$), Best Western Carlton Suites (205-940-9990, $–$$), and the Hilton Garden Inn (205-314-0274, $$).

## CAMPUS AT ITS BEST!

Hometown Birmingham offers guests countless attractions and entertainment options. Consider visiting the Birmingham Civil Rights Institute, which stands as a living testament to heroes who fought against racism and bigotry. For more lighthearted fare, visit Alabama Adventure. This water and theme park will soon feature a sports complex and stock car racing zone. Prospective students visiting in October will be able to attend the city's annual Oktoberfest celebration.

# SEWANEE—THE UNIVERSITY OF THE SOUTH

735 University Avenue, Sewanee, TN 37383-1000
**Telephone:** 931-598-1238 • **E-mail:** collegeadmission@sewanee.edu
**Hours:** Monday–Friday, 8:00 A.M.–4:30 P.M.; Saturday, 8:15A.M.–NOON

## STUDENTS SAY

"Sewanee is simply too fulfilling. Every weekend there is a variety of outdoor activities such as caving (both wet and dry), rock climbing, kayaking, hiking, biking, and countless other things."

## FODOR'S SAYS

"From the Great Smoky Mountains to the rippling waters of the Holston, French Broad, Nolichucky, and Tennessee rivers, East Tennessee offers a cornucopia of scenic grandeur and recreational opportunities."

## ABOUT THE SCHOOL

Sewanee—The University of the South is a small university in Tennessee that places a strong emphasis on tradition as well as highly challenging academics. Students practically live at the library during the week to keep up with the heavy course load but most students loosen up on the weekends when the social scene comes alive.

## GETTING THERE

**BY AIR:** Nashville International Airport, 90 miles from campus, and Chattanooga Metropolitan Airport, 50 miles from campus, are the closest airports to campus. Groome Transportation Shuttle (800-896-9928) provides shuttle service from the airport.

**BY TRAIN:** Amtrak stops in Atlanta, three hours away.

**BY BUS:** Greyhound buses serve Monteagle, which is four miles from Sewanee. If you make arrangements with the admissions office, the school will provide transportation to and from the bus station.

**BY CAR:** From I-24: Take Exit 134 (Monteagle) to Highway 41 North. After about four miles, turn right onto University Avenue and follow it until you see the university. From Route 41 South: Sewanee is six miles East of Cowan. At the top of the mountain, make a left onto University Avenue and follow it until you see the university.

**LOCAL:** If you don't have a car on campus, some ways to get around town include Absolute Brown's Taxi Cab (931-728-7392), ABCD Delivery & Taxi Svc (931-393-0500), and A D C Taxi (931-967-0044).

## WHERE TO STAY

If you're planning on staying for a few days, the Sewanee Inn (931-598-1686, $$) is conveniently located on campus. Other options include the Best Western Smoke House (913-924-2091, $), the Monteagle Inn (931-924-3869, $), and the Edgeworth Inn (931-924-2669, $$).

| SCHOOL AT A GLANCE | |
| --- | --- |
| Type of School | Private |
| Environment | Rural |
| Tuition | $28,910 |
| Enrollment | 1,465 |
| % Male/Female | 46/54 |
| Student/Faculty Ratio | 11:1 |

| FRESHMAN PROFILE | |
| --- | --- |
| Range SAT | |
| Critical Reading | 588-670 |
| Range SAT Math | 570-660 |
| Range ACT Composite | 25-29 |
| Average HS GPA | 3.62 |

| ON-CAMPUS APPOINTMENTS | |
| --- | --- |
| Advance Notice | Yes, 1 week |
| Appointment | Required |
| Saturdays | Sometimes |
| Average Length | 60 min |
| Info Sessions | Yes |
| Class Visits | Yes |

| CAMPUS TOURS | |
| --- | --- |
| Appointment | Required |
| Times | M–F 10:00 A.M. and |
| | 2:00 P.M.; Sat 11:30 A.M. |
| Average Length | 60 min |

## CAMPUS AT ITS BEST!

Hiking the Perimeter Trail allows visitors to observe Sewanee from a distance. Portions of the trail along the bluff expose university landmarks like the Memorial Cross and Morgan's Steep. Of course, you'll want to actually hit the campus at some point. When you do, be sure to stop by Stirling's Coffee House. A great atmosphere for quiet conversation or heady intellectual debate, Stirling also hosts art exhibits, improv performances, and poetry readings.

# SPELMAN COLLEGE

350 Spelman Lane, South West, Atlanta, GA 30314
**Telephone:** 404-270-5193 • **E-mail:** admiss@spelman.edu
**Website:** www.spelman.edu • **Hours:** Monday–Friday, 9:00 A.M.–5:00 P.M.

## STUDENTS SAY

"Spelman seeks to empower the total person who appreciates the many cultures of the world and commits to positive social change."

## FODOR'S SAYS

"The Zoo Atlanta has nearly 1,000 animals living in naturalistic habitats, such as the Ford African Rainforest, Flamingo Plaza, Masai Mara (re-created plains of Kenya), and Sumatran tiger exhibits. The gorillas are always hits, as are the giant pandas: two precocious bears named Yang Yang and Lun Lun."

## ABOUT THE SCHOOL

With only 2,000 students, Spelman College offers a small college experience with big university connections. All students are free to join programs at any college in the Atlanta University Center. This large consortium of colleges in the area includes Morehouse College and Clark Atlanta University, both conveniently located right across the street.

## GETTING THERE

**BY AIR:** Hartsfield-Jackson International Airport, the second busiest in the world, is only 11 miles away from Spelman.

**BY TRAIN:** Take Amtrak to Atlanta's Brookwood Station.

**BY BUS:** There is a Greyhound station one mile away from campus at 232 Forsyth Street Southwest, and another station at Hartsfield-Jackson airport.

**BY CAR:** From I-75/85 North and South: Take I-20 West and take Exit 55B at Lee Street. Turn right onto Lee Street and continue through the next traffic light (Westview Drive). Turn right into the first driveway of a large parking lot and you will approach the gates of Spelman College. From I-20 West: Take Exit 55A at Lowery Boulevard. Cross Lowery Boulevard and continue on Oak Street. Turn left onto Lee Street and cross the bridge over I-20. Turn right into the first driveway of a large parking lot and you will approach the gates of Spelman College. From I-20 East: Take Exit 55B at Lee Street. Turn right onto Lee Street and continue through the next traffic light (Westview Drive). Turn right into the first driveway of a large parking lot and you will approach the gates of Spelman College. From Downtown Atlanta: Take Peachtree Street South to Martin Luther King Jr. Drive and turn right. Continue on MLK Jr. Drive to Northside and turn left. Continue on Northside through the next three traffic lights. Turn right onto Greensferry Avenue, and turn left to go through the gates of Spelman College.

**LOCAL:** MARTA (Metropolitan Atlanta Rapid Transit Authority) is a short walk away from campus and services most destinations in metropolitan Atlanta and the surrounding areas. For local taxi service try Atlanta Checker Cab (404-351-1111), American Cab Co. (404-873-1410), and Atlanta Lenox Taxi (404-872-2600). The Atlanta University Center shuttle travels to some clubs and areas of interest in the city.

## WHERE TO STAY

The Days Inn (404-523-1144, $) in downtown Atlanta is only a few blocks from a MARTA train station and close to the airport and campus. Other lodging options include the Grand Hyatt Atlanta in the Buckhead area (404-237-1234, $$) and the Marriott Marquis Atlanta Downtown (404-521-0000 or 800-932-2198, $$$).

---

## CAMPUS AT ITS BEST!

Students study hard and enjoy Spelman's beautiful campus in their downtime, but most of the excitement seems to be off campus. The university's proximity to downtown Atlanta ensures that there is something to do at all times: great museums, restaurants, and socializing with students from other nearby colleges. When Spelman students want to stay closer to home, they hang out on the Strip, an area between the Spelman campus and its neighboring colleges.

# TULANE UNIVERSITY

6823 St. Charles Avenue, New Orleans, LA 70118
**Telephone:** 504-865-5731 • **E-mail:** undergrad.admission@tulane.edu
**Website:** www.tulane.edu • **Hours:** Monday–Friday, 8:30 A.M.–5:00 P.M.

| SCHOOL AT A GLANCE | |
| --- | --- |
| Type of School | Private |
| Environment | City |
| Tuition | $28,900 |
| Enrollment | 7,952 |
| % Male/Female | 47/53 |
| **FRESHMAN PROFILE** | |
| Range SAT | |
| Critical Reading | 628-725 |
| Range SAT Math | 603-700 |
| Range ACT Composite | 28-32 |
| Average HS GPA | 3.6 |
| **ON-CAMPUS APPOINTMENTS** | |
| Info Sessions | Yes |
| Class Visits | Yes |
| **CAMPUS TOURS** | |
| Appointment | Preferred |
| Dates | Year Round |
| Times  M–F 2 tours daily; Sat 1 tour | |
| Average Length | 120 min |

## STUDENTS SAY

"Tulane attracts a wide spectrum of people who are all really laid-back and easy to get along with."

## FODOR'S SAYS

"Also known as Maison LeMonnier, the 'First Skyscraper' was so called because it was once the tallest building in the French Quarter. It was built between 1796 and 1811 for Dr. Yves LeMonnier, whose initials can be seen worked into the second-floor balcony."

## ABOUT THE SCHOOL

Tulane University is a school that embodies the rich culture and relaxed spirit of its hometown New Orleans despite the fact that most of its students are from outside the state. Students at Tulane quickly learn that they have to party hard and study harder to take full advantage of the school's academic and social offerings.

## GETTING THERE

**BY AIR:** Louis Armstrong New Orleans International Airport is the closest airport to campus. Taking a taxi or airport shuttle (504-522-3500) might be the easiest way to get from the airport to the university, since parking near campus can be extremely limited.

**BY TRAIN:** Amtrak trains stop at Union Station in New Orleans on Loyola Avenue. Take a cab to campus.

**BY BUS:** Greyhound buses stop at the Downtown Bus Station in New Orleans on Loyola Avenue. Take a taxi to the campus.

**BY CAR:** From I-10 East: Head toward the Central Business District. Follow signs to Highway 90 Business/West Bank. Get off at St. Charles Avenue/Carondelet Street. At the second traffic light, turn right onto St. Charles Avenue. Take St. Charles Avenue for four miles and the university will be on your right. From I-10 West: Follow the signs to Highway 90 Business/West Bank. Get off at St. Charles Avenue/Carondelet Street. At the second traffic light, turn right onto St. Charles Avenue. Take St. Charles Avenue for four miles and the university will be on your right.

**LOCAL:** New Orleans Regional Transit Authority provides bus and streetcar service throughout New Orleans. Jefferson Transit provides bus service to downtown New Orleans and Jefferson county. If you'd rather take a taxi around the city, some local companies include Coleman Cab Company (504-586-0222), United Cabs Inc (504-522-9771), Veterans Cab Company (504-367-6767), and White Fleet & Rollins Cabs (504- 822-3800).

## WHERE TO STAY

If you're planning on staying a while in New Orleans, some local accommodations include Mandevilla Bed and Breakfast (504-862-6396, $$), Hampton Inn Garden District (504-899-9990, $$), and Loews New Orleans Hotel (504-595-5314, $$$).

## CAMPUS AT ITS BEST!

Musical theater devotees who visit Tulane during the summer months should definitely take in a performance at the Summer Lyric Theatre. Among the best theatrical opportunities in the Gulf South region, past shows have included *Guys and Dolls*, *Victor/Victoria*, and *Damn Yankees*. Visitors with a passion for music will want to investigate the Hogan Jazz Archive, part of the university's Special Collections Division. This renowned resource houses oral histories, recorded music, photographs, sheet music, film, and orchestrations. Of course, it'll be difficult to resist the allure of New Orleans itself. Take advantage of some of the city's more unique attractions such as a swamp tour or the Voodoo Spiritual Temple.

## SCHOOL AT A GLANCE

| | |
|---|---|
| Type of School | Public |
| Environment | City |
| In-state Tuition | $5,278 |
| Out-of-state Tuition | $15,294 |
| Enrollment | 17,372 |
| % Male/Female | 47/53 |
| Student/Faculty Ratio | 19:1 |

### FRESHMAN PROFILE

| | |
|---|---|
| Range SAT | |
| Critical Reading | 500-630 |
| Range SAT Math | 500-630 |
| Range ACT Composite | 21-27 |
| Average HS GPA | 3.4 |

### ON-CAMPUS APPOINTMENTS

| | |
|---|---|
| Advance Notice | No, other |
| Appointment | Not Required |
| Saturdays | Yes |
| Average Length | 60 min |
| Info Sessions | Yes |
| Class Visits | Yes |

### CAMPUS TOURS

| | |
|---|---|
| Appointment | Required |
| Dates | Year Round |
| Times | M–F 10:00 A.M. |
| | and 2:00 P.M., Sat 10:00 A.M. |
| Average Length | 60 min |

# THE UNIVERSITY OF ALABAMA AT TUSCALOOSA

Box 870132, Tuscaloosa, AL 35487-0132
**Telephone:** 205-348-5666 • **E-mail:** admissions@ua.edu
**Hours:** Monday–Friday, 8:00 A.M.–4:45 P.M.; Saturday, 8:00 A.M.–NOON

## STUDENTS SAY

"The whole town is immersed in Alabama spirit."

## FODOR'S SAYS

"The Paul W. 'Bear' Bryant Museum follows the University of Alabama's 100-year tradition of football preeminence. The museum has many of Coach Bryant's personal belongings, as well as those of others who have laid the foundation for the University of Alabama football program."

## ABOUT THE SCHOOL

The University of Alabama at Tuscaloosa is a large Southern university where Southern hospitality makes up for the impersonality typically found in universities of this size. Great academics, Greek life, and pride for the Crimson Tide sports teams are some of this school's standout features.

## GETTING THERE

**BY AIR:** Birmingham International Airport is more than 60 miles from campus. Take the Birmingham Door to Door shuttle service from the airport to campus. Call 205-591-5550 to arrange a pickup.

**BY TRAIN:** Amtrak services Tuscaloosa. Take a taxi to get to the campus.

**BY BUS:** Greyhound and Trailways bus lines stop in Tuscaloosa. Take a taxi to get to the campus.

**BY CAR:** From Birmingham: Take I-59/20 to I-359 into Tuscaloosa. I-359 turns into Lurleen B. Wallace Boulevard. Make a right at University Boulevard and go East through downtown Tuscaloosa to the university. From Jasper: Take Highway 69 South to University Boulevard. Turn left on University Boulevard. Go East through downtown Tuscaloosa to the university. From Moundville: Go North on Highway 69, which turns into I-359 at the I-59/20 interchange. I-359 turns into Lurleen B. Wallace Boulevard. Make a right at University Boulevard and head East through downtown Tuscaloosa to the university. From Fayette: Take U.S. 43 South to U.S. 82. Make a left onto McFarland Boulevard. Take the University Boulevard exit. Make a right onto University Boulevard and travel West to the university. From Montgomery: Take U.S. 82 West to Tuscaloosa. Get off at the University Boulevard exit. At University Boulevard make a right and drive West to the university. From Columbus: Take U.S. 82 East. Take the University Boulevard exit and make a right onto University Boulevard. Travel West to the university.

**LOCAL:** If you don't have your car on campus, some ways to get around include Bama Taxi Service (205-345-5111), Druid Cab Service (205-758-9011), and Radio Cab Service (205-758-2831).

## WHERE TO STAY

If you plan on spending the night, some hotel accommodations include Four Points on campus (205-752-3200, $$), La Quinta Inn (205-349-3270, $), and Tuscaloosa Courtyard by Marriott (205-750-8384, $$).

## CAMPUS AT ITS BEST!

When preparing for your visit to the University of Alabama, remember to pack a bathing suit. The Student Recreation Center features an incredible outdoor aquatic area complete with a lazy river, large water slide, and plenty of deck space. Towel off and head back in time with a ride on the Bama Belle Riverboat. This replica of an early twentieth century paddlewheel riverboat is perfect for sightseeing and dinner cruises. Return to campus for one of University Programs exciting events. You can learn tips from the Date Doctor, hear former *Real World* cast members speak, or watch the Ultimate Fan Competition.

# UNIVERSITY OF ARKANSAS— FAYETTEVILLE

232 Silas Hunt Hall, Fayetteville, AR 72701
Telephone: 479-575-5346 • E-mail: uofa@uark.edu
Website: www.uark.edu • Hours: Monday–Friday, 8:00A.M.–5:00P.M.

## STUDENTS SAY

"[At UA,] all things Southern are the way of life."

## FODOR'S SAYS

"The University of Arkansas, home of the hallowed Razorback teams, has museums and a lively arts calendar. Former president Bill Clinton and Hilary Rodham Clinton taught law here."

## ABOUT THE SCHOOL

Life at Arkansas is all about finding a healthy balance between academics and socializing. The university prides itself on strong programs in engineering, business, and nursing. Honors students especially highlight great preparation for postgraduate work. However, it's not all work all the time; parties can be found virtually everywhere.

## GETTING THERE

**BY AIR:** Northwest Arkansas Regional is the closest airport to the campus. Rental cars, taxis, and shuttles are accessible to take you to the campus.

**BY TRAIN:** Unfortunately, there is no Amtrak service within 150 miles of Fayetteville. It is best to find alternate transportation.

**BY BUS:** Greyhound offers service to Fayetteville. Take a taxi to get to the campus.

**BY CAR:** From the South: Follow I-40 to I-540 North (Exit 7). Proceed from I-540 North to Razorback Road (Exit 61). Make a right onto Razorback Road, driving North. You'll find the entrance to the campus located at the corner of Razorback and Sixth Street. From the North: After Bella Vista, follow I-540 South to Fayetteville. From I-540, continue to Highway 112 (Exit 66). Make a right onto Highway 112 and drive South for two miles. You'll find the entrance to campus at the corner of Garland Avenue and Cleveland Street. After crossing the North Street intersection, Highway 112 becomes Garland Avenue. From the East: Follow Highway 412 to I-540. Follow the "From the North" directions above. From the West: Follow Highway 412 East via Cherokee Turnpike (from Tulsa, OK) to I-540 South. Follow the "From the North" directions above.

**LOCAL:** For local cab service call C&H Taxi Service (479-521-1900), Dynasty Taxi (479-521-8294), or Tony CS Taxi Cab Co. (479-872-6600).

## WHERE TO STAY

Moderately priced lodging can be found at the Quality Inn (479-444-9800, $), Clarion Hotel (479-521-1166, $–$$), or the Comfort Inn (479-695-2121, $–$$).

### SCHOOL AT A GLANCE

| | |
|---|---|
| Type of School | Public |
| Environment | Town |
| In-state Tuition | $4,590 |
| Out-of-state Tuition | $12,724 |
| Enrollment | 17,938 |
| % Male/Female | 51/49 |
| Student/Faculty Ratio | 18:1 |

### FRESHMAN PROFILE

| | |
|---|---|
| Range SAT | |
| Critical Reading | 510–640 |
| Range SAT Math | 520–640 |
| Range ACT Composite | 22–28 |
| Average HS GPA | 3.6 |

### ON-CAMPUS APPOINTMENTS

| | |
|---|---|
| Advance Notice | Yes, 1 week |
| Appointment | Preferred |
| Saturdays | Yes |
| Average Length | 30 min |
| Info Sessions | Yes |
| Class Visits | Yes |

### CAMPUS TOURS

| | |
|---|---|
| Appointment | Preferred |
| Dates | Year Round |
| Times | 8:30 A.M.; 10:30 A.M.; 12:30 P.M., 2:30 P.M. |
| Average Length | 120 min |

## CAMPUS AT ITS BEST!

Razorback fans surely won't want to miss the Jim Lindsey/Jerry Jones Hall of Champions in Broyles Athletic Center. This facility honors Arkansas football, displaying trophies, memorabilia, and an interactive video. Additionally, the Tommy Boyer Hall of Champions boasts exhibits on a variety of UA sports, including basketball and track and field. Visitors not as enamored with athletics should attend a University Programming event. Activities range from stand-up comics, such as Daniel Tosh, to poetry slams and a fright film fest.

# UNIVERSITY OF CENTRAL FLORIDA

PO Box 160111, Orlando, FL 32816-0111
**Telephone:** 407-823-3000 • **E-mail:** admission@mail.ucf.edu
**Website:** www.ucf.edu • **Hours:** Monday–Friday; see website

## STUDENTS SAY

"UCF is a growing school in size and prestige and offers many different extracurricular activities and a modern yet classic atmosphere, but does not make you feel like just another number."

## FODOR'S SAYS

"Walt Disney World was created because of Walt Disney's dream of EPCOT, the Experimental Prototype Community of Tomorrow, which would reap the miraculous harvest of technological achievement. The permanent community that he envisioned has not yet come to be."

## ABOUT THE SCHOOL

Many UCF undergrads claim that their school achieves the impossible: It manages to maintain a student body of more than 37,000 students without anyone getting lost in the shuffle. A laid-back attitude permeates the campus, and students appreciate the absence of cutthroat competition. Opportunities for hands-on research abound, especially within computer science and engineering. Hometown Orlando provides a fantastic escape from academics, offering up an exciting night life and, of course, the country's favorite theme park.

## GETTING THERE

**BY AIR:** Orlando International is a major airport fielding flights from all over the world. Travelers have access to taxis, shuttles, and rental cars so they can get to the campus.

**BY TRAIN:** Amtrak provides service to Orlando. To reach the campus from the station it is best to take a taxi.

**BY BUS:** Visitors wishing to travel via bus may take Greyhound directly to Orlando. Take a taxi to get to the campus.

**BY CAR:** From the North: Follow the Florida Turnpike South to 408 East. Proceed on 408 East to 417 North (408 and 417 merge). Take Exit 417 to University Boulevard East. Continue on University Boulevard for two miles, which takes you to the main entrance of the campus. Take a right turn at the first light, which is Gemini Boulevard. You will see a visitors information booth at the first stop sign. From the South (Melbourne): Follow the Florida Turnpike North, exiting onto I-4 East. Continue until you reach 408 East. Follow the "From the North" directions above. From the East (Titusville and Daytona): Follow Highway 50 West to Alafaya Trail. Make a right onto Alafaya Trail, driving North for two miles. Make a right onto University Boulevard. Continue on University Boulevard for two miles, which takes you to the main entrance of the campus. Take a right turn at the first light, which is Gemini Boulevard. You will see a visitors information booth at the first stop sign. From Tampa: Follow I-4 East to 408 East. Follow the "From the North" directions above.

**LOCAL:** For local taxi service call Star Taxi (407-857-9999), City Cab Co. (407-422-5151), or Diamond Cab Co. (407-523-3333).

## WHERE TO STAY

As a major tourist destination, Orlando has many hotel options, including Crestwood Suites (407-249-0044, $), Hampton Inn and Suites (407-282-0029, $–$$), and the Courtyard by Marriott (407-277-7676, $–$$$).

## CAMPUS AT ITS BEST!

UCF's reflecting pond, located between Millican Hall and the library, is a great place to relax and be entertained. Surrounded by lush lawns and comfortable benches, the pond is equipped with a computer programmed to provide water theatrics. Should that novelty wear thin, consider attending one of the Campus Activities Board special events. Especially popular with undergrads are the annual Haunted Arboretum and Mystery Dinner Theater, which are held during the spring semester.

# UNIVERSITY OF FLORIDA

201 Criser Hall, Box 114000, Gainesville, FL 32611-4000
**Telephone:** 352-392-1365 • **E-mail:** ourwebrequests@registrar.ufl.edu
**Website:** www.ufl.edu • **Hours:** Monday–Friday, 8:00 A.M.–5:00 P.M.

## STUDENTS SAY

"Despite the students' overwhelming commitment to sports and their social lives, the school is still very strong academically. Only Florida's best and brightest are allowed through UF's doors."

## FODOR'S SAYS

"About 10,000 years ago an underground cavern collapsed and created a geological treat. At Devil's Milhopper State Geological Site, see the botanical wonderland of exotic subtropical ferns and trees growing in the 500-foot-wide and 120-foot-deep sinkhole. You pass a dozen small waterfalls as you head down 232 steps to the bottom."

## ABOUT THE SCHOOL

The gargantuan University of Florida is known for more than being the place where Gatorade was invented. UF offers its 33,000 undergrads challenging academics, excellent resources, not to mention the super-talented Gators football team. When students want to head off campus for fun, the incredible diversity of hometown Gainesville beckons.

## GETTING THERE

**BY AIR:** Gainesville Regional Airport, which is about five miles away, is the closest airport to the university. You might also consider arriving through Jacksonville International Airport or Orlando International Airport. Take a taxi to get to the campus.

**BY TRAIN:** Amtrak trains stop in Gainesville. Take a taxi to get to the campus.

**BY BUS:** Greyhound provides bus service to Gainesville. Take a taxi to get to the campus.

**BY CAR:** From I-75: Take Exit 387, Newberry Road. Go East on Newberry Road, which turns into University Avenue. Make a right onto 13th Street, and you should see the college shortly thereafter. From I-95: Get out at I-295. Take I-295 to I-10. Follow I-10 West (toward Tallahassee) to I-75. Take I-75 to Exit 387. Follow the "From I-75" directions above. From I-275: Take I-275 until it merges with I-75. Take I-75 to Exit 387. Follow the "From I-75" directions above.

**LOCAL:** Regional Transit System (RTS) provides bus service on campus and in Gainesville. Call 352-334-2600 for route and schedule information. If you'd rather get around by taxi, some local companies include Safety Cabs (352-372-1444), Gainesville Cab Co. (352-371-1515), and Bestway Cab (352-367-8222).

## WHERE TO STAY

Some of the most popular nearby hotels include the Budget Inn (352-352-2525, $), Holiday Inn (352-332-7500, $$), and Hilton University of Florida Conference Center (352-371-3600, $$).

## CAMPUS AT ITS BEST!

The Marston Science Library at the University of Florida allows visitors to get a great look at the skies. Among the library's many holdings is a unique collection of NASA Kennedy Space Center film rolls. If you're curious about some of the university's more earthly pursuits, check out the Ben Hill Griffin Stadium. Home to the Gator football team, the stadium is always packed on game days. Also held there is the Gator Growl, the largest student-run pep rally in the world. Student and alumni gather on the Friday night of homecoming for cheers, skits, and amazing stand-up comics.

## SCHOOL AT A GLANCE

| Type of School | Public |
|---|---|
| Environment | City |
| In-state Tuition | $3,892 |
| Out-of-state Tuition | $16,968 |
| Enrollment | 24,791 |
| % Male/Female | 43/57 |
| Student/Faculty Ratio | 18:1 |

### FRESHMAN PROFILE

| Range SAT | |
|---|---|
| Critical Reading | 560-660 |
| Range SAT Math | 570-670 |
| Range ACT Composite | 24-29 |
| Average HS GPA | 3.74 |

### ON-CAMPUS APPOINTMENTS

| Class Visits | No |
|---|---|

### CAMPUS TOURS

| Appointment | Required |
|---|---|
| Dates | Year Round |
| Times | Schedule available online |
| Average Length | 60 min |

# UNIVERSITY OF GEORGIA

Terrell Hall, Athens, GA 30602

**Telephone:** 706-542-8776 • **E-mail:** visetr@uga.edu

**Hours:** Monday–Friday, 8:00 A.M.–5:00 P.M.; Saturday, 9:00 A.M.–5:00 P.M.;Sunday, 1:00 P.M.–5:00 P.M.

## STUDENTS SAY

"UGA has an amazing social scene and an extremely high level of school spirit. Athens is an amazing college town. Also, the facilities and meal plan are superb."

## FODOR'S SAYS

"Athens, an artistic jewel of the American South, is known as a breeding ground for such famed rock groups as the B-52s and REM. Because of this distinction, creative types from all over the country flock to its trendy streets."

## ABOUT THE SCHOOL

The University of Georgia offers students a solid education at a reasonable price, with many of the perks of a more expensive university. The school's 24,600 undergraduates are almost all from Georgia, due in part to a HOPE scholarship system that makes the tuition even more affordable for Georgia students. There are many opportunities for research and small discussion-style classes at the honors level, but students need to be proactive about seeking out and utilizing the school's many resources.

## GETTING THERE

**BY AIR:** Ben Epps Airport in Athens offers connecting flights via USAir to and from Charlotte. Take a taxi to the University of Georgia campus. Hartsfield International Airport in Atlanta is one-and-a-half hours from Athens. There is scheduled ground shuttle service between Hartsfield International Airport and the University of Georgia's Georgia Center for Continuing Education. Call 800-354-7874 for more information.

**BY TRAIN:** Athens is an hour and a half drive from Gainesville, Georgia, the nearest Amtrak station.

**BY BUS:** Greyhound stops in downtown Athens. The campus is two blocks away.

**BY CAR:** From I-85 North: Travel on I-85 North to GA 316 (Exit 106). Follow 316 East. Proceed on GA 316 East for approximately 40 miles. Make sure not to exit at the first exit for Athens/Monroe at Highway 78, but continue until you see signs for the Athens Perimeter (Loop 10). Bear right onto the Athens Perimeter (GA Loop 10) traveling East. After approximately five miles on the Perimeter, exit onto College Station Road (Exit 7).Take a left onto College Station Road. After passing under the bypass bridge, go through two traffic lights and the Visitors Center will be on your right in the Four Towers Building. From the East via U.S. 78: Exit right onto GA 316 at the stoplight (there will be a sign for South Athens), and proceed on GA 316 to the Athens Perimeter. Follow the "From I-85 North" directions above. From the West via U.S. 78 West: In Athens, travel under the Athens Perimeter (GA Loop 10) and make a left at the next traffic light onto the Perimeter going Westbound. Exit the Perimeter at the next exit, which is College Station Road (Exit 7). Turn right onto College Station Road and continue through one traffic light. The Visitors Center is on the right in the Four Towers Building. From the South on GA 106: GA 106 joins Loop 10 (Athens Perimeter). Follow Loop 10 West to the College Station Road Exit 7. Exit at College Station Road and turn right. Go through one traffic light. After the traffic light, the Visitors Center will be on the right in the Four Towers Building.

**LOCAL:** University of Georgia students ride campus transit and Anthens public transit free with a valid student ID. There is no Athens transit service most evenings and Sundays. For local taxi service call Athens Cab (740-594-7433) or Top Dawg Taxi Service (706-552-0744).

## WHERE TO STAY

There are many hotel options in Athens. There's the Georgia Center Hotel right on campus, open to all University of Georgia guests (888-295-8894, $–$$). For other lodging options, please see UGA.edu/visit.

## CAMPUS AT ITS BEST!

On the University of Georgia campus, football is the main attraction. Attend a UGA football game (and tailgate) to get an idea of the university's school spirit. Meanwhile, Athens is a college student's dream with its clubs, bars, and cutting edge music scene that has been dubbed "live music central." AthFest in late June is a must-see if you're in the area. The weekend-long music festival features indoor and outdoor live performances by more than 120 bands.

# UNIVERSITY OF KENTUCKY

100 Funkhouser Building, Lexington, KY 40506
**Telephone:** 859-257-2000 • **E-mail:** admission@uky.edu
**Hours:** Monday–Friday and Saturday, 9:00 A.M.–4:30 P.M.

## STUDENTS SAY

"Everyone is very easy to get along with. I swear people at UK are probably the nicest people I've ever seen or met in my life."

## FODOR'S SAYS

"Lexington, the world capital of racehorse breeding and burley tobacco was named by patriotic hunters who camped here in 1775 shortly after hearing news of the first battle of the Revolutionary War at Lexington, Massachusetts."

## ABOUT THE SCHOOL

The University of Kentucky offers its 18,000 undergrads excellent resources, fantastic sports teams to root for, and a very active Greek life. When students want to experience life away from campus, hometown Lexington offers a variety of great restaurants and nightlife.

## GETTING THERE

**BY AIR:** Bluegrass Airport is a small airport in Lexington. The Louisville International Airport and the Cincinnati/Northern Kentucky Airport are both about 90 miles away from the campus.

**BY TRAIN:** Amtrak stops in Louisville, an hour-and-a-half drive away.

**BY BUS:** Greyhound buses stop in Lexington. A taxi can get you to the campus.

**BY CAR:** From the North: Take I-275 East (or South) to I-75 South. Stay on I-75 South all the way to Lexington. After I-64 merges with I-75, follow exits for the university. From the South: Take I-75 North into Lexington and exit at Athens-Boonesboro Road (Exit 104), and turn left after the ramp onto Richmond Road, which will bring you into downtown. Follow signs for the university. From the East: Take I-64 West. Then head South on I-75. Take I-75 and follow exits for the university. From the West: Take I-64 East about 75 miles. Look for exits on I-64 (after it merges with I-75) for the university.

**LOCAL:** The Lextran (859-253-4636) is an intra-city bus system that will get you around town. If you'd rather take a taxi, call Yellow Cab Taxicabs (859-231-8294).

## WHERE TO STAY

If you are planning on staying for a while, some lodging options in the area include Lexington-Days Inn (859-299-1202, $), Sleep Inn Lexington (859-543-8400, $), and Lexington Knights Inn (859-299-8481, $$$).

### SCHOOL AT A GLANCE

| | |
|---|---|
| Type of School | Public |
| Environment | City |
| In-state Tuition | $5,782 |
| Out-of-state Tuition | $13,242 |
| Enrollment | 18,416 |
| % Male/Female | 48/52 |
| Student/Faculty Ratio | 17:1 |

### FRESHMAN PROFILE

| | |
|---|---|
| Range SAT | |
| Critical Reading | 510–630 |
| Range SAT Math | 520–640 |
| Range ACT Composite | 22–27 |
| Average HS GPA | 3.55 |

### ON-CAMPUS APPOINTMENTS

| | |
|---|---|
| Advance Notice | 2 weeks |
| Appointment | Required |
| Saturdays | No |
| Info Sessions | Yes |
| Class Visits | Yes |

### CAMPUS TOURS

| | |
|---|---|
| Appointment | Required |
| Dates | Year Round |
| Times | M–F 10:00 A.M. |
| | and 2:00 P.M.; Sat 11:00 A.M. |
| Average Length | 120 min |

---

## CAMPUS AT ITS BEST!

Prospective Kentucky students should aim to have their visit coincide with Theoretical Thursdays. This entertaining series is designed to provoke discussion about uncommon topics such as the possibility of living on Mars or UFO conspiracies. After you've fed your mind, think about nourishing your body at the K-Lair Grill, a campus favorite. Here patrons can feast on burgers and fries while they check their e-mail. If you're looking for fresher fare, head into Lexington for a tour of the Farmer's Market. Open from mid-April through early December, the market offers fresh fruit, flowers, local fare, and more.

# UNIVERSITY OF LOUISIANA AT LAFAYETTE

PO Drawer 41210, Lafayette, LA 70504
**Telephone:** 337-482-6457 • **E-mail:** admissions@louisiana.edu
**Website:** www.louisiana.edu

## STUDENTS SAY

Hometown Lafayette is "very welcoming to outsiders, with a rich Cajun/francophone culture."

## FODOR'S SAYS

"Lafayette is a major center of Cajun lore and life... Its excellent restaurants and B&Bs make it a good jumping-off point for exploring the region."

## ABOUT THE SCHOOL

The University of Louisiana at Lafayette (ULL) boasts a large honors programs, more than 100 programs of study, some of the best research facilities and opportunities in the state, and small average class size. Once you factor in the very low tuition and the fun-filled city of Lafayette, the whole package is a great deal.

## GETTING THERE

**BY AIR:** Lafayette Regional Airport is just two miles from campus. Take an airport shuttle or taxi to the ULL campus.

**BY TRAIN:** There is an Amtrak station in Lafayette, which is within walking distance of the ULL campus.

**BY BUS:** Greyhound stops in Lafayette, which is within walking distance of the ULL campus.

**BY CAR:** From Lafayette Regional Airport: Drive North on Terminal Drive, and turn left onto Blue Boulevard followed by a left turn onto Surrey Street. Cross U.S. Highway 90 at the light. Surrey Street becomes University Avenue. Cross under railroad overpass, cross Pinhook Road at the light, and then turn left onto McKinley Street at the light. Drive one block; turn right into Visitors' Lot behind Union. From the North (e.g., Alexandria): Drive South on I-49. Drive under the I-10 overpass. At the seventh light, turn right onto Johnston Street. Cross the railroad tracks. Go through three traffic lights. At the fourth light, turn left onto University Avenue. At the second light, turn right onto McKinley Street. Drive one block; turn right into Visitors' Lot behind Union. From the South (e.g., Houma/Thibodaux): Drive North on U.S. Highway 90 When approaching Lafayette, watch for Lafayette Regional Airport on right. After spotting the Airport, shift into the inside (left) lane. Turn left onto University Avenue (marked by traffic light). At the fourth light, turn left onto McKinley Street. Drive one block; turn right into Visitors' Lot behind Union. From the East (e.g., Baton Rouge): Drive West on I-10. Exit at Lafayette/Carencro (Exit #101). Turn left onto University Avenue. Drive through ten traffic lights. Turn right at McKinley Street (marked by traffic light). Drive one block; turn right into Visitors' Lot behind Union. From the West (e.g., Lake Charles): Drive East on I-10. Exit at Lafayette/Carencro (Exit #101). Turn onto University Avenue. Drive through ten traffic lights. Turn right at McKinley Street (marked by traffic light). Drive one block; turn right into Visitors' Lot behind Union.

**LOCAL:** Lafayette transit serves the city and the University of Louisiana at Lafayette. ULL also has campus transit.

## WHERE TO STAY

Options for accommodations in Lafayette include the Hilton & Towers Lafayette (337-235-6111, $$), and the Lafayette Comfort Inn (337-232-9000, $). Ask about special rates for guests of the University of Louisiana at Lafayette.

## CAMPUS AT ITS BEST!

The Ragin' Cajuns are a big part of the school's community feeling, so be sure to stop by a game and see how the lively ULL students support their teams! Lafayette is a true college town, providing the standard bars and clubs, but also a host of festivals and celebrations, such as the International Music Festival and local Mardi Gras events in the spring.

# UNIVERSITY OF MARY WASHINGTON

1301 College Avenue, Fredericksburg, VA 22401
Telephone: 540-654-2000 • E-mail: admit@umw.edu

## STUDENTS SAY

"Campus safety is great, the library resources are excellent, the campus is beautiful, and since this is a small university, it has a tight, friendly feel."

## FODOR'S SAYS

"Just outside the Fredericksberg Battlefield Park Visitor Center is Sunken Road, where from December 11 to 13, 1862, General Robert E. Lee led his troops to a bloody but resounding victory over Union forces attacking across the Rappahannock."

## ABOUT THE SCHOOL

The University of Mary Washington—the new incarnation of Mary Washington College—has the community feel of a much smaller school, and the academic strength of a much larger one. It's rare to see a school of UMW's size offer so many strong programs of study and so many opportunities for funded research. Not to mention an atmosphere on campus so collegial that students feel safe leaving their doors unlocked! This combination of warmth and rigorous academics has solidified UMW's status as a strong up-and-coming university, and it still seems to be on an upswing.

## GETTING THERE

**BY AIR:** Reagan National Airport is about 50 miles from the UMW campus, and Washington Dulles International Airport is about 70 miles from UMW. Take a cab or airport shuttle to the campus.

**BY TRAIN:** There is an Amtrak station about 1.2 miles from campus. Ride a public transit bus to campus or take a taxi.

**BY BUS:** There is a Greyhound depot about 1.8 miles away from campus. Ride a public transit bus to campus or take a taxi.

**BY CAR:** From I-95: The University of Mary Washington is located in Fredericksburg, Virginia, 50 miles South of Washington, DC, and 50 miles North of Richmond. To reach the campus from Interstate 95, take Exit 130-A. Follow Route 3 East business to the traffic light for William Street. Make a left at the light. Follow William Street to the next traffic light, and make a left onto College Avenue. Proceed to the university gates, located at the next traffic light. Directions from U.S. 1: When you see the Park and Shop shopping center, turn left (if you are headed South) or right (if you are headed North) onto College Avenue and proceed to the university gates, located at the next traffic light.

**LOCAL:** Students with a valid ID ride free on FRED, the Fredericksburg Regional Transit bus system. Call 540-372-1222 for route and schedule info.

## WHERE TO STAY:

Options for accommodations in Fredericksburg include the Hilton Garden Inn (540-548-8822, $$), the Best Western Central Plaza (540-786-7404, $), and the Hampton Inn and Suites Fredericksburg (540-898-5000, $$). Ask about special rates for University of Mary Washington guests.

## SCHOOL AT A GLANCE

| | |
|---|---|
| Type of School | Public |
| Environment | City |
| In-state Tuition | $5,634 |
| Out-of-state Tuition | $14,776 |
| Enrollment | 3,952 |
| % Male/Female | 34/66 |
| Student/Faculty Ratio | 14:1 |

### FRESHMAN PROFILE

| | |
|---|---|
| Range SAT | |
| Critical Reading | 580-670 |
| Range SAT Math | 560-640 |
| Range ACT Composite | 25-29 |
| Average HS GPA | 3.67 |

### ON-CAMPUS APPOINTMENTS

| | |
|---|---|
| Saturdays | No |
| Info Sessions | Yes |
| Class Visits | Yes |

### CAMPUS TOURS

| | |
|---|---|
| Appointment | Preferred |
| Dates | Year Round |
| Times | M–F; 10:30 A.M. |
| | and 2:00 P.M. |
| Average Length | 60 min |

## CAMPUS AT ITS BEST!

At UMW, many students take advantage of the school's proximity to several major cities and to the nature sports and activities available in the Shenandoah area. The bulk of student life on campus is wrapped up in athletics and student organizations, so stop by a basketball game (or any of UMW's many varsity teams) and see the students in action! Fredericksburg offers a plethora of antique shops and historic sites, so set aside some time to explore the area.

# UNIVERSITY OF MIAMI

Office of Admission, PO Box 248025, Coral Gables, FL 33124-4616

**Telephone:** 305-284-4323 • **E-mail:** admissions@miami.edu

**Website:** www.miami.edu • **Hours:** Monday–Saturday, 8:30 A.M.–5:00 P.M. and by appointment

## STUDENTS SAY

"At UM there is an ideal balance of being able to enjoy an absolutely beautiful environment while also pursuing a first-rate education."

## FODOR'S SAYS

"At Haulover Beach Park, far from the action of SoBe, see the Miami of 30 years ago. Pack a picnic, use the barbecue grills, or grab a snack at the concession stand. There are tennis and volleyball courts and paths designed for walking and bicycling."

## ABOUT THE SCHOOL

The University of Miami, with its ample resources, great facilities, variety of majors, fantastic Hurricanes football team, and great weather, has a lot to offer its students. World-class faculty and innumerable research and internship opportunities across disciplines attract many ambitious undergraduates to UM's campus. Not many schools can claim to offer students a great education in a gorgeous, resort-like environment.

## GETTING THERE

**BY AIR:** Miami International Airport and Fort Lauderdale Hollywood International Airport are the closest airports to campus. Taxi service is available from the airport.

**BY TRAIN:** Amtrak trains stop in Miami. Take a taxi to get to the campus.

**BY BUS:** Greyhound buses stop in Miami. Take a taxi to get to the campus.

**BY CAR:** From Miami International Airport: Take LeJeune Road South to Ponce de Leon Boulevard. Make a right on Ponce de Leon and take it to Stanford Drive, and you will see the university ahead. From Fort Lauderdale Hollywood International Airport: Take 595 West to I-95 South. Take I-95 South (which turns into U.S. 1) to Stanford Drive. Make a right on Stanford Drive and you will see the university ahead. From the North: Take I-95 South (which turns into U.S. 1). Take it to Stanford Drive. Make a right on Stanford Drive and you will see the university ahead. From the Florida Turnpike: Take the turnpike to Bird Road (Southwest 40th Street). Go East on Bird Road to Red Road (Southwest 57th Street). Make a right onto Red Road and take it to Miller Road (Southwest 56 Street). Turn left turn and take Miller Road until you reach San-Amaro Drive. Turn right and take this road to Ponce de Leon. Turn left on Ponce and take it Stanford Drive and you will see the university ahead. From I-75: Take I-75 to the 826 West Exit. 826 West becomes 826 South. Take 826 South to the Miller Drive Exit (Southwest 56 Street). Go East on Miller to Red Road (Southwest 57 Avenue). Make a right onto Red Road and take it to Ponce de Leon Boulevard. Make a left on Ponce and go to Stanford Drive and you will see the university ahead.

**LOCAL:** The Metrorail, Miami's 22-mile rapid transit system, will get you around the area. If you'd rather take a taxi to get around town, call Yellow Cab (305-444-4444).

## WHERE TO STAY

If you plan on staying overnight, some local hotel accommodations include the Holiday Inn-University of Miami (305-667-5611, $$), which is on campus, and the nearby Biltmore Hotel (305-445-1926, $$$) and Marriott Hotel-Dadeland (305-670-1035, $$$).

---

## CAMPUS AT ITS BEST!

Those who happen to tour Miami during Homecoming weekend will be privy to some of the university's most treasured traditions. One such event is the Boat Burning Ceremony which, as the name implies, involves burning a wooden boat in Lake Osceola. A spectacular fireworks display follows the burning. For another taste of student life, simply stop by the UC Patio, an open area between the food court and first floor of the University Center. A hotspot during lunch, the patio also hosts a variety of events such as Patio Jams, concerts performed by student bands every Thursday.

# UNIVERSITY OF MISSISSIPPI

145 Martindale, University, MS 38677
**Telephone:** 662-915-7226 • **E-mail:** admissions@olemiss.edu
**Website:** www.olemiss.edu • **Hours:** Monday–Friday and Saturday by appointment

### SCHOOL AT A GLANCE

| | |
|---|---|
| Type of School | Public |
| Environment | Village |
| In-state Tuition | $4,602 |
| Out-of-state Tuition | $10,566 |
| Enrollment | 12,117 |
| % Male/Female | 47/53 |
| Student/Faculty Ratio | 19:1 |

### FRESHMAN PROFILE

| | |
|---|---|
| Range SAT | |
| Critical Reading | 480–580 |
| Range SAT Math | 490–600 |
| Range ACT Composite | 20–26 |
| Average HS GPA | 3.25 |

### ON-CAMPUS APPOINTMENTS

| | |
|---|---|
| Class Visits | Yes |

### CAMPUS TOURS

| | |
|---|---|
| Appointment | Required |
| Dates | Year Round |
| Times | See website |
| Average Length | Varies |

## STUDENTS SAY

"Tradition and school spirit are a part of everything we do, whether it's walking to class, going to a football game, or just relaxing in the Grove, the most exquisite piece of land I have ever seen."

## FODOR'S SAYS

"Oxford and Lafayette County were immortalized as Jefferson and Yoknapatawpha County in the novels of Oxford native William Faulkner."

## ABOUT THE SCHOOL

In recent years, Ole Miss has concentrated much of its energy on strengthening academics. Great results have followed and the college boasts solid programs in journalism, pharmacy, accounting, music, and engineering. Additionally, the university remains steeped in tradition and Southern charm. Many undergrads eagerly embrace the extremely healthy Greek scene. For those looking for off-campus fun, Oxford offers many great restaurants, live music, and poetry readings.

## GETTING THERE

**BY AIR:** Those guests wishing to travel by air should fly into Memphis International Airport. Limos, taxis, and rental cars are available for additional transportation needs.

**BY TRAIN:** Amtrak does not offer service to Oxford.

**BY BUS:** Unfortunately, Greyhound does not provide service to Oxford. Visitors wishing to travel by bus may take Greyhound to either Tupelo or Batesville.

**BY CAR:** From Memphis, TN (via Highway 78): Follow U.S. 78 for 52 miles. You will exit U.S. 78 at the Holly Springs/Oxford exit. At Holly Springs, proceed on MS-7 South for 31 miles. When you reach Oxford, take the fourth exit onto MS-6 and continue West. Take the third exit, Coliseum Drive, to the campus. From Jackson, MS: Follow I-55 North for 150 miles. You will take the Batesville/Oxford exit off I-55. Continue East on MS-6 for 26 miles, heading toward Oxford. When you reach Oxford, take the second exit, Coliseum Drive, to the campus. From Tupelo, MS: Follow MS-6 West for 53 miles. When you reach Oxford, take the sixth exit, Coliseum Drive, to the campus.

**LOCAL:** For local taxi service call Oxford City Cab (662-234-2250).

## WHERE TO STAY

Choices in Oxford include Holiday Inn Express (662-236-2500, $–$$), the Colonel's Quarters (662-236-9601, $–$$), and the Downtown Oxford Inn and Suites (662-234-3031, $$).

---

## CAMPUS AT ITS BEST!

Ole Miss is awash in tradition. One annual event that evokes the Ole Miss spirit is Red and Blue Week. Typically celebrated in April, students participate in activities that involve a bungee trampoline, mechanical bull rides, rock walls, and more. The week culminates in an intra-squad football game. Speaking of football, definitely try to catch a game if you're visiting the campus in the fall. You'll get to see Ole Miss school spirit in action and you'll also get to check out the Grove, where you can participate in some great tailgating. Visitors looking for more intellectual pursuits should pay a visit to the Rowan Oak. Originally owned by William Faulkner, his daughter sold it the university 1972. It currently stands as a testament to the renowned author and his work.

# UNIVERSITY OF NEW ORLEANS

AD 103, Lakefront, New Orleans, LA 70148
**Telephone:** 504-280-6595 • **E-mail:** admissions@uno.edu
**Website:** www.uno.edu

## STUDENTS SAY

"University of New Orleans is a great school in the heart of the best city in the South."

## FODOR'S SAYS

"At the 1850 House, you can see what life was like for upscale nineteenth-century Creole city dwellers on a guided tour of this restored apartment, which belongs to the Louisiana State Museum."

## ABOUT THE SCHOOL

The University of New Orleans boasts strong academic programs in business, engineering, and psychology. It also has a racially and culturally diverse study body. Most of the students on campus are commuters, and they know how to take full advantage of the perks that come with their hometown N'awlins location.

## GETTING THERE

**BY AIR:** Louis Armstrong New Orleans International Airport is the closest airport to campus. Take a taxi or use the Airport Shuttle (504-522-3500) to arrange convenient transportation to the campus.

**BY TRAIN:** Amtrak trains stop at Union Station in New Orleans on Loyola Avenue. Take a taxi or public transit to get to the campus.

**BY BUS:** Greyhound buses stop at the Downtown Bus Station in New Orleans on Loyola Avenue. Take a taxi or public transit to get to the campus.

**BY CAR:** From the North via I-55: Take I-55 South to I-10 East. Follow I-10 and exit at I-610 (left exit). Take the Elysian Fields Avenue Exit and make a left onto Elysian Fields. Go North for about three miles until you see the university. From the North via I-59: Take I-59 South to I-10 West. Get onto I-610 West and drive toward the Elysian Fields Avenue Exit and make a right. Go North for about three miles until you see the university. From New Orleans International Airport and the West: Take I-10 East to I-610 East (left exit). Take I-610 to the Elysian Fields Avenue Exit. Turn left onto Elysian Fields, and go North for about three miles until you see the university. From the East: Take I-10 West to I-610 West. Exit at the Elysian Fields Avenue and make a right. Go North for about three miles until you see the university.

**LOCAL:** New Orleans Regional Transit Authority provides bus and streetcar service throughout the city. Jefferson Transit provides bus service to downtown New Orleans and Jefferson county. If you'd rather take a taxi around the city, some local companies include Coleman Cab Company (504-586-0222), United Cabs Inc (504-522-9771), Veterans Cab Company (504-367-6767), and White Fleet & Rollins Cabs (504-822-3800).

## WHERE TO STAY

If you're planning on staying a while in New Orleans, some local accommodations include Hotel St. Marie (504-561-8951, $), Hampton Inn—Garden District (504-899-9990, $$), and Loews New Orleans Hotel (504-595-5314, $$$).

## CAMPUS AT ITS BEST!

The University of New Orleans Naval Architecture Ship Testing Facility offers students a priceless, hands-on experience. Consisting of an above ground tank 125 feet long, this teaching and research facility has a variable depth of up to seven feet. While you're on campus, remember to take a stroll along Lake Pontchartrain which borders the campus and offers some great views. Guests touring the university on a Tuesday or Friday might also choose to attend Flambeau After Five. These free concerts are held in the Flambeau Room on the first floor of the University Center.

# THE UNIVERSITY OF NORTH CAROLINA AT ASHEVILLE

CPO #2210, 117 Lipinsky Hall, Asheville, NC 28804-8510
**Telephone:** 828-251-6481 • **E-mail:** admissions@unca.edu

## STUDENTS SAY

"UNCA is about getting to know the people around you in your classes through arts, nature, and entertainment of all forms, while still getting a rewarding education."

## FODOR'S SAYS

"Famed Black Mountain College (1933–1956), 16 miles east of Asheville, was important in the development of several groundbreaking twentieth-century art, dance, and literary movements. A museum and gallery dedicated to the history of the radical college occupies a small space in downtown Asheville."

## ABOUT THE SCHOOL

The University of North Carolina at Asheville strives to combine a challenging program of study with room for freedom of expression. To this end, classes are kept small, all professors teach undergraduate courses, and administrators spend time interacting with students, to stay in tune with the needs of the undergraduates. A core curriculum that covers a broad spectrum of ideas—including health and fitness—and a myriad of student organizations ensure that students enjoy a well-rounded college experience.

## GETTING THERE

**BY AIR:** Asheville Regional Airport is the nearest airport to campus, and Asheville Transit number 6 bus travels from the airport into town. Take the number 18 bus to the UNCA campus. The Asheville Airport Express shuttle is also available for direct transport to campus.

**BY TRAIN:** The nearest Amtrak station is 55 miles away in Greenville, South Carolina. Greyhound provides limited service between Asheville and Greenville.

**BY BUS:** There is a Greyhound depot two miles from downtown Asheville. Take the number 4 or number 13 buses of the Asheville Transit System to the UNCA campus.

**BY CAR:** From the North on U.S. 19-23: Take the NC 251/UNCA Exit. Turn left at the traffic light at the bottom of the ramp. Proceed approximately half a mile to the second traffic light; turn left onto W. T. Weaver Boulevard. Proceed approximately a third of a mile to the second left-hand turn for the main entrance road to the UNCA campus. From the East on I-40: Take Exit 53B for I-240. Follow I-240 for approximately 4.5 miles. Take Exit 5A for Merrimon Avenue. Turn right at the light at the bottom of the ramp. Proceed for approximately one mile to third light; turn left onto W. T. Weaver Boulevard. Proceed for approximately a quarter of a mile to the right-hand turn for the main entrance road to the UNCA campus. From the South or West on I-26 or I-40: Take I-240 for Asheville. As you cross the river, move into the left-hand lane. Take U.S. 19-23 North. Proceed for approximately one mile to the UNCA Exit. Turn right at bottom of exit ramp. Proceed for approximately a third of a mile to the second traffic light; turn left onto W. T. Weaver Boulevard. Proceed for approximately a third of a mile to the second left-hand turn for the main entrance road to the UNCA campus.

**LOCAL:** Several bus routes in the Asheville Transit System serve the UNCA campus. Call 828-253-5691 for route and schedule info. For local taxi service in Asheville call Yellow Cab Company (828-253-3311) or A Red Cab Company (828-232-1112).

## WHERE TO STAY

For hotel accommodations in Asheville, try the Sleep Inn Biltmore, just a few minutes drive from the campus (828-277-1800, $$) and the Comfort Suites Biltmore Square Mall (828-665-4000). The Doubletree Biltmore hotel is also nearby (828-274-1800, $$$).

### SCHOOL AT A GLANCE

| | |
|---|---|
| Type of School | Public |
| Environment | Town |
| In-state Tuition | $2,172 |
| Out-of-state Tuition | $12,287 |
| Enrollment | 3,124 |
| % Male/Female | 42/58 |
| Student/Faculty Ratio | 13:1 |

### FRESHMAN PROFILE

| | |
|---|---|
| Range SAT | |
| Critical Reading | 540-660 |
| Range SAT Math | 540-640 |
| Range ACT Composite | 22-27 |
| Average HS GPA | 3.8 |

### ON-CAMPUS APPOINTMENTS

| | |
|---|---|
| Advance Notice | Yes, 2 weeks |
| Appointment | Not Required |
| Saturdays | Sometimes |
| Average Length | 30 min |
| Info Sessions | Yes |
| Class Visits | Yes |

### CAMPUS TOURS

| | |
|---|---|
| Appointment | Required |
| Dates | Year Round |
| Times | Varies |
| Average Length | 60 min |

## CAMPUS AT ITS BEST!

The University of North Carolina at Asheville is set in the Blue Ridge Mountains and lies about a mile from downtown Asheville. While you're on campus, plan to attend one of the Office of Cultural & Special Events shows. These take place throughout the year and showcase entertainers as diverse as gospel choirs, dance companies, and guitar quartets.

**FRESHMAN PROFILE**

| | |
|---|---|
| Range SAT | |
| Critical Reading | 600-690 |
| Range SAT Math | 610-700 |
| Range ACT Composite | 25-31 |
| Average HS GPA | 4.33 |

**ON-CAMPUS APPOINTMENTS**

| | |
|---|---|
| Info Sessions | Yes |
| Class Visits | Yes |

**CAMPUS TOURS**

| | |
|---|---|
| Appointment | Preferred |
| Dates | Year Round |
| Times | M–F 10:00 A.M. and 2:30 P.M. |
| Average Length | 60 min |

# THE UNIVERSITY OF NORTH CAROLINA AT CHAPEL HILL

Office of Undergraduate Admissions, Jackson Hall 153A—Campus Box #2200, Chapel Hill, NC 27599-2200

**Telephone:** 919-966-3621 • **E-mail:** unchelp@admissions.unc.edu

**Hours:** Monday–Friday, 9:00 A.M.–5:00 P.M.

## STUDENTS SAY

"This is by far the best combination of academics, athletics, and social life anywhere in the country."

## FODOR'S SAYS

"Morehead Planetarium, where the original Apollo astronauts and many since have trained, is one of the largest in the country. You can learn about the constellations and take in laser-light shows."

## ABOUT THE SCHOOL

The University of North Carolina at Chapel Hill, highly regarded for its top-notch academic programs and hugely popular Tar Heel sports teams, provides the perfect combination of quality and affordability to its students. The enthusiasm doesn't stop with sports and academics; UNC nightlife has endless possibilities, with tons of restaurants and clubs from which to choose in the university's hometown of Chapel Hill.

## GETTING THERE

**BY AIR:** Raleigh-Durham International Airport, a 20-minute drive, is the closest airport to the campus. Take a taxi to your final destination.

**BY TRAIN:** Amtrak trains stop in Raleigh. Take a taxi to get to the campus.

**BY BUS:** Greyhound and Carolina Trailways stop in Raleigh. Take a taxi to get to the campus.

**BY CAR:** From the East: Take I-40 West to Exit 273-B (Highway 54) toward Chapel Hill. Go straight on Highway 54 until you see the university. From the West: Take I-40 East toward Raleigh. Take Exit 273 and make a right after the exit ramp. Follow Highway 54 to the university. From the North: Take I-85 to its intersection with Highway 15-501 South. Take Follow 15-501 South toward Chapel Hill. The highway will split. Stay on 15-501 South bearing left, away from Franklin Street. Make a right at the Highway 54 Exit and take the highway to the university.

**LOCAL:** Chapel Hill Transit (919-968-2769) offers local public transit service. Triangle Transit Authority (919-549-9999) provides airport shuttle and regular bus service in the area. Orange Public Transportation (919-245-2008) provides bus service in the area. If you'd rather use a taxi to get around, some local companies include Ike's Taxi (919-961-2477), Main Street Taxi (919-923-1479), and Tar Heel Taxi (919-933-1255).

## WHERE TO STAY

Some local hotel accommodations include the Carolina Inn on the campus of UNC (919-933-2001, $$$) and nearby Courtyard by Marriott (919-883-0700, $$). Holiday Inn Express (919-644-7997, $$) is another popular choice.

## CAMPUS AT ITS BEST!

UNC students tend to congregate at the Pit, the sunken courtyard adjacent to the Student Union. A great place to catch up with friends, it's also often the site of speeches and performances. Another Carolina landmark is the Morehead Planetarium, one of the largest in the United States. The thousands of visitors who pass through each year learn about lunar landings, the Big Bang, black holes, and more. Certainly, the Dean E. Smith Center is close to every UNC student's heart. Home to UNC's successful basketball team, visitors will most assuredly catch Tar Heel fever should they attend a game.

# THE UNIVERSITY OF NORTH CAROLINA AT GREENSBORO

1400 Spring Garden Street, Greensboro, NC 27402-6170
**Telephone:** 336-334-5243 • **E-mail:** admissions@uncg.edu
**Website:** www.uncg.edu

## STUDENTS SAY

"Academics and internships give very good opportunities for learning. You feel like you are respected in the community when you tell someone that you are a student at UNCG."

## FODOR'S SAYS

"The Weatherspoon Art Museum, on the campus of The University of North Carolina at Greensboro, consists of six galleries and a sculpture courtyard. It is nationally recognized both for its permanent collection, which includes lithographs and bronzes by Henri Matisse, and for its changing exhibitions of twentieth-century American art."

## ABOUT THE SCHOOL

The University of North Carolina at Greensboro has been gaining national recognition as a great choice for students looking for a midsize college with excellent academic and study abroad opportunities and a hands-on approach to learning. At UNCG, students receive lots of personal attention; most classes have fewer than 30 students and almost all are taught by professors. Outside of class, students have access to a wealth of networking and internships opportunities. To top it all off, Greensboro will be introducing its new Lloyd International Honors College for the 2006–2007 academic year.

## GETTING THERE

**BY AIR:** The Piedmont Triad International Airport (PTI) is located 10 miles away from the UNCG campus. Take a PART Express shuttle to the PART Regional Hub and a PART Express bus from there to downtown Greensboro. Take a Greensboro Transit Authority bus from downtown Greensboro to the campus.

**BY TRAIN:** Amtrak stops at the Galyon Transportation Center in Greensboro. Take a Greensboro Transit Authority bus or a taxi to the campus.

**BY BUS:** There is a Greyhound depot in downtown Greensboro. Take a Greensboro Transit Authority bus or a taxi to the UNC—Greensboro campus.

**BY CAR:** From the North and East (Burlington, Raleigh/Durham, Richmond, VA): From I-40/85, follow I-40/Business 85 toward Greensboro/Winston-Salem. Take the Freeman Mill Road/Coliseum Area Exit, and turn right on Freeman Mill Road. Turn left at the first stoplight onto Coliseum Boulevard. Follow for approximately 1.5 miles and turn right at third stoplight onto Spring Garden Street. The campus is ahead. From the South (Salisbury, Charlotte, Atlanta, GA): From I-85 North, follow Business 85 toward Greensboro, take the Holden Road Exit, and turn right on Holden Road. Follow Holden for approximately 4.5 miles and turn right on Market Street. Turn right on Aycock Street South. At the second light, turn left on Spring Garden Street. The campus is ahead. From the West (Winston-Salem, Asheville, Knoxville, TN): From I-40 East, take the Wendover Avenue East Exit. Follow Wendover to the exit for Market Street (3.5 miles). Turn right on Market Street and stay on it for less than one mile. Turn right on Aycock Street South. At the second stoplight, turn left on Spring Garden Street. The campus is ahead.

**LOCAL:** The campus is served by several Greensboro Transit Authority bus routes, and the Piedmont Authority for Regional Transit's PART Express buses and shuttles go to the PTI airport and nearby cities for a reasonable fare. For local taxi service call Blue Bird Taxi (336-272-5112).

## WHERE TO STAY

For lodging in Greensboro, options include the Battleground Inn (336-272-4737, $) and the Greensboro Marriott Downtown (336-379-8000, $$), both of which offer special pricing to university guests. The very comfortable O. Henry Hotel is also nearby (336-544-9609, $$$).

## CAMPUS AT ITS BEST!

The University of North Carolina at Greensboro is about a mile from downtown Greensboro and within driving distance of six other colleges, so there are many options for things to do in the area. On campus, be sure to visit the Weatherspoon Art Museum or catch a soccer or baseball game. In Greensboro, take advantage of the many fall outdoor events, including the Music for a Sunday Evening in the Park concert series and the annual Greek Food Festival.

| SCHOOL AT A GLANCE | |
| --- | --- |
| Type of School | Public |
| Environment | Metropolis |
| In-state Tuition | $2,211 |
| Out-of-state Tuition | $13,964 |
| Enrollment | 13,069 |
| % Male/Female | 42/58 |
| Student/Faculty Ratio | 22:1 |

| FRESHMAN PROFILE | |
| --- | --- |
| Range SAT | |
| Critical Reading | 510-610 |
| Range SAT Math | 500-600 |
| Range ACT Composite | 20-24 |
| Average HS GPA | 3.46 |

| ON-CAMPUS APPOINTMENTS | |
| --- | --- |
| Advance Notice | Yes, 1 week |
| Appointment | Preferred |
| Saturdays | Sometimes |
| Average Length | 60 min |
| Info Sessions | Yes |
| Class Visits | Yes |

| CAMPUS TOURS | |
| --- | --- |
| Appointment | Preferred |
| Dates | Year Round |
| Times | 9:00 A.M., 1:00 P.M. |
| Average Length | 60 min |

# UNIVERSITY OF NORTH FLORIDA

4567 St. Johns Bluff Road, South, Jacksonville, FL 32224-2645
**Telephone:** 904-620-2624 • **E-mail:** admissions@unf.edu
**Website:** www.unf.edu • **Hours:** Monday–Friday, 8:00 A.M.–6:00 P.M.

## STUDENTS SAY

"UNF's greatest strength is the openness of the administrators. They don't stay up in their offices all day. They come out and talk to us. How many college presidents do that?"

## FODOR'S SAYS

"The world-famous Wark Collection of early eighteenth-century Meissen porcelain is just one reason to visit the Cummer Museum of Art and Gardens, which includes 12 permanent galleries with more than 5,000 items spanning more than 8,000 years and 3 acres of gardens reflecting Northeast Florida's blooming seasons and indigenous varieties."

## ABOUT THE SCHOOL

University of North Florida is a college committed to the success of its undergraduates. Students have access to passionate and distinguished faculty who offer engaging and enlightening classes. Fifty majors and 115 areas of concentration ensure that the academic needs and interests of all students are met. The beautifully maintained campus and the amazing Florida sun ensures a tremendous four years for Florida's 14,000 students.

## GETTING THERE

**BY AIR:** Those traveling by air may fly into Jacksonville International Airport. Shuttles and taxis are available for transportation to the campus.

**BY TRAIN:** Amtrak does provide service to Jacksonville. Local public buses and taxis are available.

**BY BUS:** Greyhound also offers direct service into Jacksonville. To reach campus, visitors may either use local transportation or take a taxi.

**BY CAR:** From I-95 North: Follow I-95 South. Merge onto J. Turner Butler Boulevard E (SR-202) via Exit 344 at St. Johns Bluff Road (9A). Be sure to stay in the left-hand lane. Make a left at the fork in the ramp (North). Exit on the right and merge onto UNF Drive. The campus is ahead. From I-95 South: Follow I-95 North. Exit right onto SR-9A North (Jax Beaches). Continue on SR-9A for roughly nine miles. You'll drive past J. Turner Butler Boulevard. Exit on the right and merge onto UNF drive. The campus is ahead. From I-10 (Eastbound): Follow I-10 East to I-95 South. Merge onto J. Turner Butler Boulevard E (SR-202) via Exit 344 at St. Johns Bluff Road (9A). Be sure to stay in the left-hand lane. Make a left at the fork in the ramp (North). Exit on the right and merge onto UNF Drive. The campus is ahead.

**LOCAL:** The Jacksonville Transportation Authority (904-630-3100) offers bus service throughout Jacksonville and the Northeast Florida region. For local taxi service call Yellow Cab (904-260-1111) or Gator City Taxi (904-355-TAXI).

## WHERE TO STAY

For accommodations within four miles of campus, try Homewood Suites (904-641-7988, $$), Hilton Garden Inn (904-997-660, $$), and the Residence Inn (904-996-8900, $$–$$$).

---

## CAMPUS AT ITS BEST!

Osprey Productions is the arm of UNF's student government responsible for entertaining the undergraduate masses. And entertain they do! The group promotes many on-campus concerts featuring A-list performers such as The Roots, Ludacris, Dave Chappelle, and Lewis Black. The Jacksonville area also contains numerous attractions, and visitors should set aside some time to explore. For some typical Floridian character, stop by the St. Augustine Alligator Farm. Surrounded by lush wildlife, guests are privy to glimpses of the rare white alligator.

# UNIVERSITY OF RICHMOND

28 Westhampton Way, Richmond, VA 23173
**Telephone:** 804-289-8640 • **E-mail:** admissions@richmond.edu

## STUDENTS SAY

"A fabulous institution where you'll get a top-notch education, be extremely well prepared for postgraduation opportunities, and have a lot of fun in a beautiful setting while you're at it!"

## FODOR'S SAYS

"Richmond's historic attractions lie north of the James River, which bisects the city with a sweeping curve. The heart of old Richmond is the Court End district downtown. This area, close to the capitol, contains seven National Historic Landmarks, three museums, and 11 additional buildings on the National Register of Historic Places—all within eight blocks."

## ABOUT THE SCHOOL

The University of Richmond offers its 2,900 undergraduates every advantage to ensure a successful future: rigorous and excellent pre-professional programs, undergraduate research opportunities (often paid), skills centers, free tutoring, and a network of successful alumni. The undergraduates are divided into two colleges that are governed separately but share dining halls and classes: Richmond for men and Westhampton for women. Classes are small, and a beautiful campus adds to the school's attraction.

## GETTING THERE

**BY AIR:** Richmond International Airport is 19 miles away from the University of Richmond campus. The GRTC Transit System has limited bus service to the airport area. Otherwise, take a taxi or airport shuttle to the campus.

**BY TRAIN:** The local Amtrak station is approximately five miles Northeast of campus. Take a GRTC transit bus or taxi to the campus.

**BY BUS:** Greyhound's North Boulevard station is six miles Northeast of the campus. Take a GRTC transit bus or taxi to the campus.

**BY CAR:** From the West via I-64: Take Exit 183/Glenside Drive South. Continue South on Glenside Drive to the fourth traffic light (Three Chopt Road). Turn left on Three Chopt Road. Continue straight for 0.8 mile. Turn right onto Boatwright Drive. At the bottom of the hill, make a left onto Campus Drive. From U.S. 60 (Midlothian Turnpike): Turn left on State Route 147 (Huguenot Road) and continue approximately eight miles to Three Chopt Road. Turn left on Three Chopt Road, and left on Towana Drive. The main entrance is on the left. From the Southwest via U.S. 360 (Hull Street Road): Take Route 288 North to the Powhite Parkway (toll road). Continue for nine miles to State Route 150 (Chippenham Parkway) North. After two miles, exit onto State Route 147 (Huguenot Road). Turn right on State Route 147. You will pass over the James River on the Huguenot Bridge. Proceed to the second traffic light after the bridge (Three Chopt Road). Turn left on Three Chopt Road, and turn left again on Towana Drive. The main entrance is on the left. From the North via I-95: Take Exit 79 off I-95 to I-64 West, and continue West on I-64. Take Exit 183-A/Glenside Drive South. Continue South on Glenside Drive to the fifth traffic light (Three Chopt Road). Turn left on Three Chopt Road, and continue straight for 0.8 mile. Turn right onto Boatwright Drive. At the bottom of the hill, make a left onto Campus Drive. From the East via I-64: West on I-64. As you approach Richmond, I-64 West merges with I-95 North. Take I-95 North to Exit 79 back onto I-64 West. Take Exit 183-A/Glenside Drive South. Continue South on Glenside Drive to the fifth traffic light (Three Chopt Road). Turn left on Three Chopt Road, and continue straight for 0.8 mile. Turn right onto Boatwright Drive. At the bottom of the hill, make a left onto Campus Drive. From the South via I-85 to I-95: Take Exit 79 off I-95 North to I-64 West, continue West on I-64. Take Exit 183-A/Glenside Drive South. Continue South on Glenside Drive to the fifth traffic light (Three Chopt Road). Turn left on Three Chopt Road, and continue straight for 0.8 mile. Turn right onto Boatwright Drive. At the bottom of the hill, make a left onto Campus Drive.

**LOCAL:** GRTC transit buses (804-358-GRTC) serve the Richmond campus and city of Richmond. For local taxi service call Flex Taxi Service (804-868-8294).

## WHERE TO STAY

Richmond has many choices for lodging just a short ride from the University of Richmond campus. Options include the Embassy Suite Hotel-Richmond, just two miles away (804-672-8585, $$), the Days Inn (804-282-3300, $), and the Jefferson Hotel (800-424-8014, $$$). Ask about special rates for University of Richmond guests before you make a reservation.

## CAMPUS AT ITS BEST!

University of Richmond students consistently use words such as "gorgeous" and "beautiful" to refer to their campus and they're right. Take a walk through the campus's beautiful pine trees along its 10-acre lake when you visit. Attend a sports event to get a feel for U of R's school spirit. In nearby Richmond, plan to attend one of the outdoor theater or concert events that happen year-round.

# UNIVERSITY OF SOUTH CAROLINA— COLUMBIA

Office of Undergraduate Admissions, University of South Carolina, Columbia, SC 29208
**Telephone:** 803-777-7700 • **E-mail:** admissions@sc.edu
**Hours:** Monday–Friday, 8:30 A.M.–5:00 P.M.; Saturday, 9:00 A.M.–2:00 P.M. by appointment

## STUDENTS SAY

"The typical student is a typical Southerner: warm and friendly and can cook like they made a deal with the devil."

## FODOR'S SAYS

"Six bronze stars on the Western wall of the State House mark where direct hits were made by General Sherman's cannons. The capitol building, started in 1851 and completed in 1907, is made of native blue granite in the Italian Renaissance style."

## ABOUT THE SCHOOL

The University of South Carolina offers its students an attractive combination of great academic programs and research opportunities at an affordable price. Students tend to work hard, particularly when it comes to reaching out to professors and registering for classes in the large school, but find that the extra effort is worth it. The highly competitive Honors College is a great alternative for students looking for a more intimate learning experience.

## GETTING THERE

**BY AIR:** Columbia Metropolitan Airport is the closest airport to campus. Taxi service is available from the airport.

**BY TRAIN:** Amtrak trains stop in Columbia. Take a taxi to get to the campus.

**BY BUS:** Greyhound buses service Columbia. Take a taxi to get to the campus.

**BY CAR:** From I-20 West: Take the SC 277 Exit (Exit 73) toward Columbia. SC 277 turns into Bull Street. Take Bull Street to Pendleton Street, and you will see the university shortly thereafter. From I-20 East: Get onto I-26 East. Follow I-26 East to the Elmwood Avenue Exit. Make a right onto Bull Street and take Bull Street to Pendleton Street. You will see the university ahead. From I-26 East: Take I-26 East to U.S. 126 toward downtown Columbia and exit at Elmwood Avenue. Make a right onto Bull Street and take Bull Street to Pendleton Street. You will see the university ahead. From I-26 West: Take I-26 to U.S. 126 toward downtown Columbia and exit at the Elmwood Avenue Exit. Make a right onto Bull Street and take Bull Street to Pendleton Street. You will see the university ahead.

**LOCAL:** Central Midlands Regional Transit Authority runs local bus service throughout Columbia. Call 803-255-7100 for route and schedule info. If you'd rather take a taxi to get around town, some local companies include Capitol City Cab (803-233-8294), Checker Yellow Cab Company Inc. (803-799-3311), or Classic Cab (803-348-0662).

## WHERE TO STAY

Local hotel accommodations include the Inn at USC (803-779-7779, $$), which is on campus. The Clarion Townhouse (803-771-8711, $$) and Holiday Inn-Coliseum/City Center (803-799-7800, $$) are nearby options.

## CAMPUS AT ITS BEST!

Housing accommodations are an important aspect of college life. To get a sense of dorm life at the University of South Carolina, stop by the 18-story Capstone House. The most distinct aspect of this residence hall is Top of Carolina, a revolving restaurant on the top floor. You can also visit the Greek Village, home to 15 fraternity and sorority houses. Each house has a variety of amenities, including full kitchens, rooms for dining and entertaining, and exquisitely manicured lawns. Those who visit during football season should go support the Gamecocks. Tailgating before the game is extremely popular, especially during homecoming.

# THE UNIVERSITY OF TENNESSEE AT KNOXVILLE

320 Student Service Building, Circle Park Drive, Knoxville, TN 37996-0230
**Telephone:** 865-974-2184 • **E-mail:** admissions@tennessee.edu
**Hours:** Monday–Friday, 8:00 A.M.–5:00 P.M.

## STUDENTS SAY

"UT has all types of majors, cares for its students, has tremendous spirit, and embodies the torch-bearer creed: 'One who beareth the torch, shadowth oneself to give light to others.'"

## FODOR'S SAYS

"Founded in 1786, Knoxville became the first state capitol when Tennessee was admitted to the Union in 1796."

## ABOUT THE SCHOOL

Like many big schools, the University of Tennessee at Knoxville offers its 19,000 undergrads nearly every activity and academic program there is. It's up to the students to determine how challenging or enlightening their academic career at UT will be. UT's fun-loving students also share an interest in cheering for the school's popular sports teams.

## GETTING THERE

**BY AIR:** McGhee Tyson Airport, 12 miles Southwest of Knoxville, is the closest airport to campus. Taxis are available to get to the campus.

**BY TRAIN:** The only stops Amtrak makes in Tennessee are at stations in Newburn and Memphis.

**BY BUS:** Greyhound buses stop in Knoxville. Taxis are available to get to the campus.

**BY CAR:** From the Atlanta/Chattanooga Area: Take I-75 North to I-40 East and exit at the James White Parkway Exit 388 A. Take 158 West (Neyland Drive/University of Tennessee) to the third traffic light. Stay right onto Lake Loudon Boulevard and take Lake Loudon to the second traffic light and then make a right onto Volunteer Boulevard. Take Volunteer Boulevard to the second traffic light and make a right onto Cumberland Avenue. Then, turn right onto Phillip Fulmer Way and you will see the university shortly. From the Nashville Area: Take I-40 East to the James White Parkway Exit 388 A. From there, proceed according to "From Atlanta" directions above. From the Lexington/Cincinnati Area: Take I-75 South to 275 South (Knoxville). Take 275 South to I-40 East (Asheville). Take I-40 East to the James White Parkway Exit 388 A. From there, proceed according to "From Atlanta" directions above. From the North Carolina Area: Take I-40 West to the James White Parkway Exit 388 A. From there, proceed according to "From Atlanta" directions above. From the Tri-Cities, TN Area: Take I-81 South to I-40 West and exit at the James White Parkway Exit 388 A. From there, proceed according to "From Atlanta" directions above.

**LOCAL:** The Knoxville Area Transit (KAT) provides bus service throughout the area. If you'd rather use a taxi to get around the area, some local companies include Yellow Cab (865-523-5151) and Service Cab Co. (865-522-2121).

## WHERE TO STAY

If you're planning on staying in Knoxville overnight, some local hotel accommodations include Quality Inn Knoxville (865-689-9896, $), Hilton Knoxville Hotel (865-523-2300, $$), and Holiday Inn Select (865-522-2800, $$).

## CAMPUS AT ITS BEST!

One of the University of Tennessee's greatest traditions is the Volunteer Navy event. Taking advantage of the school's proximity to the Tennessee River, approximately 200 boating enthusiasts take to the water for a giant, floating tailgating party.

# UNIVERSITY OF VIRGINIA

Office of Admission, PO Box 400160, Charlottesville, VA 22906
**Telephone:** 434-982-3200 • **E-mail:** undergradadmission@virginia.edu
**Website:** www.virginia.edu • **Hours:** Monday–Friday, 8:00 A.M.–5:00 P.M.

## STUDENTS SAY

"Virginia honors tradition and offers a great balance between hard work and recreation that creates a great atmosphere for students and faculty alike."

## FODOR'S SAYS

"Monticello, the most famous of Jefferson's homes, was constructed from 1769 to 1809. Throughout the house are Jefferson's inventions, including a seven-day clock and a two-pen contraption that allowed him to copy his correspondence as he wrote it—without having to show it to a copyist. On-site are re-created gardens, the plantation street where his slaves lived, and a gift shop. Arrive early to avoid a long wait for a tour of the house."

## ABOUT THE SCHOOL

The University of Virginia is about balance: the balance between a large research university and a small liberal arts college, balance between tradition and progress, and balance between work and play. UVA embodies the spirit of its founder, Thomas Jefferson, in its commitment to developing students' independence and initiative. Hands-on learning opportunities are limitless, and funding is readily available for study abroad and research opportunities. Considering that you get all this for a public school sticker price, it's no wonder UVA students can't stop singing their school's praises.

## GETTING THERE

**BY AIR:** Charlottesville-Albemarle Airport, approximately eight miles away, is the closest airport to campus. Take a taxi to get to the campus.

**BY TRAIN:** Amtrak stops in Charlottesville, approximately two miles away from campus. Take a taxi to get to the campus.

**BY BUS:** Greyhound Buses stop at the Charlottesville bus station approximately two miles away from campus. Take a taxi to get to the campus.

**BY CAR:** From I-64: Take Exit 118B onto the 29/250 Bypass. Take the second exit (250 East Business). Turn right after the ramp and make another right, about a mile later, onto Emmet Street. The university is ahead. From I-495: Get onto I-66 West. Take the U.S. 29 South Exit. From U.S. 29, follow signs to Business 29, which turns to Emmet Street. The university is ahead.

**LOCAL:** JAUNT (434-296-6174) provides public transportation for central Virginia, including Charlottesville. Charlottesville Transit Service or CTS (434-296-7433) provides local bus service. If you'd rather take a taxi around the area, some local companies include Charlottesville Cab Co. (434-981-9594), Skyline Cab (434-981-0473), and Yellow Cab (434-295-4131).

## WHERE TO STAY

Local hotel accommodations include the Quality Inn (434-971-3746, $), Holiday Inn (434-977-7700, $$), and Residence Inn by Marriott (434-923-0300, $$$).

---

## CAMPUS AT ITS BEST!

When they're not engaged in a lively classroom debate, many UVA students can be spotted at the Corner. Located on University Avenue, this collection of shops, bookstores, and cafés is a great place to study, meet with professors, or simply people-watch. Charlottesville also has many charming attractions. Locals always come out in droves for the annual spring Dogwood Festival and Parade. Also a hit is Fridays After Five, a concert series held at the historic downtown mall every summer.

# VANDERBILT UNIVERSITY

2305 West End Avenue, Nashville, TN 37203
**Telephone:** 615-322-2561 • **E-mail:** admissions@vanderbilt.edu • **Website:** www.vanderbilt.edu
**Hours:** Monday–Friday, 8:00 A.M.–5:00 P.M.; Saturday, 9:00 A.M.–1:00 P.M.

## Students Say

"Vanderbilt, in addition to having a beautiful campus, also has excellent professors, a great social scene, and just about any extracurricular activity you can think of—and some you can't."

## Fodor's Says

"An exact copy of the Athenian original, Nashville's Parthenon was constructed to commemorate Tennessee's 1897 centennial. Across the street from Vanderbilt University's campus, in Centennial Park, it's a magnificent sight, perched on a gentle green slope beside a duck pond."

## About the School

Vanderbilt University is a Southern school that manages to balance the personal touch of a small college with the great resources of a large university. Professors are extremely accessible, and it's not uncommon for students to be invited over to dinner at a professor's house. Hometown Nashville offers great music and plenty of entertainment for students when they want to take a break from the lively social scene on campus.

## Getting There

**BY AIR:** Nashville International Airport is the closest airport to the campus. Visitors take a taxi or the Metropolitan Transit Authority to the university.

**BY TRAIN:** The only stops Amtrak makes in Tennessee are in Newbern and Memphis.

**BY BUS:** Greyhound provides bus service to Nashville. A taxi can provide access to the campus.

**BY CAR:** From the North: Take I-65 to I-40 West to Exit 209B, and make a right on Broadway. Driving on Broadway, go right to West End Avenue where the campus is. From the East or South: Follow I-40 West to Exit 209A and make a left on Broadway. From there, proceed accordingly to "From the North" directions above. From the West: Follow I-40 East to Exit 209B and a make a right on Broadway (U.S. 70 South). From there, proceed accordingly to "From the North" directions above.

**LOCAL:** The Metropolitan Transit Authority (MTA) provides local bus service in Nashville. If you'd rather use a taxi or a car rental around the city, some local companies include Allied Cab (615-244-7433) and Yellow Cab Metro, Inc. (615-256-0101).

## Where to Stay

If you're planning on staying overnight, some local hotel accommodations that are within walking distance of the campus include Hampton Inn (615-329-1144, $), Nashville Marriott (615-321-1300, $$), and Loews-Vanderbilt Plaza (615-320-1700, $$$).

| SCHOOL AT A GLANCE | |
|---|---|
| Type of School | Private |
| Environment | Metropolis |
| Tuition | $32,620 |
| Enrollment | 6,286 |
| % Male/Female | 48/52 |
| Student/Faculty Ratio | 9:1 |

| FRESHMAN PROFILE | |
|---|---|
| Range SAT | |
| Critical Reading | 640-730 |
| Range SAT Math | 660-740 |
| Range ACT Composite | 29-33 |

| ON-CAMPUS APPOINTMENTS | |
|---|---|
| Class Visits | Yes |

| CAMPUS TOURS | |
|---|---|
| Appointment | Preferred |
| Dates | Year Round |
| Times | Varies; call for schedule |
| Average Length | 60 min |

## CAMPUS AT ITS BEST!

Many adjectives can be applied to Vanderbilt students but "bored" is certainly not among them. The ever-industrious Programming Board sponsors Sarratt Live, bringing free entertainment to the Overcup Oak and the Sarratt Student Center. Popular activities include hypnotists, cooking shows, and the annual Casino Night. Students also often venture into Nashville. Historic 2nd Avenue features a variety of shops, restaurants, and nightclubs. Prior to a night on the town, you can visit the Country Music Hall of Fame and Museum or catch a Tennessee Titans or Nashville Predators game.

# VIRGINIA COMMONWEALTH UNIVERSITY

821 West Franklin Street, PO Box 842526, Richmond, VA 23284
**Telephone:** 804-828-1222 • **E-mail:** upgrad@vcu.edu

## STUDENTS SAY

"VCU is the best place to be: People are friendly, professors are interesting and accessible, the city is exciting, and the student body is extremely diverse."

## FODOR'S SAYS

"Richmond's oldest residence, the Old Stone House in the Church Hill Historic District just east of downtown, now holds a museum honoring Edgar Allan Poe. Poe grew up in Richmond, and although he never lived in this early-to-mid-eighteenth-century structure, his disciples have made it a shrine with some of the writer's possessions on display."

## ABOUT THE SCHOOL

VCU is one of Virginia's most comprehensive colleges, offering numerous courses of study (including 44 programs unique within the state). Admitted students are welcomed into a top research university where diversity is valued and where undergrads are committed to making a difference. The city of Richmond provides an ideal setting, enhancing students' college experience with access to art galleries, museums, riverfront parks, and sports facilities.

## GETTING THERE

**BY AIR:** Richmond International Airport receives flights from several major airlines. Taxis, shuttles, and public buses are all available for further transit.

**BY TRAIN:** Amtrak does indeed provide service to Richmond. Take a taxi to get to the campus.

**BY BUS:** Visitors may take Greyhound directly into Richmond. Take a taxi to get to the campus.

**BY CAR:** From the East or South by Interstate 64 West/95 North: Take Exit 76A to Chamberlayne Avenue. At the next light, make a right onto Leigh Street. When you reach the next light, take a left onto Belvidere Street. Continue for six blocks until you hit Main Street. Make a right onto Main and turn left onto Laurel Street. You'll find the entrance to the Main Street Parking Deck on your right. From the West or North by Interstate 64 East/95 South: Take Exit 76B to Belvidere Street. At the first light, turn left on Leigh Street. At the next light, turn right on Belvidere Street. Continue for six blocks until you hit Main Street. Make a right onto Main and turn left onto Laurel Street. You'll find the entrance to the Main Street Parking Deck on your right.

**LOCAL:** The Greater Richmond Transit Company provides public buses for travel around the Richmond area. For local taxi service call Metro Taxi Service at 804-353-5000.

## WHERE TO STAY

Hotels that offer discounts to VCU guests include the Fairfield Inn (804-672-8621, $), Linden Row Inn (804-783-7000, $), and the Jefferson Hotel (804-788-8000, $$).

---

## CAMPUS AT ITS BEST!

VCU is a university ripe with traditions, and there are many annual events to celebrate and enjoy. Attend the fall step show and become mesmerized by some amazing dance moves. Guests touring campus during the spring semester should aim to participate in Spring Fest. This week-long event typically features dances, films, concerts, and novelty acts. Richmond also offers numerous attractions. Literary fiends might want to investigate the Edgar Allen Poe Museum and history buffs St. John's Church, the site of Patrick Henry's famous speech.

# VIRGINIA TECH

Undergraduate Admissions, 201 Burruss Hall, Blacksburg, VA 24061
**Telephone:** 540-231-6267 • **E-mail:** vtadmiss@vt.edu
**Hours:** Monday–Friday, 8:00 A.M.–NOON, 1:00 P.M.–5:00 P.M.

## STUDENTS SAY

"Campus unity is among the greatest strengths of Virginia Tech. The student body is proud to show off its Hokie spirit. Just come to any football game."

## FODOR'S SAYS

"The Virginia Museum of Natural History presents rotating exhibits on local and national wildlife; a separate geology museum in Derring Hall displays gems and minerals."

## ABOUT THE SCHOOL

Virginia Polytechnic and State University specializes in real-world education, and its more than 21,000 undergraduates appreciate the balance between academics and practical application. Classes are usually fewer than 30 students, and accessible and helpful professors teach about three quarters of them. Tech's seven colleges emphasize technology, incorporating the latest into every class and department, which makes students highly employable upon graduation.

## GETTING THERE

**BY AIR:** Roanoke Regional Airport in Roanoke, Virginia, is served by major domestic airlines. Take the Smart Way Bus from the airport to the Squires Student Center on the Blacksburg campus.

**BY TRAIN:** The nearest Amtrak station is in White Sulfur Springs, 40 miles away.

**BY BUS:** Greyhound bus lines serve the Blacksburg area; there is a stop in Roanoke at the Campbell Court bus station downtown. Take the Smart Way Bus from the Campbell Court bus station to the Squires Student Center on the Blacksburg campus.

**BY CAR:** From Interstate 81 (South and Northbound): Take Exit 118 to reach the exit ramps for all three of the exits at this location. There is only one exit ramp serving the exits; missing the ramp means a trip North to Exit 128 or South to Exit 114, where you will have to turn around. Take Exit 118B onto U.S. 460 West. This exit connects directly to the Christiansburg Bypass. Follow the signs for Blacksburg/Virginia Tech. The U.S. 460 bypass between Blacksburg and Christiansburg is a limited-access highway from I-81 to the campus entrance at Southgate Drive. Watch signs carefully for routes and directions. From the bypass, take the Business U.S. 460—South Main Street exits to the right (take South Main Street to reach downtown Blacksburg). Stay on U.S. 460 West, and follow the signs for Virginia Tech, Bluefield to continue directly to the university. Drive for 2.5 miles on U.S. 460 to the traffic light at VA 314, Southgate Drive. Turn right onto Southgate Drive. There is a campus map a quarter of a mile on the right and the Visitor Information Center is half a mile from U.S. 460 on the right.

**LOCAL:** Students with a valid ID ride Blacksburg transit buses free. Smart Way Bus charges three dollars for transportation to the airport or nearby cities. For local taxi service call Blacksburg Taxi (540-552-6671).

## WHERE TO STAY

Blacksburg has many options for accommodations. The The Inn at Virginia Tech and Skelton Conference Center is right on the Virgina Tech campus (540-231-8000, $$). The Ramada Ltd. Blacksburg is about three miles away from campus (540-951-1330, $) and the AmeriSuites Blacksburg University is within walking distance of the campus (540-552-5636, $).

| SCHOOL AT A GLANCE | |
| --- | --- |
| Type of School | Public |
| Environment | Town |
| In-state Tuition | $5,450 |
| Out-of-state Tuition | $17,406 |
| Enrollment | 21,938 |
| % Male/Female | 58/42 |
| Student/Faculty Ratio | 16:1 |

| FRESHMAN PROFILE | |
| --- | --- |
| Range SAT | |
| Critical Reading | 540-630 |
| Range SAT Math | 570-660 |
| Average HS GPA | 3.80 |

| ON-CAMPUS APPOINTMENTS | |
| --- | --- |
| Appointment | Not Required |
| Info Sessions | Yes |
| Class Visits | Yes |

| CAMPUS TOURS | |
| --- | --- |
| Appointment | No |
| Dates | Year Round |
| Times | Varies |
| Average Length | 60 min |

## CAMPUS AT ITS BEST!

Hokie football and basketball are big draws on the Virginia Tech campus, so be sure to attend a game when you visit; it's a good place to see the fun-loving undergraduates in action. For a small town, Blacksburg has quite a lively social scene. Head downtown to listen to live music, watch sports TV while you eat a plate of wings, or sing at karaoke night.

# WAKE FOREST UNIVERSITY

Box 7305, Reynolda Station, Winston-Salem, NC 27109
**Telephone:** 336-758-5201 • **E-mail:** admissions@wfu.edu
**Website:** www.wfu.edu • **Hours:** Monday–Friday, 8:30 A.M.–5:00 P.M.; Saturday mornings

## STUDENTS SAY

"The strength of Wake Forest is the tremendous sense of community on campus. As a Wake student, you really feel like you belong to something."

## FODOR'S SAYS

"The SciWorks complex includes a 120-seat planetarium, a 15-acre Environmental Park, and 45,000 square feet of interactive and hands-on exhibits, including the Coastal Encounters wet lab."

## ABOUT THE SCHOOL

Wake Forest University offers its 4,100 undergraduates the same amenities as a large college with the personal touch of a small one. WFU's rigorous classes are often fewer than 20 students, and professors teach all of them. Students find the administrators to be just as accessible and happy to help as the professors. WFU's state-of-the-art facilities help ease the pressure of its tough classes; the school provides computers and printers to each incoming student.

## GETTING THERE

**BY AIR:** The Piedmont Triad International Airport is just 24 miles away from the campus. From there, take an airport shuttle or a taxi.

**BY TRAIN:** Amtrak provides service to Greensboro, about 20 minutes away. Take a taxi to get to the campus.

**BY BUS:** Greyhound offers regular service to Winston Salem, about five minutes away from the campus. Take a Winston-Salem Transit Authority bus or a cab to campus.

**BY CAR:** From Washington, DC, and points North: Take I-95 South to I-85 South to I-40 West. In Winston-Salem take Business 40 to the Silas Creek Parkway North Exit and follow the signs to Wake Forest. From Atlanta and points South: Take I-77 North to I-40 East. In Winston-Salem take Business 40 to the Silas Creek Parkway North Exit and follow the signs to Wake Forest. From Raleigh and points East: Take I-40 West to Winston-Salem. Take Business 40 to the Silas Creek Parkway North Exit and follow the signs to Wake Forest. From Asheville and points West: Take I-40 East to Winston-Salem. Take Business 40 to the Silas Creek Parkway North Exit and follow the signs to Wake Forest.

**LOCAL:** The Winston Salem Transit Authority (910-727-2000) serves the Wake Forest campuses. For local taxi service call Willard's Cab Company (336-725-2227) or Blue Bird Cabs (336-722-7121).

## WHERE TO STAY

Downtown Winston Salem has many lodging options for visitors. Ask for the Wake Forest University guest price when reserving. Options include the Brookstown Inn (336-725-1120, $$), the Hawthorne Inn (336-777-3000, $), and the Wingate Inn (336-714-2800, $$).

## CAMPUS AT ITS BEST!

Wake Forest's campus is gorgeous in the opinion of its undergraduate occupants. A perfect example is the Reynolda Gardens, whose walkways, flowers, and exotic plants are also open to the public. Attend a game while you're at Wake Forest University. School spirit for the Demon Deacons brings the whole campus together!

# WASHINGTON AND LEE UNIVERSITY

Letcher Avenue, Lexington, VA 24450-0303
**Telephone:** 540-458-8710 • **E-mail:** admissions@wlu.edu
**Website:** admissions.wlu.edu • **Hours:** Monday–Friday, 8:30 A.M.–5:00 P.M.; Saturday, 8:00 A.M.–NOON

## STUDENTS SAY

"Washington and Lee is a school where you are surrounded by people who, like you, are very focused academically and on [their] future but are also eager to go out and have a great time."

## FODOR'S SAYS

"The inventor of the first mechanical wheat reaper is honored at the Cyrus McCormick Museum, which sits about a mile off I-81. Follow the signs to Walnut Grove farm; now a livestock research center, this mill farmstead is where McCormick did his work."

## ABOUT THE SCHOOL

Washington and Lee University's much-respected honor system directs its students to comport themselves like gentlemen (or ladies). These simple guidelines govern Washington and Lee campus life; students don't lie, steal, or cheat, and it's not uncommon for them to leave their dorm rooms unlocked or take unproctored tests. As a small school in a small town, finding stuff to do outside of class often means partaking of the school's lively Greek scene. Students looking for other entertainment options take advantage of the many outdoor activities available in the area.

## GETTING THERE

**BY AIR:** Visitors should fly into the Roanoke Regional Airport, about an hour's drive away from Lexington. Take a Roanoke Limo shuttle (540-345-7710) to get to the campus.

**BY TRAIN:** Amtrak serves Staunton, Virginia, which is about 30 miles north of Lexington on I-81. No public transportation is available from the Amtrak station to Lexington.

**BY BUS:** The Greyhound bus line passes through Buena Vista, which is about seven miles from Lexington. Take a taxi to get to the campus.

**BY CAR:** From the North, South, or East: Take I-81 to Exit 191. This exit will take you onto I-64. Next, take I-64 at Exit 55. Make a left onto Route 11 South at the stop sign. Stay on Route 11 South through three stoplights. Then, bear right onto Route 11 Business and you will see the university shortly thereafter on your left. From the West: Take I-64 to Exit 55. Make a right on Route 11 South at the stop sign. Stay on Route 11 South through three stoplights. Bear right onto Route 11 Business and you will see the university shortly thereafter on your left.

**LOCAL:** If you want to take a taxi around the area, some local companies include Dunn's Taxi Service (540-463-1056) and Frank's Cab Co. (540-464-3198).

## WHERE TO STAY

If you plan on spending the night, some local hotel accommodations include the Wingate Inn (540-464-8100, $$), Best Western Lexington Inn (540-458-3020, $$), and Sheridan Livery Inn (540-464-1887, $$).

### SCHOOL AT A GLANCE

| | |
|---|---|
| Type of School | Private |
| Environment | Village |
| Tuition | $31,175 |
| Enrollment | 1,745 |
| % Male/Female | 50/50 |
| Student/Faculty Ratio | 10:1 |

### FRESHMAN PROFILE

| | |
|---|---|
| Range SAT | |
| Critical Reading | 650–740 |
| Range SAT Math | 650–740 |
| Range ACT Composite | 28–31 |

### ON-CAMPUS APPOINTMENTS

| | |
|---|---|
| Advance Notice | Yes, 2 weeks |
| Appointment | Required |
| Saturdays | Yes |
| Average Length | 45 min |
| Info Sessions | Yes |
| Class Visits | Yes |

### CAMPUS TOURS

| | |
|---|---|
| Appointment | Not Required |
| Dates | Year Round |
| Times | M–F 10:00 A.M.–3:00 P.M.; |
| | Sat NOON |
| Average Length | 60 min |

## CAMPUS AT ITS BEST!

The John W. Elrod University Commons is truly the heart of student life at Washington and Lee. The building is equipped with many amenities, from dining facilities and a convenience store, to lounge spaces, meetings rooms, and a movie theater. There are also a myriad of activities to keep you entertained outside of the Commons. Consider attending the annual Battle of the Bands or ThinkFast, a trivia game show where you can walk away with cold hard cash.

# WESLEYAN COLLEGE

4760 Forsyth Road, Macon, GA 31210-4462

**Telephone:** 478-477-1110 • **E-mail:** admissions@wesleyancollege.edu • **Website:** www.wesleyancollege.edu

**Hours:** Monday–Friday, 8:30 A.M.–5:00 P.M.; Saturday by appointment

## SCHOOL AT A GLANCE

| | |
|---|---|
| Type of School | Private |
| Environment | City |
| Tuition | $14,500 |
| Enrollment | 561 |
| % Male/Female | 0/100 |
| Student/Faculty Ratio | 8:1 |

### FRESHMAN PROFILE

| | |
|---|---|
| Range SAT | |
| Critical Reading | 500-630 |
| Range SAT Math | 490-600 |
| Range ACT Composite | 21-26 |
| Average HS GPA | 3.5 |

### ON-CAMPUS APPOINTMENTS

| | |
|---|---|
| Advance Notice | No |
| Appointment | Preferred |
| Saturdays | Yes |
| Average Length | 30 min |
| Info Sessions | Yes |
| Class Visits | Yes |

### CAMPUS TOURS

| | |
|---|---|
| Appointment | Preferred |
| Dates | Year Round |
| Times | M–F 8:30 A.M. to 5:00 P.M. |
| Average Length | Varies |

## STUDENTS SAY

"Wesleyan College is a place where girls from around the world come together to accomplish their goals in a very challenging, yet relaxed, atmosphere."

## FODOR'S SAYS

"The Macon Museum of Arts and Sciences and Mark Smith Planetarium displays everything from a whale skeleton to fine art."

## ABOUT THE SCHOOL

Wesleyan College, one of the oldest women's colleges in the nation, places a high premium on tradition and sisterhood, all in a charming Southern setting. Students are drawn to the school's mission to teach women to think analytically, independently, and confidently. With fewer than 600 undergraduates on campus, Wesleyan is able to offer its students small classes and incredible one-on-one attention in the classroom. It's a good thing, too, because academics at Wesleyan are intense. Fortunately, accessible professors and plenty of resources for extra help make the workload that much more manageable.

## GETTING THERE

**BY AIR:** Middle Georgia Regional Airport in Macon is the closest airport to campus. The Hartsfield Atlanta International Airport is an hour and a half away. Rental car, taxi, and shuttle service are all available from the airport.

**BY TRAIN:** Amtrak stops in Atlanta, which is about an hour and a half from Macon.

**BY BUS:** The Greyhound bus station is located at 65 Spring Street in Macon. Take a taxi to get to the campus.

**BY CAR:** From the North: Go South on I-75, through Forsyth. Bear right onto I-475 South. Take Exit 9, Zebulon Road, and turn left onto Zebulon Road, which ends at Forsyth Road. Make a right at Forsyth Road, and you will see the college shortly thereafter. From the West: Take U.S. 80 or GA Highway 22. Get onto I-475 North and take it to Exit 9, Zebulon Road. Make a right onto Zebulon Road and follow it to Forsyth Road. Make a right at Forsyth Road, and you will see the college shortly thereafter. From the South: Take I-75 North. Head left onto I-475, the Macon Bypass, and take it to Exit 9, Zebulon Road. Take Exit 9 and make a right onto Zebulon Road and follow it to Forsyth Road. Make a right at Forsyth Road, and you will see the college shortly thereafter. From the East: Take I-16 West to I-75 North. Take I-75 and take Exit 169, Arkwright Road. Make a left, and head straight until you hit Northside Drive, where you will make a right. Go straight through the light at Forest Hill Road. At the caution light, make a left onto Wesleyan Drive. Turn left on Forsyth Road, and take it to the college.

**LOCAL:** The Macon-Bibb County Transit Authority provides downtown trolley and county bus service in the area. For local taxi service, try Yellow Cab (478-742-6464), Radio Cab Inc. (478-781-0076), or Safety Cab (478-621-0789).

## WHERE TO STAY

Popular lodging choices include the Best Western Inn (478-743-6311, $), Holiday Inn Express Macon (478-743-1482, $$), and Crowne Plaza Hotel Macon (478-738-2460, $$$).

---

## CAMPUS AT ITS BEST!

Foster Lake is one of Wesleyan College's most picturesque locations. An ecologically diverse habitat, the area serves as a preserve and is utilized for biology field study work. The well-maintained trails provide excellent recreational opportunities, from biking and jogging, to horseback riding. The college has many traditions, and one of the most beloved is STUNT. At this annual event, students write and produce their own skits, raising money for scholarships in the process.

# WEST VIRGINIA UNIVERSITY

Admissions Office, PO Box 6009, Morgantown, WV 26506-6009
**Telephone:** 304-293-2121 • **E-mail:** wvuadmissions@arc.wvu.edu
**Hours:** Monday–Friday, 8:00 A.M.–5:00 P.M.; Saturday, 9:00 A.M.–4:00 P.M.

| SCHOOL AT A GLANCE | |
| --- | --- |
| Type of School | Public |
| Environment | Town |
| In-state Tuition | $4,476 |
| Out-of-state Tuition | $13,840 |
| Enrollment | 27,115 |
| % Male/Female | 52/48 |
| Student/Faculty Ratio | 23:1 |

| FRESHMAN PROFILE | |
| --- | --- |
| Range SAT | |
| Critical Reading | 460–560 |
| Range SAT Math | 480–580 |
| Range ACT Composite | 20–26 |
| Average HS GPA | 3.3 |

| ON-CAMPUS APPOINTMENTS | |
| --- | --- |
| Class Visits | Yes |

| CAMPUS TOURS | |
| --- | --- |
| Appointment | Required |
| Dates | Year Round |
| Times | M–F 10:30 A.M. and |
| | 2:00 P.M.; Sat 10:00 A.M. |
| | and 12:30 P.M. |
| Average Length | 120 min |

## STUDENTS SAY

"The greatest strength of our school is its homey environment, with its relaxed small-town atmosphere."

## FODOR'S SAYS

"Morgantown [is] an industrial and educational center known internationally for its glass. It is home of West Virginia University, where the world's first fully automated transportation system has carried students between campuses since the 1970s."

## ABOUT THE SCHOOL

Depending on what a student is looking for, WVU can be the ultimate party school or an academically rigorous experience in which students are challenged by the school's strong programs in forensics, engineering, journalism, the sciences, and business. Whatever their educational philosophy, all students benefit from WVU's caring approach and excellent resources. WVU's state-of-the-art recreation center and nationally ranked sports teams offer plenty of fun outside of class.

## GETTING THERE

**BY AIR:** Pittsburgh International Airport, which is 78 miles away from campus, is the closest airport.

**BY TRAIN:** The closest Amtrak station is in Connellsville and is 32 miles away. Take a taxi to get to the campus.

**BY BUS:** The MountainLine bus system connects the closest Greyhound bus station in downtown Pittsburgh to the station at the Pittsburgh Airport. From there, students can connect to another bus that will take them into Morgantown.

**BY CAR:** From I-68 West: Exit at I-68 West, make a left after the exit ramp onto Route 119 North. Go through three stoplights, and you should see the university shortly thereafter. From I-79: If you take the I-79 Exit onto I-68 East, make a left at the light on Route 119 North. Go straight through three stoplights, and you should see the university shortly thereafter.

**LOCAL:** Personal Rapid Transit (PRT) provides the primary mode of transportation between downtown Morgantown and the university. The MountainLine bus system also gets students around town. If you'd rather use a taxi to get around the area, call Yellow Cab (304-292-7441).

## WHERE TO STAY

Some local hotel accommodations include the Hampton Inn (304-599-1200, $$) and Waterfront Place Hotel (887-477-5817, $$).

## CAMPUS AT ITS BEST!

Crime House is perhaps West Virginia University's most impressive resource. Crime House is officially referred to as the Forensic Identification Laboratory; professors stage murders, kidnappings, and other crimes that allow students to hone their forensic techniques.

# WOFFORD COLLEGE

429 North Church Street, Spartanburg, SC 29303-3663
**Telephone:** 864-597-4130 • **E-mail:** admissions@wofford.edu

## STUDENTS SAY

"Although Wofford is small, it is a big part of every student and alumnus's life. Wofford is all about building meaningful relationships with friends and professors while learning crucial, lifelong academic and social skills."

## FODOR'S SAYS

"Many local restaurants serve 'meat and three,' which is your choice of a meat main and three side dishes. Macaroni and cheese, rice and gravy, mashed potatoes, and Jell-O are popular sides."

## ABOUT THE SCHOOL

The 1,150 undergraduates at Wofford College have to work very hard for each grade. The academic demands are rigorous, but fortunately the college provides easily accessible tutors and professors. Wofford College's location in Spartanburg, South Carolina, is another plus: Students are surrounded by a beautiful natural landscape, yet can easily visit nearby Greenville, Asheville, and Charlotte, all great destinations for awesome restaurants and nightlife.

## GETTING THERE

**BY AIR:** The Greenville/Spartanburg International Airport (GSP) is a 25-minute drive away. Take a taxi to the Wofford campus.

**BY TRAIN:** Amtrak stops in Spartanburg. Ride the SPARTA (Spartanburg Area Regional Transit Agency) bus to get to the Wofford campus.

**BY BUS:** There is a Greyhound station in Spartanburg. Ride SPARTA to the Wofford campus.

**BY CAR:** From Charlotte via I-85 South: Continue Southbound on I-85 to Exit 75 (SC-9), marked "To Wofford College." At the top of the ramp, turn left. After the fourth traffic signal, SC-9 turns left down a ramp to join I-585. Do not turn there, but follow the sign straight ahead to Wofford via North Church Street (U.S. 221). Church Street curves to the left at its intersection with the Asheville Highway. The front gate to the campus is on the left, 0.4 miles beyond that point. From Atlanta via I-85 North: Leave I-85 at Exit 69, the Spartanburg Business I-85 spur. Follow the freeway to Exit 4 (Asheville Highway/ SC-56), marked "To Wofford College." At the bottom of the ramp, you will be on Hearon Circle. The second exit off the circle is Asheville Highway and is marked with a Wofford sign. Continue toward downtown Spartanburg for 2.7 miles. The front gate to the campus is on the left, 0.4 miles after the intersection with North Church Street (U.S. 221). From Asheville and I-40 via I-26 East: Take Exit 15 (Spartanburg via U.S. 176), marked "To Wofford College." At the top of the cloverleaf ramp, 8.2 miles from the college, turn right. Be sure to bear left and stay on U.S. 176/ I-585. Take Exit 25-B, North Church Street (U.S. 221). Church Street curves to the left at its intersection with the Asheville Highway; the front gate to the campus is on the left, 0.4 miles beyond that point. From Columbia and I-20 via I-26 West: Take Exit 28 (U.S. 221), marked "To Wofford College." At the bottom of the ramp, 8.9 miles from the college, turn right. This becomes South Church Street and leads directly to Wofford. The main gate is on the right just past Spartanburg Memorial Auditorium.

**LOCAL:** The SPARTA #5 bus serves the Wofford campus and connects to other buses at various points on the route. For local taxi service call Checker Cab & Locksmith (864-583-2724) or Merry Travelers (864-591-1050).

## WHERE TO STAY

There are many hotel choices in Spartanburg. Nearby options include The Holiday Express Hotel & Suites (864-699-7777, $), the Fairfield Inn Spartanburg (864-542-0333, $), and the Residence Inn Greenville-Spartanburg (864-627-0001, $$).

---

### CAMPUS AT ITS BEST!

When visiting Wofford College, make plans to attend a campus athletic event. Wofford's football and basketball teams are extremely popular, and at the game you'll get to see where a lot of Wofford's fun happens. Spartanburg also offers great entertainment; its spring and summer outdoor concert series Music on Main features live performances and great food.

---

# THE WEST

If you approach the Western United States from the East, the first thing you'll be struck by is its contrast with the region you just left (the Midwest). The Rocky Mountains rise abruptly from the Great Plains, stretching from New Mexico to Alaska to create the Continental Divide. Rivers to the east of the Divide drain into the Atlantic or Arctic Oceans, while rivers to the west drain into the Pacific Ocean. Colorado contains the highest peaks and, as a result, fabulous ski resorts, though Utah, Idaho, and Wyoming have world-renowned ski resorts of their own.

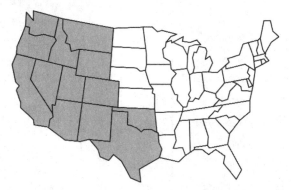

As you move west from the Rockies, the landscape changes from mountains to plateaus and basins. Nevada is known as the "Great Basin," and if you aren't sure what that implies, imagine a seemingly endless expanse of desert or grassy plains with far-off, unreachable mountains lingering in the background, interrupted by the glittering neon lights of the Vegas strip. A road trip through Arizona will reveal a mix of canyons, desert, and mountains. (Hey, if it was good enough for Georgia O'Keefe, it's definitely worth a look.) California, Oregon, and Washington State all border the Pacific Ocean, offering miles of dramatic and diverse ocean vistas. Alaska is untamed wilderness at its best (it boasts an average of just one person per square mile!) and Hawaii, well…Hawaii is beaches, volcanoes, sun, and surf. Enough said.

Check out a map of the region and eye-popping national parks seem to be just about everywhere: Yellowstone (Wyoming), Yosemite (California), Glacier (Montana), Canyonlands (Utah), Olympic (Washington), and the Grand Canyon (Arizona), just to name a few. And don't forget the Redwood Forest and the inspiring rocks at Joshua Tree, both in California.

Millions of migrants came to the region during America's era of expansion. Some were brought by the Gold Rush, others came to find the land of milk and honey promised by wagon trail organizers, while still others were the early explorers, hunters, and trappers who paved the way for the rest.

During the period of U.S. expansion into the West, the Spanish, Mexicans, and Native Americans were the primary forces to be reckoned with, and their cultural influence is still obvious, particularly in Southern California, Arizona, New Mexico, and Texas. Asian influence is obvious in Northern California, the Pacific Northwest, and Hawaii, where large immigrant populations from all over Asia settled. Native American life—past and present—can be experienced by visiting Anasazi ruins or stopping at one of the many reservations dotted throughout the region. The American frontier feel is still going strong in areas of Montana, Wyoming, Colorado, Texas, and Nevada.

If urban life is what you crave, big cities like Los Angeles, Phoenix, San Francisco, San Diego, Seattle, Portland, Salt Lake City, and Denver each have a flavor of their own. The cities of Texas (and indeed the entire Lone Star State), have created a distinct culture of their own.

To sum up, a person can fit pretty much any mold and be happy in the West. Whether you are a new age type (check out Sedona, Arizona), feel most at home with a backpack and water bottle (see any national park area), have a future as a high-roller (viva Las Vegas), dig the alternative life (check out Seattle or Portland), or want to be a movie star (stop by Hollywood or even Aspen), you can find a comfortable niche here.

# WESTERN MILEAGE MATRIX

| | Tempe | Phoenix | Sacramento | Claremont | Los Angeles | Malibu | Berkeley | San Diego | Santa Barbara |
|---|---|---|---|---|---|---|---|---|---|
| Tempe, Arizona | – | 14 | 767 | 353 | 384 | 418 | 756 | 366 | 481 |
| Phoenix, Arizona | 14 | – | 756 | 342 | 372 | 406 | 751 | 354 | 469 |
| Sacramento, California | 767 | 756 | – | 411 | 385 | 469 | 78 | 506 | 405 |
| Claremont, California | 353 | 342 | 411 | – | 33 | 68 | 402 | 121 | 125 |
| Los Angeles, California | 384 | 372 | 385 | 33 | – | 36 | 374 | 121 | 97 |
| Malibu, California | 418 | 406 | 469 | 68 | 36 | – | 400 | 155 | 67 |
| Berkeley, California | 756 | 751 | 78 | 402 | 374 | 400 | – | 554 | 334 |
| San Diego, California | 366 | 354 | 506 | 121 | 121 | 155 | 554 | – | 220 |
| Santa Barbara, California | 481 | 469 | 405 | 125 | 97 | 67 | 334 | 220 | – |
| Santa Cruz, California | 744 | 732 | 154 | 372 | 363 | 338 | 75 | 493 | 273 |
| San Francisco, California | 762 | 750 | 87 | 408 | 381 | 402 | 13 | 501 | 337 |
| Colorado Springs, Colorado | 853 | 840 | 1252 | 1052 | 1082 | 1119 | 1326 | 1186 | 1171 |
| Boulder, Colorado | 907 | 937 | 1174 | 1004 | 1034 | 1070 | 1248 | 1100 | 1123 |
| Boise, Idaho | 1072 | 1149 | 556 | 995 | 940 | 957 | 630 | 1086 | 976 |
| Missoula, Montana | 1187 | 1333 | 1128 | 1180 | 1211 | 1269 | 1173 | 1271 | 1312 |
| Las Vegas, Nevada | 305 | 293 | 588 | 240 | 270 | 311 | 563 | 331 | 359 |
| Reno, Nevada | 899 | 887 | 135 | 545 | 518 | 536 | 208 | 637 | 545 |
| Albuquerque, New Mexico | 478 | 465 | 1089 | 756 | 786 | 839 | 1079 | 810 | 875 |
| Tulsa, Oklahoma | 1095 | 1171 | 1741 | 1407 | 1437 | 1474 | 1746 | 1462 | 1526 |
| Portland, Oregon | 1373 | 1332 | 580 | 990 | 964 | 981 | 626 | 1083 | 953 |
| Salem, Oregon | 1299 | 1287 | 535 | 945 | 919 | 936 | 581 | 1038 | 907 |
| Houston, Texas | 1295 | 1297 | 2058 | 1639 | 1669 | 1704 | 2048 | 1792 | 1771 |
| Dallas, Texas | 1062 | 1065 | 1731 | 1425 | 1435 | 1470 | 1722 | 1357 | 1544 |
| College Station, Texas | 1119 | 1121 | 1926 | 1462 | 1527 | 1527 | 1885 | 1414 | 1595 |
| Austin, Texas | 1003 | 1005 | 1765 | 1346 | 1411 | 1411 | 1756 | 1298 | 1479 |
| Salt Lake City, Utah | 676 | 812 | 652 | 656 | 690 | 730 | 725 | 749 | 778 |
| Provo, Utah | 622 | 768 | 694 | 614 | 644 | 686 | 767 | 706 | 734 |
| Olympia, Washington | 1494 | 1454 | 692 | 1112 | 1085 | 1102 | 738 | 1204 | 1065 |
| Seattle, Washington | 1572 | 1513 | 752 | 1171 | 1145 | 1153 | 797 | 1264 | 1124 |
| Spokane, Washington | 1425 | 1571 | 933 | 1343 | 1317 | 1334 | 978 | 1463 | 1305 |
| Laramie, Wyoming | 975 | 1054 | 1040 | 1040 | 1071 | 1112 | 1113 | 1137 | 1161 |

# WESTERN MILEAGE MATRIX

| | Santa Cruz | San Francisco | Colorado Springs | Boulder | Boise | Missoula | Las Vegas | Reno | Albuquerque |
|---|---|---|---|---|---|---|---|---|---|
| Tempe, Arizona | 744 | 762 | 853 | 907 | 1072 | 1187 | 305 | 899 | 478 |
| Phoenix, Arizona | 732 | 750 | 840 | 937 | 1149 | 1333 | 293 | 887 | 465 |
| Sacramento, California | 154 | 87 | 1252 | 1174 | 556 | 1128 | 588 | 135 | 1089 |
| Claremont, California | 372 | 408 | 1052 | 1004 | 995 | 1180 | 240 | 545 | 756 |
| Los Angeles, California | 363 | 381 | 1082 | 1034 | 940 | 1211 | 270 | 518 | 786 |
| Malibu, California | 338 | 402 | 1119 | 1070 | 957 | 1269 | 311 | 536 | 839 |
| Berkeley, California | 75 | 13 | 1326 | 1248 | 630 | 1173 | 563 | 208 | 1079 |
| San Diego, California | 493 | 501 | 1186 | 1100 | 1086 | 1271 | 331 | 637 | 810 |
| Santa Barbara, California | 273 | 337 | 1171 | 1123 | 976 | 1312 | 359 | 545 | 875 |
| Santa Cruz, California | – | 73 | 1363 | 1317 | 709 | 1281 | 550 | 287 | 1065 |
| San Francisco, California | 73 | – | 1335 | 1257 | 639 | 1183 | 570 | 218 | 1086 |
| Colorado Springs, Colorado | 1363 | 1335 | – | 97 | 898 | 963 | 815 | 1118 | 378 |
| Boulder, Colorado | 1317 | 1257 | 97 | – | 820 | 885 | 758 | 1040 | 475 |
| Boise, Idaho | 709 | 639 | 898 | 820 | – | 368 | 756 | 422 | 1276 |
| Missoula, Montana | 1281 | 1183 | 963 | 885 | 368 | – | 941 | 928 | 1460 |
| Las Vegas, Nevada | 550 | 570 | 815 | 758 | 756 | 941 | – | 447 | 572 |
| Reno, Nevada | 287 | 218 | 1118 | 1040 | 422 | 928 | 447 | – | 1246 |
| Albuquerque, New Mexico | 1065 | 1086 | 378 | 475 | 1276 | 1460 | 572 | 1246 | – |
| Tulsa, Oklahoma | 1719 | 1737 | 676 | 711 | 1511 | 1576 | 1224 | 1731 | 651 |
| Portland, Oregon | 700 | 635 | 1324 | 1246 | 430 | 548 | 1152 | 578 | 1755 |
| Salem, Oregon | 655 | 590 | 1370 | 1292 | 475 | 593 | 1100 | 533 | 1800 |
| Houston, Texas | 2034 | 2055 | 961 | 1039 | 1937 | 2002 | 1555 | 2308 | 882 |
| Dallas, Texas | 1708 | 1728 | 724 | 801 | 1622 | 1762 | 1214 | 1967 | 645 |
| College Station, Texas | 1871 | 1891 | 875 | 952 | 1773 | 1838 | 1377 | 2118 | 796 |
| Austin, Texas | 1742 | 1762 | 876 | 976 | 1778 | 1842 | 1395 | 1913 | 720 |
| Salt Lake City, Utah | 805 | 735 | 601 | 523 | 339 | 524 | 420 | 518 | 970 |
| Provo, Utah | 846 | 777 | 548 | 492 | 382 | 566 | 376 | 556 | 563 |
| Olympia, Washington | 812 | 747 | 1430 | 1352 | 535 | 516 | 1288 | 690 | 1860 |
| Seattle, Washington | 866 | 807 | 1399 | 1321 | 501 | 475 | 1257 | 750 | 1557 |
| Spokane, Washington | 1047 | 988 | 1160 | 1082 | 426 | 197 | 1138 | 793 | 1658 |
| Laramie, Wyoming | 1193 | 1123 | 214 | 136 | 686 | 844 | 802 | 906 | 592 |

# WESTERN MILEAGE MATRIX

| | Tulsa | Portland | Salem | Houston | Dallas | College Station | Austin | Salt Lake City | Provo |
|---|---|---|---|---|---|---|---|---|---|
| Tempe, Arizona | 1095 | 1373 | 1299 | 1295 | 1062 | 1119 | 1003 | 676 | 622 |
| Phoenix, Arizona | 1171 | 1332 | 1287 | 1297 | 1065 | 1121 | 1005 | 812 | 768 |
| Sacramento, California | 1741 | 580 | 535 | 2058 | 1731 | 1926 | 1765 | 652 | 694 |
| Claremont, California | 407 | 990 | 945 | 1639 | 1425 | 1462 | 1346 | 656 | 614 |
| Los Angeles, California | 1437 | 964 | 919 | 1669 | 1435 | 1527 | 1411 | 690 | 644 |
| Malibu, California | 1474 | 981 | 936 | 1704 | 1470 | 1527 | 1411 | 730 | 686 |
| Berkeley, California | 1746 | 626 | 581 | 2048 | 1722 | 1885 | 1756 | 725 | 767 |
| San Diego, California | 1462 | 1083 | 1038 | 1792 | 1357 | 1414 | 1298 | 749 | 706 |
| Santa Barbara, California | 1526 | 953 | 907 | 1771 | 1544 | 1595 | 1479 | 778 | 734 |
| Santa Cruz, California | 1719 | 700 | 655 | 2034 | 1708 | 1871 | 1742 | 805 | 846 |
| San Francisco, California | 1737 | 635 | 590 | 2055 | 1728 | 1891 | 1762 | 735 | 777 |
| Colorado Springs, Colorado | 676 | 1324 | 1370 | 961 | 724 | 875 | 876 | 601 | 548 |
| Boulder, Colorado | 711 | 1246 | 1292 | 1039 | 801 | 952 | 976 | 523 | 492 |
| Boise, Idaho | 1511 | 430 | 475 | 1937 | 1622 | 1773 | 1778 | 339 | 382 |
| Missoula, Montana | 1576 | 548 | 593 | 2002 | 1762 | 1838 | 1842 | 524 | 566 |
| Las Vegas, Nevada | 1224 | 1152 | 1100 | 1555 | 1214 | 1377 | 1395 | 420 | 376 |
| Reno, Nevada | 1731 | 578 | 533 | 2308 | 1967 | 2118 | 1913 | 518 | 556 |
| Albuquerque, New Mexico | 651 | 1755 | 1800 | 882 | 645 | 796 | 720 | 970 | 563 |
| Tulsa, Oklahoma | – | 1938 | 1983 | 495 | 256 | 443 | 452 | 1215 | 1172 |
| Portland, Oregon | 1938 | – | 47 | 2363 | 2048 | 2199 | 2248 | 765 | 808 |
| Salem, Oregon | 1983 | 47 | – | 2408 | 2093 | 2244 | 2294 | 811 | 853 |
| Houston, Texas | 495 | 2363 | 2408 | – | 239 | 95 | 162 | 1794 | 1740 |
| Dallas, Texas | 256 | 2048 | 2093 | 239 | – | 181 | 196 | 1325 | 1204 |
| College Station, Texas | 443 | 2199 | 2244 | 95 | 181 | – | 107 | 1476 | 1355 |
| Austin, Texas | 452 | 2248 | 2294 | 162 | 196 | 107 | – | 1480 | 1277 |
| Salt Lake City, Utah | 1215 | 765 | 811 | 1794 | 1325 | 1476 | 1480 | – | 45 |
| Provo, Utah | 1172 | 808 | 853 | 1740 | 1204 | 1355 | 1277 | 45 | – |
| Olympia, Washington | 2044 | 114 | 159 | 2469 | 2154 | 2305 | 2309 | 871 | 913 |
| Seattle, Washington | 2012 | 173 | 219 | 2438 | 2162 | 2273 | 2277 | 837 | 879 |
| Spokane, Washington | 1774 | 352 | 397 | 2199 | 1960 | 2035 | 2039 | 721 | 763 |
| Laramie, Wyoming | 828 | 1112 | 1157 | 1253 | 1014 | 1068 | 1072 | 389 | 407 |

# WESTERN MILEAGE MATRIX

| | Olympia | Seattle | Spokane | Laramie |
|---|---|---|---|---|
| Tempe, Arizona | 1494 | 1572 | 1425 | 975 |
| Phoenix, Arizona | 1454 | 1513 | 1571 | 1054 |
| Sacramento, California | 692 | 752 | 933 | 1040 |
| Claremont, California | 1112 | 1171 | 1343 | 1040 |
| Los Angeles, California | 1085 | 1145 | 1317 | 1071 |
| Malibu, California | 1102 | 1153 | 1334 | 1112 |
| Berkeley, California | 738 | 797 | 978 | 1113 |
| San Diego, California | 1204 | 1264 | 1463 | 1137 |
| Santa Barbara, California | 1065 | 1124 | 1305 | 1161 |
| Santa Cruz, California | 812 | 866 | 1047 | 1193 |
| San Francisco, California | 747 | 807 | 988 | 1123 |
| Colorado Springs, Colorado | 1430 | 1399 | 1160 | 214 |
| Boulder, Colorado | 1352 | 1321 | 1082 | 136 |
| Boise, Idaho | 535 | 501 | 426 | 686 |
| Missoula, Montana | 516 | 475 | 197 | 844 |
| Las Vegas, Nevada | 1288 | 1257 | 1138 | 802 |
| Reno, Nevada | 690 | 750 | 793 | 906 |
| Albuquerque, New Mexico | 1860 | 1557 | 1658 | 592 |
| Tulsa, Oklahoma | 2044 | 2012 | 1774 | 828 |
| Portland, Oregon | 114 | 173 | 352 | 1112 |
| Salem, Oregon | 159 | 219 | 397 | 1157 |
| Houston, Texas | 2469 | 2438 | 2199 | 1253 |
| Dallas, Texas | 2154 | 2162 | 1960 | 1014 |
| College Station, Texas | 2305 | 2273 | 2035 | 1068 |
| Austin, Texas | 2309 | 2277 | 2039 | 1072 |
| Salt Lake City, Utah | 871 | 837 | 721 | 389 |
| Provo, Utah | 913 | 879 | 763 | 407 |
| Olympia, Washington | – | 61 | 321 | 1218 |
| Seattle, Washington | 61 | – | 280 | 1187 |
| Spokane, Washington | 321 | 280 | – | 1041 |
| Laramie, Wyoming | 1218 | 1187 | 1041 | – |

# WEST SAMPLE ITINERARIES

Beaches, sunshine, mountains, desert—you name it, the West has got it. Road-tripping through the West is an experience in itself; you'll get to see some of the most breathtaking and awe-inspiring landscapes in the country. It's no surprise, then, that many of the colleges you'll be visiting in this region routinely land on The Princeton Review's "Most Beautiful Campus" ranking list. Try to set aside some time to explore the natural beauty of the surrounding area during your visit. Distances between campuses can be long, so focus on having more substantive visits over quantity. Before you head out, be sure to gather maps to and from schools and hotels, driving directions, and all the phone numbers you may need. Research any local dining and shopping establishments you're interested in visiting and print out their names, addresses, and telephone numbers. Finally, be realistic: You're not going to cover all the ground you want to cover in just a few days. In general, try not to see more than two (three at most) colleges a day; too many visits in one day and your brain will start to atrophy. The itineraries listed below are just suggestions—you can and should modify them to suit your individual needs.

## IF YOU'VE GOT SEVEN DAYS:

**Starting Point:** San Diego, California

**Saturday:** Claremont-McKenna College, Harvey Mudd College, Pitzer College, Pomona College, Scripps College
Drive to Los Angeles. Stay overnight in Los Angeles.

**Sunday:** University of California—Los Angeles, Occidental College, University of Southern California, Whittier College
Stay overnight in Los Angeles.

**Monday:** California Institute of Technology, Pepperdine University, University of California—Irvine
Drive to San Francisco. Stay overnight in San Francisco.

**Tuesday:** University of San Francisco, Mills College, St. Mary's College of California
Stay overnight in San Francisco.

**Wednesday:** University of California—Berkeley, Stanford University
Drive Seattle, Washington. Stay overnight in Seattle.

**Thursday:** University of Washington, Seattle University
Stay overnight in Seattle.

**Friday:** University of Puget Sound, The Evergreen State College
Head home.

## IF YOU'VE GOT THREE DAYS:

**Starting Point:** Dallas, Texas

**Friday:** University of Dallas, Southern Methodist University, Texas Christian University, Baylor University
Drive to San Antonio, Texas. Stay overnight in San Antonio.

**Saturday:** Trinity University
Drive to Austin, Texas.

**Saturday PM:** University of Texas at Austin
Drive to College Station, Texas. Stay overnight in College Station.

**Sunday:** Texas A&M University—College Station
Drive to Houston, Texas.

**Sunday PM:** Rice University
Head home.

# WESTERN SCHOOLS

# ALBERTSON COLLEGE

2112 Cleveland Boulevard, Caldwell, ID 83605
**Telephone:** 208-459-5305 • **E-mail:** admission@albertson.edu

## STUDENTS SAY

"The wireless network is awesome! The school is very technically oriented."

## FODOR'S SAYS

Idaho's longest river, the Snake, carves a steely-blue course of nearly 1,000 miles through southern Idaho.

## ABOUT THE SCHOOL

With just under 700 undergrads, a 13:1 student/faculty ratio, and an average class size of 10–20, Albertson College makes sure every student gets individual attention. Students laud the dedication and accessibility of the faculty. Mountains and rivers for every sort of outdoors activity surround the town of Caldwell, and the state's capital, Boise, is just a half hour away.

## GETTING THERE

**BY AIR:** Boise airport is the closest, about 25 miles away. A cab, shuttle service, or rental car is the best way to get to campus. As an added perk of the small school experience: The college's alumni organization can make arrangements for new students, parents, visiting students, and those returning from breaks to be picked up at the airport. Contact the Admissions Office for more information.

**BY TRAIN:** Nampa, nine miles away, has an Amtrak station. Take a cab to the Albertson campus.

**BY BUS:** Greyhound has a station in Caldwell, and a cab is the best way to campus from there.

**BY CAR:** From Interstate I-84: Take Exit 29 (Franklin Road). Turn South off the ramp towards Caldwell. After half a mile, you'll come to a fork in the road. Bear left onto 21st Avenue. In just under one mile this road will end in front of the college. Turn left onto Cleveland Boulevard. Proceed 200 yards and turn right onto Indian Street. Follow the signs to visitor parking. The Admissions Office is located in Hendren Hall.

**LOCAL:** There is no public transit in Caldwell, so most students drive their own cars. Options for cabs include A B Taxi (208-468-3939) and Kool Kab (208-454-9982).

## WHERE TO STAY

For accommodations in Caldwell, check out: La Quinta Inn Caldwell (208-454-2222, $$), the Best Western Inn (208-454-7225, $$) and the Sundowner Motel (208-459-1585, $).

## CAMPUS AT ITS BEST!

During your visit, make time to attend some of the Program Council's events on campus: Bowling Night and Midnight Movie are popular. The Caldwell Night Rodeo is certainly worth a visit while you're in town. And the dining, arts, and entertainment options of nearby Boise are only 30 minutes away.

# ARIZONA STATE UNIVERSITY AT THE TEMPE CAMPUS

Box 870112, Tempe, AZ 85287-0112
**Telephone:** 480-965-7788 • **E-mail:** ugradinq@asu.edu
**Hours:** Monday–Friday, 8:00 A.M.–5:00 P.M.

## STUDENTS SAY

"Many students pay . . . attention to the college lifestyle and partying more so than studying, at least for the first year or two. As they get older, they take their studies more seriously and seek internships and professional development."

## FODOR'S SAYS

"Excellent hiking, golf, shopping, and dining and some of the best luxury resorts in the country make the Valley of the Sun one of the country's leading business and vacation destinations."

## ABOUT THE SCHOOL

A city inside a city, Arizona State University's Tempe campus offers students a high-quality, low-cost education as well as a rich student lifestyle. Whether they're gushing over the perpetual sunshine, the glut of hands-on research opportunities, or the widely varied options for R&R, undergrads at ASU tend to agree that life is good in Tempe.

## GETTING THERE

**BY AIR:** Phoenix Sky Harbor International Airport sees traffic from all major airlines. The airport, which is just 15 minutes from ASU's Tempe campus, is easily accessible by car, taxi, or bus.

**BY TRAIN:** Amtrak services the Sky Harbor International Airport and the Greyhound station in downtown Phoenix.

**BY BUS:** Greyhound operates the Phoenix Station, located in downtown Phoenix and within easy access of ASU's Tempe campus via car.

**BY CAR:** From Phoenix Sky Harbor International Airport: Get on the Red Mountain Freeway Loop 202 East and follow it to the exit for Scottsdale/Rural Road (Exit 7). Make a right onto Rural Road. Take Rural Road until you reach Apache Boulevard—turn right. Follow Apache until you reach College Avenue—turn left. Take the first left into the lot for metered parking. From I-10 West (Southern Arizona): Follow I-10 West to U.S. 60 East (Superstition Freeway). Turn off U.S. 60 at the Rural Road Exit. Make a left onto Rural Road and continue North until you reach Apache Boulevard. Turn left onto Apache Boulevard. Make another left onto College Avenue. Make your first left into the lot for metered parking. From I-10 East (Northern Arizona): Follow I-10 East to the Red Mountain Freeway Loop 202 East (Exit 147). Follow this to the exit for Scottsdale/Rural Road (Exit 7). Make a right onto Rural Road. At Apache Boulevard turn right. Make a left (South) onto College Avenue. Take the first left into the lot for metered parking.

**LOCAL:** Valley Metro bus routes run in and around the Tempe campus and the surrounding metro area, including ASU's West Downtown, Phoenix, and Polytechnic campuses. Students are eligible for the Unlimited Access Bus Pass for Valley Metro transit. In addition, university-operated shuttle systems provide free transportation between the ASU campuses and around the university's Tempe campus. Taxi services in Tempe include Taxi Express (480-557-7000) and City Cab (480-635-0911).

## WHERE TO STAY

The many lodgings options around ASU's Tempe campus include the Ramada Limited of Tempe (800-272-6232, $), the Best Western Inn of Tempe at ASU (800-784-2811, $$), and the Twin Palms Hotel (800-367-0835, $$$).

| SCHOOL AT A GLANCE | |
| --- | --- |
| Type of School | Public |
| Environment | City |
| In-state Tuition | $4,591 |
| Out-of-state Tuition | $15,750 |
| Enrollment | 48,303 |
| % Male/Female | 47/53 |
| Student/Faculty Ratio | 22:1 |

| FRESHMAN PROFILE | |
| --- | --- |
| Range SAT | |
| Critical Reading | 490-610 |
| Range SAT Math | 500-620 |
| Range ACT Composite | 20-26 |
| Average HS GPA | 3.3 |

| ON-CAMPUS APPOINTMENTS | |
| --- | --- |
| Info Sessions | No |
| Class Visits | Yes |

| CAMPUS TOURS | |
| --- | --- |
| Appointment | Not Required |
| Dates | Year Round |
| Times | Contact Admissions Office |
| | at 480-727-7013 |
| Average Length | 60 min |

## CAMPUS AT ITS BEST!

Described by *Art in America* magazine as "the most impressive venue for contemporary art in Arizona," the ASU Art Museum is not to be missed. Boasting a diverse collection of modernist and contemporary Latin American works, the Art Museum draws visitors from around the country. The surrounding area also offers students numerous cultural options; every spring and fall the Tempe Arts Festival showcases artists' creations in woodwork, ceramics, and photography.

# AUSTIN COLLEGE

900 North Grand Ave, Suite 6N, Sherman, TX 75090-4400
**Telephone:** 903-813-3000 • **E-mail:** admission@austincollege.edu
**Website:** www.austincollege.edu

## STUDENTS SAY

"The [school's] emphasis on international travel and the acceptance of international students leaves students with a thrilling experience they savor for the rest of their lives."

## FODOR'S SAYS

"In the northern panhandle, I-27 from Lubbock to Amarillo carries you through the buffalo grass and high, flat lands of the Llano Estacado, or Staked Plains."

## ABOUT THE SCHOOL

Austin College is a gem of a small college located an hour outside of Dallas, Texas. The premed program is especially strong, and the school encourages an informed approach to choosing a concentration via class requirements in a variety of areas and a study abroad program with many destination options. At Austin College, personal attention is the norm, and all students benefit from a mentoring program which assigns students a mentor throughout their undergraduate experience.

## GETTING THERE

**BY AIR:** Both Dallas-Fort Worth International Airport and Dallas Love Field Airport are about 70 miles away from Austin College. ATP Limousine & Sedan Service will pick up and drop off at the campus with 24 hours advance notice and a credit card deposit.

**BY TRAIN:** The closest Amtrak station is in Gainesville, Texas. Take a car or taxi to campus.

**BY BUS:** Greyhound's station is located about four and a half miles from Austin College. Take a car or taxi to campus, or call the Texoma Area Paratransit System (TAPS), which will drive you curb to curb within the city. TAPS requires one-day advance notice for all rides and charges by distance (903-893-5257).

**BY CAR:** From the East (U.S. Highway 82 or State Highway 11): Take State Highway 56 West, turn right on Grand Avenue. Austin College is 1/2 mile on the left. From the West (U.S. Highway 82): Take Exit 21 for State Highway 91 (Texoma Parkway), turn right on Texoma Parkway and proceed to the third traffic light (Grand Avenue). Turn left on Grand Avenue and continue on Grand across the overpass. Austin College is 1/2 mile on the right. From the North (U.S. Highway 75): Take Exit 63 to U.S. Highway 82. Travel East on U.S. Highway 82 and take Exit 21 for State Highway 91 (Texoma Parkway), turn right on Texoma Parkway, and proceed to third traffic light (Grand Avenue). Turn left on Grand Avenue and continue on Grand across the overpass. Austin College is 1/2 mile on the right. From the South (U.S. Highway 75): Take Exit 61 for State Highway 91 (Texoma Parkway). Turn right at the second traffic light on Grand Avenue. Continue on Grand across the overpass. Austin College is 1/2 mile on the right.

**LOCAL:** TAPS will drive you curb to curb within the city. Otherwise, taking cabs and driving your own car are the most convenient options for getting around. For cab service, call Sherman Taxi (903-892-1544) or Prime Time Limousine (903-870-3569).

## WHERE TO STAY

Only one mile from Austin College and close to downtown Sherman is the Days Inn (903-892-0433, $). The La Quinta Inn & Suites (903-870-1122, $$) is just north of downtown Sherman. The Three Sisters Victorian Inn is only two blocks from the Austin College Campus (903-868-4697, $).

## CAMPUS AT ITS BEST!

Students at Austin College tend to make their own fun on campus, as Sherman is a small, somewhat sedate city: The Greek party scene and sports events are popular entertainment options. The school also organizes tons of activities for students including movie nights, performances, and bowling nights. Head into the nearby city of Dallas for countless dining, dancing, and shopping options.

# AZUSA PACIFIC UNIVERSITY

901 East Alosta Avenue, Azusa, CA 91702
**Telephone:** 626-812-3016 • **E-mail:** admissions@apu.edu
**Website:** www.apu.edu

## STUDENTS SAY

"APU is about love—love for learning, love for God, and love for helping the world."

## FODOR'S SAYS

"When winter snow brings droves of Angelenos to the mountains for skiing, expect to pay sky-high prices for any kind of room. Most establishments require a two-night stay on weekends."

## ABOUT THE SCHOOL

Azusa Pacific University is a midsize school of 4,100 traditional undergraduates located in the San Gabriel Valley. APU has a strong Christian, evangelical tradition, and focuses on turning out successful students through commitment to its Christian worldview and partnering with the community. For the nonreligious student, its statements of belief may be stifling, but for the student in search of a top-notch education with an evangelical bent, this is the place to be.

## GETTING THERE

**BY AIR:** There are many airports within an hour's drive of APU: Ontario International Airport is the closest at 22 miles away; The Bob Hope Airport (BUR) is 33 miles away; Long Beach Airport (LGB) is 32 miles away; and Los Angeles International (LAX) is 41 miles away from campus. Shuttle vans are available from the airport and fares range from $35 to $55 one way. Try Prime Time Shuttle's shared van service (Primetimeshuttle.com, 800-RED-VANS).

**BY TRAIN:** The closest Amtrak station is located in Pomona, 10 miles away from campus. Take a taxi to campus.

**BY BUS:** Greyhound services a station in nearby El Monte. Take a taxi to campus.

**BY CAR:** From 210 Freeway: Take the 210 Freeway to the Citrus Avenue exit. Travel north on Citrus Avenue, cross Alosta Avenue, and enter the campus, turning right on University Avenue at 901 East Alosta Avenue.

**LOCAL:** Taking cabs and driving your own or a rental car are the most convenient options for getting around. For cab service in the Azusa area, call Yellow Cab: Azusa (626-301-0011), City Cab (626-815-0733), or Bell Cab Company (626-258-1310).

## WHERE TO STAY

Azusa Pacific University has special rates with many area hotels, so be sure to mention the college when reserving. Five minutes from APU's campus is the Guest House Inn (626-963-9361, $). The Covina Embassy Suites is another option, located 10 minutes from campus (626-915-3441, 800-EMBASSY, $$). In nearby Pomona, about a 15-minute drive away, is the Sheraton Suites Fairplex (909-622-2220, $$$).

## CAMPUS AT ITS BEST!

If you're visiting Azusa Pacific in March, stop by the "Night of Champions" event, a university-sponsored evening showcase for team competitions, live concerts, athletic exhibitions, and musical performances, all by prominent Christian artists and athletes. During the fall, don't miss APU's Homecoming weekend, which brings APU students, faculty, staff, alumni, family, and friends to campus for a variety of events including the annual Red Races and Homecoming football game.

# BAYLOR UNIVERSITY

One Bear Place #97056, Waco, TX 76798-7056
**Telephone:** 254-710-3435 • **E-mail:** admissions@baylor.edu
**Website:** www.baylor.edu • **Hours:** Monday–Friday, 8:00 A.M.–5:00 P.M.

## SCHOOL AT A GLANCE

| | |
|---|---|
| Type of School | Private |
| Environment | City |
| Tuition | $20,574 |
| Enrollment | 11,751 |
| % Male/Female | 42/58 |
| Student/Faculty Ratio | 16:1 |

### FRESHMAN PROFILE

| | |
|---|---|
| Range SAT | |
| Critical Reading | 540-650 |
| Range SAT Math | 550-660 |
| Range ACT Composite | 22-27 |

### ON-CAMPUS APPOINTMENTS

| | |
|---|---|
| Advance Notice | Yes, 2 weeks |
| Appointment | Preferred |
| Saturdays | Sometimes |
| Average Length | 60 min |
| Info Sessions | Yes |
| Class Visits | Yes |

### CAMPUS TOURS

| | |
|---|---|
| Appointment | Preferred |
| Dates | Year Round |
| Times | M–F 8:30 A.M., 10:30 A.M., |
| | 1:30 P.M., 3:00 P.M. |
| Average Length | 120 min |

## STUDENTS SAY

"Baylor is great for churchy folk."

## FODOR'S SAYS

"In every way, East Texas—a region once dependent on cotton—feels more Southern than Western."

## ABOUT THE SCHOOL

At the nation's largest and best-known Baptist university, students find a balanced regimen of religion and academics. And let's not forget good old-fashioned fun. Plentiful extracurricular activities, a strong Greek system, and the distractions of Waco ensure that the undergrads are happy, deep in the heart of Texas.

## GETTING THERE

**BY AIR:** Waco Regional Airport is serviced by American Airlines/American Eagle and Continental Connections for Sky West. Transportation from the airport is provided by many hotel shuttles. Taxi service is also available. For a wider airline selection, see Dallas-Fort Worth International Airport, which is a two-hour drive from campus.

**BY TRAIN:** The nearest Amtrak station is in McGregor, about 15 miles from Waco.

**BY BUS:** Greyhound maintains a Waco depot (254-753-4534).

**BY CAR:** From I-35 South: Follow I-35 to Exit 335B. Turn left onto University Parks Drive. The campus is just ahead. From I-35 North: Follow I-35 to Exit 335B. Turn right onto University Parks Drive. The campus is just ahead. From U.S 290 West: Follow U.S. 290 West until it meets TX-6. Take TX-6 going north. Merge onto TX-434 SPUR North. Next, turn onto the U.S. 77 Business South ramp. Make a right onto University Parks Drive. The campus is up ahead.

**LOCAL:** Local bus service operates regularly through Waco Transit. Waco's taxi companies include Waco Yellow Cab (254-756-1861) and Waco Streak (800-460-0430).

## WHERE TO STAY

Waco offers a range of lodging options. Among these are the Super 8 Motel (254-754-1023, $), the Best Western Old Main Lodge (254-753-0316, $$), and the Cotton Palace Bed and Breakfast (254-753-7294, $$$).

---

## CAMPUS AT ITS BEST!

Prospective Baylor students should set aside some time to explore the Mayborn Museum Complex. The diversity of exhibits in areas ranging from optics and simple machines to bubbles and Native Americans is sure to delight everyone. The university also has a number of popular cultural events. The springtime festival, Fiesta on the River, is a campus favorite and features mariachis and piñatas. You might also want to attend Baylor's Chinese New Year Celebration, complete with free food and dragon dances.

# BRIGHAM YOUNG UNIVERSITY (UT)

A-153 ASB, Provo, UT 84602-1110
**Telephone:** 801-422-2507 • **E-mail:** admissions@byu.edu
**Website:** www.byu.edu • **Hours:** Monday–Friday, 8:00 A.M.–5:00 P.M.

## STUDENTS SAY

"BYU has a good academic reputation and doesn't charge high tuition. The value of the education you can receive here is incredible."

## FODOR'S SAYS

"Dinosaurs left their remains in these mountains, and Butch Cassidy and other outlaws stashed caches of 'loot' as they fled through the canyons."

## ABOUT THE SCHOOL

Brigham Young University's flagship campus in Provo, Utah, boasts a wide range of classes, majors, and research opportunities. While enjoying the perks of a mammoth university, students at BYU also find a comfortable environment enriched by the Mormon values of the university and many of its students.

## GETTING THERE

**BY AIR:** Salt Lake City International Airport is 45 minutes north of the BYU campus. Transit options to Provo include taxi service and Utah Transit Authority bus service.

**BY TRAIN:** Amtrak maintains a station in Provo, about three miles from campus. Travel from the station to campus is available by car, cab, or bus.

**BY BUS:** Greyhound offers regular service through its Provo station. Trips to Salt Lake City run numerous times daily and take less than an hour.

**BY CAR:** From I-15 South: Follow I-15 South to Exit 272 (University Parkway). Go East on University Parkway. At University Avenue, make a right. After a block, turn left onto the campus. From I-15 North: Follow I-15 North to Exit 266 (University Avenue). Go North on University Avenue. At 1230 North (Bulldog Avenue), take a right and enter the campus ahead.

**LOCAL:** Utah Transit Authority provides local bus service. Provo taxi companies include 24/7 Affordable Cab & Limousine & Taxi Service (801-375-0000) and Yellow Cab (801-377-7070).

## WHERE TO STAY

Provo's hotels include the Best Western Cotton Tree Inn (801-373-7044, $) and Provo Marriott Hotel (801-377-4700, $$). Lodging options are available in neighboring Orem as well.

### SCHOOL AT A GLANCE

| | |
|---|---|
| Type of School | Private |
| Environment | City |
| Tuition | $3,620 |
| Enrollment | 30,798 |
| % Male/Female | 51/49 |
| Student/Faculty Ratio | 21:1 |

### FRESHMAN PROFILE

| | |
|---|---|
| Range SAT | |
| Critical Reading | 550-660 |
| Range SAT Math | 570-670 |
| Range ACT Composite | 25-29 |
| Average HS GPA | 3.73 |

### ON-CAMPUS APPOINTMENTS

| | |
|---|---|
| Advance Notice | Yes, other |
| Appointment | Preferred |
| Saturdays | No |
| Average Length | 60 min |
| Info Sessions | Yes |
| Class Visits | Yes |

### CAMPUS TOURS

| | |
|---|---|
| Appointment | Preferred |
| Dates | Year Round |
| Times | M–F, 9:00 A.M. , 10:00 A.M., |
| | 11:00 A.M.; NOON, 1:00 P.M., |
| | 2:00 P.M., 3:00 P.M., and 4:00 P.M. |
| Average Length | 60 min |

## CAMPUS AT ITS BEST!

Future anthropologists and archeologists will appreciate Brigham Young's Museum of Peoples and Cultures. Its remarkable collection spans the globe, from Navajo rugs to Polynesian basketry. Those who thrive on competition or enjoy model cars should try to tour the campus in the summer, during BYU's annual Pinewood Derby. Other popular activities include the Spring Freshmen Dance and dollar movie night at the Varsity Theatre.

# CALIFORNIA INSTITUTE OF TECHNOLOGY

1200 East California Boulevard, Mail Code 1-94, Pasadena, CA 91125
**Telephone:** 626-395-6341 • **E-mail:** ugadmissions@caltech.edu
**Hours:** Monday–Friday, 8:00 A.M.–5:00 P.M.

## STUDENTS SAY

"The classes are the hardest you'll ever take, but at the end of the day, you look around at the friends you're working on a problem set with and you realize you wouldn't change schools for the world."

## FODOR'S SAYS

"If you have time for only one stop in the Pasadena area, it should be the Huntington, built in the early 1900s as the home of railroad tycoon Henry E. Huntington. Henry and his wife Arabella voraciously collected rare books and manuscripts, botanical specimens, and eighteenth-century British art. The institution they established became one of the most extraordinary cultural complexes in the world."

## ABOUT THE SCHOOL

Students come to Caltech to work hard—and work hard they do. At this highly selective school (about 900 undergrads total), rigorous academics, heavy workloads, and sky-high expectations combine to ensure that students graduate with a degree worth its weight in gold. After graduation, students enjoy healthy rewards for their efforts.

## GETTING THERE

**BY AIR:** Los Angeles International Airport is less than half an hour away. Smaller airports are nearby as well: Bob Hope Airport (20 minutes) and Ontario International Airport (40 minutes). Take a taxi or a shuttle service from any of these airports to the Caltech campus.

**BY TRAIN:** Amtrak services Los Angeles. For the most convenient travel to campus, take a taxi from the Amtrak station.

**BY BUS:** Greyhound offers regular service to the Los Angeles area. Limited departures are available from Pasadena's Walnut Street Station.

**BY CAR:** From the I-110 (Harbor Freeway): Take the 110 Freeway North until it turns into the Arroyo Parkway. Follow the Arroyo Parkway North until it interests with California Boulevard. Turn right (East) onto California Boulevard. Go straight for a little more than a mile. The Caltech campus is visible on your left-hand side. Make a left onto Hill Avenue, another left onto San Pasqual Street, then a right onto Holliston Avenue, which will lead you to the Holliston Parking Structure (right-hand side). From I-210 (Foothill Freeway): Follow the 210 Freeway until exiting at Hill Avenue. Go South on Hill Avenue and proceed to San Pasqual Street, where you'll make a right. Turn right onto Holliston Avenue, which will lead you to the Holliston Parking Structure (right-hand side).

**LOCAL:** Foothill Transit and the MTA regional transit authority both service Pasadena and the surrounding area. The City of Pasadena also operates two free, limited service Area Rapid Transit Service (ARTS) shuttle bus lines. The Downtown ARTS bus stops on Wilson, within walking distance of campus.

## WHERE TO STAY

Pasadena's accommodations include Econo Lodge (626-792-3700, $), Best Western Pasadena Royale (626-793-0950, $$), and the Ritz Carlton, Huntington Hotel (626-568-3900, $$$+).

## CAMPUS AT ITS BEST!

Literature fiends and Elizabethan scholars might want to visit during Caltech's annual Shakespeare Read-a-thon. During this springtime event, members of the Caltech community and the general public attempt to read the Bard's entire repertoire in a mere 24 hours. For those who want to explore life off campus (although it's not likely that you'll have much downtime as a student here), check out the myriad street performers in Venice Beach or enjoy some window-shopping on Rodeo Drive during your stay.

# CALIFORNIA POLYTECHNIC STATE UNIVERSITY—SAN LUIS OBISPO

Admissions Office, Cal Poly, San Luis Obispo, CA 93407

Telephone: 805-756-2311 • E-mail: admissions@calpoly.edu • Website: www.calpoly.edu

## STUDENTS SAY

"Cal Poly is my idea of a perfect campus—the location is perfect, the weather is usually pleasant, and the living arrangements are also very good. People here are friendly and always ready with a smile."

## FODOR'S SAYS

"The San Luis Obispo Mozart Festival takes place in late July and early August. Not all the music is Mozart; you'll also hear Haydn and other composers."

## ABOUT THE SCHOOL

"Learn by doing" is the philosophy of the California Polytechnic State University—San Luis Obispo or "Cal Poly—SLO." The undergraduates at Cal Poly profit from hands-on engagement in every discipline, and enjoy a sense of community in each university department that balances the impersonality of a large school. Living in the San Luis Obispo region is the perfect antidote to over-work: The beach is less than 10 miles away and students find the school's moniker "SLO" fitting given the quiet, relaxing atmosphere of the area.

## GETTING THERE

**BY AIR:** The San Luis Obispo County regional airport (SBP) is five miles away. Take a taxi to get to campus.

**BY TRAIN:** The Amtrak station in San Luis Obispo is located at 1011 Railroad Avenue. A designated Amtrak California bus picks passengers up outside the train and takes them to the Cal Poly—SLO campus. Take SLO Regional Transit, the San Luis Obispo Regional Rideshare (Rideshare.org), or a cab to the station.

**BY BUS:** Greyhound has a depot in San Luis Obispo and also makes some stops at the Amtrak station. Take SLO Regional Transit, the San Luis Obispo Regional Rideshare (Rideshare.org), or a cab to the station.

**BY CAR:** From Los Angeles on Route 101: Travel North on Route 101 to San Luis Obispo. Go through much of San Luis Obispo and exit at the Grand Avenue/Cal Poly Exit. Turn left onto Grand Avenue and go (uphill) approximately a quarter mile to the south entrance of the campus. From San Francisco on Route 101: Travel South on Route 101 to San Luis Obispo. As you approach San Luis Obispo, exit at Monterey Street (the first exit in SLO). Make a right turn, then an immediate left turn onto the Frontage Road (you will be going the same direction you were on the Freeway). Go approximately three blocks to Grand Avenue. Turn right (going uphill) and go approximately a quarter mile to the South entrance of the campus. From Monterey via scenic Route 1: The Pacific Coast Highway: Travel South on Highway 1. As you approach San Luis Obispo, turn left at the first stop light on the edge of town—Highland Avenue—this is the Northwest entrance to the campus. Follow Highland Ave as it goes under the train trestle and into the lower parking lot area. Continue straight until you reach a stop sign. Turn right and go to the next stop sign. At the next stop sign turn left onto North Perimeter Drive and proceed until you reach the third stop sign (you will be going downhill). Turn left and proceed to the South entrance of the campus where you will find the Campus Information Center.

**LOCAL:** San Luis Obispo's SLO Regional Transit serves Cal Poly—SLO via the 6A and 6B routes. Ride-On Transportation provides transportation options for getting to airports, restaurants, and hospitals and whom to call (Ride-on.org). For an eco-friendly option, ride the San Luis Obispo Regional Rideshare, a bus initiative "dedicated to reducing the number of single occupant vehicles on San Luis Obispo's roads and highways, conserving fuel, reducing air pollution."

## WHERE TO STAY

The Days Inn—Morro Bay in San Luis Obispo is about 14 miles from the Cal Poly—SLO campus (805-772-2711, $). In downtown SLO, options include the Ramada Inn Olive Tree (805-544-2800, $$) and the Garden Street Inn (805-545-9802, $$$).

### SCHOOL AT A GLANCE

| | |
|---|---|
| Type of School | Public |
| Environment | Town |
| In-state Tuition | $0 |
| Out-of-state Tuition | $10,170 |
| Enrollment | 17,385 |
| % Male/Female | 57/43 |
| Student/Faculty Ratio | 20:1 |

### FRESHMAN PROFILE

| | |
|---|---|
| Range SAT | |
| Critical Reading | 540-630 |
| Range SAT Math | 570-670 |
| Range ACT Composite | 23-28 |
| Average HS GPA | 3.73 |

### ON-CAMPUS APPOINTMENTS

| | |
|---|---|
| Info Sessions | Yes |
| Class Visits | No |

### CAMPUS TOURS

| | |
|---|---|
| Appointment | Required |
| Dates | Year Round |
| Times | M, W, F 10:10 A.M. |
| | and 2:10 P.M. |
| Average Length | 120 min |

## CAMPUS AT ITS BEST!

The University Art Gallery on Cal Poly—SLO's campus is a must-see during your visit. The gallery hosts five exhibitions and many other events throughout the year and mixes student pieces with those of nationally and internationally known artists. The Thursday evening Farmer's Market in SLO is also very popular; it boasts fresh produce, live music, and local delicacies.

# CALIFORNIA STATE UNIVERSITY— LONG BEACH

1250 Bellflower Boulevard, Long Beach, CA 90840
**Telephone:** 562-985-5471 • **E-mail:** eslb@csulb.edu

## STUDENTS SAY

"The strange thing about CSULB is that it's a small world. You are loosely connected to everyone through three people, even though the campus population is huge."

## FODOR'S SAYS

While you're in Long Beach, check out the "Queen Mary. Very few places are able to make you feel as lost in time as this gracious passenger ship. Its teak decks, elegant parlors, and fading staterooms strongly evoke its Art Deco past."

## ABOUT THE SCHOOL

Cal State—Long Beach offers students a solid education at an affordable price. As a large university, numerous resources and opportunities are available, although high enrollment numbers can sometimes result in limited interaction with professors for less assertive students. The student body's laid-back attitude means there is little academic pressure or competition on campus. Many students take advantage of the school's location, often venturing to the beach for some sun and sand.

## GETTING THERE

**BY AIR:** Visitors can either fly into Los Angeles International Airport (LAX) or Long Beach Airport (LGB). Taxis are available to campus from both locations.

**BY TRAIN:** Amtrak stops in Long Beach. To reach campus from the station, visitors can either use local transportation or call a cab.

**BY BUS:** Visitors can take Greyhound bus service directly to Long Beach. From there, call a taxi or take public transportation to campus.

**BY CAR:** From 405 Freeway Southbound (LAX, Santa Monica, West LA): Exit at Bellflower Boulevard. Turn left from the off-ramp and then make an immediate right on Bellflower Boulevard. Continue to Beach Drive and turn left onto campus. The Visitor Information Center will be on your right side after passing the first stop sign. From the 405 Freeway Northbound/22 Freeway West/605 Freeway South (Orange County, Downtown, East LA): Exit at 7th Street and continue to Bellflower Boulevard. Turn right at Bellflower Boulevard and make another right at Beach Drive. See above for the remainder of the directions.

**LOCAL:** Long Beach offers plenty of public transportation options. The Passport Shuttle provides free transit to a variety of downtown attractions. There is also an extensive local bus system. Of course, traditional taxis are also available: Call Long Beach Yellow Cab (310-715-1968).

## WHERE TO STAY

For local hotel accommodations, consider: Coast Long Beach Hotel (562-435-7676, $$), Courtyard by Marriott (562-435-8511, $$), or the Hyatt Regency (562-491-1234, $$–$$$).

## CAMPUS AT ITS BEST!

Students in search of their own little Zen retreat often stop by the Earl Burns Miller Japanese Garden. Equipped with a koi pond and traditional teahouse, this one-and-a-half-acre oasis offers plenty of peace and solitude. Once you've recharged, you might think about attending some of Long Beach's annual events. Check out the latest style trends at the hip-hop fashion show (and concert).

# CALIFORNIA STATE UNIVERSITY— SACRAMENTO

6000 J Street, Lassen Hall, Sacramento, CA 95819-6048
**Telephone:** 916-278-3901 • **E-mail:** admissions@csus.edu
**Website:** www.csus.edu • **Hours:** Monday–Friday, 8:00 A.M.– 5:00 P.M.

### SCHOOL AT A GLANCE

| | |
|---|---|
| Type of School | Public |
| Environment | Metropolis |
| In-state Tuition | $3,072 |
| Out-of-state Tuition | $13,242 |
| Enrollment | 23,028 |
| % Male/Female | 43/57 |
| Student/Faculty Ratio | 22:1 |

### FRESHMAN PROFILE

| | |
|---|---|
| Range SAT | |
| Critical Reading | 420–540 |
| Range SAT Math | 440–550 |
| Range ACT Composite | 17–22 |
| Average HS GPA | 3.2 |

### ON-CAMPUS APPOINTMENTS

| | |
|---|---|
| Class Visits | Yes |

### CAMPUS TOURS

| | |
|---|---|
| Appointment | Required |
| Dates | Varies |
| Times | Varies |
| Average Length | 60 min |

## Students Say

"The biggest strength would have to be the beauty of our campus."

## Fodor's Says

Check out the "California State Indian Museum. Among the interesting displays at this well-organized museum is one devoted to Ishi, the last Yahi Indian to emerge from the mountains, in 1911. Ishi provided scientists with insight into the traditions and culture of this group of Native Americans."

## About the School

Professors at Sacramento garner rave reviews. Undergrads stress that their teachers express a genuine interest in their students and often make themselves accessible outside of the classroom. Although CSUS is largely a commuter school, an active Greek system allows for plenty of social interaction. For those students that are looking to get off campus, San Francisco, Tahoe, and Reno are all just over an hour away.

## Getting There

**BY AIR:** Sacramento International Airport receives flights from 13 major airlines and one commuter line. Rental cars, shuttles, taxis, and public buses are all accessible for further transportation needs.

**BY TRAIN:** Amtrak provides service directly to Sacramento. Take local transit or call a cab to get to campus.

**BY BUS:** Greyhound offers service to Sacramento. Take local transit or call a cab to get to campus.

**BY CAR:** From the East via I-80 (Auburn and Reno): Follow I-80 West into Sacramento. When the road splits, take Business 80 West (Capitol City Freeway). Continue to the J Street Exit, making a left onto J. You will follow J Street for roughly three miles through East Sacramento. This will take you to the North entrance of campus. Make a right into the North gate at the intersection of J Street and Carlson Drive. You will find an information booth on the right-hand side, where a campus directory and further assistance is available. From the South via I-5 (Stockton, Los Angeles): Proceed on I-5 North into Sacramento. Follow the signs to the Highway 50 East Exit. Continue onto Highway 50, driving East to the Howe Avenue/Power Inn Road Exit. You will want to stay to the far right as you exit and merge onto Hornet Drive. Make a left when the road becomes a dead end at College Town Drive. Continue through the second stop light at State University Drive. After you drive through the intersection you will see an information booth on your right-hand side. Further assistance will be available. From the North via I-5 (Woodland, Redding, Sacramento International Airport): Follow I-5 South into Sacramento. Follow "From the South" directions above. West via I-80 (Davis, San Francisco): Follow I-80 East, heading towards Sacramento. As the road splits between I-80 and Bus 80/Highway 50 in West Sacramento, be sure to stay on Bus 80/Highway 50. You will take this into Sacramento. After crossing the Sacramento River, I-80 becomes Highway 50. Follow "From the South" directions above.

**LOCAL:** The Sacramento Regional Transit District provides the city bus and light rail service. Bus routes 30, 31, 34, 79, 82, and 87 make stops at the Sacramento State Transit Center located at the North end of campus. Light Rail runs South to Meadowview Road, and East to Matherfield Road through downtown. Passengers can catch a bus connection to Sacramento State at the 65th Street Station.

## Where to Stay

Sacramento has a number of lodging options, including: Days Inn (916-488-4100, $), Larkspur Landing (916-646-1212, $$), and the Hilton Sacramento Arden West (916-922-4700, $$–$$$).

## CAMPUS AT ITS BEST!

Sleep, though often hard to come by in college, is a favorite pastime of many students at Sacramento State. Stop by Sacramento's sleep lab in Amador Hall to learn more about this valued commodity. The lab includes EEG equipment and a counseling center. Prospective students who are wide awake and looking for fun should attend the annual Festival of New American Music. Organized every fall by the music faculty, this event is the West Coast's largest showcase for contemporary music.

## SCHOOL AT A GLANCE

| Type of School | Private |
|---|---|
| Environment | Village |
| Tuition | $33,000 |
| Enrollment | 1,140 |
| % Male/Female | 54/46 |
| Student/Faculty Ratio | 9:1 |

### FRESHMAN PROFILE

| | |
|---|---|
| Range SAT | |
| Critical Reading | 630–740 |
| Range SAT Math | 640–740 |
| Range ACT Composite | 28–33 |

### ON-CAMPUS APPOINTMENTS

| | |
|---|---|
| Advance Notice | Yes, 2 weeks |
| Appointment | Required |
| Saturdays | Sometimes |
| Average Length | 45 min |
| Info Sessions | Yes |
| Class Visits | Yes |

### CAMPUS TOURS

| | |
|---|---|
| Appointment | Not Required |
| Dates | Year Round |
| Times | 10:00 A.M., 11:00 A.M., |
| | 2:30 P.M., 3:30 P.M. |
| Average Length | 60 min |

# CLAREMONT MCKENNA COLLEGE

890 Columbia Avenue, Claremont, CA 91711
**Telephone:** 909-621-8088 • **E-mail:** admission@claremontmckenna.edu
**Website:** www.cmc.edu • **Hours:** Monday–Friday, 8:00 A.M.–5:00 P.M.

## STUDENTS SAY

"Claremont students definitely subscribe to the 'work hard, party hard' motto. But unlike many colleges, these two mindsets are constantly in conjunction. Intellectual debates about philosophy or Supreme Court justices often happen at school parties or while sunbathing on the quad."

## FODOR'S SAYS

Check out Claremont's Rancho Santa Ana Botanical Gardens, "a living museum and research center dedicated to the conservation of more than 2,800 native-California plant species."

## ABOUT THE SCHOOL

The liberal arts specialist of the powerhouse Claremont consortium, Claremont McKenna offers students a traditional education with cutting-edge pre-professional options in fields such as law, business, and medicine. And with a campus that sits within an easy drive of Pacific beaches and downtown LA, CMC's undergrads officially have nothing to complain about.

## GETTING THERE

**BY AIR:** Ontario International Airport is only 10 miles from campus. Traffic permitting, Los Angeles International, Bob Hope Airport, and John Wayne Airport are all within an hour's drive of campus. For easiest transportation to and from any of these airports, take a taxi.

**BY TRAIN:** Amtrak services LA's Union Station. The station can be most conveniently accessed by taxi.

**BY BUS:** Greyhound runs direct service to Claremont via the Indian Hill Boulevard station. The Greyhound station in downtown Los Angeles offers extended hours and more wide-ranging destinations.

**BY CAR:** From I-10 West: Take I-10 West toward LA At the Indian Hill/Claremont Exit, make a left onto Indian Hill Boulevard. After one and a half miles, you come to 10th Street, where you turn right. When 10th Street reaches Columbia Avenue, it ends. Go right onto Columbia and keep an eye out for the Admissions Office ahead on the left. From I-10 East: Take I-10 East in the direction of San Bernardino. At the Indian Hill/Claremont Exit, make a right onto Indian Hill Boulevard. After one and a half miles, you come to 10th Street, where you turn right. When 10th Street reaches Columbia Avenue, it ends. Go right onto Columbia and keep an eye out for the Admissions Office ahead on the left. From I-210 East: Travel along I-210 East toward San Bernardino. At the Towne Avenue Exit, make a right. Stay on Towne Avenue for a mile. At Foothill Boulevard, turn left and go straight for a mile. Then go right onto Dartmouth Avenue and continue ahead for three blocks. At 10th Street, turn left. When 10th Street reaches Columbia Avenue, it ends. Go right onto Columbia and keep an eye out for the Admissions Office ahead on the left.

## WHERE TO STAY

Accommodations close to campus include AmeriSuites (909-980-2200, $$), the Claremont Inn (800-854-5733, $$), and the Doubletree Hotel (909-937-0900, $$$).

## CAMPUS AT ITS BEST!

Looking to soak up some California sun and campus vibes simultaneously? Take a moment to visit Flamson Plaza, a central hangout spot at Claremont McKenna. If you're lucky, you might even witness someone getting "ponded," a campus tradition of pushing an unsuspecting soul into the fountain. Afterwards, head over to The Marian Miner Cook Athenaeum where you can join in an afternoon tea and peruse a number of periodicals. The Ath, as it's affectionately known, also features speakers four nights a week. Previous guests have included Daniel Patrick Moynihan, Michael Ondaatje, and P.J. O'Rourke.

# COLORADO COLLEGE

14 East Cache la Poudre Street, Colorado Springs, CO 80903
**Telephone:** 719-389-6344 • **E-mail:** admission@coloradocollege.edu • **Website:** www.coloradocollege.edu
**Hours:** Monday–Friday, 8:30 A.M.–5:00 P.M.; Saturday, 10:00 A.M.–NOON

## STUDENTS SAY

"We are intense about everything, whether it be studying, mountaineering, or demonstrating."

## FODOR'S SAYS

"The Garden of Gods has picnic spots and hikes among 1,350 acres of weird, windswept re-rock formations and unusual plant life."

## ABOUT THE SCHOOL

Colorado College offers its students "a unique intellectual adventure"—and that's not simply a slogan. Undergrads at this small liberal arts college take one class at a time in three-and-a-half week blocks. And with the Colorado wilderness all around them, these students have no problem finding intense experiences inside and outside of the college gates.

## GETTING THERE

**BY AIR:** Colorado Springs Airport, 20 minutes from campus, is serviced by eight airlines. Take a cab or shuttle for the easiest transportation to campus. For a larger flight selection, try Denver International Airport, about an hour and a half from the college. Use shuttle service to and from the airport.

**BY TRAIN:** The nearest Amtrak rail service is in Denver, about 70 miles away. Amtrak offers connection service via bus to Colorado Springs.

**BY BUS:** The Colorado Springs TNM & O/Greyhound station is a little more than a mile South of campus.

**BY CAR:** From I-25: Stay on I-25 (traveling North or South) to Exit 143 for Uintah Street. Drive East until you come to Cascade Avenue, where you make a right. You are now on campus. From U.S. 24 West: Follow U.S. 24 West, continuing straight as it merges into East Platte Avenue. In Colorado Springs, make a right onto North Nevada Avenue. Half a mile later, make a left onto East Cache la Poudre Street. You are now at the edge of campus.

**LOCAL:** The Mountain Metropolitan Transit Buses (that's just Metro to the locals) services the greater Colorado Springs area. Catch the #9 bus for Colorado College. Peak Transit offers shuttle service to the Colorado Springs and Denver airports (call in advance: 719-687-3456). For taxi service, try Yellow Cab (719-634-5000).

## WHERE TO STAY

Lodging options in Colorado Springs include the Radisson North (719-598-5770, $), Antler's Hilton Hotel (719-473-5600, $$), and the five-star Broadmoor Hotel (719-634-7711, $$–$$$+). If you're looking for a bed and breakfast, try the Crescent Lily Inn (719-442-2331, $$) and the Lennox House (719-471-9265, $$); mention you're with Colorado College and receive a discount at these B&Bs.

### SCHOOL AT A GLANCE

| | |
|---|---|
| Type of School | Private |
| Environment | Metropolis |
| Tuition | $30,048 |
| Enrollment | 1,928 |
| % Male/Female | 46/54 |
| Student/Faculty Ratio | 9:1 |

### FRESHMAN PROFILE

| | |
|---|---|
| Range SAT | |
| Critical Reading | 610-710 |
| Range SAT Math | 610-690 |
| Range ACT Composite | 27-31 |

### ON-CAMPUS APPOINTMENTS

| | |
|---|---|
| Advance Notice | Yes, 2 weeks |
| Appointment | Required |
| Saturdays | Sometimes |
| Average Length | 30 min |
| Info Sessions | Yes |
| Class Visits | Yes |

### CAMPUS TOURS

| | |
|---|---|
| Appointment | Preferred |
| Dates | Year Round |
| Times | Varies |
| Average Length | 60 min |

## CAMPUS AT ITS BEST!

Colorado College's Worner Center isn't your average student union. While it does have the obligatory dining hall and bookstore, the Center also offers a wide array of arts resources. Students can work in mediums such as ceramics, batik, and stained glass. If you're able to get off campus, think about traveling 35 miles west to the Stabler Gilmore cabin. Classes and campus organizations use this cabin as a retreat destination. Finally, those visiting the school in early summer should try to get tickets to a chamber concert at the annual summer music festival.

# COLORADO SCHOOL OF MINES

Weaver Towers, 1811 Elm Street, Golden, CO 80401-1842
**Telephone:** 303-273-3220 • **E-mail:** admit@mines.edu
**Website:** www.mines.edu • **Hours:** Monday–Friday, 8:00 A.M.–5:00 P.M.

## STUDENTS SAY

"Mines is about getting a very hands-on education. . .[for] a successful career in engineering."

## FODOR'S SAYS

"The drive up Lookout Mountain to the Buffalo Bill Grave and Museum affords a sensational panoramic view of Denver."

## ABOUT THE SCHOOL

This is not your typical research university. With 2,700 undergrads and a 3:1 student/faculty ratio, CSM dishes up a small-school atmosphere with big-school research opportunities. But small does not exactly equal cozy. The undergrads in Golden, Colorado will be the first to tell you that when they stop working hard, it's because they start working harder.

## GETTING THERE

**BY AIR:** Denver International Airport is 35 miles from CSM. Golden West Commuter shuttle service is available for transit to campus (303-342-9300). Cabs also offer easy transportation.

**BY TRAIN:** Amtrak offers train service to downtown Denver. Take a taxi from the station to campus.

**BY BUS:** Denver's full service Greyhound station is about 15 miles from Golden. Use taxi service to travel between the station and campus.

**BY CAR:** From I-25 South: Follow I-25 South toward Denver. Turn off at Exit 216B onto I-76 West toward Grand Junction. After six miles, I-76 West turns into I-70 West. Take Exit 265 onto Route 58 West toward Golden/Central City. Exit at Washington Avenue and turn left. Half a mile later, turn right onto 14th Street. Then make a left onto Illinois Street. From I-25 North: Take I-25 North to Exit 194 for Route 470 West/E-470 Tollway. Move left to merge onto Route 470 West toward Grand Junction. Travel for 27 miles, then turn left onto Route 6 West/West 6th Avenue. Next, turn right onto 19th Street. Then make a left onto Illinois Street. From I-70 West: From I-70 West, take Exit 265 onto Route 58 West toward Golden/Central City. Exit at Washington Avenue and turn left. Half a mile later, turn right onto 14th Street. Then make a left onto Illinois Street. From I-70 East: Travel on I-70 East to Exit 260 for Route 470 East toward Colorado Springs/U.S. 6 West. Stay left to merge onto Route 470 East, going toward 6th Avenue. About a mile later, exit left onto U.S. 6 West/West 6th Avenue. After two miles, turn right onto 19th Street. Then make a left onto Illinois Street.

**LOCAL:** Regional Transportation District (RTD) provides bus service to CSM and all of Golden. For taxi service, try Yellow Cab (303-777-7777).

## WHERE TO STAY

Golden lodging includes the Residence Inn by Marriott (303-279-4930, $$), the Golden Hotel (303-279-0100, $$), and the Table Mountain Inn (303-277-9898, $$–$$$).

## CAMPUS AT ITS BEST!

Among CSM's unique resources is the Edgar Mine, which functions as an underground laboratory. Here students gain hands-on experience in an array of operations including mine surveying, geological mapping, and rock fragmentation and blasting practice. Tours are available and are led by both students and staff. Not surprisingly, students' interest in rocks and geology also extends to recreational activity. Many are avid climbers and the school sponsors "Wednesday Wall Nights" at a nearby gym. Another increasingly popular event is the weekly pull-up contest. Winners receive a highly coveted t-shirt and the admiration of their peers.

# DEEP SPRINGS COLLEGE

Applications Committee, HC 72 Box 45001, Dyer, NV 89010
**Telephone:** 760-872-2000 • **E-mail:** apcom@deepsprings.edu
**Website:** www.deepsprings.edu

| SCHOOL AT A GLANCE | |
| --- | --- |
| Type of School | Private |
| Environment | Rural |
| Tuition | $0 |
| Enrollment | 26 |
| % Male/Female | 100/0 |
| Student/Faculty Ratio | 4:1 |

| FRESHMAN PROFILE | |
| --- | --- |
| Range SAT | |
| Critical Reading | 750-800 |
| Range SAT Math | 700-800 |

| ON-CAMPUS APPOINTMENTS | |
| --- | --- |
| Advance Notice | Yes, other |
| Appointment | Required |
| Saturdays | Sometimes |
| Average Length | 60 min |
| Info Sessions | No |
| Class Visits | Yes |

| CAMPUS TOURS | |
| --- | --- |
| Appointment | Required |
| Dates | Varies |
| Average Length | Varies |

## Students Say

"The three pillars of a Deep Springs education—labor, academics, and self-governance—combine to produce the most intense experience you will ever have."

## Fodor's Says

"The 'Loneliest Road in America' is U.S. 50 in Nevada, which winds across the central part of the state from Lake Tahoe to Great Basin National Park."

## About the School

A highly selective, two-year college for men, Deep Springs is more than a school: It's a home, a job, and a way of life for the 26 students who attend. Students become fully immersed in the daily rigors of running their isolated ranch near the Sierra Nevadas, while simultaneously probing broad philosophical questions both in and outside of the classroom. Accepted students receive full scholarships, and at the completion of the program, they typically move on to colleges like Harvard, Yale, and Oxford.

## Getting There

**BY AIR:** McCarren International Airport in Las Vegas, Nevada, is a four-hour drive away from campus. Rent a car to get to campus.

**BY TRAIN:** Amtrak trains stop in Las Vegas. Rent a car to get to campus.

**BY BUS:** Greyhound buses service Las Vegas. Rent a car to get to campus.

**BY CAR:** Deep Springs is on Highway 168 in Inyo County, California. Its postal address is just over the state line in Dyer, Nevada. The nearest gas station is in Big Pine, and the nearest town is Bishop, California, 40 miles away. From Los Angeles (via I-405 North): Take I-405 North to I-5 North. Follow I-5 North to Route 14 North. Route 14 North will change into Route 395 North. Just North of Big Pine, take Route 168 East. From Las Vegas (via I-15 North): Take I-15 North to U.S. 95 North. Make a left onto Route 266. Take Route 266 to Route 168.

## Where to Stay

An hour and 100,000 acres away, Bishop is home to the closest hotels to campus. Some options include: The Holiday Inn Express (760-872-2423, $$), Best Western Bishop Holiday Spa Lodge (760-873-3543, $$), and Bishop Days Inn (760-872-1095, $$).

## CAMPUS AT ITS BEST!

When it comes to a unique experience in higher education, Deep Springs is second to none. The school's philosophy of labor, academics, and self-governance is deeply embedded in the campus life. Just outside the laundry room guests will find the Bonepile, a communal wardrobe often used by the student body. In fact, every year the college challenges new students to come to campus with no luggage.

# THE EVERGREEN STATE COLLEGE

2700 Evergreen Parkway Northwest, Office of Admissions, Olympia, WA 98505
**Telephone:** 360-867-6170 • **E-mail:** admissions@evergreen.edu
**Website:** www.evergreen.edu • **Hours:** Monday–Friday, 8:00 A.M.–5:00 P.M.

## STUDENTS SAY

"I love the freedom of having no required courses and the feedback with an evaluation (rather than a letter grade)."

## FODOR'S SAYS

"The Olympic Flight Museum, housed in a hangar at the Olympic Regional Airport south of town, brings to life an ever-changing collection of vintage aircraft. On the annual schedule are winter lectures, weekly tours, monthly flights, and the Gathering of Warbirds event each June."

## ABOUT THE SCHOOL

Evergreen State College is quite the alternative school with its lack of prerequisites for classes, letter grades, or even majors. Students are given written evaluations as opposed to grades, are encouraged to learn rather than memorize, and are in charge of developing their own education.

## GETTING THERE

**BY AIR:** SeaTac Airport in Seattle is the closest airport to campus. Visitors can take the Capital Aeroporter transportation (800-962-3579) and be dropped off at campus or a hotel. It takes about an hour and costs around $40.

**BY TRAIN:** Amtrak stops in nearby Lacey.

**BY BUS:** Greyhound bus line stops in Olympia.

**BY CAR:** From the North or South: Take Interstate 5 to Olympia. Get off at Exit 104 onto Highway 101. Proceed West on 101 North for three miles. Take the Evergreen State College Exit. Proceed two miles North on the Evergreen Parkway to the college. From the West: Go East on 101 North toward Olympia. Take the Aberdeen/Shelton Exit. Make a left at the stop sign onto 2nd Avenue Southwest, which becomes Mud Bay Road. Follow the road's curve to the right and go up the hill. At the hill's top, just beyond the overpass, make a left at the Evergreen State College Exit. Merge onto Evergreen Parkway. Proceed two miles north until you reach the college.

**LOCAL:** Intercity Transit, a local bus service with five major transit centers including Olympia, can get you around town easily. Local taxi service includes City Cab (360-705-8294) and DC Cab (360-786-5226). For car rental, Enterprise Rent-A-Car (360-956-3714) and Hertz Rent a Car: Olympia (360-352-0171) are popular choices.

## WHERE TO STAY

Some of the most popular lodging choices near campus include the Days Inn (360-493-1991, $), Holiday Inn Express (360-412-1200, $$), and AmeriTel Inn (360-459-8866, $$$).

## CAMPUS AT ITS BEST!

Visitors with a passion for the finer arts will definitely want to stop in Lab II, Evergreen's arts and sciences building. Despite the lackluster name, the facility features a glassblowing shop and printmaking studio. Afterwards, follow the half-mile path down to the organic farm where students learn about sustainable agriculture and can even acquire a plot of land where they grow their own produce. Be sure to inquire as to whether the farm is sponsoring anything that day, as it often hosts potlucks and cultural events.

# GONZAGA UNIVERSITY

502 East Boone Avenue, Spokane, WA 99258
**Telephone:** 509-323-6572 • **E-mail:** admissions@gonzaga.edu
**Website:** www.gonzaga.edu

## STUDENTS SAY

"The greatest strength GU has is the students. The general guideline most students live by is study hard, play hard."

## FODOR'S SAYS

"Among the large cats living near campus, at the Cat Tales Zoological Park are lions, tigers, ligers (a combination of lions and tigers), leopards, puma, and lynx. Guided tours give background on the animals, and there's also a petting zoo."

## ABOUT THE SCHOOL

Gonzaga University is a Jesuit university with a high regard for academic ethics and particularly strong programs in business, science, and history. The small university has seen a rise in its enrollment and school spirit due to the success of its basketball team.

## GETTING THERE

**BY AIR:** Most visitors will fly into the Spokane International Airport. The best way to get to Gonzaga University from the airport is to take a taxi.

**BY TRAIN:** Amtrak trains stop in Spokane, and from there you can take a taxi to campus.

**BY BUS:** Greyhound buses service Spokane.

**BY CAR:** From I-90 Westbound: take Exit 281 (Newport-Colville/Highway 395 North/Division Street Exit). Turn right after the ramp and take this road until you reach Sharp Avenue. Make a right on Sharp Avenue. Turn right on Addison Street and you will see the college shortly. From I-90 Eastbound: take Exit 281 (Division Street/Newport-Colville/Highway 395 North Exit). Turn left after the ramp and take this road until you reach Sharp Avenue. Follow directions above.

**LOCAL:** Spokane Transit Authority (STA) provides bus service throughout the area surrounding the university. If you'd rather take a taxi or rent a car, some local companies include Transx (509-536-1666), Spokane Cab (509-568-8000), Yellow Cab (509-535-6151), Avis (800-331-1212), and Budget (800-527-0700).

## WHERE TO STAY

If you're planning on spending the night, some popular nearby hotels include Spokane Downtown Travelodge (509-623-9727, $), Courtyard By Marriott (509-456-7600, $$), and Red Lion River Inn (509-326-5577, $$).

| SCHOOL AT A GLANCE | |
| --- | --- |
| Type of School | Private |
| Environment | City |
| Tuition | $24,590 |
| Enrollment | 4,060 |
| % Male/Female | 46/54 |
| Student/Faculty Ratio | 12:1 |

| FRESHMAN PROFILE | |
| --- | --- |
| Range SAT | |
| Critical Reading | 540-640 |
| Range SAT Math | 550-650 |
| Range ACT Composite | 24-29 |
| Average HS GPA | 3.63 |

| ON-CAMPUS APPOINTMENTS | |
| --- | --- |
| Advance Notice | Yes, 2 weeks |
| Appointment | Required |
| Saturdays | Sometimes |
| Average Length | 30 min |
| Info Sessions | Yes |
| Class Visits | Yes |

| CAMPUS TOURS | |
| --- | --- |
| Appointment | Preferred |
| Dates | Year Round |
| Times | Varies |
| Average Length | Varies |

## CAMPUS AT ITS BEST!

Music enthusiasts and Bing Crosby fanatics should make a point of visiting the Crosbyana Room in Gonzaga's student center. This mini-museum has over 200 artifacts on display from their famous singing alumnus. Off campus, Lake Coeur d'Alene is a frequent student destination, offering alluring beaches and boat cruises. Those who visit the school in May might be able to partake in the annual Spokane Lilac Festival, a perennial favorite that celebrates local spirit.

# HARVEY MUDD COLLEGE

301 Platt Boulevard, Claremont, CA 91711-5990
**Telephone:** 909-621-8011 • **E-mail:** admission@hmc.edu
**Hours:** Monday–Friday and Saturday, 8:00 A.M.–5:00 P.M. and 9:00 A.M.–NOON

## STUDENTS SAY

"People in general are overloaded with work, but because of that we seek out positive ways to unwind. There's a really strong sense of camaraderie in that we're all in this together, so this is an extremely trusting and friendly environment."

## FODOR'S SAYS

"Today, Claremont Village harks back to the 1950s with its main streets and hot-rod shows. The downtown district is a beautiful place to visit with citrus- and oak-lined streets and Victorian, Craftsman, and Colonial buildings."

## ABOUT THE SCHOOL

If we think of the five Claremont schools as siblings, Harvey Mudd is the precocious older brother with a hankering for math, engineering, technology—anything, basically, under the umbrella of science. Known worldwide for the strength of its students and professors, Harvey Mudd is the setting for extreme academic rigor and high intellectual reward.

## GETTING THERE

**BY AIR:** Ontario International Airport is about 10 miles from campus, offering the easiest commute to Harvey Mudd. In good traffic, Los Angles International, Bob Hope Airport, and John Wayne Airport are all within an hour's drive of the campus. Take a shuttle or taxi from any airport to the campus.

**BY TRAIN:** Amtrak services LA's Union Station. Take a taxi from the station to the campus.

**BY BUS:** Greyhound's direct service to Claremont arrives at the Indian Hill Boulevard station. The Greyhound station in downtown L.A. has extended hours and wider service.

**BY CAR:** From I-10 East: Follow I-10 East (San Bernardino Freeway) to Exit 47 for Indian Hill Boulevard. Travel North, and make a right at Foothill Boulevard. After half a mile, turn right onto Dartmouth Avenue. Then turn left onto Platt Blvd. From I-10 West: Follow I-10 West (San Bernardino Freeway) to Exit 47 for Indian Hill Boulevard. Travel North, and make a right at Foothill Boulevard. After half a mile, turn right onto Dartmouth Avenue. Then turn left onto Platt Blvd. From I-210 East: Follow I-210 East toward San Bernardino. Make a right at the exit for Towne Avenue. Then turn left at Foothill Boulevard. Drive about two miles before turning right onto Dartmouth Avenue. At Platt Blvd., make a left.

**LOCAL:** MetroLink (commuter rail) offers service to Claremont via the Red Line. Super Shuttle provides easy transportation from local airports to campus (800-258-3826; make reservations in advance). For taxi service, try Yellow Cab (909-622-1313).

## WHERE TO STAY

Nearby lodging options include AmeriSuites (909-980-2200, $$), Howard Johnson Express Inn (909-626-2431, $–$$), and the Doubletree Hotel (909-626-2411, $$$).

---

## CAMPUS AT ITS BEST!

When there's a spare moment between classes, Harvey Mudd students often retreat to breathtaking Hixon Court. The Venus Fountain, the courtyard's centerpiece, will have you feeling as though you're sitting in an Italian palazzo. For a glimpse into Mudd academics, attend Presentation Days. This annual spring event celebrates students' achievements and scholarly endeavors. Finally, no visit to the college would be complete without watching the Gonzo Unicycle Madness's annual Foster's Run. Every April, on the weekend of daylight savings time, the members of Harvey Mudd's unicycle club ride down to Donut Man, covering an impressive 8.7 miles.

# IDAHO STATE UNIVERSITY

Admissions Office, Campus Box 8270, Pocatello, ID 83209-8270
**Telephone:** 208-282-2475 • **E-mail:** info@isu.edu
**Website:** www.isu.edu • **Hours:** Monday–Friday, 8:00 A.M.–5:00 P.M.; Tuesday 8:00 A.M.–7:00 P.M.

## STUDENTS SAY

"The school's administration is pretty good at attending to the students' needs."

## FODOR'S SAYS

"With 40 percent of its acreage in trees, Idaho is the most heavily forested of the Rocky Mountain States."

## ABOUT THE SCHOOL

Tucked away in the mountains of southeastern Idaho, ISU offers undergraduates a solid education. Nationally recognized programs include business, pharmacy, education, and engineering. The university also maintains some unbelievable resources such as the ISU Business and Research Park and the Idaho Museum of Natural History. Additionally, the surrounding area supplies many opportunities for outdoor recreation, including hiking and skiing.

## GETTING THERE

**BY AIR:** Visitors may opt to fly into Pocatello Regional Airport. Skywest Airlines provides connecting flights to Salt Lake City. Furthermore, Big Sky Air will connect passengers to Northwest, Alaska Air, and America West via Boise.

**BY TRAIN:** Amtrak does not offer service within 150 miles of Pocatello.

**BY BUS:** Greyhound offers service to Pocatello. Take a cab to get to campus

**BY CAR:** From American Falls West: Drive east on I-86 until you get to Pocatello. Take the I-15 South Exit (number 63A) towards Salt Lake. Take the Clark Street/Idaho State University Exit (number 69). From Idaho Falls: Drive South on I-15 until you get to Pocatello. Continue on I-15 to the Clark Street/Idaho State University Exit (number 69). From Utah: Drive North on I-15 until you get to Pocatello. Continue on I-15 to the Clark Street/Idaho State University Exit (number 69).

**LOCAL:** Pocatello Urban Transit offers bus service throughout the area.

## WHERE TO STAY

For overnight accommodations, consider: Ramada Inn (208-237-0020, $), Super 8 Motel (208-234-0888, $), or the Holiday Inn (208-237-1400, $–$$).

### SCHOOL AT A GLANCE

| | |
|---|---|
| Type of School | Public |
| Environment | Town |
| In-state Tuition | $0 |
| Out-of-state Tuition | $7,700 |
| Enrollment | 10,376 |
| % Male/Female | 44/56 |
| Student/Faculty Ratio | 14:1 |

### FRESHMAN PROFILE

| | |
|---|---|
| Range SAT | |
| Critical Reading | 440-570 |
| Range SAT Math | 470-610 |
| Range ACT Composite | 18-24 |
| Average HS GPA | 3.3 |

### ON-CAMPUS APPOINTMENTS

| | |
|---|---|
| Advance Notice | Yes, 2 weeks |
| Appointment | Preferred |
| Saturdays | No |
| Average Length | 60 min |
| Info Sessions | Yes |
| Class Visits | Yes |

### CAMPUS TOURS

| | |
|---|---|
| Appointment | Preferred |
| Dates | Varies |
| Times | M–F by appt. |
| Average Length | 120 min |

---

## CAMPUS AT ITS BEST!

The student activities calendar at ISU is always chock-full of fantastic events. Even the busiest undergrads clamor to attend activities like bonfires, fishing workshops, and Guitars Unplugged. If you're growing weary of college tours, think about getting off campus for awhile and visit the Lava Hot Springs, just south of Pocatello. The 110-degree natural springs are guaranteed to soothe your body and mind.

# LEWIS & CLARK COLLEGE

0615 Southwest Palatine Hill Road, Portland, OR 97219-7899
**Telephone:** 503-768-7040 • **E-mail:** admissions@lclark.edu • **Website:** www.lclark.edu
**Hours:** Monday–Friday, 8:30 A.M.–5:00 P.M.; Saturday, 10:00 A.M.–NOON, by appointment

## Students Say

"People here are very accepting . . . they'll ask you your story and ask questions to make sure they understand. Discussion is common."

## Fodor's Says

"The main mast of the battleship Oregon, which served in three wars, stands at the foot of Oak Street. The exterior of the Oregon Maritime Center and Museum incorporates fine street-level examples of cast-iron architecture. Inside are models of ships that once plied the Columbia River."

## About the School

Lewis & Clark College offers students a well-rounded package. Great professors, a beautiful campus, and limitless opportunities create a great learning environment for students. Committed to academics, the outdoors, and improving the world through education, the college boasts especially strong programs in psychology, biology, premedical sciences, and international affairs.

## Getting There

**BY AIR:** Portland International Airport is near the campus and services all the major airlines. The Raja Tour and Airporter (503-524-4386) offers shuttle service to campus for about $25.

**BY TRAIN:** Amtrak makes a stop at Union Station in Portland. Take a car or local transit to the campus.

**BY BUS:** Greyhound stops in downtown Portland. Take a car or local transit to the campus.

**BY CAR:** From the North: Take I-5 South and make a right onto Terwilliger Boulevard (297). Continue on Terwilliger for 1.6 miles until you get to a roundabout. Make the third right off the roundabout. The main campus will be ahead on your left. From the South: Take I-5 North, get off at Terwilliger Boulevard (297), and stay to the right. At the stoplight, make a right onto Terwilliger Boulevard. From there, proceed according to "From the North" directions above.

**LOCAL:** Visitors can hop a ride to the campus with the Pioneer Express Shuttle, a free service operated by the college. Catch it downtown at the South West Broadway and South West Morrison Street (Pioneer Courthouse Square) stop. TriMet, the Portland area's public transportation system, also offers bus, light rail, and streetcar services. It travels from the airport to downtown and can be used to reach the college's free shuttle. Those wanting to take a taxi to get around town can call Broadway Cab (503-227-1234) or Radio Cab (503-227-1212).

## Where to Stay

If you're looking for someplace to spend the night, some popular options near campus include Days Inn City Center (503-221-1611, $), Lakeshore Inn (503-636-9679, $$), and the Four Points by Sheraton Portland Downtown (503-221-0711, $$).

## CAMPUS AT ITS BEST!

There's no dearth of serene, beautiful natural scenery on Lewis and Clark's campus. To fully appreciate the surroundings, make sure to visit the Estate Gardens. This spectacular structure includes four terraces, a reflecting pool, and a breathtaking view of Mt. Hood. Hometown Portland also provides countless opportunities for excitement and distraction. It houses numerous quirky attractions like Velveteria, a museum whose entire collection consists of velvet paintings

# LOYOLA MARYMOUNT UNIVERSITY

One LMU Drive, Suite 100, Los Angeles, CA 90045
**Telephone:** 310-338-2750 • **E-mail:** admissions@lmu.edu
**Website:** www.lmu.edu

## STUDENTS SAY

"LMU is about growing intellectually and spiritually in a community that truly cares about one another and about the world."

## FODOR'S SAYS

"Topping this art-loving city's museum list are the Getty Center; the Los Angeles County Museum of Art in the mid-Wilshire district; the two sites of the Museum of Contemporary Art; the Huntington Library, Art Collections, and Botanical Gardens in San Marino; and the Norton Simon Museum in Pasadena."

## ABOUT THE SCHOOL

As a Jesuit institution, Loyola Marymount's philosophy is geared toward educating the whole person. Undergrads complete a thorough core curriculum and graduate as well-rounded scholars. Social justice is also heavily promoted, and roughly 90 percent of the student body participates in community service. Students rave about LMU's locale and take advantage of the beaches and entertainment that hometown Los Angeles has to offer.

## GETTING THERE

**BY AIR:** Los Angeles International Airport is a mere four miles from LMU's campus. There are numerous options for additional transportation, including taxis, rental cars, and public transportation.

**BY TRAIN:** Amtrak offers service to Los Angeles's Union Station as well as multiple other points throughout the county. Take a taxi or public transportation to get to the campus.

**BY BUS:** Greyhound makes multiple stops within the LA area. Take a taxis or public transportation from the terminal to the campus.

**BY CAR:** From the 105 Freeway: Follow I-105 West to the Sepulveda Boulevard North/Airport Exit. It is best to stay to your left as you exit onto Sepulveda. Drive North on Sepulveda, through the tunnel, past the airport, bearing left onto Lincoln. Remain on Lincoln for approximately two miles. Cross Manchester and pass through a small commercial strip. Following the traffic light at West 83rd Street, drive down the hill toward Marina del Rey. You will find Loyola's Lincoln entrance on your right. There is a fountain right at the entrance.

**LOCAL:** The Los Angeles Metro (1-800-COMMUTE) maintains 200 bus lines and 4 rail lines, making almost any destination in LA county accessible. For local taxi service call City Cab (323-666-1200) or United Independent Taxi (213-385-2227).

## WHERE TO STAY

For accommodations that are within five miles of Loyola Marymount, try the Hilton Garden Inn (310-726-0100, $$), Embassy Suites (310-215-1000, $$–$$$), or the Courtyard Marriott (310-822-8555, $$–$$$).

## CAMPUS AT ITS BEST!

Every November LMU sponsors a special Open House and Preview Day. This program allows prospective students to meet with undergrads and professors as well as tour both the campus and residence halls. You should sign up on LMU's mailing list to receive updated information regarding this event. The surrounding L.A. area is also bursting with cultural attractions. Home to more than 800 museums and galleries, consider visiting the Getty Museum or getting tickets to the Los Angeles Philharmonic.

# MILLS COLLEGE

5000 MacArthur Boulevard, Oakland, CA 94613
**Telephone:** 510-430-2135 • **E-mail:** admission@mills.edu
**Website:** www.mills.edu • **Hours:** Monday–Friday, 8:30 A.M.–5:00 P.M.

## STUDENTS SAY

"Living and studying with women who are committed to developing their voice and using it to impact the world in positive ways is an amazing opportunity."

## FODOR'S SAYS

"In addition to bus and van tours of [nearby] San Francisco, most tour companies run excursions to various Bay Area and Northern California destinations."

## ABOUT THE SCHOOL

The life of the liberal arts student is pretty good at Mills College. Small classroom numbers and devoted professors provide this all-female student population with a safe space to exchange opinions, test ideas, and enhance creativity. With the Bay Area at their fingertips, Mills students enjoy life off campus as well.

## GETTING THERE

**BY AIR:** Oakland International Airport is less than half hour away. Take a cab to get to the campus.

**BY TRAIN:** Amtrak's Capitol Corridor, Coast Starlight, and San Joaquin lines service Oakland's central station on Second Street. The station is about four miles away from the campus. It's best to take a taxi to Mills.

**BY BUS:** Greyhound arrives in Oakland at its San Pablo Avenue terminal, less than two miles from campus. Take a taxi to Mills.

**BY CAR:** From I-80 East: Follow I-80 East across the Bay Bridge. After the bridge, merge onto I-580 East (also called the MacArthur Freeway). Once you are just past the High Street Exit, turn onto the MacArthur Boulevard Exit. Go right off the ramp. Then, at the first light, turn left to enter campus. From I-80 West: Follow I-80 West to I-580 East (also called the MacArthur Freeway). Once you are just past the High Street Exit, turn onto the MacArthur Boulevard Exit. Go right, off the ramp. Then, at the first light, turn left to enter campus. From I-580 West: Follow I-580 West to the exit for MacArthur Boulevard/High Street. At the stop sign, make a left. After passing below the underpass, make a left at the light. At the next light, you'll see Mills to the left. From I-880 (Nimitz Freeway) North: Follow I-880 North into Oakland, where you turn off at the High Street Exit (a few exits after passing the turnoff for the Oakland International Airport). Make a right onto High Street. Three miles later, make another right onto MacArthur Boulevard. After passing below the underpass, bear right. Look for Mills on the left-hand side of the road.

**LOCAL:** Local bus service stops at the campus gates. For taxis, try Veterans Cab (510-533-1900) or Yellow Cab (510-251-0222).

## WHERE TO STAY

Nearby lodging include the San Leandro Marina Inn (510-895-1311, $$), The Washington Inn (510-452-1776, $$), and Executive Inn and Suites (510-536-6633, $$–$$$).

---

## CAMPUS AT ITS BEST!

In addition to its immense beauty, the Mills campus provides many incredible resources for its students. The Mills College Art Museum boasts more than 8,000 pieces—including works by Cezanne, Degas, Manet, and Renoir—making it the largest permanent collection of any liberal arts college on the West Coast. And the College's close proximity to San Francisco, Berkeley, and the entire Bay Area ensures that there is always plenty to do and see off campus as well.

# NEW MEXICO INSTITUTE OF MINING & TECHNOLOGY

Campus Station, 801 Leroy Place, Socorro, NM 87801
**Telephone:** 505-835-5424 • **E-mail:** admission@admin.nmt.edu
**Website:** www.nmt.edu

## STUDENTS SAY

"Tech is very difficult, meaning that you are going to learn the material and be an expert by the time you graduate. Everyone at Tech has to work hard, so distractions are few."

## FODOR'S SAYS

"No trip to northern New Mexico is complete without the 100-mile trip along the Enchanted Circle, a breathtaking panorama of deep canyons, passes, alpine valleys, and towering mountains of the verdant Carson National Forest."

## ABOUT THE SCHOOL

As evidenced by its not-so-subtle name, New Mexico Tech is primarily focused on geological science, engineering, and computers. Classes are demanding, forcing students to develop a strong work ethic. Fortunately, the tremendous workload is tempered by affable professors and regular help sessions. While Tech's rural location offers little excitement, students often partake in outdoor activities such as mountain biking and rock climbing.

## GETTING THERE

**BY AIR:** Guests should fly into Albuquerque International Sunport, roughly 72 miles from New Mexico Tech. It is serviced by most major airlines and car rentals are available.

**BY TRAIN:** Amtrak does have a station in Socorro. Take a taxi to get to campus.

**BY BUS:** Visitors who wish to travel via bus may take Greyhound to either Albuquerque or El Paso. Local commercial bus service to Socorro is available from either of those cities.

**BY CAR:** From I-25: Take Exit 150. As you leave the exit ramp, drive south on California Street (Socorro's main street). Make a right onto Bullock Avenue. You will now be driving west toward "M" Mountain. Continue through the first stop sign. When you reach the second stop sign, take a left. Tech will be on your right, at the corner of Bullock and Leroy.

**LOCAL:** Need a taxi? Try calling Socorro Taxi at 505-835-4276.

## WHERE TO STAY

For affordable accommodations in Socorro, try: Days Inn (505-835-0230, $), Econo Lodge (505-835-1500, $), or the San Miguel Motel (505-835-0211, $).

## CAMPUS AT ITS BEST!

Housing is a key component to college life, regardless of what school you choose to attend. Consider visiting the Ben D. Altamirano Student Apartments to gauge residential options at Tech. This cushy complex is replete with study lounges, landscaped courtyards, and 24-hour security. Afterwards, purchase tickets to one of the shows in PAS, the Performing Arts Series. This program nets renowned acts like Arlo Guthrie and the Shangri-La Chinese Acrobats.

# OCCIDENTAL COLLEGE *Pasadena*

1600 Campus Road, Office of Admission, Los Angeles, CA 90041
**Telephone:** 323-259-2700 • **E-mail:** admission@oxy.edu • **Website:** www.oxy.edu
**Hours:** Monday–Friday, 8:00 A.M.–5:00 P.M.; Saturday, 9:00 A.M.–NOON

## SCHOOL AT A GLANCE

| | |
|---|---|
| Type of School | Private |
| Environment | Metropolis |
| Tuition | $32,800 |
| Enrollment | 1,825 |
| % Male/Female | 44/56 |
| Student/Faculty Ratio | 10:1 |

### FRESHMAN PROFILE

| | |
|---|---|
| Range SAT | |
| Critical Reading | 600-690 |
| Range SAT Math | 610-690 |

### ON-CAMPUS APPOINTMENTS

| | |
|---|---|
| Advance Notice | Yes, 2 weeks |
| Appointment | Required |
| Saturdays | Sometimes |
| Average Length | 45 min |
| Info Sessions | Yes |
| Class Visits | Yes |

### CAMPUS TOURS

| | |
|---|---|
| Appointment | Not Required |
| Dates | Varies |
| Times | Contact Admissions Office |
| Average Length | 60 min |

## STUDENTS SAY

"Occidental has a 'rising star' quality to it. Pomona and Claremont McKenna are the heavyweight liberal arts colleges on the West Coast, and Oxy often finds itself in their shadows. Nonetheless, the tide is changing and Oxy is stepping up its game. This constant striving to become something better embodies the ethos of Oxy."

## FODOR'S SAYS

"The Norton Simon Museum is one of the finest small museums anywhere, with an excellent collection that spans more than 2,000 years of Western and Asian art. . . . It is richest in works by Rembrandt, Goya, Picasso, and, most of all, Degas: This is one of the only two U.S. institutions to hold the complete set of the artist's model bronzes."

## ABOUT THE SCHOOL

While often in the shadows of its West Coast peers, Occidental provides a remarkable education. The college attracts intelligent, motivated students and retains a faculty deeply committed to teaching. Undergrads are a hardworking, left-leaning lot, though there is little competition and even less room for cliques. Students frequently take advantage of the surrounding area, often venturing into Hollywood, Pasadena, and Glendale.

## GETTING THERE

**BY AIR:** Visitors can fly into either Los Angeles International or Burbank Airports. Taxis, shuttles, and rental cars are all available for any other transportation needs.

**BY TRAIN:** Amtrak offers service to Los Angeles' Union Station as well as multiple other points throughout the county. Taxis and public transportation may take you to your final destination.

**BY BUS:** Greyhound makes multiple stops within the LA area. Taxis and public transit are available for transportation from the terminal.

**BY CAR:** From Downtown Los Angeles: Follow the Golden State Freeway (I-5) North towards Bakersfield. Remain on the Golden State Freeway (I-5) North until you hit the Glendale Freeway (I-2). From the Glendale Freeway (I-2) North, you will take the Verdugo Road Exit. Make a left at the end of the off-ramp onto Eagle Rock Boulevard. Drive straight through five stoplights to Westdale Avenue. Make a right at Westdale Avenue. You will follow the street until it ends at Campus Road. Take a left at Campus Road and follow the signs to Visitor Parking. From Northern California: Follow U.S. I 101 South or the Golden State Freeway (I-5) South to the Ventura Freeway (I-134) East. Continue to the Ventura Freeway East (I-134) through Glendale, taking the Harvey Drive Exit. Make a right at the end of the off-ramp followed by a left (at the light) onto Broadway. Broadway will merge into Colorado Boulevard. Proceed on Colorado Boulevard to Eagle Rock Boulevard. Take a right onto Eagle Rock Boulevard and drive through four traffic lights to Westdale Avenue. Make a left at Westdale Avenue. You will follow Westdale until it ends at Campus Road. Turn left onto Campus and follow the signs to Visitors' Parking.

**LOCAL:** The Los Angeles Metro maintains 200 bus lines and four rail lines, making almost any destination in LA County accessible.

## WHERE TO STAY

These hotels all offer Occidental guests a special rate: Best Western Eagle Rock Inn (323-256-7711, $–$$), Courtyard by Marriott—Los Angeles/Old Pasadena (626-403-7600, $$), or the Sheraton Inn—Pasadena (626-449-4000, $$).

---

## CAMPUS AT ITS BEST!

Thorne Hall, located just off the quad, is Occidental's largest auditorium. As a student, you are likely to attend frequent events here, such as convocation and performances by the renowned Occidental Glee Club. Additionally, Thorne often hosts the Music Circle's Indian music concerts (which were once graced by George Harrison). Visitors might also want to investigate Occidental's First Tuesday speaker series. This program promotes thought-provoking presentations and has included, in the past, guests such as Anne Lamott, Jane Goodall, and Michael Lerner.

# OKLAHOMA STATE UNIVERSITY

324 Student Union, Stillwater, OK 74078
**Telephone:** 800-233-5019 • **E-mail:** admit@okstate.edu

| SCHOOL AT A GLANCE | |
| --- | --- |
| Type of School | Public |
| Environment | Town |
| In-state Tuition | $3,263 |
| Out-of-state Tuition | $11,835 |
| Enrollment | 18,773 |
| % Male/Female | 52/48 |
| Student/Faculty Ratio | 19:1 |

| FRESHMAN PROFILE | |
| --- | --- |
| Range SAT | |
| Critical Reading | 500-610 |
| Range SAT Math | 510-620 |
| Range ACT Composite | 22-27 |
| Average HS GPA | 3.53 |

| ON-CAMPUS APPOINTMENTS | |
| --- | --- |
| Class Visits | Yes |

| CAMPUS TOURS | |
| --- | --- |
| Appointment | Required |
| Dates | Year Round |
| Times | 10:00 A.M. and 1:00 P.M. |
| Average Length | 60 min |

## STUDENTS SAY

"Oklahoma State is all about academic, athletic, and personal excellence."

## FODOR'S SAYS

"More than half of Oklahoma's state parks can be found in northeastern Oklahoma, where the western boundaries of the Ozark and Ouachita mountains lie. Beautiful, unspoiled scenery is kept a vibrant green by the many lakes, rivers, and creeks."

## ABOUT THE SCHOOL

OSU, the state's flagship land-grant institution, provides a world-class education ripe with opportunity and challenges. Undergrads are taught by leading scientists, artists, and intellectuals who craft the scholars of tomorrow. Impressively, the university offers a unique undergraduate research scholarship that allows students to develop their own projects in university labs. Furthermore, recent renovations to residence halls ensure comfortable housing with modern amenities.

## GETTING THERE

**BY AIR:** Stillwater Regional Airport is closest to OSU. Guests may also fly into the Will Rogers World Airport in Oklahoma City, a little more than an hour from campus.

**BY TRAIN:** Amtrak does not provide service to Stillwater. The closest station is located in Guthrie, approximately 26 miles away. Take a taxi to get to the campus.

**BY BUS:** Unfortunately, Greyhound does not offer service to Stillwater. Visitors may take the bus to either Oklahoma City or Tulsa. It is recommended you rent a car from either location.

**BY CAR:** From Oklahoma City (Will Rogers Airport): Make a left onto Terminal Drive. Follow the ramp toward I-44/downtown. Get onto Airport Road and then merge onto I-44 East/OK-3 West/OK-74 North via the exit on the left (you should be heading toward Tulsa/downtown). Follow the I-44 East Exit toward I-35/Tulsa/Wichita. Continue onto OK-66 East and proceed to I-35 North. Take the OK-51 Exit 174 heading toward Stillwater/Hennessey. Take OK-51 East in the direction of Stillwater/Oklahoma State. Make a left onto South Western Road. South Western becomes West Hall of Fame Avenue. This will be a half mile from campus. From Tulsa: Proceed Northeast on SR-266 East. Take the U.S. 169 South ramp, driving onto U.S. 169 South. Follow the I-244 West/U.S. 412 West Exit toward Tulsa. Continue onto I-244 West, and take the U.S. 412 West/U.S. 64 West/OK-51 West Exit. You will then merge onto U.S. 412 Toll West. Take the exit toward OSU/Stillwater. Proceed onto Cimarron Turnpike Toll. Take the second exit (U.S. 177 South), and continue onto U.S. 177. Drive straight onto North Washington Street and it becomes Boomer Drive, which becomes South Main Street. Make a right onto Hall of Fame Avenue, and stay on it for half a mile until you reach the campus.

**LOCAL:** For local taxi service guests may call Roy's Taxi (405-743-1700) or Anytime Taxi (405-743-8131).

## WHERE TO STAY

Hotels in the area include Motel 6 (405-624-0433, $), Dancing Deer Lodge Bed and Breakfast (405-743-8743, $–$$), and the Atherton Hotel (405-744-6835, $–$$).

## CAMPUS AT ITS BEST!

Oklahoma State's Gardiner Gallery is an important resource for art students and a fantastic setting for visitors to appreciate the visual arts. Exhibits vary widely, from student and faculty shows to Japanese and German prints—even a sand painting created by Tibetan monks. The permanent collection includes work by such luminaries as Jasper Johns, Alexander Calder, and Salvador Dalí. Those who are curious about OSU traditions should attend the Orange Peel. Sponsoring the largest student-produced concert in the country, the group has netted performers like the Barenaked Ladies, Faith Hill, Bill Cosby, and Jeff Foxworthy.

# OREGON STATE UNIVERSITY

104 Kerr Administration Building, Corvallis, OR 97331-2106
**Telephone:** 541-737-4411 • **E-mail:** osuadmit@oregonstate.edu
**Website:** oregonstate.edu • **Hours:** Monday–Friday, 8:00 A.M.–5:00 P.M.

## STUDENTS SAY

"From the nerd to the partier, OSU is a diverse campus. However, you'll see the cheerleader hanging out with the art student or the drama person having coffee with an engineering major. There's a place for everyone here."

## FODOR'S SAYS

"Oregon has 400 miles of white-sand beaches, not a grain of which is privately owned."

## ABOUT THE SCHOOL

With total enrollment exceeding 19,000 and hosting scholars from across the United States and 90-plus countries, OSU offers its students the chance to interact with an incredibly diverse campus population. The university offers a number of majors, and programs in forestry, pharmacy, and environmental sciences are especially strong. Additionally, its core curriculum emphasizes world cultures, creative thinking, and writing skills, and fosters global awareness in students.

## GETTING THERE

**BY AIR:** Visitors flying to OSU have three airport options. Corvallis has its own little airport 10 minutes from campus. You might also fly into Eugene, approximately 45 minutes from OSU. Lastly, Portland airport is roughly 90 minutes from campus. Taxis and shuttles are accessible for transport to campus.

**BY TRAIN:** Unfortunately, there is no train service leading directly into Corvallis. Visitors may take Amtrak to Albany, approximately 30 minutes from campus.

**BY BUS:** Guests may take Greyhound into Corvallis. The station is a just five minutes away from campus.

**BY CAR:** From Interstate 5: Take the Highway 34 Exit (this reads Corvallis/Oregon State University—Exit Number 228). Proceed West on Highway 34 for approximately 10 miles to Corvallis. Cross the Willamette River Bridge onto Harrison Boulevard. Two blocks after the bridge, make a left onto 4th Street. Proceed on 4th Street until you reach Jefferson Avenue and turn right. The next right after 11th Street will lead to a campus parking lot and information booth.

**LOCAL:** For airport transportation from Corvallis to Portland, call the Hut Airport Shuttle (888-257-0126).

## WHERE TO STAY

For hotels in Corvallis, try: Hilton Garden Inn (541-752-5000, $–$$), Nutcracker Sweet (541-752-0702, $–$$), or the Hanson Country Inn (541-752-2919, $$).

## CAMPUS AT ITS BEST!

Oregon's O.H. Hinsdale Wave Research Laboratory is one of the campus highlights. This facility is a leader in coastal engineering and near-shore science. Equipment includes a Tsunami Basin with multi-directional wavemaker, a Circular Wave Basin for littoral transport, and a large wave flume. Tours are available. Those interested in exploring the surrounding area might want to attend the annual Corvallis Fall Festival. The largest arts and crafts festival in the vicinity, it showcases handcrafted ceramics, leather goods, woodworking, and paintings.

# PEPPERDINE UNIVERSITY

24255 Pacific Coast Highway, Malibu, CA 90263
**Telephone:** 310-506-4392 • **E-mail:** admission-seaver@pepperdine.edu
**Website:** www.pepperdine.edu • **Hours:** Monday–Friday, 8:00 A.M.–5:00 P.M.

## STUDENTS SAY

"While trying to uphold Christian values, Pepperdine offers a wonderful education to students with many different beliefs studying a wide range of subjects in a beautiful part of the country."

## FODOR'S SAYS

"Eateries, souvenir shops, a psychic adviser, arcades, and Pacific ark are all part of the truncated Santa Monica Pier at the foot of the Colorado Boulevard below Palisades Park. The pier's trademark 46-horse Looff carousel, built in 1922, has appeared in many films, including *The Sting*."

## ABOUT THE SCHOOL

Pepperdine University is a small Christian university in the gorgeous and expensive Malibu that could well be the perfect vacation spot. Students discover quickly that the price of such beautiful surroundings is hard work and challenging classes. But with that view, who could complain?

## GETTING THERE

**BY AIR:** The Los Angeles International Airport, which is 25 miles and 45 minutes away, is the closest airport to Pepperdine. There are a number of public and private transportation options from the airport to the campus.

**BY TRAIN:** Amtrak trains service Los Angeles.

**BY BUS:** Greyhound buses service Los Angeles.

**BY CAR:** From the South: Head North on I-405 to I-10. Head West on I-10 until it merges with the Pacific Coast Highway (Highway 1). Head North on Highway 1 for about 14 miles into Malibu. Make a right on Malibu Canyon Road. Make a left at Seaver Drive. From the East: Head West on I-10 until it merges with the Pacific Coast Highway (Highway 1). Head North on Highway 1 and follow above directions. From the North: Head South on I-5 and go South on I-405 into the San Fernando Valley. At the Ventura Freeway (U.S. Highway 101) go North toward Ventura. Get off at Malibu Canyon/Las Virgenes Road. Make a left after the ramp and go nine miles through Malibu Canyon. Make a right at Seaver Drive.

**LOCAL:** If you'd rather take a taxi or use a rental car around town, some local companies include Malibu Cab (310-456-0500), Malibu A Taxi (310-317-0048), and Yellow Cab (310-456-5303).

## WHERE TO STAY

Some local lodging options include Villa Graziadio (310-506-1100, $$$), located on campus, and the nearby Casa Malibu Inn (310-456-2219, $$) and Malibu Beach Inn (310-456-6444, $$$).

### SCHOOL AT A GLANCE

| | |
|---|---|
| Type of School | Private |
| Environment | Village |
| Tuition | $32,620 |
| Enrollment | 2,957 |
| % Male/Female | 42/58 |
| Student/Faculty Ratio | 12:1 |

### FRESHMAN PROFILE

| | |
|---|---|
| Range SAT | |
| Critical Reading | 550–660 |
| Range SAT Math | 570–670 |
| Range ACT Composite | 24–35 |
| Average HS GPA | 3.67 |

### ON-CAMPUS APPOINTMENTS

| | |
|---|---|
| Advance Notice | Yes, 1 week |
| Appointment | Required |
| Saturdays | No |
| Average Length | 30 min |
| Info Sessions | Yes |
| Class Visits | Yes |

### CAMPUS TOURS

| | |
|---|---|
| Appointment | Preferred |
| Dates | Year Round |
| Times | M–F, 9:00 A.M.–3:00 P.M. |
| Average Length | 60 min |

---

## CAMPUS AT ITS BEST!

When students tire of studying in Pepperdine's Payson Library, they head to the Cyber Café in the Tyler Campus Center. In addition to a juice and coffee bar, the café has computer stations, a stage, and a television lounge. After an intellectually rigorous day, students kick back at the Battle of the Bands or one of the other events happening around campus.

# PITZER COLLEGE

1050 North Mills Avenue, Claremont, CA 91711-6101
**Telephone:** 909-621-8129 • **E-mail:** admission@pitzer.edu
**Website:** www.pitzer.edu • **Hours:** Monday–Friday, 8:00 A.M.–5:00 P.M.; Saturday, 9:00 A.M.–NOON

## STUDENTS SAY

"The typical Pitzer student is well-informed and intelligent while also being relaxed and easygoing."

## FODOR'S SAYS

"In winter, ski resorts offer great snow and challenging terrain, along with often crowded conditions. Summer brings opportunities for hiking the Pacific Crest Trail, fishing in streams or lakes such as Silverwood and Big Bear, and camping at thousands of sites peppered through the mountains."

## ABOUT THE SCHOOL

A Pitzer education is rather unconventional and individualized. Many students design their own course work so self-motivation is important. The school resonates with an inclusive spirit, whether in regards to participating in important committee decisions or attending an open party (the frat scene is nonexistent). The Claremont College Consortium also guarantees a wealth of social options. When campus life grows weary, students have both Los Angeles and the beach at their fingertips.

## GETTING THERE

**BY AIR:** Ontario International Airport, located 20 minutes away from campus, is your best bet for air travel.

**BY TRAIN:** The nearest Amtrak station is located on Garey Avenue in Pomona, about three miles away from campus. Service is provided daily.

**BY BUS:** The closest Greyhound depot is located on Indian Hill Boulevard, just South of the I-10 freeway.

**BY CAR:** From San Diego: Take I-15 North. Take I-10 West (toward Los Angeles). Exit on Indian Hill Boulevard going North (toward the mountains) for about two miles. Turn right onto Foothill Boulevard. Turn right onto Claremont Boulevard, which should be the third stoplight you encounter. Turn right onto Ninth Street. The Pitzer Visitor Parking Lot will be directly on your right (East Mesa Parking Lot). From Interstate 10: Exit North on Indian Hill Boulevard going North (toward the mountains) for about two miles. Turn right onto Foothill Boulevard. Turn right onto Claremont Boulevard, which should be the third stoplight you encounter. Turn right onto Ninth Street. The Pitzer Visitor Parking Lot will be directly on your right (East Mesa Parking Lot). From Orange County: Take the CA-57 freeway North (toward Pomona). Take I-10 East. Exit on Indian Hill Boulevard going North (toward the mountains) for about two miles. Turn right onto Foothill Boulevard. Turn right onto Claremont Boulevard, which should be the third stoplight you encounter. Turn right onto Ninth Street. The Pitzer Visitor Parking Lot will be directly on your right (East Mesa Parking Lot).

**LOCAL:** Claremont has a Transit Center with commuter rail service (Monday to Saturday) and bus service to Union Station in downtown Los Angeles and many other southern California destinations. The transit center is located on First Street between Yale and College Avenues, about 12 blocks away from campus.

## WHERE TO STAY

For overnight accommodations consider the Red Roof Inn (909-988-8466, $), Double Tree Claremont (909-626-2411, $–$$), or Embassy Suites (626-915-3441, $$).

---

## CAMPUS AT ITS BEST!

Pitzer students are constantly revolving in and out of Grove House. A comfortable place to meet with a professor or relax with friends, undergrads can enjoy homemade lunches and freshly baked cookies. The house also maintains an ecology center, a poetry room, an art gallery, and a women's center. Curious about social outlets at Pitzer? Try visiting during the annual Kohoutek Music Festival. This event sponsors 12 straight hours of live music, food, and art displays from the Claremont Colleges.

# POMONA COLLEGE

333 North College Way, Claremont, CA 91711-6312
**Telephone:** 909-621-8134 • **E-mail:** admissions@pomona.edu
**Website:** www.pomona.edu • **Hours:** Monday–Friday, 8:00 A.M.–4:30 P.M.; Saturday, 9:00 A.M.–NOON

## Students Say

"Pomona receives its strength from the friendliness and collaboration of its students and faculty; everyone who I've met is fun and interesting outside of the classroom, but has a genuine desire to learn."

## Fodor's Says

"Raging Waters, a tropical-theme water park in San Dimas (10 miles West of Claremont), has 17 chutes and slides with such names as Neptune's Fury, Thunder Rapids, and Dragon's Den. When you're ready for a break, head over to the sandy beach lagoon and relax, or go to the Tropical Bar for a fruit drink or funnel cake."

## About the School

Students at Pomona College work hard to keep up with their challenging courses, always managing to still find time to enjoy the beautiful southern California weather and charming town of Claremont. The school is the founding member of the Claremont Colleges, a consortium of five undergraduate and two graduate institutions, meaning that students have plenty of options of what and where they want to study.

## Getting There

**BY AIR:** Ontario International Airport is nine miles away from the campus and, therefore, the closest option. Los Angeles International Airport is 50 miles away and John Wayne International Airport is 45 miles away from Claremont. Car rentals, taxis, and a shuttle van are available from both airports.

**BY TRAIN:** Amtrak stops at 200 West First Street at the Metrolink Station in Claremont. From the Metrolink station, walk four blocks North on College Avenue to Bonita Avenue. Turn right and travel four blocks to the Sumner Hall (Admissions Office) parking lot.

**BY BUS:** Greyhound Bus service stops at 888 South Indian Hill Boulevard in Claremont, which is less than two miles away from campus.

**BY CAR:** From Pasadena and the San Fernando Valley: Take the 210 Freeway East to Towne Avenue. Turn right onto Towne, continue, and turn left on Foothill Boulevard. Travel East on Foothill to Indian Hill Boulevard, turn right, and proceed South eight blocks, turning left on Sixth Street, then right on College Avenue. Take the first left onto Fourth Street to the Sumner Hall (Admissions Office) parking lot. From Orange County: Take the Orange Freeway (Route 57) to I-10 East. Exit at Indian Hill Boulevard. Continue and turn right on First Street. Take First to College Avenue and turn left. Proceed on College Avenue and turn right on Bonita Avenue. Follow Bonita Avenue to the Sumner Hall (Admissions Office) parking lot. From the Long Beach area: Take the San Gabriel River Freeway (I-605) or the Long Beach Freeway (I-710) to I-10 East. Follow the "From Orange County" directions above. From Ontario Airport or the Inland Empire: Take I-10 West to the Indian Hill exit. Follow the "From Orange County" directions above.

**LOCAL:** Foothill Transit and Metrolink service Claremont and the greater area. For a taxi, try Yellow Cab (909-621-0699) or Byrd Limousine Services (909-621-3502).

## Where to Stay

Popular places to crash near the college include the Doubletree Hotel (909-626-4111, $–$$; ask for Claremont Colleges rate), and Sheraton Suites Fairplex (866-716-8130, $$$).

---

## CAMPUS AT ITS BEST!

Rest your weary feet at Pomona's recently restored Sontag Greek Theatre. This stunning outdoor venue is utilized for everything from classes and informal gatherings to special performances. When you're done with all things theatrical, hit the road and discover the Southland. Those imbued with a sense of adventure might consider a visit to the shark petting pools at the Aquarium of the Pacific. To conclude your evening, take in a performance at The Groundlings, arguably LA's best improv theater.

---

# REED COLLEGE

3203 Southeast Woodstock Boulevard, Portland, OR 97202-8199 • **Telephone:** 503-777-7511
**E-mail:** admission@reed.edu • **Website:** www.reed.edu • **Hours:** Monday–Friday, 8:30 A.M.–5:00 P.M.

| SCHOOL AT A GLANCE | |
|---|---|
| Type of School | Private |
| Environment | Village |
| Tuition | $34,300 |
| Enrollment | 1,340 |
| % Male/Female | 45/55 |
| Student/Faculty Ratio | 10:1 |

| FRESHMAN PROFILE | |
|---|---|
| Range SAT | |
| Critical Reading | 660–760 |
| Range SAT Math | 620–710 |
| Range ACT Composite | 29–32 |
| Average HS GPA | 3.9 |

| ON-CAMPUS APPOINTMENTS | |
|---|---|
| Advance Notice | Yes, 1 week |
| Appointment | Required |
| Saturdays | No |
| Average Length | 30 min |
| Info Sessions | Yes |
| Class Visits | Yes |

| CAMPUS TOURS | |
|---|---|
| Appointment | Preferred |
| Dates | Year Round |
| Times | M–F morning and afternoon |
| Average Length | 60 min |

## STUDENTS SAY

"The Honor Principle makes the Reed experience. It's only after you leave campus that you learn how much freedom you have, which in itself rocks."

## FODOR'S SAYS

"Step back 400 years to China's Ming era in [Portland's] peaceful Classical Chinese Garden. It's the largest Suzhou-style garden outside China, with a large lake, bridged and covered walkways, statues, waterfalls, courtyards, and plenty of bamboo."

## ABOUT THE SCHOOL

Reed College is known as a place where students and teachers are into learning for learning's sake. With fewer than 1,400 undergrads total, classes at Reed are rarely larger than 10 students and are always discussion-based. Students thrive on the challenging workload but they know how to relax, too. The hustle and bustle of hometown Portland provides students with a break from the academic strain, while the university-owned ski cabin on Mt. Hood is a popular destination for more elaborate getaways.

## GETTING THERE

**BY AIR:** Reed College is 12 miles away from Portland International Airport. Take the Redline Tri-Met MAX light rail and the number 75 bus to the campus. Taxi service is also available to the campus for about $35 or airporter van for $26.

**BY TRAIN:** Amtrak stops at Union Station in downtown Portland. Take a bus or taxi to the campus. A free "transportation mall" is available from central downtown.

**BY BUS:** Greyhound's terminal is located next door to Amtrak's Union Station. Take a bus or taxi to the campus. A free "transportation mall" is available from central downtown.

**BY CAR:** From the North on I-5: Take the I-84 East Exit (Exit 301) and the 39th Avenue Exit (Exit 2). Turn right and Travel 3.5 miles until you reach Southeast Woodstock Boulevard and make a right. Reed College is on the right. From the South on I-5: Take the Ross Island Bridge Exit and follow the signs to cross the bridge. At the East end of the bridge, take the 99 East /Milwaukee Exit. Follow 99E (McLoughlin Boulevard) to the Eastmoreland/Reed College Exit. Just off the exit, turn right onto Southeast Bybee Boulevard. Veer left onto Southeast 28th Avenue and drive North to the intersection of Southeast 28th Avenue and Southeast Woodstock Boulevard. Reed is directly ahead. From the North on I-205: Take the Southeast Powell Boulevard Exit. Travel West on Powell to Southeast 39th Avenue. Turn left on 39th Avenue, passing through several intersections until you reach Southeast Woodstock Boulevard. Turn right on Woodstock. Reed will be on the right-hand side. From the South on I-205: Take the Southeast Powell Boulevard Exit. Travel West on Powell to Southeast 39th Avenue. Turn left on 39th Avenue, passing through several intersections until you reach Southeast Woodstock Boulevard. Turn right on Woodstock. Reed will be on the right-hand side. From the East on I-84: Take the I-205 South Exit. Take the Southeast Powell Boulevard Exit (Exit 19). Travel West on Powell to and turn left on Southeast 39th Avenue, and right on Southeast Woodstock Boulevard. Reed is on the right.

**LOCAL:** Portland's Tri-Met public transportation system services the three counties in the Portland metro area (503-238-RIDE) and the number 19 bus (Woodstock) takes you to downtown Portland. For local taxi service try Radio Cab at 503-227-1212 or New Rose City Cab at 503-282-7707.

## WHERE TO STAY

Portland and the surrounding areas have many accommodations. Fifteen minutes away from Reed are the Portland International Hostel (503-236-3380, $–$$) and the Best Western Sunnyside Inn (503-652-1500, $). In downtown Portland, lodging options include the Benson Hotel (503-228-2000, $$) and The Heathman Hotel (503-241-4100, $$$). Check the university's website for codes to get the Reed discounted rates.

## CAMPUS AT ITS BEST!

Paideia takes place a few days before the start of the spring semester and is a purely for fun tradition of informal courses and lectures on topics of interest. Other traditions include Canyon Day, where Reed students work on preserving the canyon on campus and party while they do it, and RAW (Reed Arts Week), a week long arts festival open to the public, and Greek tradgedies performed in the outdoor amphitheater.

# RICE UNIVERSITY

MS 17 PO Box 1892, Houston, TX 77251-1892
**Telephone:** 713-348-7423
**Hours:** Monday–Friday, 8:30 A.M.–5:00 P.M.; Saturday, 9:00 A.M.–NOON

## STUDENTS SAY

"The residential colleges system and lack of Greek life make Rice an incomparably tight-knit, unique, spirited school."

## FODOR'S SAYS

"The Menil Collection is one of [Houston's] premier cultural treasures. Italian architect Renzo Piano designed the spacious building, with its airy galleries. John and Dominique de Menil collected the eclectic art, which ranges from tribal African sculptures to Andy Warhol's painting of Campbell's soup cans."

## ABOUT THE SCHOOL

Rice University has it all: a great academic reputation, awesome research facilities, caring professors, a welcoming campus community, and an unbeatable location in one of the great cities in the United States. The intellectually curious and hardworking students at Rice know how to balance studying with fun. The university's much-respected honor code helps foster an environment of mutual respect on campus.

## GETTING THERE

**BY AIR:** The closest airports to campus are Houston's Bush Intercontinental Airport and Hobby Airport. Take a taxi or the Houston Metropolitan Transit Authority (METRO) to get to the campus.

**BY TRAIN:** Amtrak stops at in Houston. Take a taxi or the METRO to get to the campus.

**BY BUS:** Greyhound stops in Houston. Take a taxi or the METRO to get to the campus.

**BY CAR:** From the North: Take U.S. 59 South and take the Fannin Street Exit. Travel South on Fannin until you reach Sunset Boulevard. Make a right on Sunset and an immediate left onto Main Street. Turn right into the college. From the South: Take U.S. 59 North and exit at Greenbriar. Turn right (South) on Greenbriar. Take Greenbriar to the light at Rice Boulevard. Make a left onto Rice Boulevard. Stay on Rice Boulevard until it turns into Sunset. Make a right on Main Street, and make an immediate right into the college. From the West on I-10 East: Take 610 South to 59 North and exit at Greenbriar. Follow the "From the South" directions above. From the East on I-10 West: Take the U.S. 59 South Exit. Take the Fannin Street Exit, and follow the "From the North" directions above.

**LOCAL:** METRO offers bus service in and around Houston, including from the airport to the campus. Call 713-635-4000 for route and schedule info. Visitors can also hail a taxi to get around the city. Some local companies include Liberty Cab Co Inc (713-695-6700) and Yellow Cab (713-236-1111).

## WHERE TO STAY

There are tons of hotels in the Houston metro area. Some popular choices include the Holiday Inn Express Hotels & Suites Downtown (713-652-9400, $$), Warwick Hotel (713-526-1991, $$), and Hilton Houston Plaza (713-313-4000, $$$).

### SCHOOL AT A GLANCE

| | |
|---|---|
| Type of School | Private |
| Environment | Metropolis |
| Tuition | $26,500 |
| Enrollment | 2,988 |
| % Male/Female | 52/48 |
| Student/Faculty Ratio | 5:1 |

### FRESHMAN PROFILE

| | |
|---|---|
| Range SAT | |
| Critical Reading | 660–760 |
| Range SAT Math | 670–780 |
| Range ACT Composite | 30–34 |

### ON-CAMPUS APPOINTMENTS

| | |
|---|---|
| Advance Notice | Yes, 2 weeks |
| Appointment | Required |
| Saturdays | Sometimes |
| Average Length | 30 min |
| Info Sessions | Yes |
| Class Visits | Yes |

### CAMPUS TOURS

| | |
|---|---|
| Appointment | Not Required |
| Dates | Year Round |
| Times | M–F 11:00 A.M. |
| | and 3:00 P.M.; Sat 10:30 A.M. |
| Average Length | 60 min |

---

## CAMPUS AT ITS BEST!

Interaction with current Rice students is perhaps the best way to gain insight into university life. Visitors should therefore take advantage of the Lunch Program. This affords guests the opportunity to dine with a student representative in one of the residential colleges. Visitors who are eager to see Houston might want to visit the Hermann Park Conservancy, where you can enjoy a free show at the outdoor theater, get sprayed by a geyser, or simply take a nap in the shade.

## SCHOOL AT A GLANCE

| Type of School | Private |
|---|---|
| Environment | Village |
| Tuition | $28,900 |
| Enrollment | 3,291 |
| % Male/Female | 37/63 |
| Student/Faculty Ratio | 12:1 |

### FRESHMAN PROFILE

| | |
|---|---|
| Range SAT | |
| Critical Reading | 490-600 |
| Range SAT Math | 490-600 |
| Average HS GPA | 3.33 |

### ON-CAMPUS APPOINTMENTS

| Advance Notice | Yes, 1 week |
|---|---|
| Appointment | Preferred |
| Saturdays | No |
| Average Length | 30 min |
| Info Sessions | Yes |
| Class Visits | Yes |

### CAMPUS TOURS

| Appointment | Preferred |
|---|---|
| Dates | Year Round |
| Times | E-mail |
| | smcadmit@stmarys-ca.edu |
| Average Length | 60 min |

# SAINT MARY'S COLLEGE OF CALIFORNIA

PO Box 4800, Moraga, CA 94575-4800

**Telephone:** 925-631-4224 • **E-mail:** smcadmit@stmarys-ca.edu

**Website:** www.stmarys-ca.edu • **Hours:** Monday–Friday, 8:30 A.M.–4:30 P.M.; Saturday, 9:00 A.M.–1:00 P.M.

## STUDENTS SAY

"Saint Mary's has an unbelievably nurturing environment with a beautiful campus."

## FODOR'S SAYS

"The Bay Area Discovery Museum fills five former military buildings with entertaining and enlightening hands-on exhibits related to science and the arts. Kids and their families can fish from a boat at the indoor wharf, imagine themselves as marine biologists in the Wave Workshop, and play outdoors at Lookout Cove, a 2.5-acre bay-in-miniature made up of scaled-down sea caves, tide pools, and even a re-created shipwreck."

## ABOUT THE SCHOOL

Saint Mary's College reflects its Lasallian foundation, educating undergraduates on the tenets of Western thought. Professors are exceedingly dedicated to their students and truly want to see them succeed. The college encourages undergrads to expand their horizons and many opt to study abroad. The student body, primarily religious and conservative, is overwhelmingly friendly and inclusive.

## GETTING THERE

**BY AIR:** Saint Mary's is accessible from both Oakland and San Francisco International Airports (23 and 34 miles South, respectively). Both airports receive flights from most U.S. cities. For shuttle service from either airport call Airport Connection (650-401-8300), Bayporter Express (510-864-4000), or East Bay Connection (925-609-1920).

**BY TRAIN:** The closest Amtrak station is located in Oakland, roughly seven miles from Moraga. Taxis and public transportation can take you to Saint Mary's.

**BY BUS:** Greyhound offers service to nearby Oakland and San Francisco. From the bus depot visitors may either take taxis or public transportation to get to the campus.

**BY CAR:** From San Francisco Bay Bridge or San Rafael/Richmond Bridge: Take Highway 580 toward Hayward then Highway 24 toward Walnut Creek. Once through the Caldecott Tunnel, take the third exit, which will be marked Orinda/Moraga. Turn right and follow Moraga Way about five miles. Make a left onto Moraga Road, and make a right onto Saint Mary's Road. The college is about one mile down on the right. From Walnut Creek/Highway 680: Take Highway 24 West (Oakland) to the Central Lafayette Exit. Go right under the freeway, right onto Mt. Diablo Boulevard, left onto Moraga Road, and left onto Saint Mary's Road. The college will be on your left about four miles up.

**LOCAL:** From BART (Bay Area Rapid Transit): Take the Pittsburg/Bay Point train to either the Orinda or the Lafayette station. From there, take the County Connection bus (Route 106) to Saint Mary's College.

## WHERE TO STAY

For overnight accommodations within 20 minutes of campus try the Holiday Inn Walnut Creek (925-932-3332, $–$$), Embassy Suites Hotel (925-934-2500, $$), or the Marriott Walnut Creek (925-934-2000, $$).

## CAMPUS AT ITS BEST!

Saint Mary's undergrads are a proactive lot. Gallery 160, a student-run art gallery, mounts seven different exhibitions each academic year. Students may propose group or solo shows and the space provides curatorial experience for those interested in art management and curation. For more culture, consider attending the Creative Writing Reading Series. This program has featured authors such as Michael Chabon, Tony Kushner, Maxine Hong Kingston, and Michael Cunningham.

# SAN FRANCISCO STATE UNIVERSITY

1600 Holloway Avenue, San Francisco, CA 94132
**Telephone:** 415-338-6486 • **E-mail:** ugadmit@sfsu.edu
**Hours:** Monday–Friday, 9:00 A.M.–5:00 P.M.

## STUDENTS SAY

"Most people try to enjoy the environment that San Francisco provides."

## FODOR'S SAYS

"Local artist Ruth Asawa's sculpture, a wonderland of real and mythical creatures, honors the city's hills, bridges, and architecture. Children and friends helped Asawa shape the hundreds of tiny figures from baker's clay; these were assembled on 41 large panels from which molds were made for the bronze casting."

## ABOUT THE SCHOOL

San Francisco State is a leading public university that encourages students to be proactive about their education. Undergrads have the opportunity to design their own majors, participate in faculty research, and hone problem-solving skills. SFSU is also deeply committed to the Bay Area community, and many students undertake service-learning projects. The city itself, with its cultural offerings and professional resources, complements your education greatly.

## GETTING THERE

**BY AIR:** SFSU is accessible via the San Francisco, San Jose, and Oakland international airports. Public transportation, taxis, and rental cars are all available.

**BY TRAIN:** Amtrak offers service to nearby Emeryville and Oakland. Taxis and local public transportation are available.

**BY BUS:** Greyhound stops in San Francisco. Taxis and local public transportation are available.

**BY CAR:** From the North: Proceed on Highway 101 South and cross the Golden Gate Bridge. Take the 19th Avenue/Highway 1 Exit and continue along 19th Avenue to campus (at Holloway Avenue). From the South: Follow I-280 North and exit at 19th Avenue. Proceed to Junipero Serra Boulevard, taking a left onto Holloway Avenue. You'll find SFSU's campus at the intersection of Holloway and 19th Avenue. From the East: Follow I-80 West across the Bay Bridge to Highway 101 South. Proceed on 101 South to I-280 toward Daly City. Take the San Jose Avenue/Mission Street Exit (immediately after the Ocean Avenue Exit). Bear right onto Sagamore Street and take this to Brotherhood Way. Brotherhood leads to Junipero Serra Boulevard North. Follow the "From the South" directions above.

**LOCAL:** Take any San Francisco-bound BART train to the Daly City BART station. SFSU runs a free shuttle to campus from the Daly City BART station during the academic year (weekdays only). Call 415-989-2278 for route and schedule info.

## WHERE TO STAY

Hotels within close proximity to campus include the Days Inn (415-665-9000, $–$$), Seal Rock Inn (415-752-8000, $$), and the Hampton Inn (650-755-7500, $$).

### SCHOOL AT A GLANCE

| | |
|---|---|
| Type of School | Public |
| Environment | Metropolis |
| In-state Tuition | $2,724 |
| Out-of-state Tuition | $12,894 |
| Enrollment | 23,074 |
| % Male/Female | 41/59 |
| Student/Faculty Ratio | 20:1 |

### FRESHMAN PROFILE

| | |
|---|---|
| Range SAT | |
| Critical Reading | 440-560 |
| Range SAT Math | 450-570 |
| Range ACT Composite | 17-23 |
| Average HS GPA | 3.18 |

### ON-CAMPUS APPOINTMENTS

| | |
|---|---|
| Info Sessions | Yes |
| Class Visits | Yes |

### CAMPUS TOURS

| | |
|---|---|
| Appointment | Not Required |
| Dates | Year Round |
| Times | Varies |
| Average Length | 60 min |

## CAMPUS AT ITS BEST!

SFSU's Sutro Egyptian collection contains artifacts spanning 5,000 years, from pre-dynastic times to the Greco-Roman period. Classical archaeology and museum studies students coordinate yearly exhibits. Additionally, the artifacts are used in courses regarding conservation. When you've finished examining these ancient relics you might decide to pay a visit to the Depot, a campus hotspot. This venue, located in the Cesar Chavez Student Center, hosts many events from concerts/DJs to film screenings, televised sports games, and even a free henna night.

# SANTA CLARA UNIVERSITY

500 El Camino Real, Santa Clara, CA 95053
**Telephone:** 408-554-4700 • **E-mail:** ugadmissions@scu.edu
**Website:** www.scu.edu • **Hours:** Monday–Friday, 8:00 A.M.–5:00 P.M.; Saturday, 9:00 A.M.–NOON

## STUDENTS SAY

"Quality community with good academics and people who love to have fun."

## FODOR'S SAYS

"At the gigantic theme park, Paramount's Great America, each section recalls a familiar part of North America: Hometown Square, Yukon Territory, Yankee Harbor, or Country Fair. Popular attractions include the Drop Zone Stunt Tower, the tallest free-fall ride in North America; a *Top Gun* movie-theme roller coaster, whose cars travel along the outside of a 360-degree loop track; and Nickelodeon Splat City, three acres of obstacle courses apparently designed for kids who love to get wet and dirty."

## ABOUT THE SCHOOL

Santa Clara is a vibrant Jesuit university located in the heart of Silicon Valley. The nationally recognized faculty emphasizes the exploration of morals and ethics in their goal of developing each student's potential. Santa Clara's prime location provides access to some amazing places, including San Francisco, Monterey Bay, Santa Cruz, and of course, the Pacific Ocean.

## GETTING THERE

**BY AIR:** Santa Clara is a mere minute from San Jose International Airport and only 30 minutes South of San Francisco International Airport.

**BY TRAIN:** Amtrak provides service to Santa Clara. Take public transportation or a taxi to reach the campus.

**BY BUS:** Greyhound does not offer direct service to Santa Clara. However, guests can take the bus service to nearby San Jose.

**BY CAR:** From U.S. Highway 101: Take the De La Cruz Boulevard/Santa Clara Exit. Proceed on De La Cruz Boulevard toward El Camino Real (stay in the right lane). When De La Cruz Boulevard splits, you'll want to bear right split and drive over the overpass. Next, make a right onto Lafayette Street (stay in the right lane). Make another right at El Camino Real. The main entrance to Santa Clara University is on the right-hand side of the road. From Interstate 880: Take the Alameda Exit. Continue driving North on The Alameda. This will eventually become El Camino Real. The main entrance to Santa Clara University is on the left-hand side of the road. From Interstate 280: Follow Interstate 880 North toward Oakland. Exit at The Alameda and turn left. The Alameda eventually turns into El Camino Real. You will find the main entrance to Santa Clara University on the left-hand side of the road.

**LOCAL:** The Altamont Commuter Express provides rail service between Stockton and San Jose. The VTA (the Santa Clara Valley Transportation Authority) offers bus and light rail service around Santa Clara.

## WHERE TO STAY

For accommodations that are within three miles of campus try Madison Street B&B Inn (408-249-5541, $–$$), Hawthorn Suites (408-241-6444, $$), or Hotel De Anza (408-286-1000, $$–$$$).

---

## CAMPUS AT ITS BEST!

Visit Santa Clara on a Wednesday to see the Music at Noon concert series. The series features some of the world's finest performers and presents a variety of musical genres ranging from Samba and Tango to Delta Blues and Bluegrass. Concerts are free and open to the public. For some college night life, head over to The Bronco, a continually packed venue that hosts a variety of events such as Date Auctions, talent shows, Oktoberfest, and Monday night football.

# SCRIPPS COLLEGE

1030 Columbia Avenue, Claremont, CA 91711
**Telephone:** 909-621-8149 • **E-mail:** admission@scrippscollege.edu
**Website:** www.scrippscollege.edu • **Hours:** Monday–Friday, 8:00 A.M.–5:00 P.M.

## STUDENTS SAY

"I love the Claremont Consortium; [it has] all the advantages of a small school with many of the opportunities of a larger one, plus you get an expanded diversity of people, not just ethnically but also in terms of political and intellectual interests."

## FODOR'S SAYS

"The 10,064-foot mountain's real name is Mount San Antonio, but Mount Baldy Ski Resort—the oldest ski area in Southern California—takes its name from the treeless slopes. It's known for its steep triple diamond runs, though the facilities could use some updating."

## ABOUT THE SCHOOL

Scripps is composed of thoughtful, intelligent women bent on improving themselves and the world around them. While the school maintains a decidedly feminist perspective, the college community is far from militant. Enrollment hovers at slightly more than 800 students, creating a nurturing, family-like atmosphere. However, as a member of the Claremont Consortium, undergrads have the academic and social resources of a larger school.

## GETTING THERE

**BY AIR:** At only a 15-minute drive away, the nearest airport to Scripps is Ontario International, served by most major airlines with direct or connecting flights to major cities nationwide. Los Angeles International Airport (50 miles) and the John Wayne Airport (40 miles) are good alternatives.

**BY TRAIN:** Amtrak offers service to Claremont. To reach the campus from the station it's best to call a taxi.

**BY BUS:** Greyhound provides service to Claremont. For additional transportation visitors may use local transportation or call a taxi.

**BY CAR:** From Orange County: Follow the Orange Freeway (I-57) North to the San Bernardino Freeway (I-10) East. Take the exit at Indian Hill Boulevard. You will make a left onto the Boulevard and then a right onto Tenth Street. Continue driving East to the corner of Tenth and Columbia. From Long Beach: Follow the San Gabriel Freeway (I-605) North to the San Bernardino Freeway (I-10) East. Follow the "From Orange County" directions above. From West and Southwest Los Angeles: Follow the Pomona Freeway (I-60) East to the Orange Freeway (I-57) North. Proceed to the San Bernardino Freeway (I-10) East. Follow the "From Orange County" directions above. From Pasadena and the San Fernando Valley: Follow the I-210 freeway East exiting on Towne Avenue. Make a right onto Towne and a left onto Foothill Boulevard. Proceed on Foothill for approximately one mile and make a right onto Dartmouth Avenue. Continue South to Tenth Street and make a left. Remain on Tenth Street until it terminates at Columbia Avenue.

**LOCAL:** Claremont's Transit Center offers commuter rail and bus service to Union Station in downtown Los Angeles, as well as many other Southern California destinations.

## WHERE TO STAY

For special Scripps College rates, call Sheraton Ontario Airport (909-937-8000, $), Sheraton Suites Fairplex (909-622-2220, $$), or the Doubletree Hotel Claremont (909-626-2411, $$).

### SCHOOL AT A GLANCE

| | |
|---|---|
| Type of School | Private |
| Environment | Town |
| Tuition | $33,506 |
| Enrollment | 879 |
| % Male/Female | 0/100 |
| Student/Faculty Ratio | 11:1 |

### FRESHMAN PROFILE

| | |
|---|---|
| Range SAT | |
| Critical Reading | 650-740 |
| Range SAT Math | 620-710 |
| Range ACT Composite | 26-31 |
| Average HS GPA | 4.07 |

### ON-CAMPUS APPOINTMENTS

| | |
|---|---|
| Advance Notice | Yes, 2 weeks |
| Appointment | Required |
| Saturdays | Sometimes |
| Average Length | 30 min |
| Info Sessions | Yes |
| Class Visits | Yes |

### CAMPUS TOURS

| | |
|---|---|
| Appointment | Preferred |
| Dates | Year Round |
| Times | Varies |
| Average Length | 60 min |

---

## CAMPUS AT ITS BEST!

Every Wednesday Scripps holds an afternoon tea, where members of the college community gather for refreshments, relaxation, and conversation. Further adventures for hot beverage enthusiasts can be found at the Motley Coffeehouse. This student-run café serves up delectable breakfast burritos, baked goods, and of course, a variety of coffees. As a socially responsible organization, they purchase only fair-trade products and support local vendors.

# SEATTLE UNIVERSITY

Admissions Office, 900 Broadway, Seattle, WA 98122-4340
**Telephone:** 206-296-2000 • **E-mail:** admissions@seattleu.edu
**Website:** www.seattleu.edu

| SCHOOL AT A GLANCE | |
|---|---|
| Type of School | Private |
| Environment | Metropolis |
| Tuition | $22,905 |
| Enrollment | 4,110 |
| % Male/Female | 39/61 |
| Student/Faculty Ratio | 13:1 |

| FRESHMAN PROFILE | |
|---|---|
| Range SAT | |
| Critical Reading | 520-630 |
| Range SAT Math | 530-620 |
| Range ACT Composite | 23-27 |
| Average HS GPA | 3.55 |

| ON-CAMPUS APPOINTMENTS | |
|---|---|
| Advance Notice | Yes, 2 weeks |
| Appointment | Required |
| Saturdays | Sometimes |
| Average Length | 60 min |
| Info Sessions | Yes |
| Class Visits | Yes |

| CAMPUS TOURS | |
|---|---|
| Appointment | Preferred |
| Dates | Year Round |
| Times | Varies |
| Average Length | 60 min |

## STUDENTS SAY

"It's impossible not to find something to do on or off campus. Whether designer shopping, strong coffee, or indie concerts are your scene, Seattle truly brings something for everyone."

## FODOR'S SAYS

"[The Odyssey Maritime Discovery Center hosts a variety of] cultural and educational exhibits on Puget Sound [where you can] learn all about the Northwest's fishing traditions with hands-on exhibits that include kayaking over computer-generated waters, loading a container ship, and listening in on boats radioing one another on Elliott Bay just outside. You can also shop the on-site fish market, dine on the catch of the day at the seafood restaurant, or spy on boaters docking at the marina or cruise ships putting into port."

## ABOUT THE SCHOOL

Seattle University is a midsize Jesuit school with strong academics, dedicated to community service and awareness. Classes are kept small and undergraduates are taught by sharp, well-liked professors who favor an interactive approach to learning. Known as the most ethnically diverse school in the Northeast, Seattle U. stresses the importance of a "whole-life education": Students are engaged in volunteer efforts for the environment and community as well as academics.

## GETTING THERE

**BY AIR:** The Seattle-Tacoma International Airport (aka "Sea Tac") is only 15 miles from downtown Seattle and the Seattle University campus. From the airport catch bus 194 to downtown Seattle. Take bus 2, 3, or 4 on Third Avenue or bus 12 on First Avenue or Marion Street to the campus.

**BY TRAIN:** From the King Street Station at 303 South Jackson in Seattle, walk three blocks to Third Avenue. Take bus 2, 3, or 4 to the campus.

**BY BUS:** Greyhound has a station at 811 Stewart in Seattle. From the station walk three blocks South to Third Avenue. Take bus 2, 3, or 4 to the campus.

**BY CAR:** From I-5 (Northbound): Take the James St. Exit off I-5 (Exit 164A). Turn right on James Street and follow it until you reach 12th Avenue. Turn left at the light on 12th Avenue and turn left on East Marion Street. The visitor parking lot information booth will be directly ahead. From I-5 (Southbound): Take the James St. Exit off I-5 (Exit 165). Follow the "From I-5" directions above. From I-90: Take the Rainier Avenue North Exit (3B) and merge onto Rainier Avenue South (you will be heading Northbound). Follow Rainier Avenue South to the intersection of Rainier Avenue South and Boren Avenue South. Turn slightly left onto Boren Avenue South, and turn right onto 12th Avenue. Follow 12th Avenue (0.7 miles) to East Marion Street and turn left. The visitor parking lot information booth will be directly ahead. From Highway 520: Take 520 Westbound to I-5 South. Take the James Street Exit off I-5 (Exit 165a). Follow the "From I-5" directions above.

**LOCAL:** King County's Metro Transit buses serve Kings County, including Seattle and the Seattle University campus.

## WHERE TO STAY

Seattle offers many choices for accommodations to the Seattle University visitor. The deluxe Silver Cloud Hotel is right across the street (206-325-1400, $$$) and the Baroness Hotel (206-624-0787, $) is only a few blocks away and offers a Seattle University discount. The Crown Plaza Seattle is a half mile away (206-464-1980, $$).

---

## CAMPUS AT ITS BEST!

Seattle University is right in downtown Seattle, so the city is part of the larger campus. On campus, visit the Wismer Gallery at Seattle University, founded to show exclusively women's art. In Seattle, attend the Northwest Folklife Festival in early May to experience music, dancing, food, and art from all over the world.

# SONOMA STATE UNIVERSITY

1801 East Cotati Avenue, Rohnert Park, CA 94928
**Telephone:** 707-664-2778 • **E-mail:** admitme.@sonoma.edu
**Website:** www.sonoma.edu

### SCHOOL AT A GLANCE

| | |
|---|---|
| Type of School | Public |
| Environment | Town |
| In-state Tuition | $0 |
| Out-of-state Tuition | $10,170 |
| Enrollment | 8,274 |
| % Male/Female | 36/64 |
| Student/Faculty Ratio | 22:1 |

### FRESHMAN PROFILE

| | |
|---|---|
| Range SAT | |
| Critical Reading | 450-550 |
| Range SAT Math | 450-560 |
| Range ACT Composite | 18-23 |
| Average HS GPA | 3.19 |

### ON-CAMPUS APPOINTMENTS

| | |
|---|---|
| Class Visits | No |

### CAMPUS TOURS

| | |
|---|---|
| Appointment | Preferred |
| Dates | Year Round |
| Average Length | Varies |

## STUDENTS SAY

"[At Sonoma State, you feel] surrounded by a tight-knit community that will embrace you if you're out there trying to experience things; [it's] not a big party school, good for the laid-back, chill kind of people."

## FODOR'S SAYS

"Although the Sonoma Valley may not have quite the cache of the neighboring Napa Valley, wineries here entice with their unpretentious attitude and smaller crowds."

## ABOUT THE SCHOOL

Sonoma's rural campus provides a serene and attractive locale for academic pursuits. The prominent Hutchins School of Liberal Studies offers a unique interdisciplinary approach that strengthens critical thinking skills. Other recognized programs include psychology, business, and health sciences. The laid-back students appreciate the equally laid-back setting, and when they are anxious for more entertainment, they typically venture into San Francisco.

## GETTING THERE

**BY AIR:** Visitors may fly into either San Francisco or Oakland International airports. For shuttle service to and from either airport call the Sonoma County Airport Express (707-837-8700).

**BY TRAIN:** Amtrak provides service to Rohnert Park. It's best to take a taxi to Sonoma State.

**BY BUS:** Unfortunately, Greyhound does not offer transportation to Rohnert Park. Visitors may take Greyhound to nearby Santa Rosa or to San Francisco (roughly an hour away).

**BY CAR:** From the San Francisco Bay Area: Follow Highway 101 North to the Rohnert Park Expressway Exit. Make a right onto Rohnert Park Expressway and continue to the end at Petaluma Hill Road. Turn right onto Petaluma Hill Road and proceed to the stoplight at East Cotati Avenue. Make a right onto East Cotati. You will see Sonoma's main entrance on your right. There is an information booth at the end of the drive. From Sacramento: Follow Interstate 80 West to Vallejo. Proceed to Highway 37 West and onto Highway 101 North. Follow the "From the San Francisco Bay Area" directions above. From Oakland East Bay Area: Follow Interstate 580 across the Richmond-San Rafael Bridge to Highway 101 North. Follow the "From the San Francisco Bay Area" directions above.

**LOCAL:** Sonoma Country Transit provides local bus service. For taxi service call Rohnert Park Taxi (707-585-0211).

## WHERE TO STAY

Visitors will find a variety of hotels in Rohnert Park, including the Good Nite Inn (707-584-8180, $), Ramada Inn Limited (707-584-5690, $), and the Doubletree Hotel (707-584-5466, $$).

## CAMPUS AT ITS BEST!

The Sonoma Film Institute screens more than 50 films a year, ranging from silent and avant-garde to contemporary Hollywood fare. SFI also has held a long-running discussion and lecture series featuring some of cinema's most influential and colorful characters, such as Nicholas Ray, Michael Powell, and Thelma Schoonmaker. If film holds no appeal, check out Sonoma's events calendar. You're likely to discover tons of activities from Trivia Night to Energy Limbo.

# SOUTHERN METHODIST UNIVERSITY

PO Box 750181, Dallas, TX 75275-0181

**Telephone:** 214-768-3417 • **E-mail:** enrol_serv@smu.edu

**Website:** www.smu.edu • **Hours:** Monday–Friday, 9:00 A.M.–5:00 P.M.; Saturday, 9:30A.M.–NOON

## STUDENTS SAY

"SMU is about getting a good education while making connections to help you succeed later in life."

## FODOR'S SAYS

"Minutes north of Dallas lies one of the city's most enduring landmarks, Southfork Ranch. Built in 1970, the ranch became one of the city's best-known symbols when the TV show Dallas premiered in 1978. You can still tour the mansion, have lunch at Miss Ellie's Deli, and try to remember who shot J. R."

## ABOUT THE SCHOOL

Southern Methodist University (SMU) feels strongly about having its students feel at home on campus and having them receive personal attention from professors. Freshmen undergo an in-depth orientation to the school and always meet with professors one-on-one at some point in the class. Undergraduates even have a voting presence on the Board of Trustees. SMU's academic programs are challenging. When students tear themselves away from the school's lively social scene, they benefit from resources such as honors programs, internships, research opportunities, and study abroad.

## GETTING THERE

**BY AIR:** Dallas Fort Worth International Airport is 26 miles away. Take a DART (Dallas Area Rapid Transit) bus to the campus.

**BY TRAIN:** Amtrak stops at the Dallas Union station. Take a DART (Dallas Area Rapid Transit) rail to the campus.

**BY BUS:** Greyhound stops in Dallas. Take a DART (Dallas Area Rapid Transit) rail to the campus.

**BY CAR:** Northbound on I-35: Take I-35 East North to I-30. Go East on I-30 to U.S. 75 North (Central Expressway). Go North on Central Expressway to the Mockingbird Lane exit. Continue through the light at 75 and Mockingbird, and turn left (West) onto SMU Boulevard to enter the campus. Southbound on I-35: Take I-35E to I-635 (LBJ Freeway). Go East on I-635 to U.S. 75S (Central Expressway). Go South on U.S. 75 and take Exit Lovers Lane/SMU Boulevard. Continue South on the access road through the lights at Lovers Lane and at University, and turn right (West) onto SMU Boulevard to enter the campus. Northbound on I-45: I-45 becomes U.S. 75 (Central Expressway) in downtown Dallas. Follow Sherman-U.S. 75N (Central Expressway) North to the Mockingbird Lane Exit. Continue through the light at 75 and Mockingbird, and turn left (West) onto SMU Boulevard to enter the campus. Eastbound on I-30: Take I-30 East East to U.S. 75 North (Central Expressway). Stay in the left lane and follow the signs to Sherman-U.S. 75 North. Exit at Mockingbird Lane. Continue through the light at U.S. 75 and Mockingbird, and turn left (West) onto SMU Boulevard to enter the campus. Westbound on I-30: Take I-30 West to U.S. 75 North (Central Expressway). Go North on Sherman-U.S. 75. Exit at Mockingbird Lane. Continue through the light at 75 and Mockingbird, and turn left (West) onto SMU Boulevard to enter the campus.

**LOCAL:** DART offers local bus service to the Hughes-Trigg Student Center. The closest train stations to the campus are the Mockingbird Station and the Lovers Lane Station.

## WHERE TO STAY

Accommodations are plentiful near SMU. Hotels offering special rates for SMU visitors include the Hotel Lumen (214-219-2400, $$), the Courtyard by Marriott Central Expressway (800-321-2211, $), and the Melrose Hotel (214-521-5151, $$$).

## CAMPUS AT ITS BEST!

If you're visiting SMU on a football Saturday, be sure to stop by the Boulevard, a pre-game tailgate gathering on the Main Quad, with food, music, and children's activities. For art on campus, visit the university's Meadows Museum, which has a large collection of fine Spanish art. SMU is just five miles from downtown Dallas, so take a DART bus into town. The neighborhood of Deep Ellum is a good place to see live music and dance and eat great food.

# SOUTHWESTERN UNIVERSITY

Office of Admission, PO Box 770, Georgetown, TX 78627-0770
**Telephone:** 512-863-1200 • **E-mail:** admission@southwestern.edu
**Website:** www.southwestern.edu

## STUDENTS SAY

"The teachers and administrators are so easy to get in touch with, it's silly."

## FODOR'S SAYS

"In far southwest Texas, Route 170 from Lajitas through Presidio and into the Chinati Mountains is one of the most spectacular drives in the state, plunging over mountains and through canyons along the Rio Grande."

## ABOUT THE SCHOOL

Southwestern University (SU) is a small school with the academic opportunities of a much larger university. Professors are very accessible, but expect hard work in return. In classes that are often fewer than 10 students, absence is not an option. Southwestern's new Paideia program is an intense, three-year, integrative course of study available to sophomores in which students work in small groups on practical applications of the rigorous curriculum.

## GETTING THERE

**BY AIR:** SU is approximately 45 minutes away from the Austin-Bergstrom International Airport in Austin. Taxis and shuttles service are also available.

**BY TRAIN:** The nearest Amtrak station is about 15 miles away. Take a taxi to the campus.

**BY BUS:** Greyhound has a terminal in Round Rock. Take a taxi to the campus.

**BY CAR:** From Interstate 35: Take Exit 261 (Texas Highway 29). Follow Highway 29 East (University Avenue) into Georgetown, approximately 1.3 miles. Turn left at Maple, the first street beyond the train tracks. Visitor parking is available along the West side of the Cullen Building and in the parking lot on the North side of the building.

**LOCAL:** For local taxi service call Ace Taxi (512-930-9800).

## WHERE TO STAY

Accommodations are plentiful in Georgetown and nearby and include the San Gabriel House (512-930-0070, $$) and the Harper-Chesser Historic Inn (512-864-1887, $$), which are both within walking distance of SU. The Holiday Inn Express Georgetown (512-868-8555, $) and the Comfort Suites of Georgetown (512-863-7544, $) are fewer than five miles away.

| SCHOOL AT A GLANCE | |
| --- | --- |
| Type of School | Private |
| Environment | Town |
| Tuition | $23,650 |
| Enrollment | 1,296 |
| % Male/Female | 41/59 |
| Student/Faculty Ratio | 10:1 |

| FRESHMAN PROFILE | |
| --- | --- |
| Range SAT | |
| Critical Reading | 560-670 |
| Range SAT Math | 570-660 |
| Range ACT Composite | 24-29 |

| ON-CAMPUS APPOINTMENTS | |
| --- | --- |
| Advance Notice | Yes, 2 weeks |
| Appointment | Preferred |
| Saturdays | Yes |
| Average Length | 60 min |
| Info Sessions | Yes |
| Class Visits | Yes |

| CAMPUS TOURS | |
| --- | --- |
| Appointment | Preferred |
| Dates | Year Round |
| Times | 10:00 A.M., 11:00 A.M., |
| | 1:00 P.M., 2:00 P.M. |
| Average Length | 60 min |

---

## CAMPUS AT ITS BEST!

Southwestern University students spend a lot of time off campus in nearby Round Rock and Austin. Be sure to stop by the busy, trendy city of Austin during your visit. A few fun activities for you to check out include First Thursdays: on the first Thursday of every month, an event in which stores stay open late and vendors and artists congregate to sell/show food, arts and crafts. Also, the bats under the Congress Avenue Bridge taking flight every day at dusk should not be missed!

# STANFORD UNIVERSITY

Undergraduate Admission, Montag Hall, 355 Galvez Street, Stanford, CA 94305-3020
**Telephone:** 650-723-2091 • **E-mail:** admission@stanford.edu
**Website:** www.stanford.edu • **Hours:** Monday–Friday, 8:30 A.M.–5:00 P.M.

## STUDENTS SAY

"Stanford is where gorgeous weather meets amazing, intelligent, and laid-back people who want to learn in an environment where the professors are all known worldwide and yet supremely approachable."

## FODOR'S SAYS

"Tucked into a small, heavily wooded plot is the Papua New Guinea Sculpture Garden, filled with tall, ornately carved poles, drums, and stones—all created in the 1990s by 10 artists from Papua, New Guinea. Complementing them are plants from Melanesia, including a huge, gorgeous Silk Oak tree."

## ABOUT THE SCHOOL

Stanford University is the West Coast's answer to the Ivies. Take a challenging academic curriculum and world-renowned professors, and combine that with the beauty and temperate climate of Northern California, and you have the makings for a truly impressive school and college experience. Stanford students work during the week and play hard on the weekend: partying, swimming, sunbathing, and any other outdoor activity imaginable.

## GETTING THERE

**BY AIR:** Both the San Jose International Airport and San Francisco International Airport Stanford are about the same distance from the university. The Sam Trans' Route KX bus can get you to and from the San Francisco airport. It connects to the Marguerite, Stanford's free shuttle.

**BY TRAIN:** Amtrak stops in Santa Clara. From there, you can take the light rail line in Santa Clara, which is operated by The Valley Transportation Authority.

**BY BUS:** Greyhound buses stop in San Francisco and San Jose.

**BY CAR:** From Highway 101 North and South: Take Embarcadero Road (which turns into Galvez Street) West until you see the university. From Highway 280 North and South: Take Sand Hill Road East. Turn right on Santa Cruz Avenue. Then make a left onto Junipero Serra Boulevard. Make a left at Campus Drive East. Take Campus Drive until you reach Palm Drive, where you'll make a left. Continue until you reach the university.

**LOCAL:** Stanford has ample public transportation, including Caltrain, a commuter rail between Gilroy and San Fransisco, and BART (Bay Area Rapid Transit), which provides regional rail service in the San Francisco Bay area. The Valley Transportation Authority (VTA) provides service bus and light rail service South of Stanford. The SamTrans runs buses in Stanford and North of Stanford. The Dumbarton Express, used by many East Bay commuters, also provides transportation near and in Stanford. The Stanford Shuttle, called Marguerite, meets most trains at their stops in Stanford. If you'd rather take a taxi or use a rental car to get around Stanford, some local companies include Yellow Cab (650-325-0310), Palo Alto Car Service (650-323-7878), Luxury Discount Auto Rental Company (800-462-5266), and Enterprise Rent-a-Car (650-833-8060).

## WHERE TO STAY

Some popular lodging choices near campus include the Coronet Motel (650-326-1081, $), the Best Western Riviera Inn (650-321-8772, $$), and the Sheraton Palo Alto (650-328-2800, $$).

## CAMPUS AT ITS BEST!

Once filled with winter rains and heated by the summer sun, Lake Lagunita becomes the destination of choice for many Stanford students. An ideal spot for sunbathing, barbecues, and even windsurfing lessons. Elsewhere, explore the Frank Lloyd Wright–designed Hanna House, which served as the provost's residence in the past. Also be sure to catch the annual Jazz Festival that runs from the end of June through the beginning of August and promises a variety of lively concerts.

# TEXAS A&M UNIVERSITY— COLLEGE STATION

Admissions Counseling, College Station, TX 77843-1265
**Telephone:** 979-845-3741 • **E-mail:** admissions@tamu.edu • **Website:** www.tamu.edu
**Hours:** Monday–Friday, 8:00 A.M.–5:00 P.M.; Saturday, 10:00 A.M.–4:00 P.M.; Sunday, 1:00 P.M.–4:00 p.m.

## STUDENTS SAY

"Texas A&M is all about fidelity, faith, family, and learning."

## FODOR'S SAYS

"Route 87 takes you over several dramatic lakes and through one of the huge pine forests for which east Texas is famous."

## ABOUT THE SCHOOL

The 36,000-plus undergraduates at Texas A&M University love the deep-rooted traditions that make up A&M culture. Those traditions include 12th Man, Aggie Spirit, Aggie football, Aggie Men's and Women's basketball, Aggie baseball, and the Aggie school ring. Sports and school spirit are huge; hometown College Station comes out in full support on game days.

## GETTING THERE

**BY AIR:** Houston's Bush Intercontinental Airport is an hour and a half drive away.
**BY TRAIN:** Amtrak trains stop in Houston.
**BY BUS:** Greyhound provides service to nearby Bryan. Take a taxi to get to the campus.
**BY CAR:** From North Austin: Take 290 East to Highway 21 East. Take Highway 21 to Highway 47. Go East on Highway 21 to Highway 47, which will eventually become Highway 60. Turn left on George Bush Drive. Take this street to Houston Street. Make a left on Houston Street and you should see the university shortly thereafter. From South Austin: Take Highway 183 South to Highway 71. Go East on Highway 71 to Highway 21. Stay on Highway 21 until you reach Highway 57. Follow the "From North Austin" directions above. From Dallas: Take I-35 South to Waco. Take Exit 339 to 340. Take Highway 6 Exit to Bryan. Make a right at Highway 60 (University Drive). Turn left on Texas Avenue. Turn right on George Bush Drive. Follow the "From North Austin" directions above. From San Antonio: Take I-35 North to San Marcos. Take Exit 205, Highway 21 toward Bastrop/Luling. Stay on Highway 21 East until you reach Highway 47. Follow the "From North Austin" directions above.
**LOCAL:** The District, the Bryan/College Station city transit service, can get you around town. Call 979-778-4480 for route and schedule info. If you'd rather take a taxi, some local companies include AA-Aggieland Cab (979-846-2285) and AAA University Taxi (979-268-2233).

## WHERE TO STAY

Some local hotel accommodations include La Quinta Inn (800-531-5900, $), College Station Hilton and Conference Center (979-693-7500, $$), and the Ramada Inn (979-693-9891, $$).

### SCHOOL AT A GLANCE

| | |
|---|---|
| Type of School | Public |
| Environment | City |
| In-state Tuition | $4,371 |
| Out-of-state Tuition | $12,621 |
| Enrollment | 36,227 |
| % Male/Female | 51/49 |
| Student/Faculty Ratio | 20:1 |

### FRESHMAN PROFILE

| | |
|---|---|
| Range SAT | |
| Critical Reading | 530-640 |
| Range SAT Math | 560-670 |
| Range ACT Composite | 23-28 |

### ON-CAMPUS APPOINTMENTS

| | |
|---|---|
| Class Visits | Yes |

### CAMPUS TOURS

| | |
|---|---|
| Appointment | Preferred |
| Dates | Year Round |
| Times | Varies |

## CAMPUS AT ITS BEST!

Prospective students should definitely contemplate attending Aggieland Saturday, Texas A&M's premier open house. This is a fantastic way to see the campus and learn about life as an Aggie. Take a moment to relax and bask in the shade of the Century Tree located in the Academic Plaza. It's a great place for conversations with friends or quiet contemplation. For those visitors who can spare the time, you'll find it's worth your while to stick around for the Midnight Yell. This awe-inspiring event happens every midnight before each home football game.

# TEXAS CHRISTIAN UNIVERSITY

Office of Admissions, TCU Box 297013, Fort Worth, TX 76129
**Telephone:** 817-257-7490 • **E-mail:** frogmail@tcu.edu
**Hours:** Monday–Friday, 9:00 A.M.–5:00 P.M.; Saturday, 10:00 A.M.–NOON

## STUDENTS SAY

"The school has many different highly ranked programs, which is appealing to students who can't decide on a major."

## FODOR'S SAYS

"Architect Louise Kahn's last and finest building was the Kimbell Art Museum, made up of six long concrete vaults with skylights running the length of each. Here are top-notch collections of both early twentieth-century European art and old masters, including Munch's *Girls on a Bridge*, and Goya's *The Matador Pedro Romero*."

## ABOUT THE SCHOOL

Texas Christian University offers its students an entire growth experience that encompasses an excellent academic education as well as an education in how to be an ethical person. TCU offers close to 100 undergraduate majors, including innovative programs like entrepreneurship and nurse anesthesia. Hometown Fort Worth offers a lively mix of business, culture, and entertainment opportunities.

## GETTING THERE

**BY AIR:** Dallas/Fort Worth International Airport is 25 miles from TCU. Shuttle, bus service, taxi, and car rental services are available at the terminal.

**BY TRAIN:** Amtrak trains stop in Fort Worth. Take a taxi to get to the campus.

**BY BUS:** Greyhound buses stop in Fort Worth. Take a taxi to get to the campus.

**BY CAR:** From the South: Take I-35 West to I-20 West. Exit Hulen Street. Then proceed North. Head East on Bellaire South and you will see the university shortly therefore. From the North: Take I-35 West to I-30 West. Drive for 2.6 miles before exiting University Drive South (Exit 12). Once on University Drive, you will see the university up ahead. From the East or West: Take I-30 to University Drive South. Follow the "From the North" directions above.

**LOCAL:** The Dallas Area Rapid Transit (DART) services 13 cities with rail and bus service. Call 214-979-1111 for route and schedule info. Visitors can also take a taxi to get around town. Some local companies include Yellow Cab (817-426-6262), Executive Taxi (817-877-1212), and Cowboy Cab Co (817-428-0202).

## WHERE TO STAY

Fairfield Inn (817-335-2000, $$) is a popular hotel choice located only one mile away from the college. La Quinta Inn (817-370-2700, $) and Renaissance Worthington Hotel (817-361-9797, $$$) are other nearby options.

## CAMPUS AT ITS BEST!

Studying is a principal aspect of college life. Therefore, think about spending a few minutes perusing the impressive stacks at TCU's Burnett Library. When you tire of reading, grab a bite to eat in the library's bistro. Visitors should inquire as to whether the Fogelson Lecture is taking place while they are on campus. Past speakers have included David McCullough and James Carville.

# TEXAS STATE UNIVERSITY—SAN MARCOS

429 North Guadalupe St., San Marcos, TX 78666
**Telephone:** 512-245-2364 • **E-mail:** admissions@txstate.edu
**Website:** www.txstate.edu • **Hours:** Monday–Friday, 8:00 A.M.–5:00 P.M.

## STUDENTS SAY

"The school's greatest strength is in targeting a variety of students. I also feel that if I need help in a subject I have a million options as far as free tutors, study groups, or note takers go!"

## FODOR'S SAYS

The drive back to San Antonio on U.S. 281 is pleasant, but if you have time, go by way of San Marcos on Route 32. This road, which skips along parts of a ridge called the Devil's Backbone, lead through classic Hill Country landscapes."

## ABOUT THE SCHOOL

San Marcos is the largest campus in the Texas State University system and holds the distinction of being the only university in the state of Texas that can claim an ex-president of the United States as one of its alumnus (Lyndon B. Johnson). Once a teachers college, Texas State has grown into a vast multipurpose university that offers more than 110 undergraduate degree programs, more than 90 graduate programs, and one of the top three teacher education programs in the country.

### SCHOOL AT A GLANCE

| | |
|---|---|
| Type of School | Public |
| Environment | Town |
| In-state Tuition | $4,140 |
| Out-of-state Tuition | $12,390 |
| Enrollment | 22,986 |
| % Male/Female | 45/55 |
| Student/Faculty Ratio | 24:1 |

### FRESHMAN PROFILE

| | |
|---|---|
| Range SAT | |
| Critical Reading | 490–580 |
| Range SAT Math | 500–590 |
| Range ACT Composite | 21–25 |

### ON-CAMPUS APPOINTMENTS

| | |
|---|---|
| Class Visits | No |

### CAMPUS TOURS

| | |
|---|---|
| Appointment | Preferred |
| Dates | Varies |
| Times | 1:00 A.M.–NOON, 2:00 P.M. |
| Average Length | 60 min |

## GETTING THERE

**BY AIR:** Visitors may fly into Austin-Bergstrom International Airport or San Antonio International Airport. Taxis and rental cars are available at the terminal.

**BY TRAIN:** Amtrak stops in San Marcos. Take a taxi to get to the campus.

**BY BUS:** Greyhound also offers service to San Marcos. Take a taxi to get to the campus.

**BY CAR:** From Austin/Dallas/Waco and the I-35 Corridor North: Follow I-35 South to San Marcos, taking Exit 206. You want to remain on the access road. Merge right onto Aquarena Springs Drive/Loop 82. Drive through two traffic lights and cross over a railroad track. You will see Bobcat Stadium on your left-hand side. Proceed through another traffic light and then over the San Marcos River. Make a right onto Sessom Drive. Continue past another three lights, driving to the top of the hill and taking a left at the three-way stop onto Comanche Street. Make another left at the first street, Student Center Drive. Then take a right before the stop sign to enter the public parking garage. From San Antonio/Corpus Christi/Laredo and I-35 Corridor South: Proceed along I-35 North to San Marcos, taking Exit 206 (Aquarena Springs Drive/Loop 82). Make a left onto Aquarena Springs Drive/Loop 82 going under I-35 toward the university. Drive through three traffic lights and cross over a railroad track. Follow the "From Austin/Dallas/Waco" directions above.

**LOCAL:** For taxi service call Corridor Cab (512-392-2222).

## WHERE TO STAY

For affordable accommodations call the Red Roof Inn (512-754-8899, $), Days Inn (512-353-5050, $), or the Holiday Inn Express (512-754-6621, $).

## CAMPUS AT ITS BEST!

Try to time your visit to coincide with Texas State's Family Weekend. Hosted by the Student Center, it's the largest parent and family event to take place in the fall semester. The weekend includes various campus tours, glass bottom boat rides, an 18-hole golf tournament, a barbecue lunch, and performances by various campus groups, including the Harambee singing group, Double Portion and Hip-Hop Congress, and the Bobcat Marching Band.

# TRINITY UNIVERSITY

One Trinity Place, San Antonio, TX 78212
**Telephone:** 210-999-7207 • **E-mail:** admissions@trinity.edu • **Website:** www.trinity.edu
**Hours:** Monday–Friday, 8:00 A.M.–5:00 P.M.; Saturday, 9:00 A.M.–1:00 P.M.

## STUDENTS SAY

"The broad requirements of the curriculum make for a great base. You can still complete your area of study, all the while learning things you never thought you would, taking classes in subjects you are interested in."

## FODOR'S SAYS

"Leading German merchants settled the King William Historic Area in the late nineteenth century. The Victorian mansions, set in a quiet, leafy neighborhood, are a pleasure to behold; Madison, Guenther, and King William streets are particularly pretty for a stroll or drive."

## ABOUT THE SCHOOL

Trinity University is committed to providing its students with an excellent and well-rounded education and is meeting that goal at an affordable price and with the perks of a larger, more expensive school. The academic programs are rigorous in every department, yet concerned teachers ensure that students are successful and are even open to sharing their research opportunities with undergraduates. Trinity supports study abroad and makes the experience accessible for students. All this combined with a prime location in the bustling city of San Antonio, and it's no wonder no one's complaining.

## GETTING THERE

**BY AIR:** San Antonio International Airport is about seven minutes from the Trinity campus. Take a taxi or VIA Metropolitan transit from the airport to campus.

**BY TRAIN:** Amtrak services a station at 350 Hoefgen Street. Take a taxi or VIA Metropolitan transit to campus.

**BY BUS:** Greyhound has a station at 500 North St. Mary's Street. Take a cab or VIA Metropolitan transit to campus.

**BY CAR:** From the South on Highway 281 (Downtown/Riverwalk and Corpus Christi): Travel North on Interstate 281 North/37 North. Exit St. Mary's/Stadium Drive. Stay on the access road through two stoplights. Veer to the right onto Stadium Drive (do not re-enter the highway). Go over the highway, making a U-turn where Stadium Drive forks just over the freeway. You should now be proceeding South on the access road of Highway 281. Exit at the Trinity University Exit sign (for Hildebrand Avenue). The campus is ahead. From the North on I-35 (Austin): Travel South on Interstate 35 and Exit Highway 281 North. On Highway 281 North, Exit St. Mary's/Stadium Drive. Follow the "From the South" directions above. From the East on I-10 (Houston): Travel West on Interstate 10 and Exit Interstate 281 North/37 North. From Highway 281, Exit St. Mary's/Stadium Drive. Stay on the access road through two stoplights. Follow the "From the South" directions above. From the West on I-10 (El Paso): Travel East on Interstate 10 into San Antonio. Exit at Hildebrand Avenue (Exit 566B). Turn left on Hildebrand and travel approximately two miles. At the intersection of Hildebrand and Devine Road/Stadium Drive, Trinity will be located on your right.

**LOCAL:** VIA Metropolitan transit services Trinity University and most points in San Antonio. Call 210-362-2020 for route and schedule info.

## WHERE TO STAY

There are several options for accommodations near Trinity and throughout San Antonio. Bonner Garden Bed & Breakfast is the closest to Trinity and offers a 10 percent Trinity discount most of the time (210-733-4222, $$). There's a Day's Inn in downtown San Antonio (210-271-3334, $) and a Marriott right on the Riverwalk (210-224-4555, $$$).

## CAMPUS AT ITS BEST!

Trinity students get really involved in on-campus extracurriculars, so plan to attend an event or two: A student-run musical or a concert is a good place to meet current students and get a feel for campus life. Nearby San Antonio is a haven for the city-minded student: Take a stroll on the famous Riverwalk and visit its gardens, theaters, and restaurants.

# UNIVERSITY OF ARIZONA

PO Box 210040, Tucson, AZ 85721-0040
**Telephone:** 520-621-3237 • **E-mail:** appinfo@arizona.edu
**Website:** www.arizona.edu • **Hours:** Monday–Friday, 8:00 A.M.–5:00 P.M.

## STUDENTS SAY

"UA does a great job constantly improving the looks of the campus and ensuring student awareness by means of a solid campus newspaper."

## FODOR'S SAYS

"Near Saguaro National Park West is the Arizona-Sonora Desert Museum, where birds and animals busy themselves in a desert microcosm."

## ABOUT THE SCHOOL

The University of Arizona offers its students the perfect combination of affordable tuition, solid academics, and fantastic social scene. Students take their academics seriously and put a lot of effort into succeeding in UA's rigorous classes. The university's incredible basketball team and wealth of campus activities keep students from ever feeling bored.

## GETTING THERE

**BY AIR:** Tucson International Airport is the closest airport to campus. Shuttle service is available from many companies, including Arizona Stagecoach (520-881-4111). Sky Harbor International Airport in Phoenix is about two hours away from campus. Shuttle, bus, and train service is available from the airport.

**BY TRAIN:** Amtrak stops in Tucson. Take a taxi to get to the campus.

**BY BUS:** Greyhound services a station in Tucson. Take a taxi to get to the campus.

**BY CAR:** From North or South bound I-10: Exit I-10 at Exit 257 (the university's exit) Take Speedway Boulevard East (a right for Northbound travelers and a left for Southbound travelers). Stay East on Speedway Boulevard to Park Avenue. The university will be on both the North and South side of Speedway Boulevard.

**LOCAL:** Sun Tran, Tucson's public bus service, operates several routes near campus. In the downtown area, you can catch a free ride on the Tucson Inner City Express Transit (T.I.C.E.T.) every day but Sunday. You can also take a taxi to get around. Some local companies include Fiesta Taxi (520-622-7777) and ABC Taxi (520-623-7979).

## WHERE TO STAY

Four Points by Sheraton (520-327-0276, $$) is a popular hotel choice for visitors and is located next to the university. Embassy Suites Tucson Williams Centre (800-362-2779, $$$) and Viscount Suite Hotel (800-527-9666, $) are also nearby.

### SCHOOL AT A GLANCE

| | |
|---|---|
| Type of School | Public |
| Environment | Metropolis |
| In-state Tuition | $4,594 |
| Out-of-state Tuition | $14,800 |
| Enrollment | 28,023 |
| % Male/Female | 47/53 |
| Student/Faculty Ratio | 19:1 |

### FRESHMAN PROFILE

| | |
|---|---|
| Range SAT | |
| Critical Reading | 500-620 |
| Range SAT Math | 500-630 |
| Range ACT Composite | 21-26 |
| Average HS GPA | 3.38 |

### ON-CAMPUS APPOINTMENTS

| | |
|---|---|
| Advance Notice | Yes, 1 week |
| Appointment | Required |
| Saturdays | Yes |
| Average Length | 30 min |
| Info Sessions | Yes |
| Class Visits | Yes |

### CAMPUS TOURS

| | |
|---|---|
| Appointment | Required |
| Dates | Year Round |
| Times | 10:00 A.M.–2:00 P.M. |
| Average Length | 60 min |

## CAMPUS AT ITS BEST!

"Monotony" is a word that University of Arizona students don't understand. Recreational opportunities abound on campus—the only difficult part is deciding what to do. Balloon Glo, which occurs the second Friday of December, is one such remarkable event. Open to the public, visitors can stroll down University Mall and watch hot air balloon pilots fire their burners. Another great tradition is Spring Fling. With more than 30,000 attendees and more than 25 rides, this is the largest student run carnival in the United States.

# UNIVERSITY OF CALIFORNIA—BERKELEY

Office of Undergraduate Admissions, 110 Sproul Hall #5800, Berkeley, CA 94720-5800
**Telephone:** 510-642-3175 • **E-mail:** ouars@uclink.berkeley.edu
**Hours:** Monday–Friday, 10:00 A.M.–NOON, 1:00 P.M.–4:00 P.M.

## STUDENTS SAY

"UC—Berkeley is so friggin' awesome with its superior faculty, beautiful campus, diverse student body, rigorous academics, and the California-cation of everyone who even visits."

## FODOR'S SAYS

"At the fortress-like Lawrence Hall of Science, a dazzling hands-on science center, kids can look at insects under microscopes, solve crimes with chemical forensics, and explore the physics of baseball."

## ABOUT THE SCHOOL

As one of the nation's premiere research institutions, Berkeley cultivates an intellectually charged atmosphere. Students know that they've been welcomed into an academic mecca permeated with world-class professors. Courses are incredibly demanding and undergraduates will not be coddled. When time permits a study break, students can easily find a party to attend. Undergrads also frequently patronize Berkeley's many restaurants and often venture into nearby San Francisco for fun.

## GETTING THERE

**BY AIR:** Visitors may fly into San Francisco International Airport, serviced by all major carriers. Rental cars, taxis, and shuttles as well as public transportation are all available for travel to campus.

**BY TRAIN:** Amtrak stops in Berkeley. To reach campus from the station, visitors may either take public transportation or take a taxi.

**BY BUS:** Greyhound does not have a station in Berkeley. Guests may take the bus service to San Francisco and switch to local public transportation to get to Berkeley's campus.

**BY CAR:** From San Francisco, the San Francisco airport, and points South on Northbound Highway 101: Follow U.S. 101 North to I-80 East. Then take I-80 across to the San Francisco/Oakland Bay Bridge. Stay to the left as you exit the bridge. Continue on I-80 East heading to Berkeley and Sacramento. Exit onto University Avenue. Proceed East on University Avenue for approximately 1.5 miles to Oxford Street at the Western edge of the campus. From Oakland, the Oakland airport, Hayward or San Jose on Northbound I-880: Remain in the left center lanes on I-880 when you reach downtown Oakland. Exit I-80 East (to Berkeley). Take the exit at University Avenue. Follow the "From San Francisco" directions above.

**LOCAL:** Guests may take BART (Bay Area Rapid Transit) trains to reach campus. The Berkeley Bart station is only 1.5 blocks West of campus. For service from San Francisco transfer at the 12th Street or MacArthur station to a Richmond train or for direct passage (except on Sundays)—board a Richmond train in San Francisco. Additionally, AC Transit provides commuter bus service from San Francisco and throughout Alameda and Western Contra Costa County. Bus lines that come near the campus area include numbers 65, 52, 51, 43, 40, 15, and 9, and U and F. For local taxi service call American Yellow Cab (510- 655-2233) or Yellow Taxi Cab (510-528-9999).

## WHERE TO STAY

For overnight accommodations guests should call Golden Bear Inn (510-525-6770, $–$$), Bancroft Hotel (510-549-1000, $$), or the Beau Sky Hotel (510-540-7688, $$).

## CAMPUS AT ITS BEST!

If you're serious about securing acceptance to Berkeley, you might want to stop by the 4.0 ball. This stone sphere, sitting outside the Campanile, is known to bring luck to those who give it a little rub. After the ball has worked its charm, you might attend a SUPERB Productions event. This student programming board entertains the Berkeley campus with a variety of activities such as comedy competitions, chess tournaments, and the ongoing Friday Film Series.

# UNIVERSITY OF CALIFORNIA—DAVIS

178 Mrak Hall, 1 Shields Ave, Davis, CA 95616
**Telephone:** 530-752-2971 • **E-mail:** undergraduateadmissions@ucdavis.edu
**Hours:** Monday–Friday, 9:00 A.M.–NOON and 1P.M.–5:00 P.M.

## Students Say

"Life at school is great. Everyone is very friendly. And during the entire year you can have fun. Play sports, go bowling, horseback ride, or even milk cows. It's all at UC—Davis."

## Fodor's Says

"The work by Northern California craftspeople displayed at the Artery, an artists' cooperative, includes decorative and functional ceramics, glass, wood, jewelry, fiber arts, painting, sculpture, drawing, and photography."

## About the School

UC—Davis is well recognized for its strong life sciences program. The university churns out an impressive number of biology majors each year. Research opportunities are plentiful, and professors are, by and large, accessible. The campus is always abuzz with activity, be it intramural sports, a film screening, or a performance in the premier Mondavi Performing Arts Center.

## Getting There

**BY AIR:** Visitors should fly into Sacramento International Airport. Rental cars and taxis are both available for any other transportation needs.

**BY TRAIN:** Amtrak's Capitol Corridor line provides direct service to Davis. Take a taxi to get to the campus.

**BY BUS:** Guests may take Greyhound to Davis. To reach campus it's easiest to call a taxi.

**BY CAR:** From Sacramento and San Francisco: Follow Interstate 80 exiting at UC—Davis. Those exiting Westbound will make a right onto Old Davis Road. Those traveling Eastbound will take a left onto Old Davis Road. Proceed for three quarters of a mile, driving past the Visitor Information Kiosk and parking structure. Drive through the traffic light of Mark Hall Drive, making a left at the T. You will then drive counter-clockwise around the park and pull into a 30-minute visitor parking space in front of the Walter A. Buehler Alumni & Visitors Center. From Southern California: Follow Interstate 5 North to Sacramento. Proceed to Interstate 80 West toward San Francisco. Take the UC—Davis Exit. Make a right onto Old Davis Road. Follow the "From Sacramento" directions above.

LOCAL: For local cab service call Checker Cab Co. (530-750-7979), Village Cab (530-753-8294), or University Cab (530-792-8000).

## Where to Stay

For overnight accommodations in Davis call Aggie Inn (530-756-0352, $–$$), Davis Inn (530-753-9611, $–$$), or the Best Western Palm Court (530-753-7100, $$).

| SCHOOL AT A GLANCE | |
| --- | --- |
| Type of School | Public |
| Environment | Town |
| Out-of-state Tuition | $27,007 |
| Enrollment | 22,618 |
| % Male/Female | 45/55 |
| Student/Faculty Ratio | 19:1 |

| FRESHMAN PROFILE | |
| --- | --- |
| Range SAT | |
| Critical Reading | 500-630 |
| Range SAT Math | 560-670 |
| Range ACT Composite | 21-27 |
| Average HS GPA | 3.73 |

| ON-CAMPUS APPOINTMENTS | |
| --- | --- |
| Class Visits | No |

| CAMPUS TOURS | |
| --- | --- |
| Appointment | Required |
| Dates | Varies |
| Times | M–F 10:00 A.M. |
| | and 2:00 P.M.; |
| | Sat–Sun 11:30 A.M. and 1:30 P.M. |
| Average Length | Varies |

## CAMPUS AT ITS BEST!

Prospective students should aim to attend Picnic Day, a springtime event that showcases the best of Davis. The festivities open with a parade and are followed by a myriad of exhibits from fashion shows to Dachshund races. Dance troupes and musical groups also perform throughout the day. Visitors who'd like to get off campus may indulge their sweet tooth by taking a tour of the Jelly Belly Factory. You'll be able to watch the candy makers in action and enjoy free samples.

# UNIVERSITY OF CALIFORNIA—IRVINE

Office of Admissions & Relations with Schools, 204 Administration Building, Irvine, CA 92697-1075

**Telephone:** 949-824-6703 • **E-mail:** admissions@uci.edu

**Hours:** Monday–Friday, 8:00 A.M.–5:00 P.M.

## SCHOOL AT A GLANCE

| | |
|---|---|
| Type of School | Public |
| Environment | City |
| In-state Tuition | $6,141 |
| Out-of-state Tuition | $24,825 |
| Enrollment | 19,930 |
| % Male/Female | 49/51 |
| Student/Faculty Ratio | 19:1 |

### FRESHMAN PROFILE

| | |
|---|---|
| Range SAT | |
| Critical Reading | 540-630 |
| Range SAT Math | 570-680 |
| Average HS GPA | 3.72 |

### ON-CAMPUS APPOINTMENTS

| | |
|---|---|
| Class Visits | Yes |

### CAMPUS TOURS

| | |
|---|---|
| Appointment | Not Required |
| Dates | Year Round |
| Times | M–F NOON |
| Average Length | 60 min |

## STUDENTS SAY

"UC—Irvine is all about students who are relaxed enough to have lots of fun, but who are studious enough to have made it to a UC school."

## FODOR'S SAYS

"Wild Rivers Water Park has more than 40 rides and attractions, including a wave pool, daring slides, and an inner-tube river ride."

## ABOUT THE SCHOOL

UC—Irvine is a research-oriented university that encourages hands-on learning. Although it is best known for its stellar biology program, in recent years the economics and sociology departments have also earned great acclaim. While TAs might be the norm, especially in lower level classes, undergrads grant them high marks. Outside of class, students make the most of Irvine's superb locale, a short jaunt to both Los Angeles and the beach.

## GETTING THERE

**BY AIR:** Those traveling by air should fly into Orange County's John Wayne Airport. Rental cars, shuttles, and taxis are all available at the airport.

**BY TRAIN:** Visitors may ride Amtrak directly to Irvine. Taxis and local buses are available for further transportation needs.

**BY BUS:** Unfortunately, Greyhound does not provide service to Irvine. Guests may take Greyhound to nearby Santa Ana. Take a taxi to the campus.

**BY CAR:** 405 Freeway from the North: Exit at Jamboree Road. You will make a right onto Jamboree and then a left onto Campus Drive. Lastly, take a right onto West Peltason, which takes you to UCI. 405 Freeway from the South: Exit at University Drive. You'll make a left onto University followed by another left onto Campus Drive. Lastly, turn right onto West Peltason. 5 Freeway from the North: Take 5 South to 55 South. From there proceed to the 73 South exit at Bison Avenue. Make a left onto Bison. This will take you to UCI. 5 Freeway from the South: Follow 5 North to 405 North. Exit at University Drive. You'll make a left onto University followed by another left onto Campus Drive. Turn right onto West Peltason.

**LOCAL:** OCTA (the Orange Country Transportation Authority) offers local bus service around the area. Call 714.560.OCTA for route and schedule info. If you're looking for taxi service in the area try Super Taxis (949-653-8294), Star Taxi Company (949-653-9449), or VIP Taxis (949-256-2222).

## WHERE TO STAY

The Irvine area is home to a number of hotels, including the Hyatt Regency Irvine (949-975-1234, $$), Atrium Hotel (949-833-2770, $$–$$$), or the Fairmont Newport Beach (949-476-2001, $$$+).

## CAMPUS AT ITS BEST!

The Bren Events Center presents a variety of programming that keeps the Irvine community entertained year-round. Past performances have ranged from a WCW wrestling match to a Blink 182 concert and a Rock 'n Jock basketball game. Nearby Laguna Beach also provides a wealth of recreational opportunities. Its breathtaking beaches are perfect for picnics, volleyball, and admiring beautiful sunsets. The town is also renowned for its festivals and art galleries.

# UNIVERSITY OF CALIFORNIA— LOS ANGELES

405 Hilgard Avenue, Box 951436, Los Angeles, CA 90095-1436
**Telephone:** 310-825-3101 • **E-mail:** ugadm@saonet.ucla.edu
**Website:** www.ucla.edu • **Hours:** Monday–Friday, 9:00 A.M.–5:00 P.M.

## STUDENTS SAY

"There's a certain magic about UCLA that can't be accurately explained. It's in a beautiful location, it's great on an academic level, and the sports teams are very good."

## FODOR'S SAYS

"With its curving walls and isolated hilltop perch, the Getty Center resembles a pristine fortified city of its own. You may be lured up by the beautiful views of LA (on a clear day stretching all the way to the Pacific Ocean), but the architecture, the uncommon gardens, and the fascinating art collections are more than enough to capture your attention."

## ABOUT THE SCHOOL

The students at UCLA, a large public school with top-ranked programs in almost every area, never have a chance to get bored. The university's size, tremendous resources, and unbeatable location provide something for everyone—you'd be hard-pressed to find a better combination of great academics and awesome social life.

### SCHOOL AT A GLANCE

| | |
|---|---|
| Type of School | Public |
| Environment | Metropolis |
| In-state Tuition | $6,141 |
| Out-of-state Tuition | $25,432 |
| Enrollment | 24,811 |
| % Male/Female | 44/56 |
| Student/Faculty Ratio | 18:1 |

### FRESHMAN PROFILE

| | |
|---|---|
| Range SAT | |
| Critical Reading | 570-680 |
| Range SAT Math | 610-720 |
| Range ACT Composite | 24-30 |
| Average HS GPA | 4.14 |

### ON-CAMPUS APPOINTMENTS

| | |
|---|---|
| Saturdays | No |
| Class Visits | Yes |

### CAMPUS TOURS

| | |
|---|---|
| Appointment | Required |
| Dates | Year Round |
| Times | Varies |
| Average Length | 60 min |

## GETTING THERE

**BY AIR:** The Los Angeles International Airport is the closest airport to campus. Take a taxi or public transportation to get to the campus.

**BY TRAIN:** Amtrak trains stop at Union Station in Los Angeles. Take a taxi or public transportation to get to the campus.

**BY BUS:** Greyhound bus lines stop in Los Angeles. Take a taxi or public transportation to get to the campus.

**BY CAR:** From North or South: Take Route 405 (San Diego Freeway) to Wilshire Boulevard East. Go East three blocks to Westwood Boulevard and make a left. Stay on it until you see the university. From the East via 10 (Santa Monica Freeway): Take 10 (Santa Monica Freeway) to 405 (San Diego Freeway) North. Travel down 405 (San Diego Freeway) to Wilshire Boulevard. East. Drive East three blocks to Westwood Boulevard, and make a left on it. Travel five blocks to the Parking and Information kiosk.

**LOCAL:** Campus Express Shuttle System, Wilshire Center Express, and Northwest Shuttle provide transportation service around the university. The Los Angeles County Metropolitan Transportation Authority (Metro or MTA) provides bus and rail service around the city. If you'd rather take a taxi, call City Yellow Cab (323-666-1200).

## WHERE TO STAY

If you plan on spending the night, some local accommodations include the UCLA Guest House on campus (310-825-2923, $$), LAX Plaza Hotel (310-484-7000, $$), and the Beverly Hilton (310-274-7777, $$$).

## CAMPUS AT ITS BEST!

Convince your parents that there's intellectual merit in watching a *Sopranos* marathon with a visit to UCLA's Film and Television Archive at the Powell Library. The archive has amassed more than 200,000 television programs and films along with 27 million feet of newsreel footage. You'll probably want to head outdoors and take advantage of Southern California's fantastic weather. Try making your way over to Westwood Plaza, a central campus meeting locale, where students often hold political rallies and cultural fairs.

# UNIVERSITY OF CALIFORNIA—RIVERSIDE

1120 Hinderaker Hall, Riverside, CA 92521
**Telephone:** 951-827-3411 • **E-mail:** discover@ucr.edu
**Hours:** Monday–Friday, 8:00 A.M.–5:00 P.M.

## STUDENTS SAY

"UCR gives each student every possible opportunity to excel that other colleges offer, yet there is a strong focus by the university on the individual student that is hard to find elsewhere."

## FODOR'S SAYS

"California Citrus State Historic Park—A celebration of California's citrus-growing history, this Victorian-style park occupies 337 well-kept acres of working citrus groves. The grounds, developed in 1880, are perfect for a leisurely afternoon picnic."

## ABOUT THE SCHOOL

Smaller than most of its UC peers, Riverside provides its students with the opportunity to become well acquainted with their professors. The school encourages undergraduate research, and students have access to great study abroad, internship, and interuniversity programs. While largely a commuter school, there are plenty of social opportunities available on campus through clubs and an active Greek scene. Furthermore, Riverside is within driving distance from both the mountains and the beach.

## GETTING THERE

**BY AIR:** Ontario International Airport is the closest facility to campus. Guests may also choose to fly into Los Angeles International Airport. Car rentals, shuttles, and taxis are available at both locations.

**BY TRAIN:** Amtrak does indeed maintain a station in Riverside. Public buses and taxis are available for additional transportation.

**BY BUS:** Greyhound offers service to Riverside. To reach campus you may either take public transportation or call a taxi.

**BY CAR:** From the 91 Freeway (from LA County): Follow the 91 Freeway East to the 60 Freeway East. Exit at University Avenue and make a left. Proceed to the second light and make a right onto Campus Drive. From the 10 Freeway (from LA County): Follow the 10 Freeway East to Interstate 15 South. Continue on to the 60 Freeway East. Exit at University Avenue and make a left. Follow the "From 91 Freeway" directions above. From the 60 Freeway (from LA County): Follow the 60 Freeway East. Follow the "From 91 Freeway" directions above. From Palm Springs: Follow the 10 Freeway West to the junction with the 60 Freeway and continue driving West. You will exit at University Avenue and follow the "From 91 Freeway" directions above. From San Diego County: Follow the 15 Freeway North to the 215 North. Next, proceed to the 60 Freeway West. You will exit at University Avenue and follow the "From 91 Freeway" directions above. From San Bernardino: Follow the 215 Freeway South to the junction with the 60 Freeway and continue driving East. Follow the "From 91 Freeway" directions above.

**LOCAL:** The RTA (Riverside Transit Agency) offers local bus service around the city. Visitors in need of a taxi might call Yellow Cab of Riverside (951-684-1234) or Checker Cab of Riverside (951-637-6667).

## WHERE TO STAY

For hotels that are within close proximity to campus, try Dynasty Suites (951-369-8200, $–$$), Comfort Inn (951-683-6000, $–$$), or the Mission Inn (951-784-0300, $$–$$$+).

## CAMPUS AT ITS BEST!

Students looking to unwind often head over to the main lounge of the University Commons. Undergrads congregate to shoot pool, play video games, or flick through the TV channels. Those in search of more cultural entertainment should get tickets to a UC—Riverside Presents show. Past seasons have attracted artists such as the Kronos Quartet, Meredith Monk and Vocal Ensemble, and Garrison Keillor. Another popular event, the International Food Faire/World Fest, always draws a crowd. Come sample some international treats and see who wins the food contest.

# UNIVERSITY OF CALIFORNIA—SAN DIEGO

9500 Gilman Drive, 0021, La Jolla, CA 92093-0021
Telephone: 858-534-4831 • E-mail: admissionsinfo@ucsd.edu
Website: www.ucsd.edu • Hours: Monday–Friday, 8:00 A.M.–4:30 P.M.

## STUDENTS SAY

"The greatest strength of UCSD is the academics, especially biology and research-related fields."

## FODOR'S SAYS

"The Fleet Center's clever interactive exhibits are artfully educational. You can reconfigure your face to have two left sides, or, by replaying an instant video clip, watch yourself coming and going at different speeds."

## ABOUT THE SCHOOL

At this large university of more than 20,000 undergraduates, the hard sciences dominate. Premeds profit from top-notch chemistry and biology departments, and earth and environmental science students benefit from the school's affiliation with the Scripps Institute of Oceanography. Classes at UCSD are demanding, and studying eats up the majority of time. When students need to take a study break and relax, they typically venture to the beach for surfing, snorkeling, and sun bathing.

## GETTING THERE

**BY AIR:** San Diego International Airport services a number of major airlines. Take a taxi to get to the campus.

**BY TRAIN:** Amtrak does provide service to San Diego and, more specifically, La Jolla. Take a taxi to get to the campus.

**BY BUS:** Greyhound stops in San Diego. Take a taxi to get to the campus.

**BY CAR:** From North of La Jolla: Follow Interstate 5 South, exiting onto Genesee Avenue West. Drive to the top of the hill. When you reach the third light, make a left onto North Torrey Pines Road. Make a left onto North Point Drive and continue until you see a UCSD Visitor Information Center on the right. From South of La Jolla: Follow Interstate 5 North exiting onto Gilman Drive, where you make a left. Drive for approximately another 1.5 miles and you'll come upon a UCSD Visitor Center on your right-hand side.

**LOCAL:** San Diego offers a number of public transportation options. Metropolitan Transit System (MTS) provides local bus service. San Diego also has a trolley system that offers service through many neighborhoods and city landmarks. Lastly the Amtrak Intercity and Coaster lines provide commuter rail service to downtown San Diego and locales as far as Los Angeles and Orange Counties. For local taxi service call Village Transportation Inc. (858-459-2470) or Hooman's Luxury Cab (858-775-1868).

## WHERE TO STAY

Possible accommodations include Travelodge (619-297-2271, $), Bankers Hill Manor (619-297-3212, $$), or the Balboa Park Inn (619-298-0823, $$–$$).

## SCHOOL AT A GLANCE

| | |
|---|---|
| Type of School | Public |
| Environment | Metropolis |
| In-state Tuition | $6,685 |
| Out-of-state Tuition | $18,684 |
| Enrollment | 21,361 |
| % Male/Female | 48/52 |
| Student/Faculty Ratio | 19:1 |

### FRESHMAN PROFILE

| | |
|---|---|
| Range SAT | |
| Critical Reading | 590-660 |
| Range SAT Math | 600-700 |
| Range ACT Composite | 23-29 |
| Average HS GPA | 3.93 |

### ON-CAMPUS APPOINTMENTS

| | |
|---|---|
| Class Visits | No |

### CAMPUS TOURS

| | |
|---|---|
| Appointment | Preferred |
| Dates | Year Round |
| Times | Mon-Sat 11:00 A.M. |
| Average Length | 120 min |

---

## CAMPUS AT ITS BEST!

Visitors should most definitely take advantage of UCSD's proximity to the Pacific Ocean. While scuba diving and beach parties are a favorite of UC students, the area is also prime for fishing, whale watching, waterskiing, year-round surfing, and kayaking.

## SCHOOL AT A GLANCE

| | |
|---|---|
| Type of School | Public |
| Environment | City |
| In-state Tuition | $0 |
| Out-of-state Tuition | $18,684 |
| Enrollment | 18,077 |
| % Male/Female | 45/55 |
| Student/Faculty Ratio | 17:1 |

### FRESHMAN PROFILE

| | |
|---|---|
| Range SAT | |
|   Critical Reading | 530–650 |
| Range SAT Math | 560–670 |
| Range ACT Composite | 22–28 |
| Average HS GPA | 3.76 |

### ON-CAMPUS APPOINTMENTS

| | |
|---|---|
| Advance Notice | No |
| Appointment | Not Required |
| Saturdays | No |
| Info Sessions | Yes |
| Class Visits | Yes |

### CAMPUS TOURS

| | |
|---|---|
| Appointment | Not Required |
| Dates | Year Round |
| Times | M–F 12:00 P.M., 2:00 P.M. |
| Average Length | Varies |

# UNIVERSITY OF CALIFORNIA—SANTA BARBARA

Office of Admissions, 1210 Cheadle Hall, Santa Barbara, CA 93106-2014
**Telephone:** 805-893-2881 • **E-mail:** admissions@sa.ucsb.edu
**Website:** www.ucsb.edu • **Hours:** Monday–Friday, 9:00 A.M.–NOON and 1:00 P.M.–5:00 P.M.

## STUDENTS SAY

"UCSB is all about a healthy mixture of exceptional education and ample opportunities for fun and relaxation, all in a beautiful location."

## FODOR'S SAYS

"Andree Clark Bird Refuge—This peaceful lagoon and gardens sits north of East Beach. Bike trails and footpaths, punctuated by signs identifying native and migratory birds, skirt the lagoon."

## ABOUT THE SCHOOL

Santa Barbara students profess to being extremely happy, and why shouldn't they be? This solid UC school combines great academics and a beautiful setting. Undergrads are challenged intellectually in the classroom and encouraged to pursue research interests. Students are also quick to take advantage of the university's unbeatable locale, frequently surfing and bike-riding and enjoying the lively downtown scene.

## GETTING THERE

**BY AIR:** Santa Barbara Airport offers direct service to and from San Francisco, San Jose, Los Angeles, Phoenix, Denver, and Las Vegas. Guests may also choose to fly into Los Angles International Airport, which is roughly two hours away from Santa Barbara. Taxi service is available from both airports.

**BY TRAIN:** Amtrak serves both downtown Santa Barbara and nearby Goleta. You may reach campus by taxi or the SuperRide Shuttle (800-977-1123).

**BY BUS:** Greyhound stops in Santa Barbara. Take a taxi to or from the terminal.

**BY CAR:** From Highway 101 North: Take the Airport/UCSB Exit (Highway 217) and continue for approximately one mile to the campus. From Highway 101 South: Follow the Storke Road/Glen Annie Road Exit off U.S. 101 (roughly 12 miles North of Santa Barbara). Make a right onto Storke Road and drive for two more miles to El Colegio Road and proceed to campus.

**LOCAL:** If you are in need of local taxi service call Blue Dolphin Cab Company (805-962-6886) or Rose Cab (805-564-2600).

## WHERE TO STAY

For local accommodations consider the Super 8 Motel (805-967-5591, $), Bath Street Inn (805-682-9680, $$–$$$), or the Country Inn (805-963-4471, $$–$$$).

---

## CAMPUS AT ITS BEST!

Not surprisingly, there is always fun and excitement to be found on the Santa Barbara campus. The UCSB After Dark calendar is chockfull of delightful events such as Rock 'n Bowl, Jimmy Buffet concerts, and performances from the Bulgarian National Theatre. There are also numerous off-campus attractions for those seeking a respite from academics. Consider visiting El Presidio de Santa Barbara, a military fortress built by the Spanish the 1700s. It is currently the site of an active archaeological dig.

# UNIVERSITY OF CALIFORNIA—SANTA CRUZ

Office of Admissions, Cook House, 1156 High Street, Santa Cruz, CA 95064
**Telephone:** 831-459-4008 • **E-mail:** admissions@ucsc.edu
**Website:** admissions.ucsc.edu • **Hours:** Monday–Friday, 9:00 A.M.–5:00 P.M.

## STUDENTS SAY

"The typical student at UCSC is, well, atypical. I've lost all fear of looking out of place, because even if I do look weird, somebody always looks weirder."

## FODOR'S SAYS

"About [one and three-quarter] miles west of the lighthouse is secluded Natural Bridge State Beach, a stretch of soft sand with tidal pools and a natural rock bridge nearby. From October to early March a colony of monarch butterflies resides here."

## ABOUT THE SCHOOL

UC—Santa Cruz provides rigorous academics in a laid-back environment. Enthusiastic students consistently praise the engineering, marine biology, and astrophysics departments. Research and job opportunities are plentiful, and many undergrads laud professors for helping them network. Avid outdoorsmen will especially appreciate the school's lush surroundings, which offer ample hiking, climbing, and surfing options.

## GETTING THERE

**BY AIR:** Santa Cruz is accessible from both San Francisco and San Jose International Airports. A wide variety of ground transportation is available for additional travel needs.

**BY TRAIN:** Amtrak does provide service to Santa Cruz. Taxis and local buses are recommended for further transportation.

**BY BUS:** Greyhound also offers direct service to Santa Cruz. Take a taxi to reach the campus.

**BY CAR:** From San Francisco: Follow Highway 101 South or Interstate 280 South to Highway 85 South. Continue on 880 South, which becomes Highway 17, to Santa Cruz. When you reach the outskirts of Santa Cruz, take Highway 1 North (toward Half Moon Bay). You will then drive for roughly a mile North on Business Highway 1 (Mission Street) to Bay Street in Santa Cruz. Make a right onto Bay and drive up the hill to the main campus entrance. From Sacramento: Follow Interstate 80 West to the exit for Interstate 680 (toward San Jose). In San Jose, Interstate 680 becomes Interstate 280 North. Proceed to Highway 17 South. When you reach the outskirts of Santa Cruz, take Highway 1 North. Follow the "From San Francisco" directions above. From Los Angeles: Follow Interstate 5 North. Proceed to Highway 152 West to Watsonville. Take Highway 1 North to Santa Cruz. Follow the "From San Francisco" directions above. From Santa Barbara: Follow Highway 101 North to Highway 129 to Watsonville until you reach Business Highway 1 (Mission Street). Follow the "From San Francisco" directions above.

**LOCAL:** The Santa Cruz Metropolitan Transit District maintains a public transit system for the county. Call 831-425-8600 for schedule and route information. For local taxi service call Yellow Cab (831-423-1234) or Deluxe Cab (831-462-6063).

## WHERE TO STAY

For overnight accommodations in the Santa Cruz area consider Knights Inn (831-423-6020, $), Hampton Inn (831-457-8000, $$), or the Ramada Limited Fisherman's Wharf (831-423-7737, $$).

## SCHOOL AT A GLANCE

| | |
|---|---|
| Type of School | Public |
| Environment | Town |
| In-state Tuition | $0 |
| Out-of-state Tuition | $17,304 |
| Enrollment | 13,588 |
| % Male/Female | 46/54 |
| Student/Faculty Ratio | 19:1 |

### FRESHMAN PROFILE

| | |
|---|---|
| Range SAT | |
| Critical Reading | 520-630 |
| Range SAT Math | 530-640 |
| Range ACT Composite | 21-27 |
| Average HS GPA | 3.51 |

### ON-CAMPUS APPOINTMENTS

| | |
|---|---|
| Saturdays | No |
| Info Sessions | Yes |
| Class Visits | Yes |

### CAMPUS TOURS

| | |
|---|---|
| Appointment | Required |
| Dates | Year Round |
| Times | Varies |
| Average Length | 120 min |

## CAMPUS AT ITS BEST!

UC—Santa Cruz's Living Writers Series is a fantastic way to learn about writing and the creative process. The series attracts highly regarded critics, journalists, and published authors, including Joshua Clover, poetry editor for the Village Voice Literary Supplement. The readings are held every Wednesday and are free to the public. Visitors interested in exploring the surrounding area might appreciate Santa Cruz's coastal location. Nicknamed Surf City, Santa Cruz is an excellent place for kayaking, fishing, kite-boarding, and windsurfing.

# UNIVERSITY OF COLORADO—BOULDER

552 UCB, Boulder, CO 80309-0552
**Telephone:** 303-492-6301 • **E-mail:** apply@colorado.edu
**Hours:** Monday–Friday, 9:30 A.M. and 1:30 P.M.; Saturday, 10:30 A.M.

## SCHOOL AT A GLANCE

| | |
|---|---|
| Type of School | Public |
| Environment | City |
| In-state Tuition | $4,554 |
| Out-of-state Tuition | $21,900 |
| Enrollment | 25,205 |
| % Male/Female | 53/47 |
| Student/Faculty Ratio | 16:1 |

### FRESHMAN PROFILE

| | |
|---|---|
| Range SAT | |
| Critical Reading | 530-630 |
| Range SAT Math | 550-650 |
| Range ACT Composite | 23-28 |
| Average HS GPA | 3.53 |

### ON-CAMPUS APPOINTMENTS

| | |
|---|---|
| Advance Notice | Yes, 2 weeks |
| Appointment | Required |
| Saturdays | No |
| Average Length | 30 min |
| Info Sessions | Yes |
| Class Visits | Yes |

### CAMPUS TOURS

| | |
|---|---|
| Appointment | Required |
| Dates | Year Round |
| Times | See |
| http://www.colorado.edu/visit/ | |
| Average Length | 120 min |

## STUDENTS SAY

"There are always pick up ultimate Frisbee and basketball games and everyone is always going skiing or snowboarding during the winter. In Boulder, it's hard to not find an outdoor sport you can enjoy."

## FODOR'S SAYS

"Pearl Street Mall is a see-and-be-seen pedestrian street with benches, grassy spots, great shopping, and outdoor cafés."

## ABOUT THE SCHOOL

The University of Colorado has a lot to offer its students, including strong programs in the sciences and a stellar journalism program. Students love hometown Boulder and support the school's popular Division I sports programs. During their downtime, students break out the skis and hit the slopes.

## GETTING THERE

**BY AIR:** Denver International Airport is the closest airport to campus and is about 60 to 90 minutes away from Boulder.

**BY TRAIN:** Amtrak trains provide service to Boulder. Take a taxi to the campus

**BY BUS:** Greyhound offers limited service to Boulder. Take a taxi to the campus.

**BY CAR:** From the East: Go West on U.S. 36 (from I-25 or I-270) and exit at Baseline Road. Make a left on Baseline Road. Then make a right on Broadway to campus. From the North: Take U.S. 287 South to Highway 119 (Diagonal Highway). Highway 119 turns into Highway 157 (Foothills Parkway) just North of Boulder. Make a right from Foothills Parkway onto Baseline Road. Go West on Baseline to Broadway. Then make a right on Broadway to campus. From the West: Take I-70 East to U.S. 6. Head East on U.S. 6 to CO-58. Make a right on CO-58 to CO-93. Make a left onto CO-93 toward Boulder. CO-93 becomes Broadway in Boulder. Continue on Broadway (West) and you will see the campus shortly thereafter.

**LOCAL:** The Regional Transportation District (RTD) provides bus service in Boulder and its surrounding areas. You can also take a taxi to get around town. Some local companies include Boulder Yellow Cab Bus Office (303-442-2279) and Budget Car Rental (303-444-9054).

## WHERE TO STAY

If you're planning on spending the night, some popular hotel options in the area include the Days Inn (303-499-4422, $), Boulder Outlook Hotels & Suite (303-443-3322, $$), and Boulder Marriott (303-440-8877, $$).

---

## CAMPUS AT ITS BEST!

Many Boulder students would agree that Varsity Lake is one of the most scenic spots on campus. A refreshing counterpoint to the bustle of college life, it's a great place to study or simply take a walk. Of course, when students want to embrace the bustle they can always rely on the Cultural Events Board for thought-provoking and fascinating programs. Past events have included Waffle Day, complete with traditional Scandinavian performances, Afghan Culture Night, and a lecture by Paul Rusesabagina, the inspiration behind *Hotel Rwanda*.

# UNIVERSITY OF DALLAS

1845 East Northgate Drive, Irving, TX 75062
**Telephone:** 972-721-5266 • **E-mail:** ugadmis@udallas.edu
**Hours:** Monday–Friday and Saturday by appointment, 8:00 A.M.–5:00 P.M.

| SCHOOL AT A GLANCE | |
| --- | --- |
| Type of School | Private |
| Environment | Metropolis |
| Tuition | $20,780 |
| Enrollment | 1,058 |
| % Male/Female | 42/58 |
| Student/Faculty Ratio | 12:1 |

| FRESHMAN PROFILE | |
| --- | --- |
| Range SAT | |
| Critical Reading | 580-700 |
| Range SAT Math | 540-650 |
| Range ACT Composite | 23-29 |
| Average HS GPA | 3.59 |

| ON-CAMPUS APPOINTMENTS | |
| --- | --- |
| Advance Notice | Yes, 2 weeks |
| Appointment | Preferred |
| Saturdays | Sometimes |
| Average Length | 90min |
| Info Sessions | Yes |
| Class Visits | Yes |

| CAMPUS TOURS | |
| --- | --- |
| Appointment | Preferred |
| Dates | Year Round |
| Times | Varies |
| Average Length | Varies |

## Students Say

"Where else can you find students discussing casually over lunch, as if it were the most normal thing in the world, Plato's *Republic*, the concept of divine love in Dante's *Commedia*, or the effects of the French Revolution in modern society?"

## Fodor's Says

"Downtown is one of the most remarkable flowerings of skyscraping architecture anywhere—that same skyline familiar to the world from the television show Dallas—and a multitude of restaurants and shops in the West End, a former warehouse district."

## About the School

The University of Dallas (UD) offers its 1,080 undergraduates a rigorous academic program with excellent support and attention from its passionate professors. A much-lauded core curriculum, which emphasizes Western civilization's great texts and ideas, offers students a solid introduction to areas of study and thought outside of their major. UD facilitates and encourages study abroad, and a large number of the students spend a semester away, especially at the university's campus in Rome.

## Getting There

**BY AIR:** Dallas Fort Worth International Airport is 11.5 miles away from the campus. Take a taxi or DART (Dallas Area Rapid Transit) bus to the campus.

**BY TRAIN:** Amtrak stops at Dallas' Union station. Take a taxi or DART bus to the campus.

**BY BUS:** Greyhound stops 969 East Irving Boulevard. Take a taxi or DART bus to the campus.

**BY CAR:** From Dallas-Fort Worth International Airport: Take South exit from the airport onto Highway 183 East. Take the Carl Road exit, turn left at the signal, turn right onto Northgate Drive. The campus is ahead. From North of the DFW Metroplex: From U.S. 75 South (Central Expressway) or the North Dallas Tollway, take I-635 West (LBJ) to I-35 South. I-35 South will merge into Loop 12 towards Irving. Take the DFW/Grapevine Exit and turn right heading on the service road parallel to E. John W Carpenter Freeway/Highway 114. At the first stoplight, turn left onto Tom Braniff Drive and then right onto East Northgate Drive. The campus is ahead. From West of the DFW Metroplex: Take I-820 East to Highway 183 East. Exit Carl Road and take a left under Highway 183. At the end of Carl Road, turn right onto Northgate Drive. The campus is ahead. From Dallas: Take I-35 East North to Highway 183 West to Highway 114 West. Take the Loop 12/Tom Braniff Exit, turn left onto Tom Braniff Drive at the second stop light. Turn right onto Northgate Drive. The campus is ahead.

**LOCAL:** DART serves Irving, Dallas, and the neighboring areas. Call 214-979-1111 for route and schedule info. Some local taxi companies include Yellow Cab (817-426-6262), Executive Taxi (817-877-1212), and Cowboy Cab Co (817-428-0202).

## Where to Stay

There are many hotel options in Irving and Dallas. During the official visit weekends, many hotels provide special rates and free transportation to the campus for its guests. Contact The Irving Wyndham Hotel (972-650-1600, $), the Sterling Hotel Dallas (214-634-8550, $$), and the Hilton Homewood Suites Irving (972-556-0665, $) for the specials.

---

## CAMPUS AT ITS BEST!

Students are very active in student organizations and activities on the UD campus. Popular activities involve concerts and dances, so be sure to attend one on your visit. The Groundhog Day celebration on campus is legendary, with games, a bonfire, live music, and even a Groundhog King and Queen! Students drive or take public transit into Dallas for off-campus fun. There is always something to do in Dallas.

# UNIVERSITY OF DENVER

University Hall, Room 110, 2197 South University Boulevard, Denver, CO 80208
**Telephone:** 303-871-2036 • **E-mail:** admission@du.edu
**Website:** www.du.edu/admission

## STUDENTS SAY

"The University of Denver is the perfect size: Small enough to offer a personalized education and large enough to offer everything you could possibly want or need!"

## FODOR'S SAYS

"An average of 10 billion coins are stamped yearly at the U.S. Mint, which has several exhibits on the history of money and a restored version of Denver's original mint."

## ABOUT THE SCHOOL

The University of Denver has strong programs in a variety of majors, but its business and pre-MBA program is the most popular; almost one-third of the school's 4,700 undergraduates major in this area. The small size of the school allows professors to give students a lot of individual attention and support. The fantastic weather in Denver is an added bonus.

## GETTING THERE

**BY AIR:** Denver International Airport is located about 23 miles from downtown Denver. Take RTD—Regional Transportation Division's SkyRide to downtown Denver. SkyRide buses stop at the Market Street Station (16th Street Mall and Market Street) or the Denver Bus Center (19th & Arapahoe Streets). Take the RTD light rail to the DU campus.

**BY TRAIN:** Amtrak stops at Union station and at the Denver Bus Center. Take an RTD bus to the campus.

**BY BUS:** Greyhound stops at the Market Street Station, the Denver Bus Center, and Union Station. Take the RTD light rail to the campus.

**BY CAR:** From I-25: Take the University Boulevard for the South exit—Exit 205. Turn right on East Warren Avenue for access to Carnegie Green. The campus is ahead. From the airport: Exit the airport going West on Peña Boulevard. Merge onto I-70 West / U.S. 36 West. Merge onto I-25 South toward Denver / Colorado Springs. Take the University Boulevard Exit 205. Turn right onto South University Boulevard and drive South for approximately half a mile. Turn right onto East Warren Avenue. The campus is ahead.

**LOCAL:** RTD—Regional Transportation Division serves the University of Denver campus and the city of Denver, including the Denver International Airport.

## WHERE TO STAY

There are many hotel options in Denver. The Fairfield Inn & Suites Denver Cherry Creek is close to the DU campus (303-691-2223, $). The Four Points by Sheraton Denver Cherry Creek is about 3 miles from campus (303-757-3341, $$), and the Denver Loew's hotel is less than 3 miles from DU (303-782-9300, $$). Ask for the Denver University rate when reserving.

## CAMPUS AT ITS BEST!

While you're on the University of Denver campus, be sure to attend a hockey game, where many of the students turn out to support the school. Students spend a lot of time off campus for internships and entertainment, so factor in some time to get to know downtown Denver, eight miles away—the Cheery Creek district in particular is great for dining and other entertainment.

# UNIVERSITY OF IDAHO

UI Admissions Office, PO Box 444264, Moscow, ID 83844-4264
**Telephone:** 208-885-6326 • **E-mail:** admappl@uidaho.edu
**Hours:** Monday–Friday, 8:00 A.M.–5:00 P.M.

## STUDENTS SAY

"Life here is small-town America. Downtown on Saturday mornings is live entertainment at the farmer's market, along with a vast array of artistic endeavors, home-cooked and foreign foods, and, obviously, fresh produce."

## FODOR'S SAYS

"Water reigns supreme in wooded Northern Idaho, which claims more than 140 lakes and 2,000 miles of streams and rivers."

## ABOUT THE SCHOOL

The University of Idaho, a state school with a reputation for providing a great education at an affordable price, is set in the laid-back, quiet setting of small-town Moscow. For social activities, many students participate in the Greek system and root for the university sports teams.

## GETTING THERE

**BY AIR:** Most visitors fly into Spokane International Airport, which is one hour Northwest of the campus. The Wheatland Express (1-800-334-2207) offers shuttle service from the airport to the university. Pullman-Moscow Regional Airport and Lewiston Airport are other nearby airport options.

**BY TRAIN:** Amtrak trains provide service to Moscow. A taxi can provide transportation to the campus.

**BY BUS:** Greyhound buses stop in Moscow. A taxi can provide transportation to the campus.

**BY CAR:** From Spokane: Take Highway 195 South to Pullman. Make a left at signs to Pullman. Then, turn right on Davis Way (Highway 270). Stay on Davis Way until it intersects with North Grand Avenue in downtown Pullman. Make a right on North Grand Avenue and get into the left lane. Make a left at the second stop light and follow signs to Moscow. At Moscow, 270 turns into Highway 8. Turn right on Perimeter Drive, make a left on 6th Street, and go to the first stop light. Make a right on Deakin Avenue and the university will be on your right. From Boise: Take Highway 55 North to New Meadows. Turn right onto Highway 95 and go North, toward Moscow. At Moscow, make a left at Sweet Avenue. Make a right at Deakin Avenue and drive until you see the university. From Pocatello: Take I-86 East to I-15 North. Take I-15 to I-90 West and exit at I-90 at Coeur d'Alene. Take Coeur d'Alene to Exit 12. Make a left here onto Highway 95 and head South for 84 miles to Moscow. Follow Highway 95 until you reach 6th Street, and make a right on 6th Street followed by a left on Deakin Avenue. You should see the university ahead.

**LOCAL:** The Moscow Valley Transit provides regional bus service throughout the area surrounding the university. A-Z Taxi (208-882-6141), Blue Water Taxi (208-883-2800), and Moscow Pullman Taxi Service (208-883-4744) are some local taxi companies.

## WHERE TO STAY

If you're planning on staying overnight, some nearby hotel options include La Quinta Inn (208-882-5365, $), Best Western University Inn (208-882-0550, $$), and Holiday Inn Express (509-334-4437, $$).

### SCHOOL AT A GLANCE

| | |
|---|---|
| Type of School | Public |
| Environment | Town |
| In-state Tuition | $0 |
| Out-of-state Tuition | $9,660 |
| Enrollment | 8,978 |
| % Male/Female | 54/46 |
| Student/Faculty Ratio | 20:1 |

### FRESHMAN PROFILE

| | |
|---|---|
| Range SAT | |
|   Critical Reading | 490-610 |
| Range SAT Math | 490-610 |
| Range ACT Composite | 20-26 |
| Average HS GPA | 3.36 |

### ON-CAMPUS APPOINTMENTS

| | |
|---|---|
| Advance Notice | Yes, 1 week |
| Appointment | Not Required |
| Saturdays | No |
| Average Length | 45 min |
| Info Sessions | Yes |
| Class Visits | Yes |

### CAMPUS TOURS

| | |
|---|---|
| Appointment | Preferred |
| Dates | Year Round |
| Times | M–F 9:30 A.M. and 1:30 P.M. |
| Average Length | 60 min |

---

## CAMPUS AT ITS BEST!

University of Idaho is a close-knit and welcoming community. Simply take a stroll down "Hello Walk" and this attribute will become palpable. Indeed, students continually greet each other on this walkway, located across from the Administration Lawn. Afterwards, head over to the Recreation Center. Here you'll find a 55-foot freestanding climbing wall, the tallest wall to be found at any domestic university. Those touring Idaho in the summer will have the opportunity to attend the Fresh Aire Concert Series in downtown Moscow. This annual series promotes local musicians with music ranging from classical and jazz to Celtic and bluegrass.

# UNIVERSITY OF MONTANA—MISSOULA

Lommasson Center 101, Missoula, MT 59812
**Telephone:** 406-243-6266 • **E-mail:** admiss@umontana.edu

## SCHOOL AT A GLANCE

| | |
|---|---|
| Type of School | Public |
| Environment | City |
| In-state Tuition | $4,978 |
| Out-of-state Tuition | $14,484 |
| Enrollment | 13,602 |
| % Male/Female | 46/54 |
| Student/Faculty Ratio | 19:1 |

### FRESHMAN PROFILE

| | |
|---|---|
| Range SAT | |
| Critical Reading | 508-585 |
| Range SAT Math | 486-578 |
| Range ACT Composite | 20-25 |
| Average HS GPA | 3.24 |

### ON-CAMPUS APPOINTMENTS

| | |
|---|---|
| Advance Notice | Yes, 2 weeks |
| Appointment | Preferred |
| Saturdays | Sometimes |
| Average Length | 60 min |
| Info Sessions | Yes |
| Class Visits | Yes |

### CAMPUS TOURS

| | |
|---|---|
| Appointment | Preferred |
| Dates | Year Round |
| Times | M–F, 11:00 A.M. and 2:00 P.M. |
| Average Length | 60 min |

## STUDENTS SAY

"[UM] is a complete package. Nice people, good programs, fun extracurricular action. There are things to do here no matter what kind of a person you are, or what your interests are."

## FODOR'S SAYS

"Montana's heartland is open grasslands and, rising abruptly from the plains, the sheer escarpment of the Rocky Mountain Front."

## ABOUT THE SCHOOL

The University of Montana—Missoula has a little bit of everything—friendly students and faculty, a great sense of community, a variety of educational opportunities, as well as a beautiful campus. While everything seems to revolve around Grizzly football in the fall, the rest of the social scene is up to each student to create, since there isn't a lively Greek scene to fall back on at this university.

## GETTING THERE

**BY AIR:** The Missoula International Airport is the closest airport to the campus. Take a taxi or shuttle to get to the campus.

**BY TRAIN:** The closest train station to Missoula is the station in Whitefish, MT, which is 109 miles from Missoula. From Whitefish, you will need to rent a car or take the Rimrock Trailways Bus (406-862-6700) to Missoula.

**BY BUS:** Greyhound buses stop in Missoula. Take a taxi to get to the campus.

**BY CAR:** From I-90 West: Exit at Van Buren Street and turn left at the stop sign. Make a right onto Broadway Street and make a left onto Madison. Drive over the bridge, stay in the left lane, and head left at the fork in the road. After the fork, make a left at the stop light. You should see the university shortly. From I-90 East: Exit at Van Buren Street, and turn right at the stop sign. From there, proceed according to "From I-90 West" directions above. From Highway 12 and 93 North: Both highways turn into Brooks Street through Missoula. Take Brooks Street through Missoula to Higgins Avenue. Turn right onto Sixth Street. Follow Sixth Street to the university.

**LOCAL:** The Mountain Line provides bus service throughout the area and to the university. The Airport Shuttler (406-543-9416) can take you from the airport to your hotel or the local area. If you'd rather take a taxi, one of the local companies is Yellow Cab Inc. (406-543-6644).

## WHERE TO STAY

If you're planning on staying overnight, some popular hotel accommodations include Campus Inn (800-232-8013, $$), Holiday Inn Express (406-549-7600, $$), and Double Tree Edgewater (406-728-3100, $$$).

---

## CAMPUS AT ITS BEST!

With its unparalleled beauty and outdoor recreational opportunities, nascent environmentalists will love the University of Montana—Missoula. The school's Forest Sciences Laboratory retains several research units that are part of the U.S. Forest Service Rocky Mountain Research station. Those with an appreciation for the arts will enjoy the Noon Performance Series at the University Center. These events feature a variety of entertainment, from singer-songwriters to cooking demonstrations.

# UNIVERSITY OF NEVADA—LAS VEGAS

4505 Maryland Parkway, Box 451021, Las Vegas, NV 89154-1021
**Telephone:** 702-774-8658 • **E-mail:** Undergraduate.Recruitment@ccmail.nevada.edu
**Website:** www.unlv.edu

## Students Say

"[UNLV has] a good atmosphere, a very nice campus with good facilities, and lots of activities organized by the campus."

## Fodor's Says

"At 1,149 feet, the Stratosphere Tower is the tallest building west of the Mississippi. High-speed elevators whisk you to a 12-story pod with a revolving restaurant, bar, and meeting rooms. The tower's most unusual features, however, are its roller coaster (which runs 900 feet above ground!) and the Big Shot thrill ride, which thrusts up and free-falls down the needle. Only in Las Vegas."

## About the School

UNLV is a fairly young institution that is making great strides in cementing its academic reputation. While undergrads readily admit that professor quality varies, students maintain that all of them are extremely approachable. Though largely a commuter school, UNLV's Greek scene is incredibly active and students love supporting Rebel athletics. Of course, Vegas itself is renowned for some of the best entertainment options in the world, and many an undergrad can be found strolling the strip between study sessions.

## Getting There

**BY AIR:** Visitors may fly into McCarran International Airport. The airport receives flights from every major airline. Taxis, car rentals, shuttles, and public buses are all available.

**BY TRAIN:** Amtrak provides service to Las Vegas, including one stop at the airport. Take a taxi to get to the campus.

**BY BUS:** Greyhound also provides direct service to Las Vegas. For additional transportation visitors may either use local buses or call a cab.

**BY CAR:** From Reno: Take I-80 East. You will take Exit 48 toward Fernley/ Fallon/Ely/ Great Basin National Park. Make a right onto U.S. 95 ALT/ NV-343 followed by a left onto U.S. 50 ALT. This becomes U.S. 50. Make a right onto South Taylor Street / U.S. 95. Continue to follow U.S. 95. Make a left onto U.S. 95 Truck/ NV-359 and another left onto U.S. 95. Make yet another left onto South Second Street/South U.S. 95/U.S. 95. Take the Las Vegas Boulevard Exit, Exit 75A, toward Cashman Field. Turn Left onto North Las Vegas Boulevard/ NV-604. Finally, make a right onto East Bonanza Road.

**LOCAL:** Las Vegas does maintain a public bus system known as CAT (Citizens Area Transit). The system consists of 51 routes and is served by 365 vehicles. Call 800-228-3911 for schedule and route information. For local cab service try Desert Cab Co. (702-386-9102) or Ace Cab Co. (702-736-8383).

## Where to Stay

For accommodations located within three miles of campus, try AmeriSuites (702-369-3366, $$), La Quinta Inn (800-531-5900, $$), and the Alexis Park Resort (800-453-8000, $$–$$$).

---

## CAMPUS AT ITS BEST!

UNLV sponsors a number of cultural events that are guaranteed to enrich your educational experience. The Charles Vanda Masters Series brings high-caliber performers such as Itzhak Perlman and the London Symphony to campus. Additionally, the Barrick Lecture Series has attracted a variety of luminaries, including Walter Cronkite, Tom Wolfe, and Henry Kissenger. The surrounding area also offers plenty of entertainment and excitement. The Hoover Dam is an easy day trip from UNLV as are the trails of Mount Charleston.

# UNIVERSITY OF NEW MEXICO

Office of Admissions, PO Box 4895, Albuquerque, NM 87196-4895
**Telephone:** 505-277-2446 • **E-mail:** apply@unm.edu
**Hours:** Monday–Friday, 8:00 A.M.–5:00 P.M.

## SCHOOL AT A GLANCE

| | |
|---|---|
| Type of School | Public, HSI |
| Environment | Metropolis |
| In-state Tuition | $4,336 |
| Out-of-state Tuition | $14,177 |
| Enrollment | 18,725 |
| % Male/Female | 42/58 |
| Student/Faculty Ratio | 20:1 |

### FRESHMAN PROFILE

| | |
|---|---|
| Range SAT | |
| Critical Reading | 480-600 |
| Range SAT Math | 470-600 |
| Range ACT Composite | 19-24 |
| Average HS GPA | 3.34 |

### ON-CAMPUS APPOINTMENTS

| | |
|---|---|
| Advance Notice | Yes, 2 weeks |
| Appointment | Preferred |
| Saturdays | Sometimes |
| Average Length | 120 min |
| Info Sessions | Yes |
| Class Visits | Yes |

### CAMPUS TOURS

| | |
|---|---|
| Appointment | Preferred |
| Dates | Year Round |
| Times | 9:00 A.M.–2:00 P.M. |
| Average Length | 60 min |

## STUDENTS SAY

"UNM is a place where people can feel free to be themselves and further their education in a fun way."

## FODOR'S SAYS

"Spend an afternoon at Albuquerque Biological Park, an environmental museum that includes the Albuquerque Aquarium, Rio Grande Zoo, and Rio Grande Botanic Garden. The eel cave and shark tank are real kid-pleasers, and the zoo houses more than 1,000 animals, including elephants, bison, koalas, and endangered Mexican wolves, known as lobos."

## ABOUT THE SCHOOL

The University of New Mexico (UNM) offers its 17,440 undergraduates a rigorous academic program taught by top-notch professors, and then goes the extra mile to help students find their area of interest. Students participate in a core curriculum that gets everyone up to the UNM standard, and can then choose to join a freshman interest group, which expands on the core classes, take interdisciplinary classes, and join freshman learning communities. The beautiful city of Albuquerque adds to the school's allure.

## GETTING THERE

**BY AIR:** Albuquerque Sunport International Airport is three miles from the UNM campus. Take the Route #50 ABQ Ride bus from the airport to the UNM campus.

**BY TRAIN:** The nearest Amtrak station is in downtown Albuquerque. Take an ABQ Ride public transit bus to the campus.

**BY BUS:** There is a Greyhound depot in downtown Albuquerque. Take an ABQ Ride public transit bus to the campus.

**BY CAR:** From I-25 Southbound: Take Exit 224B, Dr. Martin Luther King Jr./Central. Turn left onto Dr. Martin Luther King Jr. You will enter the UNM campus at Dr. Martin Luther King Jr. and University. Turn left onto Redondo Road and right onto Las Lomas. This will turn into Campus Boulevard. Continue on Campus Boulevard until you reach Redondo. Turn right onto Redondo at the stop sign. Continue on Redondo—it will curve to the right. Turn right to enter Visitor Parking Structure. From I-25 Northbound: Take Exit 224B, Dr. Martin Luther King Jr./Central. Turn right onto Dr. Martin Luther King Jr. From there, proceed according to "From I-25 Southbound" directions above. From I-40 Eastbound: Take Exit 160, Carlisle. Turn right onto Carlisle. Continue on Carlisle until you reach Lomas. Turn right onto Lomas and enter the UNM campus by turning left at the University Hospital/Lomas light. Turn left onto Campus Boulevard. Turn right onto Redondo. Continue on Redondo—it will curve to the right. Turn right to enter Visitor Parking Structure. From I-40 Westbound: Take Exit 160, Carlisle. Turn left onto Carlisle. From there, proceed according to "From I-40 Eastbound" directions above.

**LOCAL:** Albuquerque's ABQ Ride buses serve the UNM campus.

## WHERE TO STAY

For lodging options in Albuquerque, check out The Plaza Inn, just a few minutes from the UNM campus (505-243-5693, $) and The Doubletree Hotel downtown (505-247-3344, $$). The Hilton is also nearby (505-884-2500, $$).

## CAMPUS AT ITS BEST!

The University of New Mexico has recently built a new student union on campus; this is a great place to get a feel for the student body when you visit. Athletics are big at UNM, so be sure to attend one of the rousing football games. Nearby Albuquerque provides endless entertainment, with cultural activities and festivals taking place year round: The New Mexico State Fair in early September is a great place to unwind during your visit.

# UNIVERSITY OF OKLAHOMA

660 Parrington Oval, Norman, OK 73019-4076
**Telephone:** 405-325-2151 • **E-mail:** admrec@ou.edu
**Hours:** Monday–Friday, 8:00 A.M.–5:00 P.M.; Saturday, 9:00 A.M.–NOON

## STUDENTS SAY

"OU is casual, fun, and friendly; it's a school that is good at academics and sports, and it's a place where it is easy to get involved."

## FODOR'S SAYS

"Many towns in central Oklahoma, including Guthrie, Oklahoma City, and Norman, share a common heritage: They were born in a single day. The land run of April 22, 1889 opened parcels of land in central Oklahoma to non-Indian settlements. Would-be homesteaders lined up on the borders and literally raced to stake their claims."

## ABOUT THE SCHOOL

The University of Oklahoma is a large school with more than 20,000 undergrads that offers its students an exceptional academic experience. Great facilities, a wide variety of academic majors, plentiful internships, and research opportunities galore help create an enriching academic experience for students. OU is no slacker in the social department either. The Greek organizations on campus work with other student groups to sponsor co-programmed events, and the whole campus comes together when it's time to pack the stadium in support of Sooner football.

## GETTING THERE

**BY AIR:** Will Rogers World Airport in Oklahoma City is the closest to campus. Take the Airport Express (405-681-3311) shuttle to get to the campus.

**BY TRAIN:** Amtrak trains stop in Norman. Take a taxi to get to the campus.

**BY BUS:** Greyhound stops in Norman. Take a taxi to get to the campus.

**BY CAR:** From I-35: Take the Main Street Downtown Exit and head East. Take Main Street to University Boulevard. Make a right (South) on University Boulevard. Follow this street to the university.

**LOCAL:** Students can easily get around Norman using Cleveland Area Rapid Transit or CART (405-325-2278), a public transportation system serving the campus and the surrounding area. City Metro Transit (405-235-RIDE) provides bus service in the Oklahoma City area.

## WHERE TO STAY

Some local hotel accommodations include the Days Inn (800-329-7466, $), Holiday Inn Norman (405-364-2882, $$), and Hampton Inn Norman (405-366-2100, $$).

| SCHOOL AT A GLANCE | |
| --- | --- |
| Type of School | Public |
| Environment | City |
| In-state Tuition | $3,006 |
| Out-of-state Tuition | $11,295 |
| Enrollment | 20,967 |
| % Male/Female | 49/51 |
| Student/Faculty Ratio | 22:1 |

| FRESHMAN PROFILE | |
| --- | --- |
| Range ACT Composite | 23-28 |
| Average HS GPA | 3.63 |

| ON-CAMPUS APPOINTMENTS | |
| --- | --- |
| Advance Notice | Yes, 2 weeks |
| Appointment | Preferred |
| Saturdays | Sometimes |
| Average Length | 30 min |
| Info Sessions | Yes |
| Class Visits | Yes |

| CAMPUS TOURS | |
| --- | --- |
| Appointment | Preferred |
| Dates | Year Round |
| Times M–F 9:00 A.M. and 2:00 P.M.; | |
| | Sat 9:30 A.M. |
| Average Length | 120 min |

## CAMPUS AT ITS BEST!

University of Oklahoma's Museum of Natural History is a fantastic destination for students and parents alike. It offers a wide range of exhibits, allowing visitors to explore evolution, Oklahoma's Native American population, and more. For a taste of Oklahoma's social scene, check out the Big Red Rally in early fall. On this occasion, thousands of Sooners fans gather together for one big mega-pep rally before OU's first home football game.

# UNIVERSITY OF THE PACIFIC

3601 Pacific Avenue, Stockton, CA 95211
**Telephone:** 209-946-2211 • **E-mail:** admissions@pacific.edu • **Website:** www.pacific.edu
**Hours:** Monday–Friday, 8:30 A.M.–5:00 P.M.; Saturday, 9:00 A.M.–NOON, and by appointment

| SCHOOL AT A GLANCE | |
| --- | --- |
| Type of School | Private |
| Environment | City |
| Tuition | $26,920 |
| Enrollment | 3,535 |
| % Male/Female | 44/56 |
| Student/Faculty Ratio | 14:1 |

| FRESHMAN PROFILE | |
| --- | --- |
| Range SAT | |
| Critical Reading | 500-620 |
| Range SAT Math | 540-670 |
| Range ACT Composite | 22/27 |
| Average HS GPA | 3.46 |

| ON-CAMPUS APPOINTMENTS | |
| --- | --- |
| Advance Notice | Yes, 1 week |
| Appointment | Required |
| Saturdays | Usually |
| Average Length | 45 min |
| Info Sessions | Yes |
| Class Visits | Yes |

| CAMPUS TOURS | |
| --- | --- |
| Appointment | Required |
| Dates | Year Round |
| Times | Call for times |
| Average Length | 60 min |

## STUDENTS SAY

"The strength of this school is academics. You can be sure that you will be well advised in class-es, and professors are always available outside of class."

## FODOR'S SAYS

"If you're here in late April, don't miss the Stockton Asparagus Festival at the Downtown Stockton Waterfront. The highlight of the festival is the food; organizers try to prove that almost any dish can be made with asparagus."

## ABOUT THE SCHOOL

University of the Pacific manages to attract a number of strong students, and many come to the campus to take advantage of the school's accelerated programs in pharmacy and dentistry. Pacific also boasts extraordinary departments in international studies, music, and engineering. Outside of the classroom, undergrads enjoy a healthy Greek scene and are quick to demonstrate their school spirit at Pacific's well-attended athletic events.

## GETTING THERE

**BY AIR:** The four international airports are San Jose, San Francisco, Oakland, and Sacramento. Airport shuttles and taxis are available.

**BY TRAIN:** Amtrak's San Joaquin route travels between Oakland and Los Angeles, stopping along the way in Stockton. Take a taxi to get to the campus.

**BY BUS:** Greyhound provides transportation to Stockton. It is best to take a taxi to the campus.

**BY CAR:** From San Francisco: Take I-80 East to Bay Bridge/Oakland. Proceed to I-580 East, heading in the direction of Downtown Oakland (CA-24)/Hayward-Stockton. Continue to I-205 East toward Tracy/Stockton. Take the I-5 North ramp. You will take the Pershing Avenue Exit. Continue on North Pershing until you reach Larry Heller Drive. Make a right onto Heller followed by a left onto Baxter Way. Make a right at President Drive. Lastly, turn right at Pacific Avenue. From Sacramento: Follow I-80 West, heading in the direction of San Francisco. Proceed to I-5 South toward Sacramento/Lost Angeles. Take the March Lane Exit. Make a left at West March Lane. Finally, turn right at Pacific Avenue.

**LOCAL:** The Altamont Commuter Express provides rail service from Stockton to San Jose during weekday rush hour. Additionally the San Joaquin Regional Transit offers local bus service around the city. For local taxi service call Yellow Cab (209-465-5721) or Valley Transport Services (209-234-7603).

## WHERE TO STAY

For accommodations relatively close to campus, try La Quinta Inn (209-952-7800, $–$$), Comfort Inn (209-478-4300, $–$$), and Radisson Hotel (800-333-3333, $$)

## CAMPUS AT ITS BEST!

The annual Resident Artist Series, presented by the Conservatory of Music, continually offers fresh and innovative programming. Past performers have included the New Pacific Trio and the Pacific Arts Woodwind Quartet. Hometown Stockton also has a lot to offer. The new Stockton Arena is home to hockey, indoor soccer, and arena football teams. In addition, the arena hosts concerts, including recent performances by Bob Dylan and Neil Diamond.

# UNIVERSITY OF PORTLAND

5000 North Willamette Boulevard, Portland, OR 97203-7147
**Telephone:** 503-943-7147 • **E-mail:** admission@up.edu
**Website:** www.up.edu

## STUDENTS SAY

"A great blend of academics, athletics, and college fun in a large city on a smaller campus."

## FODOR'S SAYS

"Pittock Mansion, 1,000 feet above the city [and] about two miles West of downtown, yields superb views of the skyline, rivers, and Cascade Mountains. Set in its own scenic park, the opulent manor is filled with art and antiques of the 1880s."

## ABOUT THE SCHOOL

University of Portland is a Catholic institution tucked away in one of the West's most luminous cities. The relatively small student body enjoys an intimate setting and close-knit community. It's not unusual for professors to meet with undergrads over coffee and invite them to participate in research projects. While the university hosts many spiritual activities, students say there is no pressure to participate. When looking for more secular fun, Portland offers fantastic culture and entertainment.

## GETTING THERE

**BY AIR:** Portland International Airport receives flights from a number of major airlines. Public transportation, taxis, and rental cars are all accessible for transportation to the campus.

**BY TRAIN:** Visitors wishing to travel by train will be delighted to know that Amtrak services Portland as well as nearby Vancouver and Oregon City.

**BY BUS:** Greyhound does offer direct service to Portland. To reach campus guests may either take local buses/trains or taxi service.

**BY CAR:** From Interstate Highway 5 (heading North): Driving on I-5, take the Portland Boulevard Exit (304). Make a left onto Portland Boulevard, continuing to Willamette Boulevard. Make a right onto Willamette and proceed for roughly 1.5 miles. You'll find the main entrance to the university on your left-hand side. From Interstate Highway 5 (heading South): Driving on I-5, you will take the Portland Boulevard Exit (304). Make a right onto Portland followed by a right onto Willamette Boulevard. Follow the "From Interstate Highway 5" directions above. From Portland International Airport: Driving on the Portland Airport Exit road (Airport Way), turn right onto 82nd Avenue. Make another right onto Columbia Boulevard and proceed for roughly seven miles. Make a left onto Portsmouth Avenue followed by another left onto Willamette Boulevard. You will find the main entrance to campus on your right-hand side.

**LOCAL:** Portland is often referred to as an environmentally conscious city and, not surprisingly, offers a variety of public transportation. The city operates both the TriMet system (which covers both the city and surrounding suburbs) as well as the MAX light rail (which conveniently stops at the airport). Additionally, tourists and residents alike can enjoy Portland's streetcar service. For local taxi service call Portland Taxi (503-256-5400).

## WHERE TO STAY

For hotels located reasonably close to campus try the Delta Inn (503-289-1800, $), Fifth Avenue Suites Hotels (503-222-0001, $$), and the Benson Hotel (503-228-2000, $$–$$$).

| SCHOOL AT A GLANCE | |
|---|---|
| Type of School | Private |
| Environment | Metropolis |
| Tuition | $26,000 |
| Enrollment | 2,860 |
| % Male/Female | 38/62 |
| Student/Faculty Ratio | 13:1 |

| FRESHMAN PROFILE | |
|---|---|
| Range SAT | |
| Critical Reading | 540-640 |
| Range SAT Math | 540-640 |
| Average HS GPA | 3.63 |

| ON-CAMPUS APPOINTMENTS | |
|---|---|
| Advance Notice | Yes, 1 week |
| Appointment | Preferred |
| Saturdays | Yes |
| Average Length | 60 min |
| Info Sessions | Yes |
| Class Visits | Yes |

| CAMPUS TOURS | |
|---|---|
| Appointment | Preferred |
| Dates | Year Round |
| Times | Continuously |
| Average Length | 60 min |

## CAMPUS AT ITS BEST!

The Office of Student Activities endeavors to assemble programs that appeal to a diverse student body. Their calendar always has a variety of events on tap, featuring everything from College Bowl to outdoor drive-in movies and barn dances. Portland itself is a vibrant city well worth exploring. The Hat Museum offers quirky displays of U.S. costume and cultural heritage. Portland's Blue Heron Cheese Company is another great destination. Come sample some brie and local Oregon wines while the kids enjoy the petting farm.

# UNIVERSITY OF PUGET SOUND

1500 North Warner Street, Tacoma, WA 98416-1062
**Telephone:** 253-879-3211 • **E-mail:** admission@ups.edu • **Website:** www.ups.edu
**Hours:** Monday–Friday, 8:00 A.M.–5:00 P.M.; Saturday mornings by appointment only

## STUDENTS SAY

"The University of Puget Sound is an unpretentious school that provides an excellent liberal arts education as well as a place to live, work, and play."

## FODOR'S SAYS

Don't miss the International Museum of Glass whose "showpiece is the 500-foot-long Chihuly Bridge of Glass, a tunnel of glorious color and light that stretches above I-705. Cross it to reach the building grounds, which sit above the bay and next to a shallow reflecting pool dotted with large modern-art sculptures."

## ABOUT THE SCHOOL

The University of Puget Sound combines strong academic programs with smart professors that care about undergraduates. The school boasts small class sizes of 10–20 students, almost all of which are taught by professors. The University of Puget Sound encourages the application of knowledge through its study abroad program, opportunities for community service, and special interdisciplinary majors can tailor classes to their areas of interest.

## GETTING THERE

**BY AIR:** The Seattle-Tacoma International Airport (AKA Sea-Tac) is located between Seattle and Tacoma, just 18 miles from Tacoma. Take an airport shuttle to the University of Puget Sound campus.

**BY TRAIN:** There is an Amtrak station at 1001 Puyallup Avenue. Take a Pierce County Transit bus or taxi to the University of Puget Sound campus.

**BY BUS:** There is a Greyhound depot at 510 Puyallup Avenue and Greyhound stops at the Amtrak Station at 1001 Puyallup Avenue. Take a taxi or the Pierce County Transit bus to campus.

**BY CAR:** From I-5, take Exit 133, Interstate 705 North, City Center Exit. Exit at Schuster Parkway and continue for approximately one mile and stay to the left. Exit to the left (Schuster Parkway), and follow Schuster along the water. Stay to the right and proceed approximately 1.5 miles. Exit right onto North 30th. Continue through the traffic signal in Old Town and up the hill.

**LOCAL:** Pierce County Transit operates a bus system throughout Tacoma, which includes service from campus to major shopping areas in Tacoma and buses to Seattle every day. For taxi service call Yellow Cab at (253-472-3303).

## WHERE TO STAY

For lodging options near the University of Puget Sound, options include Keenan House (253-752-0702, $), just seven blocks from the UPS campus and the luxury Chinaberry Inn (253-272-1282, $$), less than two miles away. Thornewood Castle B&B, an impressive mansion with stained glass and an English Garden, is about 12 miles away (253-584-4393, $$$).

## CAMPUS AT ITS BEST!

The University of Puget Sound is surrounded by nature at its most glorious: Washington State Commencement Bay, the Cascades, the Olympic Rain Forest, Mount Rainer, Point Defiance Park, and several beaches. With this setting, it's no wonder that nature-oriented sports and activities reign supreme on campus. To unwind, attend a sporting event to see many of the 2,600 undergraduate unite in cheering for the varsity teams or visit the popular Tacoma Aquarium and Zoo.

# UNIVERSITY OF REDLANDS

1200 East Colton Avenue, Redlands, CA 92373
**Telephone:** 800-455-5064 • **E-mail:** admissions@redlands.edu
**Website:** www.redlands.edu • **Hours:** Monday–Saturday, Monday–Friday, 8:00 A.M.–5:00 P.M.

## STUDENTS SAY

"Friendliness, social life, the weather, and independent study at the Johnston Center are definitely the school's main strengths, followed by great intramural programs and good academics."

## FODOR'S SAYS

"In 1897 Cornelia A. Hill built Kimberly Crest House and Gardens to mimic the chateaux of France's Loire Valley. Surrounded by orange groves, lily ponds, and terraced Italian gardens, the mansion has a French Revival parlor, a mahogany staircase, a glass mosaic fireplace, and a bubbling fountain in the form of Venus rising from the sea."

## ABOUT THE SCHOOL

The University of Redlands offers students programs of study in both traditional majors through the College of Arts and Sciences, or individualized programs through the Johnston Center for Integrative Studies. Either way, students face a rigorous workload tempered by the high accessibility and involvement of professors. The school also encourages study abroad by offering the programs around the world at the same rate as a semester at home.

## GETTING THERE

**BY AIR:** Ontario International Airport is 25 miles from campus and Los Angeles International Airport is 65 miles away. Take an airport shuttle to the University of Redlands campus.

**BY TRAIN:** There is a local commuter rail service, Metrolink, that runs from LA Union Station to San Bernardino, which is 11 miles away.

**BY BUS:** There is a Greyhound depot in Riverside, about 16 miles away. Take a taxi to the University of Redlands campus.

**BY CAR:** From the Los Angeles area: Take the I-10 East to University Street Exit. Turn left on University Street and then turn right on Colton Avenue. From the Palm Springs area: Take the I-10 West to Cypress Avenue Exit. Go through the first stop sign to Cypress Avenue and turn left on Cypress Avenue. From there turn right on University Street, and then a right on Colton Avenue.

**LOCAL:** The Redlands Trolley provides limited service around Redlands. Take a taxi to get around outside the Trolley service area. For taxi service in Redlands, try calling Yellow Cab Co. (909-793-6151), Taxi of Redlands (909-798-1111), and Yucaipa Empire Taxicab Service (909-790-2332).

## WHERE TO STAY

For lodging options near University of Redlands choices in the town of Redlands include the Dynasty Suites Redlands (909-793-6648, $–$$) and Comfort Suites (909-335-9988, $). Nearby San Bernardino also has lodging available at the Fairfield Inn (909-382-4560, $$).

### SCHOOL AT A GLANCE

| | |
|---|---|
| Type of School | Private |
| Environment | Town |
| Tuition | $28,476 |
| Enrollment | 2,358 |
| % Male/Female | 41/59 |
| Student/Faculty Ratio | 12:1 |

### FRESHMAN PROFILE

| | |
|---|---|
| Range SAT | |
| Critical Reading | 530-620 |
| Range SAT Math | 540-630 |
| Range ACT Composite | 21-26 |
| Average HS GPA | 3.58 |

### ON-CAMPUS APPOINTMENTS

| | |
|---|---|
| Advance Notice | Yes, 1 week |
| Appointment | Required |
| Saturdays | Sometimes |
| Average Length | 60 min |
| Info Sessions | Yes |
| Class Visits | Yes |

### CAMPUS TOURS

| | |
|---|---|
| Appointment | Preferred |
| Dates | Year Round |
| Times | 10:00 A.M., 1:00 P.M., and 4:00 P.M. |
| Average Length | 60 min |

## CAMPUS AT ITS BEST!

It doesn't hurt to be situated in the place Theodore Roosevelt once called "a sight for the gods." Students at Redlands love their campus's beautiful buildings and proximity to the great outdoors, so be sure to take a leisurely tour of the campus. Take in a concert at the Summer Redlands Bowl, or if it's Thursday night, try Market Night, a weekly entertainment and food festival. Palm Springs and Los Angeles are both less than an hour away.

# UNIVERSITY OF SAN DIEGO

5998 Alcala Park, San Diego, CA 92110-2492
**Telephone:** 619-260-4506 • **E-mail:** admissions@sandiego.edu
**Hours:** Monday–Friday, 8:30 A.M.–5:00 P.M.; Saturday, 10:00 A.M.–2:00 P.M. and by appointment

## STUDENTS SAY

"USD is a small school where students are people and not just numbers; it is a safe community with many great opportunities and friends waiting for you to find them."

## FODOR'S SAYS

"Maritime Museum: A must for anyone with an interest in nautical history—or who has ever read a Patrick O'Brian novel—this collection of six restored ships affords a fascinating glimpse of San Diego during its heyday as a commercial seaport."

## ABOUT THE SCHOOL

Famed for its strikingly beautiful and well-maintained campus, the University of San Diego has created a near-perfect environment for the driven student who thrives under personal attention. Professors go out of their way to get to know students and are extremely accessible outside of class. Students feel invested in the school's vision of a "community accentuated by a spirit of freedom and charity" via the "community service learning" that is a part of many departments' curriculum. The coursework is rigorous, but the helpful professors, perfect weather, and unbeatable location in vibrant San Diego make it all worthwhile.

## GETTING THERE

**BY AIR:** San Diego International Airport at Lindbergh Field is located about 15 minutes West of campus. Take MTS bus Route 992 from the airport to downtown San Diego and bus Route 44 to the USD campus. Taxi service is also available from the airport.

**BY TRAIN:** There are a few Amtrak stations in San Diego, but the nearest is Old Town Train station at 4005 Taylor Street, just half a mile away. Walk or take a cab or bus to the USD campus.

**BY BUS:** Greyhound has a bus stop at 120 West Broadway. Take a cab or MTS bus to the USD campus.

**BY CAR:** From the North: Use I-5 South, exit at Sea World Drive and Tecolote Road. Proceed left at the stoplight toward Morena Boulevard. Turn right on Morena, left on Napa, and left on Linda Vista Road. Travel to the second stoplight to USD's East entrance, turn left, and enter campus. From the South (or the airport): Use I-5 North, exit at Morena Boulevard. Signs will say Morena Boulevard; use I-8 East. Stay to the right and follow the signs for Morena Boulevard. Make the first right onto Linda Vista Road. Travel to the third stoplight to USD's East entrance, turn left, and enter campus. From the East: Use I-8 West, exit at Morena Boulevard. Make a right onto Linda Vista Road. Travel to the third stoplight to USD's East entrance, turn left, and enter campus.

**LOCAL:** MTS buses, trolleys, and coasters serve San Diego County. Bus Route 44 stops at the USD campus. For local taxi service call Orange Cab at 619-291-3333.

## WHERE TO STAY

San Diego has a wide selection of hotels and bed and breakfasts for visitors. Ask about special rates for USD guests before reserving. In the Hotel Circle/Mission Valley area, 10 minutes away from the USD campus, options include the King's Inn (619-297-2231, $), and the Town and Country Hotel (619-291-7131, $$). The ritzy San Diego Paradise Point (858-274-463, $$$+) in Mission Bay is 5 to 10 minutes away. For additional info about discounted room rates, visit BartellHotels.com/USDpartnership.

---

## CAMPUS AT ITS BEST!

The beauty of USD's campus is a definite point in its favor. Take a stroll through the manicured grounds and beautiful buildings to see what the students are so happy about. Greater San Diego offers much to do, but be sure to visit the historic San Diego Zoo during your stay! The Gaslamp district has great restaurants and nightlife, and Tijuana, Mexico, is nearby for people who are interested in a quick day trip across the border.

# UNIVERSITY OF SAN FRANCISCO

2130 Fulton Street, San Francisco, CA 94117 • **Telephone:** 415-422-6563
**E-mail:** admission@usfca.edu • **Website:** www.usfca.edu • **Hours:** Monday–Friday, 8:30 A.M.–5:00 P.M.

## STUDENTS SAY

"One of the greatest strengths about USF is that our college town is not just little shops and restaurants located around our campus. It is the whole entire city of San Francisco!"

## FODOR'S SAYS

"San Francisco is an outdoor person's dream. Golden Gate Park with more than 1000 acres of trails and fields, is especially popular with cyclists and in-line skaters."

## ABOUT THE SCHOOL

The University of San Francisco pledges in its Mission Statement a commitment to establishing a "diverse, socially responsible learning community of high-quality scholarship and academic rigor sustained by a faith that does justice." Students at USF embrace this ideal wholeheartedly, getting involved in community service (often built into the curriculum) and often studying abroad. In addition to socially responsible leadership, USF offers its 5,400 undergraduates the perks of much larger school, including great research and internship opportunities, while maintaining the personal attention and commitment to quality of a small college.

## GETTING THERE

**BY AIR:** The San Francisco International Airport (SFO) is only 15 miles away from campus. Take Bay Area Rapid Transit (BART) from the airport to downtown San Francisco and a cab or MUNI bus (lines #31, #5 or #38) to the USF campus. Cabs and airport shuttles are also available at the airport.

**BY TRAIN:** The nearest Amtrak station is in Emeryville, CA, but Amtrak's Thruway connecting bus service transports riders between the Emeryville station and San Francisco. Take a MUNI bus to the SFU campus.

**BY BUS:** Greyhound stops in San Francisco. Take a MUNI bus to the USF campus.

**BY CAR:** From the Golden Gate Bridge/North Bay: After crossing the Golden Gate Bridge, stay in the right lane and take the 19th Avenue Exit. Turn right on Cabrillo Street and left onto 14th Avenue. Proceed to Fulton Street and turn left. At the top of the hill, turn left onto Parker Avenue and right onto Golden Gate Avenue. Proceed to the visitor's entrance on Golden Gate between Kittredge Terrace and Roselyn Terrace. From the Bay Bridge/East Bay: After crossing the Bay Bridge, take the "101 North, Golden Gate Bridge" Exit to the Fell/Octavia Streets Exit (434B). Proceed straight through five signals and turn left onto Fell Street. Travel approximately one mile to Masonic Avenue. Turn right on Masonic and travel three blocks. Turn left onto Fulton and continue four blocks to Parker Avenue. Turn right onto Parker, and go one block to Golden Gate Avenue. Turn right onto Golden Gate and proceed to the visitors entrance (located to your right between Kittredge Terrace and Roselyn Terrace). From the Peninsula/South Bay: Take Highway 280 Northbound. Take the 19th Avenue Exit and stay in the left lane. Stay on 19th Avenue for approximately three miles. Turn right onto Fulton Street. At the top of the hill, turn left onto Parker Avenue and right onto Golden Gate Avenue. Proceed to the visitors entrance on Golden Gate between Kittredge Terrace and Roselyn Terrace. From Highway 101 Northbound (Peninsula/San Jose/South Bay): Take Highway 101 Northbound. Once in San Francisco, stay in the left lane and follow "101 North, Golden Gate Bridge" then take the Fell/Octavia Streets Exit (434B). Proceed straight through five signals and turn left onto Fell Street. Travel approximately one mile to Masonic Avenue. Follow "From the Bay Bridge/East Bay" directions above.

**LOCAL:** San Francisco's MUNI lines 5, 21, 31, 38, and 43 and the Bay Area Rapid Transit (BART) serve the university. For local taxi service call the Yellow Cab Cooperative at 415-626-2345.

## WHERE TO STAY

There are many options for accommodations near the University of San Francisco. Try the Laurel Inn (415-567-8467, $$), the Carl Hotel (415-661-5679, $), or the Baker at Jackson (415-921-3088, $$$). All three are within reasonable walking distance of USF.

## CAMPUS AT ITS BEST!

The USF campus is small and about half of the student body lives off campus, so San Francisco is definitely the campus-by-extension of the university. A tourist attraction in itself, students benefit from the great food, culture, and architecture of the city. Plan your trip around events such as ArtsFest in May, a showcase for art in different media from many cultures, or take a duck tour to get familiar with the city.

# UNIVERSITY OF SOUTHERN CALIFORNIA

Admissions Office: Student Administrative Services, 700 Childs Way, Los Angeles, CA 90089-0911
**Telephone:** 213-740-1111 • **E-mail:** admitusc@usc.edu
**Hours:** Monday–Friday, 8:30 A.M.–5:00 P.M.

## STUDENTS SAY

"You will be treated like gold while you are here. USC is committed to making happy alumni who love the Trojan Family. The best way to make happy alumni is to make happy students—and USC knows this."

## FODOR'S SAYS

"From surfing to whale-watching, LA has an enviable scope of activities. Given the right weather conditions, it's possible to choose between skiing and a trip to the beach. A word to the wise, though: the air is dry, so no matter where your adventures take you, bring bottled water and lip balm."

## ABOUT THE SCHOOL

The University of Southern California offers its students a great package—a hip environment; strong school pride, including a shared love for the cardinal and gold Trojans sports teams; and a wide range of academic programs, including one of the country's best film schools. With the city of Los Angeles at their fingertips, USC students are never bored.

## GETTING THERE

**BY AIR:** Los Angeles International Airport is the closest airport to the campus.

**BY TRAIN:** Amtrak provides service to Los Angeles. Take a taxi to get to the campus.

**BY BUS:** Greyhound makes several stops in Los Angeles. Take a taxi to get to the campus.

**BY CAR:** From 110 (Harbor Freeway) North: Take the Exposition Boulevard Exit. Take this road until you see signs for the university. From 110 (Harbor/Pasadena Freeway) South: Take the Exposition Boulevard Exit to the university. From 10 (Santa Monica Freeway) East: Take the Hoover Street Exit. Make a right at the light. Take Hoover Street to Jefferson Boulevard. Make a left on Jefferson Boulevard, and turn right on Figueroa Street. Take Figueroa Street to Exposition Boulevard, and make a right and follow signs for the university. From 10 (Santa Monica Freeway) West: Take the Hoover Street Exit. Turn right at the light onto Hoover Street. Follow the "From 10 East" directions above.

**LOCAL:** The DASH provides public transportation between Downtown Los Angeles and the university. The Los Angeles County Metropolitan Transportation Authority (Metro or MTA) provides bus and rail service that can get you around the city. If you'd rather take a taxi, call City Yellow Cab (323-666-1200).

## WHERE TO STAY

If you're planning on staying overnight, some local hotel accommodations include the Inn at 657 (213-741-2200, $$$), which is a charming bed and breakfast located close to USC. Other nearby options include the Radisson Hotel (213-381-7411, $$) and LAX Plaza Hotel (310-484-7000, $$).

## CAMPUS AT ITS BEST!

Every Monday, Wednesday, and Friday the Office of Admission sponsors Meet USC programs, designed especially for prospective freshmen. These half-day campus visits include information sessions with admissions counselors, campus tours, and meetings with representatives from academic departments. With the rest of your day free, you'll want to go off campus and explore LA. The Museum of Neon Art features the best examples of electric media and neon signs (naturally). The Ahmanson Theatre is one of the region's premier venues, presenting the works of leading U.S. playwrights such as Wendy Wasserstein and John Guare.

# THE UNIVERSITY OF TEXAS AT AUSTIN

PO Box 8058, Austin, TX 78713-8058
**Telephone:** 512-475-7440
**Hours:** Monday–Friday, 8:30 A.M.–4:30 P.M.

## Students Say

"Basically at UT the attitude is: If you can fit it in within four years and you meet the prerequisites, go for it. And if they don't offer what you want, figure out how to take it and it's yours."

## Fodor's Says

"The Austin Nature and Science Center, adjacent to the botanical gardens, has 80 acres of trails, interactive exhibits teaching about the environment, and animal exhibits."

## About the School

The University of Texas at Austin, one of the largest universities in the country, offers its 50,000 students state-of-the-art technology, fantastic athletic and library facilities, incredible academics, and student programs galore. It's up to students to decide how challenging they want their academic life at UT—Austin to be—the school has limitless resources for students who have the drive and initiative to take advantage of them. When students feel like having some fun off campus, they have the great city of Austin with its amazing music scene and incredible restaurants right at their fingertips.

## Getting There

**BY AIR:** Austin-Bergstrom International Airport, the closest airport to the university, is about 15 miles from campus.

**BY TRAIN:** Amtrak trains provide service to Austin Station. Use a taxi to get to campus.

**BY BUS:** Greyhound Bus Lines stop in Austin. Use a taxi to get to campus.

**BY CAR:** From I-35: Take MLK Boulevard Exit West for the South campus and it will be on your right. If you take I-35 to the 26th Street (Dean Keeton Street) Exit heading West for the North campus, then the campus will be on your left. From MoPac/Loop 1: Take the Windsor Road Exit East. It turns into 24th Street, which turns into Guadalupe Street, the Western border of campus. From Highway 71: If you're coming from the East, take I-35 North. From there, proceed according to "From I-35" directions above. From the West, take MoPac/Loop 1 North. From there, proceed according to "From MoPac/Highway 1" directions above. From I-290: If you're coming from the East, take I-35 South and from there, proceed according to "From I-35" directions above. From the West, proceed according to "From Highway 71" directions above.

**LOCAL:** Capital Metro Transit offers public bus service throughout the area. Call 512-474-1200 for route and schedule information. For local taxi service try American Yellow Checker Cab (512-452-9999), Austin Cab (512- 478-2222), or the SuperShuttle (512-258-3826).

## Where to Stay

If you're planning on spending the night, some popular nearby hotel options include the Super 8 Motel, Austin South (512-441-0143, $), the Radisson Hotel & Suites (512-478-9611, $$), and the Holiday Inn North (512-459-4251, $$).

## CAMPUS AT ITS BEST!

Are your college visits becoming slightly pedestrian? Shake up your search by taking the Moonlight Prowl, a nighttime tour of the campus. This program combines the standard sites with personal anecdotes and university lore. As you'll no doubt learn, UT is a school steeped in tradition. The annual Torchlight Parade continually brings out the masses in support of Longhorn football. The city of Austin itself also provides a good deal in the way of entertainment. Zilker Park is a local favorite, covering 351 acres and offering a multitude of recreational opportunities, including bike trails, a golf course, and even a kite festival.

# UNIVERSITY OF UTAH

201 South 1460 East, Room 250 South, Salt Lake City, UT 84112
**Telephone:** 801-581-7281 • **E-mail:** admissions@sa.utah.edu
**Website:** www.sa.utah.edu/admiss/index.htm • **Hours:** Monday–Friday, 8:00 A.M.–5:00 P.M.

## STUDENTS SAY

"The education here is really top-notch; [there are] tons of opportunities for undergraduate research."

## FODOR'S SAYS

"The Utah Museum of Natural History has Native American artifacts, dinosaur skeletons, and hands-on science adventures."

## ABOUT THE SCHOOL

The University of Utah provides a solid yet affordable education for its self-motivated students. The school is large, with 21,600 undergraduates, but the administration goes out of its way to make sure that the personal needs of each student are met. Honors-level classes provide greater access to U of U's excellent professors, and the school's 101-plus majors, excellent honors and research programs, and nationally-ranked sports teams ensure that students get a well-rounded experience.

## GETTING THERE

**BY AIR:** The Salt Lake City International Airport (SLC) is 11 miles away from the campus. Take a taxi or ride a Utah Transit bus and/or Trax train to get to the campus.

**BY TRAIN:** Amtrak has a station in Salt Lake City. Take a taxi or ride a Utah Transit bus and/or Trax train to get to the campus.

**BY BUS:** Greyhound stops in Salt Lake City. Take a taxi or ride a Utah Transit bus and/or Trax train to get to the campus.

**BY CAR:** From the Salt Lake City International Airport: Take I-80 East approximately 1.5 miles to the North Temple Exit. Follow North Temple approximately 3 miles to State Street (1 block beyond the Mormon Temple). Turn right on State Street, and go South 5 blocks to 400 South. Turn left, proceeding East on 400 South for approximately 1.5 miles until you reach the University of Utah campus. From I-15 Northbound: Take the Eastbound 600 South Exit. At State Street turn left, proceeding 2 blocks North until you reach 400 South. Turn right, proceeding East on 400 South for approximately 2 miles until you reach the University of Utah campus. From I-15 Southbound: Take the Eastbound 600 North Exit. At 300 West turn right, proceeding approximately 1.5 miles South until you reach 400 South. Turn left, proceeding East on 400 South for approximately 2 miles until you reach the University of Utah campus.

**LOCAL:** Salt Lake City's transit buses and Trax trains serve the University of Utah campus. Call 801-RIDE-UTA for route and schedule info.

## WHERE TO STAY

The University of Utah's Guest House is a comfortable and affordable place to stay right on campus (801-587-1000, $). In Salt Lake City there are many options for accommodations. Try the Sheraton City Centre Hotel (801-401-2000, $$) or the Hotel Monaco Salt Lake City (800-805-1801, $$–$$$).

## CAMPUS AT ITS BEST!

Only 7 percent of undergraduates live on campus, so in many ways Salt Lake City is the extended campus of the University of Utah. Students and residents of Salt Lake City alike attend concerts at the university's Red Butte Botanical Garden and Arboretum. Salt Lake City is known for its skiing, so try to get in a day on the slopes when you visit.

# UNIVERSITY OF WASHINGTON

1410 Northeast Campus Parkway, 320 Schmitz Box 355840, Seattle, WA 98195-5840
**Telephone:** 206-543-9686
**Hours:** Monday–Friday, 8:00 A.M.–5:00 P.M.

## STUDENTS SAY

"Students on this campus have a friendly, laid-back attitude. It's a casual atmosphere where you could talk to anyone about anything. We all have opinions, but they're well respected."

## FODOR'S SAYS

For the science-fiction connoisseur, check out The Science Fiction Experience whose "interactive multimedia museum takes you 'out there' with spaceship rooms and a science-fiction hall of fame. *Fantastic Voyages* focuses on time travel, *Them!* illustrates the fear of aliens, and *Brave New Worlds* explores the future."

## ABOUT THE SCHOOL

The University of Washington has everything its 26,000 bright undergraduates could want in a college: a gorgeous campus set in a vibrant city, state-of-the-art facilities/technology, and professors that want students to learn and grow, not just pass. The proximity of the mountains, lakes, and beaches are icing on the cake, since Seattle itself offers a variety of shopping, dining, and entertainment for students.

| SCHOOL AT A GLANCE | |
| --- | --- |
| Type of School | Public |
| Environment | Metropolis |
| In-state Tuition | $5,985 |
| Out-of-state Tuition | $17,592 |
| Enrollment | 25,469 |
| % Male/Female | 49/51 |
| Student/Faculty Ratio | 11:1 |
| **FRESHMAN PROFILE** | |
| Range SAT | |
|    Critical Reading | 530-650 |
| Range SAT Math | 570-670 |
| Range ACT Composite | 23-28 |
| Average HS GPA | 3.69 |
| **ON-CAMPUS APPOINTMENTS** | |
| Class Visits | No |
| **CAMPUS TOURS** | |
| Appointment | Required |
| Dates | Year Round |
| Times | M–F 2:30 P.M. |
| Average Length | 60 min |

## GETTING THERE

**BY AIR:** The Seattle-Tacoma International Airport (SEA) or "Sea Tac" is only 18 miles from the University of Washington's Seattle campus. From the airport, board bus 194 to downtown Seattle. Once in downtown, depart at any stop on Third Avenue. Transfer to either the 71, 72, or 73 bus to the University District. Exit the bus at Northeast Campus Parkway stop.

**BY TRAIN:** From the King Street Station at 303 South Jackson in Seattle, walk three blocks to Third Avenue. Board the 71, 72, or 73 bus to the University District and exit at the Northeast Campus Parkway stop, which is one block from the main campus.

**BY BUS:** Greyhound has a station at 811 Stewart in Seattle. From the station walk three blocks south to Third Avenue. Board the 71, 72, or 73 bus to the University District and exit at the Northeast Campus Parkway stop, which is one block from the main campus.

**BY CAR:** Take I-90 or U.S. 151 to Highway 12/18. Follow Highway 12/18 exit at Park Street Exit 261 B. Proceed North on Park Street about 5 miles to Langdon Street and turn right. Proceed one block to Lake Street and turn right.

**LOCAL:** King County's Metro Transit buses serve Kings County, the UW campus and Seattle.

## WHERE TO STAY

Seattle offers many choices for accommodations to the University of Washington visitor. The Chambered Nautilus bed and breakfast is within walking distance (206-522-2536, $$) and the Seattle University Travelodge is just two blocks away (206-525-4612, $). The Admiral Arms Bed and Breakfast is also only a few blocks from the campus (206-528-7800, $$$)

---

## CAMPUS AT ITS BEST!

There never seems to be a bad time to take in the University of Washington and its 700 acres of well-maintained greenery. Tour the Suzzallo library, an impressive three-wing structure described by a student as "straight out of a Harry Potter movie," or attend an Ethnic Cultural Theatre event on campus. Seattle itself offers tons of entertainment, and the surrounding areas provide venues for boating, sea kayaking, skiing, and hiking.

# WASHINGTON STATE UNIVERSITY

PO Box 641067, Pullman, WA 99164-1067
**Telephone:** 509-335-5586 • **E-mail:** admiss2@wsu.edu
**Hours:** Monday–Friday, 7:00 A.M.–4:00 P.M.

## STUDENTS SAY

"The student camaraderie is outstanding, especially at football or basketball games."

## FODOR'S SAYS

"Kamiak Butte County Park has a 3,360-foot-tall butte that's part of a mountain chain that was here long before the lava flows of the Columbia basin erupted millions of years ago. Ten miles north of Pullman, the park has great views of the Palouse hills and Idaho's snow-capped peaks to [the] east as well as nice primitive campsites, a picnic area, and one mile trail to the top of the butte."

## ABOUT THE SCHOOL

Washington State University is a big university with the personalized learning and perks of a small school. The 18,000 undergraduates are divided into 10 smaller colleges, which keeps the class size under 20, and students are happy with their professors' accessibility and the advising system. Students from the different colleges bond when it comes time to support the Cougars at this Pac-10 school.

## GETTING THERE

**BY AIR:** Horizon Airlines flies direct into the Pullman-Moscow Airport (4 miles). Otherwise, try Spokane International Airport (80 miles away). WSU recommends Wheatland Express Airport Shuttle Bus (800-334-2207).

**BY TRAIN:** The Amtrak Station in Pullman is less than 1 mile from campus.

**BY BUS:** Northwestern Trailways offers regular service to Pullman (also only one mile from campus).

**BY CAR:** From Seattle/Tacoma: Travel East on Interstate-90 to Vantage. Cross over Columbia River and take Exit 137 to Highway 26. Take Highway 26 approximately 130 miles to Colfax. At Colfax, turn right onto Main Street (Highway 195). Continue to Pullman. Turn left at signs to Pullman, then right on Davis Way. Follow Davis Way until it intersects with North Grand Avenue in downtown Pullman. From Portland/Vancouver: Travel East on Interstate 84 to Interstate 82 (Exit 179). Go North on Interstate 82 to Kennewick. Take Highway 395 North and cross bridge to Pasco. Proceed West on Interstate 182. Turn left onto Highway 395 at the intersection of I-182, Highway 12, and 395. Take 395 North, turn right on Highway 260 at Connell. At Washtucna, turn right on Highway 26 and continue to Colfax. From there, proceed according to "From Seattle/Tacoma" directions above. From Spokane: Take Interstate 90 to Colfax/Pullman Exit 279. Take the Pullman/Colfax Exit 279 and then take Highway 195 South to Pullman. From there, proceed according to "From Seattle/Tacoma" directions above. From Missoula: Take Interstate 90 West to Spokane. Take the Pullman/Colfax Exit to Highway 195. From there, proceed according to "From Seattle/Tacoma" directions above. From Boise: Take Interstate 84 West. At Pendleton, take Oregon-Washington Highway 11. At Walla Walla, get on Highway 12 East. At Dusty, turn right onto Highway 26. At Colfax, turn right onto Main Street (Highway 195) and continue to Pullman. From there, proceed according to "From Seattle/Tacoma" directions above.

**LOCAL:** Washington State University students ride free on Pullman Transit. Pullman transit serves Pullman and the WSU campus, going between campus and remote housing as well.

## WHERE TO STAY

The city of Pullman and its neighbors have many accommodations options in Pullman, including the Holiday Inn Express (509-334-4437, $$) and Hawthorn Inn & Suites (509-332-0928, $). La Quinta Inn (208-882-5635, $) is just 8 miles outside of Pullman in Moscow.

## CAMPUS AT ITS BEST!

The Washington State University Creamery is a must-see on the WSU campus. The Creamery turns out cheeses and ice creams in many unique favors and offers tours and short cheese-making courses. Take a look at the Bill Chipman Trail, 6.3 miles of paved path in the wheat fields between Pullman and Moscow, Idaho where you can blade, skate, jog, and even sometimes ski! And don't forget to join in and cheer the Cougars on to victory!

# WHITMAN COLLEGE

345 Boyer Ave, Walla Walla, WA 99362-2083
**Telephone:** 509-527-5176 • **E-mail:** admission@whitman.edu
**Website:** www.whitman.edu • **Hours:** Monday–Friday, 8:30 A.M.–4:30 P.M.;  Saturday, 9:00 A.M.–1:00 P.M.

## Students Say

"Demanding classes that challenge and develop one's ability to think analytically and critically all in a non-competitive, supportive, fun environment."

## Fodor's Says

"Ft. Walla Walla Museum, a few miles west of Walla Walla, occupies a museum building. Before the U.S. Army established Ft. Wall Walla at this site, five fur-traders forts bearing that name were built near Wallula, above the mouth of the Walla Walla River. . . . All of them were destroyed by flood waters."

## About the School

Students sometimes refer to school as the Whitman Bubble due to the constant flurry of class, community service, and recreational activities on campus. At this tiny college of just 1,450 undergraduates the student/faculty ratio of 10:1 and the approachability of the professors make the rigorous workload bearable. Whitman College keeps students involved in the administrative life of the college as well; students review teachers and give feedback on the selection of new presidents.

## Getting There

**BY AIR:** Horizon Airlines flies direct from Seattle Tacoma International to Walla Walla Airport. Another option is Tri-Cities Airport in Pasco (45 miles away).

**BY TRAIN:** The Amtrak station is less than a mile away from campus. Take Valley Transit to the Whitman Campus.

**BY BUS:** There is a Greyhound depot in Pasco (45 miles). It's best to rent a car or take a taxi to the Whitman campus.

**BY CAR:** From Northwest (Seattle): Take Interstate 90 East, and exit onto I-82 East/U.S. 97 South. Follow Interstate 82. Exit at I-182 East/U.S.-12 East. Take Interstate 182, which becomes U.S. 12 East, for 10 miles. In Walla Walla, take the Clinton Street Exit to the right. Turn right on Boyer Avenue. From Western Oregon (Portland): Follow Interstate 84 East. Take Exit 210, the OR-11 exit, toward Pendleton/Milton-Freewater. Turn left onto Oregon-Washington Highway/OR-11. Turn right onto SE Court Avenue/OR-11/Oregon-Washington Highway/Pendleton Highway/U.S. 30. Follow OR-11/Oregon-Washington Highway. OR-11 North becomes WA-125 North after 33 miles. WA-125 North brings you into Walla Walla. WA-125 becomes Ninth Street. Turn right on Main Street. At the five-point intersection, veer right onto Boyer Avenue. From Northeast (Spokane): Take Interstate 90 West. Exit on U.S. 395 South and follow for 75 miles. Exit U.S. 12 East and follow for 30 miles. In Walla Walla take the Clinton Street exit to the right. Turn right on Boyer Avenue. From East (Boise): Follow Interstate 84 West. Take Exit 216 toward Walla Walla. Turn right off of the exit ramp. Follow this road past Mission until you reach OR-11. OR-11 North becomes WA-125 North. WA-125 North brings you into Walla Walla. WA-125 becomes Ninth Street. Turn right on Main Street. At the five-point intersection, veer right onto Boyer Avenue.

**LOCAL:** Valley Transit stops at Whitman College and serves the Walla Walla Valley.

## Where to Stay

There are several options for lodging within walking distance of the Whitman College Campus. Try the Green Gables Inn (509-525-5501, $$), the Travelodge Walla Walla (509-529-4940, $), and the Howard Johnson Express (509-529-4360, $).

| SCHOOL AT A GLANCE | |
| --- | --- |
| Type of School | Private |
| Environment | Town |
| Tuition | $28,400 |
| Enrollment | 1,488 |
| % Male/Female | 46/54 |
| Student/Faculty Ratio | 10:1 |

| FRESHMAN PROFILE | |
| --- | --- |
| Range SAT | |
| Critical Reading | 620-750 |
| Range SAT Math | 620-700 |
| Range ACT Composite | 27-31 |
| Average HS GPA | 3.77 |

| ON-CAMPUS APPOINTMENTS | |
| --- | --- |
| Advance Notice | Yes, 2 weeks |
| Appointment | Preferred |
| Saturdays | Sometimes |
| Average Length | 60 min |
| Info Sessions | Yes |
| Class Visits | Yes |

| CAMPUS TOURS | |
| --- | --- |
| Appointment | Preferred |
| Dates | Year Round |
| Times | M–F 9:00 A.M., 10:00 A.M., and 2:30 P.M. |
| Average Length | 60 min |

## CAMPUS AT ITS BEST!

At Whitman College, students make their own fun on campus, since nearby Walla Walla is pretty quiet. Attend a performance by one of the very popular a cappella groups or go to a sports event. If you're there on a Friday be sure to stop by the Friday night Coffeehouse, a showcase for Whitman College's different musical talents.

# WHITTIER COLLEGE

13406 East Philadelphia Street, PO Box 634, Whittier, CA 90608
**Telephone:** 562-907-4238 • **E-mail:** admission@whittier.edu
**Website:** www.whittier.edu • **Hours:** Monday–Friday, 8:00 A.M.–5:00 P.M.

## STUDENTS SAY

"Whittier is a great place to be—close to the city, the beach, the mountains—and a great place to learn with small class sizes and some serious one-on-one attention."

## FODOR'S SAYS

"California has more mall space, by far, than any other state. Since distances between shopping districts can be vast in this notoriously car-dependent city, don't try to hit too many shopping areas in one day or you'll spend more time driving than spending."

## ABOUT THE SCHOOL

Whittier College's greatest strengths lie in its professors' dedication and the small student/faculty ratio of 12:1. Whittier's 1,300 undergraduates usually find themselves in classes of 10 to 20 students, being taught discussion-style by full professors. The individual attention continues outside the classroom where students can find help from a professor or administrator with everything from writing a paper to time management. When students need a break from studying, the beach and Los Angeles are just 20 to 30 minutes away.

## GETTING THERE

**BY AIR:** Los Angeles International Airport (LAX) is 26 miles away. Take an airport shuttle or taxi to the Whittier campus.

**BY TRAIN:** There is an Amtrak station 10 miles away in Fullerton. Take a taxi to the campus.

**BY BUS:** There is a Greyhound depot in Norwalk, about six miles away from the Whittier campus. Take a taxi to the campus.

**BY CAR:** From the San Gabriel Freeway (605): Exit 605 Freeway on Beverly Boulevard East. Proceed on Beverly Boulevard to Painter Avenue for approximately 2.5 miles. Turn right. Proceed on Painter Avenue for approximately half a mile to Whittier College. From the Pomona Freeway (60): Exit 60 Freeway on Azusa Avenue. Go South. Proceed on Azusa Avenue to Colima Road (0.5 miles). Turn right. Proceed on Colima Road for five miles to Mar Vista Street. Turn right. Proceed on Mar Vista Street for two miles to Painter Avenue. Turn right. Proceed on Painter Avenue for two blocks to Whittier College.

**LOCAL:** Routes 1 and 2 of Whittier Transit (800-266-6883) stop at Whittier College. For local taxi service, call All Brother Cabs (562-698-0666) or 1 Airport Taxi Services (562-693-5050).

## WHERE TO STAY

There are many options for accommodations in Whittier or in nearby Los Angeles. Ask about special Whittier rates at local hotels and bed and breakfasts when reserving. The Vagabond Inn is about two miles off campus (562-698-9701, $) and the Radisson Hotel Whittier is only a half mile away (562-945-8511, $$). Nearby Rosemead has the Double Tree Hotel (323-201-3461, $–$$).

## CAMPUS AT ITS BEST!

If you are there in the fall, attend Whittier College's three-day fall SportsFest, a college-wide Olympics whose proceeds benefit a blood drive. There's always something to do in the surrounding area as well: a 20-minute drive gets you to the beach or to busy Los Angeles, and uptown Whittier—just a few blocks away—has entertainment movie houses and restaurants for those who can't drive off-campus.

# WILLAMETTE UNIVERSITY

900 State Street, Salem, OR 97301
**Telephone:** 503-370-6303 • **E-mail:** libarts@willamette.edu
**Website:** www.willamette.edu • **Hours:** Monday–Friday, 8:00 A.M.–5:00 P.M.

## STUDENTS SAY

"Almost all of the students at Willamette are smart and serious about their studies, even though they like to have fun too. Interests outside of classes vary widely, as do values. Everyone is welcomed."

## FODOR'S SAYS

"[Salem's] Deepwood Estate, on the National Register of Historic Places, encompasses [five and a half] acres of lawns, formal English gardens, and a fanciful 1894 Queen Anne mansion with splendid interior woodwork and original stained glass."

## ABOUT THE SCHOOL

The 1,875 undergraduates at Willamette seem to have found the trifecta for a balanced college experience: rigorous academics with accessible professors, a beautiful campus near a fun city, and excellent sports and study abroad opportunities. The classes are usually seminar-style, and struggling students find professors to be very accessible and tuned in to student needs. The Willamette students take the university's motto "Not Unto Ourselves Alone Are We Born" seriously, and engage in a wide variety of community service both in the Salem area and throughout the country.

## GETTING THERE

**BY AIR:** Portland International Airport (PDX) is 60 miles away. Take the HUT Airport Shuttle to the Red Lion Hotel (3301 Market Street Northeast) in Salem. From there, take a cab or ride Cherriots (Salem's public transit) to the campus.

**BY TRAIN:** Amtrak services a station at the Southeast corner of the campus.

**BY BUS:** There is a Greyhound depot just six blocks away from the Willamette campus.

**BY CAR:** From I-5 (North or South): Take the Highway 22 Exit (253). At the first light, head West (a left turn for those coming from the South and a right when coming from the North). As you pass 17th street you'll start up an overpass. At the top of this overpass, take the exit to the right (Willamette University is indicated on the sign). Keep left as the exit divides. After passing through the stoplight, you will see a Willamette U. sign and entrance to the right. Pass and make a right at the next stoplight (Winter Street). Pull into the Guest Parking lot immediately on the right. From the Oregon Coast: Take Highway 18 from Lincoln City (off Highway 101) East. Stay on Highway 18 for about 27 miles. Take the Salem Exit (Highway 22). Stay on Highway 22 for about 26 miles. Highway 22 will take you into downtown Salem, crossing a bridge over the Willamette River, onto Center Street. Turn right on High Street. Turn left on State Street. Turn right on Winter Street (this is the Northwest corner of campus). Just before the stoplight (Bellevue Street), turn left into the Guest Parking lot. From the Cascade Mountains: Take Highway 22 West. After your pass I-5, follow the "From I-5" directions above.

**LOCAL:** Students with a valid ID ride free on Cherriots, Salem's public transit bus. The number 6 bus stops at the university.

## WHERE TO STAY

Salem has plenty of accommodations for visitors, and even the inexpensive options have great amenities. Ask about special Willamette rates before reserving. Try either the Phoenix Inn (888-239-9593) or the Red Lion Hotel (503-370-7888, $). Both are just 2.5 miles from the Willamette campus and have a pool, wireless high-speed access, and a spa and fitness center. The fancy Phoenix Grand Hotel is half a mile away in downtown Salem. A two night stay is required (503-540-7800, $$).

## CAMPUS AT ITS BEST!

Take advantage of the outdoor activities in the Salem area when you visit. The Cascade Mountains are only an hour east and the beaches are an hour west. Both make great day or weekend trips for Willamette students. While you're on campus, visit the Hallie Ford Museum of Art. It boasts a wide collection of European, Asian, Native American, and historic and contemporary regional art on display throughout the year.

# THE MIDWEST

The Midwest is a pretty neat stretch of country, aptly nick-named the "breadbasket" of the United States. It has acres and acres of farmland, envelops most of the Great Lakes, and boasts fantastic architecture, world-class cities, and all the best features of small-town life.

Much of the Midwest is flat, and you can drive for hours in a straight line without hitting a hill. But did you know that Minnesota is known as the "Land of 10,000 Lakes" (though the number of lakes is actually much higher)? Michigan, on the other hand, is the "Great Lakes State" because it touches four of the five Great Lakes in addition to playing host to 11,000 inlands lakes of its very own.

Wisconsin, Michigan, Illinois, and Indiana all have miles of Lake Michigan shoreline that, as many Midwesterners would say, rival that of any ocean state. Illinois, on the other hand, is largely made up of prairie fields, hence its nickname, the "Prairie State."

Missouri and Nebraska are marked by rolling hills, (yep, we said hills), and open, fertile plains. South Dakota has the Black Hills, home to famed Mount Rushmore, and the Badlands.

While the Midwest is often thought of as the gateway to the West (St. Louis played a pivotal role in the westward migration of settlers as the starting point for the Oregon and Santa Fe trails) there are enough things to see and plenty of things to do in the region to cause you to want to stop and stay awhile.

One of the Midwest's biggest highlights is the big, modern city of Chicago. Chicago is the hub of activity and excitement in the Midwest. But, though they are often overlooked by folks outside the area, there are plenty of other cities that provide those looking for an urban experience with a destination to enjoy some good ol' fashioned city living, including the Twin Cities of St. Paul and Minneapolis, Kansas City, Indianapolis, and Cleveland (home to the Rock and Roll Hall of Fame), to name just a few.

If you're into architecture, a visit to the Midwest is mandatory to see the numerous Frank Lloyd Wright buildings alone, not to mention others designed by Mies van der Rohe and Louis Sullivan. If music is more your thing, you can hear great blues in Chicago and Kansas City, while the classic sound of Motown (plus a little Eminem) still prevails in Detroit. Chicago has great theater (Steppenwolf anyone?), museums, and other performing arts venues that rival those of any large U.S. city.

The region's demographic breakdown is quite interesting. While the Dakotas are both sparsely populated, averaging around 9 to 10 people per square mile, and predominantly white, they also report above-average percentages of American Indian/Native Alaskan people in their borders. In general, as you head further west, the region's population decreases in both density and diversity, especially outside of the major urban areas (Chicago and Detroit).

The Midwest also has a reputation of a place where business gets done. The automobile industry got its start with Henry Ford in Michigan, cereal companies are dominant in Michigan (Kellogg) and Minnesota (General Mills), and breweries gained ground in and around Milwaukee (Pabst) and St. Louis (Annheuser Busch).

So, while there are plenty of cows in the Midwest, there's a lot more to see and do during your spare time than learning how to become a pro cow-tipper. (Besides, the cows are not big fans of that.) If you're considering attending college in the Midwest, plan a visit and spend some time in the region. Just remember that as you head further and further north, you'd better get used to the idea of some really long winters.

# MIDWEST MILEAGE MATRIX

| | Chicago | Carbondale | Urbana | Greencastle | Bloomington | Terre Haute | Cedar Rapids | Iowa City | Wichita |
|---|---|---|---|---|---|---|---|---|---|
| Chicago, Illinois | — | 330 | 139 | 175 | 226 | 181 | 250 | 221 | 737 |
| Carbondale, Illinois | 330 | — | 198 | 232 | 246 | 190 | 466 | 437 | 536 |
| Urbana, Illinois | 139 | 198 | — | 102 | 162 | 88 | 272 | 243 | 620 |
| Greencastle, Indiana | 175 | 232 | 102 | — | 45 | 34 | 372 | 343 | 648 |
| Bloomington, Indiana | 226 | 246 | 162 | 45 | — | 59 | 416 | 387 | 659 |
| Terre Haute, Indiana | 181 | 190 | 88 | 34 | 59 | — | 359 | 330 | 605 |
| Cedar Rapids, Iowa | 250 | 466 | 272 | 372 | 416 | 359 | — | 31 | 562 |
| Iowa City, Iowa | 221 | 437 | 243 | 343 | 387 | 330 | 31 | — | 507 |
| Wichita, Kansas | 737 | 536 | 620 | 648 | 659 | 605 | 562 | 507 | — |
| Topeka, Kansas | 598 | 403 | 485 | 512 | 526 | 469 | 385 | 369 | 139 |
| Grand Rapids, Michigan | 177 | 479 | 283 | 292 | 347 | 319 | 412 | 384 | 888 |
| East Lansing, Michigan | 220 | 519 | 327 | 306 | 307 | 335 | 456 | 427 | 931 |
| Ann Arbor, Michigan | 259 | 538 | 348 | 326 | 327 | 354 | 487 | 445 | 951 |
| Detroit, Michigan | 303 | 581 | 391 | 365 | 366 | 393 | 528 | 498 | 992 |
| Minneapolis, Minnesota | 409 | 721 | 515 | 636 | 680 | 600 | 274 | 303 | 647 |
| Saint Paul, Minnesota | 400 | 713 | 530 | 629 | 673 | 616 | 278 | 306 | 641 |
| St. Louis, Missouri | 294 | 132 | 184 | 210 | 224 | 168 | 349 | 320 | 442 |
| Kansas City, Missouri | 533 | 341 | 432 | 450 | 464 | 407 | 323 | 307 | 202 |
| Columbia, Missouri | 383 | 218 | 299 | 327 | 341 | 284 | 287 | 254 | 320 |
| Lincoln, Nebraska | 520 | 535 | 554 | 645 | 658 | 602 | 317 | 301 | 279 |
| Omaha, Nebraska | 467 | 528 | 489 | 637 | 651 | 594 | 264 | 248 | 376 |
| Grand Forks, North Dakota | 723 | 1059 | 828 | 927 | 971 | 914 | 587 | 616 | 864 |
| Bismark, North Dakota | 834 | 1171 | 939 | 1039 | 1083 | 1025 | 780 | 771 | 976 |
| Cleveland, Ohio | 343 | 580 | 471 | 365 | 366 | 393 | 579 | 550 | 1055 |
| Cincinnati, Ohio | 295 | 338 | 233 | 157 | 128 | 185 | 519 | 476 | 784 |
| Columbus, Ohio | 380 | 438 | 292 | 224 | 225 | 252 | 574 | 545 | 855 |
| Sioux Falls, South Dakota | 574 | 746 | 627 | 727 | 795 | 714 | 357 | 386 | 551 |
| Rapid City, South Dakota | 913 | 1049 | 966 | 1066 | 1150 | 1100 | 697 | 725 | 897 |
| Milwaukee, Wisconsin | 93 | 423 | 231 | 268 | 324 | 316 | 292 | 264 | 770 |
| Madison, Wisconsin | 148 | 447 | 255 | 353 | 413 | 339 | 163 | 178 | 689 |

# MIDWEST MILEAGE MATRIX

| | Topeka | Grand Rapids | East Lansing | Ann Arbor | Detroit | Minneapolis | Saint Paul | Saint Louis | Kansas City |
|---|---|---|---|---|---|---|---|---|---|
| Chicago, Illinois | 598 | 177 | 220 | 259 | 303 | 409 | 400 | 294 | 533 |
| Carbondale, Illinois | 403 | 479 | 519 | 538 | 581 | 721 | 713 | 132 | 341 |
| Urbana, Illinois | 485 | 283 | 327 | 348 | 391 | 515 | 530 | 184 | 432 |
| Greencastle, Indiana | 512 | 292 | 306 | 326 | 365 | 636 | 629 | 210 | 450 |
| Bloomington, Indiana | 526 | 347 | 307 | 327 | 366 | 680 | 673 | 224 | 464 |
| Terre Haute, Indiana | 469 | 319 | 335 | 354 | 393 | 600 | 616 | 168 | 407 |
| Cedar Rapids, Iowa | 385 | 412 | 456 | 487 | 528 | 274 | 278 | 349 | 323 |
| Iowa City, Iowa | 369 | 384 | 427 | 445 | 498 | 303 | 306 | 320 | 307 |
| Wichita, Kansas | 139 | 888 | 931 | 951 | 992 | 647 | 641 | 442 | 202 |
| Topeka, Kansas | — | 749 | 793 | 812 | 855 | 499 | 500 | 310 | 64 |
| Grand Rapids, Michigan | 749 | — | 72 | 132 | 161 | 585 | 576 | 446 | 685 |
| East Lansing, Michigan | 793 | 72 | — | 62 | 89 | 628 | 619 | 489 | 728 |
| Ann Arbor, Michigan | 812 | 132 | 62 | — | 43 | 655 | 646 | 508 | 749 |
| Detroit, Michigan | 855 | 161 | 89 | 43 | — | 697 | 387 | 551 | 791 |
| Minneapolis, Minnesota | 499 | 585 | 628 | 655 | 697 | — | 9 | 668 | 436 |
| Saint Paul, Minnesota | 500 | 576 | 619 | 646 | 687 | 9 | — | 669 | 438 |
| St. Louis, Missouri | 310 | 446 | 489 | 508 | 551 | 668 | 669 | — | 247 |
| Kansas City, Missouri | 64 | 685 | 728 | 749 | 791 | 436 | 438 | 247 | — |
| Columbia, Missouri | 188 | 535 | 606 | 624 | 668 | 555 | 557 | 124 | 125 |
| Lincoln, Nebraska | 167 | 681 | 724 | 743 | 785 | 432 | 434 | 442 | 191 |
| Omaha, Nebraska | 170 | 629 | 672 | 691 | 744 | 377 | 379 | 434 | 184 |
| Grand Forks, North Dakota | 723 | 899 | 942 | 969 | 1012 | 314 | 324 | 926 | 676 |
| Bismark, North Dakota | 774 | 1010 | 1053 | 1080 | 1122 | 430 | 437 | 1038 | 788 |
| Cleveland, Ohio | 917 | 305 | 229 | 176 | 169 | 751 | 742 | 612 | 855 |
| Cincinnati, Ohio | 652 | 376 | 309 | 246 | 256 | 744 | 735 | 352 | 590 |
| Columbus, Ohio | 719 | 323 | 261 | 192 | 202 | 813 | 804 | 417 | 657 |
| Sioux Falls, South Dakota | 349 | 758 | 801 | 820 | 861 | 245 | 252 | 614 | 363 |
| Rapid City, South Dakota | 691 | 1097 | 1140 | 1159 | 1201 | 614 | 610 | 955 | 704 |
| Milwaukee, Wisconsin | 629 | 269 | 312 | 340 | 395 | 336 | 327 | 380 | 567 |
| Madison, Wisconsin | 551 | 324 | 367 | 392 | 433 | 269 | 259 | 360 | 488 |

# MIDWEST MILEAGE MATRIX

| | Columbia | Lincoln | Omaha | Grand Forks | Bismark | Cleveland | Cincinnati | Columbus | Sioux Falls |
|---|---|---|---|---|---|---|---|---|---|
| Chicago, Illinois | 383 | 520 | 467 | 723 | 834 | 343 | 295 | 380 | 574 |
| Carbondale, Illinois | 218 | 535 | 528 | 1059 | 1171 | 580 | 338 | 438 | 146 |
| Urbana, Illinois | 299 | 554 | 489 | 828 | 939 | 471 | 233 | 292 | 627 |
| Greencastle, Indiana | 327 | 645 | 637 | 927 | 1039 | 365 | 157 | 244 | 727 |
| Bloomington, Indiana | 341 | 658 | 651 | 971 | 1083 | 366 | 128 | 225 | 795 |
| Terre Haute, Indiana | 284 | 602 | 594 | 914 | 1025 | 393 | 185 | 252 | 714 |
| Cedar Rapids, Iowa | 287 | 317 | 264 | 587 | 780 | 579 | 519 | 574 | 357 |
| Iowa City, Iowa | 254 | 301 | 248 | 616 | 771 | 550 | 476 | 545 | 386 |
| Wichita, Kansas | 320 | 279 | 376 | 864 | 976 | 1055 | 784 | 855 | 551 |
| Topeka, Kansas | 188 | 167 | 170 | 723 | 774 | 917 | 652 | 719 | 349 |
| Grand Rapids, Michigan | 535 | 681 | 629 | 899 | 1010 | 305 | 376 | 323 | 758 |
| East Lansing, Michigan | 606 | 724 | 672 | 942 | 1053 | 229 | 309 | 261 | 801 |
| Ann Arbor, Michigan | 624 | 743 | 691 | 969 | 1080 | 176 | 246 | 192 | 820 |
| Detroit, Michigan | 668 | 785 | 744 | 1012 | 1122 | 169 | 256 | 202 | 861 |
| Minneapolis, Minnesota | 555 | 432 | 377 | 314 | 430 | 751 | 744 | 813 | 245 |
| Saint Paul, Minnesota | 557 | 434 | 379 | 324 | 437 | 742 | 735 | 804 | 252 |
| St. Louis, Missouri | 124 | 442 | 434 | 926 | 1038 | 612 | 352 | 417 | 614 |
| Kansas City, Missouri | 125 | 191 | 184 | 676 | 788 | 855 | 590 | 657 | 363 |
| Columbia, Missouri | — | 320 | 312 | 804 | 916 | 729 | 467 | 534 | 492 |
| Lincoln, Nebraska | 320 | — | 58 | 550 | 662 | 848 | 786 | 839 | 237 |
| Omaha, Nebraska | 312 | 58 | — | 495 | 607 | 795 | 722 | 788 | 182 |
| Grand Forks, North Dakota | 804 | 550 | 495 | — | 271 | 1074 | 1058 | 1127 | 321 |
| Bismark, North Dakota | 916 | 662 | 607 | 271 | — | 1176 | 1170 | 1239 | 432 |
| Cleveland, Ohio | 729 | 848 | 795 | 1074 | 1176 | — | 243 | 142 | 924 |
| Cincinnati, Ohio | 467 | 786 | 722 | 1058 | 1170 | 243 | — | 101 | 904 |
| Columbus, Ohio | 534 | 839 | 788 | 1127 | 1239 | 142 | 101 | — | 969 |
| Sioux Falls, South Dakota | 492 | 237 | 182 | 321 | 432 | 924 | 904 | 969 | — |
| Rapid City, South Dakota | 833 | 582 | 524 | 620 | 351 | 1263 | 1249 | 1266 | 349 |
| Milwaukee, Wisconsin | 470 | 561 | 508 | 650 | 761 | 434 | 386 | 446 | 500 |
| Madison, Wisconsin | 448 | 483 | 430 | 583 | 702 | 490 | 447 | 507 | 440 |

# MIDWEST MILEAGE MATRIX

| | Rapid City | Milwaukee | Madison |
|---|---|---|---|
| Chicago, Illinois | 913 | 93 | 148 |
| Carbondale, Illinois | 1049 | 423 | 447 |
| Urbana, Illinois | 966 | 231 | 255 |
| Greencastle, Indiana | 1066 | 268 | 353 |
| Bloomington, Indiana | 1150 | 324 | 413 |
| Terre Haute, Indiana | 1100 | 316 | 339 |
| Cedar Rapids, Iowa | 697 | 292 | 163 |
| Iowa City, Iowa | 725 | 264 | 178 |
| Wichita, Kansas | 897 | 770 | 689 |
| Topeka, Kansas | 691 | 629 | 551 |
| Grand Rapids, Michigan | 1097 | 269 | 324 |
| East Lansing, Michigan | 1140 | 312 | 367 |
| Ann Arbor, Michigan | 1159 | 340 | 392 |
| Detroit, Michigan | 1201 | 395 | 433 |
| Minneapolis, Minnesota | 614 | 336 | 269 |
| Saint Paul, Minnesota | 610 | 327 | 259 |
| St. Louis, Missouri | 955 | 380 | 360 |
| Kansas City, Missouri | 704 | 567 | 488 |
| Columbia, Missouri | 833 | 470 | 448 |
| Lincoln, Nebraska | 582 | 561 | 483 |
| Omaha, Nebraska | 524 | 508 | 430 |
| Grand Forks, North Dakota | 620 | 650 | 583 |
| Bismark, North Dakota | 351 | 761 | 702 |
| Cleveland, Ohio | 1263 | 434 | 490 |
| Cincinnati, Ohio | 1249 | 386 | 447 |
| Columbus, Ohio | 1266 | 446 | 507 |
| Sioux Falls, South Dakota | 349 | 500 | 440 |
| Rapid City, South Dakota | — | 838 | 779 |
| Milwaukee, Wisconsin | 838 | — | 79 |
| Madison, Wisconsin | 779 | 79 | — |

# MIDWEST SAMPLE ITINERARIES

College touring in the Midwest is going to involve a lot of time on the road—there are tons of great colleges in the region to check out, but covering the distances between them can be somewhat daunting. For that reason, it's best to start in a major city like Chicago, Cincinnati, or Minneapolis, covering as much ground as you can in the surrounding area. Focus on quality of visit rather than quantity; non-Midwesterners considering schools in the region should make sure they are comfortable with the area's (sometimes very different) pace of life. This means saving time to explore life off campus during your visit, finding out about availability of public transportation, hometown entertainment options, distance to the nearest major city, and so on. Before you head out, be sure to gather maps to and from schools and hotels, driving directions, and all the phone numbers you may need. Research any local dining and shopping establishments you're interested in visiting and print out their names, addresses, and telephone numbers. Finally, be realistic: You're not going to cover all the ground you want to cover in just a few days. In general, try not to see more than two (three at most) colleges a day; too many visits in one day and your brain will start to atrophy. The itineraries listed below are just suggestions—you can and should modify them to suit your individual needs.

## IF YOU'VE GOT SEVEN DAYS:

**Starting Point:** Chicago, Illinois

**Saturday:** University of Chicago, University of Illinois at Chicago, DePaul University, Loyola University—Chicago
Stay overnight in Chicago.

**Sunday:** Illinois Institute of Technology, Northwestern University, Lake Forest College, Wheaton College
Drive to Lafayette, Indiana. Stay overnight in Lafayette.

**Monday:** Purdue University—West Lafayette, Wabash College, DePauw University
Drive to Cincinnati, Ohio. Stay overnight in Cincinnati.

**Tuesday:** Miami University (OH), University of Dayton, Antioch College
Drive to Columbus, Ohio. Stay overnight in Columbus.

**Wednesday:** Ohio State University, Ohio Wesleyan, Denison University, Kenyon College
Drive to Ann Arbor, Michigan. Stay overnight in Ann Arbor.

**Thursday:** University of Michigan—Ann Arbor, Eastern Michigan University, Wayne State University
Drive to Grand Rapids, Michigan. Stay overnight in Grand Rapids.

**Friday:** Calvin College, Michigan State University
Head home.

## IF YOU'VE GOT THREE DAYS:

**Starting Point:** Minneapolis, Minnesota

**Friday:** University of Minnesota—Twin Cities, Macalester College, Carleton College, St. Olaf College
Drive to Ames, Iowa. Stay overnight in Ames.

**Saturday:** Iowa State University, Grinnell College
Drive to Columbia, Missouri. Stay overnight in Columbia.

**Sunday:** University of Missouri—Columbia, William Jewell College
Head home.

# MIDWEST SCHOOLS

# ALBION COLLEGE

611 East Porter, Albion, MI 49224
**Telephone:** 517-629-0321 • **E-mail:** admissions@albion.edu
**Website:** www.albion.edu

## SCHOOL AT A GLANCE

| | |
|---|---|
| Type of School | Private |
| Environment | Village |
| Tuition | $25,668 |
| Enrollment | 1,953 |
| % Male/Female | 44/56 |
| Student/Faculty Ratio | 13:1 |

### FRESHMAN PROFILE

| | |
|---|---|
| Range SAT | |
|   Critical Reading | 520-645 |
| Range SAT Math | 540-670 |
| Range ACT Composite | 22-27 |
| Average HS GPA | 3.55 |

### ON-CAMPUS APPOINTMENTS

| | |
|---|---|
| Advance Notice | Yes, 1 week |
| Appointment | Preferred |
| Saturdays | Sometimes |
| Average Length | 30 min |
| Info Sessions | Yes |
| Class Visits | Yes |

### CAMPUS TOURS

| | |
|---|---|
| Appointment | Preferred |
| Dates | Year Round |
| Times | M–F 8:30 A.M.–4:00 P.M.; |
| | Sat 9:00 P.M. |
| Average Length | 60 min |

## STUDENTS SAY

"Albion College is truly dedicated to its students and their futures—the academics are excellent, the faculty top-notch, and the opportunities are amazing."

## FODOR'S SAYS

"Michigan has 96 state parks, including 21 in the Upper Peninsula, many with spectacular waterfalls."

## ABOUT THE SCHOOL

Albion's students describe the school as a caring and nurturing institution; the president even knows the majority of the student body by name. Students are also quick to praise the school's academic opportunities, especially within the pre-professional programs. While many are underwhelmed by hometown Albion, undergrads are kept entertained by a lively campus Greek scene and a plethora of extracurricular activities. Many also escape to nearby Kalamazoo or Ann Arbor on the weekends.

## GETTING THERE

**BY AIR:** Visitors traveling by air have three different options. The cities of Kalamazoo, Lansing, and Detroit all have airports within a reasonable distance from Albion. Rental cars or taxis are your best options for getting to campus.

**BY TRAIN:** Amtrak trains running between Chicago and Detroit stop in Albion daily. Take a taxi to get to campus.

**BY BUS:** Greyhound services a station in Albion. Take a taxi to get to campus.

**BY CAR:** From Eastbound I-94: Take Exit 121 (Eaton Avenue/28 Mile Road) and turn right. Follow southbound Business I-94 to Michigan Avenue (M-99 East). Make a left onto M-99. The campus will be to your right, between Huron and Mingo Streets. From Westbound I-94: Take Exit 124 (M-99) and turn right. Follow M-99 for roughly three miles into town. The campus will be on your left, between Mingo and Huron Streets. From Northbound M-99: Follow the highway into downtown Albion. Turn right onto Erie Street. The main part of campus will be on your left, between Huron and Mingo Streets.

**LOCAL:** For local taxi service call Limos.com at 866-546-6726.

## WHERE TO STAY

Visitors who require overnight lodging should investigate these charming accommodations: Wilde Oaks Guest Suites (517-629-4678, $), Albion Heritage Bed and Breakfast (517-629-3550, $–$$), or Palmer House Inn (517-629-0001, $–$$).

## CAMPUS AT ITS BEST!

The Kellogg Center is arguably the foundation of student life at Albion. From the Living Room and the Eat Shop to the game area and campus radio station, students flock here for relaxation, extracurricular activities, and receptions. The center is even equipped with a grand piano available for anyone who wants to entertain. If you choose to dine on campus, think about joining an Odd Topics Society Luncheon. These delightful events, occurring every fourth Wednesday of the month, allow individuals to share unusual interests with others in the Albion community.

# ANTIOCH COLLEGE

795 Livermore Street, Yellow Springs, OH 45387
**Telephone:** 937-769-1100 • **E-mail:** admissions@antioch-college.edu
**Website:** www.antioch-college.edu • **Hours:** Monday–Friday, 9:00 A.M.–5:00 P.M.

## STUDENTS SAY

"The professors and administrators are fantastically dedicated to the students."

## FODOR'S SAYS

"Southeast of Dayton, the National Afro-American Museum and Cultural Center is one of the largest African American museums in the United States—and the only such museum chartered by Congress."

## ABOUT THE SCHOOL

Antioch expects its students to be active, engaged citizens of the world, and it nurtures this goal from the beginning of freshman year. The college prides itself on operating as a democracy, and undergrads are involved in all important decisions. Students design their own majors and must participate in three co-ops, many of which take place abroad. Many continually boast that these real-world experiences are invaluable when it comes to transitioning into the workforce.

## GETTING THERE

**BY AIR:** Dayton International Airport, roughly 25 miles from Yellow Springs, is the most convenient for Antioch visitors. Take a taxi to get to campus.

**BY TRAIN:** The closest Amtrak station is located in Cincinnati, nearly 60 miles from Yellow Springs.

**BY BUS:** The Dayton Bus terminal, approximately 25 miles from Yellow Springs, is serviced by Greyhound. Once in Dayton, it's best to call a taxi to reach Antioch.

**BY CAR:** From I-675 Bypass: Take Exit 20, making a right onto Dayton-Yellow Springs Road. You'll stay on this street for roughly six miles and take a right on South Walnut Street. You'll pass an elementary school on your right. Proceed to the end of the street, taking a left onto Limestone Street. Drive through the traffic light at Xenia Avenue and make the first right onto President Street. You'll find the Office of Admissions and Financial Aid at the end of the street, inside Weston Hall. From I 70: Take Exit 52A and proceed south on Route 68 toward Xenia and Yellow Springs. After approximately six miles you'll enter Yellow Springs. Route 68 then turns into Xenia Avenue, the main street through Yellow Springs. When you hit the second traffic light, make a left onto East Limestone Street. Next, make the first right onto President Street. You'll find the Office of Admissions and Financial Aid at the end of the street, inside Weston Hall.

**LOCAL:** For local taxi service, try Charter Vans (937-898-4043) or Checker Cabs (937-222-4011).

## WHERE TO STAY

These hotels are all within a 15-minute drive to Antioch: Arthur Morgan House Bed & Breakfast (937-767-1761, $–$$), Comfort Suites (800-517-4000, $–$$) or Hampton Inn (800-HAMPTON, $$).

## SCHOOL AT A GLANCE

| | |
|---|---|
| Type of School | Private |
| Environment | Rural |
| Tuition | $26,000 |
| Enrollment | 379 |
| % Male/Female | 42/58 |
| Student/Faculty Ratio | 11:1 |

### FRESHMAN PROFILE

| | |
|---|---|
| Range SAT | |
| Critical Reading | 60-710 |
| Range SAT Math | 520-630 |
| Average HS GPA | 3.23 |

### ON-CAMPUS APPOINTMENTS

| | |
|---|---|
| Advance Notice | Yes, 1 week |
| Appointment | Required |
| Saturdays | Sometimes |
| Average Length | 30 min |
| Info Sessions | Yes |
| Class Visits | Yes |

### CAMPUS TOURS

| | |
|---|---|
| Appointment | Required |
| Dates | Academic Year |
| Times | M–F 10:30 A.M. |
| Average Length | 60 min |

## CAMPUS AT ITS BEST!

Antioch offers students and visitors alike numerous occasions to expand their cultural horizons. Herndon Gallery presents five contemporary art exhibitions each year and hosts a variety of events. Additionally, every Wednesday at noon the Antioch community is invited to attend the Faculty Lecture Series. Professors speak on a range of topics, from Mozart to the stigma of weight. Of course, many recreational opportunities are available as well. Prospective students might enjoy checking out the college's new Frisbee golf course.

# BALL STATE UNIVERSITY

Office of Admissions, 2000 University Avenue, Muncie, IN 47306
**Telephone:** 765-285-8300 • **E-mail:** AskUs@bsu.edu
**Website:** www.bsu.edu

| SCHOOL AT A GLANCE | |
|---|---|
| Type of School | Public |
| Environment | City |
| In-state Tuition | $6,360 |
| Out-of-state Tuition | $16,736 |
| Enrollment | 17,269 |
| % Male/Female | 48/52 |
| Student/Faculty Ratio | 17:1 |

| FRESHMAN PROFILE | |
|---|---|
| Range SAT | |
| Critical Reading | 470-570 |
| Range SAT Math | 470-570 |
| Range ACT Composite | 19-25 |

| ON-CAMPUS APPOINTMENTS | |
|---|---|
| Advance Notice | No |
| Appointment | Preferred |
| Saturdays | Sometimes |
| Average Length | 30 min |
| Info Sessions | Yes |
| Class Visits | Yes |

| CAMPUS TOURS | |
|---|---|
| Appointment | Preferred |
| Dates | Year Round |
| Times | 11:00 A.M. and 2:00 P.M.; |
| | Sat 11:00 A.M. |
| Average Length | 120 min |

## STUDENTS SAY

"Professors are willing to go above and beyond for their students' needs. They make sure students really understand material and are there to help if they don't."

## FODOR'S SAYS

"A living-history farm and a replica of Abraham Lincoln's boyhood home are the lures at the Lincoln Boyhood National Memorial."

## ABOUT THE SCHOOL

Ball State is a dynamic institution offering over 170 baccalaureate majors within seven academic colleges. The university has exceptionally strong programs in education and telecommunications. When class is out, many students partake in Muncie's healthy social scene. For big-city entertainment, those with cars sometimes head to nearby Indianapolis, Chicago, or Cincinnati.

## GETTING THERE

**BY AIR:** Both Indianapolis and Fort Wayne International Airports are close to campus. From there, take a taxi.

**BY TRAIN:** For train travel, take Amtrak to either Connersville or Indianapolis. These stations are approximately 40 and 50 miles from Muncie, respectively.

**BY BUS:** Greyhound does not provide service to Muncie. Instead, guests can take the bus line to either Fort Wayne or Indianapolis.

**BY CAR:** From Chicago, Northern Illinois, and Northwestern Indiana: Follow I-80 East to I-65 South. Proceed on I-65 South to I-865 East (just outside of Indianapolis). From I-865 East (which turns into I-465 East), take I-69 North (the Fort Wayne Exit). Continue on I-69 North to Exit 41 (Muncie/Frankton) at Highway 332, making a right turn onto said highway. You'll continue driving East on Highway 332 for roughly eight miles until you reach Tillotson Avenue (the fourth stoplight). Make a right onto Tillotson. Stay on the road until you come to the fourth stoplight. This will be University Avenue. Take a left onto University and go past Ball Memorial Hospital (located on the right). This road will take you to the South part of campus where the Visitors Center and Administration Building are located. From Indianapolis and Central Indiana: Follow I-69 North (which originates on the Northeast side of I-465). You'll take I-69 North to Exit 41 (Muncie/Frankton) at Highway 332. Turn right onto the highway and follow "From Chicago" directions above. From Cleveland, Akron, and Northeastern Ohio: Follow I-71 South to I-270 West (just outside of Columbus). Proceed on I-270 West (which becomes I-270 South) to I-70 West. Follow I-70 West to Richmond, Indiana and get on Highway 35 North. Highway 35 North will take you to Muncie. The highway will exit to your right and merge with Highways 67 and 3 into a bypass around the East side of Muncie. (Note: Drivers should ignore the sign directing you to go straight to Ball State.) Follow the bypass until you reach the McGalliard Road Exit. Make a left onto McGalliard Road and follow for around four miles until you come to Tillotson Avenue. Take a left onto Tillotson. Follow "From Chicago" directions above.

**LOCAL:** MITS, Muncie's city bus system, provides transportation from Ball State to many downtown destinations. Students ride for free.

## WHERE TO STAY

For hotels in Muncie, consider: Super 8 Motel (765-286-4333, $), Lees Inn (765-282-7557, $–$$) or Fairfield Inn (765-282-6666, $–$$).

---

## CAMPUS AT ITS BEST!

Prospective students who want to secure admittance to Ball State might want to pay a quick visit to the Frog Baby (a statue in the fountain next to Bracken Library). In the past, undergrads would rub her nose for luck prior to an exam. Today students have fun dressing her up during the cold winter months. Sports fans should think about touring the campus during one of the Football Saturdays. Come learn about university life and get a taste of Division I action.

---

# BELOIT COLLEGE

700 College Street, Beloit, WI 53511
**Telephone:** 608-363-2500 • **E-mail:** admiss@beloit.edu
**Website:** www.beloit.edu • **Hours:** Monday–Friday; 8:00 A.M.–4:30 P.M.; Saturday, 9:00 A.M.–NOON

## STUDENTS SAY

"Beloit is all about close relationships with other students and professors, meaningful class work, and figuring out who exactly you are."

## FODOR'S SAYS

"One of the state's foremost natural attractions is the Wisconsin Dells, nearly 15 miles of soaring, eroded rock formations created over thousands of years as the Wisconsin River cut into soft sandstone."

## ABOUT THE SCHOOL

Creativity. Community. Interdisciplinary learning. These are among the words most fitting to describe a Beloit education. Students at Beloit are encouraged to constantly challenge their imaginations, their curiosities, and their intellects. As a result, Beloit is the home of a vibrant study body that's active both inside and outside of the classroom.

## GETTING THERE

**BY AIR:** O'Hare International Airport in Chicago (70 miles from campus) is serviced by all major airlines. Van Galder Bus Lines offers regular service between O'Hare and the Beloit campus (608-752-5407). Other options include the General Mitchell International Airport in Milwaukee (70 miles from campus) and the Dane County Regional Airport in Madison (55 miles from campus), although be aware that there is no regular public transit between Beloit and these airports.

**BY TRAIN:** Amtrak service operates regionally out of South Beloit, Rockford, and Madison. Van Galder Bus Lines offers transportation from Amtrak's central station in Chicago.

**BY BUS:** Greyhound stops in Beloit. Van Galder Bus Lines also offers service between Beloit and numerous regional destinations.

**BY CAR:** From I-90: Travel on I-90 until you're near Beloit. Take Exit 185A on the Southernmost end of I-43 and go West. I-43 becomes Milwaukee Road. Stay on Milwaukee Road (which bears left after the railroad crossing) until you reach Chapin Street. Make a right onto Chapin. Five blocks later you'll come to College Street and see the college in front of you. From I-43 West: On the outskirts of Beloit, I-43 turns into Milwaukee Road. Stay on Milwaukee Road (which bears left after the railroad crossing) for two miles until you reach Chapin Street. Make a right onto Chapin. Five blocks later you'll come to College Street and see the college in front of you.

**LOCAL:** For taxi service, try Yellow Cab of Beloit (608-365-8855), Flying AJ's Taxi Service (608-368-7000), or Call-Me-A-Cab Incorporated (608-758-4004).

## WHERE TO STAY

A number of hotels sit within minutes of campus, including the Ramada Inn (815-389-3481, $), the Holiday Inn Express (608-365-6000, $$), and the Beloit Inn (608-362-5500, $$$).

| SCHOOL AT A GLANCE | |
| --- | --- |
| Type of School | Private |
| Environment | Town |
| Tuition | $28,130 |
| Enrollment | 1,328 |
| % Male/Female | 41/59 |
| Student/Faculty Ratio | 11:1 |

| FRESHMAN PROFILE | |
| --- | --- |
| Range SAT | |
| Critical Reading | 580-700 |
| Range SAT Math | 560-660 |
| Range ACT Composite | 25-29 |
| Average HS GPA | 3.52 |

| ON-CAMPUS APPOINTMENTS | |
| --- | --- |
| Advance Notice | Yes, 2 weeks |
| Appointment | Required |
| Saturdays | Yes |
| Average Length | 60 min |
| Info Sessions | No |
| Class Visits | Yes |

| CAMPUS TOURS | |
| --- | --- |
| Appointment | Required |
| Dates | Year Round |
| Times | Varies |
| Average Length | 60 min |

## CAMPUS AT ITS BEST!

For a small college tucked away in a cozy Wisconsin town, Beloit buzzes with a surprising amount of entertainment and opportunity. Students touring the college in the fall might be lucky enough to catch Folk and Blues, a yearly on-campus music festival. Those contemplating a springtime visit might want to try Jello wrestling at Beloit's annual Spring Day festival. The Logan Museum of Anthropology is another must-see, and is home to a notable collection of Mesoamerican ceramics, Paleolithic art, and Native North American basketry.

# BRADLEY UNIVERSITY

1501 West Bradley Avenue, Peoria, IL 61625
**Telephone:** 309-677-1000 • **E-mail:** admissions@bradley.edu
**Website:** www.bradley.edu

## STUDENTS SAY

"Our Greek system is probably one of the greatest strengths of Bradley University."

## FODOR'S SAYS

"If you want downhill skiing in Illinois, try Chestnut Mountain Resort, with 19 runs that overlook the Mississippi."

## ABOUT THE SCHOOL

During March Madness 2006, the Bradley men's basketball team helped put the spotlight on this small university out in the Midwest. But, as many people have known for quite some time, small classes and personal attention have long marked Bradley as one of the Midwest's worthiest educational destinations. And, as the old saying goes, it's fun to "play in Peoria."

## GETTING THERE

**BY AIR:** The Greater Peoria Regional Airport receives daily flights from Atlanta, Chicago, Denver, Las Vegas, Minneapolis-St. Paul, and St. Louis. A wider selection of flights and destinations is available through Chicago's O'Hare and Midway airports. The Peoria Charter Coach Company provides transportation to and from Chicago airports (309-688-9523).

**BY TRAIN:** The nearest Amtrak station is in Bloomington-Normal, approximately 30 miles from campus.

**BY BUS:** Greyhound stops at the Greater Peoria Regional Airport. The Peoria Charter Coach Service offers regional bus service.

**BY CAR:** From I-74: Follow I-74 toward Peoria. Turn at Exit 91 (University Street) toward Bradley. Continue South on University as you pass through two stoplights. Then make a right onto the Bradley campus.

**LOCAL:** CityLink provides mass transit in and around Peoria. Among Peoria's taxi options are Airport City River Cab Company (309-685-2227), Peoria Cab Company (309-673-9101), and Elite Taxi Service (309-674-8294).

## WHERE TO STAY

Peoria's wide range of hotels includes Red Roof Inn (309-685-3911, $), Comfort Suites (309-688-3800, $$), and Staybridge Suites (309-673-7829, $$$).

## CAMPUS AT ITS BEST!

When it's time to put down the books, Bradley students know how to have a good time. The Activities Council always has something going on. While on campus, consider going to a performance by Bradley's premier improv troupe, Barbeque Kitten. The surrounding area also offers a ton of fun things to do. Seasonal Riverfront festivals like Bluesfest are especially popular with visitors.

# CALVIN COLLEGE

3201 Burton Street Southeast, Grand Rapids, MI 49546
**Telephone:** 616-526-6106 • **E-mail:** admissions@calvin.edu • **Website:** www.calvin.edu

## STUDENTS SAY

"Calvin's greatest strength is its commitment to godliness. It is also good at encouraging student growth in all areas. The academics are excellent."

## FODOR'S SAYS

"The Lake Michigan shoreline, which extends from the southwestern corner of the state up to the Mackinac Bridge, is one of Michigan's greatest natural resources. Its placid waters, cool breezes, and sugary beaches (including some of the largest sand dunes in the world) have attracted generations of tourists."

## ABOUT THE SCHOOL

Although Calvin bills itself as a Christian institution, students and administrators are quick to note that indoctrination has no place on campus. Students are encouraged to think for themselves and decide how to integrate faith into their lives. Undergrads assert that academics here are rigorous, and slacking isn't really an option. Fortunately, a number of engaging professors make studying palatable.

## GETTING THERE

**BY AIR:** The Gerald R. Ford International Airport is located approximately five miles from the campus. Call a cab to get to campus.

**BY TRAIN:** Amtrak provides daily rail service between Grand Rapids and Chicago. Call 800-USA-RAIL for reservations and/or information.

**BY BUS:** Greyhound offers service to Grand Rapids. Take a taxi to get to campus.

**BY CAR:** From Lansing: Take I-96 West to the 28th Street Exit (Exit 43A). Proceed West on 28th Street for approximately three miles until you hit the East Beltline. You'll pass the CenterPointe Mall and Toys R us on your right (Note: If you pass the Woodland Mall, also on your right, you've gone too far). Take a right onto the East Beltline and go North for roughly a mile (three traffic lights) to Burton Street. Calvin College is on the Northwest corner of the East Beltline and Burton Street. From Muskegon: Take I-96 East to the East Beltline Exit (Exit 38). Careful—this exit can be confusing as you'll need to get off soon after I-196 merges onto I-96. After exiting, take a right at the traffic light and go South on the East Beltline for nearly three miles (four traffic lights). You'll find the entrance to campus is on the West side of the East Beltline, past Lake Drive (the fourth traffic light). From Holland: Take I-196 East to the East Beltline Exit (Exit 38). You'll approach the exit soon after I-196 merges onto I-96. At the top of the ramp, make a right and go south on the East Beltline for approximately three miles (four traffic lights). The entrance to the campus is on the West side of the East Beltline, past Lake Drive (the fourth traffic light). From Kalamazoo: Take U.S. 131 North to the Burton Street Exit (Exit 82). Go East on Burton Street for roughly four miles, just before the East Beltline (10 traffic lights from the Expressway). The entrance to Calvin College will be on your left.

**LOCAL:** If you're looking for taxi options, consider calling: Calder City Taxi (616-454-8080), Yellow Cab (616-459-4646), or Port City Cab (616-243-5314).

## WHERE TO STAY

Grand Rapids offers a number of great lodging options, many of which are conveniently located near campus. The following grant special rates to parents of Calvin students: Best Western Midway Hotel (616-942-2550, $), Baymont Inn (616-956-3300, $), or Hilton Hotel Grand Rapids Airport (616-957-0100, $$).

### SCHOOL AT A GLANCE

| | |
|---|---|
| Type of School | Private |
| Environment | Metropolis |
| Tuition | $20,245 |
| Enrollment | 4,040 |
| % Male/Female | 46/54 |
| Student/Faculty Ratio | 12:1 |

### FRESHMAN PROFILE

| | |
|---|---|
| Range SAT | |
| Critical Reading | 540-663 |
| Range SAT Math | 550-670 |
| Range ACT Composite | 23-28 |
| Average HS GPA | 3.57 |

### ON-CAMPUS APPOINTMENTS

| | |
|---|---|
| Advance Notice | Yes, 1 week |
| Appointment | Preferred |
| Saturdays | Sometimes |
| Average Length | 45 min |
| Info Sessions | Yes |
| Class Visits | Yes |

### CAMPUS TOURS

| | |
|---|---|
| Appointment | Preferred |
| Dates | Varies |
| Times | M–F 8:00 A.M.–5:00 P.M.; |
| | Sat 9:00 A.M.–1:00 P.M. |
| Average Length | Varies |

## CAMPUS AT ITS BEST!

Prospective students interested in the arts should definitely trek over to the Center Art Gallery. The facility features works from the Calvin community as well as celebrated religious and secular artists. Afterwards, stop by the Student Activities Office and investigate all the events being sponsored on campus. Past events have included a masquerade party, Old School Video Gaming Night, and an All Night Extravaganza featuring inflatable games and a pool party.

# CARLETON COLLEGE

100 South College Street, Northfield, MN 55057
**Telephone:** 507-646-4190 • **E-mail:** admissions@acs.carleton.edu • **Website:** www.carleton.edu
**Hours:** Monday–Friday, 8:00 A.M.–5:00 P.M.; Saturday, 8:30 A.M.–NOON

## SCHOOL AT A GLANCE

| | |
|---|---|
| Type of School | Private |
| Environment | Village |
| Tuition | $34,083 |
| Enrollment | 1,936 |
| % Male/Female | 48/52 |
| Student/Faculty Ratio | 9:1 |

### FRESHMAN PROFILE

| | |
|---|---|
| Range SAT | |
| Critical Reading | 660-760 |
| Range SAT Math | 660-740 |
| Range ACT Composite | 27-32 |

### ON-CAMPUS APPOINTMENTS

| | |
|---|---|
| Advance Notice | Yes, 2 weeks |
| Appointment | Required |
| Saturdays | Sometimes |
| Average Length | 60 min |
| Info Sessions | Yes |
| Class Visits | Yes |

### CAMPUS TOURS

| | |
|---|---|
| Appointment | Required |
| Dates | Year Round |
| Times | M–F varying times; Sat mornings |
| Average Length | 60 min |

## STUDENTS SAY

"The Carleton campus is beautiful and everyone here is really nice. Once you're on campus, you're in the 'Carleton Bubble' and you can do whatever."

## FODOR'S SAYS

"Pipestone National Monument, in southwestern Minnesota, protects the red stone quarry, mined for centuries by Native Americans for material to carve their ceremonial pipes."

## ABOUT THE SCHOOL

Making a recent appearance on our "Best Overall Academic Experience for Undergraduates" list, Carleton College is a small liberal arts college that packs a big academic punch. Demanding workloads, dedicated professors, a strong sense of community, and quaint Minnesotan surroundings give the Carleton experience an enviable flair.

## GETTING THERE

**BY AIR:** The Minneapolis/St. Paul International Airport is half an hour from campus. The campus, at the beginning and end of each trimester, provides limited shuttle service. Otherwise, taxis provide the easiest transit between the airport and Carleton.

**BY TRAIN:** Amtrak services Minneapolis. Be aware that most trains arrive at night; transport or overnight lodging near the station should be considered prior to traveling.

**BY BUS:** Greyhound and Jefferson Lines offer service to and from Northfield.

**BY CAR:** From I-35 North/South: Follow I-35 to Exit 69 (Highway 19 East/Northfield). Follow Highway 19 for seven miles, into Northfield. At the first light (the intersection of Highways 19 and 3), make a left and go North for three blocks. Turn right on 2nd Street and continue up the hill. Take a left at College Street and enter campus.

**LOCAL:** Northfield Transit offers regular bus service Monday–Friday, and limited service on Saturday. The weekday evening Intercampus Shuttle (between and around Carleton and nearby St. Olaf College) and the weekend Co-op Bus (traveling to St. Olaf and the Twin Cities) offer additional transit options. Among the taxi options is Northfield Taxi (507-645-4447).

## WHERE TO STAY

Local lodging includes the Super 8 Motel (507-663-0371, $), the Archer House (507-645-5661, $$), the Froggy Bottoms River Suites (507-650-0039, $$), and the Magic Door Bed and Breakfast (507-581-0445, $$$).

## CAMPUS AT ITS BEST!

Intellectual and social opportunities abound at Carleton. Prospective students who visit the campus on a Friday will be privy to one such option—convocation. This weekly event brings distinguished speakers, such as Maya Angelou and Stephen Jay Gould, to the college for a lecture and lunch. Visitors interested in gaining a greater understanding of campus life should aim to attend Mai Fete. This annual weekend arts festival features a number of student bands. Those seeking additional social outlets should investigate The Cave, the oldest college-owned and -operated club.

# CASE WESTERN RESERVE UNIVERSITY

103 Tomlinson Hall, 10900 Euclid Avenue, Cleveland, OH 44106-7055
**Telephone:** 216-368-4450 • **E-mail:** admission@case.edu
**Website:** admission.case.edu • **Hours:** Monday–Friday 8:30 A.M.–5:00 P.M.; Saturday by appointment

## STUDENTS SAY

"One of the most underrated schools in the country, Case provides a top-notch learning environ-ment that is both enjoyable and challenging."

## FODOR'S SAYS

"In recent years, Cleveland has emerged with a new cultural identity. Major attractions such as the Rock and Roll Hall of Fame and Museum, the Great Lakes Science Center, and the Gateway sports ven-ues have been the main catalysts, along with a world-class orchestra, a stunning art museum, a fully restored downtown theater district, and blooming gardens on the east side of town."

## ABOUT THE SCHOOL

A longtime champion of technology-oriented learning, Case Western continues to broaden its offerings in the traditional arts and sciences as well. While the urban campus doesn't boast the feel of a tight-knit community, it does provide plenty of opportunities for undergrads to get out and enjoy the social and cultural diversions of Cleveland.

## GETTING THERE

**BY AIR:** The Cleveland Hopkins International Airport offers wide-ranging airline service. For most convenient travel to and from campus, take the RTA Rapid Transit red line train from the air-port to University Circle. A free University Circle shuttle provides transportation to campus.

**BY TRAIN:** Amtrak services Cleveland. For most convenient travel to and from campus, take the RTA Rapid Transit.

**BY BUS:** Greyhound and Trailways service downtown Cleveland.

**BY CAR:** From I-90 West: Take I-90 to the Martin Luther King Jr. Boulevard Exit. Proceed South on MLK Jr. Boulevard for a mile. Just after the light at East 105th, bear right through the traffic circle, continuing on MLK Jr. Boulevard until reaching Euclid Avenue. Make a left on Euclid Avenue and proceed to the Case Western information booth on the right. From I-80 (Ohio Turnpike) West: Follow I-80 West to I-480 West (Exit 187). Drive West on I-480, which merges with I-271 North. Remain on I-271 until exiting at Cedar Road. Take Cedar Road Westbound toward Cleveland. (Case Western is still 25 minutes away at this point.) Eventually, at the intersection of Cedar Road and Murray Hill Road, you'll see a sign for the university. Continue on Cedar Road under the bridge, veering right at the next light. This puts you on Martin Luther King Jr. Boulevard. Turn right from MLK Jr. Boulevard onto Euclid and proceed to the Case Western information booth on the right. From I-80 (Ohio Turnpike) East: Take I-80 East to Exit 142, where you turn onto I-90 East. After the downtown exits you'll come to the exit for Martin Luther King Jr. Boulevard (I 80); exit at Exit 142 and follow I 90 East. Shortly after passing the downtown exits, exit at Martin Luther King Jr. Boulevard. Proceed South on MLK Jr. Boulevard for a mile. Just after the light at East 105th, bear right through the traffic circle, continuing on MLK Jr. Boulevard until reaching Euclid Avenue. Make a left on Euclid Avenue and proceed to the Case Western information booth on the right. From I-71 or I-77 North: Follow I-71 (or I-77) North until it merges with I-90. Proceed on I-90 East to the Martin Luther King Jr. Boulevard Exit. Proceed South on MLK Jr. Boulevard for a mile. Just after the light at East 105th, bear right through the traffic circle, continuing on MLK Jr. Boulevard until reaching Euclid Avenue. Make a left on Euclid Avenue and proceed to the Case Western information booth on the right.

**LOCAL:** RTA provides regular bus and light rail service. Taxi companies include Ace Taxi (216-361-4700) and Americab (216-881-1111).

## WHERE TO STAY

Nearby lodging includes the InterContinental Hotel (216-707-4300, $$) and the Glidden House (216-231-8900, $$–$$$).

| SCHOOL AT A GLANCE | |
| --- | --- |
| Type of School | Private |
| Environment | Metropolis |
| Tuition | $30,240 |
| Enrollment | 3,824 |
| % Male/Female | 60/40 |
| Student/Faculty Ratio | 9:1 |

| FRESHMAN PROFILE | |
| --- | --- |
| Range SAT | |
| Critical Reading | 600-700 |
| Range SAT Math | 640-740 |
| Range ACT Composite | 27-31 |

| ON-CAMPUS APPOINTMENTS | |
| --- | --- |
| Advance Notice | Yes, 2 weeks |
| Appointment | Required |
| Saturdays | Selected |
| Average Length | 45 min |
| Info Sessions | Yes |
| Class Visits | Yes |

| CAMPUS TOURS | |
| --- | --- |
| Appointment | Required |
| Dates | Year Round |
| Times | M–F 10:30 A.M., 11:30 A.M., |
| | 1:30 P.M., and 2:30 P.M. |
| Average Length | 60 min |

## CAMPUS AT ITS BEST!

Music lovers will want to attend a performance at Case Western's Chapel, Court and Countryside. This early music series features artists from around the world as well as Case's distinguished faculty. Following the performance, stop by the university's radio station, WRUW FM. This student-operated station presents the most diverse programming available in the Cleveland area. To experience social life at Case, try visiting during Springfest, an annual celebration that features barbeque, bands, and naturally, an inflatable obstacle course.

1220 First Avenue Northeast, Cedar Rapids, IA 52402
**Telephone:** 319-399-8500 • **E-mail:** admission@coe.edu
**Website:** www.coe.edu

## STUDENTS SAY

"[Coe] encompasses everything someone would want out of a college: close relationships between students and faculty, a supportive surrounding community, and a curriculum that is flexible to fit each student."

## FODOR'S SAYS

"Cedar Rapids is on U.S. 151 in east-central Iowa, just north of the Amana Colonies. In the nineteenth and early twentieth centuries, waves of Czechoslovakian immigrants settled in this manufacturing town. A sampling of Czech heritage is on view at the National Czech and Slovak Museum and Library."

## ABOUT THE SCHOOL

Nestled away in Cedar Rapids, Coe really exemplifies the liberal arts experience. With undergraduate enrollment hovering around 1,300, students are welcomed into an intimate and supportive community. Close relationships with professors are the norm and academic opportunities abound. The Coe Plan, a significant educational component, requires students to perform community service and a practicum.

## GETTING THERE

**BY AIR:** The Eastern Iowa Airport is located within Cedar Rapids borders. Taxis, shuttle buses, and rental cars are all available for travel to and from the airport.

**BY TRAIN:** The closest Amtrak station is located roughly 65 miles outside of Cedar Rapids in Davenport, IA. If you choose to travel by train you'll probably want to rent a car for the final leg of the trip.

**BY BUS:** Greyhound does offer service to Cedar Rapids. You'll need to arrange for a rental car or taxi to get to your final destination.

**BY CAR:** From East or West via I-80: Exit onto I-380 North near Iowa City and proceed to Cedar Rapids. Continue as directed below—From the North or South via I-380. From the North or South via I-380: Take Exit 20B (Coe College exit) and proceed to First Avenue (second traffic light). Take First Avenue East (turn left) to College Drive (13th Street) and turn left to enter the campus. From North or South via Highway 151: Highway 151 becomes First Avenue in Cedar Rapids. Proceed to College Drive (13th Street) and turn left (from the South) or right (from the North) to enter the campus.

**LOCAL:** For local taxi service call Century Cab Inc. at 319-365-0505.

## WHERE TO STAY

Cedar Rapids offers visitors many affordable accommodations including Crowne Plaza Five Seasons Hotel (319-363-8161, $; inquire about special rates for Coe College visitors), Clarion Hotel and Convention Center (319-366-8671, $), and Best Western Longbranch Hotel (319-377-6386, $$).

## CAMPUS AT ITS BEST!

Students at Coe are active and engaged, with good reason. There's always an intriguing lecture or event happening on campus. Late Night Fridays promise fun times with activities like roller skating, board games, and late-night concerts. Undergrads also frequent Charlie's Coffeehouse. This student-managed shop is a great place to enjoy a gourmet coffee and dessert. Clubs and organizations often reserve the venue for parties and events.

# COLLEGE OF THE OZARKS

Office of Admissions, Point Lookout, MO 65726
**Telephone:** 417-334-6411 • **E-mail:** admiss4@cofo.edu
**Website:** www.cofo.edu • **Hours:** Monday–Friday, 8:00 A.M.–5:00 P.M.

| SCHOOL AT A GLANCE | |
| --- | --- |
| Type of School | Private |
| Environment | Rural |
| Tuition | $0 |
| Enrollment | 1,333 |
| % Male/Female | 45/55 |
| Student/Faculty Ratio | 16:1 |
| **FRESHMAN PROFILE** | |
| Range ACT Composite | 20-24 |
| Average HS GPA | 3.34 |
| **ON-CAMPUS APPOINTMENTS** | |
| Advance Notice | Yes, 2 weeks |
| Appointment | Preferred |
| Saturdays | Sometimes |
| Average Length | 60 min |
| Info Sessions | Yes |
| Class Visits | Yes |
| **CAMPUS TOURS** | |
| Appointment | Preferred |
| Dates | Year Round |
| Times | 9:00 A.M.–11:00 A.M., 1:00 P.M.–4:00 P.M. |
| Average Length | 60 min |

## STUDENTS SAY

"C of O is a wonderful place to go to school. I think the greatest benefit is the work program; I will graduate completely debt-free."

## FODOR'S SAYS

"The Ozark hill region of central and southern Missouri is famed for its wooded mountaintops; clear, spring-fed streams; and water playgrounds, the Lake of the Ozarks and the Table Rock Lake."

## ABOUT THE SCHOOL

Those in search of an affordable education might want to explore College of the Ozarks. The school offers students a tuition-free education in exchange for weekly work-study hours, as part of its Work-for-Tuition Program. Christian ideals are heavily emphasized on campus and Bible studies are well attended. When they're not studying, C of O students are busy participating in the many extracurricular activities the campus offers.

## GETTING THERE

**BY AIR:** The Springfield Branson Regional Airport, approximately an hour away, is the closest airport to the college. Visitors can also fly into Tulsa International Airport, roughly 3.5 hours away from the campus.

**BY TRAIN:** Unfortunately, there is no train service to Point Lookout.

**BY BUS:** There is no direct bus service to Point Lookout. Guests who wish to travel by bus can take Greyhound to nearby Branson Hollister, and take a taxi to the campus.

**BY CAR:** From Springfield Branson Regional Airport: Make a right out of the airport onto West Kearney Street/ MO-744 East. Make a left onto U.S. 160 West/ West Bypass. Merge onto I-44 East and proceed onto U.S. 65 South (via Exit 82A) toward Branson. Make a right onto MO-V. The campus is ahead. From Tulsa International Airport: Travel South on Airport Drive, heading toward East Young Place. Make a right onto East Virgin Street. Merge onto OK-11 via the ramp on the left. Drivers should head toward I-244/ Tulsa/ Joplin. Take U.S. 412 East, merging onto I-44 East in the direction of Joplin. Merge onto James River Freeway, via Exit number 69, driving toward Route 60. (Note: the James River Freeway becomes U.S. 60 East). Merge onto U.S. 65 South toward Branson. Make a right onto MO-V. The campus is ahead.

**LOCAL:** For local taxi service try Branson City Cab (417-334-5678) and Jerry's Shuttle Service and Taxi (417-348-1419).

## WHERE TO STAY

There are a few hotels located in nearby Branson. The most popular choices are The Best Western Landing View Inn & Suites (417-334-6464, $), Holiday Inn (417-3362100, $–$$), and Fall Creek Resort (800-562-6636, $–$$$). Visitors may also stay on campus at a student-operated lodge called The Keefer Center (417-239-1900, $–$$$).

## CAMPUS AT ITS BEST!

While touring the campus, make a point of visiting the Fruitcake and Jelly Kitchen. These baked goods are legendary, with student workers (along with supervisors) creating more than 40,000 cakes a year. Try a tasty treat for yourself but be careful: They can be addictive! After your snack, head over to the greenhouses, home to the beautiful Clint McDade orchid collection. Individual orchids and other plants are available for purchase.

# THE COLLEGE OF WOOSTER

847 College Avenue, Wooster, OH 44691
**Telephone:** 330-263-2322 • **E-mail:** admissions@wooster.edu
**Website:** www.wooster.edu
**Hours:** Monday–Friday, 8:00 A.M.–5:00 P.M.; Saturday, 8:00 A.M.–NOON

## STUDENTS SAY

"The campus is beautiful, the people are friendly, the professors are great, and the senior capstone program is among the best in the nation."

## FODOR'S SAYS

"Spring is damp and clammy, with erratic weather and temperatures ranging from the 30s to the 60s."

## ABOUT THE SCHOOL

From the day they enroll to the day they pocket those diplomas, undergrads at the College of Wooster assert and explore their independence. This liberal arts school's innovative curriculum culminates in senior capstone, an original independent study project produced through one-on-one work with a faculty advisor. This translates into soaring expectations, a strenuous workload, and some very intelligent Fighting Scots.

## GETTING THERE

**BY AIR:** The closest major airport is the Cleveland Hopkins International Airport, about an hour from campus. The Akron-Canton Regional Airport is about 50 minutes from campus. Both airports can be accessed by shuttle. Call the college Admissions Office (800-877-9905) to arrange transportation.

**BY TRAIN:** There is no direct train service to Wooster. Amtrak's Capitol Limited and Lake Shore Limited lines run through Elyria, Cleveland, and Sandusky, all within 60 miles of campus.

**BY BUS:** Greyhound operates a station in Wooster that is a little over a mile from campus.

**BY CAR:** From I-76 West: Follow I-76 West to Exit 13A for Route 21 South toward Massillon. After about three miles, merge onto Route 585 West toward Wooster. Take Route 585 for 21 miles into Wooster, then turn right onto Wayne Avenue. Make a left onto Bever Street. Make another left onto Pine Street to enter campus. From I-71 South: Take I-71 South to Exit 204 for Route 83 South toward Wooster. After 14 miles, turn right at Friendsville Road. Merge onto Burbank Road, which connects with Bever Street. Turn left onto Pine Street to enter campus. From I-71 North: Follow I-71 North to Exit 176 for Route 30 East toward Wooster. After about 30 miles, turn onto Madison Avenue, going right at the end of the exit ramp. Follow Bever Street to Pine Street and turn right into campus. From Route 30 West: Take the Madison Avenue Exit. Make a right onto Bever Street. Make another right onto Pine Street to enter campus.

**LOCAL:** For local taxi service, call Miller Cab (330-262-8294). For shuttle service to and from regional airports, contact the college Admissions Office (800-877-9905).

## WHERE TO STAY

Area hotels include the Econo Lodge (330-264-8883, $) and the Hilton Garden Inn (330-202-7701, $$). Cozy, locally owned options such Harbor Hill's Black Squirrel Inn (330-262-3803, $$), Leila Bell Inn Bed and Breakfast (330-262-8866, $$), and Mirabelle Bed and Breakfast (330-264-6006, $$) are also available.

## CAMPUS AT ITS BEST!

When students at the College of Wooster are looking for good place to study, they typically head over to the Wired Scot. This cyber café offers computer workstations, plasma TV screens, and wireless Internet access. Conversely, when it's time to relax, students make a beeline for the Underground. This campus club hosts a variety of entertainment, from comedians to live bands. If you'd like to attend a specific event, think about visiting in September. The Party on the Green, an annual outdoor concert, is a perennial favorite.

# CORNELL COLLEGE

600 First Street West, Mount Vernon, IA 52314-1098

**Telephone:** 319-895-4477 • **E-mail:** admissions@cornellcollege.edu • **Website:** www.cornellcollege.edu
**Hours:** Monday–Friday and Saturday, 8:00 A.M.–4:30 P.M. and by appoinment

## STUDENTS SAY

"The greatest strengths of my school are the attention an individual student receives and the overall friendliness of the campus."

## FODOR'S SAYS

"East of Des Moines, this region is a mix of historic towns, trim farmsteads, and forested river valleys. Cedar Rapids is the largest town in the area."

## ABOUT THE SCHOOL

Start at one and count to 18. That's the number of days undergrads at Cornell College devote to each class. The college's One-Course-at-a-Time (OCAAT) curriculum lets students sink their teeth into a subject without distraction. Lively class discussions and always-accessible professors contribute to this one-of-a-kind education.

## GETTING THERE

**BY AIR:** Eastern Iowa Airport, about 20 miles from campus, is serviced by Allegiant, American, Delta, NWA, and United Airlines. Shuttle buses offer transportation between the airport and campus. Try Airport Shuttle Service (319-337-2340) or Airport Super Shuttle (800-383-2219). For more extensive service, see Des Moines International Airport, which is about two and a half hours from Mount Vernon.

**BY TRAIN:** The nearest Amtrak rail stop is in Mount Pleasant, more than 60 miles south.

**BY BUS:** Greyhound stops at a number of regional destinations, including nearby Cedar Rapids. Airport Shuttle Service (listed above) also offers transportation from the bus station. Make arrangements in advance.

**BY CAR:** From Route 1 North: Follow Route 1 North into Mount Vernon. Turn left at First Street West. The campus is just ahead. From I-380 North/South: Take I-380 to Exit 16A for Route 30 East toward Mount Vernon. After 13 miles, make a left at Route 1/First Avenue South. Soon after, go left onto First Street West. The campus is just ahead. From Route 30 West: Follow Route 30 West toward Mount Vernon. Make a right onto First Street East. The college is less than a mile ahead on your left.

**LOCAL:** For taxi service, try Yellow Cab (319-365-1444) or Century Cab (319-365-0505), both based in nearby Cedar Rapids.

## WHERE TO STAY

The small town of Mount Vernon offers a few overnight options. For a standard hotel, try the Sleep Inn and Suites (319-895-0055, $$). Several bed and breakfasts are available as well, including the Blythe Cottage Inn (319-895-0188, $) and the Brackett House (319-895-4425, $–$$). Cedar Rapids, about 20 minutes west, hosts a wider selection of accommodations.

| SCHOOL AT A GLANCE | |
|---|---|
| Type of School | Private |
| Environment | Rural |
| Tuition | $23,500 |
| Enrollment | 1,171 |
| % Male/Female | 45/55 |
| Student/Faculty Ratio | 11:1 |

| FRESHMAN PROFILE | |
|---|---|
| Range SAT | |
| Critical Reading | 560-680 |
| Range SAT Math | 550-680 |
| Range ACT Composite | 23-29 |
| Average HS GPA | 3.54 |

| ON-CAMPUS APPOINTMENTS | |
|---|---|
| Advance Notice | Yes, 2 weeks |
| Appointment | Preferred |
| Saturdays | Sometimes |
| Average Length | 60 min |
| Info Sessions | Yes |
| Class Visits | Yes |

| CAMPUS TOURS | |
|---|---|
| Appointment | Preferred |
| Dates | Year Round |
| Average Length | Varies |

---

## CAMPUS AT ITS BEST!

Those who are serious about attending Cornell will want to spend some time in The Commons. The Commons is at the center of student life, housing everything from dining halls, conference and game rooms, to computer kiosks and even the school's radio station. For further evidence of Cornell ingenuity, simply visit College Hall. Students constructed this building when the college was too poor to hire an architect. Also, think about attending a Fireside Chat. During these monthly events, professors and staff members stop by residence halls to share their hobbies and interests, lecturing on everything from beekeeping to cooking.

# DENISON UNIVERSITY

PO Box 740, Granville, OH 43023
**Telephone:** 740-587-6276 • **E-mail:** admissions@denison.edu
**Website:** www.denison.edu
**Hours:** Monday–Friday, 8:30 A.M.–4:00 P.M.; Saturday, 8:45 A.M.–NOON

| SCHOOL AT A GLANCE | |
| --- | --- |
| Type of School | Private |
| Environment | Village |
| Tuition | $29,860 |
| Enrollment | 2,100 approx. |
| % Male/Female | 45/55 |
| Student/Faculty Ratio | 11:1 |

| FRESHMAN PROFILE | |
| --- | --- |
| Range SAT | |
| Critical Reading | 580-680 |
| Range SAT Math | 590-670 |
| Range ACT Composite | 25-30 |
| Average HS GPA | 3.6 |

| ON-CAMPUS APPOINTMENTS | |
| --- | --- |
| Advance Notice | Yes, 1 week |
| Appointment | Preferred |
| Saturdays | Sometimes |
| Average Length | 60 min |
| Info Sessions | No |
| Class Visits | Yes |

| CAMPUS TOURS | |
| --- | --- |
| Appointment | Preferred |
| Dates | Year Round |
| Times | Varies |
| Average Length | 60 min |

## STUDENTS SAY

"Professors at Denison are generally fantastic. They are very engaged with their students and their work, and they love teaching."

## FODOR'S SAYS

"Of Ohio's 73 state parks, 8 are classified as Ohio State Park Resorts, which have rooms for rent and facilities for swimming, boating, golf, tennis, and dining."

## ABOUT THE SCHOOL

Denison University, a small liberal arts Ohio school, provides its students with a rigorous curriculum and easily accessible professors. The university has a strict on-campus policy, which allows students to form stronger connections with each other and to take advantage of Denison's incredible apartment-style dorms.

## GETTING THERE

**BY AIR:** Port Columbus International Airport is about 22 miles from campus. Visitors can arrange to have student drivers pick them up at the airport. Call the Admissions Office for more info (800-DENISON or 740-587-6276).

**BY TRAIN:** Amtrak stops in Toledo, which is about 150 miles, or three hours, away from campus.

**BY BUS:** Greyhound Bus Line stops in Columbus, about 35 miles away from campus.

**BY CAR:** The university is located 27 miles east of Columbus in Granville, Ohio. From the South, East, and West: Take I 70, Exit 126 on Route 37. From the North: Take I 71 Exit at Bellville. Take State Route 13 South into Mt. Vernon. From there take Route 661 South to the college.

**LOCAL:** The best way to get around locally is by taking a taxi. Local taxi companies include: Yellow Cab (740-344-1014), Buckeye Lake Taxi (740-928-0666), New Albany Taxi (614-657-6499), and West Side Taxi (614-374-1617).

## WHERE TO STAY

Some of the best lodging choices near campus include the Holiday Inn Express Hotel & Suites Newark-Heath (740-522-0778, $$), Courtyard by Marriott Newark Granville (740-344-1800, $$), and Cherry Valley Lodge (740-788-1200, $$$).

## CAMPUS AT ITS BEST!

Denison's Vail Series certainly makes a stop in Granville worthwhile. This celebrated music series, now in its 25th season, brings a number of accomplished artists to campus every year. Previous concerts have featured Yo Yo Ma, Wynton Marsalis, Béla Fleck, and the Pittsburgh Symphony Orchestra. Don't fret if you miss a show; the Student Activities Council is always sponsoring some form of entertainment. Perhaps you'll be on campus for a drive-in movie or sumo wrestling. If you're looking for a comfortable place to reflect on your thoughts, stop by the Bandersnatch Coffee House. This student-run establishment is a great place to study or simply unwind with friends.

# DEPAUL UNIVERSITY

1 East Jackson Boulevard, Chicago, IL 60604-2287
**Telephone:** 312-362-8300 • **E-mail:** admission@depaul.edu

## STUDENTS SAY

"Depaul strongly supports multiculturalism; we even have to take a class on it."

## FODOR'S SAYS

"Mayor Daley's goal is to make Chicago the most bike-friendly city in the United States—120 miles of designated bike routes run throughout the city."

## ABOUT THE SCHOOL

DePaul University doesn't just think about the undergraduate experience, it also focuses on turning out highly employable graduates by using the latest technology across the board, and having professors spend more time on student development than outside research. The 14,200 well-prepared undergraduates at DePaul often find they can put their education to use immediately in the city of Chicago, where job and internship opportunities abound.

## GETTING THERE

**BY AIR:** Chicago O'Hare International Airport (ORD) is 19 miles away, about a half-hour's drive. Chicago's Transit Authority Blue Line runs 24 hours between the airport and downtown Chicago. From downtown, several Rapid Transit trains, CTA buses, and Metra Trains serve the various campuses. Airport shuttles and taxicabs are also available at the airport.

**BY TRAIN:** Amtrak goes through Chicago's Union Station at 225 South Canal Street. Ride Chicago public transportation to the DePaul downtown "Loop" campus.

**BY BUS:** There is a Greyhound station at 630 West Harrison Street, one mile from the downtown Chicago "Loop" campus of DePaul University. Ride Chicago public transportation to the DePaul campus.

**BY CAR:** (To the downtown "Loop" campus) From the North and Northwest: From the Kennedy Expressway (I-90/I-94), exit at Jackson Boulevard and turn East. The Loop campus is approximately one mile from the Expressway on Jackson Boulevard at State Street. From the West: From the Eisenhower Expressway (I-290), continue toward downtown. As you approach the downtown area, the Expressway becomes Congress Parkway. Turn left (North) on Dearborn Street, go two blocks to Jackson Boulevard, and turn right (East). The Loop campus is one block East on Jackson Boulevard at State Street. From the South: From the Dan Ryan Expressway (I-90/I-94), exit at Jackson Boulevard and turn East. The Loop campus is approximately one mile from the Expressway on Jackson Boulevard at State Street. From Lake Shore Drive (North or South): Exit on Lake Shore Drive at Jackson Boulevard and turn West. Proceed to Michigan Avenue (100 East). Turn right on Michigan Avenue, go one block to Adams Street (200 South) and turn left. Go one block to Wabash Avenue (50 East) and turn left. Go one block to Jackson Boulevard.

**LOCAL:** The best way to get around is using Chicago's many public transit options. For service from the Loop Campus downtown, use any of the six Rapid Transit Train lines: 1, 3, 14, 29, 36, 60, 6, 99, 129, 146, 147, 151, or 162 CTA buses, or Metra Trains.

## WHERE TO STAY

There are many hotel options near the downtown Loop and uptown Lincoln Park campuses; most, however, are over $100/night. Try the Days Inn—Lincoln Park (773-525-7010, $) near the Lincoln Park Campus; The Palmer House Hilton (877-865-5321, $$) less than five blocks from the Loop campus; or The Ritz-Carlton Chicago (800-621-6906, $$$) within 10 minutes of both.

## CAMPUS AT ITS BEST!

Students do most of their socializing in Chicago, since many commute and Chicago offers a plethora of entertainment options. Be sure to visit the Chicago Jazz Festival in late summer, where most concerts are free, and local and nationally known musicians perform live. Chicago Artists' Month takes place in October all over the city; visiting the shows and exhibitions in the different neighborhoods is a fun way to experience social life in the area.

# DEPAUW UNIVERSITY

101 East Seminary, Greencastle, IN 46135
**Telephone:** 765-658-4006 • **E-mail:** admission@depauw.edu
**Website:** www.depauw.edu
**Hours:** Monday–Friday, 8:00 A.M.–4:30 P.M.; Saturday 8:00 A.M.–4:00 P.M.

## STUDENTS SAY

"The greatest strengths of the school are that we all feel safe here, we have good academic programs, we know we will get jobs or graduate placement, and we can all learn as much as we want to learn."

## FODOR'S SAYS

"Trace Indiana's early frontier history along the Chief White Eyes Trail from Madison to Dillsboro on Route 62."

## ABOUT THE SCHOOL

When the university says, "Uncommon success begins at DePauw," it's referring to the combination of intellectual intensity and real-world work experience that characterizes the undergraduate experience at DePauw. Through a network of internships and study abroad opportunities, DePauw ensures that in Greencastle, Indiana, student learning extends beyond the university walls.

## GETTING THERE

**BY AIR:** The Indianapolis International Airport is less than an hour from campus. Campus Life offers shuttle service to and from the airport for $15 each way. Call 765-658-4850 to make reservations. Also try Castle Cab, a long-distance transportation service based in Greencastle, at 765-653-8294.

**BY TRAIN:** Crawfordsville and Indianapolis, both less than an hour from campus, are serviced by Amtrak. Take a car or cab to campus.

**BY BUS:** Indianapolis and Terre Haute are regularly serviced by Greyhound. Crawfordsville has limited service as well.

**BY CAR:** From I-65 South: Take I-65 South to Exit 178 for Route 43 South. Follow Route 43 South into Lafayette, where it meets with Route 231 South. Stay on Route 231 South into Greencastle, passing through the town square. Make a right on Locust Street, then another right on Seminary Street. From I-65 North: Take I-65 North until merging onto I-465 West at the edge of Indianapolis. Exit I-465 West onto I-70 West and follow the "From I-70 West" directions below. From I-70 West: Follow I-70 West to Exit 41 for Route 231 North, which leads you into Greencastle. Make a left on Seminary Street and proceed onto campus. From I-70 East: Follow I-70 East to Exit 41 for Route 231 North, which leads you into Greencastle. Make a left on Seminary Street and proceed onto campus.

**LOCAL:** For local transport, traveling by car is the best option.

## WHERE TO STAY

Budget-friendly options in Greencastle include the College Inn (765-653-4167, $) and the Greencastle Inn (765-653-8424, $). For a little more money, rooms are available at the on-campus Walden Inn (765-653-2761, $$). A range of chain hotels can be found 10 miles south of Greencastle at the I-70/Route 231 intersection.

## CAMPUS AT ITS BEST!

When visiting DePauw, think about trekking over to the F.W. Olin Biological Sciences Building. You don't have to be a botany enthusiast to be impressed by the climate-zone and computer-operated greenhouse. Of course, if you really want to feel like an honorary DePauw student, stop at Marvin's for a meal. Known for their garlic cheeseburgers, this culinary establishment caters to late-night cravings and will keep you satiated during those all-night cram sessions. If you want to work up an appetite, attend the Little 5 Bike Race. This annual event, initially begun as a fundraiser, also includes plenty of other activities such as mud volleyball and tomato dodgeball.

# EARLHAM COLLEGE

801 National Road West, Richmond, IN 47374-4095
**Telephone:** 765-983-1600 • **E-mail:** admission@earlhA.M..edu
**Website:** www.earlham.edu
**Hours:** Monday–Friday, 8:00 A.M.–5:00 P.M.

## STUDENTS SAY

"I love the 'feel' of Earlham—the people are amazing and it's not just lots of carbon copies of people walking around; no one is trying to fit into some made up mold."

## FODOR'S SAYS

"Beginning in the 1820s, historic Centerville and Richmond, on the Ohio state line, saw as many as 200 wagons pass daily on the National Road, a western immigration trail and America's first federally funded highway."

## ABOUT THE SCHOOL

Earlham College, a Quaker-affiliated school, encourages its students in the pursuit of truth and demands that its students show genuine respect for one another. This all adds up to an ideal place for individual learning and community building. Socially and intellectually, students report that life is good in Richmond, Indiana.

## GETTING THERE

**BY AIR:** Dayton International Airport, about 40 minutes away, is the nearest option. Indianapolis International Airport is an hour and half from campus. Take a shuttle from the Dayton airport to campus. To make shuttle arrangements, contact the Admissions Office at 765-983-1600.

**BY TRAIN:** Amtrak's Cardinal/Hoosier State line stops in Connersville, about 20 miles away from campus. Take a cab from the station to campus.

**BY BUS:** Greyhound operates a station in Richmond. Contact the Admissions Office (765-983-1600) to arrange for an Earlham driver to meet you at the depot.

**BY CAR:** From I-70 West: Follow I-70 West to Exit 156A for Route 40 West, which will take you through Richmond. After about five miles, the campus entrance is on your left. From I-70 East: Follow I-70 East to Exit 145 for Centerville. Make a right at the end of the exit and continue straight until you come to Route 40 (or National Road) in Centerville. Turn left onto Route 40 East. After about four miles, the campus is on your right. From Route 35 South: Follow Route 35 South into Richmond, continuing straight as the road turns into Williamsburg Pike/Northwest 5th Street. Eventually, Williamsburg Pike/Northwest 5th Street ends. Make a right at the stoplight onto Route 40 West (or National Road). Proceed two blocks. The campus is on your left.

**LOCAL:** For taxi service, call City of Roses (765-939-9000), Old Richmond Taxi (765-939-7311).

## WHERE TO STAY

Richmond is home to a variety of popular hotel chains such as Lee's Inn (765-966-6559, $), Hampton Inn (765-939-9500, $$), and Holiday Inn—Holidome (765-966-7511, $$). Bed and breakfast patrons can check out the Philip W. Smith Bed and Breakfast (765-966-8972, $$) or the Historic Lantz House Inn (765-855-2936, $$).

| SCHOOL AT A GLANCE | |
| --- | --- |
| Type of School | Private |
| Environment | Town |
| Tuition | $28,600 |
| Enrollment | 1,248 |
| % Male/Female | 43/57 |
| Student/Faculty Ratio | 11:1 |
| **FRESHMAN PROFILE** | |
| Range SAT | |
| Critical Reading | 570-700 |
| Range SAT Math | 530-650 |
| Range ACT Composite | 23-29 |
| Average HS GPA | 3.5 |
| **ON-CAMPUS APPOINTMENTS** | |
| Advance Notice | Yes, 1 week |
| Appointment | Required |
| Saturdays | No |
| Average Length | 60 min |
| Info Sessions | Yes |
| Class Visits | Yes |
| **CAMPUS TOURS** | |
| Appointment | Required |
| Dates | Year Round |
| Times | Varies |
| Average Length | 60 min |

## CAMPUS AT ITS BEST!

A visit to Earlham's campus wouldn't be complete without stopping at the Joseph Moore Museum, the college's renowned natural history museum. Its extensive collection includes an Egyptian mummy, a mastodon, the most complete giant beaver in the world, and a planetarium. For some insight into Earlham's social life, visit Runyan Center and find out what the Student Activities Board is promoting that day. Past events have featured bands, comedians, dances, escape artists, and free movie nights.

# EASTERN MICHIGAN UNIVERSITY

400 Pierce Hall, Ypsilanti, MI 48197
**Telephone:** 734-487-3060 • **E-mail:** admissions@emich.edu
**Website:** www.emich.edu

## STUDENTS SAY

"[At Eastern] I personally have met a diverse group students from all different backgrounds. We are an odd bunch, but we are tons of fun."

## FODOR'S SAYS

"In winter, Michigan has the only significant downhill skiing in the region."

## ABOUT THE SCHOOL

For a large state university, Eastern Michigan has managed to carve out a close-knit community. Students highlight caring professors, a laid-back campus, and an affordable price tag as reasons enough for enrolling. Education is the most popular major followed closely by psychology and marketing. Although largely a commuter school, many undergrads are quick to point out that there's always fun to be found on campus.

## GETTING THERE

**BY AIR:** Detroit Metro Airport is only 25 miles from Eastern Michigan's campus. The airport is serviced by a number of national and international airlines. Take a taxi to get to campus.

**BY TRAIN:** There is no direct service to Ypsilanti. Those wishing to travel by train can take Amtrak to nearby Ann Arbor. From there, take a taxi to campus.

**BY BUS:** Greyhound stops in Ann Arbor, roughly six miles from Ypsilanti. Take a taxi to campus.

**BY CAR:** From Eastbound (via I-94): Take Exit 181 (Michigan Avenue) and turn left at the end of the ramp. At the first traffic signal, turn left onto Hewitt Road. Go 1.4 miles and turn right at the light onto Washtenaw Avenue and follow to campus.

From Westbound (via I-94): Take Exit 183 (Huron Street) and turn right at the end of the ramp. After passing Michigan Avenue, stay in the left lane. At the next traffic light, the left lane will go left onto Cross Street. Take Cross Street to campus. From US 23: Take Exit 37A (Ypsilanti–Washtenaw Avenue East). Follow Washtenaw Avenue approximately 3 miles to campus. Detailed directions for parking and reaching the appropriate Admissions Office location are available on the university's website.

**LOCAL:** For local cab service call Argus Cab Co. (734-477-0997) or Airport Transportation Service (734-930-0600).

## WHERE TO STAY

A wide range of hotels are available in the Ypsilanti/Ann Arbor area.

## CAMPUS AT ITS BEST!

With hundreds of activities and organizations on campus, there's always a fabulous event to attend. Consider trying your luck at the Texas Hold 'Em Tournament. Guests can also find plenty of entertainment in downtown Ypsilanti. The annual Elvisfest attracts a crowd, entertaining visitors with a tribute concert, impersonators, and memorabilia. The Riverside Arts Center is another fantastic destination, with a private gallery and performance space.

# GRINNELL COLLEGE

Grinnell, IA 50112-1690

Telephone: 641-269-3600 • E-mail: askgrin@grinnell.edu

Website: www.grinnell.edu • Hours: Monday–Friday, 8:00 A.M.–5:00 P.M.; Saturday, 9:00 A.M.–NOON

## STUDENTS SAY

"Grinnell is a place where you will be accepted for just being yourself . . . but you'll need to stay focused or the course work will eat you alive."

## FODOR'S SAYS

"Iowa's most beautiful scenic drive may be the series of roads that take you south along the high bluffs and verdant banks of the Mississippi River on the state's eastern border."

## ABOUT THE SCHOOL

Students at this highly respected liberal arts school have no problem sinking their teeth into their academics. Grinnell's undergrads attack a formidable workload with the help of a concerned and accessible faculty. This all adds up to what the college calls "a challenging yet cooperative environment" in which to learn.

## GETTING THERE

**BY AIR:** The nearest airport is about an hour away in Des Moines. Contact Hamilton Shuttle (641-236-3600) for information on transport between the airport and campus.

**BY TRAIN:** Amtrak's California Zephyr line stops in Ottumwa, about an hour from Grinnell.

**BY BUS:** Greyhound stops in Des Moines and Marshalltown, each about an hour from Grinnell.

**BY CAR:** From I-80 East/West: Follow I-80 to Exit 182. Take Highway 146 North. At Sixth Avenue (Highway 6), turn right. Continue ahead on Sixth Avenue until you come to Grinnell. From Highway 151 South: Follow I-151 South to I-380 South at Cedar Rapids. After about 16 miles, merge onto I-80 West and proceed according to "From I-80 East/West" directions above. From Highway 63 South: Follow Highway 63 South to the junction with Highway 6. Take Highway 6 West, continuing as Highway 6 turns into Sixth Avenue. Eventually, Grinnell College is on your right. From I-35 South: Follow I-35 South to Des Moines, where you pick up I-80 East. From there, proceed according to "From I-80 East/West" directions above. From I-70 West: Follow I-70 West until exiting onto Highway 63 North in Columbia, Missouri. In the town of New Sharon, Missouri, continue straight through the stop sign, which puts you on Highway 146 North. At Sixth Avenue (Highway 6), turn right. Continue ahead until you reach Grinnell.

**LOCAL:** Grinnell, a town of about 9,000, offers no major public transportation. For transportation to and from the Des Moines International Airport, contact Hamilton Shuttle (641-236-3600).

## WHERE TO STAY

Overnight accommodations in Grinnell include Clayton Farms Bed and Breakfast (641-236-3011, $) and Country Inn and Suites (800-456-4000, $$).

### SCHOOL AT A GLANCE

| | |
|---|---|
| Type of School | Private |
| Environment | Village |
| Tuition | $28,566 |
| Enrollment | 1,546 |
| % Male/Female | 46/54 |
| Student/Faculty Ratio | 9:1 |

### FRESHMAN PROFILE

| | |
|---|---|
| Range SAT | |
| Critical Reading | 640-750 |
| Range SAT Math | 640-730 |
| Range ACT Composite | 29-33 |

### ON-CAMPUS APPOINTMENTS

| | |
|---|---|
| Advance Notice | Yes, 2 weeks |
| Appointment | Required |
| Saturdays | Yes |
| Average Length | 60 min |
| Info Sessions | Yes |
| Class Visits | Yes |

### CAMPUS TOURS

| | |
|---|---|
| Appointment | Required |
| Dates | Year Round |
| Times | M–F 8:00 A.M.–5:00 P.M., |
| | Sat 9:00 A.M.–NOON |
| Average Length | 60 min |

---

## CAMPUS AT ITS BEST!

You'll have your finger on the pulse of life at Grinnell after a trip to the Student Publications building. This facility is the campus media hub, and houses the student newspaper, literary magazine, and yearbook, as well as the college's radio station. After perusing the latest issue of *The Scarlet & Black*, journey over to the Faulconer Gallery where you can view prints by Goya and Picasso. Those that want to test their physical prowess should investigate the Grinnell Outdoor Recreation Program (GORP). GORP sponsors on-campus, open climbs five days a week. Strap on a harness and get ready to rappel.

# GUSTAVUS ADOLPHUS COLLEGE

800 West College Avenue, Saint Peter, MN 56082
**Telephone:** 507-933-7676 • **E-mail:** admission@gustavus.edu
**Website:** www.gustavus.edu

## STUDENTS SAY

"Gustavus is about giving the student the tools to succeed in the world as a service-oriented and self-aware individual."

## FODOR'S SAYS

"Sudden snowstorms can make winter driving unpredictable and treacherous."

## ABOUT THE SCHOOL

In the small town of Saint Peter, Minnesota, the biggest name around is Gustavus Adolphus College. Gustavus, a Lutheran liberal arts school, aims to educate its students both academically and civically, and prepare them for well-rounded success after they graduate. The five key components of the Gustavus experience are: academic excellence, community, justice, service, and faith.

## GETTING THERE

**BY AIR:** The Minneapolis-St. Paul International Airport is about an hour from campus. Mankato Land to Air Express (507-625-3977) is the best option for transport between Saint Peter and the airport.

**BY TRAIN:** The nearest Amtrak service is in Minneapolis-St. Paul. Take a cab to the airport and catch the Mankato Land to Air Express from there.

**BY BUS:** Both Greyhound and Jefferson Lines bus services operate out of the Freedom Value Center in Saint Peter.

**BY CAR:** From Route 169 South: Follow Route 169 South, continuing ahead until it becomes Minnesota Avenue. At College Avenue, turn right. Proceed up the hill and onto campus. From Route 169 North: Follow Route 169 North, continuing ahead until it becomes Minnesota Avenue. At College Avenue, turn left. Proceed up the hill and onto campus. From Highway 99 West: Follow Highway 99 West into Saint Peter. Highway 99 becomes Highway 99/Broadway Avenue. At the intersection of Broadway Avenue and Minnesota Avenue, turn left onto Minnesota Avenue. Then turn right onto College Avenue and proceed up the hill to campus. From Highway 99 East: Follow Highway 99 East into Saint Peter. At Minnesota Avenue, make a left. At College Avenue, take a left and drive up the hill onto campus.

**LOCAL:** For local taxi service Monday through Saturday, try Saint Peter Transit (507-934-0668). This service is not available after 8:00 P.M. Senate Shuttle, operated by Gustavus's student senate, runs late-night service.

## WHERE TO STAY

Overnight lodging in Saint Peter includes Viking Jr. Motel (507-931-3081, $), St. Peter Motel (507-931-3081, $), and AmericInn Motel and Suites (507-931-6554, $$). For a larger selection of accommodations, drive to nearby Mankato, located about 20 minutes from Saint Peter.

## CAMPUS AT ITS BEST!

You'll want to practice your backhand before visiting Gustavus Adolphus. The college's striking Swanson Tennis Center covers 44,000 square feet and has a 65-foot air-supported fabric ceiling. Impressively, the courts have the same surface as those used at the U.S. Open. After your match, take a leisurely stroll through the Linnaeus Arboretum and enjoy Minnesota's natural beauty. Visitors who tour the campus in the fall might also have the opportunity to brush shoulders with the truly brilliant. The annual Nobel Conference brings world-class scientists and researchers to campus for lectures on everything from medicine to economics.

# HANOVER COLLEGE

PO Box 108, Hanover, IN 47243-0108
**Telephone:** 812-866-7021 • **E-mail:** admission@hanover.edu

## STUDENTS SAY

"I like to call Hanover College the 'Hillbilly Harvard.' It's like an Ivy League school in the Midwest."

## FODOR'S SAYS

"Dense stands of oak, hickory, and maple crown the rolling terrain that dominates southern Indiana. Tucked among the hills and valleys are nineteenth-century riverfront towns, caves that beg to be explored, and vast stretches of clear blue water."

## ABOUT THE SCHOOL

Hanover College, a small liberal arts college based in a quiet Indiana town, offers students a family-like atmosphere in which it's not uncommon for faculty to invite their classes over to dinner. Hometown Hanover isn't known for having a ton of social outlets, but the administration makes up for it by bringing a variety of events and activities to campus. A thriving campus Greek scene keeps students entertained on the weekends.

## GETTING THERE

**BY AIR:** Louisville International Airport is the closest airport to campus. Prospective students can call the Admissions Office at 812-866-7021 to arrange transportation from the airport.

**BY TRAIN:** The closest stop Amtrak services is in Connersville, which is located over 90 miles away from campus.

**BY BUS:** Greyhound stops in Evansville, which is over 150 miles away from campus.

**BY CAR:** From the Northwest: Take I-65 South to Highway 56, and Exit 29. Go East on Highway 56 until you reach the college. From the Southwest: Take I-65 North from the Indiana state line to Highway 56. Get off at Exit 29 in Scottsburg. Take Highway 56 East 19 miles to the college entrance. From the Northeast: Take I-71 South to Highway 227, and Exit 44. Take Highway 227 North three miles to Highway 36. Take Highway 36 West 13 miles to Highway 421. Go North on Highway 421 across the Madison-Milton Bridge to Indiana. Make a left on Second Street. Drive one block to Baltimore Street. Turn right on Baltimore Street and then drive one block to Main Street (Highway 56). Go west on Main Street (Highway 56) five miles until you reach the college entrance.

**LOCAL:** Visitors can get around town by calling Yellow Taxi (812-265-2374) or Hilltop Taxi (812-265-3337).

## WHERE TO STAY

Some popular lodging choices near campus include Best Western (812-273-5151, $), Holiday Inn Express (800-465-4329, $$), and Hampton Inn & Suites (812-752-1999, $$).

| SCHOOL AT A GLANCE | |
|---|---|
| Type of School | Private |
| Environment | Rural |
| Tuition | $22,200 |
| Enrollment | 999 |
| % Male/Female | 44/56 |
| Student/Faculty Ratio | 10:1 |

| FRESHMAN PROFILE | |
|---|---|
| Range SAT | |
| Critical Reading | 540-650 |
| Range SAT Math | 550-650 |
| Range ACT Composite | 23-29 |

| ON-CAMPUS APPOINTMENTS | |
|---|---|
| Advance Notice | Yes, 1 week |
| Appointment | Preferred |
| Saturdays | Sometimes |
| Average Length | 60 min |
| Info Sessions | Yes |
| Class Visits | Yes |

| CAMPUS TOURS | |
|---|---|
| Appointment | Preferred |
| Dates | Year Round |
| Times | Varies |
| Average Length | 60 min |

## CAMPUS AT ITS BEST!

While touring Hanover College, treat yourself to a quiet moment at The Point. This picturesque spot overlooking the Ohio River is an ideal place for introspection and relaxation as you watch the paddleboats and barges drift by. Located just up the river is the town of Madison, which offers a number of attractions. Students visiting in the summer should check out the annual Madison Regatta featuring hydroplanes from all over the world.

# HIRAM COLLEGE

PO Box 96, Hiram., OH 44234

**Telephone:** 330-569-5169 • **E-mail:** admission@hiram.edu • **Website:** www.hiram.edu
**Hours:** Monday–Friday, 9:00 A.M.–4:00 P.M.; Saturday, 9:00 A.M.–NOON

## STUDENTS SAY

"At Hiram, you really get the sense that the staff and faculty want you to be the greatest student and person you can. They take a personal interest in your development."

## FODOR'S SAYS

"Ohio is a leading producer of astronauts. At the Neil Armstrong Air and Space Museum, you can begin to identify with these explorers."

## ABOUT THE SCHOOL

Hiram College is a small school where students enjoy the safety, peacefulness, and personal attention that comes with college life in a small town. Students say the greatest strengths of the college are its challenging academic programs and supportive faculty and administration.

## GETTING THERE

**BY AIR:** Cleveland Hopkins International Airport is a 45-minute drive away from campus and services all the major airlines. The Akron-Canton Airport is also nearby and offers slightly cheaper fares.

**BY TRAIN:** Amtrak stops in Cleveland, which is less than an hour from campus.

**BY BUS:** Greyhound stops in Cleveland, Akron, and Youngstown, which are all less than an hour away from campus.

**BY CAR:** Hiram College is located at the intersection of State Routes 82/700 and Route 305. It's less than an hour's drive from Cleveland, Akron, and Youngstown. From the West: Take the Indiana Toll Road (I-80/90) East to the Ohio Turnpike (I-80). Go East on I-80 to Exit 193 (Ravenna). Go North on Route 44. Go East on Route 82 to Hiram. From the East: Proceed South on I-271 and then East to Route 422 (toward Solon). Go East on Route 422 to Route 700. Proceed South for five miles on Route 700 into Hiram. From the North: Take I-77 South to I-480. Take I-480 East to Route 422. Go East on Route 422 to Route 700. Proceed South for five miles on Route 700 into Hiram. From the South: Take I-71 North to I-271. Go North on I-271. Get off at Route 82 and travel east to Hiram.

**LOCAL:** Getting around town is easy with any of these taxi services: Emerald Transportation (330-673-9258), OK & USA Taxi & Service (330-395-3226), and Carrier Cab Co (330-467-5100).

## WHERE TO STAY

The on-campus hotel, the Hiram Inn (888-447-2646, $), and The Lily Ponds Bed and Breakfast (800-325-5087, $$), a five-minute walk from campus, are two popular lodging choices. Another good hotel choice not too far from campus is the Best Western Woodlands Inn (330-562-9151, $$).

## CAMPUS AT ITS BEST!

Vegetarians need not subsist on cereal at Hiram. Visit Booth-Centennial Hall and you'll find the Stone Soup Co-op, a student-run operation where members do all the cooking and (unfortunately) cleaning. This is a popular dining alternative for vegetarians, vegans, and those with special dietary needs. Another student-run favorite is the B-side Café. This not-for-profit coffee shop provides a welcome atmosphere for studying, relaxing with friends, or playing games. It also hosts open mic nights along with poetry slams. If you'd like to check out the social scene, think about attending the annual IF (Intercultural Forum) Dinner and Talent Show, always a highly anticipated event.

# ILLINOIS INSTITUTE OF TECHNOLOGY

10 West Thirty-third Street, Chicago, IL 60616
**Telephone:** 312-567-3025 • **E-mail:** admission@iit.edu
**Hours:** Monday–Friday, 8:30 A.M.–5:00 P.M.; Saturday, 9:00 A.M.–NOON

## STUDENTS SAY

"The student population at IIT is very diverse, but we all have one thing in common, which is a love for engineering."

## FODOR'S SAYS

"For a waterfront detour and a great view of the skyline, make a stop at Navy Pier, a former shipping pier that now has shops, restaurants, and bars."

## ABOUT THE SCHOOL

IIT is not for the academically indolent. An architecture and engineering powerhouse, these programs are especially demanding. However, undergrads stress that close interaction with professors makes the work more palatable. The institute takes a decidedly professional approach to education, requiring "Interprofessional Projects" that are sponsored by outside companies and government agencies. While IIT is ethnically diverse, the college is populated by self-professed nerds.

## GETTING THERE

**BY AIR:** IIT is accessible via both O'Hare International and Midway Airports. Taxis, limousines, and public transit can take you to campus.

**BY TRAIN:** Guests can take Amtrak into Chicago's Union Station. Public transportation and taxis are accessible to help you reach your final destination.

**BY BUS:** Both Greyhound and Continental Trailways offer service to Chicago. To reach campus, visitors can either hail a cab or use public transportation.

**BY CAR:** From the North: Follow the Dan Ryan Expressway East to the 31st Street Exit. Proceed South to 33rd Street and make a left. The campus is ahead. From the South: Take the Dan Ryan Expressway West to the 35th Street Exit. Proceed North to 33rd Street and make a right. The campus is ahead. From Lake Shore Drive: Take the exit at 31st Street. Drive inland to State Street, making a left. The campus is ahead.

**LOCAL:** Those wishing to use public transit can take the following: CTA Red Line (Howard-95th/Dan Ryan) to Sox-35th station, CTA Green Line (Ashland-63rd or 63rd-Cottage Grove) to 35th-Bronzeville-IIT station, or the CTA Bus lines with stops on Main Campus (#29-State, #35-35th, #24-Wentworth, #4-Cottage Grove).

## WHERE TO STAY

As a significant center for both business and tourism, Chicago offers a plethora of hotel options. Here are a few: Best Western River North (312-467-0819, $–$$), Sheraton Chicago (800-325-3535, $$), and Holiday Inn Chicago City Center (312-787-6100, $$–$$$).

| SCHOOL AT A GLANCE | |
|---|---|
| Type of School | Private |
| Environment | Metropolis |
| Tuition | $23,329 |
| Enrollment | 2,156 |
| % Male/Female | 75/25 |
| Student/Faculty Ratio | 13:1 |

| FRESHMAN PROFILE | |
|---|---|
| Range SAT | |
| Critical Reading | 560-660 |
| Range SAT Math | 620-720 |
| Range ACT Composite | 25-30 |
| Average HS GPA | 3.87 |

| ON-CAMPUS APPOINTMENTS | |
|---|---|
| Advance Notice | Yes, other |
| Appointment | Preferred |
| Saturdays | Yes |
| Average Length | 30 min |
| Info Sessions | Yes |
| Class Visits | Yes |

| CAMPUS TOURS | |
|---|---|
| Appointment | Preferred |
| Dates | Year Round |
| Times | M–F 9:00 A.M.–5:00 P.M. |
| Average Length | 60 min |

## CAMPUS AT ITS BEST!

IIT is only minutes from downtown Chicago, and guests should take advantage of the school's proximity to some phenomenal attractions. The Buckingham Fountain, found inside Grant Park, is designed to symbolize Lake Michigan. Every hour, beginning at dusk, the fountain's water display is accompanied by a music and light show. Those visiting during the summer months should plan to attend a concert at the Grant Park Music Festival. The festival is the nation's only remaining free outdoor classical music series.

# ILLINOIS STATE UNIVERSITY

Admissions Office, Campus Box 2200, Normal, IL 61790-2200
**Telephone:** 309-438-2181 • **E-mail:** admissions@ilstu.edu
**Website:** www.ilstu.edu

## STUDENTS SAY

"Life at Illinois State is so much fun. There is always something to do if you are bored."

## FODOR'S SAYS

"Starved Rock State Park on the Illinois river between LaSalle and Ottawa has 18 canyons, formed during the melting of the glaciers."

## ABOUT THE SCHOOL

Illinois State defies large university stereotypes. Although the administration must cater to the needs of thousands, undergrads are continually surprised by the accessibility of faculty and staff. Praise is virtually unanimous for the education, English, and music departments, and many students report forming friendships with professors. The social scene is dominated by fraternities and sororities.

## GETTING THERE

**BY AIR:** Central Illinois Regional Airport receives daily commuter flights from Chicago, Detroit, Atlanta, and Orlando. Taxi service and rental cars are both available for transport to campus.

**BY TRAIN:** Amtrak does offer service to Bloomington/Normal. The station, on the Chicago-St. Louis route, is only two blocks from campus.

**BY BUS:** Visitors can ride Greyhound to nearby Bloomington. To reach ISU it is best to call a cab.

**BY CAR:** From the North: Follow I 55 South to the Normal-Business 51 Exit (#165). After the exit ramp you'll approach a stoplight where you will take a left onto Main Street. As you near the Illinois State campus, you will continue on Main, passing stoplights at Raab Road, Orlando Avenue, and Gregory Street. The next stoplight will be at the intersection of Willow and Main. Make a left here. Drive two blocks to Normal Avenue and take a right. You will see gates for the Bone Student Center parking lot directly in front of you. From the South: Exit I 55 North at the Normal-Business 51 Exit (#165-A). The ramp exits onto Main Street (heading South). Continue traveling on Main. Follow "From the North" directions above. From the East and West: Take I 74 to I 55 North. Exit I 55 at the Normal-Business 51 exit (#165-A). The ramp exits onto Main Street (heading south). Continue traveling on Main. Follow "From the North" directions above.

**LOCAL:** For local car service, try calling Cassano Limousine (309-452-2237).

## WHERE TO STAY

For local accommodations, check out Best Western University Inn (309-454-4070, $), Super 8 Motel (309-454-5858, $), or the Bloomington Courtyard (309-862-1166).

## CAMPUS AT ITS BEST!

At Illinois State, the sky is indeed the limit. Pay a visit to the university's planetarium and spend an enjoyable afterNOON learning about the solar system. For more earthly pursuits, stop by the Bone Student Center for bowling and billiards. Each year, the Illinois Shakespeare Festival draws audiences from all over the country. The productions are performed in an open air theater constructed in the Elizabethan style.

# ILLINOIS WESLEYAN UNIVERSITY

PO Box 2900, Bloomington, IL 61702-2900
**Telephone:** 800-332-2498 • **E-mail:** iwuadmit@iwu.edu
**Website:** www.iwu.edu • **Hours:** Monday–Friday, 8:30 A.M.–4:30 P.M.; Saturday, 10:00 A.M.–NOON

## STUDENTS SAY

"The professors are fantastic. They make students want to attend class by making class interactive, fun, and often humorous."

## FODOR'S SAYS

"Shawnee National Forest blankets the southern tip of Illinois with 275,000 acres."

## ABOUT THE SCHOOL

Although IWU might be under the radar, this top-tier liberal arts university provides its students with a stellar education. Undergrads applaud nearly all academic departments, from biology and chemistry to political science and music. Professors imbue their classes with energy and humor, resulting in engaged students who are eager to learn. Hometown Bloomington is a little on the quiet side, but undergrads don't seem to mind, as there's always plenty to do on campus.

## GETTING THERE

**BY AIR:** Central Illinois Regional Airport receives daily commuter flights from Chicago, Detroit, Atlanta, and Orlando. Taxi service and rental cars are both available for additional transportation needs.

**BY TRAIN:** Amtrak does offer service to Bloomington/Normal. The station, on the Chicago-St. Louis route, is only one mile north of campus.

**BY BUS:** Visitors can take Greyhound directly to Bloomington. To reach IWU it's best to take a cab.

**BY CAR:** From Chicago: Follow I-55 South to Veterans Parkway South (Business 55—exit #167). Drive for roughly four miles and make a right onto Route 9 (Pekin West exit). Continue for another two miles to Park Street and take a right. From Madison, WI: Follow I-39/90 South to Rockford, IL and proceed on I-39 South. You'll then turn onto Route 51 South (Business Exit #2), making a left at the end of the ramp. Continue for approximately six miles to Emerson Street and take a left at the light. Next, make a right onto Franklin Street, and finally a left onto Beecher Street. From Indianapolis, IN: Follow I-74 West to Route 51 (North Business Exit #135). Drive for roughly two miles to Veterans Parkway North (Business 55 Chicago) exit. Continue for three and a half miles, taking a left turn onto Route 9 (Pekin West exit). Follow "From Chicago" directions above. From St. Louis, MO: Follow I-55 North to Veterans Parkway North (Business 55 Exit #157B). You'll drive for approximately six miles, making a left onto Route 9 (Pekin West Exit). Follow "From Chicago" directions above.

**LOCAL:** For local taxi service, try the Checker Cab Co. (309-828-0123) or Red Top Cab (309-827-9707).

## WHERE TO STAY

Overnight guests should consider these charming accommodations: The Burr House (309-828-7686, $–$$), The Vrooman Mansion (309-828-8816, $–$$), or The Chateau (309-662-2020, $$).

---

## CAMPUS AT ITS BEST!

When you've finished touring Illinois Wesleyan's campus, backtrack to the Hansen Student Center. Here you can reward yourself with a scrumptious meal at Tommy's Grille and Patio. A popular student hangout, you'll also be able to admire the center's impressive architecture and resources. Following your meal, you can attend any number of events typically happening around campus. The Titan Film Series always offers thought-provoking fare, and musical groups such as Naturally 7 can often be heard performing.

# INDIANA STATE UNIVERSITY

Office of Admissions, Erickson Hall 114, Terre Haute, IN 47809
**Telephone:** 812-237-2121 • **E-mail:** admisu@isugw.indstate.edu

## STUDENTS SAY

"My school is about learning and having fun, all while feeling comfortable in the surroundings."

## FODOR'S SAYS

"Dense stands of oak, hickory, and maple crown the rolling terrain that dominates southern Indiana. Tucked among the hills and valleys are nineteenth-century riverfront towns, caves that beg to be explored, and vast stretches of clear, blue water."

## ABOUT THE SCHOOL

Prospective students in search of an educational bargain should consider Indiana State. A mid-size university, ISU offers over 100 majors, ranging from criminology and aerospace technology to sports and recreation management. With so much variety, even the most ambivalent students are likely to find their passion. Most importantly, opportunities for both intellectual and personal growth are abundant. Undergraduates often conduct research alongside professors and are encouraged to study abroad.

## GETTING THERE

**BY AIR:** Indianapolis International, a 60-minute drive from Terre Haute, is the most convenient airport for visitors. Car rentals and taxi service are both available for transportation to ISU.

**BY TRAIN:** The nearest Amtrak station is located in Crawfordsville, approximately 47 miles from campus. Those who choose to travel by train will need to arrange for car rental or taxi service to reach ISU.

**BY BUS:** Greyhound stops in Terre Haute. Take a taxi to get to campus.

**BY CAR:** From I-70: Take the U.S. 41 (Third Street) Exit (turning North) and proceed roughly 2.7 miles to Chestnut Street (Note: Wolf Field and Marks Field will be on your right). Take a right onto Chestnut. Continue for two blocks and you will arrive at the Commons paid parking area. This lot serves as short-term parking (two hours or less). For half-day or all-day parking, make a left at the intersection of Fifth and Chestnut. Drive one block and make a right onto Spruce Street. Here you will find the university pay lot.

**LOCAL:** Terre Haute has a city bus system that provides service to the campus. For local cab service, call: Terre Haute Cab (812-232-1313) or Yellow Cab Company (812-478-5000).

## WHERE TO STAY

If you are looking for overnight accommodations, consider: Drury Inn, (812-238-1206, $), The Pear Street Inn (812-234-4268, $), or the Holiday Inn (812-232-6081, $$).

## CAMPUS AT ITS BEST!

The Sycamore Lounge, found in Hulman Memorial Student Union, is often teeming with students. From billiards and board games to wireless access and comfortable conversation areas, the lounge is ideal for work or play. Try to time your visit to coincide with ISU's annual Mardi Gras celebration. Held close to the official Fat Tuesday, the Student Union is transformed with music, mask decorating, beads, mocktails, and more! The Indiana State Tricycle Derby (otherwise known as Trike) also generates excitement. This event features men's and women's teams racing on specially built tricycles at the new Simmons Student Activity Center.

# INDIANA UNIVERSITY—BLOOMINGTON

300 North Jordan Avenue, Bloomington, IN 47405-1106
**Telephone:** 812-855-0661 • **E-mail:** iuadmit@indiana.edu
**Hours:** Monday–Friday, 8:00 A.M.–5:00 P.M.; Saturday, 10:00 A.M.–4:00 P.M.; Sunday, NOON–3:00 P.M.

## STUDENTS SAY

"My school is about everyone and everything—if you can't find a place and group to call home, you aren't looking."

## FODOR'S SAYS

"In Bloomington, home of Indiana University, ethnic restaurants, boutiques, galleries, and shops surround the courthouse square and fill Fountain Square, a block-long mall distinguished by historic storefront facades."

## ABOUT THE SCHOOL

Size does matter—or so say the undergrads at IU. The wealth of academic, social, and networking resources available at Indiana's flagship institution can be attributed to the sheer size of the university. And the university's host city of Bloomington enjoys a reputation as one of the best college towns in the Midwest.

## GETTING THERE

**BY AIR:** Indianapolis International Airport is about an hour from campus. A number of companies offer transportation between the airport and campus, including Bloomington Shuttle Service (800-589-6004), Classic Touch Limousine Service (812-339-7269), and Carey Indiana (800-888-4639).

**BY TRAIN:** Amtrak's Cardinal/Hoosier State line, though very limited, stops about 45 miles away in Indianapolis.

**BY BUS:** Bloomington is no longer serviced by Greyhound. For daily runs to the Indianapolis Greyhound depot, call 812-339-9744.

**BY CAR:** From Route 37 South: Follow Route 37 South. Turn at the first Bloomington Exit for Walnut Street/College Avenue. Drive three and a half miles before taking a left onto State Road 45/46. Less than a mile later, go right onto Fee Lane. Then make a left onto Tenth Street. At Jordan Avenue, turn right. After the stop sign, the Office of Admissions is on your left. From Route 37 North: Follow Route 37 North until exiting onto routes 45 North/46 East. At the fourth light, make a right onto Fee Lane. Then make a left onto Tenth Street. At Jordan Avenue, turn right. After the stop sign, the Office of Admissions is on your left. From Route 46 West: Follow Route 46 West into Bloomington, where Route 46 becomes East Third Street. At Jordan Avenue, make a right. After the traffic circle, the Office of Admissions will be on your right.

**LOCAL:** Several Bloomington Transit bus lines stop on campus, including the 1 North, 6, and C routes. For taxi service, contact White Cab Company (812-334-8294) and Yellow Cab Company (812-339-9744).

## WHERE TO STAY

Bloomington's overnight accommodations include Econo Lodge (812-332-9453, $), Holiday Inn Express Hotel and Suites (812-334-8800, $$), and Grant Street Inn (B&B, 812-334-2353, $$–$$$).

### SCHOOL AT A GLANCE

| | |
|---|---|
| Type of School | Public |
| Environment | Town |
| In-state Tuition | $7,460 |
| Out-of-state Tuition | $20,472 |
| Enrollment | 29,120 |
| % Male/Female | 48/52 |
| Student/Faculty Ratio | 18:1 |

### FRESHMAN PROFILE

| | |
|---|---|
| Range SAT | |
| Critical Reading | 490-610 |
| Range SAT Math | 500-620 |
| Range ACT Composite | 21-27 |
| Average HS GPA | 3-4 |

### ON-CAMPUS APPOINTMENTS

| | |
|---|---|
| Advance Notice | Yes, 2 weeks |
| Appointment | Required |
| Saturdays | Sometimes |
| Average Length | 90min |
| Info Sessions | Yes |
| Class Visits | Yes |

### CAMPUS TOURS

| | |
|---|---|
| Appointment | Required |
| Dates | When classes are in session; summer; some Sat. |
| Times | M–F, varies |
| Average Length | Varies |

---

## CAMPUS AT ITS BEST!

If your time at IU is limited, a visit to Indiana Memorial Union will offer ample insight into university life. The building, practically a microcosm of Bloomington, contains everything from eateries, hair salons, and even travel agents, to a bowling alley, arcade, a 400-seat theater, and a student activities tower. As might be expected, there's always something going on here. Try to catch a Jazz Night performance or one of the Union Board films. The bustle at the Union can be overwhelming, so take a moment to unwind at Rose Well House. This open-air pavilion is listed on the National Register of Historic Places.

# IOWA STATE UNIVERSITY

100 Alumni Hall, Ames, IA 50011-2011
**Telephone:** 515-294-5836 • **E-mail:** admissions@iastate.edu
**Website:** www.iastate.edu • **Hours:** Monday–Friday, 8:00 A.M.–5:00 P.M.; Saturday, 9:00 A.M.–1:00 P.M.

## SCHOOL AT A GLANCE

| | |
|---|---|
| Type of School | Public |
| Environment | Town |
| In-state Tuition | $5,086 |
| Out-of-state Tuition | $15,580 |
| Enrollment | 20,364 |
| % Male/Female | 57/43 |
| Student/Faculty Ratio | 15:1 |

### FRESHMAN PROFILE

| | |
|---|---|
| Range SAT | |
| Critical Reading | 530-660 |
| Range SAT Math | 550-690 |
| Range ACT Composite | 22-27 |
| Average HS GPA | 3.49 |

### ON-CAMPUS APPOINTMENTS

| | |
|---|---|
| Advance Notice | Yes, 2 weeks |
| Appointment | Preferred |
| Saturdays | Yes |
| Average Length | 60 min |
| Info Sessions | Yes |
| Class Visits | Yes |

### CAMPUS TOURS

| | |
|---|---|
| Appointment | Preferred |
| Dates | Year Round |
| Times | M–F 10:00 A.M. and 2:00 P.M. |
| Average Length | 60 min |

## STUDENTS SAY

"The students here have great attitudes about life."

## FODOR'S SAYS

"The Iowa Great Lakes lie in the northwest corner of the state. The region has six lakes (including West Okoboji—one of only three true blue-water lakes in the world) and dozens of vacation resorts."

## ABOUT THE SCHOOL

Low tuition and highly ranked programs in agriculture, engineering, and journalism, among others, are the qualities that entice undergrads to rural Ames, Iowa. Whether students are in the classrooms, in the stadium bleachers, or just walking around campus, a strong sense of community pervades ISU.

## GETTING THERE

**BY AIR:** The Des Moines International Airport is 40 miles from Ames. To get to campus, take a car or shuttle. Try Out of Town Limo (515-266-4469) for shuttle service.

**BY TRAIN:** The nearest Amtrak stop is about 70 miles away in Osceola. Amtrak's California Zephyr line services Osceola.

**BY BUS:** Greyhound operates regular service in Ames.

**BY CAR:** From Route 30 East: Follow Route 30 East to Exit 142; from there turn onto Lincoln Way toward Napier. Continue East on West Lincoln Way until you see the campus on your left. From Route 30 West: Follow Route 30 West, Exit 146, for Elwood Drive. Turn off Route 30 and onto Elwood Drive (following signs indicating ISU). A mile and a half later, turn left onto Lincoln Way. Before long, you'll see ISU on your right. From I-35 North: Follow I-35 North to Exit 111B toward Ames/Iowa State University. At the end of the ramp, merge onto Route 30 West and proceed according to "From Route 30 West" directions above. From I-35 South: Follow I-35 South to Exit 111B toward Ames. At the end of the ramp, merge onto Route 30 West heading toward ISU. From there, proceed according to "From Route 30 West" directions above.

**LOCAL:** The city bus system for Ames, CyRide, offers regular service on and around campus. The #3 line hits a number of campus halls. If you're looking for a cab, call Ames Taxi (515-232-1343) or Cyclone Cab (515-232-1343). On nice days, try Bikes at Work rickshaw service (515-233-6120).

## WHERE TO STAY

If you plan to stay overnight in Ames, try Heartland Inn (515-232-2300, $), Country Inn & Suites (515-233-3935, $$), or the Hotel at Gateway Center (515-292-8600, $$).

---

## CAMPUS AT ITS BEST!

The Farm House Museum is a popular Iowa State attraction. This 14-room structure offers insight into archetypal nineteenth-century home life. Students especially appreciate the museum, as it often provides free hot cider and lemonade. Continuing on your intellectual journey, visit the butterfly wing at the Reiman Gardens. The 2,500-square-foot tropical garden is filled with both native and exotic butterflies from six continents. If you're touring the university on a Friday, you can cap off your visit with a show at the Iowa State Center. The Stephens Auditorium, located within the Center, sponsors "Festive Fridays," which feature dinner and a performance.

# KALAMAZOO COLLEGE

1200 Academy Street, Kalamazoo, MI 49006
**Telephone:** 269-337-7166 • **E-mail:** admission@kzoo.edu
**Website:** www.kzoo.edu
**Hours:** Monday–Friday, 8:00 A.M.–5:00 P.M.; Saturday, 9:00 A.M.–NOON

## STUDENTS SAY

"Kalamazoo College is about personalized attention: From the personalized acceptance letter each prospective student receives in the winter, to the small classes and accessible professors, students are always recognized as important individuals."

## FODOR'S SAYS

"Summer is the most popular time to visit the Midwest and the Great Lakes. Generally the farther North you go, the fewer people you'll find."

## ABOUT THE SCHOOL

The K-Plan at K-Zoo is the blueprint for an education rich in liberal arts study, career prep, civic awareness, individual motivation, and leadership development. Add to all of this an active extracurricular scene and a steady supply of campus-wide events, and what you have is a happy and well-rounded crew of Kalamazoo undergrads.

## GETTING THERE

**BY AIR:** Kalamazoo/Battle Creek International Airport is on the edge of town. Catch a taxi to campus or contact the Office of Admission for pick-up information (800-253-3602).

**BY TRAIN:** Amtrak's Michigan Services line stops in Kalamazoo several times daily. The station is about a mile from campus. For maximum convenience, take a taxi to campus.

**BY BUS:** Greyhound and Indian Trails bus lines operate out of the Kalamazoo Transportation Center, about a mile from campus..

**BY CAR:** From Route 131 North: Follow Route 131 North to Exit 38A, which puts you on West Main Street (or Route 43) East. Drive ahead for 3.5 miles. When you come to the Dow Science Center, make a right onto Thompson Street. From I-94 East: Follow I-94 East toward Kalamazoo/Portage to Exit 75 for Oakland Drive. Make a left onto Oakland Drive heading North. After 3 miles, Oakland Drive turns into Stadium Drive. Shift to the left lane as the 2 roads merge. Make a sharp left turn onto Academy Street and proceed to campus. From I-94 West: Follow I-94 East toward Kalamazoo/Portage to Exit 75 for Oakland Drive. Make a right onto Oakland Drive heading North. After 3 miles, Oakland Drive turns into Stadium Drive. Shift to the left lane as the 2 roads merge. Make a sharp left turn onto Academy Street and proceed to campus.

**LOCAL:** Kalamazoo's downtown district and Western Michigan University are just a quick walk away. Metro buses offer transportation to most local destinations. If you're looking for a taxi, try Checker Cab (269-345-0177) or Bright Day Taxi Cab (269-720-7200).

## WHERE TO STAY

Among the lodging options for overnight visitors try Super 8 Motel (269-345-0146, $), Hall House Bed and Breakfast (269-343-2500, $$), and the Radisson Plaza Hotel (269-343-3333, $$$). Wherever you stay, be sure to inquire about discounts for Kalamazoo College visitors.

### SCHOOL AT A GLANCE

| | |
|---|---|
| Type of School | Private |
| Environment | City |
| Tuition | $27,054 |
| Enrollment | 1,345 |
| % Male/Female | 43/57 |
| Student/Faculty Ratio | 12:1 |

### FRESHMAN PROFILE

| | |
|---|---|
| Range SAT | |
| Critical Reading | 600-720 |
| Range SAT Math | 600-690 |
| Range ACT Composite | 26-31 |
| Average HS GPA | 3.62 |

### ON-CAMPUS APPOINTMENTS

| | |
|---|---|
| Advance Notice | Yes, 2 weeks |
| Appointment | Preferred |
| Saturdays | Sometimes |
| Average Length | 60 min |
| Info Sessions | Yes |
| Class Visits | Yes |

### CAMPUS TOURS

| | |
|---|---|
| Appointment | Preferred |
| Dates | Year Round |
| Times | Call for times |
| Average Length | 60 min |

---

## CAMPUS AT ITS BEST!

Visitors touring Kalamazoo near end-of-term finals will be able to enjoy Exam Week Extravaganza. This biannual event allows students to let loose before hitting the books. Some featured activities have included themed events like Monte Carlo night, Comedy Club, and hypnotist shows. For an evening of culture, you can attend a performance at the Kalamazoo Bach Festival. This group sponsors concerts throughout the year, playing music by J. S. Bach and that of contemporary composers. If you're looking to spend some time outdoors, visit the Lillian Anderson Arboretum. The arboretum is utilized for many purposes, from experiential learning to hiking, bird watching, and contemplation.

# KANSAS STATE UNIVERSITY

119 Anderson Hall, Manhattan, KS 66506
**Telephone:** 785-532-6250 • **E-mail:** kstate@ksu.edu
**Website:** www.consider.k-state.edu

## STUDENTS SAY

"Kansas State University is all about purple power, purple pride, and Wildcat tradition!"

## FODOR'S SAYS

"Heading west from Kansas City across east central Kansas, you'll follow in the footsteps of pioneers who blazed the Oregon and Santa Fe trails, and you'll cross the paths of those who followed by [way of] the Smoky Hill and Chisholm trails. Native American history, Civil War sites, and the Old West loom large along this 150-mile stretch of prairie."

## ABOUT THE SCHOOL

Kansas State's academic strengths lie in its especially outstanding agriculture, architecture, interior design, ecology, biology, and engineering programs. Research opportunities are plentiful, and classes present students with opportunities to interact with industry professionals. As a state school in the heartland, K-State attracts a fair share of conservative Midwesterners. However, undergrads are overwhelmingly friendly, and the student body always joins together in support of Wildcat athletics.

## GETTING THERE

**BY AIR:** Guests traveling via plane should fly into Kansas City International Airport. There is taxi service available for transportation to campus.

**BY TRAIN:** Amtrak does not offer service to Manhattan. The nearest station is located in Topeka, approximately 50 miles away. Your best option to reach campus from there is to rent a car.

**BY BUS:** Guests can ride Greyhound to Topeka, roughly 55 miles from Manhattan. Your best option to reach campus from there is to rent a car.

**BY CAR:** From the East: Follow I-70 West, and make a right at Exit 313 (K-177 North). After driving over the Kansas River Bridge, take the Fort Riley Boulevard Exit. The Town Center Mall will be in front of you. Make a right at the stoplight onto Fort Riley Boulevard. Make another right at the 17th Street stoplight. Continue for 11 blocks to the Anderson Avenue stoplight. The campus will be in front of you. From the West: Follow I-70 East, and take Exit 303 (K-18 North). Make a left onto K-18. Stay on K-18 for approximately 10 minutes; K-18 becomes Ft. Riley Boulevard at the edge of Manhattan. Make a left at the 17th Street stoplight. Follow the "From the East" directions above. From the North: Follow Highway 13 South to Highway 113, and make a left onto 113, which becomes Seth Childs Road. Drive South to Anderson Avenue. Make a left onto Anderson and another left onto 17th Street. From the South: Follow K-177 North to Manhattan. Follow the "From the East" directions above.

**LOCAL:** For local taxi service call Bell Taxi Transportation Inc. (785-537-2080) or ABC Union Cab Co. (785-537-1295).

## WHERE TO STAY

Manhattan features many affordable accommodations such as the Econo Lodge (785-539-5391, $), Best Western (785-537-8300, $), or Fairfield Inn (785-539-2400, $$).

---

## CAMPUS AT ITS BEST!

If you're curious about agriculture, K-State is the place to visit. For example, the sheep unit offers an adorably fun time. You can admire some baby lambs or witness shearing in all its glory. Think you feel more kinship with cows? Go over to the dairy unit where you'll be able to observe the milking process. Of course, interaction with human members of the Kansas State community is important as well. Consider attending a pep rally where you can enjoy the pep band, get some free food, and meet some of the coaches and athletes.

# KENT STATE UNIVERSITY—
# KENT CAMPUS

161 Michael Schwartz Center, Kent, OH 44242-0001
**Telephone:** 330-672-2444 • **E-mail:** admissions@kent.edu

## STUDENTS SAY

"The library is something of a wonder—all 13 stories."

## FODOR'S SAYS

"The Cuyahoga Valley National Park Recreation Area is on 33,000 acres of forested valley between Cleveland and Akron along the Cuyahoga River and follows the path of the historic Ohio and Eerie Canal."

## ABOUT THE SCHOOL

As a relatively large public institution, Kent State runs the gamut both academically and socially. The majority of professors are readily accessible and always willing to assist students. The university offers an abundance of extracurricular activities for students, although much fun can also be found off campus, too.

## GETTING THERE

**BY AIR:** Kent State is accessible via both the Cleveland Hopkins and Akron-Canton Airport. Taxis, car rentals, shuttles, and limousines are available for transportation to and from campus.

**BY TRAIN:** Amtrak provides service to both Alliance and Cleveland. Take a taxi to get to campus.

**BY BUS:** Greyhound stops in Cleveland. Take a taxi to get to campus.

**BY CAR:** From I-76: Drivers should take the Kent/Route 43 Exit (actual Exit 33) and continue North to Route 261. Make a right onto Route 261 and follow for a quarter mile to Campus Center Drive. Make a left onto Campus Center Drive and follow it to the stop sign at the junction of East Campus Center Drive and West Campus Center Drive. Follow the signs to your destination. From I-80 (Ohio Turnpike): Take Exit 187/13 (Streetsboro). Following the toll booth, continue straight (follow Ravenna sign) onto Route 14 (Southeast). You will go past Route 303, getting onto Route 43. Make a right on Route 43 and drive South for roughly 6 miles until you come to the traffic light at the dead end at Haymaker Parkway (you'll have reached Kent at this point). Make a left onto Haymaker and continue until you reach the traffic light at the intersection of Lincoln and Haymaker. Follow the signs to your destination. From I-90: Head in the direction of Cleveland. Proceed onto I-271 South to I-480 East. You'll continue on I-480 until it becomes Route 14 in Streetsboro. Next you'll make a right on Route 43. From there, proceed according to "From I-80" directions above.

**LOCAL:** For local taxi service call ABC Taxi at 330- 678-7433.

## WHERE TO STAY

Consider these hotel options in and around the Kent area: Hampton Inn Kent (330-673-8555, $), Bertram Inn (330-995-7628, $$), and Sheraton Suites (330-929-3000, $$–$$$).

### SCHOOL AT A GLANCE

| | |
|---|---|
| Type of School | Public |
| Environment | Village |
| In-state Tuition | $8,430 |
| Out-of-state Tuition | $15,862 |
| Enrollment | 18,365 |
| % Male/Female | 40/60 |
| Student/Faculty Ratio | 19:1 |

### FRESHMAN PROFILE

| | |
|---|---|
| Range SAT | |
| Critical Reading | 460-570 |
| Range SAT Math | 460-570 |
| Range ACT Composite | 19-24 |
| Average HS GPA | 3.16 |

### ON-CAMPUS APPOINTMENTS

| | |
|---|---|
| Class Visits | No |

### CAMPUS TOURS

| | |
|---|---|
| Appointment | Preferred |
| Dates | Year Round |
| Average Length | 120 min |

## CAMPUS AT ITS BEST!

Budding fashionistas will definitely want to spend some time exploring the Kent State University Museum. Also serving as a teaching lab, this premier museum is home to one of the finest collections of costumes in the country. Visitors wishing to kick back a bit should check out an event such as FlashFest. From musical performers and inflatable games to "Pie Your Professor," this festivity is sure to give you a taste of life as a Kent student.

# KENYON COLLEGE

Admissions Office, Ransom Hall, Gambier, OH 43022-9623
**Telephone:** 740-427-5776 • **E-mail:** admissions@kenyon.edu
**Website:** www.kenyon.edu
**Hours:** Monday–Friday, 8:30 A.M.–4:30 P.M.; Saturday, 9:00 A.M.–NOON

## STUDENTS SAY

"Kenyon College is all about the student. When you're here, you're considered part of a greater community. The classes are small and the professors rock, and people here all seem to be fantastic. You occasionally get the grumpy individual, but she is one who did not get a good night's sleep."

## FODOR'S SAYS

Ohio "national monuments include the Hopewell Culture National Historic Park, with its earthen wall enclosures built in geometric patterns and mounds of various shapes."

## ABOUT THE SCHOOL

Despite the rigor of its academic programs, Kenyon College is the type of school where students learn together. At Kenyon, the focus is on supporting each other rather than competing for the highest grades. On this inclusive and community-oriented campus, even the social scene is nondiscriminating: all students having a standing invite to every campus activity—even the frat parties are open to everyone.

## GETTING THERE

**BY AIR:** Port Columbus International Airport is an hour drive from Gambier. Taxis are available between the airport and Mount Vernon or Gambier (taxis must be pre-arranged). During the school year, students traveling alone can arrange to be picked up by the school's shuttle.

**BY BUS:** Greyhound stops in Mansfield, which is just under 32 miles from campus.

**BY CAR:** From the North or Northwest: Take I-75 South to Findlay and exit at U.S. 23/Ohio 15 South. Take 23 South to Ohio 95 East in Marion, and continue on 95 East to Ohio 13 South in Fredericktown. Take 13 South to Mount Vernon. From the East or Northeast: Take I-71 South and exit at Ohio 13 South at Mansfield. Take 13 South to Mount Vernon. From the East or Southeast: Take I-70 West and exit at Ohio 13 North at Newark. Take 13 North to Mount Vernon. From the West or Southwest: Take I-71 North from Columbus and exit at U.S. 36 East. Take 36 East to Mount Vernon.

**LOCAL:** Visitors using taxis to get around town may call Knox Taxi 740-392-7433 and Yellow Cab Co. 740-345-1111.

## WHERE TO STAY

Nearby hotels include The Kenyon Inn (740-427-2202, $$) and The Gambier House (740-427-2668, $$). Another good option, albeit slightly farther away, is the Holiday Inn Express (740-392-1900, $$).

## CAMPUS AT ITS BEST!

Do you want to convene with literary gods? Does language excite you? Then tell your Kenyon guide to make sure you make a stop at Sunset Cottage. This building is home to Kenyon's nationally-renowned English department, long associated with the prominent *Kenyon Review*. Afterwards, stop by for a meal at the Middle Ground Café. Packed with students day and night, this establishment has become a central gathering place for social and academic activities. Those touring the college in February should attempt to have their visit coincide with Philander's Phebruary Phling, a popular weekend event designed to keep the winter blues at bay.

# KNOX COLLEGE

2 East South Street, Galesburg, IL 61401
**Telephone:** 309-341-7100 • **E-mail:** admission@knox.edu
**Website:** www.knox.edu **Hours:** Monday–Friday, 8:00 A.M.–4:00 P.M.; Saturday, 9:00 A.M.–NOON

## Students Say

"Knox College gives students the freedom to pursue virtually any personal interest, academically or otherwise, in a healthy and diverse environment with just the right amount of cultural activity and distraction."

## Fodor's Says

"Illinois has more than 260 state parks, conservation areas, fish and wildlife areas, and recreation areas."

## About the School

Intellectual freedom, academic challenge, and community engagement—these are among the principles at work in Knox College of Galesburg, Illinois. A liberal arts college, Knox brings together a highly touted faculty, an attentive administration, and an ambitious undergrad population. The result? One Knox-out of an education.

## Getting There

**BY AIR:** Greater Peoria Regional Airport and Moline's Quad City International Airport are each about 45 minutes from campus and together offer flights on a half dozen airlines. Call the Admissions Office to arrange a pick up.

**BY TRAIN:** Amtrak's California Zephyr, Southwest Chief, and Illinois Zephyr lines arrive daily in Galesburg. The station is five blocks from campus. Walk or take a taxi.

**BY BUS:** Greyhound runs regular service to and from Galesburg. The station is less than half a mile from campus.

**BY CAR:** From I-74 East: Follow I-74 East to Exit 48 toward Galesburg. Turn right onto East Main Street and proceed nearly two miles before turning left onto South Cherry Street. From I-74 West: Follow I-74 West to Exit 46A toward Galesburg and exit on Seminary Street. Proceed nearly two miles before turning right on Main left onto South Cherry Street. From Route 34 East: Follow Route 34 East to the exit for Seminary. On the ramp, turn left on Seminary Street. After two miles, make a right onto Main Street. Two blocks later, make a left onto Cherry Street.

**LOCAL:** Galesburg Transit's #2 Green Central bus line provides transportation from Knox to a number of local destinations. Galesburg's local cab companies include Courtesy Cab (309-341-1077), Ace Cab (309-343-4444), and City Cab Incorporated (309-341-6161).

## Where to Stay

Galesburg has a number of local accommodations, from cozy B&Bs to well-known chain hotels. These include the Fairfield Inn (309-344-1911, $), Country Inn and Suites (309-344-4444, $$), and the Fahnestock House (B&B, 309-344-0270, $$). Be sure to ask about discounts for visitors to the college.

## CAMPUS AT ITS BEST!

Students visiting during the winter months should stick around to witness one of Knox's most sacred traditions—"traying" in "the Bowl." Every year courageous students grab a cafeteria tray and go sledding down the 16 foot drop on their bowl-shaped football field. Afterwards, warm up at McGillacudy's with the Knox Jazz Combo. If you're looking for a good meal, stop by the Landmark Café and Creperie. Knox students rave about the café's world-famous spinach bisque.

# LAKE FOREST COLLEGE

555 North Sheridan Road, Lake Forest, IL 60045
**Telephone:** 847-735-5000 • **E-mail:** admissions@lakeforest.edu • **Website:** www.lakeforest.edu
**Hours:** Monday–Friday, 8:30 A.M.–5:00 P.M.; Saturday by appointment

## STUDENTS SAY

"Life at Lake Forest is quite laid back. Students are generally really nice to one another. Chicago is a great asset to the school and many students travel into the city to go to shows, sporting events, or just to walk around."

## FODOR'S SAYS

Nearby Chicago is "the country's biggest convention town, and accommodations can be tight when major events are scheduled. Most hotels run weekend specials when no big shows are on."

## ABOUT THE SCHOOL

Lake Forest College, a liberal arts school with fewer than 1,400 undergraduates, offers its students plenty of personal attention. Students here enjoy flexible course requirements that allow them to explore classes in their different areas of interest. When they need a break from the books, Lake Forest students take the train into nearby Chicago, where all the distractions of big-city life await.

## GETTING THERE

**BY AIR:** O'Hare International Airport is located approximately 25 miles from the campus. Visitors can call the Airport Express Shuttle Service (312-454-7800) for transportation to the campus. Midway Airport is closer to downtown Chicago. Visitors can take the Omega Shuttle Service (773-483-6634) from Midway to O'Hare, then take Airport Express or American Taxi to the college.

**BY TRAIN:** Amtrak's Chicago Union Station stops in downtown Chicago. From there, go to the Ogilvie Transportation Center, at the intersection of Madison and Canal Streets. This is where you will transfer to the METRA Union Pacific North Line commuter train, which will take you to the campus. Call 312-836-7000 for more information.

**BY BUS:** From the Greyhound Bus Depot on Harrison Street in Chicago, take a taxi to the Ogilvie Transportation Center to catch the METRA train.

**BY CAR:** From Chicago: Take I-94 (Edens Expressway) North. I-94 splits off toward Milwaukee. Stay on the Edens, which will become U.S. Route 41. Exit at Deerpath Road. Make a right onto Deerpath and continue through the town of Lake Forest and toward the school. Once in Lake Forest on Deerpath Road, go East through the business district and across the railroad tracks. Continue through a residential area until you reach a stop sign at Sheridan Road, which is the entrance to the North Campus. From the North: Take I-94 South from Milwaukee. Just South of the Wisconsin-Illinois line, get in the left lane and follow U.S. Route 41. Exit at Deerpath Road, turn left onto Deerpath, and continue through the town of Lake Forest and toward the school. From there, proceed according to "From Chicago" directions above. From the West and Southwest: Take I-294 (Tri-State Tollway), which becomes I-94, North to Illinois 60 (Town Line Road). Exit and turn right on Route 60. Continue East to Route 43 (Waukegan Road). Turn left and drive for 1/2 mile to Deerpath Road. Turn right onto Deerpath and continue through the town of Lake Forest and toward the school. From there, proceed according to "From Chicago" directions above.

**LOCAL:** Local taxi service includes American Taxi (847-566-3131) and Blue Line Limousine (0-548-7771). The METRA Union Pacific North Line train is another way to get around town.

## WHERE TO STAY

Some of the most popular hotel choices near the campus include Sleep Inn at Great Lakes (847-578-9900, $), Holiday Inn Gurnee-Convention Center (847-336-6300, $$), and Courtyard by Marriott Lincolnshire (847-634-9555, $$$).

## CAMPUS AT ITS BEST!

Students considering Lake Forest should aim to attend one of the scheduled Campus Visit Days. These specially designed programs include campus tours, meetings with admissions counselors, faculty panel discussions, and perhaps most importantly, lunch. Save some time after the tour to meander over to Lake Forest Beach only a few blocks from the South Campus. A frequent destination for students, they come here to enjoy all the recreational opportunities afforded by the school's close proximity to Lake Michigan.

# LAWRENCE UNIVERSITY

PO Box 599, Appleton, WI 54912-0599
**Telephone:** 800-227-0982 • **E-mail:** excel@lawrence.edu
**Website:** www.lawrence.edu • **Hours:** Monday–Friday; 8:00 A.M.–5:00 P.M.; Saturday, 9:00 A.M.–NOON

## Students Say

"This school is an incredibly challenging school without any grade inflation. To do well here you cannot rest on your laurels."

## Fodor's Says

"South of Wisconsin Dells is Baraboo, former site of an early nineteenth-century fur-trading post run by a Frenchman named Baribault. It is best known as the place where the five Ringling brothers began their circus careers." Baraboo is not far from Lawrence University's campus.

## About the School

Undergrads at Lawrence University, a small liberal arts school in Wisconsin, tend to have a few things in common: 1) They're not afraid of hard work. 2) They love the unwavering attention they get from their professors. 3) Though they admit Appleton, Wisconsin, may not be the world's most exciting town, there's nowhere else they'd rather be.

## Getting There

**BY AIR:** Nearby Outagamie County Airport is serviced by four airlines. Take a taxi to the campus. Expect to pay around $15.

**BY TRAIN:** Amtrak offers thruway bus service to Appleton.

**BY BUS:** Greyhound offers regular service to Appleton. The bus station is within walking distance of the campus.

**BY CAR:** From South of Appleton: Follow Highway 41 North and take Exit 137 for College Avenue. Proceed East (right) on College Avenue for four miles through downtown Appleton to the campus. From North of Appleton: Follow Highway 41 South and take Exit 137 for College Avenue. Proceed East (left) on College Avenue for 4 miles through downtown Appleton to the campus.

**LOCAL:** Valley Transit, Appleton's public transportation system, offers wide-ranging service throughout the area. For information, contact Valley Transit at 920-832-5800. If you're looking for a taxi in Appleton, try Fox Valley Cab (920-734-4546), Appleton Taxi (920-733-4444), or Kidz Kab (920-830-2067).

## Where to Stay

On-campus guest housing is available at the Alumni House at a rate of $45 per room, per night. Space is limited, so contact the university as soon as possible to secure reservations (920-832-6601). Other overnight accommodations within four miles of the campus include the Hampton Inn (920-954-9211, $), the Copper Leaf Boutique Hotel and Spa (920-749-0303, $$), and the Radisson Paper Valley Hotel (920-733-8000, $$–$$$).

## CAMPUS AT ITS BEST!

For a firsthand look at Lawrence University's exceptional resources, stop by the Seeley G. Mudd Library. The library contains the Lincoln Reading Room, home to an outstanding collection on Abraham Lincoln, Slavery, the American Civil War, and Reconstruction, and the Milwaukee-Downer Room which contains over 3,400 rare books. On your way to the Memorial Union for a bite to eat at the Union Grill, stop by the Wriston Art Center to see the Ancient and Byzantine Coin Collection, and the outdoor amphitheater. For a taste of the campus social scene, attend a basketball game at the Alexander Gymnasium, hear a concert in the Memorial Chapel, or warm up at the Coffeehouse while listening to a poetry reading.

# LOYOLA UNIVERSITY—CHICAGO

820 North Michigan Avenue, Chicago, IL 60611
**Telephone:** 312-915-6500 • **E-mail:** admission@luc.edu
**Website:** www.luc.edu

## STUDENTS SAY

"Loyola is a Jesuit Catholic University that strives to educate the entire person through a wide variety of classes, service projects, and extracurricular activities."

## FODOR'S SAYS

Check out the Museum of Science and Industry, whose many exhibits "are hands-on, letting you walk through the caves of a human heart and study the inner workings of a coal mine from below ground."

## ABOUT THE SCHOOL

Students at Loyola University—Chicago enjoy small classes, great facilities, and a variety of cultural and professional development options available in the big city of Chicago. Students also rely on the city of Chicago for their fun as the scene on campus isn't exactly jumping. Some commuter students prefer to head home on the weekends.

## GETTING THERE

**BY AIR:** O'Hare International Airport is closest to campus and services all the major airline carriers. From there, you can take a taxi, or the Chicago Transit Authority (CTA) to get to campus.

**BY TRAIN:** Amtrak makes a stop at Union Station in downtown Chicago. Take a taxi or CTA to campus. If traveling by public transportation from Union Station, take the 1, 7, 60, 126, or 151 CTA Bus Eastbound to State Street. From there, transfer to the Red line subway on the "Northbound to Howard" platform to the Loyola stop.

**BY BUS:** Greyhound stops at the Chicago Transit Authority Building in Chicago. Take a taxi or subway to campus. If traveling by subway, take the Red Line to the Loyola stop.

**BY CAR:** From I-94 and the North: Take I-94 East to Chicago. Exit at Touhy Avenue East. Follow Touhy Avenue and go right on Sheridan Road. Take a left on Albion and then a right on Winthrop Avenue. From I-94 South and the Southeast: Take the I-55 North Exit into Chicago. From I-55 North, take the Lake Shore Drive Exit. Continue on Lake Shore Drive; go right on Sheridan Road. One more mile and you're there. From I-88 and the West: Take I-88 East into Chicago. Take Exit I-294 West North to Wisconsin. Follow I-294 until you reach the exit for I-90 East to Chicago. Take I-90 East to the Lawrence Avenue Exit. Turn left on Lawrence Avenue headed East until you reach Sheridan Road. Turn left on Sheridan and continue North on this road until you reach the college.

**LOCAL:** CTA offers bus and subway transportation around the city. Local taxi service includes American United Cab (773-248-7600), Yellow Cab Management, Inc. (312-829-4222), and Green Taxi Association (773-583-9000).

## WHERE TO STAY

There are plenty of hotel options in the Chicago area for those planning overnight stays. Some of the options closest to campus include The Lakeside Motel (773-275-2700, $), the Residence Inn by Marriott (312-943-9800, $$–$$$) and the Hilton Garden Inn Evanston (847-475-6400, $$$).

---

## CAMPUS AT ITS BEST!

With several buildings overlooking Lake Michigan, students gravitate there to study or relax with friends. They also take advantage of all the resources Chicago has to offer. Loyola students conduct research at the nearby Lincoln Park Zoo and the Field Museum, and enjoy all manner of entertainment at the Navy Pier, which showcases an IMAX Theater, the Chicago Shakespeare Theater, a Ferris wheel, carousel, and mini golf course.

# MACALESTER COLLEGE

1600 Grand Avenue, St. Paul, MN 55105
**Telephone:** 651-696-6357 • **E-mail:** admissions@macalester.edu
**Website:** www.macalester.edu
**Hours:** Monday–Friday, 8:00 A.M.–5:00 P.M.; Saturday, 9:00 A.M.–NOON

| SCHOOL AT A GLANCE | |
| --- | --- |
| Type of School | Private |
| Environment | Metropolis |
| Tuition | $30,870 |
| Enrollment | 1,843 |
| % Male/Female | 42/58 |
| Student/Faculty Ratio | 11:1 |

| FRESHMAN PROFILE | |
| --- | --- |
| Range SAT | |
| Critical Reading | 630-740 |
| Range SAT Math | 630-710 |
| Range ACT Composite | 28-32 |

| ON-CAMPUS APPOINTMENTS | |
| --- | --- |
| Advance Notice | Yes, 2 weeks |
| Appointment | Required |
| Saturdays | Sometimes |
| Average Length | 45 min |
| Info Sessions | Yes |
| Class Visits | Yes |

| CAMPUS TOURS | |
| --- | --- |
| Appointment | Required |
| Dates | Year Round |
| Times | Mon-Sat |
| Average Length | 60 min |

## STUDENTS SAY

"Not to sound corny or anything, but Mac is a great place to learn (challenging, but not stressful) and the students and teachers are some of the friendliest I've ever met."

## FODOR'S SAYS

"At the confluence of the Mississippi and Minnesota rivers is Historic Fort Snelling. As the northernmost outpost in the old Northwest Territories, it remained an active military post until after World War II."

## ABOUT THE SCHOOL

Macalester, one of the most esteemed names in liberal arts education, offers a tight-knit community amidst the expanse of St. Paul/Minneapolis. Undergrads at Macalester are bound together by their decidedly liberal leanings, a shared thirst for knowledge, and a capacity to balance strenuous workloads with healthy extracurricular lives.

## GETTING THERE

**BY AIR:** The Minneapolis-St. Paul International Airport is 15 minutes from campus and offers a wide range of airline choices. Taxis offer the easiest transport to Macalester.

**BY TRAIN:** Amtrak's Empire Builder lines stop at the St. Paul terminal, about two and a half miles from Macalester. Catch a cab to campus.

**BY BUS:** Greyhound has three stops in St. Paul: downtown, at the Amtrak station, and at the University of St. Paul. Jefferson Lines services Greyhound's downtown terminal as well. Take a taxi to campus.

**BY CAR:** From I-94 East/West: Follow I-94 to Exit 238 for Snelling Avenue. Make a left onto Snelling and drive South until reaching Grand Avenue. Take a right (heading West) onto Grand Avenue. A block later, go left onto Macalester Street and use signs to locate visitor parking. From I-35 East (heading South): Follow I-35 East toward St. Paul. Merge onto I-94 West. From there, follow "From I-94 East/West" directions above. From I-35 East (heading North): Follow I-35 East toward St. Paul. Take Exit 104B onto Ayd Mill Road. Then turn left (heading West) onto Grand Avenue. After passing over Snelling Avenue, make a left onto Macalester Street. Signs point to visitor parking.

**LOCAL:** Metro Transit bus line #63 stops at Macalester. In addition, the Associated Colleges of the Twin Cities (ACTC) provides regular daytime transit among the five participating institutions (Augsburg, Hamline, Macalester, St. Paul, and St. Thomas). If you're looking for a taxi, call Checker Taxi (651-222-2222), Citywide Cab (651-489-1111), or Airport Yellow Taxi (651-644-3212).

## WHERE TO STAY

The nearest overnight lodging is at the on-campus Macalester Alumni House Bed and Breakfast (651-696-6677, $-$$). There are only four rooms at the Alumni House, so book early. Other nearby accommodations include Holiday Inn Express (651-647-1637, $$; ask for Macalester rates) and historic downtown's Saint Paul Hotel (651-292-9292, $$-$$$).

## CAMPUS AT ITS BEST!

One need only loiter on the quad to gain an understanding of how Macalester students spend their time. This beloved spot is continually in use, and at any given moment you'll find students napping there, playing a game of Frisbee, or building a snowman. When students lack the motivation to generate their own fun, they rely on the Programming Board. While you're there, consider participating in one of the Programming Board's many events such as Fall Fest or Macalester Idol. Macalester's Twin City location also affords many entertainment options, from restaurants and cafes to annual events like the Minnesota State Fair.

# MARQUETTE UNIVERSITY

PO Box 1881, Milwaukee, WI 53201-1881

**Telephone:** 414-288-7302 • **E-mail:** admissions@Marquette.edu

**Website:** www.marquette.edu • **Hours:** Monday–Friday, 8:30 A.M.–4:30 P.M.; Saturday, 9:00 A.M.–4:30 P.M.

## STUDENTS SAY

"Marquette University is all about great people, bad food, good times, and good parties."

## FODOR'S SAYS

"Completed in 1892 for the beer baron Captain Frederick Pabst, the Pabst Mansion is one of Milwaukee's treasured landmarks. The 37-room Flemish Renaissance-style mansion, designed by the architectural firm Ferry & Clas, has a tan pressed brick exterior with carved stone and terra-cotta ornamentation."

## ABOUT THE SCHOOL

Marquette University, known for its excellent basketball program and community service opportunities, also offers an academic program so rigorous that students often end up taking 18-credit semesters. With such heavy course loads during the week, students make it a point to cut loose on the weekends. With plenty of activities on campus and with downtown Milwaukee only a stone's throw away, fun outside of class is not hard to find.

## GETTING THERE

**BY AIR:** General Mitchell International Airport is the closest airport to campus. Taxi or the airport shuttle service is a good option for getting from the airport to campus. To schedule an airport shuttle pick-up, call 800-236-5450.

**BY TRAIN:** Amtrak stops at North 5th Street and West St. Paul Avenue. From here, you can take a taxi.

**BY BUS:** Greyhound stops at 606 North James Lovell in Milwaukee. Take a taxi to campus.

**BY CAR:** From the West (I-94 East): Take I-94 East, and exit at the 35th Street ramp (309A). At the stoplight at the end of the exit ramp, turn left onto 35th Street. Go North on 35th Street for about a half mile to Wisconsin Avenue, and make a right. Take Wisconsin Avenue East one and a quarter miles to 16th Street. At 16th Street, turn left and proceed to the college. From the Northwest (I-45 South): Take I-45 South. Take Exit 39 from the left to I-94. Follow I-94 East to the 35th Street Exit ramp (309A). Follow "From the West" directions above. From the South or Southwest (I-43 North): Take I-43 North to the Kilbourn Exit (72C), which will be on the right. Take the tunnel to Sixth Street. Make a left onto Sixth and proceed to State Street. Turn left onto State Street and travel to 11th Street. At 11th Street, turn left and travel to Wells Street. Proceed towards the college.

**LOCAL:** Local taxi service includes American United Taxi Cab Service (414-220-5000) and Atta Taxi (414-587-5695).

## WHERE TO STAY

Some of the most popular nearby lodging choices are Best Western Inn Towne Hotel (414-224-8400, $$), Ambassador Hotel (414-342-8400, $$), and Astor Hotel (414-271-4220, $$).

## CAMPUS AT ITS BEST!

Feeling stressed from all this college touring? Make a pit stop at the Rec Plex, located inside Marquette's Straz Tower. Here you'll find yoga, steam rooms, saunas, and massage therapy among the Tower's other fitness equipment. There's also an abundance of campus activities to keep you distracted. The annual Winter Flurry event features everything from illusionists and wacky photos, to pre-game tailgates and stand-up comedians.

# MIAMI UNIVERSITY (OH)

301 South Campus Avenue, Oxford, OH 45056
**Telephone:** 513-529-2531 • **E-mail:** admissions@muohio.edu
**Website:** www.muohio.edu
**Hours:** Monday–Friday, 8:30 A.M.–4:30 P.M.; Saturday, 9:00 A.M.–NOON

## STUDENTS SAY

"Miami University provides students with many opportunities to grow as [people] through free speakers, challenging courses, [a] nice recreational center, amazing food, and variety of student organizations."

## FODOR'S SAYS

"Famous for its chili, Cincinnati has more good restaurants than the most ravenous traveler could sample in one visit, including riverboat restaurants and rathskellers."

## ABOUT THE SCHOOL

Miami University is a midsize school (15,000 undergrads) that offers tons of courses, a plethora of clubs, nationally competitive sports teams, and top-notch academic resources. The university maintains a small-school feel by keeping the student-faculty ratio low and the discussion level high. The university's small-town location is balanced by easy access to Cincinnati and Dayton, each an hour away.

## GETTING THERE

**BY AIR:** Cincinnati and Dayton international airports are each about an hour away. To get to campus, use a car or taxi. Shuttles are also available; just call Airport Shuttle Service (513-896-6605).

**BY TRAIN:** The closest Amtrak stops are in Hamilton (half hour away) and Cincinnati (one hour away). Oxford Limousine Service (513-523-6840) offers transportation to and from the terminals.

**BY BUS:** Greyhound services Cincinnati and Dayton.

**BY CAR:** From the East and North: Take I-70 to U.S. 127 South to 73 West to Oxford. From the Northwest: Take I-70 to U.S. 27 South, which becomes Church Street in Oxford. From the South: Take I-275 to U.S. 27 North to Oxford.

**LOCAL:** For taxi service (including airport transportation) call Uptown Taxi (513-523-8294).

## WHERE TO STAY

The Marcum Conference Center and Inn is the university's on-campus lodging (513-529-2104, $–$$). Other nearby accommodations the Elms Hotel/Holiday Inn (513-524-2002, $$) and the Hampton Inn (513-524-1147, $$).

| SCHOOL AT A GLANCE | |
|---|---|
| Type of School | Public |
| Environment | Village |
| In-state Tuition | $20,991 |
| Out-of-state Tuition | $21,011 |
| Enrollment | 14,582 |
| % Male/Female | 47/53 |
| Student/Faculty Ratio | 16:1 |

| FRESHMAN PROFILE | |
|---|---|
| Range SAT | |
| Critical Reading | 560-650 |
| Range SAT Math | 580-670 |
| Range ACT Composite | 25-29 |
| Average HS GPA | 3.8 |

| ON-CAMPUS APPOINTMENTS | |
|---|---|
| Class Visits | Yes |

| CAMPUS TOURS | |
|---|---|
| Appointment | Required |
| Dates | Year Round |
| Times | M–F 10:00 A.M., 2:00 P.M.; |
| | Sat 10:00 A.M. |
| Average Length | 120 min |

## CAMPUS AT ITS BEST!

Miami's Upham Hall combines academics with university lore. The building is home to both anthropology and zoology museums, along with an illustrious archway. Legend has it that students will marry whomever they kiss beneath the arch light at midnight. If you decide to visit on a Friday, think about staying into the evening to experience AfterDark. This student-run group sponsors a variety of events such as Beach Night, featuring sand castle building, a steel drum band, and a limbo contest.

# MICHIGAN STATE UNIVERISTY

250 Administration Building, East Lansing, MI 48824-1046
**Telephone:** 517-355-8332 • **E-mail:** admis@msu.edu
**Website:** www.msu.edu

## Students Say

"The size of MSU makes it like training wheels for the real world; every type of person, value, and belief is here, so you learn just as many street smarts as academic smarts."

## Fodor's Says

"The Midwest gets at least one subzero cold snap every year."

## About the School

Variety is truly the "spice of life" at Michigan State University. Whether looking at classes, majors, clubs, sports, or events, the 45,520 students at MSU have plenty of options to choose from. And as a major research institution, MSU possesses a wealth of top-rate resources to ensure that education in East Lansing stays strong.

## Getting There

**BY AIR:** Lansing Capital City Airport is a 20-minute drive from campus. Four airlines provide regular air transit to eight major hubs. Taxis offer the easiest transportation to campus. Local buses (#12A and #14) can take you into town; switch lines to campus.

**BY TRAIN:** East Lansing's Amtrak terminal is on the Southwest edge of campus.

**BY BUS:** Greyhound services East Lansing from its terminal a few minutes by foot from campus. A quick cab or bus ride can take you from the terminal to any destination on campus.

**BY CAR:** From I-75 South: Follow I-75 South until turning onto Route 127 South. Proceed to the exit for Trowbridge Road. Travel East on Trowbridge Road until arriving at MSU. From I-96 West: Follow I-96 West to Route 127 North toward East Lansing. Exit Route 127 at Trowbridge Road and proceed East until you reach campus. From I-96 East: From I-96 East merge onto I-69 East. Continue on I-69 East until exiting onto Route 127 South toward East Lansing. Proceed to the exit for Trowbridge Road. Travel East on Trowbridge Road until arriving at MSU. From Route 127 North/South: Follow Route 127 toward East Lansing. Exit Route 127 at Trowbridge Road and proceed East until you reach campus.

**LOCAL:** Local bus service is provided by the Capital Area Transit System (CATS). The routes servicing the MSU campus exclusively are #30, 31, 32, 33, 35, 36, 38, and 39. Routes between MSU and East Lansing destinations include #1, 20, 22, 23, 24, and 26. The campus is large, so be sure to visit the CATA website (CATA.org) prior to traveling to determine the best route. For taxi service, call Big Daddy Taxi (517-367-7474), Capitol Transit (517-482-1444), or Country Club Taxi Service (888-655-8180).

## Where to Stay

Local accommodations include the Super 8 Motel (517-337-1621, $), Howard Johnson (517-351-5500, $$), and East Lansing Marriott (517-337-4440, $$).

---

## CAMPUS AT ITS BEST!

Even students with a self-proclaimed phobia of science will want to visit the Cyclotron Laboratory at MSU. Tours of the lab allow you to witness the wild side of nuclear physics (yes, nuclear physics has a wild side). Those visiting during the winter should try to attend a Spartan's basketball game at the Breslin Center. At this Big 10 school, sports are a religious experience. If you're visiting the university during the summer, take a ride down to the Red Cedar River with the MSU Canoe Livery Service. The views are breathtaking.

# NORTHWESTERN UNIVERSITY

PO Box 3060, 1801 Hinman Avenue, Evanston, IL 60204-3060
**Telephone:** 847-491-7271 • **E-mail:** ug-admission@northwestern.edu
**Hours:** Monday–Friday, 8:30 A.M.–5:00 P.M.; Saturday, 9:00 A.M.–NOON

## STUDENTS SAY

"We were the overachievers in high school. We are used to being the best—we work hard, we are driven, we are ambitious, and [we] will succeed. Unfortunately, we get to Northwestern and realize that there are 7,999 other students that are just as brilliant and determined as we are—if not even more so."

## FODOR'S SAYS

Nearby "Chicago's arts community is world-class, and lively ethnic communities embrace immigrants from countries as disparate as Croatia and Cambodia, all of whom leave their cultural stamp on the region."

## ABOUT THE SCHOOL

Renowned for exceptional academic programs ranging from journalism to engineering, Northwestern is a prestigious private university offering a rigorous academic experience. Located just north of Chicago and only a stone's throw from Lake Michigan, Northwestern mixes intellectual rigor with exposure to one of America's great urban environments.

| SCHOOL AT A GLANCE | |
| --- | --- |
| Type of School | Private |
| Environment | Town |
| Tuition | $33,408 |
| Enrollment | 7,902 |
| % Male/Female | 47/53 |
| Student/Faculty Ratio | 7:1 |

| FRESHMAN PROFILE | |
| --- | --- |
| Range SAT | |
| Critical Reading | 650-740 |
| Range SAT Math | 670-760 |
| Range ACT Composite | 29-33 |

| ON-CAMPUS APPOINTMENTS | |
| --- | --- |
| Info Sessions | Yes |
| Class Visits | Yes |

| CAMPUS TOURS | |
| --- | --- |
| Appointment | Not Required |
| Dates | Year Round |
| Times | Varies |
| Average Length | 120 min |

## GETTING THERE

**BY AIR:** Either Chicago airport—O'Hare or Midway International Airport—offers easy transit to the city of Chicago, though O'Hare is closer to the Northwestern campus. For shuttle service from either airport, make reservations with Airport Express (800-654-7871). Taxi service is also available at the airport.

**BY TRAIN:** Amtrak's most regular Chicago service runs out of its Harrison Street terminal. A combination of bus and subway can get you to campus. Otherwise, take a cab.

**BY BUS:** A dozen bus lines stop at Chicago's Union Station. From there, walk a third of a mile North to the Ogilvie Transportation Center and board the Metra Union Pacific North Line. Get off at the Central Street Metra station. Take a cab or walk less than half a mile Northwest to campus.

**BY CAR:** From I-90 East: Follow I-90 East until merging onto I-294 North toward Wisconsin. Continue on I-294 North until exiting onto Dempster Street, driving East for about ten miles. Once in Evanston, make a left onto Chicago Avenue. Campus is less than a mile ahead. From I-94 East: Follow I-94 East (though, beginning at Milwaukee, actually traveling South) before exiting onto the Skokie Highway. Drive South on the Skokie Highway for two miles. Make a left onto Golf Road. As you enter Evanston, Golf Road becomes Emerson Road. After four miles on this road, it forks; bear right, and you will be on Clark Street. Proceed through downtown Evanston and onto campus. From I-94 (Edens Expressway) West: From points South, make your way to I-94 West, heading North into Chicago, and proceed to Exit 37B for Dempster Street, heading East. Continue on Dempster Street for five miles. Once in Evanston, make a left onto Chicago Avenue. Campus is less than a mile ahead.

**LOCAL:** Metra Union Pacific North Line stops less than half a mile from campus (Central Street Metra station). The CTA 201 bus line stops nearby. For a taxi, try Yellow Cab (312-829-4222).

## WHERE TO STAY

Lodging within walking distance of campus includes the Homestead (847-475-3300, $$), Margarita European Inn (847-869-2273, $$), and Best Western University Plaza (847-491-6400, $$$+).

## CAMPUS AT ITS BEST!

Budding literary scholars will want to visit Northwestern's Shakespeare Garden. Designed by noted landscape architect Jens J. Jensen, guests will find more than 50 plants mentioned in Shakespeare's works. Afterwards, head over to the Dearborn Observatory. This facility is equipped with one of the few remaining refracting telescopes still in use. As a Big Ten school, football factors heavily into students' social lives. If you're visiting in the fall, attend a home game and support the Wildcats.

# OBERLIN COLLEGE

101 North Professor Street, Oberlin College, Oberlin, OH 44074

**Telephone:** 440-775-8411 • **E-mail:** college.admissions@oberlin.edu • **Website:** www.oberlin.edu

**Hours:** Monday–Friday, 8:30 A.M.–5:00 P.M.; Saturday, 9:00 A.M.–NOON

## STUDENTS SAY

"Obies are the kids who never fit in back home; we're all different and unusual, which creates a common bond between students. . . . For a mere four years, 2,000 socially awkward, politically active, flaming liberal nerds experience being 'normal.'"

## FODOR'S SAYS

"The Lake Erie Circle Tour consists of nearly 200 miles of state routes and U.S. highways along the Lake Erie shoreline from Toledo to Conneaut."

## ABOUT THE SCHOOL

Oberlin is a liberal arts college in the best sense of the term. Small classes, attentive professors, a rigorous and progressive curriculum—Obie has it all. But when it comes to resources, the school has the feel of a major player. Top-notch facilities and cutting-edge programs ensure that Obies have a world of opportunity at their fingertips.

## GETTING THERE

**BY AIR:** Cleveland-Hopkins International Airport is 30 minutes from campus. Take a cab or arrange a pickup with Cleveland Limousine Service (800-543-9912). You can also take Lorain County Transit (LCT) bus #33 which runs seven trips daily between the airport and campus.

**BY TRAIN:** Amtrak services Elyria, half an hour from campus. Take a taxi to Oberlin.

**BY BUS:** Greyhound's Elyria terminal is half an hour away. Greyhound and Lakefront Trailways service downtown Cleveland as well.

**BY CAR:** From I-80 West: Follow I-80 West to Exit 140 at the Amherst-Oberlin interchange. At the end of the ramp, turn left onto Route 58, which leads to Oberlin. After arriving in town, make a right onto West Lorain Street. Make another right onto North Professor Street. From I-90 West: Follow I-90 West to I-271 South. From I-271 South, merge onto I-480 West and proceed to the left exit for Oberlin/Norwalk, where you pick up Route 10. Continue on Route 10 as it turns into Route 20. Exit onto Route 511 West, which leads to the town of Oberlin. In town, make a right onto North Professor Street. From I-80/90 East: Follow I-80/90 to Exit 140 at the Amherst-Oberlin interchange. At the end of the ramp, turn left onto Route 58, which leads to Oberlin. After arriving in town, make a right onto West Lorain Street. Make another right onto North Professor Street. From I-71 North: Follow I-71 North to Exit 186 for Route 250 toward Ashland/Wooster. At the end of the ramp, turn right onto Route 250 East and proceed until exiting (left) onto Route 89 North. After Route 58 North joins up with Route 89 North, proceed on Route 58 North. Once in town, turn left onto Lorain Street. Then make a right onto North Professor Street.

**LOCAL:** If you're looking for a taxi, try A2 Point B cab service (440-775-7222).

## WHERE TO STAY

Places to stay in the area include the on-campus Oberlin Inn (440-775-1111, $$), the Ivy Tree Inn and Garden (440-774-4510, $$), and the Hallauer House Bed and Breakfast (440-774-3400, $$).

## CAMPUS AT ITS BEST!

Oberlin students flock to The Cat in the Cream Coffeehouse for a comfortable atmosphere and a great mug of coffee. Located within Hales Annex, this student-run café often hosts free performances ranging from sketch comedy and poetry readings to religious services. After getting your caffeine fix, take in a performance from the renowned Artist Recital Series. One of the oldest continuing concert series in the country, every year it attracts highly accomplished musicians like Dave Brubeck, Yo-Yo Ma, and Denyce Graves.

# OHIO STATE UNIVERSITY—COLUMBUS

110 Enarson Hall, 154 West Twelfth Avenue, Columbus, OH 43210
**Telephone:** 614-292-3980 • **E-mail:** askabuckeye@osu.edu
**Website:** www.osu.edu • **Hours:** Monday–Friday, 9:00 A.M.–5:00 P.M.

## STUDENTS SAY

"The greatest strength of the school is it size and variety. Students can have anything they could imagine at this school."

## FODOR'S SAYS

"On the grounds of the Ohio Expo Center is the Crew Stadium, home of Major League Soccer's Columbus Crew. It's the first stadium in the country built specifically for a professional soccer team and can hold 22,500 fans."

## ABOUT THE SCHOOL

One of the big dogs in the Big Ten, OSU offers its undergrads a whole lot of everything: amazing research facilities, a wide range of majors, great courses, cultural events, clubs, and good old-fashioned parties. And they have some pretty strong sports teams, too. All of this takes place in the heart of America's fifteenth largest city, Columbus.

## GETTING THERE

**BY AIR:** Columbus International is the airport of choice when flying to OSU. Make arrangements with Urban Express Airport Shuttle (614-856-1000) in advance for terminal-to-campus service. You can also get a cab at the airport.

**BY TRAIN:** Amtrak does not service Columbus. The nearest stop is in Cincinnati, Ohio, about 110 miles away.

**BY BUS:** The Greyhound terminal is about three miles from campus. Catch a cab for easy transport to OSU.

**BY CAR:** From Route 315 South: Route 315 South can be accessed from the Northern rim of I-270. Follow Route 315 South to the exit for Lane Avenue. Make a left and proceed to campus. From I-71 North: Follow I-71 North until exiting onto Route 315 North at the edge of Columbus. Proceed on Route 315 North until turning at Lane Avenue. Make a right onto Lane Avenue and continue onto the OSU campus. From I-70 East: Follow I-70 East until merging onto I-670 East at Exit 96 (a left exit). Continue on I-670 East for about two miles. At Exit 2B, turn onto Route 315 North. Proceed on Route 315 North until turning at Lane Avenue. Make a right onto Lane Avenue and drive onto the OSU campus. From I-70 West: Follow I-70 West until exiting onto Route 315 North. Proceed on Route 315 North until turning at Lane Avenue. Make a right onto Lane Avenue and continue onto the OSU campus.

**LOCAL:** Campus Area Bus Service (CABS) offers several routes that operate exclusively on and immediately around campus. Central Ohio Transit Authority (COTA) buses also serve the campus area. If you need a cab, call Yellow Cab (614-444-4444) or Shamrock Taxi (614-784-8888).

## WHERE TO STAY

The Blackwell is an OSU-affiliated, on-campus hotel (614-247-4000, $$) and the University Plaza Hotel is an OSU-affiliated, just-off-campus hotel (614-267-7461, $$). Other nearby options include the Varsity Inn (614-291-2983, $) and Westin Great Southern Columbus (614-228-3800, $$).

### SCHOOL AT A GLANCE

| | |
|---|---|
| Type of School | Public |
| Environment | Metropolis |
| In-state Tuition | $8,667 |
| Out-of-state Tuition | $20,562 |
| Enrollment | 38,479 |
| % Male/Female | 53/47 |
| Student/Faculty Ratio | 13:1 |

### FRESHMAN PROFILE

| | |
|---|---|
| Range SAT | |
| Critical Reading | 530–640 |
| Range SAT Math | 560–670 |
| Range ACT Composite | 24–29 |

### ON-CAMPUS APPOINTMENTS

| | |
|---|---|
| Saturdays | No |
| Class Visits | Yes |

### CAMPUS TOURS

| | |
|---|---|
| Appointment | Required |
| Dates | Varies |
| Times | M–F 9:00 A.M. and 1:00 P.M. |
| Average Length | Varies |

---

## CAMPUS AT ITS BEST!

Mirror Lake is an Ohio State landmark. Originally fed by a natural spring, this body of water was a major factor when university founders were deciding where to break ground. To continue with your "landmark" theme, stop at Ohio Stadium. Home to the university's football team for over 80 years, the stadium has a capacity of 101,568. Buckeyes are fanatical about their football and you should think about visiting during Beat Michigan Week. This annual festivity promotes school spirit with a pep rally, banner signing, and everyone's favorite—Wing the Wolverines.

# OHIO UNIVERSITY—ATHENS

120 Chubb Hall, Athens, OH 45701
**Telephone:** 740-593-4100 • **E-mail:** admissions@ohio.edu
**Website:** www.ohio.edu • **Hours:** Monday–Friday, 8:00 A.M.–5:00 P.M.; Saturday, 10:00 A.M.–NOON

## STUDENTS SAY

"Ohio University is the perfect balance of academic and social excellence."

## FODOR'S SAYS

"If you're going to rural areas and small towns, go with cash; traveler's checks are best used in cities."

## ABOUT THE SCHOOL

At Ohio University there's an undeniable whiff of professional preparation in the air—and that's exactly how these undergrads like it. Small classes and accessible professors combine with a strong vocation-minded curriculum to make the students in southeastern Ohio happy about today and tomorrow.

## GETTING THERE

**BY AIR:** Columbus's Port Columbus International Airport is 80 miles from campus. Call Athens Airport Shuttle (740-592-0490) to arrange a pickup.

**BY TRAIN:** The nearest Amtrak stop is in South Portsmouth, Kentucky, about 70 miles from the university.

**BY BUS:** Greyhound/Lakefront Trailways offers limited service to Athens, stopping at the Oasis Coffee House on campus.

**BY CAR:** From Route 33 East: Follow Route 33 East into Athens. Eventually Route 33 East runs into Route 50; proceed on Route 50 West. Follow this briefly to Exit 17 for Route 682 North. At the first light, make a right onto Richland Avenue. After crossing the Hocking River, proceed onto the OU campus. The visitor's center is on the left. From I-77 South: Follow I-77 South to Exit 6 for Lower Salem/Marietta. At the end of the ramp, turn left on Route 821 South. A few miles later, when Route 821 comes to a T, make a left onto Route 60 South. Drive another few miles and turn right onto Route 7 South. In the town of Belpre, Route 7 South joins routes 32 and 50 West. Continue to follow signs for Route 50 West, which carries you into Athens. Follow this (as it combines with Route 33 East) to Exit 17 for Route 682 North. At the first light, make a right onto Richland Avenue. After crossing the Hocking River, proceed onto the OU campus. The visitor's center is on the left. From Route 32 East or Route 50 East: Proceed on either Route 32 East or Route 50 East until the two combine near Albany. Continue to Exit 17 for Route 682 North. At the first light, make a right onto Richland Avenue. After crossing the Hocking River, proceed onto the OU campus. The visitor's center is on the left.

**LOCAL:** City of Athens bus routes service campus. For a cab, try Athens Cab (740-594-7433) or Westside Cab (740-753-3535).

## WHERE TO STAY

Local lodging includes Budget Host Coach Inn (740-594-2294), Burr Oak Lodge (740-767-2112), and Ohio University Inn (740-593-6661).

---

## CAMPUS AT ITS BEST!

Cinema buffs will be thrilled to learn that Ohio has its own movie theater on campus. The Athena is used for large lecture classes during the day and operates as a commercial theater in the evenings. Additionally, sports enthusiasts will be happy to discover that the university has its own nine-hole recreational golf course on the banks of the Hocking River. After you hit the links, check out what the Program Council has in store for the evening. Past events have brought midnight movies, comedians like Al Franken, and the "Taste of Athens" food festival to campus.

# OHIO WESLEYAN UNIVERSITY

Admissions Office, 61 South Sandusky Street, Delaware, OH 43015
**Telephone:** 740-368-3020 • **E-mail:** owuadmit@owu.edu
**Website:** www.owu.edu • **Hours:** Monday–Friday, 8:30 A.M.–5:00 P.M.; Saturday, 8:30 A.M.–2:00 P.M.

## STUDENTS SAY

"The typical student at Ohio Wesleyan is goal-oriented and probably in one of the many student or service groups, though there is more emphasis on service groups than there are on other extracurriculars."

## FODOR'S SAYS

"Daily temperatures average in the 80s, though July and August heat waves can push them high into the 90s."

## ABOUT THE SCHOOL

Students at Ohio Wesleyan University have to be studious to excel in the school's challenging curriculum. An excellent science department, amazing professors, and a great education program are the standouts here. Although the administration at Wesleyan is very supportive of students, there is no coddling—students have to be proactive about taking advantage of the school's great opportunities.

## GETTING THERE

**BY AIR:** The Port Columbus Airport is the closest airport to campus. Taxi service is available from the airport to the OWU campus for approximately $50 each way.

**BY TRAIN:** The closest stop Amtrak makes near the college is in Toledo, which is over 100 miles from campus.

**BY BUS:** Greyhound stops in Marion, which is about 22 miles from campus.

**BY CAR:** From the Northeast (via I-71): Take I-71 South to Exit 131 (Route 36/37). Turn West on Route 36/37 (toward Delaware). Eventually, Route 36 and 37 will split. Continue on Route 36 (left at the split) to Sandusky Street. Turn left on Sandusky. The campus will be two blocks ahead. From the East and Southeast (via I-70): Take I-70 West to I-270 North (the Columbus outerbelt). Take I-270 North to Exit 23 (Route 23) toward Delaware. Take Route 23 North to the South Sandusky Street Exit, which is on the left. Continue on Sandusky, and the campus is six blocks ahead. From the West (via I-70): Take I-70 East to I-270 North (the Columbus outerbelt). Take I-270 North to Exit 23 (Route 23) toward Delaware. Take Route 23 North to the South Sandusky Street Exit, which is on the left. Continue on Sandusky, and the campus is six blocks ahead. From the Northwest (via I-75): Take I-75 South to Exit 156 (Route 15/23/68). Follow Route 23 South to the South Sandusky Street and Central Avenue Exit for Delaware. Turn right on Central, then left on Sandusky. The campus is four blocks ahead. From the South and Southwest (via I-71): Take I-71 North through Columbus to Exit 131 (Route 36/37). Turn West on Route 36/37 (toward Delaware). Eventually, Route 36 and 37 will split. Continue on Route 36 (left at the split) to Sandusky Street. Turn left on Sandusky, and the campus is two blocks ahead. From the South and Southeast (via I-77): Take I-77 North to I-70 West. Take I-70 West to I-270 North (the Columbus outerbelt). Take I-270 North to Exit 23 (Route 23) toward Delaware. Take Route 23 North to the South Sandusky Street Exit, which is on the left. Continue on Sandusky, and the campus is six blocks ahead.

**LOCAL:** Some local taxi companies are Yellow Cab (800-551-4222), Airport Taxi Service (614-262-8800), Acme Taxi (614-299-9990), and Northway Cab (614-299-1191).

## WHERE TO STAY

Some of the most popular lodging choices near the college include Travelodge (740-369-4421, $), AmeriHost Inn (740-363-3510, $$), and Courtyard by Marriott (614-436-7070, $$$).

### SCHOOL AT A GLANCE

| | |
|---|---|
| Type of School | Private |
| Environment | Town |
| Tuition | $29,870 |
| Enrollment | 1,956 |
| % Male/Female | 48/52 |
| Student/Faculty Ratio | 13:1 |

### FRESHMAN PROFILE

| | |
|---|---|
| Range SAT | |
| Critical Reading | 550-660 |
| Range SAT Math | 570-660 |
| Range ACT Composite | 24-29 |
| Average HS GPA | 3.3 |

### ON-CAMPUS APPOINTMENTS

| | |
|---|---|
| Advance Notice | Yes, 1 week |
| Appointment | Required |
| Saturdays | Yes |
| Average Length | 45 min |
| Info Sessions | Yes |
| Class Visits | Yes |

### CAMPUS TOURS

| | |
|---|---|
| Appointment | Required |
| Dates | Year Round |
| Times | M–F, 10:00 A.M.–4:00 P.M.; |
| | Sat 10:00 A.M.–1:00 P.M. |
| Average Length | 60 min |

## CAMPUS AT ITS BEST!

Ohio Wesleyan is home to Gray Chapel, one of the region's finest concert halls. The chapel's most prominent feature is its Rexford Keller Memorial Concert Organ, worth $1,250,000. Afterwards you'll want to journey over to the "J Walk," a landscaped pedestrian walkway. Students typically congregate here to both study and eat. The walkway also hosts popular annual events like the Greek Week Pie-Eating Contest and Chalk the Walk.

# PURDUE UNIVERSITY—WEST LAFAYETTE

470 Stadium Mall Drive, Schleman Hall, West Lafayette, IN 47907
**Telephone:** 765-494-1776 • **E-mail:** admissions@purdue.edu
**Hours:** Monday–Friday, 8:00 A.M.–5:00 P.M.; Saturday, 9:00 A.M.–NOON

## STUDENTS SAY

"There are so many opportunities to get involved. No matter what you are interested in, you are bound to find others who are interested in the same area."

## FODOR'S SAYS

"[Nearby Indianapolis'] Canal Walk, a 10.5 block vestige of the historic 400-mile canal system linking the Great Lakes and the Ohio River, is an urban haven, with benches, fountains, and wide walkways lining both sides of the canal."

## ABOUT THE SCHOOL

Purdue University, known for its strong engineering program, is a big university with a personal touch. Boasting more than 756 clubs on campus, fantastic Big Ten football, and a dominant fraternity and sorority scene, Purdue has something to offer each of its 30,000 students.

## GETTING THERE

**BY AIR:** The closest airport is the Indianapolis International Airport, 65 miles South of Lafayette. Lafayette Limo (765-497-3828) offers daily shuttle service to and from the airport.

**BY TRAIN:** Amtrak makes a stop in Lafayette. Take a taxi to get to the campus.

**BY BUS:** Greyhound bus lines provide service to Lafayette. Take a taxi to get to the campus.

**BY CAR:** From the North: Take I-65 South to Exit 178, State Road 43. Take State Road 43 seven miles to West Lafayette. You'll hit a light at the intersection of 43 and State Road 26/State Street. Make a right on 26/State Street to the second light, which is Grant Street. Make a right on Grant Street, and you will see the college shortly thereafter. From the South: Take I-65 North to Exit 178, State Road 43. Take State Road 43 seven miles to West Lafayette. You'll hit a light at the intersection of 43 and State Road 26/State Street. Make a right on 26/State Street to the second light, which is Grant Street. Make a right on Grant Street and you will see the college shortly thereafter.

**LOCAL:** Visitors can get around town by taking CityBus (765-742-RIDE), a public transportation system in Greater Lafayette, or Hoosier Bus (866-723-RIDE), which provides luxury transportation to and from the Chicago area. For local taxi service call 4 Star Taxi (765-742-8400).

## WHERE TO STAY

Some popular hotel choices include the Econo Lodge West Lafayette (765-743-9661, $), Comfort Suites (765-447-0016, $$), and Hilton Garden Inn (765-743-2100, $$).

## CAMPUS AT ITS BEST!

Students flock to the water sculpture at the center of the Purdue Mall. A beloved campus landmark, this 38-foot sculpture is a prime spot for studying and sunbathing. Occasionally, the intrepid even use it as a shower. Come crisp, fall Saturdays, however, there might be a dearth of action on the mall. As a Big 10 school, football fever takes over. Visitors should think about purchasing tickets to a game and perhaps joining a tailgate beforehand. Those who tour Purdue in the winter should inquire about sledding at Slayter Hill, a popular campus tradition.

# RIPON COLLEGE

300 Seward Street, PO Box 248, Ripon, WI 54971
**Telephone:** 800-947-4766 • **E-mail:** adminfo@ripon.edu • **Website:** www.ripon.edu

## STUDENTS SAY

"As clichéd as it sounds, the community is what makes Ripon worthwhile. Going to a professor's house for dinner or having class in the local coffee shop is common."

## FODOR'S SAYS

"Devil's Lake State Park is one of the state's most popular parks, with hiking trails, campsites, and 500-foot bluffs overlooking Devil's Lake."

## ABOUT THE SCHOOL

With a student body of just fewer than 1000, intimacy is one of Ripon's key attributes. Individual interaction with professors is not only possible, but also a priority, and the administration is quick to respond to student concerns. Although some lament the lack of diversity on campus, many praise the friendly nature of the school. Social life typically revolves around dorm living and a robust Greek community.

## GETTING THERE

**BY AIR:** If you are traveling with your family, you can fly to General Mitchell International Airport in Milwaukee and rent a car for the one-and-a-half-hour drive to Ripon. If you are traveling alone or if you prefer not to rent a car, you can fly to the Outagamie County Airport in Appleton, WI, 40 miles from Ripon (connecting flights originate from Milwaukee, Chicago and the Twin Cities). Notify the Admission office ahead of time that you are arriving at the Outagamie airport, and they will arrange to pick you up.

**BY TRAIN:** People who wish to travel by train may take Amtrak to Columbus, approximately 50 miles away. If prospective students notify the Admissions Office ahead of time, they can arrange a pick-up.

**BY BUS:** Greyhound provides service to Oshkosh, approximately 20 miles from Ripon. Prospective students can call the Admissions Office and arrange for transportation to the college.

**BY CAR:** From Chicago and Points East or South: Follow I94 North to Milwaukee. Follow 894 (bypass) around Milwaukee to Route 41/45. Follow 41 North to Fond du Lac. Exit Route 23 West (Johnson Street) to Ripon. In Ripon, 23 is Fond du Lac Street; take this to intersection with Blackburn Street. Keep going straight ahead to stop sign (at Watson Street) and straight ahead on Seward Street. From Green Bay and Points North: Follow Route 41 South to Oshkosh. Exit Route 44 West to Ripon. In Ripon, turn left at the first four-way stop onto Eureka Street. Proceed through the traffic light where Eureka turns into Blackburn Street. At the four-way stop, turn right onto East Fond du Lac Street. At next stop sign (Watson Street) go straight ahead on Seward Street. From Madison and Points South or West: Follow 151 East toward Fond du Lac. Exit Highway 26 North. In Waupun, turn onto Highway 49 North through Brandon to Ripon. In Ripon, turn left onto Fond du Lac Street. Proceed through the four-way stop to the next stop sign (Watson Street). Go straight ahead on Seward Street. From the Twin Cities and Points West: Follow I-94 East. In Mauston, take Exit Route 82 East, which turns into Route 23 East at the junction with Route 51. Follow Route 23 East to Ripon. In Ripon, go through two sets of stoplights and turn right onto Elm Street; up the hill, turn left on Seward Street.

**LOCAL:** For local taxi service try Ripon Taxi (920-748-5599).

## WHERE TO STAY

For comfortable, moderately priced accommodations consider the Comfort Suites at Royal Ridges (920- 748-5500, $–$$), or the Heidel House Resort (920-294-3344, $–$$).

| SCHOOL AT A GLANCE | |
| --- | --- |
| Type of School | Private |
| Environment | Village |
| Tuition | $22,162 |
| Enrollment | 981 |
| % Male/Female | 48/52 |
| Student/Faculty Ratio | 13:1 |

| FRESHMAN PROFILE | |
| --- | --- |
| Range SAT | |
| Critical Reading | 480–650 |
| Range SAT Math | 500–620 |
| Range ACT Composite | 21–27 |
| Average HS GPA | 3.40 |

| ON-CAMPUS APPOINTMENTS | |
| --- | --- |
| Advance Notice | Yes, other |
| Appointment | Preferred |
| Saturdays | Sometimes |
| Average Length | 30 min |
| Info Sessions | No |
| Class Visits | Yes |

| CAMPUS TOURS | |
| --- | --- |
| Appointment | Preferred |
| Dates | Varies |
| Times | Varies |
| Average Length | 60 min |

## CAMPUS AT ITS BEST!

Visitors will enjoy stopping by the campus radio station, WRPN-FM, located in the Harwood Memorial Union. The popular station provides East Central Wisconsin with a variety of impressive programming. Prospective students visiting during second semester should keep an eye out for Springfest. This annual celebration features rides such as Euro Bungee, boxing and Raging Bull, a cookout, and live music.

# ROSE-HULMAN INSTITUTE OF TECHNOLOGY

CM 15500 Wabash Avenue, Terre Haute, IN 47803-3999
**Telephone:** 812-877-8213 • **E-mail:** admis.ofc@rose-hulman.edu
**Website:** www.rose-hulman.edu

## STUDENTS SAY

"Classes are really small, so the professors know you and remember things that you are involved in and ask about them."

## FODOR'S SAYS

"Trace Indiana's early frontier history along the Chief White Eyes Trail from Madison to Dillsboro on Route 62."

## ABOUT THE SCHOOL

Emblematic of most engineering schools, Rose-Hulman demands a good deal from its students. Undergrads report rigorous academics that require 110 percent of their effort. Luckily, the heavy workload is offset by a unique group of professors who clearly love teaching. Many of the students are self-professed tech geeks who spend copious amounts of time playing video games.

## GETTING THERE

**BY AIR:** Indianapolis International, a 60-minute drive from Terre Haute, is the most convenient airport for visitors. Car rentals and taxi service are both available for transportation to Rose-Hulman.

**BY TRAIN:** The nearest Amtrak station is located in Crawfordsville, 47 miles away from Terre Haute. Visitors will need to call a taxi or limousine service for the final portion of their trip.

**BY BUS:** Greyhound provides service to Terre Haute. Take a taxi to get to the campus.

**BY CAR:** From the North via U.S. 41/State Highway 63: You will arrive in Terre Haute on Third Street. Drive South to the intersection of Third and Ohio Street (identified by signs indicating U.S. 40 East). Proceed down U.S. 40 for approximately five miles, all the way through town (signs will divert you from Ohio Street to Wabash Avenue at 11th Street). You'll find the main entrance to campus on the left-hand side (North side of U.S. 40), roughly half a mile East of the stoplight at State Highway 46. From the East via U.S. 40: Drive West toward Terre Haute through East Glenn. You'll find the main entrance to Rose-Hulman is on your right-hand side (North side of U.S. 40). From the South via State Highway 46: Proceed North on State Highway 46 until it ends at the intersection with U.S. 40 (roughly four miles). Turn East onto U.S. 40. The main entrance to Rose-Hulman will be on your left-hand side (North side of U.S. 40), approximately half a mile East of the intersection. From the South via U.S. 41/U.S. 150: Enter Terre Haute on Dixie Bee Road (Third Street). Proceed North to the intersection with I-70. Turn East onto I-70 continuing to State Highway 46 Exit (approximately four miles). Follow the "From the South via State Highway 46" directions above. From the East or West via I-70: Take the State Highway 46 Exit, and follow the "From the South via State Highway 46" directions above.

**LOCAL:** Terre Haute has a city bus system that provides local service. For taxi service, visitors may also call Terre Haute Cab (812-232-1313) or Yellow Cab Company (812-478-5322).

## WHERE TO STAY

Comfortable and modestly priced hotels include the Days Inn (812-235-3333, $), Knights Inn (812-234-9931, $), and Travelodge (812-232-7075, $).

## CAMPUS AT ITS BEST!

Chauncey's Gameroom, located in the in the Hulman Memorial Student Union, always has students milling about. Whether they're watching TV, checking e-mail, or playing Ping-Pong, Chauncey's provides students with a welcome respite from academics. It's also equipped with a DVD/video rental library. If marathon games of foosball grow old, consider investigating an event sponsored by the Student Activities Board. They've been known to throw a Las Vegas Nite themed party and campus-wide games of The Price Is Right.

# SAINT LOUIS UNIVERSITY

221 North Grand Boulevard, Saint Louis, MO 63103
**Telephone:** 314-977-2500 • **E-mail:** admitme@slu.edu
**Website:** www.slu.edu • **Hours:** Monday–Friday, 8:30 A.M.–5:00 P.M.; Saturday, 9:00 A.M.–2:00 P.M.

## STUDENTS SAY

"SLU provides a great Jesuit education with many opportunities to volunteer and participate in character-building activities."

## FODOR'S SAYS

"A ride to the top of the 630-foot Gateway Arch is a must. The centerpiece of the 91-acre Jefferson National Expansion Memorial Park, the arch was built in 1965 to commemorate the city where thousands of nineteenth-century pioneers stopped for provisions before traveling West."

## ABOUT THE SCHOOL

SLU is a Jesuit school that, not surprisingly, attracts a lot of Catholic students from the Midwest. The university has exceptionally strong programs in physical and occupational therapy, as well as a nationally ranked aviation school. Undergrads make excellent use of Saint Louis's resources and often venture into the city in search of entertainment.

## GETTING THERE

**BY AIR:** Lambert Saint Louis International Airport is the closest airport to campus. Rental cars, shuttles, taxis, and limousines are all available for transportation to and from the airport.

**BY TRAIN:** Amtrak provides direct service to Saint Louis. It's best to take a taxi from the station to the campus.

**BY BUS:** Greyhound provides service to both Saint Louis proper and Saint Louis Lambert's Field. Take a taxi to your final destination.

**BY CAR:** From I-55/70 South: Take I-55/70 South across the Poplar Street Bridge. Take I-64/40 West to the Forest Park Boulevard/Grand Exit. Make a right on Grand, and travel one block to the university. From I-55 North: Take I-55 North to I-44 West to the Grand Boulevard Exit. Make a left at the stop sign and a right on Grand. Travel one mile to the university. From I-64 East: Take I-64/40 East and exit at Forest Park Boulevard/Grand. Make a right on Grand, and travel one block to the university. From I-64 West: Take I-64/40 West to the Grand Exit. Make a right on Grand, and travel one block to the university.

**LOCAL:** Saint Louis's MetroLink and MetroBus provide light rail service and transportation to various points around the city. Call 314-231-2345 for route and schedule info. Local taxi companies include A-1 Limo and Car Service (314-576-5211), Airport Best Transportation (314-781-1515), and Harris Cab Co. (314-535-5087).

## WHERE TO STAY

Check out the Hampton Inn Union Station (314-241-3200, $$), Drury Plaza Hotel (314-231-3003, $$–$$), and Chase Park Plaza Hotel (314-633-3000, $$$) for special Saint Louis University rates.

### SCHOOL AT A GLANCE

| | |
|---|---|
| Type of School | Private |
| Environment | Metropolis |
| Tuition | $26,250 |
| Enrollment | 7,081 |
| % Male/Female | 43/57 |
| Student/Faculty Ratio | 12:1 |

### FRESHMAN PROFILE

| | |
|---|---|
| Range SAT | |
| Critical Reading | 550-650 |
| Range SAT Math | 550-670 |
| Range ACT Composite | 24-29 |
| Average HS GPA | 3.69 |

### ON-CAMPUS APPOINTMENTS

| | |
|---|---|
| Advance Notice | Yes, 2 weeks |
| Appointment | Required |
| Saturdays | No |
| Average Length | 60 min |
| Info Sessions | Yes |
| Class Visits | Yes |

### CAMPUS TOURS

| | |
|---|---|
| Appointment | Preferred |
| Dates | Year Round |
| Times | M–F 11:00 A.M., 1:00 P.M., 3:00 P.M.; Sat 10:00 A.M., NOON |
| Average Length | 60 min |

## CAMPUS AT ITS BEST!

Saint Louis is a vibrant metropolis and visitors should take advantage of all the city has to offer. The famed Gateway Arch is a definite stop for any tourist. See the city from a unique vantage point as you take the tram all the way to the top. Following your descent, go over to the Mississippi Riverfront. You can experience a piece of history with an old-time riverboat cruise or get your technology fix at the National Video Game and Co-op Museum.

# SOUTHERN ILLINOIS UNIVERSITY— CARBONDALE

MC 4710, Carbondale, IL 62901
**Telephone:** 618-536-4405 • **E-mail:** joinsiuc@siu.edu
**Hours:** Monday–Friday, 8:00 A.M.–4:30 P.M.

## STUDENTS SAY

"No one really cares what you look like or what you do, but we all get along in our own unique way."

## FODOR'S SAYS

"Rend Lake/Wayne Fitzgerald State Park has the state's second-largest inland lake, where you can fish, sail, and swim."

## ABOUT THE SCHOOL

At SIUC, the intellectual appetite of the student body often parallels the rigor of their major. Indeed, aviation management and engineering, two of the school's finest programs, demand a lot from their undergrads. Other students tend to take a laid-back approach to academics, choosing to partake of the university's extremely healthy party scene.

## GETTING THERE

**BY AIR:** Guests who would like to fly directly to Carbondale can fly to the Williamson County Airport. The airport is served by American Connections regional commuter flights. It is located 16 miles East of campus.

**BY TRAIN:** Amtrak provides train service to Carbondale. Trains serving the area leave from Amtrak's Chicago hub. Take a taxi to get to the campus.

**BY BUS:** Greyhound offers service to Carbondale. Take a taxi to get to the campus

**BY CAR:** Those traveling by car should take the most convenient route to Illinois Route 13. Route 13 takes you into Carbondale. From there turn South onto U.S. Route 51 (South University Avenue). Drive South for approximately two miles. Turn right onto Lincoln Drive (you will see IUC welcome sign).

**LOCAL:** Visitors can ride the BART (Bootheel Area Rapid Transit), a shuttle service that travels from Lambert International Airport in St. Louis to the Southern Illinois region, roughly two and a half hours away. For local cab service try the Southern Pride Cab Company (618-529-5038) or Yellow Cab (618-457-8121).

## WHERE TO STAY

For local and affordable accommodations, call the Comfort Inn (618-549-4244, $), Super 8 Motel (618-457-8822, $), or the Hampton Inn (618-549-6900, $$).

## CAMPUS AT ITS BEST!

SIUC's University Museum is not to be missed. The only encyclopedic museum in southern Illinois, patrons are privy to a diverse collection. On display are works from seminal twentieth-century artists and specimens representing geologic history and archaeological artifacts from Central and South America. If you're looking to balance your educational visit with a little fun, consider stopping by the Student Recreation Center. A popular spot for undergrads, the center hosts many events like Sport Fest, which features Tug of War, dodgeball, and flag football.

# ST. OLAF COLLEGE

1520 St. Olaf Avenue, Northfield, MN 55057
**Telephone:** 507-646-3025 • **E-mail:** admissions@stolaf.edu
**Website:** www.stolaf.edu

## STUDENTS SAY

"People [at St. Olaf] are committed to community service, whether just on campus or in the greater community."

## FODOR'S SAYS

"Minnesotans are known for the culinary traditions of their Scandinavian and German ancestors."

## ABOUT THE SCHOOL

Saint Olaf is internationally acclaimed for its music department; the college also provides a strong liberal arts program. On campus, undergrads benefit from a close-knit community in which it's not uncommon for professors to invite students over for dinner. Many Oles study abroad, solidifying St. Olaf's reputation as a leader in international education.

## GETTING THERE

**BY AIR:** Fly into Minneapolis-St. Paul International Airport and take a taxi to the campus.

**BY TRAIN:** Visitors may take Amtrak to either Red Wing or St. Paul, both fewer than 35 miles from Northfield. Take a taxi to get to the campus.

**BY BUS:** Greyhound provides limited service to Northfield. To reach the campus from the station it is easiest to take a taxi.

**BY CAR:** From I-35 (North or South): Follow I-35 to Highway 19 East (Exit 69, Northfield Exit). Drive East on Highway 19 for roughly six miles, which takes you into Northfield. You'll find the main entrance to the college on your left. From U.S. 52 (North or South): Follow U.S. 52 to Highway 19 (in Cannon Falls). Proceed West on Highway 19 into Northfield. Continue on Highway 19 until you reach the Western edge of Northfield. You'll find the main entrance to the college on your right.

**LOCAL:** For local taxi service call JJ Fairbo Taxi (507-333-4452), Taxi Connection (507-333-0090), or A&R Taxi Incorporated (507-664-9474). Additionally, Northfield Transit provides bus service between Saint Olaf and Carleton College, as well as to multiple locations in Northfield.

## WHERE TO STAY

For overnight accommodations in Northfield consider the Super 8 Motel (507-663-0371, $), AmericInn (507-645-7761, $), or Country Inn (507-645-2286, $–$$).

## SCHOOL AT A GLANCE

| | |
|---|---|
| Type of School | Private |
| Environment | Town |
| Tuition | $28,200 |
| Enrollment | 3,041 |
| % Male/Female | 44/56 |
| Student/Faculty Ratio | 13:1 |

### FRESHMAN PROFILE

| | |
|---|---|
| Range SAT | |
| Critical Reading | 580-700 |
| Range SAT Math | 590-700 |
| Range ACT Composite | 25-30 |
| Average HS GPA | 3.67 |

### ON-CAMPUS APPOINTMENTS

| | |
|---|---|
| Advance Notice | No |
| Appointment | Preferred |
| Saturdays | Sometimes |
| Average Length | 45 min |
| Info Sessions | Yes |
| Class Visits | Yes |

### CAMPUS TOURS

| | |
|---|---|
| Appointment | Preferred |
| Dates | Year Round |
| Times | Varies |
| Average Length | 60 min |

## CAMPUS AT ITS BEST!

Budding philosophers and those with a love of all things Danish will want to explore St. Olaf's Kierkegaard Library. The collection includes approximately 10,000 volumes on Kierkegaard and his writings along with microfilm of manuscripts held by the Royal Library in Copenhagen. Those desiring something more uplifting might be intrigued by the school's annual Christmas Festival. The popular event is broadcast nationwide and offers performances by the St. Olaf Choir, the Viking Chorus, and the St. Olaf Orchestra.

# STEPHENS COLLEGE

1200 East Broadway, Box 2121, Columbia, MO 65215

**Telephone:** 573-876-7207 • **E-mail:** apply@wc.stephens.edu

**Website:** www.stephens.edu

## STUDENTS SAY

"Academics at Stephens are great. Teachers are always available outside of class, and the classes are usually challenging and interesting enough to keep students motivated to work hard!"

## FODOR'S SAYS

"Route 21 from St. Louis to Doniphan, in extreme southern Missouri, passes through national forests and rugged hill country."

## ABOUT THE SCHOOL

Stephens College is a tiny, mostly women's school with very strong programs in theater, dance, and fashion design and a wide selection of non-arts majors. Classes often focus on women's issues and perspectives, and professors are extremely accessible outside of class. Stephens is committed to the idea of hands-on education and gives every student the opportunity to gain real-world experience through internships starting freshman year.

## GETTING THERE

**BY AIR:** Columbia Regional Airport is 15 minutes away from campus. Take a Mo-Express shuttle into the city and take Columbia Transit or a cab to get to the campus.

**BY TRAIN:** The nearest Amtrak station is in Jefferson City, about 25 miles away. Take a cab to get to the campus.

**BY BUS:** Greyhound stops in Columbia. Take Columbia transit or a cab to get to the campus.

**BY CAR:** From the North and South: Take Highway 63 to the Broadway Exit. Travel West on Broadway approximately two miles to the Stephens campus. From the East and West: Take I 70 to Highway 63, the Jefferson City Exit. Travel South on Highway 63 to the Broadway Exit. Travel West on Broadway approximately two miles to the Stephens campus.

**LOCAL:** Columbia Transit serves the city of Columbia and stops at Stephens College during limited hours. For route and schedule information call 573-874-7282. For local taxi service call Columbia Cab Company (573-499-3988) and Yellow Cab Company (573-446-0095).

## WHERE TO STAY

Accommodations are plentiful and very affordable in Columbia. The Regency Hotel is just one block away from campus (573-443-2090, $), and the La Quinta Inn is a little more than two miles away (573- 443-4141, $). The Courtyard by Marriott is conveniently located just five miles away (573-443-8000, $$).

---

## CAMPUS AT ITS BEST!

Many students at Stephens are either majoring in theater, dance, or fashion, or interested in them as extracurricular activities. Therefore, the best way to get a feel for the campus is to attend a performance or exhibition by one of these departments during your visit. In Columbia, check out the Columbia Festival of the Arts in September, where art in many media is displayed and performed.

# UNIVERSITY OF CHICAGO

1101 East Fifty-eighth Street, Suite 105
**Telephone:** 773-702-8650 • **Website:** www.uchicago.edu
**Hours:** Monday–Friday, 8:30 A.M.–5:00 P.M.; Saturday, 8:30 A.M.–1:00 P.M.

## STUDENTS SAY

"The academic nature of this school is evident everywhere, be it the music performed by the artist groups, the discussions during meals, or even the comments written in the bathroom stalls."

## FODOR'S SAYS

"The Magnificent Mile stretches along Michigan Avenue from the Chicago River to Oak Street. Here you'll find such high-price shops as Gucci, Tiffany & Co, and Chanel; venerable hotels such as the Drake and the Inter-Continental; and two fascinating art museums."

## ABOUT THE SCHOOL

Everything about the University of Chicago is highly intellectual. The university challenges its students from day one with a broad core curriculum in literature, philosophy, and science, taught by accomplished, tough professors. The workload is demanding, and students have to study extremely hard to keep up. The intellectual conditioning these students undergo is almost unmatched. On the rare days when students can take a break from the books, they needn't look any farther than hometown Chicago for a variety of entertainment options.

## GETTING THERE

**BY AIR:** Midway International Airport and Chicago O'Hare International Airport are the two closest airports to the campus. Omega Shuttle Service offers transportation from the airports to Hyde Park. Taxi and the Chicago Transit Authority rail and bus service are also available from the airports.

**BY TRAIN:** Amtrak stops on South Canal Street in Chicago. Take a taxi to get to the campus.

**BY BUS:** Greyhound stops on West Harrison Street in Chicago. Take a taxi to get to the campus.

**BY CAR:** From the North: Take I-90/94 to I-55 North to Lake Shore Drive South. Exit at 57th Drive. Go West and curve around the museum. Make the fourth right onto the Midway Plaisance and head West to the campus. From the West: Take the Eisenhower Expressway (I-290) to I-90/94 East. Get off on the I-55 North Exit and take I-55 North to Lake Shore Drive South. Follow the "From the North" directions above. From the South: Take the Dan Ryan Expressway (I-94) North. Get out at Stony Island Avenue. Head North on Stony Island to the Westbound Midway Plaisance (between 60th and 59th Streets). Make a left onto the Midway Plaisance, and head West to the campus.

**LOCAL:** The Chicago Transit Authority (CTA) provides rail and bus service in the Chicago area. Call 1-888-YOURCTA for route and schedule info. You'll have no trouble hailing a cab in Chicago. However, if you need to call a taxi try Checker Cab at 312-829-4222.

## WHERE TO STAY

The Ramada Inn Lake Shore Inn (773-288-5800, $$) is located very close to campus and is a popular hotel choice. Other nearby hotels are the Chicago Travelodge Downtown (312-427-8000, $$) and the Hyatt Regency McCormick Place (312-567-1234, $$).

| SCHOOL AT A GLANCE | |
| --- | --- |
| Type of School | Private |
| Environment | Metropolis |
| Tuition | $33,336 |
| Enrollment | 4,671 |
| % Male/Female | 50/50 |
| Student/Faculty Ratio | 6:1 |

| FRESHMAN PROFILE | |
| --- | --- |
| Range SAT | |
| Critical Reading | 680–770 |
| Range SAT Math | 670–760 |
| Range ACT Composite | 28–33 |

| ON-CAMPUS APPOINTMENTS | |
| --- | --- |
| Advance Notice | 1 week |
| Appointment | Required |
| Saturdays | Yes, Sept–Nov |
| Class Visits | Yes |

| CAMPUS TOURS | |
| --- | --- |
| Dates | Year-Round |
| Times | Varies |
| Average Length | 1 hour |

## CAMPUS AT ITS BEST!

With so many attractions at your fingertips, you'll surely want to maximize your time at the University of Chicago. Frank Lloyd Wright's Robie House, owned by the university, is always a popular destination. Rockefeller Chapel is another must-see during your visit. The tower features a 72-bell carillon, one of the largest musical instruments ever assembled. Visit the original Heisman trophy in the new gym, or the site of the first self-sustaining nuclear reaction. The university's Hyde Park neighborhood also provides a plethora of entertainment options. Cycling enthusiasts will want to participate in the annual Boulevard Lakefront Tour, a scenic bike tour through city streets.

# UNIVERSITY OF CINCINNATI

PO Box 210091, Cincinnati, OH 45221-0091
**Telephone:** 513-556-1100 • **E-mail:** admissions@uc.edu
**Website:** www.uc.edu

## STUDENTS SAY

"The people at UC are by far the school's greatest strength. I not only mean students, but also the teachers, faculty, and even the people that clean our dorms."

## FODOR'S SAYS

"If you have only an hour in Cincinnati, spend it at the Carew Tower, which affords sweeping views of the city from its observation deck. The building dates from 1930 and is home to dozens of shops and restaurants."

## ABOUT THE SCHOOL

As a relatively large state university, UC is equipped with a diverse course catalogue that is sure to satisfy the desires and needs of all students. An important component of the UC education is the Co-op, in which undergraduates alternate quarters of classroom study with professional experience. Many students wind up completing six co-ops during their tenure at Cincinnati, leaving them well prepared to transition into the working world.

Getting There

**BY AIR:** Guests can fly into Cincinnati/Northern Kentucky International. Taxis, rentals car, and shuttles are all accessible for travel to the university.

**BY TRAIN:** Amtrak stops in Cincinnati. Take a taxi or SORTA (local public transport) to get to the campus.

**BY BUS:** Greyhound provides service to Cincinnati. Take a taxi or local bus to get to the campus.

**BY CAR:** From the North or South via I-75: Follow I-75 to the Hopple Street Exit (Exit 3). (Note: If you are traveling North, Hopple Street exits from the left lane). Make a left off the exit onto Hopple Street. When you cross the first intersection (Central Parkway), Hopple Street will turn into Martin Luther King Drive. Proceed on Martin Luther King, driving up the hill to Clifton Avenue. Clifton Avenue borders the West edge of the West Campus. From the West via I-74: Follow I-74 East to I-75 South. From there, proceed according to "From the North" directions above. From the East via U.S. 50: Follow U.S. 50 West, taking a right on Taft Road. (Note: Taft is a one-way street heading West.) As you near campus, Taft turns into Calhoun Street. Remain on Calhoun until it ends at Clifton Avenue. Take a right onto Clifton Avenue which borders the West edge of the West Campus.

**LOCAL:** Visitors can travel around the city via metro, (Southwest Ohio Regional Transit Authority). Call 513-621-4455 for schedule and route information.

## WHERE TO STAY

For overnight stays consider Kingston Marriot Conference Hotel at the University of Cincinnati (513-487-3800, $$–$$$) Garfield Suites Hotel (513-421-3355, $–$$), Vernon Manor Hotel (513-281-3300, $$).

---

## CAMPUS AT ITS BEST!

Tangeman University Center is undoubtedly at the heart of Cincinnati's student life. Equipped with a 90-foot atrium, 600-seat food court, meeting rooms, and a movie theater, TUC is great place to escape the academic grind. The center is also home to the Catskeller, a game room and sports lounge. Every Thursday, the Catskeller hosts the Acoustic Brew, live performances from student musicians. Tuesdays lay claim to Slammin' on Main, a weekly poetry slam.

# UNIVERSITY OF DAYTON

300 College Park, Dayton, OH 45469-1300
**Telephone:** 800-837-7433 • **E-mail:** visit@udayton.edu
**Website:** www.udayton.edu
**Hours:** Monday–Friday, 8:30 A.M.–4:30 P.M.; Saturday mornings

## STUDENTS SAY

"The community and family aspect is great. I love how everyone comes together. I couldn't have asked for a more welcoming school community."

## FODOR'S SAYS

"The United State Air Force Museum, an internationally known attraction, explains the story of flight, from Icarus to the space age and features more than 300 aircrafts including Air Force One and Apollo 15."

## ABOUT THE SCHOOL

Perhaps one of Dayton's biggest assets is its moderate size. Hovering around 7,000 undergrads, the university provides big school opportunities while still offering significant interaction with professors. Though this Catholic school typically nets conservative students from the Midwest, undergrads often highlight the welcoming atmosphere on campus.

## GETTING THERE

**BY AIR:** Guests can fly into Dayton International Airport, located roughly 15 miles north of the city's center. Take a taxi to get to the campus.

**BY TRAIN:** The closest Amtrak is in Cincinnati, approximately 50 miles away. Visitors can opt to catch a connecting Greyhound bus or rent a car to reach Dayton.

**BY BUS:** Greyhound bus service is available to downtown Dayton. Take a taxi or the RTA (Regional Transit Authority) bus #16 to get to the campus.

**BY CAR:** From I-75, Southbound (from Toledo): Exit 51 at Edwin C. Moses Boulevard. Turn left and follow Edwin C. Moses Boulevard East to Stewart Street. Turn right and continue on Stewart Street to the University of Dayton entrance at College Park. From I-75, Northbound (from Cincinnati): Exit 51 at Edwin C. Moses Boulevard. Turn right and follow Edwin C. Moses Boulevard East to Stewart Street. From there, proceed according to "From Southbound" directions above. From I-70, Westbound (from Columbus): Exit I-70 at I-675. Proceed Southbound to Route 35. Go West toward Dayton to I-75. Take I-75 South one exit to 51 Edwin C. Moses Boulevard. From there, proceed according to "From Southbound" directions above. From I-70, Eastbound (from Indianapolis and Dayton Airport): Exit I-70 at I-75 South. Proceed Southbound through Dayton and exit at Edwin C. Moses Boulevard. From there, proceed according to "From Southbound" directions above.

**LOCAL:** Regional Transit Authority (RTA) provides public bus service around Dayton. The RTA bus to UD is #16. For local taxi service call Yellow Cab (937-228-1155).

## WHERE TO STAY

Dayton offers visitors a variety of lodging options like Econo Lodge South (937-223-0166, $), Crown Plaza Dayton Hotel (888-998-4683, $$), and Doubletree Hotel Dayton—Downtown (937-461-4700, $–$$).

---

### SCHOOL AT A GLANCE

| | |
|---|---|
| Type of School | Private |
| Environment | City |
| Tuition | $23,000 |
| Enrollment | 7,270 |
| % Male/Female | 51/49 |
| Student/Faculty Ratio | 14:1 |

### FRESHMAN PROFILE

| | |
|---|---|
| Range SAT | |
| Critical Reading | 520-620 |
| Range SAT Math | 540-650 |
| Range ACT Composite | 23-28 |

### ON-CAMPUS APPOINTMENTS

| | |
|---|---|
| Advance Notice | Yes, 2 weeks |
| Appointment | Preferred |
| Saturdays | Sometimes |
| Average Length | 60 min |
| Info Sessions | Yes |
| Class Visits | Yes |

### CAMPUS TOURS

| | |
|---|---|
| Appointment | Preferred |
| Dates | Year Round |
| Times | Contact the Office of Admission |
| Average Length | Varies |

---

## CAMPUS AT ITS BEST!

Are you curious about residential life at Dayton? Make sure to stop by ArtStreet, deep in the heart of the student neighborhood. This recently constructed complex combines living quarters with spaces for performances and showcasing visual art. It's also equipped with a café, radio station, and even a recording studio.

# UNIVERSITY OF ILLINOIS AT CHICAGO

Box 5220, Chicago, IL 60680
**Telephone:** 312-996-4350 • **E-mail:** uicadmit@uic.edu
**Website:** www.uic.edu

## STUDENTS SAY

"UIC is a great school because it makes every effort to relate classroom teaching to real-world experiences and it uses creative methods in the classroom to keep you engaged and challenged."

## FODOR'S SAYS

"Chicago's Little Italy is to the North of Pilsen. This traditional ethnic neighborhood has been encroached upon by the expansion of the nearby university in recent years, but there are still Italian restaurants, bakeries, groceries, and sandwich shops to explore."

## ABOUT THE SCHOOL

UIC students are quick to praise their professors and their overall academic experience. Despite its being a large public institution, UIC instructors work diligently to provide students with personal attention. Though liberal arts professors receive especially high praise, undergrads maintain you can find strong teachers in every field. Largely a commuter campus, many students turn to hometown Chicago for entertainment.

## GETTING THERE

**BY AIR:** Visitors should fly into Chicago's O'Hare International. Public transportation, taxis, and rental cars are all accessible for travel to the campus.

**BY TRAIN:** Amtrak stops in downtown Chicago at Union Station. Take local public transportation to get to the campus.

**BY BUS:** Greyhound provides service to Chicago, and the terminal is conveniently located a mere two blocks West of the campus.

**BY CAR:** From the North: Follow the Kennedy Expressway (I-90/94) to the Eisenhower Expressway (I-290), heading West. Make sure you stay to the right and take the Morgan Street Exit (the first exit from the expressway). Morgan Street will take you one block South of the campus. From the West: Follow the (I-290) Eisenhower Expressway to the Racine Avenue Exit. Proceed South onto Harrison Street and East to the campus. From the East: Follow either Harrison Street or Roosevelt Road to get to the campus. Drivers who decide to take Roosevelt Road will need to go West to Halsted Street. From the South: Follow the Dan Ryan Expressway (I-90/94) and exit onto Roosevelt Road (1200 South). You will then continue West on Roosevelt Road to Halsted Street. The campus is ahead.

**LOCAL:** The Chicago Transit Authority (CTA) maintains both rail and bus service. For El train service to the campus you may take the Blue Line to the UIC-Halsted, Racine, and Polk stops. You may also ride the Pink Line to the Polk stop. Visitors may also take the number 7 bus to Harrison, the number 8 to Halsted, the number 9 to Ashland, the number 12 to Roosevelt, X21—Cermak Express, number 37 to Sedgwick/Ogden, number 60 to Blue Island/26th, and the number 168 UIC Pilsen Express.

## WHERE TO STAY

Chicago is a booming metropolis and thus offers many hotel options. For a mere sampling consider the Red Roof Inn (312-787-3580, $$), Days Inn Lincoln Park (773-525-7010, $$), or the Swissôtel (312-565-0565, $$$+).

## CAMPUS AT ITS BEST!

UIC retains a fairly diverse student body. These differences are celebrated at Cultural Fest, an annual event sponsored by Campus Programs. The festival features an array of tasty international treats as well a night of performances. The Reading Series is another well-attended event. These presentations attract prominent writers such as John Irving and Stuart Dybek. You can follow up a reading with a stop at Java City. A popular café frequented by undergrads, come savor some gourmet coffee or a fresh panini.

# UNIVERSITY OF ILLINOIS AT URBANA-CHAMPAIGN

901 West Illinois Street, Urbana, IL 61801
**Telephone:** 217-333-0302 • **E-mail:** ugradadmissions@uiuc.edu
**Hours:** Monday–Friday, 8:30 A.M.–5:00 P.M.; Saturday by appointment

## STUDENTS SAY

"This school is academically strong across the board. The standards for grades are high; there are very few easy A's."

## FODOR'S SAYS

"Great River Road follows the Mississippi River, stretching the length of Illinois (more than 500 miles) from East Dubuque to Cairo."

## ABOUT THE SCHOOL

The gargantuan University of Illinois at Urbana-Champaign provides excellent resources and a variety of academic majors and research opportunities to its almost 29,000 undergrads. Students work hard in top-rate programs such as business and engineering, but also make sure to save time for socializing with friends and rooting for their popular athletic team.

| SCHOOL AT A GLANCE | |
| --- | --- |
| Type of School | Public |
| Environment | City |
| In-state Tuition | $7,708 |
| Out-of-state Tuition | $21,794 |
| Enrollment | 31,242 |
| % Male/Female | 53/47 |
| Student/Faculty Ratio | 14:1 |

| FRESHMAN PROFILE | |
| --- | --- |
| Range SAT | |
| Critical Reading | 560-670 |
| Range SAT Math | 620-730 |
| Range ACT Composite | 26-31 |

| ON-CAMPUS APPOINTMENTS | |
| --- | --- |
| Class Visits | Yes |

| CAMPUS TOURS | |
| --- | --- |
| Appointment | Preferred |
| Dates | Year Round |
| Times M–F 10:00 A.M. and 1:00 P.M.; | |
| | Sat 10:00 A.M. |
| Average Length | 60 min |

## GETTING THERE

**BY AIR:** Most visitors fly into the University of Illinois-Willard Airport, which is five miles south of Champaign. A taxi can provide access to the campus.

**BY TRAIN:** Amtrak provides train service to Illinois Terminal. From there, local buses will get you to the university.

**BY BUS:** Greyhound buses stop at the Illinois Terminal. Trailways and Illini Swallow also provide national and regional bus service. A taxi can provide access to the campus.

**BY CAR:** From I-190: Take I-190 to I-294, Exit 1D. Head South for 35 miles to I-80. Take I-80 West three miles and exit from the left lane onto I-57 South. Drive South to I-74 in Champaign and take I-74 East three miles and exit at Lincoln Avenue. Turn right and head South a mile where the university can be seen. From Route 9: Get onto U.S. 51/Veterans Parkway and follow it for about four miles. Exit at the U.S. 51/Main Street ramp and make a left onto U.S. 51/Main Street. Then, exit at the I-74 East ramp and follow I-74 East to Champaign-Urbana for the exit at Lincoln Avenue. Head South to the campus and you will see it to your right. From U.S. 67: Exit at I-270 and stay on I-270 for 25 miles until you reach I-70. Then go East on I-70 until you reach I-57. Take I-57 North to I-74 East. From there, proceed according to "From Route 9" directions above.

**LOCAL:** The Champaign-Urbana Mass Transit District (MTD) provides bus service throughout Champaign and Urbana. The Illini Shuttle (800-642-7388) provides bus service to and from O'Hare and Midway Airports. The Lex Express (800-223-9313) provides service from the university to the O'Hare and Midway Airports and the local area. The Suburban Express (217-344-5500) provides weekend bus service between the Chicago suburbs and the university. Local taxi service includes A and L Taxi (217-621-9906), Checker Cab (217-355-0200), Chicago Carriage Cab (312-326-2221).

## WHERE TO STAY

If you plan on staying overnight, some hotel accommodations include the Champaign Days Inn (217-356-6873, $), the Hampton Inn Champaign at the university (217-337-1100, $$), and the Holiday Inn Champaign/Urbana (217-328-0328, $$).

## CAMPUS AT ITS BEST!

University of Illinois' Japan House allows you to experience a taste of Asia without having to fight jet leg. Students can learn the art of the tea ceremony or flower arranging in a beautiful, serene environment. If you're searching for fun of a different kind, stop by the Courtyard in the Illini Union. Every night of the week is devoted to some type of performance. For example, Mondays are usually dedicated to comedy, Tuesdays to student musicians, and Wednesdays to multicultural events such as language demonstrations and ethnic dance lessons.

# UNIVERSITY OF IOWA

107 Calvin Hall, Iowa City, IA 52242

**Telephone:** 319-335-3847 • **E-mail:** admissions@uiowa.edu

**Website:** www.uiowa.edu • **Hours:** Monday–Friday, 8:30 A.M.–4:30 P.M.; Saturday, 9:00 A.M.–11:00 A.M.

## STUDENTS SAY

"Everyone who goes to Iowa talks about how they think it is the greatest school ever and how they can't see themselves anywhere else."

## FODOR'S SAYS

"Iowa City, in East-central Iowa, served as the seat of the state government until the capital moved to Des Moines in the mid-19th century. The golden dome of the Old Capitol is now the center of the beautiful, hilly campus of the University of Iowa on the banks of the Iowa River."

## ABOUT THE SCHOOL

The University of Iowa, a big state school with nearly 20,000 undergraduates, is a great institution that rewards students who have the initiative to seek personal attention from their professors. At the university, students' social lives generally revolve around Iowa City's downtown bars, Hawkeye football, and the various Christian on-campus groups.

## GETTING THERE

**BY AIR:** The university has three airports that are fairly nearby. The Eastern Iowa Airport is 25 minutes North of Iowa City. The Des Moines International Airport is two hours West of Iowa City. The Quad City International Airport is 60 miles East of Iowa City. Take a shuttle to get to the campus.

**BY TRAIN:** The nearest Amtrak station is at Mt. Pleasant, which is 60 miles South of Iowa City.

**BY BUS:** Greyhound has a bus station in Iowa City that can be used to connect with Amtrak.

**BY CAR:** From the North, East, or West: Take I-80 to the Dubuque Street exit (Exit 244). Head South on Dubuque Street to the first traffic light. Turn right on Park Road. Take the first left onto Riverside Drive, and you will see the university shortly thereafter. From the South: Take Highway 218 to the Melrose Street Exit. Take Melrose to the fourth stop light. Make a left onto Highway 6 (Riverside Drive). Get into the right-hand lane, and you will see the university shortly thereafter.

**LOCAL:** The UI Cambus system provides on-campus bus service. Iowa City Transit (319-356-5151) and Coralville Transit System (319-248-1790) provide bus service throughout the area. For local taxi service call Old Capitol Cab (319-354-7662).

## WHERE TO STAY

Some local hotel accommodations include the University of Iowa's Iowa House Hotel (319-335-3513, $$) located right on campus, as well as the nearby Travelodge (319-351-1010, $) and Sheraton Iowa City Hotel (319-337-4058, $$).

## CAMPUS AT ITS BEST!

Avid Hawkeye fans will most definitely want to stop by University of Iowa's Athletics Hall of Fame. A great destination for college sports fanatics, the facility features biographies and photos of Iowa legends as well as interactive displays. Afterward, stop by Hancher Auditorium to view one of the campus' best venues. The stage has been graced by Aretha Franklin and the Joffrey Ballet. Those who want to visit in the spring should try to have their trip coincide with RiverFest. This is a weekend-long festival featuring carnival rides, games, a River Run, an art fair, and music.

# UNIVERSITY OF KANSAS

Office of Admissions and Scholarships, 1502 Iowa Street, Lawrence, KS 66045

**Telephone:** 785-864-3911 • **E-mail:** adm@ku.edu

**Website:** www.ku.edu • **Hours:** Monday–Friday, 8:00 A.M.–5:00 P.M.; Saturday 9:00 A.M.–NOON

## STUDENTS SAY

"[At KU,] school spirit is infectious."

## FODOR'S SAYS

"About 40 miles West of Kansas City on I-70 is Lawrence. The town was rebuilt after being raided and burned by William Quantrill and a band of Confederate sympathizers for the antislavery stance of its citizens during the Civil War; many structures from this time remain."

## ABOUT THE SCHOOL

The University of Kansas is a large school with a wealth of opportunities for its 21,000 undergrads. Boasting top programs in business, engineering, and journalism, KU also offers a strong sense of community among the staff and students, and great study abroad programs. Students love hometown Lawrence with its rich culture and great restaurants. The entire campus comes together to cheer on the school's top-ranked basketball team.

| SCHOOL AT A GLANCE | |
| --- | --- |
| Type of School | Public |
| Environment | City |
| In-state Tuition | $5,513 |
| Out-of-state Tuition | $14,483 |
| Enrollment | 21,353 |
| % Male/Female | 50/50 |
| Student/Faculty Ratio | 20:1 |
| **FRESHMAN PROFILE** | |
| Range ACT Composite | 22-28 |
| Average HS GPA | 3-4 |
| **ON-CAMPUS APPOINTMENTS** | |
| Class Visits | Yes |
| **CAMPUS TOURS** | |
| Appointment | Preferred |
| Dates | Year Round |
| Average Length | 60 min |

## GETTING THERE

**BY AIR:** The Kansas City International Airport, which is an hour away, is the closest airport to campus. Special shuttles run between the airport and Lawrence. Contact Midwest Transportation Service (785-838-4500). Take a taxi to get to the campus.

**BY TRAIN:** Amtrak trains provide service to Kansas City.

**BY BUS:** Greyhound buses provide service to Kansas City. Trailways buses stop in Lawrence. Take a taxi to get to the campus.

**BY CAR:** From I-70 (the Kansas Turnpike): Take the West Lawrence Exit (#202) and follow U.S. 59 (Iowa Street) South to 15th Street (Bob Billings Parkway). Turn left onto 15th Street and the KU Visitor Center will be to your right. From U.S. 40: U.S. 40 and 6th Street are the same East/West running street in Lawrence. When U.S. 40/6th Street crosses Iowa Street (U.S. 59) turn South onto Iowa. (T intersection, no North turn possible.) Drive South to 15th Street (Bob Billings Parkway). Turn left onto 15th Street and the KU Visitor Center will be to your right. From U.S. 59: U.S. 59 and Iowa Street are the same. Drive North to 15th Street (Bob Billings Parkway). Turn right onto 15th Street and the KU Visitor Center will be to your right. From K-10: Drive West on K-10 to U.S. 59/Iowa Street. Turn North onto U.S. 59/Iowa Street. Drive North to 15th Street (Bob Billings Parkway). Turn right onto 15th Street and the KU Visitor Center will be to your right.

**LOCAL:** The Lawrence Transit System is the city's public bus transportation system. If you'd rather take a taxi to get around the city, some local companies include Midwest Transportation Service (785-842-8294), Lawrence Taxi Service (785-842-8802), and New Taxi Cab Company (785) 267-3777.

## WHERE TO STAY

Some local hotel accommodations include Econo Lodge (785-842-7030, $), Holiday Inn/Holidome (785-841-7077, $$), and Westminster Inn (785-841-8410, $$$).

## CAMPUS AT ITS BEST!

University of Kansas is filled with passionate, spirited students who possess a lot of Jayhawk pride. This is probably most evident during Late Night in the Phog, an annual party held at the start of basketball season. You can also find students congregating at Wescoe Beach, a concrete plaza in front of the humanities building. Often, you'll discover information booths flanking the area and events being held, such as talent competitions.

# UNIVERSITY OF MICHIGAN—ANN ARBOR

1220 Student Activities Building, Ann Arbor, MI 48109-1316
**Telephone:** 734-764-7433 • **E-mail:** ugadmiss@umich.edu
**Website:** www.umich.edu • **Hours:** Monday–Friday, 8:00 A.M.–5:00 P.M.; Saturday, 9:00 A.M.–NOON

## Students Say

"The fact that Michigan is a world-class research institution draws the best of the best regarding the faculty. Most students are very laid-back, happy, and enjoy their time in Ann Arbor."

## Fodor's Says

"The downtown shopping district, which extends along Main Street, is known for its funky specialty stores, run by knowledgeable, independent owners. The State Street area, closer to campus, has one of the finest concentrations of book and music stores in the country."

## About the School

The University of Michigan is a massive school with a vast array of excellent academic offerings, complemented by a plethora of extracurricular options and no shortage of parties. The entire campus shows impressive school spirit for the university's fantastic sports teams. And hometown Ann Arbor offers some great entertainment options for students.

## Getting There

**BY AIR:** Detroit Metropolitan Airport is the closest airport to the campus and is about 25 miles East of Ann Arbor.

**BY TRAIN:** Amtrak trains service a station in Ann Arbor, about a mile from the campus.

**BY BUS:** Greyhound buses stop in Ann Arbor. Take a taxi to get to the campus.

**BY CAR:** From the East: Take I-94 West to the State Street Exit 177. Make a right. Follow State Street about two miles to the university. From the West: Take I-94 East to the State Street Exit 177. Make a left, and follow State Street for about two miles to the university. From the South: Take U.S. 23 North to Exit 37B and merge onto Washtenaw. Stay to the right on Washtenaw even after the fork in the road. Make a left at Hill Street and drive toward State Street. Make a right on State Street and follow it to the university. From the North: Take I-75 South to U.S. 23 South to M-14 West. Get off at Exit 3. This will take you to downtown Ann Arbor, which will turn into Main Street. Take Main Street to William Street. Turn left at William Street and follow it to State Street toward the university.

**LOCAL:** Ann Arbor Transportation Authority (734-996-0400) provides service throughout the area. If you'd rather take a taxi, some local companies include Amazing Blue Taxi (734-846-0007), Ann Arbor Taxi (734-214-9999), and Blue Cab Co. (734- 547-2222).

## Where to Stay

If you're planning on spending the night, some local hotel accommodations include Best Value Inn & Suites (734-665-3500, $), Baymont Inn & Suites (734-477-9977, $$), and Ann Arbor Bed and Breakfast (734-994-9100, $$$).

## CAMPUS AT ITS BEST!

The Matthaei Botanical Gardens at University of Michigan are not to be missed. The 300 acres feature a variety of stunning gardens and miles of nature trails. For those that want to escape the Michigan winter, you can step inside the Conservatory. There you'll encounter displays on rain forests, Mediterranean climates, and deserts. Afterward, duck into the Michigan Union, perhaps the university's most recognizable landmark. Constantly alive with a range of activities, the Union hosts Beats n' Eats where you can dine while entertained by student performers.

# UNIVERSITY OF MINNESOTA— TWIN CITIES

240 Williamson Hall, 231 Pillsbury Drive Southeast, Minneapolis, MN 55455-0213
Telephone: 612-625-2008 • Website: www.umn.edu
Hours: Monday, 8:00 A.M.–6:00 P.M.; Tuesday–Friday, 8:00 A.M.–4:30 P.M.; Saturdays by appointment

## STUDENTS SAY

"We're definitely the school to go to if you're interested in research. Also, the cities helps to give a lot of students opportunities for jobs and internships."

## FODOR'S SAYS

"To bear the harsh winter climate, the cities have constructed several mile-long skyway systems. Using the skyway, you can drive downtown, park, walk to work, go to lunch, shop, see a show, and return to your car without once setting foot outdoors."

## ABOUT THE SCHOOL

As a Big 10 School with more than 28,000 undergraduates, the University of Minnesota—Twin Cities (UM-TC) provides everything a student needs to succeed after college: Strong academic programs, plentiful internship and research opportunities, study abroad and exchange programs, and a thriving location full of businesses just waiting to hire the school's bright graduates. The school's location in the Twin Cities of Minneapolis and St. Paul provide plenty of opportunities for entertainment and networking as well.

## GETTING THERE

**BY AIR:** Twin Cities International is the nearest airport to the UM-TC Campus. Take the Light Rail from the airport into town and connect to a bus to get to the campus.

**BY TRAIN:** The nearest Amtrak station is in St. Paul. Take Metro Transit to the UM-TC campus.

**BY BUS:** Greyhound stops at the St. Paul Student Center on the UM-TC campus.

**BY CAR:** From the North on I-35 West: Go South on I-35 West to the University Avenue South East Exit 18. At the second traffic signal, turn left onto University Avenue and drive eight blocks to 17th Avenue South East .Turn left onto 17th Avenue, go one block North, and the 4th Street Parking Ramp will be on your left. From the East on I-94: Drive West on I-94 to the Huron Boulevard Exit 235B. Follow Huron Boulevard as it curves around the campus and becomes 4th Street South East. From there, continue Westward on 4th Street to 17th Avenue South East and turn right on 17th Avenue to reach the 4th Street Parking Ramp. From the South on I-35 West: Go North onI-35 West to the University Avenue South East Exit 18. Turn right onto University Avenue and drive seven blocks to 17th Avenue South East. Turn left onto 17th Avenue, go one block North, and the 4th Street Parking Ramp will be on your left. From the West on I-94: Drive East on I-94 to the Huron Boulevard Exit 235B. Follow Huron Boulevard as it curves around the campus and becomes 4th Street South East. Continue Westward on 4th Street to 17th Avenue to reach the entrance to the 4th Street Parking Ramp.

**LOCAL:** Metro Transit and Light Rail offer frequent and convenient service in the Twin Cities and stop at many points on campus as well as the airport, Greyhound, and Amtrak stations.

## WHERE TO STAY

There are plenty of choices for lodging in the Twin Cities near the UM-TC campus. The Days Inn—University of Minnesota is close to the East bank of campus and provides complimentary shuttle service to many points on campus (612-623-3999, $). The Radisson Hotel University provides complimentary van service within five miles of the hotel as well (612-379-8888, $$).

| SCHOOL AT A GLANCE | |
|---|---|
| Type of School | Public |
| Environment | Metropolis |
| In-state Tuition | $8,854 |
| Out-of-state Tuition | $20,484 |
| Enrollment | 28,957 |
| % Male/Female | 47/53 |
| Student/Faculty Ratio | 15:1 |

| FRESHMAN PROFILE | |
|---|---|
| Range SAT | |
| Critical Reading | 540-660 |
| Range SAT Math | 570-690 |
| Range ACT Composite | 23-28 |

| ON-CAMPUS APPOINTMENTS | |
|---|---|
| Class Visits | Yes |

| CAMPUS TOURS | |
|---|---|
| Appointment | Preferred |
| Dates | Year Round |
| Times | 10:30 A.M. and 2:15 P.M. |
| Average Length | Varies |

## CAMPUS AT ITS BEST!

Given its location right in the middle of the Twin Cities, the University of Minnesota-Twin Cities blends into the surroundings, allowing students to choose at any moment between a campus or city event. On campus, take a tour of the system of tunnels and skyways that keep the widespread campus connected, and attend a Gophers game to see the UM-TC school spirit in action.

# UNIVERSITY OF MISSOURI—COLUMBIA

230 Jesse Hall, Columbia, MO 65211
Telephone: 573-882-7786 • E-mail: MU4U@missouri.edu
Hours: Monday–Friday, 8:00 A.M.–5:00 P.M.

## STUDENTS SAY

"The University of Missouri is about receiving an excellent education while also gaining a large social network of friends and making an impact on the community."

## FODOR'S SAYS

"Scenic routes in Southwestern Missouri's Ozark Mountains include Route 76, Route 248, and U.S. 65 South of Springfield."

## ABOUT THE SCHOOL

The University of Missouri, a state school with more than 21,000 undergrads, is known for its outstanding programs in journalism and the sciences, as well as for its popular Mizzou sports teams. The campus comes out in full support on game days.

## GETTING THERE

**BY AIR:** Visitors can fly into the Columbia Regional Airport. Take a Mo-Express shuttle into the city and Columbia Transit or a cab to get to the campus.

**BY TRAIN:** The closest Amtrak stop is in Jefferson City. Take a cab to get to the campus.

**BY BUS:** Greyhound buses provide service to Colombia. Take a cab to get to the campus.

**BY CAR:** From the East: Take I-70 West to the Highway 63 Exit and turn left. Follow Highway 63 South to the Stadium Boulevard Exit and turn right. Follow Stadium Boulevard to Maryland Avenue, and turn right. Follow Maryland Avenue to Conley Avenue and you should see the university shortly thereafter. From the West: Take I-70 East to the Stadium Boulevard Exit and turn right. Follow Stadium Boulevard to Maryland Avenue and turn left. Follow Maryland Avenue to Conley Avenue and you should see the university shortly. From the North: Take Highway 63 South to the Stadium Boulevard Exit and turn right. Follow Stadium Boulevard to Maryland Avenue and turn right. Follow Maryland Avenue to Conley Avenue and you should see the university shortly thereafter. From the South: Take Highway 63 North to the Stadium Boulevard Exit and turn left. Follow Stadium Boulevard to Maryland Avenue and turn right. Follow Maryland Avenue to Conley Avenue and you should see the university shortly thereafter.

**LOCAL:** Columbia Area Transit System provides bus service on fixed routes throughout the city and to the university. For route and schedule information call 573-874-7282. If you'd rather take a taxi around the area, some local companies include A-1 Express Taxi (573-442-7200) and Columbia Cab Company (573-499-3988).

## WHERE TO STAY

If you're planning on spending the night, some nearby lodging options include Quality Inn (573-449-2491, $), Candlewood Suites (573-817-0525, $), and Comfort Suites (573-443-0055, $$).

## CAMPUS AT ITS BEST!

Meet Mizzou Days offer a phenomenal introduction to life at the University of Missouri. Visitors have the opportunity to tour the campus, attend an academic fair, learn about financial aid and residential life, and enjoy a complimentary lunch. If you want a tranquil spot to digest all of your impressions, wander over to Peace Park. At one time a gathering place for anti-war protestors during the Vietnam War, the stunning park now hosts a myriad of campus and community activities.

# UNIVERSITY OF NEBRASKA—LINCOLN

1410 Q Street, Lincoln, Northeast 68588-0256
**Telephone:** 402-472-2023 • **E-mail:** admissions@unl.edu
**Website:** www.unl.edu • **Hours:** Monday–Friday, 8:00 A.M.–5:00 P.M.

## STUDENTS SAY

"The University of Nebraska, combined with the great college town of Lincoln, literally offers quality athletics, academics, variety, school spirit, and most notably a great foundation that can take anyone anywhere they so choose."

## FODOR'S SAYS

"Lincoln, home of the University of Nebraska and the state government, rises to meet you as you drive along I-80 West. You can scan the city's skyline from atop the Nebraska State Capitol Building, with its 400-foot spire that towers over the surrounding plains."

## ABOUT THE SCHOOL

The University of Nebraska—Lincoln is a large university with a small-town feel. The university manages to maintain a relatively small student to faculty ratio despite its large size and limited budget. Academically speaking, UNL's 17,000-plus undergraduates enjoy some pretty unique programs, including a highly regarded construction management program. There are excellent research opportunities and a great study abroad program.

## GETTING THERE

**BY AIR:** Lincoln Municipal Airport, a 10-minute drive from campus, and Omaha's Eppley Airfield, an hour drive away, are the closest airports to campus. Visitors can take the OMALiNK shuttle service from Eppley Airfield to the university and to downtown Lincoln. Taxi service is available from the airport.

**BY TRAIN:** Amtrak trains stop in Lincoln. Take a taxi to get to the campus.

**BY BUS:** Greyhound buses stop in Lincoln. Take a taxi to get to the campus.

**BY CAR:** From the North: Take Highway 77 South to I-80. Take I-80 to the Downtown Exit (401). Take I-180 South. Make a left on P Street and take it to 17th Street. Make a left on 17th to Q Street. Make a left on Q. Stay on Q until you see the university. From the South: Take Highway 77 North to Capitol Parkway. Make a right on Capitol Parkway (K Street). Make a left on 17th Street. Take 17th Street to Q Street. Make a left on Q Street. Stay on Q until you see the university.

**LOCAL:** StarTran, the citywide bus system, operates 19 different routes, and multiple stops are located near campus. If you'd rather take a taxi to get around the area, some local companies include Servant Cab Co LLC (402-477-4111) and Yellow Cab (402-477-4111).

## WHERE TO STAY

If you're planning on staying overnight, some local hotel accommodations include Baymont Inn & Suites (402-477-1100, $), Days Inn (402-475-3616, $), and AmericInn Lodge & Suites (402-435-1600, $$).

| SCHOOL AT A GLANCE | |
|---|---|
| Type of School | Public |
| Environment | City |
| In-state Tuition | $5,867 |
| Out-of-state Tuition | $15,317 |
| Enrollment | 17,037 |
| % Male/Female | 53/47 |
| Student/Faculty Ratio | 19:1 |

| FRESHMAN PROFILE | |
|---|---|
| Range SAT | |
| Critical Reading | 530-660 |
| Range SAT Math | 540-670 |
| Range ACT Composite | 22-28 |

| ON-CAMPUS APPOINTMENTS | |
|---|---|
| Advance Notice | Yes, 2 weeks |
| Appointment | Preferred |
| Info Sessions | Yes |
| Class Visits | Yes |

| CAMPUS TOURS | |
|---|---|
| Appointment | Required |
| Dates | Year Round |
| Times | 9:00 A.M. and 1:00 P.M. |
| Average Length | Varies |

---

## CAMPUS AT ITS BEST!

The Nebraska City Union is certainly a microcosm of university life. You can grab a bite in the food court, improve your gaming skills in the arcade, and purchase some Husker souvenirs in the bookstore. Afterward, stop by the Daily Nebraskan offices on the lower level to get the scoop on what's happening on campus guests visiting in June and July should try to attend a Fountain Frolics concert. You can enjoy some great music while munching on hot dogs and chips.

# UNIVERSITY OF NORTH DAKOTA

PO Box 8357, Grand Forks, ND 58202
Telephone: 800-225-5863 • E-mail: enrollment_services@mail.und.nodak.edu
Website: www.und.edu • Hours: Monday–Friday, 8:00 A.M.–4:30 P.M.

## STUDENTS SAY

"The attitude of the people [at UND] is amazing. Every person I have met who has come from a different state says that we are the nicest people in the world!"

## FODOR'S SAYS

"The North Dakota Museum of Art has permanent and traveling contemporary art exhibits in a building that was formerly the campus gym."

## ABOUT THE SCHOOL

The University of North Dakota gives its 10,000 undergrads a lot to brag about. With great facilities, a top-ranked aviation program, fantastic business and engineering programs, and a sensational hockey team, it is no wonder why UND students can't stop talking about how great their school is.

## GETTING THERE

**BY AIR:** Grand Forks International Airport is the closest airport to the campus. Taxi service is available from the airport.

**BY TRAIN:** Amtrak trains stop in Grand Forks. Take a taxi to get to the campus.

**BY BUS:** Greyhound buses service Grand Forks. Take a taxi to get to the campus.

**BY CAR:** From the North: Exit from I-29 on 141 (Gateway Drive or Highway 2) then turn left and proceed to Columbia Road, where you turn right. Proceed on Columbia, until you reach University Avenue. Turn right on University, and you will see Swanson Hall on the left. The Union is located right next to Swanson Hall to the West. Turn left into the parking lot located in front of Memorial Union. From the South: Exit from I-29 on 140 (Demers Avenue), turn right, and proceed to 42nd Street. Turn left proceed to University Avenue. Turn right and proceed East on University Avenue, and you will pass under the glass walkway. The Union is located approximately four blocks down the road, across from Hamline Street and the International Center. From the East: Highway 2 East becomes Gateway Drive in the city. Proceed to Columbia Road, and turn left on Columbia. Proceed on Columbia until you reach University Avenue. Turn right on University, and you will see Swanson Hall on the left. The Union is located right next to Swanson Hall to the West. Turn left into the parking lot located in front of Memorial Union. From the West: Highway 2 West becomes Gateway Drive in the city. Follow the "From the East" directions above.

**LOCAL:** You can use local taxi service to get around town. Call Grand Forks Taxi (701-775-8294) to book a ride.

## WHERE TO STAY

Some popular hotel accommodations in the area include Ramada Inn Grand Forks (701-775-3951, $), Best Value Inn (701-775-0555, $), and Comfort Inn (701-775-7503, $$).

## CAMPUS AT ITS BEST!

North Dakota's Admissions Office attempts to be as accommodating as possible, hosting ViewND Saturdays for students who can't visit during the week. This program includes a campus tour, meetings with professors, and lunch in the dining center. When you're done, make sure to swing by the North Dakota Museum of Art, featuring works by Native American artists.

# UNIVERSITY OF NOTRE DAME

220 Main Building, Notre Dame, IN 46556
**Telephone:** 574-631-7505 • **E-mail:** admissions@nd.edu
**Website:** www.nd.edu • **Hours:** Monday–Frida, 8:00 A.M.–5:00 P.M.; Saturday, 8:00 A.M.–NOON

## STUDENTS SAY

"Notre Dame is very big on the spiritual aspect of a student's life, and so there is big emphasis on religion and spirituality in general."

## FODOR'S SAYS

"Downtown South Bend's East Race Waterway attracts tubers, rafters, and Olympic kayakers."

## ABOUT THE SCHOOL

Family and tradition are hallmarks of the student experience at the University of Notre Dame. Students on campus are inducted into a large family of hardworking overachievers in an environment marked by encouragement and support. Students at Notre Dame are engaged in all aspects of university life. This involvement is clearly visible in the full classrooms, crowded libraries, and packed football stadiums.

## GETTING THERE

**BY AIR:** Notre Dame is about 15 minutes from South Bend Regional Airport. Take a taxi to get to the campus. You can also fly to Chicago, a two hour drive from O'Hare airport, and a slightly shorter ride from Midway airport, and take a rental car or limousine from there.

**BY TRAIN:** Amtrak trains stop in South Bend. Take a taxi to get to the campus.

**BY BUS:** Greyhound buses stop in South Bend. Take a taxi to get to the campus.

**BY CAR:** From the North: Take I-80/90 and take Exit 77. Turn right onto Michigan (Indiana 933). Turn left at the fourth stop light (Angela Boulevard). Turn left at the first stoplight (Notre Dame Avenue) and you will see the university shortly thereafter. From the South: Take U.S. 31 North (which turns into Indiana 933) just South of South Bend. Take Indiana 933 to Angela Boulevard, the second stoplight North of the St. Joseph River. Make a right onto Angela Boulevard and a left at the first stoplight onto Notre Dame Avenue and you will see the university shortly thereafter.

**LOCAL:** Coach USA (219-944-1200) provides charter bus service to various Indiana locations, including Notre Dame's campus in South Bend. The North Indiana Commuter Transit District's South Shore Line (574-233-3111) trains run from the Chicago area to the South Bend airport. Transpo, the municipal bus line, buses, and trolleys will get you around South Bend. Call 574-233-2131 for route and schedule information. If you'd rather take a taxi, some local companies include Ace Cab Company (574-674-0336) and Yellow Cab Company (574-233-9333).

## WHERE TO STAY

If you're planning on staying overnight, some local hotels include the Days Inn (574-277-0510, $), Hampton Inn and Suites (574-277-9373, $$), and Residence Inn by Marriott (574-289-5555, $$$).

---

## CAMPUS AT ITS BEST!

Notre Dame's Student Union Board excels at keeping the masses of Fighting Irish entertained. They sponsor everything from a Battle of the Bands to an annual literary festival, which has brought writers such as Norman Mailer and Ken Kesey to campus. They also throw the ever-popular anTostal, an annual event that occurs right before finals, typically featuring stress relievers like bouncy boxing and Laser Tag. Students also take advantage of the surrounding area. The nearby beaches of Lake Michigan are a terrific destination in good weather, and St. Patrick's Park, just a few miles from campus, offers the perfect locale for sledding.

# UNIVERSITY OF SOUTH DAKOTA

414 East Clark, Vermillion, SD 57069
**Telephone:** 605-677-5434 • **E-mail:** admiss@usd.edu
**Website:** www.usd.edu

## STUDENTS SAY

"USD is all about preparing students for their future careers; the school puts a heavy emphasis not only on the material, but [also on] how it applies to real-life situations, as opposed to a merely academic abstraction."

## FODOR'S SAYS

"Visitors to Badlands National Park, a moonscape of rugged ridgelines, deep ravines, and towering pinnacles, are often captivated by an expansive terrain that has changed but little since man first came here."

## ABOUT THE SCHOOL

With total undergraduate enrollment of fewer than 6,000, South Dakota is able to provide a level of student-professor interaction atypical of most public universities. The school places a high premium on real-life application, and all students must undertake a service learning, research, or creative project. Aside from hunting and fishing, the Vermillion area offers little in the way of entertainment. Students often choose to take road trips to Sioux Falls or Sioux City or simply head home once classes are over.

## GETTING THERE

**BY AIR:** Visitors can fly into Sioux Falls Regional Airport. Flights are available from Minneapolis-St. Paul, Chicago, Denver, Cincinnati, Las Vegas, and Orlando. Car rentals and taxis are available for further transportation.

**BY TRAIN:** Unfortunately, there is no Amtrak station within 150 miles of Vermillion.

**BY BUS:** Visitors may take Greyhound into Vermillion. To reach campus from the station it is best to take a taxi.

**BY CAR:** From the North, South and East: Take Exit 26 from I 29 and proceed West on Highway 50. You will then take Business Route 50 into Vermillion. Make a left onto Plum Street followed by a right on Clark Street. This will lead you to the Office of Admissions (in the Belbas Service's Center). From the West: Proceed East on Highway 50. Take Business Route 50 into Vermillion. Make a right onto Dakota Street and a left onto Clark Street, which leads you to the Office of Admissions.

**LOCAL:** For local taxi service call Cept Corp (605-624-7224).

## WHERE TO STAY

For local accommodations consider the Comfort Inn (605-624-8333, $), Super 8 Motel (605-624-8005, $), or the Valiant Vineyards Bed & Breakfast at Buffalo Run Resort (605-624-4117, $$).

## CAMPUS AT ITS BEST!

The National Music Museum draws thousands of visitors from all over the world. Its rich holdings include seventeenth- and eighteenth-century woodwinds from legendary craftsmen such as the Haas and Oberlender families. Also in the archives are 1,000 brass instrument mouthpieces from nearly every turn-of-the-century manufacturer. The museum frequently hosts seminars, concerts, and conventions. The more sports-minded visitor will want to attend a USD tailgate party. Football is popular on campus and school spirit is always palpable right before a big game.

# UNIVERSITY OF WISCONSIN—MADISON

Armory & Gymnasium, 716 Langdon Street, Madison, WI 53706-1481
**Telephone:** 608-262-3961 • **E-mail:** onwisconsin@admissions.wisc.edu • **Website:** www.visitbucky.wisc.edu
**Hours:** Monday–Friday, 8:00 A.M.–4:00 P.M.; Saturday, 10:00 A.M.–3:00 P.M.; Sunday, 11:00 A.M.–3:00 P.M.

## STUDENTS SAY

"We have every kind of major under the sun, every kind of club, every kind of person, every kind of activity you can imagine. All you have to do is get out there and find what's right for you."

## FODOR'S SAYS

"Capitol Square, at the center of downtown with 12 streets radiating outward, is connected to the university's campus by State Street, a mile-long tree-lined shopping district of imports shops, ethnic restaurants, and artisans' galleries."

## ABOUT THE SCHOOL

The University of Wisconsin—Madison has some of everything: majors, activities, buildings, and students (28,200 undergraduates). In addition, UW-M provides services to keep students from slipping through the cracks: free tutoring, workshops, counseling, and advising. UW-M focuses on hand-on research in many disciplines, and encourages study abroad, internships, and honors programs for its undergraduates. Madison, WI is definitely a college town, catering to students' entertainment and needs.

## GETTING THERE

**BY AIR:** Portland Dane County Regional Airport is six miles from the UW-M campus. Take a taxi or Madison's Metro Transit #24 bus into Madison and transfer to one of the many buses that stop at the campus Memorial Union.

**BY BUS:** The Greyhound/Badger Coaches, Van Galder, and Jefferson Bus Lines all stop at Memorial Union.

**BY CAR:** From I-90: Take I-90 to Highway 12/18. Follow Highway 12/18, exit at Park Street Exit 261 B, proceed North on Park Street about 5 miles to Langdon Street, and then turn right. Drive one block to Lake Street and turn right. From U.S. 151: Take U.S. 151 to Highway 12/18. Follow Highway 12/18, exit at Park Street Exit 261 B, proceed North on Park Street about 5 miles to Langdon Street, and then turn right. Drive one block to Lake Street and turn right to parking ramp.

**LOCAL:** Madison's Metro Transit system serves the University and all of Madison. Call 608-266-4466 for route and schedule information.

## WHERE TO STAY

The University of Wisconsin—Madison offers accommodations right on campus for both guests and visitors to the university. Options on campus include the Short Course Dorms on the West campus (608-262-2270, $) and the Wisconsin Union Guest Rooms (608-262-1583, $–$$—Amtrak, Greyhound, and Airport shuttles stop here). There's also plenty of lodging off-campus in Madison and the surrounding area. An interesting option is the Arbor House, an environmental inn that has won several awards for its commitment to sustainable tourism (608-238-2981, $$–$$$).

## SCHOOL AT A GLANCE

| | |
|---|---|
| Type of School | Public |
| Environment | City |
| In-state Tuition | $6,000 |
| Out-of-state Tuition | $20,000 |
| Enrollment | 28,458 |
| % Male/Female | 46/54 |
| Student/Faculty Ratio | 13:1 |

### FRESHMAN PROFILE

| | |
|---|---|
| Range SAT | |
| Critical Reading | 560–670 |
| Range SAT Math | 600–700 |
| Range ACT Composite | 26–30 |
| Average HS GPA | 3.66 |

### ON-CAMPUS APPOINTMENTS

| | |
|---|---|
| Class Visits | Yes |

### CAMPUS TOURS

| | |
|---|---|
| Appointment | Preferred |
| Dates | Year Round |
| Times | Every day, except during breaks |
| Average Length | 120 min |

## CAMPUS AT ITS BEST!

There's a lot to see on the enormous University of Wisconsin—Madison campus! Start at the Babcock Hall Dairy Store and sample the homemade ice creams and cheeses. Move on to the Allen Centennial Gardens, often referred to as UWM's largest outdoor classroom, where visitors can stroll through on brick pathways and take in the flora. Stay for a Badger's football game to see the whole campus come together in lively support of Badger athletics.

# UNIVERSITY OF WYOMING

Dept 3435, 1000 East University Avenue, Laramie, WY 82071
**Telephone:** 307-766-5160 • **E-mail:** Why-Wyo@uwyo.edu
**Website:** www.uwyo.edu

## STUDENTS SAY

"UW is well-funded. This means there are a lot of extracurricular opportunities available to everyone. Every day I hear about some amazing program that is looking for applicants."

## FODOR'S SAYS

"When John Colter's descriptions of Yellowstone were reported in St. Louis newspapers in 1810, most readers dismissed them as tall tales. His reports of giant elk roaming among fuming mud pots, waterfalls, and geysers in a wilderness of evergreens were just too far-fetched to be taken seriously."

## ABOUT THE SCHOOL

As a midsized institution, Wyoming ensures that students enjoy a lot of extracurricular and academic opportunity while maintaining manageable class sizes and ample interaction with professors. The university offers some rather unique majors like rangeland ecology and earth systems science. Outdoor recreational options are abundant and many students ski, snowboard, camp, hunt, and rock climb.

## GETTING THERE

**BY AIR:** Guests can fly into Laramie Regional Airport. Flights arrive three times a day from Denver International Airport. Rental cars are available at the airport.

**BY TRAIN:** The nearest Amtrak station is located in Cheyenne, approximately 43 miles away.

**BY BUS:** Greyhound stops in Laramie.

**BY CAR:** From Cheyenne: Take I-80 West toward Laramie. Take Exit 316/Grand Avenue. Turn right onto 15th Street. Make a left at the first light on to Ivinson Avenue.

**LOCAL:** For local car service call Elite Limousine and Taxi Service 307-760-6299. Additionally, the University of Wyoming operates three shuttles (the Union Express, the Campus Shuttle, and the Classroom Express) for transit around the college.

## WHERE TO STAY

For affordable hotel options try 1st Inn Gold (307-742-3721, $), Albany Lodge (307-745-5782, $), or the Comfort Inn (307-721-8856, $).

## CAMPUS AT ITS BEST!

It's easy to work up an appetite while visiting colleges. Following your tour of Wyoming's campus, consider grabbing a bite at the King Street Market located in the upper level of the Washakie Center. You can dine on freshly prepared sushi or sumptuous smoothies as you check your e-mail. The market also hosts a variety of events including tailgate parties and live music. For other on-campus venues, check out the University Union. From Casino Night to Comedy Night, there's always something fun going on to interest students.

# VALPARAISO UNIVERSITY

Office of Admission, Kretzmann Hall, 1700 Chapel Drive, Valparaiso, IN 46383

**Telephone:** 219-464-5011 • **E-mail:** undergrad.admissions@valpo.edu

**Website:** www.valpo.edu

| SCHOOL AT A GLANCE | |
| --- | --- |
| Type of School | Private |
| Environment | Town |
| Tuition | $23,200 |
| Enrollment | 2,918 |
| % Male/Female | 48/52 |
| Student/Faculty Ratio | 13:1 |

| FRESHMAN PROFILE | |
| --- | --- |
| Range SAT | |
| Critical Reading | 520-630 |
| Range SAT Math | 520-640 |
| Range ACT Composite | 23-28 |
| Average HS GPA | 3.36 |

| ON-CAMPUS APPOINTMENTS | |
| --- | --- |
| Advance Notice | Yes, 2 weeks |
| Appointment | Preferred |
| Saturdays | Sometimes |
| Average Length | 45 min |
| Info Sessions | Yes |
| Class Visits | Yes |

| CAMPUS TOURS | |
| --- | --- |
| Appointment | Preferred |
| Dates | Varies |
| Times | Varies |
| Average Length | 60 min |

## Students Say

"We have an open-door policy on campus, meaning that you can talk to any faculty or member of the administration at any time without an appointment all the way up to the president of the university."

## Fodor's Says

"A quaint and sometimes inexpensive option for those interested in getting to know the people as well as the local flavor of the town is to check into a bed and breakfast inn."

## About the School

Valparaiso University holds its students to strict standards: hard work in class, and respect for Lutheran traditions all over campus. Despite (or perhaps because of) these strict standards, students thrive. Caring teachers and administrators form personal relationships with the 3,040 undergraduates. Valparaiso's goal is to "prepare students to lead in both church and society" and its strong academic programs and high moral standards are certainly keeping that promise.

## Getting There

**BY AIR:** Chicago O'Hare International Airport is an hour and a half drive away. Chicago Midway International Airport (MDW) is about an hour drive from the campus. Take Coach USA or Tri-State Bus Lines from either airport to Merrillville, 15 miles West of Valparaiso, and a taxi from Merrillville to campus.

**BY TRAIN:** Amtrak has a station in Michigan City, 18 miles away. Take a taxi from Michigan City to campus.

**BY BUS:** Greyhound stops in Michigan City, 18 miles away. Take a taxi from Michigan City to campus.

**BY CAR:** From I-65: Exit at U.S. 30 East in Merrillville. Proceed approximately 12 miles East to Valparaiso. You will see the U.S. 30 entrance to the university on the left (on the North side of U.S. 30), leading toward the chapel. From I-80/90 or I-94: Exit at IN-49 South in Chesterton. Proceed approximately eight miles South to Valparaiso, and exit onto U.S. 30 West. Turn right on Sturdy Road (second stoplight). VU's Torch entrance is 100 yards on the left. From O'Hare and Midway Airport: Take I-294 South (Tri-State Tollway) to I-80/90 East, toward Indiana. When I-80 and I-94 split, you can take either highway, I-80 joins I-90 and is a toll road while I-94 remains toll free. In Chesterton, take the Indiana 49-South exit to U.S. 30 West. Turn right at the second stoplight (Sturdy Road). VU's Torch entrance is 100 yards on the left.

**LOCAL:** Drive your own car or use taxi service to get around Valparaiso. For taxi service, call Krazy Cabs, Inc. (219-962-4949).

## Where to Stay

There are many hotel options in Valparaiso and in nearby Merrillville. Try the Fairfield Inn (219-465-6225, $$) and the Residence Inn (219-791-9000, $$). The Super 8 hotel also offers low prices, even in peak season (219-464-9840, $).

---

## CAMPUS AT ITS BEST!

The design of Valparaiso University's Christopher Center Library Complex has won multiple awards; most recently it was honored in the 2006 Library Interior Design Competition. Visit the library to check out its comfy furniture in living room settings, fireplace lounges, and glass walls that let in natural light. The Union Board goes all out to plan a couple of campus-wide concerts during the school year, so call ahead for dates before your visit.

# WABASH COLLEGE

PO Box 352, 301 West Wabash Avenue, Crawfordsville, IN 47933
**Telephone:** 765-361-6225 • **E-mail:** admissions@wabash.edu
**Website:** www.wabash.edu • **Hours:** 7:00 A.M.–midnight

## STUDENTS SAY

"The all-male environment makes us more open to frank discussion of issues that would not be raised at a large coed school."

## FODOR'S SAYS

"At Spring Mill [state park] you can tour a reconstructed 1800s pioneer village and gristmill on its original site, hike an 80-acre tract of virgin hardwood forest, then explore two caves on foot or by boat."

## ABOUT THE SCHOOL

Wabash College, a small, academically rigorous men's college in the heart of the Midwest, encourages responsible action and critical thinking skills. Professors use the Socratic method in class, so students make sure they are always prepared. An amazingly simple yet wonderfully all-purpose Gentleman's Rule, which basically says "don't be an idiot," governs life inside and outside the classroom.

## GETTING THERE

**BY AIR:** The Indianapolis International Airport is the closest airport to the campus.

**BY TRAIN:** Amtrak provides train service to Crawfordsville.

**BY BUS:** Greyhound provides limited bus service to Crawfordsville. The Illini-Swallow (800-233-1344) and Trailways Bus Lines (800-992-4618) provide service in or near the city.

**BY CAR:** From the Southeast: Take I-74 to Exit 39 (Indiana 32). Make a left off the I into downtown Crawfordsville and travel for about four miles until you make a left (South) onto U.S. 231 (Washington Street). Take U.S. 231 to Wabash Avenue. Make a right on Wabash Avenue and follow it until you see the university. From the Northeast: Take I-465 North to the I-65/465 split. Go onto I-65 for about 11 miles to the Crawfordsville Exit (Indiana 32). Turn left off the I and follow Indiana 32 for 22 miles. Make a left (South) on U.S. 231 (Washington Street) to Wabash Avenue. Make a right on Wabash Avenue and follow it until you see the university. From the West: Take I-74 to Exit 34 (U.S. 231). Make a right (South) off the highway into downtown Crawfordsville (five miles). Go South to Wabash Avenue (you will see a sign for Wabash on the right). Turn right onto Wabash Avenue and follow it to the university. From the North: Get onto U.S. 231 South from I-65 and take it into downtown Crawfordsville (30 miles). Go South to Wabash Avenue and make a right onto Wabash Avenue and take it to the university.

**LOCAL:** If you don't have a car on campus, you can take a taxi to get around. Call Ben Hur Cab (765-361-9823).

## WHERE TO STAY

Some local hotel accommodations include the Days Inn (765-362-0300, $), Comfort Inn (765-361-0665, $$), and Holiday Inn (765-362-8700, $$).

## CAMPUS AT ITS BEST!

The Pioneer Chapel is a focal point for the Wabash campus and a center of student life. Although mandatory chapel has long since ended, the campus often gathers for lectures, concerts, and celebrations. If you desire more interaction with the student body, think about attending the annual spring canoe trip. Available to rising high school seniors, the trip involves a morning on the water with current Wabash students and faculty, followed by a campus cookout.

# WASHINGTON UNIVERSITY IN ST. LOUIS

Campus Box 1089, One Brookings Drive, St. Louis, MO 63130-4899
Telephone: 314-935-6000 • E-mail: admissions@wustl.edu
Website: wustl.edu • Hours: Monday–Friday, 8:30 A.M.–5:00 P.M.; Saturday, 9:00 A.M.–2:00 P.M.

## Students Say

"It's about trying to find your passion and make your way through four crazy years with the help of some good friends, great faculty and staff, and a ton of awesome opportunities.

## Fodor's Says

"Founded by the French in 1764 as a fur-trading settlement on the West bank of the Mississippi River, St. Louis is best known for the soaring silver arch that so impresses travelers entering the city from the East."

## About the School

Washington University in St. Louis provides students with a rigorous academic experience in a non-competitive, laid-back atmosphere. The university offers a balance of strong academics, good sports, a beautiful campus, and friendly people. Wash U's extremely bright (and pretty well-off) student body knows the value of a good study break. In their downtime, students head to the Loop for shops, restaurants, and movies, or and to nearby Forest Park for the skating rink, paddleboats, art museum, and paths for biking, running, and inline skating.

## Getting There

**BY AIR:** Lambert-St. Louis International Airport is approximately 10 miles from campus. Take a taxi to the campus.

**BY TRAIN:** Amtrak trains stop in St. Louis. Take a taxi to get to the campus.

**BY BUS:** Greyhound buses provide service to St. Louis. Take a taxi to get to the campus.

**BY CAR:** From I-70 and the airport: Go South on I-170 to the Delmar Boulevard Exit. Make a left on Delmar and take it to Big Bend Boulevard. Make a right onto Big Bend Boulevard and follow it approximately 0.5 miles. Make a left onto Forsyth and you should see the university shortly thereafter. From the East: Take I-64 West (Highway 40) to the Skinker/Clayton Road Exit, and make a right onto Skinker Boulevard. Head North on Skinker Boulevard for approximately one mile. Make a left on Forsyth. Head West on Forsyth, and you should see the university shortly thereafter. From the West: Take I-64 East to Exit 33D-McCausland, and make a left onto McCausland Avenue. Head North on McCausland Avenue, which becomes Skinker Boulevard, for approximately one mile to Forsyth Boulevard. Make a left onto Forsyth. Head West on Forsyth, and you should see the university shortly thereafter. Beginning in 2007, major highways in St. Louis will be under construction. Please check the "Visit Us in St. Louis: page at http://admissions.wustl.edu for up-to-date directions to campus.

**LOCAL:** Metro Link Light Rail System (314-231-2345) provides bus, rail, and paratransit service in St. Louis. If you'd rather take a taxi to get around St. Louis. call St. Louis County Cab Co Inc. (314-991-5300).

## Where to Stay

If you're planning on staying overnight, some local hotel accommodations include Best Western Inn at the Park (314-367-7500, $$), Holiday Inn (314-664-0953, $$), and Marriott St. Louis Airport (314-423-9700, $$).

## CAMPUS AT ITS BEST!

Wash U's Assembly Series brings prominent speakers to campus for weekly lectures. With guests such as Cornel West and Marian Wright Edelman, these free talks are guaranteed to be engaging. St. Louis also offers many alluring destinations. The Gateway Arch is a perennial favorite.

# WAYNE STATE UNIVERSITY

42 West Warren, Office of Admissions Welcome Center, Detroit, MI 48202
**Telephone:** 313-577-3577 • **E-mail:** Admissions@wayne.edu
**Website:** www.wayne.edu

## STUDENTS SAY

"Wayne State is extremely diverse. You can walk outside and see every color, religion, and walk of life in the spectrum."

## FODOR'S SAYS

"Greektown, one of Detroit's most popular entertainment districts, is centered on Monroe Street. It percolates day and night with markets, bars, coffeehouses, shops, and restaurants serving authentic Greek fare with an American flair."

## ABOUT THE SCHOOL

Wayne State offers students the opportunity to study nearly anything they desire. Although a large university, many nonlecture classes are relatively small and allow for ample interaction with professors. Additionally, the surrounding Detroit area offers plenty of attractions, so students never want for entertainment.

## GETTING THERE

**BY AIR:** Detroit Metro is a major airport and is serviced by a number of national and international airlines. Take a taxi to get to the campus.

**BY TRAIN:** Amtrak provides service to Detroit. To reach Wayne State, it's easiest to take a taxi.

**BY BUS:** Visitors can take Greyhound directly to Detroit. Take a taxi or use local transportation to reach Wayne State.

**BY CAR:** Lodge Freeway (from the North): Take the Lodge Freeway (M-10) South and exit at Warren-Forest. Proceed to the light and make a left, crossing over the Lodge. Make another left onto the Lodge Service Drive. Proceed on the Lodge Service Drive to Warren. Turn right at the light. Continue on Warren to Cass. Turn left. Keep going until you reach the light (Putnam) and turn right. You'll find the entrance to Parking Structure 6 on your right. Lodge Freeway (from the South): Take the Lodge Freeway (M-10) North and exit at Warren-Forest. Proceed on the Lodge Service Drive to Warren. Follow the "From the North" directions above. I-94 (from the East): Take I-94 West to John R/Woodward Exit (right side). Continue on the Service Drive and cross Woodward Avenue. Once you have crossed Woodward, you will be on Antoinette. Take Antoinette to Cass and turn left. Proceed on Cass to Putnam (third light). Turn left. Entrance to Parking Structure 6 is on the right. I-94 (from the West): Take I-94 East to Southbound Lodge Freeway (M-10). Follow the "From the North" directions above. I-96 (from the West): Take I-96 East to I-94 East (toward Port Huron). Take I-94 East to Lodge Freeway (M-10) South. Follow the "From the North" directions above. I-75 (from the North): Take I-75 South and exit at Warren. Follow the "From the South" directions above. I-75 (from the South): Take I-75 North and exit at Warren. Follow the "From the South" directions above.

**LOCAL:** People wishing to use public transportation can ride Detroit's SMART Bus. The routes cover a number of points throughout the city. Call 866-962-5515 for route info.

## WHERE TO STAY

As one of the Midwest's most vibrant metropolises, Detroit is home to a number of hotels, including Days Inn Downtown Detroit (313-568-2000, $), Hilton Garden Inn (313-967-0900, $$), and Omni Detroit River Place (313-259-9500, $$$).

## CAMPUS AT ITS BEST!

When Wayne State students are looking to be entertained they simply head in one direction: the Student Center. The Down Under, located in the lower level of the Student Center, presents diverse student programming throughout the semester. You can get rowdy at Bingo Night every Wednesday, watch your favorite movies during Thursday Matinee, see a live performance, learn to knit, or de-stress with a free mini-massage. Also held in the Student Center is the annual College Bowl. Every January, students pit their trivia knowledge against their peers in this annual tournament.

# WHEATON COLLEGE (IL)

501 College Avenue, Wheaton, IL 60187
**Telephone:** 630-752-5005 • **E-mail:** admissions@wheaton.edu
**Website:** www.wheaton.edu • **Hours:** Monday–Friday, 8:00 A.M.–5:00 P.M.; Saturday, 8:30 A.M.–NOON

## STUDENTS SAY

"The greatest strengths of Wheaton are its academic rigor and Christian focus. The Christian aspect of life at Wheaton does not hinder academic excellence, but encourages it."

## FODOR'S SAYS

"Starved Rock State Park on the Illinois River between LaSalle and Ottawa has 18 canyons formed during the melting of the glaciers. The park is about a two-hour drive from downtown Chicago."

## ABOUT THE SCHOOL

Wheaton bills itself as a nondenominational Christian institution, and the student body tends to reflect these morals and ideals. Hardworking and socially conscious undergrads readily champion their professors and often describe them as open and engaging. Wheaton is not known for its rousing party scene; Wheaton students prefer to kick back with an innocent game of sardines, a movie, or simply good conversation.

## GETTING THERE

**BY AIR:** Prospective students may fly into either O'Hare or Midway International Airports, both located in nearby Chicago. Shuttles, taxis, and rental cars are available at both locations.

**BY TRAIN:** The closest Amtrak station is located in Naperville, approximately six miles away from Wheaton. Those traveling from Chicago can take the local Metra Union Pacific West line from the Ogilvie Transportation Center. You will exit at College Avenue. Wheaton's campus is one block West.

**BY BUS:** Unfortunately, Greyhound does not provide direct service to Wheaton. Guests may take the bus to either nearby Aurora or Chicago.

**BY CAR:** From the North: Drive Northwest on I-90 (heading in the direction of Chicago). Turn South on I-355 at Schaumburg. Exit West on Roosevelt Road. Stay on Roosevelt through Glen Ellyn, driving past President Street, to Washington Street. Make a right onto Washington and cross over the Chicago and Northwestern railroad tracks. You'll find the campus a few blocks ahead. From the South: Drive Southwest on I-55 (in the direction of Chicago). Just beyond Bolingbrook, get onto I-355 North. Exit at Roosevelt Road (to the West). Follow the "From the North" directions above. From the East: Take East-West I-80/90. This becomes I-80/94 as you cross state lines from Indiana into Illinois. After several miles it connects with I-294. Follow I-294 North to I-88 at the Oak Brook (to Aurora) Exit. Continue West on I-88 to the Naperville Road Exit. Proceed North on Naperville Road. Cross Butterfield Road and continue on to Roosevelt Road. Make a right at Roosevelt and a left onto Washington Street. The campus will be a few blocks ahead, just over the railroad tracks. From the West: Drive West on I-88 (heading in the direction of Chicago). Exit North at Naperville Road, which takes you past the Danada Shopping Center at Butterfield Road and bring you to Roosevelt Road. Make a right at Roosevelt. Follow the "From the East" directions above.

**LOCAL:** For local taxi service, try American Taxi (630-790-8294) or Auto Ride Taxi (630-834-3000).

## WHERE TO STAY

For hotels that are within a reasonable distance from campus, try Exel Inn of Naperville (630-357-0022, $), Homestead Studio Suites Hotel (630-577-0200, $), or the Wyndham Lisle (630-505-1000, $$–$$$).

| SCHOOL AT A GLANCE | |
|---|---|
| Type of School | Private |
| Environment | Town |
| Tuition | $22,450 |
| Enrollment | 2,392 |
| % Male/Female | 49/51 |
| Student/Faculty Ratio | 12:1 |

| FRESHMAN PROFILE | |
|---|---|
| Range SAT | |
| Critical Reading | 630-730 |
| Range SAT Math | 620-710 |
| Range ACT Composite | 27-31 |
| Average HS GPA | 3.7 |

| ON-CAMPUS APPOINTMENTS | |
|---|---|
| Advance Notice | Yes, 2 weeks |
| Appointment | Required |
| Saturdays | Sometimes |
| Average Length | 45 min |
| Info Sessions | Yes |
| Class Visits | Yes |

| CAMPUS TOURS | |
|---|---|
| Appointment | Preferred |
| Dates | Year Round |
| Times | Varies |
| Average Length | 60 min |

## CAMPUS AT ITS BEST!

Voracious readers and lovers of all things literary are sure to view the Wade Center as Shangri-La. The facility houses collections of books by and papers from authors like G. K. Chesterton, C. S. Lewis, and J. R. R. Tolkien. In addition, the center contains personal treasures such as Tolkien's desk and Pauline Baynes's original map of Narnia. When you're ready to put the books down, head over to the Student Activities Office and see what they have cooking. Ever productive, this group frequently sponsors coffeehouses, on-campus concerts, and film series.

# WILLIAM JEWELL COLLEGE

500 College Hill, Liberty, MO 64068
**Telephone:** 816-781-7700 • **E-mail:** admission@williA.M..jewell.edu
**Website:** www.jewell.edu

## STUDENTS SAY

"William Jewell is a great place to be nurtured and grow as a young college student. You are able to discover who you are and what you want to do with your life. It's a safe place to find yourself."

## FODOR'S SAYS

"With upward of 200 fountains—more than any city except Rome—and more miles of boulevards (155) than Paris, Kansas City is attractive and cosmopolitan. The sprawling metropolitan area straddling the Missouri-Kansas line has a rich history as a frontier river port and trade center, where wagon trains were outfitted before heading West on the Santa Fe and Oregon trails."

## ABOUT THE SCHOOL

William Jewell College strives to make a personal connection with each of its 1,300 students, and students find the administrators to be genuinely concerned with their well-being, both academically and socially. WJC's Oxbridge Honors program has received national recognition and promotes active discussion as a central part of students' learning experience. WJC's beautiful campus in Liberty is just 20 minutes outside of Kansas City, where all the attractions of big-city life beckon.

## GETTING THERE

**BY AIR:** Kansas City International Airport is 22 miles away. Take the Metro to Kansas City and Liberty Express commuter bus service from Kansas City to Liberty. Otherwise, take a taxi to get to the campus.

**BY TRAIN:** Amtrak stops in Independence, 11 miles away, and Kansas City, 14 miles away. Liberty Express commuter bus service travels between downtown Liberty and Kansas City for $3 each way. Take a taxi from Liberty to the campus.

**BY BUS:** Greyhound's nearest station is in Kansas City. Take a taxi or Liberty Express to get to the campus.

**BY CAR:** From Kansas City: Drive North on I-35 to Liberty, turn right on Exit 16 /State Highway 152, which becomes Kansas Street, and continue to Lightburne (Highway 33). Make a right at the intersection of Kansas and Lightburne Street. Make a left at the intersection of Lightburne and Mill Street. You will come to a traffic light. The campus entrance is on your left. From Kansas City International Airport: Leaving the airport, you will travel on Cookingham Drive for two and a quarter miles. Exit on I-435 South (to St. Louis) and continue on I-435 to the Highway 152 East Exit (about 15 minutes). Drive East on Highway 152, which becomes Kansas Street, and continue to Lightburne (Highway 33). Follow the "From Kansas City" directions above. From I-70: Driving either East or West on I-70, take the I-435 North exit. Continue North on I-435 to I-35 North (Des Moines) exit. Take Exit 16 (State Highway 152) and turn right. Stay on Highway 152, which becomes Kansas Street, and continue to Lightburne (Highway 33). Follow the "From Kansas City" directions above.

**LOCAL:** There is no public transportation, so take a taxi or drive to get around Liberty. Liberty Express (816-221-0660) commuter bus service travels from downtown liberty to Kansas City. Take a taxi from the station to the campus. For local taxi service call Ron's Taxi (816-468-0254) or Flash Transportation (816-210-6585).

## WHERE TO STAY

Liberty and nearby Kansas City have plenty of options for accommodations at all price points. Try the Hampton Inn Kansas City/Liberty (816-415-9600, $), the Park Place Hotel (816-483-9900, $), or the Marriott Hotel Country Club Plaza (816-531-3000, $$).

## CAMPUS AT ITS BEST!

The Ruth E. Stocksdale Gallery of Art on WJC's campus is a must-see during your visit. Exhibits feature works by nationally recognized artists, in addition to works by Jewell art faculty and students. While you're on campus, check out one of the College Union Activities Board's many special events. Past hoorahs have included performances by comedians, hypnotists, musicians, and more.

# WITTENBERG UNIVERSITY

PO Box 720, Springfield, OH 45501
**Telephone:** 800-677-7558 • **E-mail:** admission@wittenberg.edu
**Website:** www.wittenberg.edu • **Hours:** Monday–Friday, 9:00 A.M.–5:00 P.M.; Saturday 9:00 A.M.–NOON

## STUDENTS SAY

"Wittenberg has a lot of opportunities, through all different venues. You just have to be willing to take advantage of them. People here are also exceedingly friendly."

## FODOR'S SAYS

"Look into discount passes to save money on park entrance fees."

## ABOUT THE SCHOOL

It's no surprise that Wittenberg students are fiercely proud of their institution. Many tend to regard the university community as an extended family. Undergrads enjoy a good balance between academics and social life. Praise is almost unanimous for the political science, biology, and education departments, as well as for Wittenberg's popular sports teams.

## GETTING THERE

**BY AIR:** Springfield is accessible via three different airports: Cincinnati/Northern Kentucky International Airport (approximately 1 hour and 30 minutes away from Wittenberg), Port-Columbus International Airport (approximately 50 minutes away from Wittenberg), and Dayton International Airport (approximately 28 minutes away from Wittenberg). You can also call A-1 taxi (937-325-3333) or the Airport Express for shuttle service (800-870-2721) to campus.

**BY TRAIN:** The closest Amtrak station to Springfield is located roughly 70 miles away in Cincinnati. Visitors will most likely want to rent a car to reach their final destination.

**BY BUS:** Greyhound does provide to Springfield. It's easiest to take a taxi to Wittenberg.

**BY CAR:** From East of Springfield: Take I-70 West, heading in the direction of Dayton. Exit onto Route 68 going North toward Urbana. Exit onto State Route 41 and make a right. Since the road turns into a dead end, turn right onto McCreight Avenue. Go straight through the first stoplight and at the next light turn right onto Fountain Avenue. You are now approaching campus. At the first stoplight turn right onto Ward Street. Follow straight through the stop sign and you will approach the main gate to campus. Drive through the gate and take the drive to the left to approach Recitation Hall and the Office of Admission. From West of Springfield: Use I-70 (East) toward Columbus. Exit onto Route 68 North, heading toward Urbana. Follow the "From East of Springfield" directions above.

## WHERE TO STAY

Springfield boasts a number of hotel options. Three of which are within five miles of campus include the Fairfield Inn (937-323-9554, $), Comfort Suites (937-322-0707, $–$$), and Simon Kenton Inn (937-399-9950, $–$$).

## SCHOOL AT A GLANCE

| | |
|---|---|
| Type of School | Private |
| Environment | Town |
| Tuition | $29,080 |
| Enrollment | 1,880 |
| % Male/Female | 43/57 |
| Student/Faculty Ratio | 12:1 |

### FRESHMAN PROFILE

| | |
|---|---|
| Range SAT | |
| Critical Reading | 520-630 |
| Range SAT Math | 500-620 |
| Range ACT Composite | 21-27 |
| Average HS GPA | 3.47 |

### ON-CAMPUS APPOINTMENTS

| | |
|---|---|
| Advance Notice | 2 weeks |
| Appointment | Required |
| Saturdays | Sometimes |
| Average Length | 45 min |
| Info Sessions | Yes |
| Class Visits | Yes |

### CAMPUS TOURS

| | |
|---|---|
| Appointment | Required |
| Dates | Academic Year |
| Times | Every hour on the hour |
| Average Length | 60 min |

## CAMPUS AT ITS BEST!

Wittenberg's Weaver Chapel is one of the campus' most exquisite buildings. The Chapel is adorned with 24 stained glass panels, which have been featured in National Geographic. The panels depict the history of Wittenberg from Germany to the current institution. Afterward, take in the beauty of Myers Hollow, a serene area on campus popular for socializing and rousing games of Frisbee. While you're there, be sure to inquire about the activities the University Union Board is promoting that particular day or week. The UB keeps students entertained with dodgeball tournaments, rock walls, and concerts.

# XAVIER UNIVERSITY (OH)

3800 Victory Parkway, Cincinnati, OH 45207-ML5311
**Telephone:** 513-745-3301 • **E-mail:** xuadmit@xavier.edu
**Website:** www.xavier.edu • **Hours:** Monday–Friday and Saturdays by appointment, 8:30 A.M.–5:00 P.M.

## STUDENTS SAY

"This is not a school where you will party your education away. You go to Xavier to meet great people and to be successful when you graduate."

## FODOR'S SAYS

"Fountain Square is the center of downtown Cincinnati and a popular lunch spot for businesspeople in fair weather. The focal point of the square is the Tyler Davidson Fountain, which was cast in 1867 at the Royal Bavarian Foundry in Munich, Germany. The square is the site of the city's annual Oktoberfest ceremony."

## ABOUT THE SCHOOL

Part of Xavier University's mission statement is to provide students with " ... an educational experience characterized by critical thinking and articulate expression with specific attention given to ethical issues and values," and its increasing recognition as a top-notch university shows it is achieving that goal. This midsize university of 3,700 undergraduates has a strong community feel and the administrators, even at the upper levels, are accessible to all students. XU offers a wide core curriculum, ensuring well-rounded graduates who are much in demand—more than 500 companies request resumes from the graduating class each year.

## GETTING THERE

**BY AIR:** The Greater Cincinnati/Northern Kentucky International Airport is only a 25-minute drive away from campus. Airport shuttles and taxis are available at the airport.

**BY TRAIN:** Amtrak stops at Cincinnati's Union Terminal. Ride the SORTA (Southwest Ohio Regional Transit Authority) number 51 bus and transfer to the number 1 bus to get to the XU campus.

**BY BUS:** There is a Greyhound station fewer than three miles away from XU's campus. Ride the SORTA (Southwest Ohio Regional Transit Authority) number 11 or 69 bus and transfer to the number 1 bus to get to the campus.

**BY CAR:** From the North or South via I-75: Take I-75 North/South to Norwood Route 562 (Exit 7) going East. Take the second exit, Route 42, Reading Road. Turn right off exit. Turn left at the third light onto Victory Parkway. Turn left at the third light onto Dana Avenue. Make a left into the Admission Office lot. From the North on I-71: Take I-71 North to Dana Avenue/Montgomery Road Exit 5. Turn left onto Duck Creek Road. At the second stop light, turn left onto Dana Avenue. After the fourth stop light (at Ledgewood Drive), turn right into the Admission Office parking lot. From the South on I-71: Take I-71 South to Dana Avenue Exit 5. Turn right off the exit. After the third stop light (at Ledgewood Drive), turn right into the Admission Office lot.

**LOCAL:** The SORTA (Southwest Ohio Regional Transit Authority) number 1 bus serves the XU Campus and connects to other buses at various points on the route.

## WHERE TO STAY

There are many hotel options in Cincinnati. Ask for the Xavier admission rate or university rate when you call to reserve. The Embassy Suites Hotel Blue Ash (513-733-8900, $$) is a 20-minute drive from campus, and the King's Island Resort and Conference Center is just 25 minutes away (800-727-3050, $).

## CAMPUS AT ITS BEST!

The Cintas Center on campus is a conveniently located venue where students can attend music, comedy, and sports events. If you're visiting in the late spring, plan to attend the Cincinnati Fringe Festival in late May, early June, where artistic performances are staged in different, sometimes untraditional, spaces.

# APPENDICES

# Appendix One: Special Tips on Visiting Military Academies, Women's Colleges, and HBCUs.

Certain types of schools—such as all-women's schools, military academies, historically Black colleges and universities, technical colleges, and sports-crazy schools—have readily identifiable distinguishing characteristics. You'll want to explore the issues associated with those characteristics during your visit; here's some information to get you started.

## MILITARY ACADEMIES

Federal military academies educate and train officers for the Army, Navy, and Air Force. These institutions require recommendation and appointment by members of Congress. There are certainly benefits associated with attending a United States military academy. In addition to free tuition, military academy students receive a top-notch education, a prestigious degree, and access to an unparalleled alumni network. Private and state-supported military institutes, however, accept applications from students interested in attending. They all offer degree programs in engineering and technology with concentrations in various aspects of military science. When visiting a military academy, these are some things you should ask about:

1. What is the length of the post-graduation commitment?

2. What percentage of graduates receives their first choice assignments after graduation?

3. What is the attrition rate for freshmen? How many leave because they "can't take it"?

4. Is the campus coeducational? How fully are women integrated on campus? How are women treated by male classmates?

5. Will the school accept your high school ROTC credit?

6. To what extent do students get a "free ride"? Does the school charge tuition? Room and board? Other fees?

7. What sort of extracurricular student activities are available? Does the average student have time to participate in these activities?

## WOMEN'S COLLEGES

Women's colleges were originally founded in the nineteenth century to meet the educational needs of women—needs that had, up until then, largely been ignored. Independent, nonprofit women's colleges were created as a counterpart to the liberal arts colleges that existed for men. Others were affiliated with religious denominations and open only to white women, while still others were founded as historically Black women's colleges. While their numbers may not be as great as they once were, women's colleges have experienced a new popularity over the last several years. Competition is fierce at the most selective women's colleges, with many women choosing single-sex education, not because it is the only option available to them, but because of the opportunities an all-women's college offers them. There are many advantages to attending a women's college.

According to the Women's College Coalition (WCC), students at women's colleges "report greater satisfaction than their coed counterparts with their college experience in almost all measures—academically, developmentally, and personally." In addition, the WCC states that women's college students "continue toward doctorates in math, science, and engineering in disproportionately large numbers." In fact, women's colleges confer a larger proportion of bachelor's degrees in traditionally male-dominated fields (mathematics, science, and engineering) than coeducational, private colleges do. Women's colleges also have a larger percentage of female faculty and administration. While many factors go into making a college choice, women's colleges are definitely worth considering. Here are some things to inquire about when you go visiting:

1. What is social life like? Many women's colleges have relatively quiet campuses, which may or may not appeal to you.

2. If you're interested in dating men, where are the closest men's and coed schools? Does the women's school traditionally have a strong social relationship with these schools?

3. What are the advantages of attending a single-sex school? Your tour guide and the leader of your information session will be more than happy to tell you!

4. Remember that most women's colleges are relatively small institutions. As with any small liberal arts college, check into the availability of programs in areas that interest you. Does the school have extensive offerings in the liberal arts? Fine arts and performing arts? How about science and mathematics? Is cross registration at other schools available to make up for absences in the school's curriculum?

5. Is there a visible LGBT population on campus? Are there organizations supporting these communities? Is there a visible heterosexual community on campus? Are there indicators of strained relations among these communities?

6. What support and advising resources are available for students interested in graduate school and/or other pre-professional programs?

## HISTORICALLY BLACK COLLEGES AND UNIVERSITIES (HBCUs)

An HBCU is, by definition, a school that was established before 1964 with the intention of serving the African American community. There are more than 100 HBCUs in the United States, and they come in all types and sizes—public and private, two-year and four-year, single-sex and coeducational. Few, if any of them, are really all-Black and some, such as Lincoln University of Missouri, actually have large white populations. The size and involvement of the African American community at any college is a factor you should weigh carefully before you apply. Dig beneath the perceptions and stereotypes, and discover for yourself which environment is best for you. Visiting the schools you are considering is a great way to assess their environments. Start by asking these questions:

1. Does the school have extensive offerings in the liberal arts? Fine arts and performing arts? How about science and mathematics? Is cross registration at other schools available to make up for absences in the school's curriculum?

2. What are the advantages of attending an HBCU? Your tour guide and the leader of your information session will be more than happy to tell you!

3. How strong is the alumni network? This has historically been one of the great strengths of HBCUs.

4. How widely available is financial aid?

5. How many companies recruit on campus? HBCUs often excel in job placement for graduates.

# Appendix Two: Special College Touring Programs

## Is A Commercial College Tour For You?

Are you intimidated by the idea of planning and executing a tour of college campuses on your own? You might want to consider signing on for a packaged college tour. Several companies offer such tours; they typically run from four to eight days in length.

There are numerous advantages to commercial tours. Commercial tours eliminate the need to create itineraries, book accommodations, and arrange travel; with a preplanned tour, all those things are done for you. College tour companies typically offer useful supplemental services, such as seminars on financial aid and the application process. Also, many students find that traveling with a busload of peers and a few high school counselors is less stressful than traveling with their parents. And because tours are chaperoned, parents can send their children off knowing that their (mis)behavior will be monitored and checked. Finally, a commercial tour can be a money saver, especially when compared to traveling with one or both parents.

Of course, there are drawbacks to commercial tours as well. Most importantly, you won't get to choose the colleges you visit. That means you'll almost certainly visit several campuses in which you have no interest. Commercial tours sometimes prioritize quantity over quality, limiting the length of a campus visit to two hours in order to squeeze three visits into a single day. That can make it hard for some students to form a definitive opinion about a campus and makes it impossible for them to explore the campus and the surrounding neighborhood independently. Also, because some tours book accommodations in hotels rather than in college dorm rooms, participants miss out on a great chance to converse in depth with current students.

Commercial campus tours are perhaps best suited for younger high school students at the very beginning of the college selection process. Commercial tours visit a variety of campus types—urban and rural, big and small, religious and secular, homogeneous and diverse, liberal and conservative—which helps students see the full spectrum of available choices.

## What to Expect

According to the website for the National Institute for Educational Planning, one of the more popular commercial campus tour companies, here's what a typical trip entails.

- Students and chaperones convene, either at the airport (if air travel is required) or at the charter bus. Everyone introduces him/herself to the group.

- The lead chaperone explains what to expect on the trip and distributes materials (including articles, worksheets, evaluation forms, etc.).

- The group travels to its first school, takes a tour, and attends an information session. Typically, there is also time to have a meal and visit the campus bookstore before boarding the bus and traveling to the next campus. During the bus ride, students participate in an organized discussion of the campus they have just visited.

- Time permitting, students are allowed to visit areas beyond campus. Visits are closely monitored by chaperones.

- At the end of the day, the bus drops participants at the hotel or residence hall at which they will be staying. Participants convene for a wrap-up session and review the following day's itinerary. Finally, ground rules for individual and group behavior in hotels is detailed. Students are warned that they will be sent home if they break the rules.

- The following day, the whole thing starts all over again.

The following companies offer prearranged campus tours:

### COLLEGE VISITS, INC.

Website: College-visits.com

215 East Bay Street, Suite 401

Charleston, SC 29401 USA

Telephone: 843-853-8149 or 800-944-2798

Fax: 843-577-2813

College Visits, Inc. organizes tours of four to eight days in duration. Their tours cover the following regions: California; the Northeast; the Middle Atlantic; and the Southeast. In 2006, prices for trips ranged from $900 to $1,800.

### COLLEGIATE EXPLORATIONS

Website: CETours.com

Collegiate Explorations

PO Box 3102

Fermington Hills, MI 48333

Telephone: 1-866-4CETOURS (423-8687)

Fax: 248-232-6524

College Explorations Tours offers regional tours in the Midwest, the Northeast, the Middle Atlantic, and the Southeast. The company offers a number of specialty tours, including tours designed for those interested in liberal arts schools, performing arts schools, visual arts and design schools, and historically Black colleges and universities. Tours typically are five to seven days long; prices were not listed at the company's website at the time of publication.

### NATIONAL INSTITUTE FOR EDUCATIONAL PLANNING

Website: NIEP.com

1601 Dove Street, Suite 299

Newport Beach, CA 92660

Telephone: 949-833-7867 or 800-888-NIEP or 714-C-O-L-L-E-G-E

NIEP offers regional tours in the Northeast, Arizona, Northern California, and Southern California. Trips are between three and seven days in duration. Prices were not listed at the company's website at the time of publication.

# INDEX

# THE NORTHEAST

# THE SOUTHEAST

# THE WEST

# THE MIDWEST

# NOTES

# NOTES

# Our Books Help You Navigate the College Admissions Process

## Find the Right School

**Best 366 Colleges, 2008 Edition**
978-0-375-76621-3 • $21.95/C$27.95
Previous Edition: 978-0-375-76558-2

**Complete Book of Colleges, 2008 Edition**
978-0-375-76620-6 • $26.95/C$34.95
Previous Edition: 978-0-375-76557-5

**College Navigator**
978-0-375-76583-4 • $12.95/C$16.00

**America's Best Value Colleges, 2008 Edition**
978-0-375-76601-5 • $18.95/C$24.95

**Guide to College Visits**
978-0-375-76600-8 • $20.00/C$25.00

## Get In

**Cracking the SAT, 2008 Edition**
978-0-375-76606-0 • $19.95/C$24.95
Previous Edition: 978-0-375-76545-2

**Cracking the SAT with DVD, 2008 Edition**
978-0-375-76607-7 • $33.95/C$42.00
Previous Edition: 978-0-375-76546-9

**Math Workout for the NEW SAT**
978-0-375-76433-2 • $16.00/C$23.00

**Reading and Writing Workout for the NEW SAT**
978-0-375-76431-8 • $16.00/C$23.00

**11 Practice Tests for the SAT and PSAT, 2008 Edition**
978-0-375-76614-5 • $19.95/C$24.95
Previous Edition: 978-0-375-76544-5

**12 Practice Tests for the AP Exams**
978-0-375-76584-1 • $19.95/C$24.95

**Cracking the ACT, 2007 Edition**
978-0-375-76585-8 • $19.95/C$24.95

**Cracking the ACT with DVD, 2007 Edition**
978-0-375-76586-5 • $31.95/C$39.95

**Crash Course for the ACT, 3rd Edition**
978-0-375-76587-2 • $9.95/C$12.95

**Crash Course for the New SAT**
978-0-375-76461-5 • $9.95/C$13.95

## Get Help Paying for It

**How to Save for College**
978-0-375-76425-7 • $14.95/C$21.00

**Paying for College Without Going Broke, 2008 Edition**
978-0-375-76630-5 • $20.00/C$25.00
Previous Edition: 978-0-375-76567-4

## Available at Bookstores Everywhere
## www.PrincetonReview.com

# AP Exams

**Cracking the AP Biology Exam,**
2006–2007 Edition
978-0-375-76525-4 • $17.00/C$24.00

**Cracking the AP Calculus AB & BC Exams,**
2006–2007 Edition
978-0-375-76526-1 • $18.00/C$26.00

**Cracking the AP Chemistry Exam,**
2006–2007 Edition
978-0-375-76527-8 • $17.00/C$24.00

**Cracking the AP Computer Science
A & AB Exams,** 2006–2007 Edition
978-0-375-76528-5 • $19.00/C$27.00

**Cracking the AP Economics (Macro &
Micro) Exams,** 2006–2007 Edition
978-0-375-76535-3 • $17.00/C$24.00

**Cracking the AP English Language and
Composition Exam,** 2006–2007 Edition
978-0-375-76536-0 • $17.00/C$24.00

**Cracking the AP English Literature Exam,**
2006–2007 Edition
978-0-375-76537-7 • $17.00/C$24.00

**Cracking the AP Environmental
Science Exam,** 2006–2007 Edition
978-0-375-76538-4 • $17.00/C$24.00

**Cracking the AP European History Exam,**
2006–2007 Edition
978-0-375-76539-1 • $17.00/C$24.00

**Cracking the AP Physics B & C Exams,**
2006–2007 Edition
978-0-375-76540-7 • $19.00/C$27.00

**Cracking the AP Psychology Exam,**
2006–2007 Edition
978-0-375-76529-2 • $17.00/C$24.00

**Cracking the AP Spanish Exam,**
2006–2007 Edition
978-0-375-76530-8 • $17.00/C$24.00

**Cracking the AP Statistics Exam,**
2006–2007 Edition
978-0-375-76531-5 • $19.00/C$27.00

**Cracking the AP U.S. Government
and Politics Exam,** 2006–2007 Edition
978-0-375-76532-2 • $17.00/C$24.00

**Cracking the AP U.S. History Exam,**
2006–2007 Edition
978-0-375-76533-9 • $17.00/C$24.00

**Cracking the AP World History Exam,**
2006–2007 Edition
978-0-375-76534-6 • $17.00/C$24.00

# SAT Subject Tests

**Cracking the SAT Biology E/M Subject
Test,** 2007–2008 Edition
978-0-375-76588-9 • $19.00/C$25.00

**Cracking the SAT Chemistry Subject Test,**
2007–2008 Edition
978-0-375-76589-6 • $18.00/C$22.00

**Cracking the SAT French Subject Test,**
2007–2008 Edition
978-0-375-76590-2 • $18.00/C$22.00

**Cracking the SAT Literature Subject Test,**
2007–2008 Edition
978-0-375-76592-6 • $18.00/C$22.00

**Cracking the SAT Math 1 and 2
Subject Tests,** 2007–2008 Edition
978-0-375-76593-3 • $19.00/C$25.00

**Cracking the SAT Physics Subject Test,**
2007–2008 Edition
978-0-375-76594-0 • $19.00/C$25.00

**Cracking the SAT Spanish Subject Test,**
2007–2008 Edition
978-0-375-76595-7 • $18.00/C$22.00

**Cracking the SAT U.S. & World History
Subject Tests,** 2007–2008 Edition
978-0-375-76591-9 • $19.00/C$25.00

# The College Dorm Survival Guide

## How to Survive and Thrive in Your New Home Away from Home

### JULIA DeVILLERS

# The Ultimate Guide to Surviving and Thriving in the Dorm

Dorm life offers you a great chance to meet new people and try new things. But entering the roommate-having, small-room-sharing, coed-bathroom-using world of the dorms can be overwhelming and intimidating. **The College Dorm Survival Guide** offers expert advice and the inside scoop on it all—from avoiding the dreaded freshman fifteen to decorating your space. This informative and funny guide gives expert advice on everything you need to know to enjoy dorm living to the fullest.

**The College Dorm
Survival Guide**

ISBN-10: 0-7615-2674-9
ISBN-13: 978-0-7615-2674-2
$12.95 PAPER
(CANADA: $16.95)

Available from
Three Rivers Press
wherever books are sold
www.crownpublishing.com